Communications
in Computer and Information Science 1415

More information about this series at http://www.springer.com/series/7899

Yuan Tian · Tinghuai Ma ·
Muhammad Khurram Khan (Eds.)

Big Data and Security

Second International Conference, ICBDS 2020
Singapore, Singapore, December 20–22, 2020
Revised Selected Papers

 Springer

Editors
Yuan Tian ⓘ
Nanjing Institute of Technology
Nanjing, China

Tinghuai Ma ⓘ
Nanjing University of Information Science
and Technology
Nanjing, China

Muhammad Khurram Khan ⓘ
King Saud Unviersity
Riyadh, Saudi Arabia

ISSN 1865-0929   ISSN 1865-0937 (electronic)
Communications in Computer and Information Science
ISBN 978-981-16-3149-8   ISBN 978-981-16-3150-4 (eBook)
https://doi.org/10.1007/978-981-16-3150-4

This Springer imprint is published by the registered company Springer Nature Singapore Pte Ltd.
The registered company address is: 152 Beach Road, #21-01/04 Gateway East, Singapore 189721, Singapore

Preface

This volume contains the papers from the Second International Conference on Big Data and Security (ICBDS 2020). The event was held at Curtin University, Singapore, and was organized by the Nanjing Institute of Technology, Oulu University, King Saud University, Curtin University, JiangSu Computer Society, Nanjing University of Posts and Telecommunications, and IEEE Broadcast Technology Society.

The International Conference on Big Data and Security brings experts and researchers together from all over the world to discuss the current status of, and potential ways to address, security and privacy regarding the use of Big Data systems. Big Data systems are complex and heterogeneous; due to their extraordinary scale and the integration of different technologies, new security and privacy issues are introduced that must be properly addressed. The ongoing digitalization of the business world is putting companies and users at risk of cyber-attacks more than ever before. Big Data analysis has the potential to offer protection against these attacks. Participation in the conference workshops on specific topics is expected to achieve progress by facilitating global networking along with the transfer and exchange of ideas.

The papers presented at ICBDS 2020 coming from researchers who work in universities and research institutions gave us the opportunity to achieve a good level of understanding of the mutual needs, requirements, and technical means available in this field of research. The topics included in this second edition of the conference covered fields connected to Big Data, Security in Blockchain, IoT Security, Security in Cloud and Fog Computing, Artificial Intelligence/Machine Learning Security, Cybersecurity, and Privacy. We received 153 submissions and accepted 52 papers. All the accepted papers were peer reviewed by three qualified reviewers chosen from our Technical Program Committee based on their qualifications and experience.

The proceedings editors wish to thank the dedicated committee members and all the other reviewers for their efforts and contributions. We also thank Springer for their trust and for publishing the proceedings of ICBDS 2020.

March 2021

Tinghuai Ma
Yi Pan
Muhammad Khurram Khan
Markku Oivo
Yuan Tian

Organization

General Chairs

Ting Huai Ma   Nanjing University of Information Science and Technology, China
Yi Pan   Georgia State University, USA
Muhammad Khurram Khan   King Saud University, Saudi Arabia
Markku Oivo   University of Oulu, Finland
Yuan Tian   Nanjing Institute of Technology, China

Technical Program Chairs

Victor S. Sheng   University of Central Arkansas, USA
Zhaoqing Pan   Nanjing University of Information Science and Technology, China

Technical Program Committee

Eui-Nam Huh   Kyung Hee University, South Korea
Teemu Karvonen   University of Oulu, Finland
Heba Abdullataif Kurdi   Massachusetts Institute of Technology, USA
Omar Alfandi   Zayed University, UAE
DongXue Liang   Tsing Hua University, China
Mohammed Al-Dhelaan   King Saud University, Saudi Arabia
Päivi Raulamo-Jurvanen   University of Oulu, Finland
Zeeshan Pervez   University of the West of Scotland, UK
Adil Mehmood Khan   Innopolis University, Russia
Wajahat Ali Khan   Kyung Hee University, South Korea
Qiao Lin Ye   Nanjing Forestry University, China
Pertti Karhapää   University of Oulu, Finland
Farkhund Iqbal   Zayed University, UAE
Muhammad Ovais Ahmad   Karlstad University, Sweden
Lejun Zhang   Yangzhou University, China
Linshan Shen   Harbin Engineering University, China
Ghada Al-Hudhud   King Saud University, Saudi Arabia
Lei Han   Nanjing Institute of Technology, China
Tang Xin   University of International Relations, China
Zeeshan Pervez   University of the West of Scotland, UK
Mznah Al Rodhaan   King Saud University, Saudi Arabia
Yao Zhenjian   Huazhong University of Science and Technology, China
Thant Zin Oo   Kyung Hee University, South Korea

Mohammad Rawashdeh	University of Central Missouri, USA
Alia Alabdulkarim	King Saud University, Saudi Arabia
Elina Annanperä	University of Oulu, Finland
Soha Zaghloul Mekki	King Saud University, Saudi Arabia
Basmah Alotibi	King Saud University, Saudi Arabia
Mariya Muneeb	King Saud University, Saudi Arabia
Maryam Hajakbari	Islamic Azad University, Iran
Miada Murad	King Saud University, Saudi Arabia
Pilar Rodríguez	The Technical University of Madrid, Spain
Zhiwei Wan	Hebei Normal University, China
Rand J.	Shaqra University, Saudi Arabia
Jiagao Wu	Nanjing University of Posts and Telecommunications, China
Mohammad Mehedi Hassan	King Saud University, Saudi Arabia
Weipeng Jing	Northeast Forestry University, China
Yu Zhang	Harbin Institute of Technology, China
Nguyen H. Tran	University of Sydney, Australia
Hang Chen	Nanjing Institute of Technology, China
Sarah Alkharji	King Saud University, Saudi Arabia
Chunguo Li	Southeast University, China
Xiao Hua Huang	University of Oulu, Finland
Babar Shah	Zayed University, UAE
Tianyang Zhou	State Key Laboratory of Mathematical Engineering and Advanced Computing, China
Manal Hazazi	King Saud University, Saudi Arabia
Jiagao Wu	Nanjing University of Posts and Telecommunications, China
Markus Kelanti	University of Oulu, Finland
Amiya Kumar Tripathy	Edith Cowan University, Australia
Shaoyong Guo	Beijing University of Posts and Telecommunications, China
Shadan AlHamed	King Saud University, Saudi Arabia
Cunjie Cao	Hainan University, China
Linfeng Liu	Nanjing University of Posts and Telecommunications, China
Chunliang Yang	China Mobile IoT Company Limited, China
Patrick Hung	University of Ontario Institute of Technology, Canada
Xinjian Zhao	State Grid Nanjing Power Supply Company, China
Sungyoung Lee	Kyung Hee University, South Korea
Zhengyu Chen	Jinling Institute of Technology, China
Jian Zhou	Nanjing University of Posts and Telecommunications, China
Pasi Kuvaja	University of Oulu, Finland
Xiao Xue	Tianjin University, China
Jianguo Sun	Harbin Engineering University, China
Farkhund Iqbal	Zayed University, UAE

Zilong Jin	Nanjing University of Information Science and Technology, China
Susheela Dahiya	University of Petroleum & Energy Studies, India
Ming Pang	Harbin Engineering University, China
Yuanfeng Jin	Yanbian University, China
Maram Al-Shablan	King Saud University, Saudi Arabia
Kejia Chen	Nanjing University of Posts and Telecommunications, China
Valentina Lenarduzzi	University of Tampere, Finland
Davide Taibi	University of Tampere, Finland
Jinghua Ding	Sungkyunkwan University, South Korea
XueSong Yin	Nanjing Institute of Technology, China
Qiang Ma	King Saud University, Saudi Arabia
Tero Päivärinta	University of Oulu, Finland
Shiwen Hu	Accelor Ltd., USA
Manar Hosny	King Saud University, Saudi Arabia
Lei Cui	Chinese Academy of Sciences, China
Yonghua Gong	Nanjing University of Posts and Telecommunications, China
Kashif Saleem	King Saud University, Saudi Arabia
Xiaojian Ding	Nanjing University of Finance and Economics, China
Irfan Mohiuddin	King Saud University, Saudi Arabia
Ming Su	Beijing University of Posts and Telecommunications, China
Yunyun Wang	Nanjing University of Posts and Telecommunications, China
Abdullah Al-Dhelaan	King Saud University, Saudi Arabia

Workshop Chairs

Jiande Zhang	Nanjing Institute of Technology, China
Ning Ye	Nanjing Forestry University, China
Asad Masood Khattak	Zayed University, UAE

Publication Chair

Vidyasagar Potdar	Curtin University, Australia

Organization Chairs

ChenRong Huang	Nanjing Institute of Technology, China
Bangjun Nie	Nanjing Institute of Technology, China
Xianyun Li	Nanjing Institute of Technology, China
Jianhua Chen	Nanjing Institute of Technology, China
Wenlong Shao	Nanjing Institute of Technology, China
Kari Liukkunen	University of Oulu, Finland

Organization Committee Members

Wei Huang	Nanjing Institute of Technology, China
Pilar Rodriguez Gonzalez	University of Oulu, Finland
Jalal Al Muhtadi	King Saud University, Saudi Arabia
Geng Yang	Nanjing University of Posts and Telecommunications, China
Qiao Lin Ye	Nanjing Forestry University, China
Pertti Karhapää	University of Oulu, Finland
Lei Han	Nanjing Institute of Technology, China
Yong Zhu	Jingling Institute of Technology, China
Päivi Raulamo-Jurvanen	University of Oulu, Finland
Bin Xie	Hebei Normal University, China
Dawei Li	Nanjing Institute of Technology, China
Jing Rong Chen	Nanjing Institute of Technology, China
Thant Zin Oo	Kyung Hee University, South Korea
Shoubao Su	JiangSu Key Laboratory of Data Science & Smart Software, China
Alia Alabdulkarim	King Saud University, Saudi Arabia
Juan Juan Cheng	Nanjing Institute of Technology, China
Rand J.	Shaqra University, Saudi Arabia
Hang Chen	Nanjing Institute of Technology, China
Jiagao Wu	Nanjing University of Posts and Telecommunications, China
Shuyang Hao	Nanjing Institute of Technology, China
Ruixuan Dong	Nanjing Institute of Technology, China

Contents

Big Data

Blockchain and Internet of Things

Artificial Intelligence/Machine Learning Security

Cybersecurity and Privacy

Application and Research of Power Communication Trusted Access Gateway

Wei-wei Kong[✉], Jie Zhang, Pei-chun Pan, and Jia Yu

NARI Group Corporation, State Grid Electric Power Research Institute, Nanjing, China
kongweiwei1@sgepri.sgcc.com.cn

Abstract. The traditional centralized access authentication method of power Internet of things terminal brings great communication pressure and computation cost to the authentication center. In view of this situation, block chain technology is introduced and applied to all kinds of power service access application scenarios through research and development. A block-chain-based power universal service access gateway is developed and tested. The test shows that it can realize terminal access authentication of typical power Internet of things systems such as distribution automation. This scheme improves the data transfer performance of power communication network and solves the bottleneck problem of network performance of power service information communication support platform.

Keywords: Access authentication · Block chain · Identity authentication · Gateway · Functional module

1 Introduction

It is necessary to integrate the infrastructure resources and the infrastructure resources of power system effectively, improve the information level of the power system, improve the utilization efficiency of the existing infrastructure of the power system, and provide important technical support for the transmission, transmission, transformation, distribution and power consumption of the power network [1–3]. In 2018, China National Network Company put forward the strategic goal of the new era company information and communication, the goal is to build the power Internet of things, build intelligent enterprises, and lead the construction of world-class energy Internet enterprises with outstanding competitiveness [4–6]. Among them, the electricity Internet of things, is the company's second network integrated with the grid development [7].

Current power communication networks are typical convergent networks. Acquisition services converge from terminal to master station, control services are sent from master station to terminal, and there is little data interaction between terminal and terminal [8, 9, 10]. The authentication of terminals depends on centralized proxy communication modes and servers, all of which are verified and connected through cloud servers with powerful running and storage capabilities. With the construction of the energy Internet, the central network will face challenges [11].

© Springer Nature Singapore Pte Ltd. 2021
Y. Tian et al. (Eds.): ICBDS 2020, CCIS 1415, pp. 3–14, 2021.
https://doi.org/10.1007/978-981-16-3150-4_1

Block-chain technology can naturally adapt to the application demand of power pan-service trusted access [12, 13, 14, 15]. Therefore, the application of block chain technology in power communication system is an inevitable requirement for the development of smart grid to the foundation of information communication support technology. A large number of studies have also shown that the current traditional information and communication infrastructure, if not improved, will not meet the development requirements of the energy Internet. In this paper, the power communication network technology in the foundation of information communication is deeply studied, and the blockchain technology is introduced. The technology is expanded, practicalized and optimized, and the service access gateway of power communication network based on block chain is developed.

2 Research on Access Authentication

2.1 Access Authentication Method for Power Communication Network

Access authentication means that the user needs to identify the user's identity according to some strategy before accessing the system, so as to ensure the legitimacy of the user's identity of the access system [16]. To record the authentication of the user, as the user in the system running identity credentials. Access authentication includes two processes, identification and authentication. Identification is the process of the user showing his identity to the system, and authentication is the process of checking the user's identity. Access authentication is an important part of platform security [17, 18]. For illegal users, access authentication mechanism limits access to platform resources. For legitimate users, access authentication permits them to access the system and generate identification for them. Access authentication is the basis of other security mechanisms of the platform. Prior to formal communication between the device and the platform, the platform authenticates visitors. After authentication, the platform authenticates and backups the equipment, the identity certificate can be checked at any time, and the identity certificate generated by the two parties through the access authentication is to prevent the occurrence of the denial behavior [19].

With the construction of smart grid, higher requirements are put forward for the confidentiality, integrity and availability of information security of enterprises. At present, the main service system of power grid enterprises has gradually adopted the access mode of mobile terminals, and the data exchange is carried out through wireless access technology such as 4G and information inside and outside network, and the number of access will continue to grow rapidly. Under this background, how to ensure that all kinds of decentralized mobile operation terminals can safely access the smart grid, and at the same time monitor and audit the access objects, so as to realize the confidentiality and controllability in the process of information transmission, has become an urgent problem to be considered and solved in the development of smart grid. In the future, with the continuous expansion of access terminals, the complexity of access environment and the diversification of access methods, the security, confidentiality and controllability of all kinds of decentralized information transmission processes will face more severe challenges.

2.2 Certification Framework for Power Communication Networks

The overall architecture of the access system for grid information security data is shown in figure. Secure access system consists of secure client, secure channel, secure access platform, PKI certificate and directory service, secure service access, etc. [20].

(1) Security client

The digital certificate, encryption chip, security module, client software and so on are deployed on the pc, portable computer terminal, PDA, smartphone terminal, meter terminal, etc.

(2) Safe access

It provides network channels between the terminal and the access platform, including all kinds of wired special lines, virtual private dial-up network of wireless special lines, access point channels, etc., encrypted tunnel connection in secure terminal layer and secure access platform layer through secure channel.

(3) Secure access platform

1) Secure access gateway system
   Provide security channel layer for security authentication and access to all kinds of decentralized terminals, set up a two-way encryption tunnel to encrypt the data of the application system. As the boundary core protection access equipment of the platform, the terminal is effectively authenticated and the data integrity, confidentiality and non-tampering are guaranteed.
2) Security exchange service system
   After authentication access, the terminal carries on the network security partition and the bare data stripping through the security exchange service system, realizes the access control and the security exchange to the service data, guarantees to the data access security, the reliability and the legitimacy.
3) Authentication server
   The server mainly has the functions of certificate online verification, terminal access arbitration, access control authority and so on.
4) Centralized supervision server
   The server mainly provides the storage of the basic data of the platform, and carries on the unified centralized management to the platform access terminal, the equipment asset information, the hardware characteristic information, the certificate information and so on, and realizes the centralized control and management of the system running state in the secure access platform through the platform bus. At the same time, it realizes the functions of platform cascade, superior and subordinate information active reporting, unified centralized configuration, security management and so on.

5) Certificate and directory services
   A digital certificate is issued by the PKI certificate service and directory system to provide the security terminal, and the online certificate verification function of the identity server is provided.
6) Security operations visits
   Security service access includes the front-end machine and the background application system of each service system, provides the service external access interface, at present mainly for the web service interface, the XML-RPC call interface and so on.

3   Design of Trusted Access Gateway for Power IoT

Based on PKI system, digital certificate, encryption and decryption algorithm and other security technologies, the management service of terminal identity certificate of power Internet of things is strengthened, and the authentication architecture of distributed access of power Internet of things terminal is realized. Users can flexibly deploy according to the business requirements of different power Internet of things.

IoT terminals contain two types of nodes. Order node is responsible for receiving the access authentication request of the power terminal, organizing the access authentication, sending the token to respond to the authentication request. Peer node is used to contact adjacent peer nodes, perform query validation, and do not perform transactions recorded. The gateway of the Internet of Things performs data reading, writing and querying. The gateway maintains the account database with the help of the consensus algorithm and consistency protocol of the block chain.

The device consists of three components,member authentication authorization module, block chain service module and business editing module. It realizes three functions, authentication of power Internet of things terminal identity, authentication certificate of power Internet of things terminal and access status certificate, authentication parameter of power Internet of things and configuration of protocol. It realizes three functions, authentication of power Internet of things terminal, authentication certificate of power Internet of things terminal and access status certificate, authentication parameter of power Internet of things and configuration of protocol, as shown below (Fig. 1).

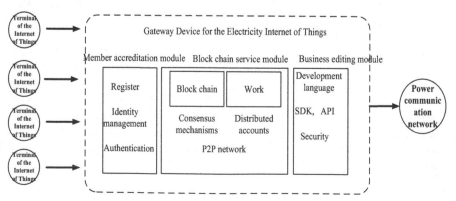

Fig. 1. Architecture diagram of gateway system based on block chain

The implementation process of block-chain-based gateway includes the following three steps.

Step 1. Each terminal authenticates to the gateway, and the gateway queries the authentication information in the block chain module to verify the identity of the terminal. A gateway opens a service access port for a validated terminal. A terminal that can not be validated will not have access to the business. For terminals that can not pass verification, if it is the first request of the terminal, the registration function of the new node is triggered, otherwise its request is ignored. The process of authentication request is shown below (Fig. 2).

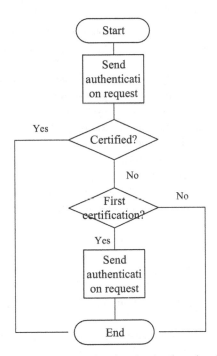

Fig. 2. Flow chart of terminal authentication based on block chain

Step 2. The service module of the block chain is responsible for maintaining the distributed account book, and the digital signature of each legal node is stored in the block chain. For newly registered nodes, the blockchain service module generates new authentication blocks by consensus algorithm.

Step 3. The business editing module realizes the authentication parameters and protocol configuration of the Internet of things through the intelligent contract of the block chain, and realizes the functions of terminal initialization according to the requirements of different Internet of things systems.

Among them, the authentication process of the terminal is as follows.

Step 1. The key system assigns keys to each terminal. Key system constructs a lightweight key based on identification for massive terminals. The system can generate the unique identification key according to the identification of the terminal, and can download the identification key safely to the terminal or its security chip online or offline. All the terminals can calculate the public key corresponding to any identity locally. The public key algorithm of the key system adopts the SM2 algorithm, and the chip selects the low power chip which supports the SM2 algorithm. The physical terminal with identification key supports end-to-end authentication and end-to-end data encryption transmission, and supports off-line authentication of terminal. The key system includes key production, application, approval, revocation, statistical analysis and other functions. The key management system stores the certificate information of the terminal in the block chain, each block stores the certificate of one terminal, and the block chain runs in the gateway node.

Step 2. The terminal sends an access request to the access gateway, which responds to the request and the terminal obtains access rights to the intranet.

Step 3. According to the characteristics of the service contained in the terminal request, the gateway selects the terminal that satisfies the threshold number to form the authentication group and initiates the distributed authentication. The nodes of the authentication group are divided into peer nodes and order nodes.

Step 4. A terminal sends the authentication request to the order node in the authentication group, order node encapsulates the authentication request and broadcasts it to the authentication group. All peer nodes in the authentication group initiate distributed authentication, which is done by voting.

Step 5. Authentication group order the node, sends the token to the access gateway, and the access gateway sends the authorization token to the terminal, so the terminal obtains access rights.

The process of the above authentication interaction is shown in the following figure (Fig. 3).

A distributed authentication process consisting of peer nodes consists of the following steps.

Step 1. M is the authentication request information broadcast by the Order node. Ballot papers submitted by the peer node voting in favour are as follows $\sigma_i = H_2(y_i)||M$. The corresponding authentication criterion is (σ_i, y_i, M). Peer node sends authentication criteria to order.

Step 2. Suppose the authentication threshold is t, order node receives t valid sub-certification criterion and obtains t point pairs $(x_1, y_1), \ldots, (x_t, y_t)$. Using Lagrange secret sharing algorithm, the formula is as follows

$$S_k = \sum_{j=i}^{t} y_j \prod_{1 < l < t, l \neq j} \frac{x_l}{x_l - x_j}$$

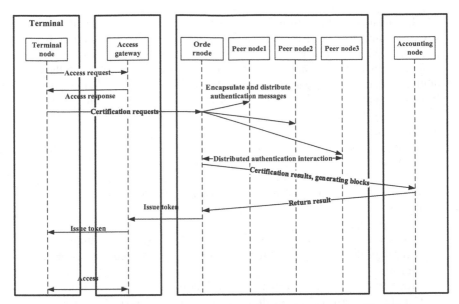

Fig. 3. Schematic diagram of distributed authentication based on blockchain

The group key S_k, the legal terminal that meets the threshold number t has confirmed the authentication of the new terminal. The sorting node submits the authentication information to the accounting node to generate new blocks.

Gateway uses the public key P to decrypt the token, and sends the information to the terminal requesting access to the network, the authentication ends.

4   Development and Test of Power Trusted Access Gateway

4.1   Development of Trusted Access Gateway

The gateway device realizes the trusted access and authentication function of the terminal based on the blockchain technology, and forms two subsystems, which are respectively the gateway system and the configuration tool of trusted access. The system mainly carries on the terminal distributed authentication and the edge authentication according to the access characteristic. The system can adapt to the power application scenarios where the physical location of each communication station is scattered, the number of service terminals is large, and each node device has many kinds of access services. The system can ensure the real-time and reliability requirements of access authentication, and can adapt the data service characteristics of different bandwidths, including discontinuous communication and burst communication, real-time service and non-real-time service, heavy load and light load, etc.

(1) Design of functional modules

Gateway system includes block chain engine, authentication module, accounting module, gateway module and configuration module and other functional modules.

Block chain module is based on super account book platform, which realizes consensus algorithm, chain code running environment, bookkeeping and query function. It interacts with the authentication algorithm through the API interface.

In the authentication module, the authentication algorithm is called by the configuration tool, the authentication algorithm is called for distributed authentication.

In the accounting module, according to the authentication results of the newly added nodes, the new block nodes are generated by sorting nodes to record the transactions.

In the gateway module, the network control instruction is output according to the authentication result, and the network port is set.

In the configuration module, the setting of authentication parameters, block chain parameters and so on is realized, and the editing, modification and execution of chain code are realized.

(2) System deployment

The block-chain certified server is connected with the power communication network through the convergent switch to verify the access request of the terminal equipment.

A demonstration verification system is divided into two segments, in which the DTU in slice 1 interworking with the convergent switch in layer 2 through the access switch, and the terminal in slice 2 interworking with the convergent switch through the public network. Before the terminal connects to the backbone communication network, it needs to authenticate through the block chain authentication server and obtain the communication token, otherwise, the communication link of the network layer can not be established (Fig. 4).

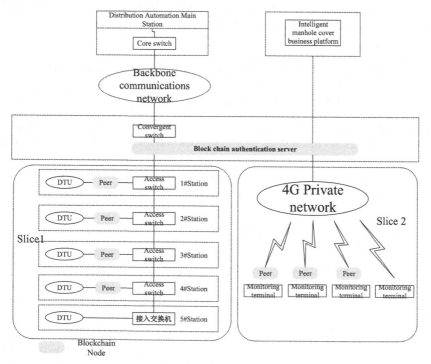

Fig. 4. Total topology of the system

(3) Composition of hardware

The hardware of the gateway includes a programmable switch, a blockchain authentication server, and a configuration terminal, as shown in the figure below (Fig. 5).

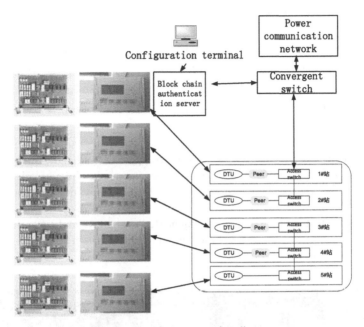

Fig. 5. Hardware connection diagram

4.2 Test Analysis of Service Access Gateway

The test scenario is the distribution automation terminal monitoring service, and the block chain authentication server is deployed in the computer room as shown in the figure (Fig. 6).

Fig. 6. Field deployment of servers and gateways

The test results are shown in the table below (Table 1).

Table 1. The results of terminal access

	Status of access	Time	Mode of communication
1	Connect	2019-09-09 10:17:21	Fibre-optical
2	Connect	2019-09-09 10:17:46	Fibre-optical
3	Disconnect		Fibre-optical
4	Connect	2019-09-09 10:18:33	Fibre-optical

It can be seen from the table that the four stations pass the authentication of the block chain, and the terminal through the authentication can access the network, which has no effect on the service, and the terminal without the authentication can not access the network.

As a contrast test, an illegal device is connected to the test, and since the authentication information of the device does not exist in the block chain and is not initialized, the following interface appears. (Fig. 7)

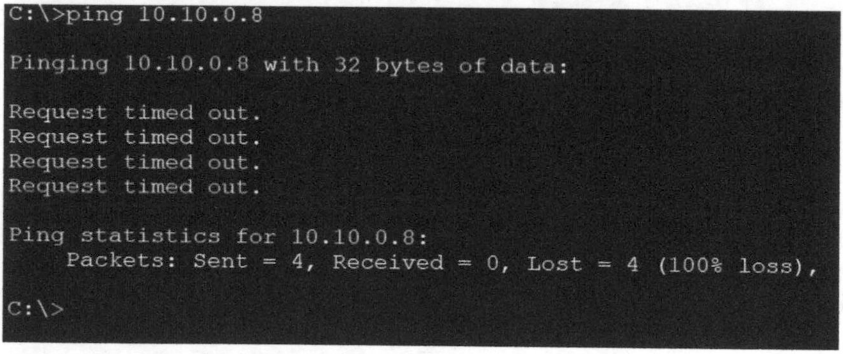

```
C:\>ping 10.10.0.8

Pinging 10.10.0.8 with 32 bytes of data:

Request timed out.
Request timed out.
Request timed out.
Request timed out.

Ping statistics for 10.10.0.8:
    Packets: Sent = 4, Received = 0, Lost = 4 (100% loss),

C:\>
```

Fig. 7. Interface display

5 Conclusion

With the further development of the technology in the field of smart grid, the power terminal puts forward higher requirements for high efficiency access. The application of block chain technology in power communication system is an inevitable requirement for the development of smart grid to support the foundation of communication technology. Based on the technology of decentralization of block chain and the characteristics of power communication network, a distributed authentication scheme for power Internet of things is proposed in this paper. The test shows that it can realize terminal access authentication of typical power Internet of things system, such as distribution automation, which has the characteristics of good universality and convenient configuration, and can significantly improve the security of terminal system without affecting the topology of original system.

Acknowledgments. The authors would like to thank the anonymous reviewers and editor for their comments that improved the quality of this paper. This work was supported by science & research project of SGCC. (Research and application of terminal layer architecture and edge eIoT agent technologies in full service ubiquitous SG-eIoT. Project No. 5700-201958240A-0-0-00.)

References

1. He, Y.-y., Pang, J.: Application prospect of block chain technology in electric power industry. Electr. Power Inf. Commun. Technol. **16**(3), 39–42 (2018)
2. Ji, B., Mo, J., Wang, J.: Study on communication reliability of weakly centralized electricity mutual transaction based on blockchain technology. Guangdong Electr. Power **32**(1), 85–92 (2019)
3. Sun, Y., Yu, Yu., Li, X., Zhang, K., Qian, H., Zhou, Y.: Batch verifiable computation with public verifiability for outsourcing polynomials and matrix computations. In: Liu, J.K., Steinfeld, R. (eds.) ACISP 2016. LNCS, vol. 9722, pp. 293–309. Springer, Cham (2016). https://doi.org/10.1007/978-3-319-40253-6_18
4. Zeng, Z., Zhang, L.: A blockchain-based smart power grid system. Electr. Power Inf. Commun. Technol. **17**(1), 31–35 (2019)
5. Fan, J., Wei, A.: Architecture of energy micro grid based on block chain. Electr. Power Inf. Commun. Technol. **16**(12), 9–13 (2018)
6. Lou, J., Zhang, Q., Qi, Z., Lei, K.: A blockchain-based key management scheme for named data networking. In: 2018 1st IEEE International Conference on Hot Information-Centric Networking (HotICN), Shenzhen, China, pp. 141–146 (2018)
7. Samaniego, M., Deters, R.: Blockchain as a service for IoT. In: 2016 IEEE International Conference on Internet of Things (iThings) and IEEE Green Computing and Communications (GreenCom) and IEEE Cyber, Physical and Social Computing (CPSCom) and IEEE Smart Data (SmartData), Chengdu, pp. 433–436 (2016)
8. Kan, L., Wei, Y., Hafiz Muhammad, A., Siyuan, W., Linchao, G., Kai, H.: A multiple blockchains architecture on inter-blockchain communication. In: 2018 IEEE International Conference on Software Quality, Reliability and Security Companion (QRS-C), Lisbon, Portugal, pp. 139–145 (2018)
9. Yuan, Y., Ni, X., Zeng, S., Wang, F.: Blockchain consensus algorithms: the state of the art and future trends. Acta Autom. Sinica **44**(11), 2011–2022 (2018)
10. Xiao, Z., Chen, N., Wei, J., Zhang, W.: A high performance management schema of metadata clustering for large-scale data storage systems. J. Comput. Res. Dev. **52**(4), 929–942 (2015)
11. Li, Y., Zheng, K., Yan, Y., et al.: EtherQL: a query layer for blockchain system. In: Proceedings of International Conference on Database Systems for Advanced Applications. Suzhou, China, pp. 556–567 (2017)
12. Yihua, D., James, W., Pradip, K., et al.: Scalable practical byzantine fault tolerance with short-lived signature schemes. In: CASCON 2018 Proceedings of the 28th Annual International Conference on Computer Science and Software Engineering, pp. 245–256 (2018)

13. Min, X.P., Li, Q.Z., Kong, L.J., et al.: Permissioned blockchain dynamic consensus mechanism based multi-centers. Chin. J. Comput. **41**(5), 1005–1020 (2018)
14. Luu, L., Narayanan, V., Zheng, C., et al.: A secure sharding protocol for open blockchains. In: CCS 2016 Proceedings of the 2016 ACM SIGSAC Conference on Computer and Communications Security, pp. 17–30 (2016)
15. Chen, X., Hu, X., Yu, J.: Research on access authentication technology of power IoT based on blockchain. Appl. Electron. Tech. **45**(5), 56–60 (2019)
16. Chen, X., Xu, X., Guo, F., Li, Y.: Research on distributed authentication of power IoT based on hyperledger blockchain. Appl. Electron. Tech. **45**(11), 77–81 (2019)
17. Castro, M., Liskov, B.: Practical byzantine fault tolerance and proactive recovery. ACM Trans. Comput. Syst. Assoc. Comput. Mach. **20**(4), 398–461 (1999)
18. Xu, Z.-H., Han, S.-Y., Chen, L.: CUB, a consensus unit-based storage scheme for blockchain system. In: Proceedings of IEEE 34th International Conference on Data Engineering, Paris, France, pp. 173–184 (2018)
19. Zhang, J.-Y., Wang, Z.-Q., Xu, Z.-L.: A regulatable digital currency model based on blockchain. J. Comput. Res. Dev. **55**(10), 127–140 (2018)
20. Wang, J., Li, L., Yan, Y., Zhao, W., Xu, Y.: Security incidents and solutions of blockchain technology application. Comput. Sci. **45**(z1), 352–355,382 (2018)

The Database Fine-Grained Access SQL Statement Control Model Based on the Dynamic Query Modification Algorithm

Ya Wei[1]([✉]), Rongyan Cai[2], Lan Zhang[1], and Qian Guo[3,4]

[1] State Grid Henan Marketing Service Center (Metrolgy Center),
Zhengzhou 450000, China
[2] State Grid Fujian Electric Power Company Limited, Fuzhou 350000, China
[3] Global Energy Interconnection Research Institute Co., Ltd., Nanjing 210000, China
[4] State Grid Key Laboratory of Information and Network Security, Nanjing 210003, China

Abstract. The SQL query technology which is the standard computer language for the processing of databases, the existing technology cannot guarantee the integrity of all SQL queries. While the fine-grained access control (FGAC) method in the DBMS shall meet the sanity attribute requirements. It means that the answer to the query obtained by this method under the FGAC shall conform to the answer without the FGAC. In this article, a new query modification algorithm is proposed . And the theory of robustness is extended and perfected, and it is pointed out that for the several SQL queries proposed, the proposed algorithm guarantees the robustness. Finally, the algorithm is implemented by the query modification and performance evaluation is carried out, which is the feasible method.

Keywords: Database security · Access control · Fine-grained access control · SQL query

1 Introduction

Through fine-grained access control (FGAC), access to tables at the granularity of individual columns, rows and cells in rows are allowed. Recently, researchers have studied new technologies for integrating FGAC into database management systems (DBMS) [1–4]. Literature [5] proposed the robustness of FGAC. If the returned answer is consistent with the answer without FGAC, the algorithm is correct, which means that with FGAC the answer will not return an error message. At the same time, it points out that the existing method cannot retain soundness as well as that when the query contains any negatives words (for example, MINUS, NOT EXISTS or NOT IN), the method in [6] will weaken soundness. To settle this situation, an algorithm is put forward in [5] to meet the soundness requirements of the MINUS queries. But for those queries that contain NOT EXISTS or NOT IN, the algorithm cannot directly retain its soundness properties. In addition, there are still many other queries, and the algorithms of these queries are not working properly. Let us look at the following example.

© Springer Nature Singapore Pte Ltd. 2021
Y. Tian et al. (Eds.): ICBDS 2020, CCIS 1415, pp. 15–26, 2021.
https://doi.org/10.1007/978-981-16-3150-4_2

Table 1. Staff

Number	Name	Age	Telephone
1(Y)	Antony(Y)	31(Y)	13111111(Y)
2(Y)	Jerry(Y)	40(N)	13222222(N)
3(Y)	Tom(Y)	35(N)	*NULL*(N)
4(N)	Jimmy(N)	22(N)	13444444(N)
5(Y)	Mike(Y)	37(N)	13555555(N)

1. Example One

Suppose there are four parameters in the table "Staff": Number, name, age, and telephone, and Number is the primary key (as shown in Table 1). This article defines an FGAC strategy P1. P1 is located above the table "Staff", and it only allows Antony to read all his own data and all Number information as well as others' names, but Antony cannot read all the data of the staff whose Number = 3. FGAC policy P1 can be defined as follows:

- Strategy P1 for Antony table "Staff":

    - The limit of row-level strategy: " Number $\neq$ 3";
    - The limit of cell-level strategy of age: " Number $=$ 1"
    - The limit of cell-level strategy of telephone: " Number $=$ 1"

Based on FGAC strategy, each cell is tagged with "(Y)" or "(N)" to indicate whether this strategy allows the cell (see Table 1). Suppose Antony issues three queries:

- Q1 = "SELECT name

    FROM Staff
    WHERE telephone IS NULL";

- Q2 = "SELECT name

    FROM Staff
    WHERE Number > (SELECT COUNT(*) FROM Staff)";

- Q3 = "SELECT name

    FROM Staff
    WHERE name IN (SELECT name FROM Staff WHERE age > 32)";

For Q1, if do not consider FGAC strategy, the answer is {Tom}. However, under the FGAC strategy P1, the answer of the algorithm in [5], [6] is {Jerry, Tom, Mike}, including Jerry and Mike whose telephone number is not NULL. Obviously, this does not conform to the soundness requirements. For Q2 and Q3, the soundness properties cannot be retained as well.

According to the example, many queries in [5], and the algorithm in [6] still cannot meet the soundness requirements.

There is no algorithm to guarantee the soundness of all queries, since SQL is easy-to-use but has lots of high-level architectures and many complicated queries can be written.

Thus, it is actually necessary to know which SQL query in all cases can definitely retain its soundness for an algorithm. But the soundness definition in the literature [5] is for all queries, and it is so strict that we cannot discover an algorithm that meets this requirement. Therefore, a definition should be proposed that only defines the soundness of query or a kind of query.

2 Related Work and Background

2.1 Related Research

The Virtual Private Database (VPD) in ORACLE supports FGAC by the functions that achieve predicates based on the FGAC strategy [7]. When a query is issued, it will be modified to enforce FGAC execution by appending the predicate obtained from the related function to the WHERE clause. Users can define access control strategies through Sybase row-level access control, which the retrieving data from the table is limited [8]. LeFevre et al. first proposed to implement FGAC with a unit-level granularity in the Hippocratic database [6]. Agrawal et al. put forward the FGAC architecture, and improved SQL statements to describe column-level, row-level, and unit-level access control strategies [9]. Chaudhuri et al. suggested a fine-grained permission architecture that adds a predicate to authorization [3]. The program supports predicate authorization for specific columns, cell-level authorization with invalidity, authorization for process/function execution, and authorization with grant options. But the robustness of FGAC is not mentioned in all the above literature.

Wang et al. [5] put forward the formal concept of FGAC rightness in the database. The concept first proposed robustness and discussed why existing methods have limitations in some cases. Then, they proposed a marking method for concealing unauthorized data items and a query valuation algorithm in relational databases for FGAC. It settles the robustness weakness caused by the MINUS operation in the SQL statement. But it can neither guarantee soundness for all queries, nor specify which types of queries it can ensure soundness.

2.2 FGAC Strategy

The FGAC strategies description approaches could be summarized into three types: view-based methods, predicate-based methods, and data log-based methods.

View-Based Method

This method can be described through the view of access control permits in the view-based method. Views describe the data that users could access in the database. It is not same as the supported conventional SQL statement views. Similarly, users cannot access the base table directly, but can only view it using conventional SQL. But users are allowed by the view here to access the base table directly.

1. Access control on the basis of INGRES

The method of implementing FGAC on the basis of INGRES view is introduced by Stonebraker and Wong. The access rights of users are described by views, and the query modification technology is used to realize the FGAC. As for query modification, its basic meaning is to dynamically and transparently modify and execute SQL statements to guarantee that users cannot access prohibited data [10].

2. Access control on the basis of Motro

A query modification algorithm resembling INGRES is put forward by Motro [11]. If a query statement S is submitted, it can be considered as a view. When the view Q is derived from the safe collection view V, the access to Q is allowed. When Q is not derived from V, but V derives the sub-view set of Q, the access to the sub-view is allowed. The disadvantages are disjoint sub views generation by the algorithm and other problems.

Method Based on Predicate

The most representative predicate-based method is Oracle Virtual Private Database (VPD). The FGAC strategy returns SQL predicates by the strategy function definition. To realize FGAC strategy functions, the strategy functions are bound to basic tables or views. However, the description of the FGAC security strategy put forward by Oracle VPD is very complicated, thus the availability and scalability are relatively low.

Method Based on Data Log

B. Purevjii et al. proposed FGAC strategies, such as methods based on data logs [15]. They used Authorization Description Language (ADL) to describe FGAC. To solve the problem of security analysis of FGAC policies, a method description based on data log rules is provided. But it cannot be used directly in the DBMS, and must be converted to be effective further.

3   Dynamic Query Modification Algorithm Based on Key Attributes

For the relation R, we use CR to represent the set of all attributes in R. A definition is introduced first before the query modification algorithm is explained.

1. Definition One (key attribute of query relationship)

- For any query Q, R is the relationship within Q.

- For any attribute $A \in CR$, if A is part of the attribute set of the WHERE clause of Q, we say that A is the key attribute for which R represents Q.

In Example One, the attribute telephone is the key attribute of Q1's Staff because telephone is in the WHERE clause of Q1. For Q3, name and age are the key attributes of Staff for Q3, and age is the only key attribute of Staff for Q3 subquery. Here, an algorithm called the key attribute-based algorithm (KAB algorithm) will be explained. There are three steps:

Step 1: Create a temporary view for each relationship within the SQL query. The key attributes of Q can be obtained based on Definition One. Then, the row-level and unit-level strategy for these key attributes could be achieved by FGAC. As below, R is the relationship within the query, P_{row} is the row-level strategy and P_{cell} is the cell-level strategy. The operational relationship will be established as:

(SELECT *
FROM *R*
WHERE P_{row} and P_{cell})

Step 2: Use temporary views to replace these relationships.
Step 3: Use the "CASE" statement [12] to change each attribute in the SQL query select list.

Literature [9] introduces the KAB algorithm for SQL query in details.

2. Example Two

In Example One, two SQL queries Q1 and Q3 under the FGAC strategy P1 are introduced, and they are used to explain the modification method also. For Q1, the telephone is the only key attribute, the row-level strategy is "Number $\neq$ 4", and the cell-level strategy of the telephone is "Number $=$ 1". Therefore, the temporary view is:

(SELECT Number, name, age, telephone
FROM Staff
WHERE Number $\neq$ 4 and Number $=$ 1)

Because no unit-level strategy on the name, there is no "CASE" statement to replace the name in the changed query. The final modified query Q1$_{modified}$ is shown below.

- Q1$_{modified} =$

SELECT name
FROM (SELECT Number, name, age, telephone
FROM Staff
WHERE Number $\neq$ 4 and Number $=$ 1)

WHERE telephone IS NULL

The same method can be used to modify the query Q3 to $Q3_{modified}$. Assuming that there is a unit-level strategy on the attribute name "Number = 1", the changed query for Q1 is $Q1_{modified}$.

- $Q3_{modified}=$

SELECT name
FROM (SELECT Number, name, age, telephone
FROM Staff
WHERE Number $\neq$ 4 and Number = 1)
WHERE name NOT IN (SELECT name
FROM (SELECT Number, name, age, telephone
FROM Staff
WHERE Number $\neq$ 4 and Number = 1)
WHERE age > 28)

- $Q1_{modified} =$

SELECT CASE
WHEN Number = 1
THEN name ELSE NULL END AS name
FROM (SELECT Number, name, age, telephone
FROM Staff
WHERE Number $\neq$ 4 and Number = 1)
WHERE telephone IS NULL

In [12], in order to maintain security, for any constant c, by replacing the value of the key attribute of these rows with NULL and the valuation rules "NULL $\neq$ NULL" and "NULL $\neq$ c", you can delete rows from the result that may break security. The put forward algorithm directly deletes these rows that may violate security based on the FGAC strategy to establish a temporary view, so that the suggested method can also retain security.

4 Algorithm Performance Evaluation

4.1 Robustness Definition

In this section, we will focus on which type of SQL query, KAB algorithm can guarantee the soundness.

The definition of robustness was first proposed in literature [5]. However, it cannot be used to determine whether the algorithm is correct for a query or for a certain kind of query.

1. Definition Two

- Given two tuples $t_x = <x_1, x_2, \cdots, x_n>$ and $t_y = <y_1, y_2, \cdots, y_n>$, we say that t_x is contained by t_y (and written as $t_x \sqsubseteq t_y$) if and only if $\forall i \in [1 \ldots n]$ makes $(x_i = y_i \vee x_i = \Phi)$.
- $\Phi \neq \Phi$.
- For any constant c, $\Phi \neq c$.

  According to the above definition, the following attributes are obviously correct:
  Property 1:

- $t_1 = t_2 \Rightarrow t_1 \sqsubseteq t_2$.

  This symbol can be expanded to the following relationship:

2. Definition Three

- Taking two simple relations R1 and R2, we say that R1 is included in R2 (represented as $R1 \sqsubseteq R2$) if and only if $\forall t1 \in R1, \exists t2 \in R2$ makes $t1 \sqsubseteq t2$.

  According to the above definition, the following lemma will be proved.
  Lemma 1:

- R1 and R2 are two relations, so $R1 = R2 \Rightarrow R1 \sqsubseteq R2$.

  Lemma 2:
  R1, R1', R2 and R2' are relations such that

- $(R1' \sqsubseteq R1) \wedge (R2' \sqsubseteq R2) \Rightarrow (R1' \cup R2') \sqsubseteq (R1 \cup R2)$.

3. Definition Four

Considering query processing algorithm A, use FGAC strategy P and query Q on database D to output the result $R = A(D, P, Q)$. Let S represents the standard query response process, and S(D, Q) denotes the answer to Q when the database status is D and there is no FGAC policy.

- If and only if the following conditions are met, A of Q is reasonable, written as Sound(A, Q) = true:
- $\forall_D \forall_P A(D, P, Q) \sqsubseteq S(D, Q)$
- If A cannot retain the robustness of Q, Sound(A, Q) = false.

  According to the above definition, the soundness definition of Algorithm A defined in [5] corresponds to the following definition.

4. Definition Five

- For query Q and query processing algorithm A, if and only if $\forall$Q is Sound (A, Q) = true, A is written as Sound (A).

The definitions of soundness and lemma have been described above. In the following sections, we will use relational algebraic expressions (they are the foundation of query statements) to analyze soundness. The KAB algorithm can ensure the rationality of which type of SQL query.

4.2 Robustness of Relational Algebra Expression

σ and π below represent queries, which mean the selection and projection of relational algebra operations, respectively. π expands to $\pi_{(A, F, \Phi)}$,

- $\pi_{(A,F,\Phi)}(R) =$

  $\{t'[A]|$
  if $F(t)$ then $t'[A] = t[A]$
  else $t'[A] = \Phi, t \in R\}$

- $\pi_{(A1,F1,\Phi),\cdots,(An,Fn,\Phi)}(R) =$

  $\{(t'[A_1], \cdots, t'[A_n])|$
  if $F_i(t)$ then $t'[A_i] = t[A_i]$
  else $t'[A_i] = \Phi, i \in [1, \cdots, n], t \in R\}$

The following symbols are introduced first:

- D is database;
- R is relationship;
- t is tuple;
- A is attribute;
- F, F', $F_1\cdots F_n$, $F_1'\cdots F_n'$ are predicates;
- $\pi_{(A,true,\Phi)}(R) = \pi_A(R)$;
- $\pi_{(A1,true,\Phi), (A2,true,\Phi),\cdots,(An,true,\Phi)} (R) = \pi_{A1, A2,\cdots, An}(R)$.

The predicate definition is explained as below, which can simplify the description.

1. Definition 6

- There are two predicates: F and F'. If F is equal to the predicate of F', then it is defined as F' $\leq$ F
- $\forall$t, F'(t) = true $\Rightarrow$ F(t) = true

4.3 Robustness of KAB Algorithm

With relational algebra, four forms of query exist. "π", "σ", " $\times$ ", "$\cup$", "-" are five basic operations and other operations can be derived from them [13]. Only one table is involved in the first, multiple tables are involved in the second. For the other tables, set operations (such as "$\cup$" and "-") are used in combination with the first and second forms shown as below:

- Form1: $Q_{form1} = \pi_{(A1,A2,\cdots,An)}(\sigma_F(R1))$;
- Form2: $Q_{form2} = \pi_{(A1,A2,\cdots,An)}(\sigma_F(R1 \times \cdots \times Rm))$;
- Form3: $Q_{form3} = Q1 \cup Q2$, Q1 and Q2 have Form1 or Form2;
- Form4: $Q_{form4} = Q1-Q2$, Q1 and Q2 have Form1 or Form2.

In literature [10], a translator that converts the relevant SQL queries subset into relational algebra was put forward. By this, the SQL queries can be mapped to relational algebra. That is, if there is a SQL query Q, an expression where the relational algebra Q is equal to Q can be found.

5 Experiment

This experiment mainly describes the KAB algorithm performance. Since the method in [5] can retain the soundness of queries including MINUS, this paper mainly compares the KAB algorithm performance. with the algorithm in [5]. The experimental method in [5] is mainly used to compare performance. First, the experimental parameters of this article are introduced as follows:

- Table Size means the tuples number in the table;
- Selectivity means the percentage of tuples selected by the query that has been issued in the table;
- Disclosure probability means the possibility that cells in sensitive attributes can be disclosed;
- Operational relationship probability means the percentage of tuples in the operating relationship of the published query in the table.

5.1 Experiment Environment

The performance is measured using a table formed on the basis of Wisconsin Benchmark [14], which is the same as the table in [5]. The query modification method is implemented using Java. The experiment needs a desktop computer with 2.8 GHz Intel Core i5-6300 CPU, 4 GB RAM and 500 GB disk, Windows 10 operating system, and Oracle 10 g DBMS.

When there is no negative in the query, modify the query with the method in [5], and it can only guarantee the soundness of the query including MINUS. Thus, only queries containing MINUS are used to measure performance in the tests of this paper. To measure the queries execution cost, each query run 6 times, and the query cache and buffer pool were refreshed between any two query executions. The following results provide the average performance for each query.

5.2 Experiment Results and Analysis

For convenience, KAB algorithm is called as KAB here, and the method in [5] is called as Sound, the method in [12] is called as Hippo, and the general query evaluation (without access control strategy) is called as Unmodified. Here only the algorithm scalability is described. This article shows the selectivity impact, the disclosure probability influence, and the operational relationship probability impact.

The query modification algorithm scalability is measured by changing the table size. In order to evaluate the cost, the case is selected with the selectivity of 100%, the probability of disclosure at 25%, and the probability of operating relationship at 100%. The experimental result is shown in Fig. 1. KAB, Hippo and Unmodified are better than Sound. For the Sound method, when the table size is 100000 and 200000, the cost is 2833 and 34495 ms, respectively. The reason why Sound is not scalable is that it employs a join operation to provide reasonable answers to MINUS. But, to preserve soundness, only predicates in the WHERE clause are added. Thus, when the table size increases, KAB is better than Sound, and the effect is similar to Hippo, and Hippo cannot retain soundness.

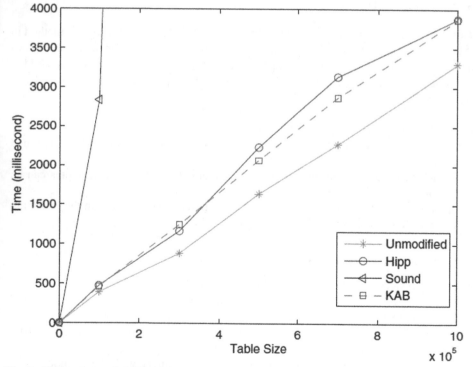

Fig. 1. Table size scalability. Selectivity = 100%, disclosure probability = 75%, operation relationship probability = 100%.

6 Conclusion

In this research, we first propose an algorithm to ensure the soundness of certain SQL query types. Then we expanded and improved the theory of robustness, and introduced new features on robustness by relational algebraic expressions. The query represented by relational algebra can be summarized into four forms, which are analyzed separately for their soundness. According to these theories, the proposed algorithm can ensure robustness for any type of SQL query. Finally, the algorithm performance evaluation is conducted. Experimental results indicate that the algorithm hardly increases the cost and is feasible.

In this article, we only study the SELECT operation. But the operations controlled by FGAC are SELECT, UPDATE, INSERT, and DELETE. Therefore, we will consider other operations in FGAC in future work.

Acknowledgement. This paper is supported by the science and technology project of State Grid Corporation of China: "Research and Application of Key Technology of Data Sharing and Distribution Security for Data Center" (Grand No. 5700-202090192A-0-0-00).

References

1. Bingyu, Z., Huanguo, Z., Xi, G., et al.: A fine-grained authorization model based on credibility in trusted network connection. J. Wuhan Univ. (Sci. Edn.) **02**, 147–150 (2010)
2. Wu, C.: Fine-grained authorization delegation method based on quantitative roles. Comput. Eng. **13**, 36–38 + 42 (2012)
3. Chaudhuri, S., Dutta, T., Sudarshan, S.: Fine grained authorization through predicated grants. In: IEEE International Conference on Data Engineering. IEEE (2007)
4. Sun, W., Shucheng, Y., Lou, W., et al.: Protecting your right: verifiable attribute-based keyword search with fine-grained owner-enforced search authorization in the cloud. In: IEEE INFOCOM 2014. IEEE (2014)
5. Wang, Q., Yu, T., Li, N., et al.: On the correctness criteria of fine-grained access control in relational databases. In: International Conference on Very Large Data Bases. DBLP (2007)
6. Calvio, A.: A simple method for limiting disclosure in continuous microdata based on principal component analysis. J. Off. Stats **33**(1) (2017)
7. Yanan, W., Yiqiu, S.: Performance optimization of oracle database application system. Manufact. Autom. **32**(008), 204–206 (2010)
8. Sybase adaptive server enterprise 12.5, System Administration Guide. Row Level Access Control. http://sybooks.sybase.com/onlinebooks
9. Agrawal, R., Bird, P., Grandison, T., et al.: Extending relational database systems to automatically enforce privacy policies. In: International Conference on Data Engineering. IEEE Computer Society (2005)
10. Xiaofeng, L., Dengguo, F., Chaowu, C., et al.: Access control model based on attributes. J. Commun. **04**, 95–103 (2008)
11. Han, Y., Zhang, Z., Wang, Y.: Access control model based on authorization view. In: Proceedings of the 2005 National Theoretical Computer Science Annual Conference (2005)
12. LeFevre, K., Agrawal, R., Ercegovac, V., Ramakrishnan, R., Xu, Y., DeWitt, D.: Limiting disclosure in hippocratic databases. In: Proceedings of VLDB, Toronto, Canada, August 2004

13. Ceri, S., Gottlob, G., et al.: Translating SQL into relational algebra: optimization, semantics, and equivalence of SQL queries. IEEE Trans. Softw. Eng. **SE-11**(4), 324–345 (2006)
14. DeWitt, D.J.: The wisconsin benchmark: past, present, and future, Technical report (1993)
15. Purevjii, B.-O., Aritsugi, M., Imai, S., Kanamori, Y., Pancake, Cherri M.: Protecting personal data with various granularities: a logic-based access control approach. In: Hao, Y., et al. (eds.) CIS 2005. LNCS (LNAI), vol. 3802, pp. 548–553. Springer, Heidelberg (2005). https://doi.org/10.1007/11596981_81

Research on Application Technology and Security of VoLTE in Power Wireless Private Network

Wei-wei Kong[1(✉)], Long Liu[1], Xing-qi Wei[2], Shan-yu Bi[1], and Xin-lei Yang[1]

[1] NARI Group Corporation, State Grid Electric Power Research Institute, Nanjing, China
[2] State Grid Jiangsu Electric Power Co., Ltd, Nanjing, China

Abstract. Based on the wireless private network established by electric power, the application of VoLTE technology in power wireless private network is studied, and through the test scheme, test the performance index of wireless power network in three voice solutions based on multiple terminals and VOLTE. The performance index includes voice and video call quality under different wireless signal intensities, as well as call quality in the process of road movement. The analysis of Volte research in power wireless private network supports the application of power wireless private network in the future, provides technical support, and lays a solid foundation for the popularization and application of power wireless private network, and the security of the power network is guaranteed.

Keywords: VoLTE · Smart grid · Road test · Voice quality · Network security

1 Introduction

Energy Internet is a new type of power network node composed of distributed energy acquisition device, distributed energy storage device and various types of load, which combines advanced power electronics technology, information technology and intelligent management technology to realize energy peer-to-peer exchange and sharing network with two-way energy flow [1–5].

Wireless communication has the advantages of ubiquitous access, flexible deployment, fast construction and so on, it has unique advantages in meeting the information and communication needs of the global energy Internet [6–9]. It makes up for the problem that optical fiber communication can not cover all the business scope of power system because of the limitation of terrain, cost and so on [9–12].

VoLTE opens the way to mobile broadband voice, which brings two aspects of value to operators, one is to improve the efficiency of wireless spectrum and reduce the network cost, and the other is to enhance user experience [13–15]. In this paper, the deployment and networking scheme of VoLTE service in power wireless private network are studied, and a pilot verification project is established.

In this paper, the deployment and networking scheme of VoLTE service in power wireless private network are studied, and a pilot verification project is established.

© Springer Nature Singapore Pte Ltd. 2021
Y. Tian et al. (Eds.): ICBDS 2020, CCIS 1415, pp. 27–40, 2021.
https://doi.org/10.1007/978-981-16-3150-4_3

According to the mobile characteristics and network coverage characteristics of the mobile terminal of the power wireless private network, the application model of the VoLTE in the power wireless special network is proposed, and the optimization direction is pointed out through analysis.

2 System Architecture of VoLTE

There are three solutions for LTE voice in the industry, which are VoLTE, CSFB and SGLTE, respectively [16]. The VOLTE and the CSFB are standardization scheme in 3GPP, and the SGLTE is the terminal implementation scheme, wherein the VoLTE is the ultimate scheme of the mobile 4G voice solution. SGLTE does not need to change the network, and both VOLTE and CSFB need to modify the network [16, 17].

In the VoLTE, it uses IMS as the business control layer system, and EPC only as the bearing layer [18]. The switching of SRVCC solves the problem of voice continuity, and the delay of call time is short. The network frame diagram of VoLTE is as follows (Fig. 1).

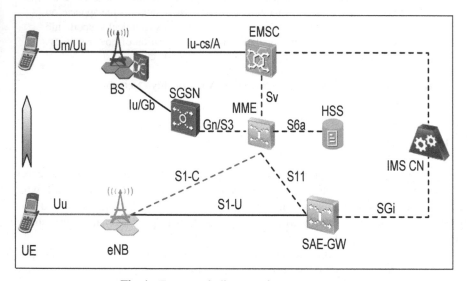

Fig. 1. Framework diagram of VoTLE network

The protocol architecture of VoLTE is as follows. As can be seen from the Fig. 2, the sip protocol only supports both the terminal and the IMS, and it's just a transmission function for wireless access networks.

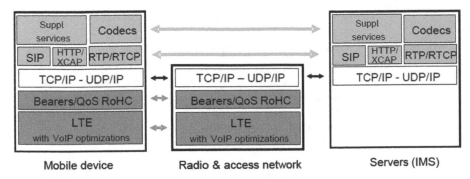

Fig. 2. Protocol architecture of VoLTE

3 Analysis of User Requirements in Power Network

The wireless special network can support the construction of smart grid, support distribution automation, marketing load control, power collection, smart home, new energy grid-connected communication, operation inspection and repair monitoring and other smart grid services, to meet the requirement of reliability, security, real-time (Tables 1 and 2).

Table 1. Demand analysis of power distribution automation services

	Department	Name of the service	Irish coefficient	Delay requirements	Quantity demand
1	Operation monitoring	Distribution automation	1	<500 ms	1000
2	Distribution transportation inspection room	Robot inspection	1	<2 s	30
3		Environmental monitoring	1	<2 s	15
4		Three-dimensional emergency repair	0.3	<2 s	15
5		Field remote management and visualization	0.3	<2 s	15

Table 2. Demand analysis of Smart grid extension service

	Department	Name of the service	Irish coefficient	Delay requirements	Quantity demand
1	Transformation and transportation room	Digitization and Informatization Management of Substation equipment	0.3	<2 s	15
2		Remote video monitoring and application of maintenance site	0.3	<2 s	15
3	Power transmission and inspection room	Intelligent Monitoring of Transmission Line Operation State	0.3	<2 s	10
4	Cable inspection room	Popularization and Application of Intelligent grounding Box for Power Cable	1	<2 s	60
5	Sales department	Intelligent building construction	0.1	<2 s	10
6		Scenery storage microgrid	1	<2 s	15
7		Smart home	1	<2 s	1000
8		Demand response information platform	0.1	<2 s	15
9		Electricity Information Collection	0.1	<2 s	5000
10		Power management service platform	0.5	<2 s	150
11		Electric automobile charging pile	1	<2 s	30
12		Shore charging pile	1	<2 s	15

(*continued*)

Table 2. (*continued*)

	Department	Name of the service	Irish coefficient	Delay requirements	Quantity demand
13		Electric load control	1	<2 s	100

4 Test Environment of VoLTE

The system is composed of wireless private network, IMS special network, administrative mobile background service and mobile soft terminal [19]. In which the IMS private network and the administrative mobile background service are deployed in the machine room, the wireless private network is deployed at the power company headquarters building, and the base station of wireless private network is in the substation. The deployed wireless private network is connected with the IMS private network and the administrative mobile background service through the SDH channel. The composition architecture of the system is as shown in the figure [20] (Fig. 3).

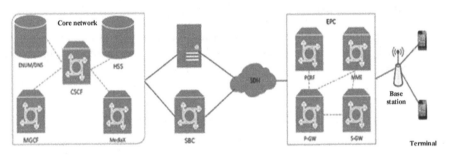

Fig. 3. Architecture of wireless private network system

The power wireless private network provides three voice solutions, the first is UC client;2, the second is administration client; the third is VoLTE. Scenarios 1 and 2 belong to the VoIP pattern, in this mode, the client software needs to be deployed on the mobile phone. The service platform is deployed on the IMS core network, and the terminal is accessed via wireless private network and registered to the service platform. Solution 3 does not need to deploy client software on power private network mobile phones. The performance indicators of voice and video under the three voice solutions are tested in this test.

Performance index refers to the quality of voice and video calls under different wireless signal intensities. The specific performance indicators are shown in the following table. The test car runs at medium speed depending on the actual road traffic conditions, and the vehicle speed is about 30 km/hour (Table 3).

Table 3. Alternative condition

	RSRP	SINR
Test point in good condition	−85 ~ −95 dBm	16–25 dB
Test points in medium condition	−95 ~ −105 dBm	11–15 dB
Test points in poor condition	−105 ~ −115dBm	3–10 dB
Test points in very poor condition	<−115dBm	<−3 dB

5 Test Result

5.1 Test of Voice Quality

The test topology diagram shows that a pair of test terminals are attached to the power wireless private network and registered to the UC background and the administrative background respectively (Fig. 4).

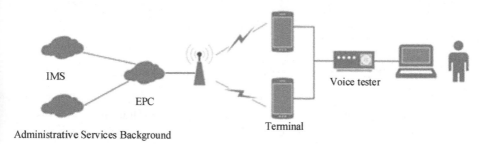

Fig. 4. Fixed-point voice test topology

Two test terminals are connected to the voice tester, and one test terminal acts as the caller and calls the other terminal. After dialing, sending the voice through the voice tester to the called terminal through the calling terminal, and returning the voice to the voice tester after being accepted by the called terminal. The test results are as follows.

(1) Voice test under good conditions

RSRP = −67 dBm and SINR = 28 dB, and the test site is 1 km from the base station by the side of the road (Tables 4 and 5)

Table 4. MOS value of speech quality (a good place)

Value of MOS / Terminal	Administrative communication	UC Client
Terminal1	4.01	4.37
Terminal2	3.43	4.06

Table 5. End-to-end call delay (a good place)

Delay / Termianl	Administrative communication（ms）	UC Client（ms）
Terminal1	430	400
Terminal2	530	420

(2) Voice test under medium conditions

RSRP = −98 dBm and SINR = 16 dB, and the test site is 3 km from the base station by the side of the road (Tables 6 and 7)

Table 6. MOS value of speech quality (a general place)

Value of MOS / Terminal	Administrative communication	UC Client
Terminal1	4.03	4.39
Terminal2	3.61	4.11

Table 7. End-to-end call delay (a general place)

Delay / Termianl	Administrative communication（ms）	UC Client（ms）
Terminal1	440	410
Terminal2	540	420

(3) Voice test under poor conditions

RSRP = −108 dBm and SINR = 11 dB, and the test site is 5.5 km from the base station by the side of the road (Tables 8 and 9)

Table 8. MOS value of speech quality (a bad place)

Value of MOS / Terminal	Administrative communication	UC Client
Terminal1	1.70	2.46
Terminal2	3.26	3.80

Table 9. End-to-end call delay (a bad place)

Delay / Termianl	Administrative communication (ms)	UC Client (ms)
Terminal1	720	680
Terminal2	590	430

(4) Voice test under very poor conditions

RSRP = −120 dBm and SINR = 0 dB, and the test site is 7 km from the base station by the side of the road (Tables 10 and 11)

Table 10. MOS value of speech quality (a very poor place)

Value of MOS / Terminal	Administrative communication	UC Client
Terminal1	无法接通	2.15
Terminal2	2.73	3.66

Table 11. End-to-end call delay (a very poor place)

Delay / Termianl	Administrative communication （ms）	UC Client （ms）
Terminal1	Unable to connect	930
Terminal2	770	560

6 Test of Video Quality

The test topology diagram shows that a pair of test terminals are attached to the power wireless private network and registered to the UC background and the administrative background respectively (Fig. 5).

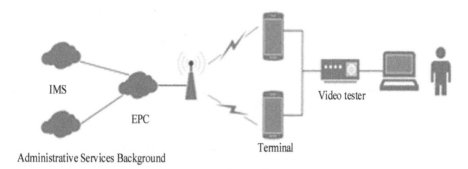

IMS

EPC

Administrative Services Background

Video tester

Terminal

Fig. 5. Fixed-point voice test topology

Two test terminals are connected to a voice tester, and one test terminal acts as a caller and calls the other terminal. After dialing, the video stream is sent to the called

Table 12. Test results of video quality index (a good place)

Quality of video / Terminal	Administrative communication	UC Client			
		MOS	Video frame rate （fps）	Frozen rate （%）	Damage rate （%）
Terminal 1	The screen is not clear	3.1	19.0	0.2	3.5
Terminal 2	Nonsupport	2.6	17.8	0.1	10.4
Terminal 3	Nonsupport	2.1	13.8	0.2	10.6
Terminal 4	Average 10 seconds, disconnect.	1.1	13.6	0.2	29.3

terminal through the calling terminal through the video quality tester, and the called terminal receives it and returns it to the video quality tester.

(1) Video test under good conditions
     RSRP = −67 dBm and SINR = 28 dB, and the test site is 1 km from the base station by the side of the road (Table 12)
(2) Video test under medium conditions
     RSRP = −98 dBm and SINR = 16 dB, and the test site is 3 km from the base station by the side of the road (Table 13)

Table 13. Test results of video quality index (a general place)

Quality of video / Terminal	Administrative communication	UC Client			
		MOS	Video frame rate (fps)	Frozen rate (%)	Damage rate (%)
Terminal 1	Nonsupport	2.1	12.2	0.5	9.9

(3) Video test under poor conditions
     RSRP = −108 dBm and SINR = 11 dB, and the test site is 5.5 km from the base station by the side of the road (Table 14)

Table 14. Test results of video quality index (a bad place)

Quality of video / Terminal	Administrative communication	UC Client			
		MOS	Video frame rate (fps)	Frozen rate (%)	Damage rate (%)
Terminal 1	Nonsupport	2.2	10.8	0	6.6

(4) Video test under very poor conditions
     RSRP = −120 dBm and SINR = 0 dB, and the test site is 7 km from the base station by the side of the road (Table 15)

Table 15. Test results of video quality index (a bad place)

Quality of video / Terminal	Administrative communication	UC Client			
		MOS	Video frame rate (fps)	Frozen rate (%)	Damage rate (%)
Terminal 1	The screen is not clear	Easy to drop line			
Terminal 2	Nonsupport	Video communication is normal.			
Terminal 3	Nonsupport	2.1	12.9	0.4	7.8
Terminal 4	Average 10 seconds, disconnect.	Video communication is normal.			

7 Road Test

(1) Test terminal is terminal 1, and the call mode is administrative communication. The road test results are shown in the figure below (Fig. 6).

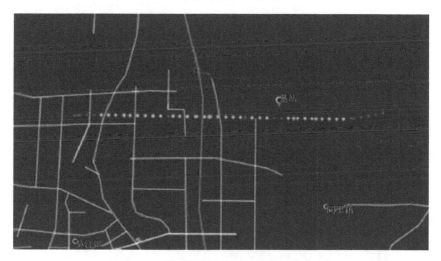

Fig. 6. Road test results

(2) Test terminal is terminal 2, and the call mode is administrative communication. The road test results are shown in the figure below (Fig. 7).
(3) Test terminal is terminal 1, and the call mode is UC Client. The road test results are shown in the figure below (Fig. 8).
(4) Test terminal is terminal 2, and the call mode is UC Client. The road test results are shown in the figure below (Fig. 9).

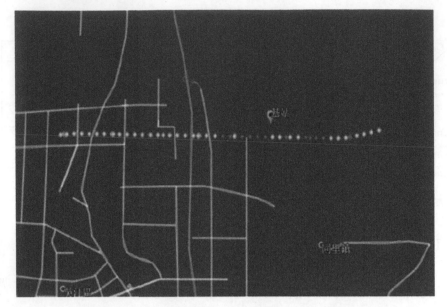

Fig. 7. Road test results

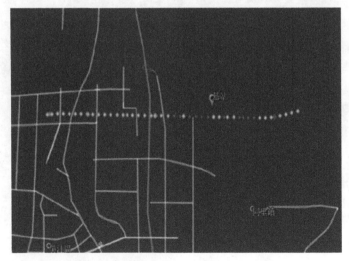

Fig. 8. Road test results

The green marker in the above test results indicates that the MOS value of voice is more than 4, the yellow marker indicates that the MOS value of voice is more than 3, and the red marker indicates that the MOS value of voice is less than 3. From the above test results, it can be seen that in the same call mode, the call performance of terminal 2 is better than that of terminal 1 at the edge far from the base station. In the UC mode,

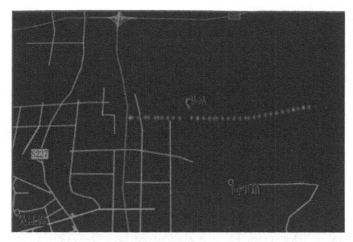

Fig. 9. Road test results

the MOS value of voice is mostly > 4, while in the administrative mode, the MOS value of voice is between 3 and 4.

8 Conclusion

In this paper, based on the wireless private network, the application of VoLTE technology in power wireless private network is studied, and the performance index of power wireless private network in three voice solutions based on multiple terminals and VOLTE is tested. The performance indexes include the voice, the video call quality under different wireless signal strengths, and the call quality in the course of road motion. The analysis of Volte research in power wireless private network supports the application of power wireless private network in the future, provides technical support, and lays a solid foundation for the popularization and application of power wireless private network.

References

1. Yao, J.: Random access technology of electric dedicated LTE network based on power priority. Autom. Electr. Power Syst. **40**(10), 127–131 (2016)
2. Cao, J., Liu, J., Li, X.: A power wireless broadband technology scheme for smart power distribution and utilization network. Autom. Electr. Power Syst. **37**(11), 76–80 (2013)
3. Yu, J., Liu, J., Cai, S.: Performance simulation on TD-LTE electric power wireless private network. Guangdong Electr. Power **30**(1), 39–45 (2017)
4. Sun, S., Chen, Y.: Research on LTE power wireless private network for service coverage. Electr. Power Inf. Commun. Technol. **13**(4), 6–10 (2015)
5. Yu, J., Liu, J., Cai, S.: Research on LTE wireless network planning in electric power system. Electr. Power Inf. Commun. Technol. **10**(2), 7–11 (2016)
6. Gao, X., Zhu, J., Chen, Y.: Research on multi-services bearing solution of LTE power wireless private network. Electr. Power Inf. Commun. Technol. **12**(12), 26–29 (2014)
7. Zhang, J.: VoLTE: leads the way of 4G voice. Commun. World **35**(1), 47–53 (2015)

8. Sedlacek, I., Lindholm, F., Holm, J.: Methods and apparatus for supporting the implementation of IMS service continuity. Biol. Blood Marrow Transplant. J. Am. Soc. Blood Marrow Transplant. **20**(8), 1104–1111 (2014)
9. Li, B., Zhou, J., Ren, X.: Research on key issues of TD-LTE network optimization. Telecom Eng. Techn. Stand. **1**, 57–61 (2015)
10. Zheng, L., Tse, D.N.C.: Diversity and multiplexing: a fundamental tradeoff in multiple antenna channels. IEEE Trans. Inf. Theor. **49**, 1073–1096 (2003). https://doi.org/10.1109/tit.2003.810646
11. Qiu, J., Ding, G., Wu, Q., et al.: Hierarchical resource allocation framework for hyper-dense small cell networks. IEEE Access **4**(99), 8657–8669 (2017)
12. Chen, X., Jiang, Y., Wang, X., et al.: Research on the development of energy internet from the perspective of internet. Autom. Electr. Power Syst. **41**(9), 2–11 (2017)
13. Gao, F., Zeng, R., Qu, L., et al.: Research on Identification of concept and characteristics of energy internet. Electr. Power, 1–6 (2018)
14. Li, W., Chen, B., Wu, Q., et al.: Applied research of TD-LTE power wireless broadband private metwork. Telecommun. Electr. Power Syst. **33**(241), 82–87 (2012)
15. Hamidi, M.M., Edmonson, W.W., Afghah, F.: A non-vooperative game theoretic approach for power allocation in interstatellite communication. In: 2017 IEEE International Conference on Wireless for Space and Extreme Environments (WISEE), pp. 13–18 (2017)
16. Li, B., Zhou, J., Ren, X.: Research on key issues of TD-LTE network optimization. Telecom Eng. Tech. Stand. **1**, 57–61 (2015)
17. Bahnasse, A., Louhab, F.E., Oulahyane, H.A., et al.: Novel SDN architecture for smart MPLS traffic engineering-Diffserv aware management. Fut. Gen. Comput. Syst. **11**(2), 212–219 (2018)
18. Zheng, L., Tse, D.N.C.: Diversity and multiplexing: a fundamental tradeoff in multiple antenna channels. IEEE Trans. Inf. Theor. (2003)
19. Fernekeb, A., Klein, A., Wegmann, B., et al.: Load dependent interference margin for link budget calculations of OFDM networks. IEEE Commun. Lett. **12**, 398–400 (2008)
20. Pickholz, P., Milstein, L., Schilling, D.: Spread spectrum for mobile communication. IEEE Trans. Veh. Technol. **VT40**, 231–233 (2001)

Semi-supervised Time Series Anomaly Detection Model Based on LSTM Autoencoder

Hui Xiao[1,2], Donghai Guan[1,2(✉)], Rui Zhao[1,2], Weiwei Yuan[1,2], Yaofeng Tu[1], and Asad Masood Khattak[3]

[1] Nanjing University of Aeronautics and Astronautics, Nanjing, China
{xiaohui822,dhguan,zrui821,yuanweiwei}@nuaa.edu.cn
[2] Collaborative Innovation Center of Novel Software Technology and Industrialization, Nanjing, China
[3] Zayed University, Abu Dhabi, UAE
Asad.Khattak@zu.ac.ae

Abstract. Nowadays, time series data is more and more likely to appear in various real-world systems, such as power plants, medical care, etc. In these systems, time series anomaly detection is necessary, which involves predictive maintenance, intrusion detection, anti-fraud, cloud platform monitoring and management, etc. Generally, the anomaly detection of time series is regarded as an unsupervised learning problem. However, in a real scenario, in addition to a large set of unlabeled data, there is usually a small set of available labeled data, such as normal or abnormal data sets labeled by experts. Only a few methods use labeled data, and the existing semi-supervised algorithms are not yet suitable for the field of time series anomaly detection. In this work, we propose a semi-supervised time series anomaly detection model based on LSTM autoencoder. We improve the loss function of the LSTM autoencoder so that it can be affected by unlabeled data and labeled data at the same time, and learn the distribution of unlabeled data and labeled data at the same time by minimizing the loss function. In a large number of experiments on the Yahoo! Webscope S5 and NAB data sets, we compared the performance of the unsupervised model and the semi-supervised model of the same network framework to prove that the performance of the semi-supervised model is improved compared to the unsupervised model.

Keywords: Time series · Anomaly detection · Semi-supervised learning · Autoencoder · LSTM

1 Introduction

With the development of technology, more and more fields have begun to carry out digital management, and various sensors are used for data monitoring. These sensors have generated a large amount of time series data. Time series data can be defined as data arranged based on time, which generally has the characteristics of large data volume and large dimensions. Detecting abnormal conditions in the time series in time can help promptly take measures to investigate the source of the abnormality and solve the

© Springer Nature Singapore Pte Ltd. 2021
Y. Tian et al. (Eds.): ICBDS 2020, CCIS 1415, pp. 41–53, 2021.
https://doi.org/10.1007/978-981-16-3150-4_4

problem. The ability to detect time series anomalies in real time is a necessary capability in today's digital industry. For example, in the monitoring of an online service system, we need to monitor various indicators. The timely detection of abnormalities represents an earlier resolution.

The research of time series anomaly detection has been developed for a long time [1, 2]. However, traditional algorithms either fail to obtain better anomaly detection accuracy, or cannot be applied well in big data scenarios. The reason for the problem is due to the unique particularity of time series compared with traditional discrete data. The particularities of time series are as follows:

1) The relationship between time series data is very complex and changeable. In addition to time dependence, there may also be trend mutations and seasonality among data.
2) The labeling cost of time series is too high. Because the abnormality determination of time series requires context analysis and comparison, manual time series labeling is a very challenging and costly work.

In recent years, the research of deep learning has made great progress [3]. In the field of time series, deep learning has gradually developed and applied. In time series anomaly detection tasks, how the algorithm learns the time dependence of the data and effectively extracts the time features from the original data is a core issue. In order to solve this core problem, recurrent neural networks (RNN) and long-short-term memory (LSTM) networks have become algorithm models suitable for extracting the time characteristics of original data. Many time series anomaly detection algorithms based on RNN and LSTM have also been proposed [4, 5], and achieved certain results in practical applications. On the other hand, due to the high cost of time series labeling, most supervised learning algorithms are not suitable for most time series anomaly detection, so unsupervised time series anomaly detection algorithms have become a further research direction. Among many algorithms, the sequence-to-sequence structure autoencoder algorithm is widely used in time series anomaly detection, and various autoencoder-based anomaly detection algorithms have been proposed. However, due to the limitations of unsupervised algorithms, unsupervised time series anomaly detection algorithms have problems in performance indicators. In view of the actual background, in addition to a large amount of unlabeled data, there may be a small amount of labeled data. Semi-supervised learning combines a small amount of labeled data that may exist with a large amount of unlabeled data to achieve improved performance indicators of the algorithm model. Semi-supervised learning uses a large amount of unlabeled data for training, and then uses a small amount of labeled data to approximate the real value, which has been proven in the improvement of algorithm model performance indicators.

This paper studies a semi-supervised time series anomaly detection algorithm based on LSTM autoencoder. The algorithm is dedicated to using a small amount of labeled data to improve the performance of autoencoder. The contributions of this article include the following aspects:

1) First, we propose a new LSTM-based autoencoder. By correspondingly changing the loss function of the autoencoder, a small amount of labeled data can further

differentiate the reconstructed data of the autoencoder through the influence on the loss function. Make the reconstruction error of abnormal data larger and the reconstruction error of normal data smaller, so as to achieve the purpose of abnormal detection.

2) Finally, the effectiveness of the model is verified by testing on three actual time series data sets. Experimental results show that compared with unsupervised algorithms, the corresponding semi-supervised algorithms have better anomaly detection accuracy.

2 Related Work

The research on time series anomaly detection has a long history. The earliest known related research is in 1972. Fox used an autoregressive prediction model and completed anomaly detection after statistical testing based on prediction errors [6]. Before the advent of machine learning technology, most of the research on time series anomaly detection was based on statistics [7, 8]. After the advent of machine learning technology, it began to be widely used in time series anomaly detection. According to several methods of time series anomaly detection, here we summarize two different ideas: one is based on prediction error, and the other is based on reconstruction error.

Methods based on prediction errors belong to the category of regression. This type of method uses some form of time series prediction model to compare actual observations with model predictions and classify them based on the prediction errors between the actual values and the predictions. There are multiple methods available for the prediction part of this method. Autoregressive moving average (ARMA) [9], which is widely used in many fields, is also used in time series anomaly detection. In order to solve the shortcomings of ARMA that it is difficult to deal with seasonal data sets, seasonal ARMA (SARMA) [10] and multilayer perceptron (MLP) methods [11] are proposed. In [12], the ARMA model and MLP are combined for sequence prediction. For prediction errors, a simple threshold is used to identify anomalies.

With the development of recurrent neural networks (RNN), LSTM and GRU can better simulate the particularity of univariate time series data. The method proposed in [13] proves that neural networks have a better ability to simulate the variability that exists in univariate systems. In [14], RNN is used for regression. Before the data is passed to the accumulator, it is compared with the threshold to determine the abnormality. When the data exceeds the threshold, it is marked as abnormal and the accumulator counts up, otherwise the accumulator decrements by a larger factor, so as to measure the collective anomaly for a long time. In [15], deep RNN was used to detect anomalies in online time series, and while normalizing the input data, the neural network was incrementally retrained so that the neural network could adapt to the drift of the data set, which proved that the neural network is Applicability in the field of sequence anomaly detection. In this method, by setting multiple different time steps, according to the prediction errors of multiple time steps, abnormal judgment is made in a way of scoring. Although RNN has made some progress in time series forecasting, there are still challenges in the work of abnormal classification based on forecast errors. In [16], Xie et al. used the Gaussian Naive Bayes model to analyze the prediction error to process the output of the RNN model, and finally output the abnormal judgment result. Bontesmps et al. [17] defined the minimum period of collective anomaly, calculated the error measurement caused by time changes, and concentrated on monitoring the collective anomaly. In [18], an indefinite, dynamically changing and unsupervised threshold method is proposed. This method does not need to make Gaussian assumptions on the past smooth prediction error distribution, and to a certain extent avoids the problems that may occur when the parameter assumptions are violated. This method determines the threshold under the influence of the current prediction error sequence by identifying the extreme value of the smooth prediction error, and uses the threshold for anomaly detection.

Methods based on reconstruction errors belong to the category of non-regression. Such methods usually use auto-encoder models to pass actual observations to a hidden layer with fewer neurons, and compress the original data. Then expand it to the output layer according to the actual observation value format, and output the reconstructed value. The reconstructed value is compared with the actual observation value, and classification is made according to the reconstruction error between the actual value and the reconstructed value. In [19], the sequential data of the mobile phone acquired from the resource-constrained sensor device for a period of time is used for the reconstruction of the autoencoder, and the abnormality is detected based on the reconstruction error of the shallow autoencoder network.

The compression of time series data by autoencoders can be divided into two categories from feature extraction: temporal feature extraction and spatial feature extraction. Most of the existing studies only consider the extraction of one of these features for anomaly detection, and some studies combine convolutional neural networks (CNN) and RNN, while considering the extraction of temporal and spatial features. The excellent effect of CNN on spatial feature extraction in other studies has led researchers to apply it to time series. However, CNN is generally used to process images, so the convolution kernel is set to two dimensions. Time series are generally univariate or multivariate sequences, which do not match the two-dimensional convolution kernel, so the time series need to be formatted. In [20], a method of projecting univariate time series onto two-dimensional images was proposed, making CNN suitable for spatial feature extraction of time series. A multivariate CNN was proposed in [21] to classify multivariate time series. These methods provide an effective way to extract the spatial features of time series and improve the performance of different classifiers. However, only extracting the spatial features of the time series will result in the loss of the time feature information of the data [22].

Because it can capture the relationship between data over a period of time, RNN is a neural network suitable for processing time series. RNN will use hidden units to retain part of the input data as historical information at each time step. However, the capacity of hidden units is limited and cannot be stored indefinitely. This will cause the loss of historical information, which will cause the gradient to disappear when the time series exceeds the maximum length of time for the RNN to capture the data relationship. In order to solve the problem of gradient disappearance caused by long-term storage, the LSTM and GRU systems simulate the memory and forgetting functions by using gate units to store new information and forget historical information. The advantages of RNN for temporal feature extraction make it very popular in time series data analysis.

In [23], Kraim et al. proposed an LSTM with an attention mechanism, which combined with CNN to jointly extract features of time series data. From the experimental results, LSTM improves the performance of the full convolutional network. In [24], Sutskever et al. proposed an RNN-based autoencoder model, which uses an encoder to extract and store temporal features of the input sequence received at each time step. The RNN-based decoder receives the encoded information and refactor it. In [25], Malhotra et al. applied LSTM-based autoencoders to time series anomaly detection for the first time, and based on experimental results proved that the performance of autoencoders for unpredictable data is better than prediction-based methods. The method of Malhotra et al. uses only normal data for the training of the autoencoder to obtain the data distribution characteristics of the normal data, so as to use the error between the decoded data and the original data for anomaly detection.

Most of the above two different directions of methods are unsupervised learning methods, so they solve the problem of time series data labeling cost in the context of big data, but unsupervised learning methods have certain problems in universality and performance. Since the data generally has partial labels, semi-supervised learning methods have emerged. Semi-supervised methods can make better use of labeled and unlabeled data, so that the model performance is better than using labeled or unlabeled data alone [26]. In [27], Cheng et al. combined semi-supervised and temporal convolutional networks (TCN) to propose a semi-supervised layered stacked TCN, and through experimental results showed that the introduction of semi-supervised learning methods improves the performance of the model. In [28], Ruff et al. proposed a semi-supervised deep support vector data description (DEEP SVDD) algorithm. In the data mapping and information entropy extraction steps, labeled data is used for improvement, thereby improving the performance of the model.

3   Proposed Anomaly Detection Scheme

In this section, we first introduce the notation used in this article and give a statement of the problem we want to study. Then, the function and realization of the model are introduced in detail. Finally, the architecture and hyperparameters are introduced.

3.1   Symbols and Problem Statement

For a time series $x = (x^1, x^2, \ldots, x^n)^T = (x_1, x_2, \ldots, x_t) \in R^{n \times t}$, where t is the timestamp of each value, n is the feature. In this article, the input sequence only considers the univariate sequence, and each time step has only one feature, so n $= 1$. In the case of a semi-supervised algorithm, there are two sets of time series: unlabeled time series x_u and labeled time series x_{label}. Therefore, the problem of semi-supervised time series anomaly detection is the reconstruction sequence $\tilde{x}_t$ obtained by auto-encoder reconstruction on each independent time series x, and the threshold is set. By comparing the threshold and the difference between x and $\tilde{x}_t$, finally output Binary output $y \in \{0, 1\}$, where $y = 1$ represents that the point is an abnormal point, and $y = 0$ represents that the point is a normal point.

3.2 Our Model

The model research proposed in this paper is based on the research in [29] and [28], including LSTM autoencoder and semi-supervised learning algorithm. Figure 1 outlines our anomaly detection algorithm, which consists of an data partition module and an LSTM autoencoder module. In this section, we will first introduce the LSTM autoencoder on the basis of unsupervised learning, and then explain how our algorithm applies the LSTM autoencoder in a semi-supervised learning scenario.

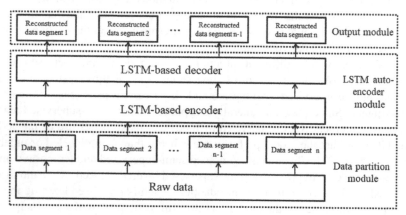

Fig. 1. A graphical illustration of the framework of a semi-supervised time series anomaly detection model based on LSTM autoencoder.

3.3 Unsupervised LSTM Autoencoder

An autoencoder (AE) consists of two parts: encoder and decoder. The encoder uses function mapping to convert the input x_t into a hidden representation h_t, and the decoder performs reconstruction through the hidden representation h_t to output the reconstruction result. The LSTM auto-encoder combines the LSTM network and AE, and hands the encoding and decoding process to the LSTM for execution. Through LSTM, the encoder extracts time features from the input time series data, and the encoder performs the conversion from feature mapping to output, as shown in Fig. 2.

The encoder of the LSTM-based autoencoder will update the time series $x = (x_1, x_2, \ldots, x_t) \in R^{n \times t}$ into the hidden state of the encoder in the following way:

$$h_t = f(h_{t-1}, x_t) \tag{1}$$

where $h_t \in R^m$ is the hidden state of the encoder corresponding to the time step t, m is the size of the hidden unit, and f is the activation function. The core of LSTM is the cell state, and the LSTM network deletes or adds information to the cell state through gates. LSTM uses forget gates, input gates and output gates to control the cell state, including determining the cell state to discard part of the information, determining the cell state to

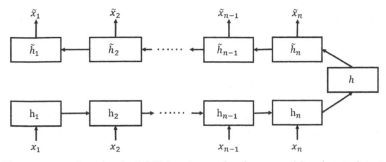

Fig. 2. The process of a simple LSTM autoencoder from acquiring input data to output reconstructing data.

add part of the information, updating the cell state, and outputting some state features in the cell. The process is as follows:

$$f_t = \sigma\left(W_f \cdot \left[h_{t-1}, x_t\right] + b_f\right) \tag{2}$$

$$i_t = \sigma\left(W_i \cdot \left[h_{t-1}, x_t\right] + b_i\right) \tag{3}$$

$$\tilde{C}_t = \tanh\left(W_C \cdot \left[h_{t-1}, x_t\right] + b_C\right) \tag{4}$$

$$C_t = f_t * C_{t-1} + i_t * \tilde{C}_t \tag{5}$$

$$o_t = \sigma\left(W_o \cdot \left[h_{t-1}, x_t\right] + b_o\right) \tag{6}$$

$$h_t = o_t \tanh(C_t) \tag{7}$$

where $\left[h_{t-1}, x_t\right] \in R^{m+n}$ is the link between the previously hidden state h_{t-1} and the current input x_t. σ is the activation function, and $*$ means element multiplication. W_f, W_i, W_o are the weights of the forget gate, input gate, and output gate, and b_f, b_i, b_o are biases. The hidden state h_t can be considered as encoding information or intermediate information containing temporal characteristics used in the decoding stage. In order to achieve the final reconstruction of the data distribution, the decoder needs to learn the mapping from h_t to x_t, output $\tilde{x}_t$ according to h_t, and minimize the error between x_t and $\tilde{x}_t$.

The principle of training the LSTM autoencoder is to minimize the reconstruction error, which can be achieved by the following loss function:

$$min\frac{1}{t}\sum\nolimits_{i=1}^{t} \|x_i - \tilde{x}_i\|_2 \tag{8}$$

In order to better extract the time features between time series, for a certain time series $x = (x_1, x_2, \ldots, x_t)$, we set a sliding window with a length of l and a step size of 1, and divide x into a set $S = \{s_1, s_2, \ldots, s_{t-l+1}\}$ composed of multiple data segments, where $s_i = (x_i, x_{i+1}, \ldots, x_{i+l})$, $1 \le i \le t - l + 1$. The processing unit of the LSTM autoencoder changes from a single data to a single data segment, so the loss function is also changed to the following formula:

$$min \frac{1}{t-l+1} \sum_{i=1}^{t-l+1} E[s_i : \tilde{s}_i] \tag{9}$$

where s_i is the i-th data segment, and $\tilde{s}_i$ is the reconstructed data corresponding to s_i. $E[s_i:\tilde{s}_i]$ represents the reconstruction error of the data segment s_i, which can be measured by mean square error or cross entropy. In this study, the vector norm between the input data segment s_i and the reconstructed data segment $\tilde{s}_i$ is used. Correspondingly, $E[s_i: \tilde{s}_i]$ can be expressed as:

$$E[s_i : \tilde{s}_i] = \frac{1}{l} \|x_j - \tilde{x}_j\|_2, \ i \leq j \leq i+l \tag{10}$$

3.4 Semi-supervised LSTM Autoencoder

Since the LSTM autoencoder strives to learn the normal data distribution by minimizing the reconstruction error, the training data needs to be as normal as possible, and the training data used in most researches based on autoencoders nowadays also uses data that does not contain anomalies. In actual scenarios, it is difficult to guarantee that the acquired data is free of abnormal data. At the same time, there will be a small part of the labeled data, so we consider using this part of the labeled data to enable the LSTM autoencoder to distinguish between normal and abnormal data.

We propose a semi-supervised LSTM autoencoder (SS-LSTM-AE) method. The unlabeled time series x_u and the labeled time series x_{label} are divided into data segments using a sliding window to obtain the unlabeled time series data segment set $S_u = \{s_1, s_2, \ldots, s_m\}$ and the labeled time series data segment set $S_{label} = \{(\tilde{s}_1, y_{s1}), (\tilde{s}_2, y_{s2}), \ldots, (\tilde{s}_n, y_{sn})\}$. In the process of transforming from $x_{label} = ((\bar{x}_1, y_1), (\bar{x}_2, y_2), \ldots, (\bar{x}_n, y_n))\}$ to labeled time series data segment set S_{label}, When y corresponding to any $\bar{x}$ in $s_i = (x_i, x_{i+1}, \ldots, x_{i+l})$ is 1, set $y_{si} = 1$, indicating that the data segment is an abnormal segment. We improve the loss function of SS-LSTM-AE according to the changes in the training data. The improved loss function is as follows:

$$min \frac{1}{m+n} \sum_{i=1}^{m} E[s_i : \tilde{s}_i] + \frac{\gamma}{m+n} \sum_{j=1}^{n} (E[\tilde{s}_j : \tilde{\tilde{s}}_j])^{(-1)^{y_{si}}} \tag{11}$$

In the loss function of our SS-LSTM-AE, for unlabeled data, the same loss term as the unsupervised LSTM autoencoder is used. When $n = 0$, that is, when there is no labeled data, the loss function will be restored to the loss function of the unsupervised LSTM autoencoder.

For labeled data, we added a new loss item, which determines how the model learns the distribution of labeled data. For the labeled normal data ($y_s = 0$), we choose the same loss item as the unsupervised LSTM autoencoder to learn the data distribution, so as to ensure that the model can learn the correct data distribution. For the marked anomaly ($y_s = 1$), we decided to punish the inverse of the reconstruction error, so that the reconstruction of the abnormal data must deviate from the original data distribution. While introducing a new loss term, we also set a weighted hyperparameter $\gamma > 0$ for the loss term, which controls the learning importance between labeled data and unlabeled data. When $\gamma > 1$, the model training will focus more on the data distribution of the labeled data, when $\gamma < 1$, the model will focus more on the data distribution of the unlabeled data.

We again define the anomaly score of SS-LSTM-AE by the reconstruction error between the reconstructed data segment and the original data segment, which is the same as the unsupervised model.

4 Experiments

In this section, we answer the following research questions by conducting experiments on three public time series data sets:

Anomaly Detection. Whether the anomaly detection performance of the autoencoder model under the semi-supervised algorithm better than the autoencoder model under the unsupervised algorithm?

Labeled Data Size. With different proportions of labeled data, can the improvement effect of the semi-supervised algorithm on the autoencoder model be maintained or increased?

4.1 Datasets

The detailed description of the three time series data sets is shown in Table 1.

Table 1. Time series data set detailed description table.

Dataset	Data	Size
Yahoo! Webscope A1Benchmark	Unlabeled dataset	17,114
	Labeled dataset	16,970
	Test dataset	10,782
Yahoo! Webscope A2Benchmark	Unlabeled dataset	17,052
	Labeled dataset	17,178
	Test dataset	22,736
NAB	Unlabeled data set	16,128
	Labeled data set	16,128
	Test dataset	8,066

The Yahoo! Webscope S5 data set is a labeled anomaly detection data set that contains real and synthetic time series data. The entire data set contains four benchmark subsets.

The A1 benchmark is the actual production flow data of some Yahoo! instances, and the remaining 3 benchmarks are based on synthetic time series. We choose A1 benchmark and A2 benchmark to evaluate the anomaly detection model. A1 benchmark has 94,866 pieces of data in total, of which only 1,669 abnormal data. In order to ensure the integrity of the experiment, for the dataset disclosed by Yahoo! Webscope, we take the dataset that has no abnormalities or a small amount of abnormality at the end, and removes the small amount of abnormal points to form an unlabeled dataset. A dataset containing both abnormal points and normal points and a relatively high number of abnormal points is taken to form a labeled dataset, and multiple files are randomly selected to form a test dataset. After screening, we got 17,114 unlabeled data, 16,970 labeled data, and 10,782 test data based on A1 benchmark, 17,052 unlabeled data, 17,178 labeled data, and 22,736 test data based on A2 benchmark.

NAB dataset is an anomaly detection dataset that does not contain labels. It consists of more than 50 real and artificial time data files without labels. We chose two datasets, artificialNoAnomaly and artificialWithAnomaly, for model evaluation. We use most of the data in the artificialNoAnomaly part as an unlabeled dataset, and the rest as a training set, and manually label the data in artificialWithAnomaly to get a labeled dataset. In this way, an unlabeled dataset containing 16,128 pieces of data, a labeled dataset containing 16,128 pieces of data, and a test dataset containing 8,066 pieces of data are generated.

4.2   Baseline Methods

This article focuses on the improvement effect of semi-supervised algorithms on unsupervised models, so we use the unsupervised LSTM autoencoder (LSTM-AE) to compare with the model under the semi-supervised algorithm, that is, the semi-supervised LSTM autoencoder (SS-LSTM-AE).

LSTM-AE. Use LSTM as the encoder and decoder of the autoencoder, and only use the unlabeled dataset and test dataset for experiments.

SS-LSTM-AE. Change the loss function of LSTM-AE, use unlabeled dataset and labeled dataset for training.

4.3   Evaluation Metrics

In our experiments, the anomaly detection problem is regarded as a classification problem, and we evaluate the accuracy, recall and F1-score of different models. For binary classification problems, if the normal situation is marked as abnormal, the error is expressed as a false positive (FP). False negative (FN) means that the abnormal instance is marked as normal. Similarly, true positive (TP) and true negative (TN) represent abnormalities, and normal conditions are correctly identified.

4.4   Result and Analysis

Anomaly Detection. Table 2 reports the performance of the same kind of autoencoders in anomaly detection tasks under unsupervised and semi-supervised. Among them, the best performance is highlighted in bold.

Table 2. Anomaly detection result table.

Model	Yahoo! A1Benchmark			Yahoo! A2Benchmark			NAB		
	pre	recall	F1-score	pre	recall	F1-score	pre	recall	F1-score
LSTM-AE	0.719	**0.999**	0.836	0.546	1.0	0.706	0.444	0.596	0.509
SS-LSTM-AE	**0.780**	0.999	**0.876**	**0.701**	**0.999**	**0.824**	**0.806**	**0.613**	**0.696**

In Table 2, we observe that under the three data sets, most of the indicators of the semi-supervised algorithm are better than the unsupervised algorithm;

Labeled Data Size. In order to further study the influence of labeled data on the model, we chose to select the corresponding percentage of the labeled dataset of each dataset, and conducted multiple experiments under different labeled data proportions. Table 3 reports the performance comparison between semi-supervised and unsupervised algorithms under different proportions.

Table 3. Model performance table under different proportions of labeled data.

Model	Yahoo! A1Benchmark			Yahoo! A2Benchmark			NAB		
	pre	recall	F1-score	pre	recall	F1-score	pre	recall	F1-score
20%标记数据占比									
LSTM-AE	0.719	0.999	0.836	0.546	1.0	0.706	0.444	0.596	0.509
SS-LSTM-AE	**0.763**	**0.999**	**0.865**	**0.546**	**1.0**	**0.707**	**0.494**	**0.597**	**0.541**
30%标记数据占比									
LSTM-AE	0.719	0.999	0.836	0.546	**1.0**	0.706	0.444	**0.596**	0.509
SS-LSTM-AE	**0.782**	**0.999**	**0.878**	**0.769**	0.987	**0.865**	**0.522**	0.594	**0.556**
50%标记数据占比									
LSTM-AE	0.719	0.999	0.836	0.546	**1.0**	0.706	0.444	0.596	0.509
SS-LSTM-AE SS-LSTM-AE	**0.780**	**0.999**	**0.876**	**0.701**	0.999	**0.824**	**0.806**	**0.613**	**0.696**

In Table 3, we observe that by increasing the proportion of labeled data in the training data set, the performance of the semi-supervised algorithm is improved compared to the unsupervised algorithm. We have also observed that as the proportion of labeled data increases, the performance of the semi-supervised algorithm is gradually improving, but as the proportion increases, the extent of algorithm performance improvement is gradually shrinking. Specifically, increasing the proportion of labeled data from 20% to 30% will improve the performance of each model much better than 30% to 50%.

5 Conclusion and Future Work

In this article, we propose a sequence-to-sequence semi-supervised deep learning framework for time series prediction. The framework uses the idea of LSTM autoencoder to explore the possibilities of the framework in depth. In order to verify that the semi-supervised learning framework can better detect anomalies in time series, we conducted experiments on three time series data sets. By comparing the performance of unsupervised and semi-supervised frameworks with the same network structure, we conclude that the semi-supervised LSTM autoencoder can perform anomaly detection more effectively than unsupervised models.

In future work, we intend to study the semi-supervised improvement method for the integrated algorithm of time series anomaly detection, and further explore the possibility of semi-supervised algorithm in the field of time series anomaly detection. The semi-supervised improvement of generative adversarial networks in the field of time series anomaly detection is also a challenging problem.

Acknowledgements. This research is supported by the key research and development program of Jiangsu province (BE2019012).

References

1. Chandola, V., Banerjee, A., Kumar, V.: Anomaly detection: a survey. ACM Comput. Surv. **41**(3), 1–58 (2009)
2. Cook, A., Misirli, G., Fan, Z.: Anomaly detection for IoT time-series data: a survey. IEEE IoT J. **7**(7), 6481–6494 (2019)
3. Goodfellow, I., Bengio, Y., Courville, A.: Deep Learning. The MIT Press, Cambridge (2016)
4. Kim, J., Kim, J., Thu, H.L.T.: Long short term memory recurrent neural network classifier for intrusion detection. In: 2016 International Conference on Platform Technology and Service (PlatCon) 2016, pp. 1–5. IEEE (2016)
5. Malhotra, P., Vig, L., Shroff, G.: Long short term memory networks for anomaly detection in time series. In: Proceedings, 2015, vol. 89, pp. 89–94. Presses universitaires de Louvain (2015)
6. Fox, A.J.: Outliers in time series. J. Roy. Stat. Soc. Ser. B (Methodol.) **34**(3), 350–363 (1972)
7. Burman, J.P., Otto, M.C.: Census bureau research project: outliers in time series. Bureau of the Census, SRD Res. Rep. CENSUS/SRD/RR-88114 (1988)
8. Vallis, O., Hochenbaum, J., Kejariwal, A.: A novel technique for long-term anomaly detection in the cloud. In: 6th USENIX Workshop on Hot Topics in Cloud Computing (HotCloud 14) (2014)
9. Wold, H.: A Study in the Analysis of Stationary Time Series. Almqvist & Wiksell, Uppsala (1938)
10. Kadri, F., Harrou, F., Chaabane, S.: Seasonal ARMA-based SPC charts for anomaly detection: application to emergency department systems. Neurocomputing **173**, 2102–2114 (2016)
11. Zhang, G.P., Qi, M.: Neural network forecasting for seasonal and trend time series. Eur. J. Oper. Res. **160**(2), 501–514 (2005)
12. Chou, J.S., Telaga, A.S.: Real-time detection of anomalous power consumption. Renew. Sustain. Energy Rev. **33**, 400–411 (2014)

13. Fu, R., Zhang, Z., Li, L.: Using LSTM and GRU neural network methods for traffic flow prediction. In: 2016 31st Youth Academic Annual Conference of Chinese Association of Automation (YAC) 2016, pp. 324–328. IEEE (2016)
14. Shipmon, D.T., Gurevitch, J.M., Piselli, P.M.: Time series anomaly detection; detection of anomalous drops with limited features and sparse examples in noisy highly periodic data (2017). arXiv preprint arXiv:1708.03665
15. Saurav, S., Malhotra, P., TV, V.: Online anomaly detection with concept drift adaptation using recurrent neural networks. In: Proceedings of the ACM India Joint International Conference on Data Science and Management of Data 2018, pp. 78–87 (2018)
16. Xie, X., Wu, D., Liu, S.: IoT data analytics using deep learning (2017). arXiv preprint arXiv: 1708.03854
17. Bontemps, L., Cao, V.L., McDermott, J., Le-Khac, N.-A.: Collective anomaly detection based on long short-term memory recurrent neural networks. In: Dang, T.K., Wagner, R., Küng, J., Thoai, N., Takizawa, M., Neuhold, E. (eds.) FDSE 2016. LNCS, vol. 10018, pp. 141–152. Springer, Cham (2016). https://doi.org/10.1007/978-3-319-48057-2_9
18. Hundman, K., Constantinou, V., Laporte, C.: Detecting spacecraft anomalies using LSTMs and nonparametric dynamic thresholding. In: Proceedings of the 24th ACM SIGKDD International Conference on Knowledge Discovery & Data Mining 2018, pp. 387–395 (2018)
19. Luo, T., Nagarajan, S.G.: Distributed anomaly detection using autoencoder neural networks in WSN for IoT. In: 2018 IEEE International Conference on Communications (ICC) 2018, pp. 1–6. IEEE (2018)
20. Wang, W., Zhu, M., Wang, J.: End-to-end encrypted traffic classification with one-dimensional convolution neural networks. In: 2017 IEEE International Conference on Intelligence and Security Informatics (ISI) 2017, pp. 43–48. IEEE (2017)
21. Liu, C.L., Hsaio, W.H., Tu, Y.C.: Time series classification with multivariate convolutional neural network. IEEE Trans. Industr. Electron. 66(6), 4788–4797 (2018)
22. Kim, T.Y., Cho, S.B.: Web traffic anomaly detection using C-LSTM neural networks. Expert Syst. Appl. 106, 66–76 (2018)
23. Karim, F., Majumdar, S., Darabi, H.: LSTM fully convolutional networks for time series classification. IEEE Access 6, 1662–1669 (2017)
24. Sutskever, I., Vinyals, O., Le, Q.V.: Sequence to sequence learning with neural networks. Adv. Neural. Inf. Process. Syst. 2014, 3104–3112 (2014)
25. Malhotra, P., Ramakrishnan, A., Anand, G.: LSTM-based encoder-decoder for multi-sensor anomaly detection (2016). arXiv preprint arXiv:1607.00148
26. Shah, M.P., Merchant, S.N., Awate, S.P.: Abnormality detection using deep neural networks with robust quasi-norm autoencoding and semi-supervised learning. In: 2018 IEEE 15th International Symposium on Biomedical Imaging 2018, pp. 568–572. IEEE (2018)
27. Cheng, Y., Xu, Y., Zhong, H.: HS-TCN: A semi-supervised hierarchical stacking temporal convolutional network for anomaly detection in IoT. In: 2019 IEEE 38th International Performance Computing and Communications Conference (IPCCC) 2019, pp. 1–7. IEEE (2019)
28. Ruff, L., Vandermeulen, R.A., Görnitz, N.: Deep semi-supervised anomaly detection (2019). arXiv preprint arXiv:1906.02694
29. Zhou, C., Sun, C., Liu, Z.: A C-LSTM neural network for text classification (2015). arXiv preprint arXiv:1511.08630

Fault Inspection of Brake Shoe Wear for TEDS Based on Machine Vision

Mengqiong Ge[1], Shengfang Lu[1], Yan Zhang[2], and Cui Qin[1(✉)]

[1] School of Information and Communication Engineering, Nanjing Institute of Technology, Nanjing 211167, China
qincui@njit.edu.cn

[2] Swissgrid Ltd, Short-Term Network Modelling, Bleichemattstrasse 31, 5001 Aarau, Switzerland

Abstract. With rapid development of high-speed railway, the automated inspection of related faults is prerequisite for ensuring the safety of the EMU movement. As similar as TFDS in moving freight trains, TEDS is also applying in fault detection of the running EMU. Brake shoe is one of the key components in brake system, and the pre-warning on wear limitation about it is very important in the fault detection on EMU. In this paper, we propose a real-time, automated inspection method to detect the wear limitation of the brake shoe. Firstly, multi-resolution pyramid template matching technology is used for fast localization of the brake shoe. Then, LSD and Hough transform are employed to detect the wear limitation of the brake shoe. The experiments demonstrate that the way is high efficiency and well real-time, and it can meet the need of practical application.

Keywords: Fault inspection · Machine vision · TEDS · LSD · Hough transform

1 Introduction

At present, train related fault diagnosis is carried out by specially trained inspectors after the train enters the warehouse. The test results are greatly affected by the quality, emotion and environment of the inspectors, and have great human subjectivity. With the increase of train speed and freight volume, the task of train detection and maintenance is becoming more and more heavy, the traditional manual detection method is time-consuming and laborious, and can't be detected in real time on line. Obviously, manual detection can't adapt to train fault diagnosis under the new situation. Along with the rapid development of visual technology, fault diagnosis based on visual detection [1, 2] has been paid more and more attention. The visual technology is applicated in the TFDS system [3] now. How to realize the fast dynamics on-line detection of the corresponding fault problems in the operation of the EMU in the TEDS system is a major challenge for the current scientific and technological workers. During the TEDS system, the wear limit detection of brake shoe is an important fault detection point. Brake shoe is an important part of EMU braking system and one of the key components to ensure the normal operation of EMU. The use of visual detection technology makes automatic real-time

Y. Tian et al. (Eds.): ICBDS 2020, CCIS 1415, pp. 54–59, 2021.
https://doi.org/10.1007/978-981-16-3150-4_5

on-line fault judgment a possibility, thus making manual maintenance into automatic machine detection, saving labor costs and improving detection efficiency. This paper mainly considers the use of a visual detection technology to achieve the EMU train brake block wear limit fault diagnosis.

TEDS system and TFDS system are similar. They are composed of image acquisition system and image processing system. TEDS (EMU running fault dynamic image detection system), which is installed high-speed acquisition equipment and electromagnetic sensors near the rail, can collect EMU pictures in high-speed operation and transmit them to the terminal server. The fault detection is judged by image processing and pattern recognition technology. A schematic diagram of the TEDS system structure is shown in Fig. 1. In front of the camera, an electromagnetic trigger detector is installed in the direction of the EMU to capture the train arrival information, and then the trigger signal is transmitted to the camera and the flash. It makes the image acquisition equipment into the acquisition state. The three cameras installed at the middle bottom of the rail are used to collect the full coverage image of the bottom of the EMU, and the two high frequency flash lights at the bottom are used to supplement the image machine. On both sides of the track, two cameras are installed to photograph the bogie and the outer compartment.

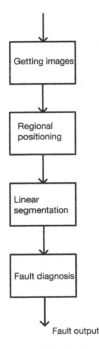

Fig. 1. Schematic diagram of brake shoe wear detection process

After obtaining the train picture of EMU, the distance between the brake pad and the brake pad in the brake pad area is judged by the quick positioning of the brake pad position. When the distance between the two is less than a certain value, the wear limit of the brake pad is judged, otherwise, the fault location realization flow chart is shown in Fig. 1.

The structure of this paper is as follows. The second part a fast positioning method is proposed for the position of the brake shoe of the EMU. The thirth part gives the method of judging the wear degree between the upper and lower brake pads of the brake shoe. Finally, the conclusion is drawn in part 4.

2 Fast Positioning of Brake Shoe

Target location is a prerequisite for fault detection. Because of the use of high-speed, high-rate cameras, the content of an image contains a lot of information. Because the wear of the brake shoe changes little relative to the whole image, an improved template matching algorithm is proposed to locate the target of the brake shoe area.

Template matching [4] algorithm referred to the use of template image slides the window in the whole image, the target position is detected through the maximum response. Supposed an image $I(x, y)$ of size $M \times N$, in which,$0 < x < M, 0 < y < N$, A template image $w(x, y)$ of size $J \times K$, in which,$0 < J < M, 0 < K < N$. Using the relevant matching principle, the response of the template in the image is defined as

$$c(x, y) = \frac{\sum_{s} \sum_{t} [I(s, t) - I'(s, t))][w(x + s, y + t) - w')]}{\left\{ \sum_{s} \sum_{t} [I(s, t) - I'(s, t))]^2 \sum_{s} \sum_{t} [w(x + s, y + t) - w')]^2 \right\}^{\frac{1}{2}}} \tag{1}$$

in which $x = 0, 1, \cdots, M - 1, y = 0, 1, \cdots, N - 1, w'$ is the average value of pixels in window w, $I'(s, t)$ is the regional average value in $I(s, t)$, which coincides with the current position in w, C is sliding window in the whole image. The algorithm is simple in principle, but when the image size is very large, the calculation will be very large and the operation will be very slow. Therefore, combined with image pyramid processing, an improved fast template matching algorithm is proposed. that is the target position is roughly located by implementing image template matching from low resolution. Then the second template matching is carried out in the rough target location area of the next pyramid image. The location result diagram is shown in Fig. 2, and the two methods match the time result pairs such as Table 1.

(a) Template Picture   (b) Location results

Fig. 2. Location of the brake pad area

Table 1. Time-consuming comparison of matching algorithms

	Original algorithm(s)	Improved algorithm(s)
Time spent	2.9296	0.2290

3 Judgment on the Wear of Brake Watt

3.1 Linear Segmentation of Image Edges

The image edge contains the most basic feature information in the image. And it is the fastest pixel in the gray value of the image.

After accurately calculating the position of the brake shoe, the wear limit of the brake shoe is judged by the distance between the brake pads. An accurate, fast linear segmentation detector LSD [3] is used to extract the edge information of an image. LSD is a fast edge extraction algorithm with linear time. It generates horizontal line interval by calculating the horizontal line angle of pixels, and then fuses pixels with the same horizontal line in the interval to form the supporting interval of edge line. Finally, the accurate extraction of image edge is realized by segmentation correction. The pseudo code of the algorithm is as follows:

By LSD algorithm, the edge segmentation image of the brake shoe is shown in Fig. 3. Because of the rigid connection between the gate and the fastening bolt, the distance between the center point of the fastening bolt at both ends of the gate can be easily judged by using the Hough transformation to realize the detection of the circle in the image of the brake shoe. When the center distance between the upper and lower two gates is less than the normal threshold between the two, the wear limit of the brake shoe is judged. Otherwise, it is judged as no fault. The detection effect of the fixed bolt is shown in Fig. 4.

Fig. 3. LSD Linear segmentation result

Fig. 4. Detection of fixed bolts at both ends of the gate

4 Conclusion

In this paper, an on-line detection method based on machine vision is proposed for fault detection of brake shoe wear limit of EMU train. By using the fast template matching algorithm and the LSD edge extraction method, the wear limit of the brake shoe is realized by identifying the center pixel distance of the fixed bolt at both ends of the brake shoe. The method has high measurement accuracy and real-time performance, and it can be applied to the on-line detection of excessive wear limit of EMU train brake shoe.

Acknowledgments. This work was supported by the Natural Science Foundation of Jiangsu Province (Grant No. BK20191012) and the Scientific Research Foundation of Nanjing Institute of Technology (Grant No. JCYJ201822).

References

1. Liu, R., Wang, Y.: Principle and Application of TFDS. China Railway Publication, Beijing (2005). (in chinese)
2. Zhou, F., Rong, Z., et al.: Dust collector localization in trouble of moving freight car detection system. J. Zhejiang Univ. C **14**(2), 98–106 (2013). https://doi.org/10.1631/jzus.C1200223
3. Gioi, R.G.V., Jakubowicz, J., Morel, J.M., et al.: LSD: a fast line segment detector with a false detection control. IEEE Trans. Pattern Anal. Mach. Intell. **32**(4), 722–732 (2010). https://doi.org/10.1109/TPAMI.2008.300
4. Gonzalez, R.C., Woods, R.E.: Digital Image Processing, 3rd edn. Prentice-Hall Inc., Upper Saddle (2007)

Android Malware Detection Method Based on App-Image Conversion

Nannan Xie[1], Hongpeng Bai[1(✉)], Yanfeng Shi[2], and Haiwei Wu[1]

[1] Changchun University of Science and Technology, Changchun 130022, China
2018100597@mails.cust.edu.cn
[2] School of Computer Engineering, Nanjing Institute of Technology,
Nanjing 211167, China

Abstract. With the rapid development of mobile internet, Android has become the most widely used mobile terminal operating system and play an increasingly important role in users' lives. However, Android malware is also bringing privacy leaks and security threats that are causing troubles to third-party markets and users. What's more, malware uses code obfuscation and camouflage to hide itself to avoid detection. Traditional malware detection techniques based on machine learning and feature matching are usually difficult to deal with this type of malware. Considering about this problem, an Android malware detection method based on app-image conversion is proposed, which maps the Android installation files to grayscale images, and employs the deep learning algorithm, CNN (Convolutional Neural Networks), for malware detection. A detection framework for Android malware is presented, which includes three parts: data set construction, app-image conversion, and deep learning detection. In the experiments, the parameters of CNN are determined through comparative analysis. It achieves the detection accuracy of 95.23%, which shows the effectiveness and feasibility of the proposed method.

Keywords: Android malware · Grayscale image · Deep learning · Convolutional Neural Networks

1 Introduction

The openness and freedom of the Android operating system allow developers all over the world to conduct secondary development and upload their own applications to the application markets. These features have promoted the rapid growth of Android applications, but they have also led to the spread of malicious applications. For example, the Android malware family DroidKungFu [6], which appeared in 2011, is a typical Trojan horse with many variants. It opens the system back door to remotely access the infected mobile phone and uses the system vulnerability to root the system. The common functions of DroidKungFu include to execute file delete commands, execute web page opening commands, download other apks, open URLs, and start other programs. These malicious behaviors have caused serious economic losses and privacy leaks.

© Springer Nature Singapore Pte Ltd. 2021
Y. Tian et al. (Eds.): ICBDS 2020, CCIS 1415, pp. 60–74, 2021.
https://doi.org/10.1007/978-981-16-3150-4_6

Smartphones with Android operating system accounted for 87% of global smartphone sales in 2019 [10]. Malware is becoming an important threat to privacy protection and network security. Kaspersky pointed out in the analysis report on the evolution of mobile malware [11], attacks on personal data have become frequent in 2019 with more Trojan horse attacks. From 2018 to 2019, the number of attacks of personal data on mobile devices increased by 50%. Public security incidents caused by mobile terminal security issues are appearing from time to time. For example, the positioning function leaks mobile phone location information, applications collect user information without notification, free wireless connection stealing device data, which resulting in the leakage of sensitive information and have caused serious security risks to social public safety and individuals' privacy. Therefore, how to detect malicious software efficiently and deal with malicious behaviors timely are still the problems that need to be solved urgently.

In the academic and industrial practice, the current Android malware detection methods mainly include rule matching and active detection. Rule matching detects the maliciousness of an application by matching its signatures with the rule base, and the rule base is maintained and updated on time. This method detects quickly but is difficult to detect new emerging malware. The active detection has high detection accuracy and can deal with unprecedented attacks by using unsupervised algorithms. Static or dynamic features are extracted, such as permissions, API calls, component information, and machine learning or other algorithms are employed to classify the malware and benign applications. There are many existing Android malware detection techniques and detection engines. However, due to the limitations of technology and regional cultures, the relevant researchers and security companies of malware detection have difficulty to share the detection results. Therefore, it is necessary to study fast and efficient detection methods.

CNN is the most widely used deep learning method with a wide range of applications in image processing since 2010. Its key concepts are "local receptive fields" and "shared weights and biases". The CNN algorithm is based on the correlation between local pixels, so the local receptive fields can be used to reduce the processed feature dimensionality and build high-level features, which make CNN more suitable for processing related features than independent features.

In this work, we propose an Android malware detection framework based on app-image conversion. The installation apk files of Android applications are converted into grayscale images in binary form, and then we employ CNN to classify the images to detect malicious applications. The theoretical basis of this method is that malware and normal applications have different behaviors in different classes while have similarities in the same class, and the grayscale images can reflect the difference between malware and normal applications to a certain extent. In addition, the detection method based on image classification try to solve the problem of malicious code deformation and confusion caused by code obfuscation and camouflage.

2 Related Work

2.1 Android Malware and Detection

As the most widely used mobile terminal system, in order to improve the security and deal with the problems caused by malware attacks, Android itself has three security mechanisms: program sandbox, software signature, and permission management. However, malware can bypass these security mechanisms to a certain extent by increasing code obfuscation, encrypting malicious payloads, or conducting secret commands communicates with remote servers, which increasing the difficulty of malware detection.

Android malware refers to applications developed for malicious purpose based on Android and circulating in the application markets. The malicious behaviors mainly include the following 6 types.

(1) Malicious deduction. It refers to the automatic deduction of fees without permission. For example, some applications automatically purchase paid services without notifying the user and deduct the fees from the user's phone account.

(2) Privacy theft. The application contains code to collect sensitive data, such as call records, contact information, location information, even account passwords, and upload them to a remote server or analyze them.

(3) Traffic data consumption. The application opens network download services in the background, which consumes data traffic and causes direct economic losses.

(4) Remote control. This kind of malicious application remotely controls the device and conducts remote operations, such as calling the camera to take pictures and upload them to a remote server.

(5) System damage. These applications delete important system files and maliciously occupy system resources, such as CPU computing resources or memory resources, which cause the system to fail to operate normally.

(6) Other behaviors. There are some other malicious behaviors, and new malware has emerged over time. For example, some applications bundle the installation of applications or automatically perform certain or illegal operations, such as playing audio. Although they do not directly damage the system, they cause confusion to users.

Android malware detection technologies mainly include static detection and dynamic detection. Static detection constructs the feature set by extracting features from system files or sentence sequences without running the source code, and use feature matching or machine learning methods to detect the maliciousness [23]. The advantages of the static detection are that it can cover the entire code and is suitable for large-scale detection, but the disadvantage is that the real operating environment cannot be simulated, so it is difficult to detect some specific behaviors. There are many studies on static methods, such as malware detection with permission features [7], behavior analysis with opcode [24], and detection with combined features of permissions and API calls [9].

Dynamic detection methods run the Android application in a sandbox or virtual environment and judge whether the application is malicious by monitoring the behaviors. This method is more practical and has a higher detection accuracy since it can simulate real running environment. Because techniques such as repacking, obfuscation, and encryption will not change the actual running behaviors of the application, dynamic method can effectively deal with the variants of malicious applications. However, dynamic detection has the disadvantage of large resource consumption. Since all working paths and functions of the application must be executed, the operation of the simulation program requires a lot of time and space.

A typical dynamic detection research is TaintDroid, which is a dynamic tool based on the detection of sensitive data flow paths in a sandbox environment [5]. By analyzing user-related activities to determine whether the user operation is an active behavior or passive one, RansomeProber [3] detected malicious behaviors in real time. In addition, Cai et al. proposed Droidcat [1], which detected the behavior of malware from the app-level, and used a combination of multiple dynamic features based on method calls and communication intentions between components to determine the maliciousness.

In addition to be used in feature matching, the features extracted by static and dynamic methods can be processed by machine learning algorithms. Machine learning algorithms, especially which based on probability statics and neural networks, are the most widely used detection methods. Probabilistic models represented by Naive Bayes have many practical applications, such as risk assessment of Android software through probability generation models [22], and construct probability discriminant models of permission features for malware detection [21].

Statistical machine learning algorithms represented by SVM and KNN are widely used because of their high accuracy and mature development. For example, Mu et al. [26] used SVM as a classifier to analyze malware risks introduced by permission features. Since a single algorithm has disadvantages, there are also researches that combine different algorithms to improve the detection result [15]. Probabilistic statistical methods have some limitations, for example, high dimensional features will take more running time and computational space. Therefore, some research combined feature selection, feature extraction or other feature dimensionality reduction methods with classification techniques, in order to achieve the balance of detection effect and detection consumption. In recent years, deep learning methods have made good attempts in this field. The correlations between Android applications are the theoretical basis for using deep learning in malware detection. Hao et al. [17] used CNN to process the extracted opcodes, while Lei et al. [2] employed Deep Belief Network to analyze multiple kinds of features.

Due to the openness of the Android system, any organizations and individuals can carry out secondary development. Malware developers may evade the detection by repackaging, resigning, and obfuscating the codes. At present, the researchers are taking attentions to the new techniques, such as knowledge graphs, artificial intelligence, to improve detection performance. In the industry, with the continuous emergence of new malware, it is important to develop detection systems with high accuracy and low consumption.

2.2 Grayscale Image and Android Malware

Grayscale image has only one sampled color per pixel and displays from the darkest black to the brightest white, with multiple levels of color depth between black and white. A complete image is usually composed of three channels of red, green, and blue, with different gray scales, which can be used to express the proportion of the three colors in the image. Grayscale image reduces the amount of original image information, but it still retains important features of the original image for processing.

There are studies attempt to combine Android malware detection with visualization, such as Android malware binary file analysis based on visualization methods. The theoretical basis of these research is that most variants of malware are generated by using automated techniques or reusing some important modules, so they have similarities in the binary codes.

In 2011, NATARAJ et al. [16] proposed a method to visualize and classify malware by image processing. Later, researchers tried different methods to visualize and detect malware, which include the method that transformed malware into images by direct conversion and opcode conversion [27]. Direct conversion is to convert the PE file of the malware into binary codes, and then generate the malware image from the binary codes, which are converted into grayscale and RGB. Opcode conversion decompiles the installation file to obtain the operation codes at first, and then the operation codes are selected and converted into a malware image. Fu et al. [8] proposed a method to convert malware into RGB color images to solve the problem of insufficient information in gray images. Zhang et al. [25] converted the opcodes into an image and achieved a better malware detection effect. Similarly to traditional malware detection, Android malicious behaviors have certain regularity, which can be distinguished from the perspective of images during the visualization process.

2.3 Convolutional Neural Networks

CNN is a deep learning algorithm with a multi-layer structure, and its related research was proposed in 1989 [12]. In the 1980s and 1990s, some researchers published related work on CNN and achieved good recognition results in several pattern recognitions and handwritten digit recognitions [13]. Utile 2012, Krizhevsky et al. used the extended depth CNN and achieved the best classification effect in the ImageNet Large Scale Visual Recognition Challenge, which make CNN to attract growing attentions. In addition, many other algorithms have emerged in deep learning, including denoising autoencoders [19], DCN [4], and sumproduct [18].

CNN is composed of input layer, convolutional layer, pooling layer, and fully connected layer. It is based on multilayer neural network structure and constructs high level abstract features by learning the original features. CNN extracts features from the input data layer by layer. After the data being operated by convolution, pooling, activation function mapping, it finally realizes the classification. The 4 layers are described as following.

(1) Convolutional layer. Through the convolution operation, the convolution kernel is used to extract the features in the local area. It uses a sliding window to extract features from the image to obtain the local information of the overall data. The size of the convolution kernel is the main parameter in this layer.

(2) Pooling layer. It performs dimensionality reduction of the up layer, and it controls the over-fitting of the model to a certain extent and optimizes the entire network. The pooling window size is the main parameter.

(3) Fully connected layer. This layer maps the features learned by the model to the classification space. In image processing, the neurons of the input are connected to the neurons of the output, and the input is the stitching of the feature maps.

(4) Activation function. The features of activated neurons are preserved and mapped out to enhance the nonlinear characteristics of convolutional neural networks. The common activation functions include Sigmoid and ReLU.

One of the characteristics of CNN is the introduction of "local perception" and "weight sharing" concepts. Local perception is a learning method that extends from local feature learning to global learning, which divides the image into several regions. Since the local features of the image are relatively stable, the overall information can be obtained after the local information is summarized. Thus, the number of connections between neurons can be greatly reduced, in other words, the model parameters are reduced. Weight sharing means to that all convolution kernels in the same layer use the same convolution kernel weights, with the purpose to effectively reduce the number of parameters required in the model training. The basic process of CNN is shown in Fig. 1.

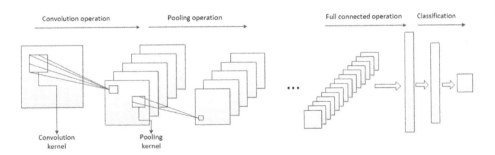

Fig. 1. Convolution Neural Networks structure.

The applications of CNN in the network security have gradually increased in recent years. Wang et al. [20] presented a hybrid Android malware detection model based on deep autoencoder and CNN, which effectively reduced the running time of the algorithm while improving the detection accuracy. Li et al. [14] proposed an Android malware detection system, which employed optimized deep Convolutional Neural Network to learn from opcode sequences. CNN is mainly employed in Android malware detection to process the extracted static or dynamic features. Considering that CNN has advantages in processing images, we employs CNN to process the converted grayscale images to achieve the malware detection in this work.

3   Malware Detection Based on App-Image Conversion

3.1   Malware Detection Framework

The proposed Android malware detection method is to convert binary Android application installation files into grayscale images, and then classify them by CNN. The detection framework is in Fig. 2, which includes data set construction, app-image conversion, and CNN detection.

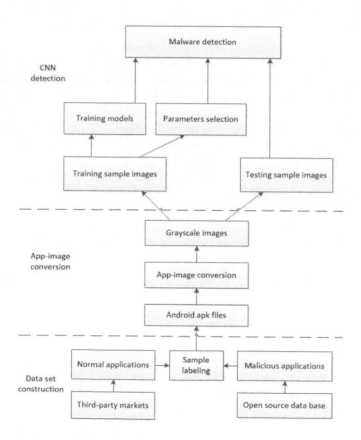

Fig. 2. Malware detection framework.

(1) Data set construction. The data set includes malicious samples and normal samples. The normal samples are collected from third-party markets, and the malicious samples come from public virus databases. The constructed data set is used to train and test CNN. In order to ensure the label purity and classification accuracy, the applications obtained are scanned by VirusTotal, the open source malware detection tool, to label the samples as accurate as possible.

(2) App-image conversion. The main work of this step is to convert the collected normal samples and malicious samples to grayscale images. At first, the apk file is read as a binary file, and then the binary file is mapped to a grayscale image. The pixels in the image represent the original Android sample.

(3) Malware detection. The Android application data set constructed above is divided into training samples and testing samples. The converted images are used to train the CNN model and test the classification results. In this process, the parameters of the model are selected, and we use the test samples to evaluate the malware detection results.

3.2 Grayscale Image Conversion

The process of grayscale image conversion adopts the function in the OpenCV library, which is an open source computer vision library that contains hundreds of computer vision algorithms of image processing. The steps of conversion are as following.

(1) The apk installation file of the Android application is read in a binary format. Every 8 bits are treated as an unsigned integer.

(2) By setting a fixed line width in advance, the binary file is converted into a two-dimensional array, and the value range of each element in the array is in [0,255].

(3) In the single channel image processing, "0" represents black and "255" represents white. The value in the array is used as the value of each pixel to generate a grayscale image. A part of the generated grayscale image is shown in Fig. 3.

4   Experiments

4.1   Environment and Data Set

The experimental part discusses the three parameters of CNN: batch size, convolution kernel size, and the number of hidden layers, and finally achieves malware detection according to the selected parameters.

The configurations used in this experiment are: Linux system, Intel Core Processor 2.4 GHz CPU, 4 GB memory, 80G hard disk, and the deep learning framework is TensorFlow-cpu 1.7.0. The data set contains 533 malware and 561

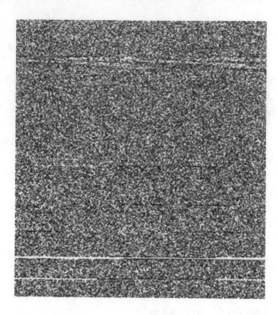

Fig. 3. Grayscale image generated by binary file (partial).

normal applications with a total of 1094 samples. The following experiments adopt five-fold cross validation.

We use accuracy to evaluate the classification results. Set P denotes the number of positive samples and N denotes the negative samples. Define the following 4 parameters: (1) TP (True Positives): the number of samples that are correctly divided into positive samples. (2) FP (False Positives): the number of samples that are wrongly divided into positive samples. (3) FN (False Negatives): the number of samples that are wrongly divided into negative samples. (4) TN (True Negatives): the number of samples that are correctly divided into negative samples.

The accuracy is defined as: Accuracy $=(TP + TN)/(P + N)$. The higher the accuracy, the better the classification effect.

4.2 Parameters of CNN

CNN needs several parameters during its execution. These parameters are related to the actual data set and operating environment. In practical, there is no effective and unified method for specific data set and environment, and experiments are usually needed to find proper parameters. Three parameters are mainly considered in the following experiments: batch size, convolution kernel size, and hidden layer.

(1) Batch size

Batch size is an important learning parameter in machine learning. In the gradient algorithm, increasing batch size within a reasonable range can improve memory utilization. It reduces the algorithm iterations, speeds up the processing of the data, and can determine the directions of decline. But the choice of batch size is not as large as possible. When it is too large, because the number of iterations required is too small, the time spend will increase greatly. Reasonable batch size selection is related to the format and quantity of data, and it is usually determined by expert experience.

In this experiment, the values of batch size are set to 10, 20, 30, 40, and the numbers of training iteration are set to 500, 1000, 2000. The experimental results are shown in Table 1 and Fig. 4.

Table 1. Training accuracy of different batch sizes

Group No.	Batch size	500 iterations	1000 iterations	2000 iterations
1	10	59.90%	54.53%	58.99%
2	20	55.00%	59.50%	79.00%
3	30	56.74%	59.97%	82.03%
4	40	56.49%	60.04%	82.60%
5	50	56.38%	59.99%	82.58%

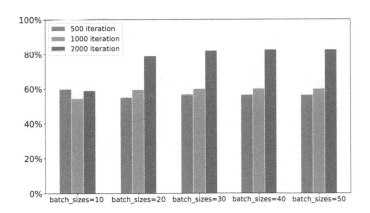

Fig. 4. Training accuracy of different batch sizes.

It can be seen from Fig. 4 that when the batch size is small, it may be insufficient training and is difficult to achieve the satisfied effect. With the batch size increasing, the improvement of accuracy is slowing down. When training 2000 iterations, batch size equals to 30 and 40, the training accuracy is 82.03% and 82.60%, and the test accuracy is 83.10% and 83.83%. When the value is 50, the accuracy drops slightly. Therefore, in the subsequent experiments, batch size is selected as 40, and the iteration is set to 2000.

(2) Convolution kernel size

The size of the convolution kernel is another key parameter of CNN. Set 5 groups of convolution kernels: 3 * 3, 5 * 5, 9 * 9, 11 * 11, 15 * 15, and the training accuracy and test accuracy are shown in Table 2 and Fig. 5.

Table 2. Accuracy of different convolution kernel sizes

Group No.	Kernel size	Training accuracy	Test accuracy
1	3 * 3	80.56%	55.23%
2	5 * 5	83.25%	55.40%
3	9 * 9	83.00%	63.12%
4	11 * 11	86.99%	94.88%
5	15 * 15	88.50%	44.30%

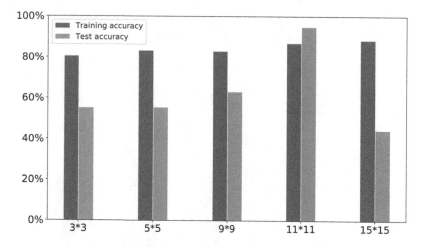

Fig. 5. Accuracy of different convolution kernel sizes.

From Table 2, we can see that as the convolution kernel size increases, the accuracy of training is gradually increasing, and the accuracy of testing also shows the same trend. However, when the convolution kernel is 15*15, the test accuracy is significantly reduce. Therefore, for the data set of this experiment, the convolution kernel of 11*11 achieves relatively best result.

(3) Hidden layers

A typical characteristic of deep learning is the multi-layer neural network, which can provide high level abstraction of data features. A hidden layer includes a convolutional layer and a pooling layer as in Fig. 1. The following 5 groups of experiments are set with the hidden layers of 1,2,3,4,5, and with the same of pooling layers. "1c-1p" refers to "1 convolution layer and 1 pooling layer". The experimental results are shown in Table 3 and Fig. 6.

Table 3. Accuracy of different hidden layers

Group No.	Hidden layers	Training accuracy	Test accuracy
1	1c-1p	85.02%	61.87%
2	2c-2p	86.99%	84.17%
3	3c-3p	87.54%	94.88%
4	4c-4p	87.62%	95.12%
5	5c-5p	87.68%	95.23%

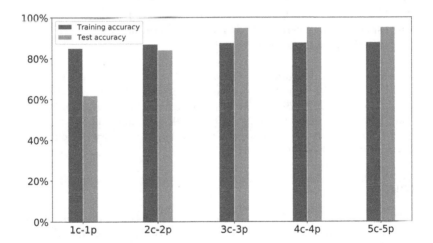

Fig. 6. Accuracy of different hidden layers.

With the number of hidden layers increasing, the training accuracy and test accuracy are both rising. However, when the number of hidden layers increases from 3 to 5, the accuracy increasing tends to be flat, reaching a relatively similar accuracy. When the hidden layer is 5, the highest test accuracy of 95.23% is achieved. However, as the hidden layer increases, the time consumption is increasing significantly. Therefore, the accuracy and time consumption need to be balanced in practical application.

5   Conclusion

Android malware detection is not only for the safety of the third-party application markets, but also for the safety of individual users who download and install the applications. With the continuous emergence of new malicious applications and the continuous updating of malicious code camouflage and obfuscation, Android malware detection is the main technology to ensure security.

An Android malware detection framework based on app-image conversion is presented in this work. It focuses on mapping the installation files of Android applications to grayscale images in binary form, and then classify the images by CNN. This method can solve the problem of malicious code deformation and confusion to a certain extent.

The experiments compare and select three parameters of CNN: batch size, convolution kernel size, and the number of hidden layers. By the constructed data set, the proposed method finally achieves a classification accuracy of 95.23%, which shows the effectiveness and feasibility of the presented method. In the future work, we will apply the proposed method to specific types of malware detection, especially malware with disguise and confusion, to verify the effectiveness and scalability if the method.

Acknowledgments. This work was supported in part by the 13th Five-Year Science and Technology Research Project of the Education Department of Jilin Province under Grant No. JJKH20200794KJ, the Innovation Fund of Changchun University of Science and Technology under Grant No. XJJLG-2018-09, the fund of Key Laboratory of Symbolic Computation and Knowledge Engineering of Ministry of Education (Jilin University) under Grant No. 93K172018K05.

References

1. Cai, H., Meng, N., Ryder, B., Yao, D.: Droidcat: effective android malware detection and categorization via app-level profiling. IEEE Trans. Inf. Foren. Secur. **14**(6), 1455–1470 (2018)
2. Cen, L., Gates, C.S., Si, L., Li, N.: A probabilistic discriminative model for android malware detection with decompiled source code. IEEE Trans. Dependable Secur. Comput. **12**(4), 400–412 (2014)
3. Chen, J., Wang, C., Zhao, Z., Chen, K., Du, R., Ahn, G.J.: Uncovering the face of android Ransomware: characterization and real-time detection. IEEE Trans. Inf. Foren. Secur. **13**(5), 1286–1300 (2017)
4. Deng, L., Yu, D.: Deep convex net: A scalable architecture for speech pattern classification. In: Twelfth Annual Conference of the International Speech Communication Association (2011)
5. Enck, W., et al.: Taintdroid: an information-flow tracking system for realtime privacy monitoring on smartphones. ACM Trans. Comput. Syst. (TOCS) **32**(2), 1–29 (2014)
6. F-Secure: Trojan: andriod/droidkungfu.c. [EB/OL] (2020). https://www.f-secure. com/vdescs/trojan_android_droidkungfu_c.shtml
7. Fang, Z., Permission based android security: Permission based Android security: issues and countermeasures. Comput. Secur. **43**, 205–218 (2014)

8. Fu, J., Xue, J., Wang, Y., Liu, Z., Shan, C.: Malware visualization for fine-grained classification. IEEE Access **6**, 14510–14523 (2018)
9. Hou, S., Ye, Y., Song, Y., Abdulhayoglu, M.: Hindroid: an intelligent android malware detection system based on structured heterogeneous information network. In: Proceedings of the 23rd ACM SIGKDD International Conference on Knowledge Discovery and Data Mining, pp. 1507–1515 (2017)
10. IDC: Smartphone challenges continue in 2019. [EB/OL] (2019). https://www.idc.com/getdoc.jsp?containerId=prUS45487719
11. Kaspersky: Mobile malware evolution 2019. [EB/OL] (2020). https://securelist.com/mobile-malware-evolution-2019/96280
12. LeCun, Y., et al.: Backpropagation applied to handwritten zip code recognition. Neural Comput. **1**(4), 541–551 (1989)
13. LeCun, Y., Bottou, L., Bengio, Y., Haffner, P.: Gradient-based learning applied to document recognition. Proc. IEEE **86**(11), 2278–2324 (1998)
14. Li, D., Zhao, L., Cheng, Q., Lu, N., Shi, W.: Opcode sequence analysis of android malware by a convolutional neural network. Concurr. Comput. Pract. Exp. **32**(18), e5308 (2020)
15. McLaughlin, N., et al.: Deep android malware detection. In: Proceedings of the Seventh ACM on Conference on Data and Application Security and Privacy, pp. 301–308 (2017)
16. Nataraj, L., Karthikeyan, S., Jacob, G., Manjunath, B.S.: Malware images: visualization and automatic classification. In: Proceedings of the 8th International Symposium on Visualization for Cyber Security, pp. 1–7 (2011)
17. Peng, H., et al.: Using probabilistic generative models for ranking risks of android apps. In: Proceedings of the 2012 ACM Conference on Computer and Communications Security, pp. 241–252 (2012)
18. Poon, H., Domingos, P.: Sum-product networks: a new deep architecture. In: 2011 IEEE International Conference on Computer Vision Workshops (ICCV Workshops), pp. 689–690. IEEE (2011)
19. Vincent, P., Larochelle, H., Lajoie, I., Bengio, Y., Manzagol, P.A., Bottou, L.: Stacked denoising autoencoders: learning useful representations in a deep network with a local denoising criterion. J. Mach. Learn. Res. **11**(12), 3371–3408 (2010)
20. Wang, W., Zhao, M., Wang, J.: Effective android malware detection with a hybrid model based on deep autoencoder and convolutional neural network. J. Ambient Intell. Humaniz. Comput. **10**(8), 3035–3043 (2018). https://doi.org/10.1007/s12652-018-0803-6
21. Wei, F., Roy, S., Ou, X.: Amandroid: a precise and general inter-component data flow analysis framework for security vetting of android apps. In: Proceedings of the 2014 ACM SIGSAC Conference on Computer and Communications Security, pp. 1329–1341 (2014)
22. Xu, K., Li, Y., Deng, R.H.: ICCDetector: ICC-based malware detection on android. IEEE Trans. Inf. Foren. Secur. **11**(6), 1252–1264 (2016)
23. Zhandi, W.: Research and application of Android malware detection based on deep learning. Guizhou Normal University (2019)
24. Zhang, H., Xiao, X., Mercaldo, F., Ni, S., Martinelli, F., Sangaiah, A.K.: Classification of Ransomware families with machine learning based on n-gram of opcodes. Fut. Gener. Comput. Syst. **90**, 211–221 (2019)
25. Zhang, J., Qin, Z., Yin, H., Ou, L., Hu, Y.: IRMD: malware variant detection using opcode image recognition. In: 2016 IEEE 22nd International Conference on Parallel and Distributed Systems (ICPADS), pp. 1175–1180. IEEE (2016)

26. Zhang, M., Duan, Y., Yin, H., Zhao, Z.: Semantics-aware android malware classi-
    fication using weighted contextual api dependency graphs. In: Proceedings of the
    2014 ACM SIGSAC Conference on Computer and Communications Security, pp.
    1105–1116 (2014)
27. Zhang, J., Chen, B., Gu, L.: Research on malware detection technology based on
    image analysis. Netinfo. Secur. **19**(10), 24–31 (2019)

Research on IMS Security Access and Mechanism in Power System

Xiao-yuan Zhang[✉], Peng Jia, and Shao-peng Wanyan

NARI Group Corporation, State Grid Electric Power Research Institute, Nanjing, China

Abstract. IMS in power system brings both multimedia services and security threats. Based on the requirements of information security and IMS architecture, an optimal access algorithm based on non-key exchange encryption and elliptic curve cryptography is proposed. The new algorithm inherits the advantages that IMS AKA mechanism can deal with attack, and solves DoS attack and SPIT attack which can not be solved. In addition, the optimized computational performance is enhanced, the cost is reduced and the authentication time is reduced.

Keywords: IMS · Secure access · Security mechanisms · Certification · Multimedia service

1 Introduction

With the construction and development of the power communication network of State Grid Company, the communication service is no longer limited to voice and data services, and a new demand for multimedia services is put forward. IP Multimedia Subsystem (IMS) is a standardized architecture introduced by 3GPP for the next generation network [1–5]. Based on full IP connections, it fuses fixed and mobile networks into packet mode. As a result, it provides a variety of multimedia services, unlimited devices or access to media [6–9]. At present, State Grid Corporation has identified IMS as the mainstream technology of the next generation grid management switching network.

The architecture of IMS consists of user device, IMS core network and application server. Although the Internet is full of novel and diverse business, but when users experience these services, they feel that the business is not integrated, the security of the business and the quality of service can not be guaranteed [10–14]. The IMS provides the control and management mechanism, and the enterprise can use the resources to provide the targeted user information, and provide the bearing quality with QoS guarantee for the contracted business through the differentiated service [15–17]. Based on security architecture of IMS network, network security of IMS is divided into two levels, that is IMS network security access and IMS core network security. Based on the above problems, this paper studies IMS safety problems [18, 19].

Y. Tian et al. (Eds.): ICBDS 2020, CCIS 1415, pp. 75–85, 2021.
https://doi.org/10.1007/978-981-16-3150-4_7

2   IMS Meeting Operational Platform

By integrating and integrating the business scope of fixed network and mobile network, IMS can be fully deployed, so that the user can access from any terminal anytime and anywhere, without being bound by fixed network and mobile network, and experience the same service [20]. Moreover, based on the IMS, carried by the ip, the business on the Internet is collected into its own business system, which expands the scope of business and allows users to have more business experience. All in all, the goal of conference building based on IMS is the integration of multi-networks to achieve multi-business integration [21]. IMS self-help conference business platform includes conference application server, resource processing server etc. The conference platform realizes the operation and management of the IMS multimedia conference by the national network company, and can also provide the functions of session control, resource management, authentication, routing, meeting notification and so on, and connect with the IMS core network through the IMS sip interface [22, 23]. Portal can provide users with self-service management functions such as conference management and venue control, provide users with direct access to web pages to participate in the meeting. A media resource service can reserve and allocate conference resources related to processing, as well as playing voice notification and receiving secondary dialing. H.323 gateway can realize the interworking between H.323 terminal and the original H.323 video conference system [24]. Short message gateway and mail server mainly forward the notice of video conference; MGCF is responsible for interconnection with PSTN terminal and mobile terminal (Fig. 1).

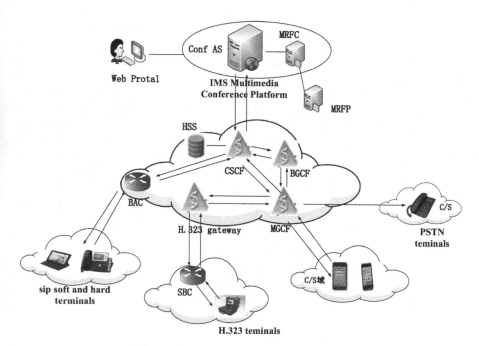

Fig. 1. IMS platform for self-help meetings

Information security protection includes production control area security protection and management information area security protection, as shown below [25]. Among them, the production control area and the management information area adopt the horizontal safety isolation device dedicated to electric power [26]. The management information is divided into information intranet and information extranet, and the information security isolation device is used between the information intranet and the information extranet. IMS administrative exchange network is deployed in the management information area, there is no business interaction with the production control area, and there is no need for special horizontal safety isolation device for electric power [27]. However, for IMS services across internal and external information networks, it is necessary to force the security isolation device to meet the requirements of information security (Fig. 2).

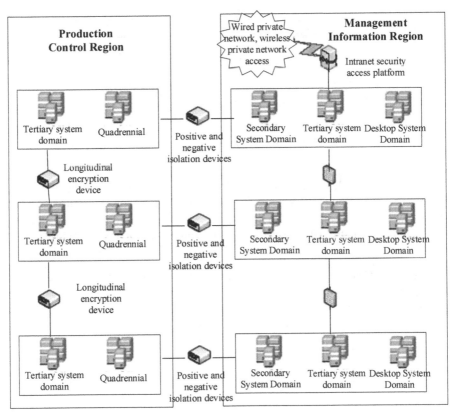

Fig. 2. Schematic diagram of security domain partition

3 Current Status of Authentication Algorithm in IMS Network

The TS33.203 specification of 3GPP defines the access security mechanism of ims network, including the authentication of network and user. The security mechanism of IMS core network protection is defined in 3GPP, which provides service protection between different network nodes. IMS network security architecture is shown in Fig. 3 [26].

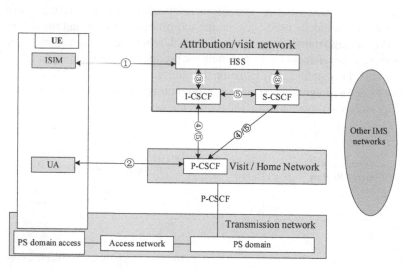

Fig. 3. Security architecture of IMS

As shown in Fig. 3, five different security dimensions defined by the 3 standards are labeled 1, 2, 3, 4, and 5. Of these, 1 and 2 represent the access security for IMS networks, while 3, 4 and 5 represent security for IMS network internetwork elements. Specific security of these five security dimensions are shown in Table 1 below.

Table 1. Concrete elements of different security dimensions of IMS networks

Order number	Security	Specific content
1	Between users and IMS networks	Realization of authentication between UE and IMS networks
2	Between user equipment and P-CSCF	Implement the security protection between terminal and access network element, execute the authentication of data source
3	Between CSCF and HSS	Provides interface security between CSCF and HSS within the network domain
4	CSCF between different networks	Secure CSCF between different networks
5	CSCF within IMS network	Secure SIP nodes within the network

The security of IMS network is divided into two levels, that is IMS network security access and IMS core network security. The connection between functional modules within the power private network is relatively secure. As a result, this paper will focus on the access security of IMS network.

Actually, IMS architecture is based entirely on various protocols. Since SIP is a text-based protocol with high activity, ignoring the privacy of users, making public and private identities unprotected, IMS networks face security risks. Effective authentication and authentication of IMS network is an important way to improve the security of IMS network access layer.

HTTPDigest authentication algorithm uses hash encryption algorithm to realize server and user authentication, but it can not ensure the two-way authentication between network and user, and lacks the integrity protection of message. The authentication and key-negotiation protocol (AKA) is designed in 3GPP designed to address sip vulnerabilities in IMS networks. IMSAKA mechanism is based on the UMTSAKA, to perform dual authentication between the terminal and the IMS core network and to establish new key pairs in terms of encryption and integrity. However, the IMSAKA algorithm does not provide authentication of intermediate network elements such as P-CSCF, and the security is not enough.

4 An Authentication Algorithm for Converting Unkey Encryption Technology and ECC

4.1 Security Gaps in IMSAKA Mechanisms

An improved access algorithm based on IMSAKA is proposed in this paper. First of all, a brief IMSAKA authentication algorithm is introduced. IMSAKA algorithm is implemented based on a long-term shared key and a serial number. It has the advantage of ensuring bidirectional authentication between users and networks and performs well at the level of integrity and confidentiality.

When an attacker sends a register request containing user identity to confuse the network and prevent legitimate users from authenticating, this increases the time for the generation of authentication vector. If a legitimate user wants to authenticate, the operation will fail, that is, the denial-of-service attack. IMSAKA does not guarantee the protection of user identity because the first register message sent by the UE is not secure and contains the IMPI and IMPU of the user. If a message is sent when the security key has not been negotiated, the eavesdropper can capture such sensitive information, thereby affecting services such as user calls. Such as DOS attacks consume network resources, spit attacks and so on, which pose a threat to the information security of users.

An attacker can extract information about UE by analyzing traffic during session initialization. For example, an attacker can get the user's information, the service, and the location of the user. Also if no Zb interface is implemented, in theory, any attacker located in an internal network can monitor the exchange of message.

4.2 Specific Flow of Improved Algorithms

Due to the security vulnerabilities of IMSAKA authentication mechanism, a new improved authentication algorithm for IMS network is proposed in this paper. This algorithm is mainly composed of two modules, one is the identity protection module, another is the authentication key negotiation module [28].

4.2.1 Identity Protection Module

The module protects the identity of the user transmitted between UE and P-CSCF. This module adopts non-key encryption technology and proposes a one-time identity mechanism. UE can generate a one-time random identity for each newly established session and respond to eavesdroppers with a fuzzy user's true identity. This scheme is based on the nature of the exchange in cryptography, which enables the communication parties to exchange data and share information without the need for a key, without any modification to the infrastructure.

For generating a one-time random identity, the user's IMPI, IMPU and the user's random key are entered into an exchange encryption function. Since users use different random keys for each newly established session, each established session generates a one-time identity.

UE generates random prime numbers p, UE and P-CSCF randomly select two random number a and b respectively in the process of fuzzy user identity module. Let a, b $\in$ $[1, p - 2]$, and maximum common divisor gcd(a, p − 1) = 1, gcd(b, p − 1) = 1, UE and P-CSCF calculate the inverse of (a − 1)mod(p − 1) and (b − 1)mod(p − 1). The process of exchanging messages is as follow, UE initiate a session to the P-CSCF, first UE randomly select a as the private secret key, and calculate the ID^a mod p. A "401 unauthorized response" with a ciphertext is sent to the UE through a public channel. UE sends a new register message to the P-CSCF according to $(ID^a)^b \bmod p = (ID^{a*(-a)})^b =$

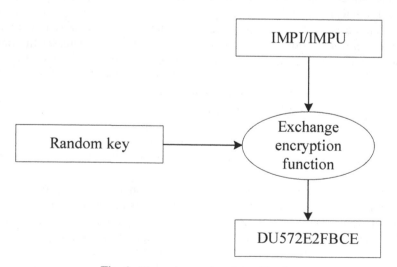

Fig. 4. Generate one-time fuzzy identity

$ID^b \bmod p$, P-CSCF extract the user's actual ID, for authentication. If the validation is successful, the agent responds with a "200 ok" message. Because the input of the encryption function is different, no new random key is needed, so is the generated ciphertext. ID represents the IMPI and IMPU. of users (Fig. 4).

UE sent to P-CSCF, $(ID^a) \bmod p$.

P-CSCF sent to UE, $(ID^a)^b \bmod p$.

UE sent to P-CSCF, $(ID^b) \bmod p$.

4.2.2 Authentication and Key Negotiation Modul

The module contains two steps. The first step is to address the need for mutual authentication between UE and HSS after user authorization. The second step is to establish confidentiality and integrity keys to implement IPSec associations in order to protect SIP messages transmitted between UE and P-CSCF. This module must also ensure that it does not replay when authentication is performed.

Because the Elliptic Curve Cryptographic Mechanism (ECC) technology meets all the requirements of the module, ECC technology is used in this module.

Step 1, Mutual authentication of UE and HSS. First it describes the meaning of parameters in the HSS execution step. P is the prime number generated, an elliptic curve equation on F_P of prime number fields is $E_p(a, b) : y^2 = x^3 + ax + b(\bmod p)a, b \in F_p 4a^3 + 27b^2 \neq 0(\bmod p)$, b is the base point on the elliptic curve; $s \in Z_p^*$ stored in HSS and UE. The $h(\cdot)$ is a secure hash function; the shared message sent by HSS is $\{E_P(a, b), B, h(\cdot)\}$.

When UE register to the IMS network, it uses HSS to perform the following steps.

1. UE select a random private key $x \in Z_p^*$ and calculate its public key $V = x * B$. Then, a register request containing its public key V is sent to the HSS.
2. When the request is received, a randomly private key $c \in Z_p^*$ is generated by HSS. The public key and the session key $AICK = c * V$ are calculated according to $W = c * B$. The HSS authentication token is calculated by $Auth_{Hss} = h(W\|s * AICK)$ and the UE authentication token is calculated by $Auth'_{UE} = h(V\|s * AICK)$. HSS then send its authentication token to the terminal UE with its public key W.
3. UE calculates the session key $AICK = c * W$ and authentication token of HSS $Auth'_{Hss}$ after receiving the message. Then, UE verifies that $Auth_{Hss} = Auth'_{Hss}$ is valid. IF established, the identity of HSS is authenticated. Next, UE compute its authentication token and send it to the HSS.
4. HSS compare the received token with the calculated token. if they are equal, the UE is authenticated.

Step 2, UE and P-CSCF should establish IPSec associations to protect sip messages after completing the mutual authentication step. This step requires two keys, the integrity key (IK) and the password key (CK). For the optimized authentication algorithm, the two keys are the abscissa and ordinate of the session key already calculated in the mutual authentication stage. Therefore, P-CSCF establish IPsec association with the UE

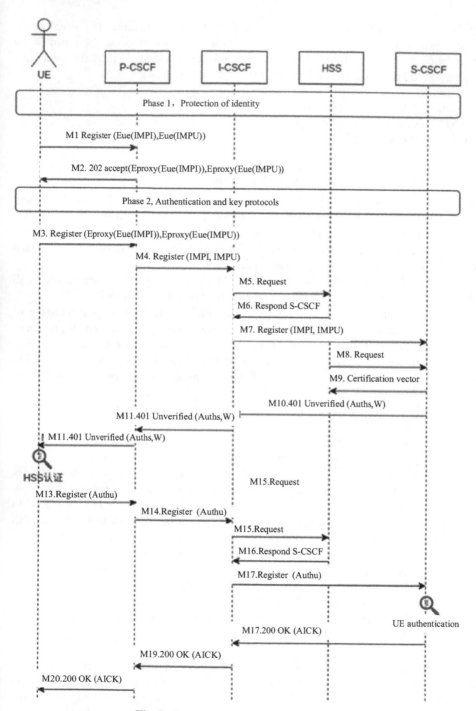

Fig. 5. Improved authentication algorithm

at the end of the mutual authentication step. Figure 5 shows the access flow chart of the improved algorithm.

5   Simulation and Analysis of Algorithm

The algorithm proposed in this paper is improved on the basis of IMS AKA, so the algorithm will be compared with IMS AKA to analyze its security and performance

5.1   Analysis of Security

IMS AKA mechanism in the registration process, the user is in the form of plaintext to provide P-CSCF with their identity. The optimization algorithm proposed in this paper ensures the user identity (IMPI and IMPU) by using the keyless encryption technology based on the mode power operation, so the attacker can never steal these identities by analyzing the packets.

The proposed optimization algorithm explicitly performs mutual authentication between UE and IMS networks. They compute their authentication tokens based on the shared key between UE and HSS to complete mutual authentication.

Only after mutual authentication, after mutual authentication, protect sip messages by establishing IPSec associations with key CK and IK calculated during the authentication phase, to ensure confidentiality and integrity of data transmitted between UE and P-CSCF.

IMS-AKA protocol can resist replay attacks and man-in-the-middle attacks, but can resist DoS synchronization and spit attacks. This paper proposes an improved algorithm to overcome these security vulnerabilities by blurring user identity and combining elliptic curve cryptography, which can deal with DoS and SPIT attacks that IMS AKA can not cope with.

Man-in-the-middle attack. UE and HSS share secret key in the proposed optimization algorithm. Mutual authentication must be performed between UE and HSS, but the attacker can neither imitate UE nor imitate when trying to attack, so it can not pass the authentication process, thus eliminating this attack.

Replay attack. Suppose the attacker intercepts the first register (V) message and simulates the UE by replay. Since the attacker has neither a secret key, nor a private key refreshed by each new session, the correct Auth can not be calculated and sent to the HSS. If the attacker tries to guess the secret key, it can not deal with the discrete logarithm problem of elliptic curve. When an attacker intercepts a message and replays it, but the information actually intercepted has expired and belongs to the old session, it is not possible to implement verification on the UE side.

SPIT attacks. A spit attack can only be triggered if you know the identity of the user. In the proposed algorithm, a private module based on non-key encryption is used to blur these identities, thus preventing such attacks.

DoS attacks. This attack is based on SQN usage and synchronization. However, the authentication algorithm proposed in this paper does not use SQN, or need synchronization process, so the attacker can not launch such an attack (Table 2).

Table 2. Comparison of imsaka algorithm and optimization algorithm's ability to combat attack

Type of attack	IMS AKA	Improved algorithm
Replay attack	Can resist	Can resist
Man-in-the-middle attack	Can resist	Can resist
SPIT attacks	Can not resist	Can resist
DoS attacks	Can not resist	Can resist

5.2 Performance Analysis

The IMS AKA authentication mechanism is based on serial number sqn, and the improved authentication mechanism proposed in this paper does not require any synchronization mechanism, thus reducing authentication time and bandwidth loss.

The authentication mechanism of IMS AKA establishes IPSec associations between UE and P-CSCF during the authentication stage, the new authentication mechanism proposed in this paper only establishes IPSec associations after mutual authentication between UE and HSS, which reduces the total authentication time.

IMS AKA mechanism uses five functions to compute authentication vectors, but this algorithm only protects user identity by generating one-off encryption. It reduces the complexity of computational.

6 Conclusion

IMS AKA is the most widely used authentication mechanism in IMS network, but there are still some vulnerabilities in its security and there is room for improvement in performance. To solve this problem, the optimization algorithm proposed in this paper uses keyless exchange encryption technology and elliptic curve cryptography (ECC) to improve the IMS AKA, which not only inherits the advantages that the IMS AKA mechanism can deal with replay attacks and MITM attacks. It can also solve the DoS attacks and SPIT attacks. Moreover, the optimized algorithm is enhanced compared with the IMS AKA, performance, which reduces the CSCF calculation cost and the authentication time. This optimization algorithm provides a good idea for ensuring the safe access of power administrative switching network used by State Grid Company.

References

1. Xue, G.A.O., Ji, Z.H.U., Yuan, C.H.E.N.: Research on multi-services bearing solution of LTE power wireless private network. Electr. Power Inf. Commun. Technol. **12**(12), 26–29 (2014)
2. Liu, C., Zhang, Y.: Application of IMS technology in power communication administrative switching network. Inf. Commun. **7**(11), 175–176 (2016)
3. Xiao-ling, P.E.N.G.: Research of an interactive voice-video response system based on IMS. Comput. Technol. Dev. **9**(2), 207–210 (2011)

4. Wang, S.-G., Sun, Q.-B.: Uncertain QoS-aware skyline service selection based on cloud model. J. Softw. **23**(6), 1397–1412 (2017)
5. Yong, Gu: Research on the application of wavelet neural network in temperature control system. Adv. Mater. Res. **12**(5), 33–49 (2014)
6. Vidal, Ivan, de la Oliva, Antonio: TRIM: an architecture for transparent IMS-based mobility. Comput. Netw. **55**(7), 1472–1486 (2017)
7. Thomas, M., Metcalf, L., Spring, J., SiLK: a tool suite for unsampled network flow analysis at scale. In: IEEE International Congress on Big Data, pp. 184–191 (2014)
8. Zhu, X., Liao, J., The, I.M.S.: IP multimedia concepts and services in the mobile domain. J. Assoc. Inf. Sci. Technol. **58**(11), 1705–1706 (2015)
9. Wang, Q., Sun, Y.: The next generation network of the soft exchange and IMS. Netw. Secur. Technol. Appl. **8**, 37–38 (2014)
10. Sun, J.: Network optimization design of NGN. Shanxi Electron. Technol. **6**, 78–83 (2014)
11. Chen, R., Tang, H., Zhao, G.: Study and implementation of user agent for SIP protocol. Commun. Technol. **2**, 163–165 (2010)
12. He, C., Yang, H., Lu, X.: Evolution scheme from soft switch to IMS in Electric Power Communication **13**(11), 1–6 (2015)
13. Yu, J., Liu, J., Cai, S.: Research on LTE wireless network planning in electric power system. Electr. Power Inf. Commun. Technol. **10**(2), 7–11 (2016)
14. You, X.H., Pan, Z.W., Gao, X.Q., et al.: The 5G mobile communication: the development trends and its emerging key techniques. Sci. Sin. **44**(5), 551 (2014)
15. Qiu, J., Ding, G., Wu, Q., et al.: Hierarchical resource allocation framework for hyper-dense small cell networks. IEEE Access **4**(99), 8657–8669 (2017)
16. Wang, K.: The application of the internet of things in the 5G era in the power system. Telecom Power Technol. **35**(5), 187–188 (2018)
17. Xia, X., Zhu, X., Mei, C., Li, W., Fang, H.: Research and practice on 5G slicing in power internet of things. Mob. Commun. **43**(1), 63–69 (2019)
18. Li, B., Zhou, J., Ren, X.: Research on key issues of TD-LTE network optimization. Telecom Eng. Tech. Stand. **1**, 57–61 (2015)
19. Fernekeß, A., Klein, A., Wegmann, B., et al.: Load dependent interference margin for link budget calculations of OFDM networks. IEEE Commun. Lett. **12**(5), 398–400 (2008)
20. Zheng, L., Tse, D.N.C.: Diversity and multiplexing: a fundamental tradeoff in multiple antenna channels. IEEE Trans. Inf. Theor. **49**(5), 1073–1096 (2003)
21. Jiming, Y.A.O.: Random access technology of electric dedicated LTE network based on power priority. Autom. Electr. Power Syst. **40**(10), 127–131 (2016)
22. Cao, J., Liu, J., Li, X.: A power wireless broadband technology scheme for smart power distribution and utilization network. Autom. Electr. Power Syst. **37**(11), 76–80 (2013)
23. Sun, J., Lin, C.: Research of smart distribution terminal communication technology based on TE-LTE. Telecommun. Electr. Power Syst. **33**(7), 80–83 (2012)
24. Li, W., Wang, J., Shao, Q., Li, S.: Efficient resource allocation algorithms for energy efficiency maximization in ultra-dense network. In: GLOBECOM 2017 - 2017 IEEE Global Communications Conference, pp. 1–6 (2017)
25. Xie, J., Liu, J.: Optimization simulation of wireless network communication coverage. Comput. Simul. **33**(6), 271–275 (2015)
26. Hamidi, M.M., Edmonson, W.W., Afghah, F.: A non-vooperative game theoretic approach for power allocation in interstatellite communication. In: 2017 IEEE International Conference on Wireless for Space and Extreme Environments (WISEE), pp. 13–18 (2017)
27. Li, W., Chen, B., Wu, Q., et al.: Applied research of TD-LTE power wireless broadband private metwork. Telecommun. Electr. Power Syst. **33**(241), 82–87 (2012)
28. Ming, L., et al.: Performance analysis and evaluation of industrial ethernet. In: International Conference on Electrical & Control Engineering. IEEE Computer Society (2010)

Research on the Role-Based Access Control Model and Data Security Method

Junhua Deng[1]([⊠]), Lei Zhao[1], Xuechong Yuan[2], Zhu Tang[2], and Qian Guo[3,4]

[1] State Grid, Jiangsu Marketing Service Center (Metrolgy Center), Nanjing 210000, China
[2] State Grid Beijing Electric Power Co., Ltd, Beijing 100000, China
[3] Global Energy Interconnection Research Institute Co., Ltd, Nanjing 210000, China
guoqian@geiri.sgcc.com.cn
[4] State Grid Key Laboratory of Information and Network Security, Nanjing 210003, China

Abstract. For management of massive data and centralized network, the data security research team has become a central issue. Role-based access control (RBAC) is a common practice to control access to sensitive data. This article uses Flex and C# to develop an RBAC model, which can make data management more flexible. Concentrating on data security, this article presents the layer structure and model design for standardized management of security access. This article also implements detailed approaches for data security by verifying parameters and codes, access control, preventing illegal users and using oracle parameters and stored procedures for database security technology. In addition, an empirical study was conducted to assess effectiveness and usefulness .

Keywords: Access control · Data Security · Hierarchical framework · Parameter · Stored procedure

1 Introductions

Recently, as the big data and the popularization of network platform technology developing, many governments and enterprises have started to devote themselves to research on data access control and data security, and to develop data and information network applications and services to realize centralized and easy management information and resources. Therefore, as the emergence of Internet and Web platform, the development mode of enterprise information system has gradually developed from C/S to B/S [1]. Using the B/S mode, the problems of the traditional C/S mode can be solved, for example, difficult system maintenance and heavy workload. For point-to-multipoint, multipoint-to-multipoint and TCP/IP B/S mode using this open architecture, its security depends on the database server to manage passwords. The security of application layer information system, especially the security of B/S mode, becomes more prominent. Therefore, in the B/S mode, how to take effective approaches to enhance the security system of basic data, solve the security problem of confidential data, and effectively provide services for the big data system, is a hot research issue [2]. This paper adopts both Flex and C#, gives the design method of authorization management, and introduces the technology and method

© Springer Nature Singapore Pte Ltd. 2021
Y. Tian et al. (Eds.): ICBDS 2020, CCIS 1415, pp. 86–96, 2021.
https://doi.org/10.1007/978-981-16-3150-4_8

to ensure data security. Through the use of Adobe Flex Builder 3 and Microsoft Visual Studio 2008 and with Oracle 10 g, the back-end database server adopts the technical route of Flex and Visual C#.Net.

2 Related Overview

2.1 Access Control

Access control (AC) is a mechanism to achieve integrity and confidentiality in software systems. It is often on the basis of access permissions (also known as authorization), and its main function is controlling the system resource permissions scope, for example, deciding which users can access which objects or perform what operations [3]. The authorization management system structure is displayed in Fig. 1. It plays a vital role in restricting users' access to confidential resources and preventing damage caused by unauthorized users' intrusion or accidental operations of legitimate users. Thus, establishing a general AC model will greatly improve the security of enterprise information systems.

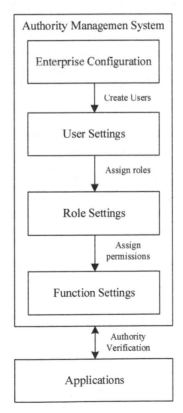

Fig. 1. Authority management system structure

Whenever the resources and users' number are high, such authorizations number becomes large. Furthermore, if the user base is highly dynamic, the number of authorization grant and revoke operations to be conducted will become very hard to manage. Traditional AC mechanisms can neither meet the requirements of fine-grained control, nor can they be implemented rapidly. Therefore, RBAC is put forward as an alternative method. At present, this form of RBAC has obvious advantages and potential, and has been widely applied to replace traditional mandatory AC (mandatory AC MAC) and Discretionary AC (DAC).

MAC security policy controls access according to the classification of objects and topics. An object is a passive entry that stores data (such as relationships), while a topic is an active entity accessing an object, usually an active process running representing the user. The access class is made up of two components: security level and a group of categories. Security levels are elements of a hierarchical ordered set. The levels usually used are top secret (TS), secret (s), secret (c) and unclassified (U), where $TS > s > C > U$.

DAC specifies rules according to which the principal can create and delete objects, and grant and revoke authorization for others to access objects. The user's access to data is managed according to the user's identity and the predefined discretionary rules determined by the security administrator. Rules specify the type of object that users are allowed to access for each object and user in the system. Check the user's request to access the object according to the specified permission; if there is authorization, it indicates that the object can be obtained in a certain mode, then the access right will be granted; otherwise, it will be rejected. These strategies are discretionary because they enable users to grant access to objects to other users. Free decision strategy is used in commercial system because of its flexibility, which makes it suitable for different protection requirements.

The AC purpose is limiting the operations that legitimate users of computer systems can conduct. AC limits the operations that users can perform directly and the programs that are allowed to execute representing users. In this method, AC attempts to block activities that could cause security violations. There are two kinds of resources in the computer system: active subject and passive object. The method a principal access an object is called access rights. Access rights enable the subject to manipulate objects (write, read, execute, etc.) or change AC information (transfer of ownership, grant and revoke rights, etc.).

AC can be on the basis of various strategies that follow different principles. The selection of security strategy is very significant since it affects the system flexibility, availability and performance. This strategy is on the basis of the following principles [3].

Principle of minimum and maximum privileges: Based on this principle, users should adopt the minimum set of privileges required for the activity. In this regard, the principle of maximum privilege is on the basis of the maximum data availability principle.

Principles of open and closed systems: For an open system, all access that is not expressly prohibited is allowed. For a closed system, all access must be permitted with explicit authorization. Closed systems are inherently safer.

Centralized and decentralized management principles: This principle addresses the issue of who is in charge of maintaining and managing permissions in the AC model. In different parts of the centralized control system, the authority of the centralized control system is different.

2.2 RBAC Model of the System

RBAC was first proposed by Ferraiolo of NIST in the 20th century [4]. After 1990s, it become the AC model mainstream gradually. Its core thought is to achieve the logical connection between users and authorization by granting role with authorization. This article offers a combined solution of operation authority, column function permission, system table authority and data table permission, so as to satisfy the centralized management organization control requirements in multi-level authority. Dynamically specify the system role based on the actual situation. The authorization administrator is only required to grant and revoke the proper role membership. The relationships defined between users, roles, and privileges are shown in Fig. 2.

There are two advantages for RBAC: (1) the change rate between user and role is higher than that between role and authorization, and the complexity of authorization management and maintenance cost can be reduced. (2) It improves the flexibility of implementing organizational AC strategies and corporate modifications.

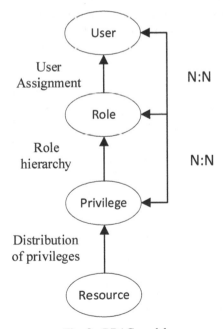

Fig. 2. RBAC model

3 RBAC Model Design

3.1 Layered System Framework

In the basic RBAC of this standard, the entire management system is on the basis of B/S and adopts a mainstream layered structure. This design's advantage is the hierarchical encapsulation of business subsystems, which reduces the degree of coupling, thereby improving the system scalability and maintainability [5].

3.1.1 The Communication Mechanism Between the Server and the Client

The Flex used in front-end user interaction is applied to solve the framework [6] by the third-party component FluourineFx, which calls C# classes directly from the server to realize the business logic layer interaction between the server and Flex.

If C# is required to interact with AS, the problem of data type conversion between the two languages shall be solved first. FlorineFx can facilitate that. The RemoteObject mechanism of AS is adopted to implement the calling approach. In the setting file, the tag [RemotingService] will be added before the called C# class, and then the following nodes will be added in file-remoting-config.xml to describe the remote call service setting file, where "source" specifies the remote object in the form of a standard name. Target decides whether the Flex Client can correctly access the remote object. This paper also suggests using struts framework model to support the development of B/S structure.

The design diagram of the role authority management system based on the Struts framework is shown in Fig. 3. The system is developed using Struts architecture, which is a classic MVC framework. The system model is composed of JavaBeans, which are

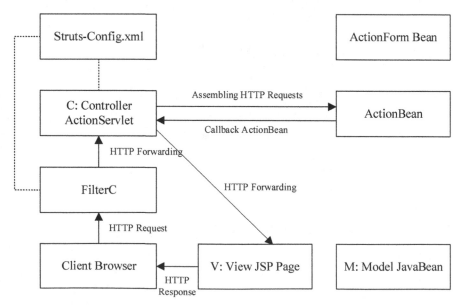

Fig. 3. Design diagram of role authority management system based on Struts framework

used to implement business logic, the controller is implemented by Action Servlet and Action, and the view is composed of a set of JSP files. In the application, Action is treated as an adapter for user request and business logic processing, and the business logic is completed by JavaBean.

When the ActionServlet controller receives a user request, it will forward the request to the corresponding Action instance.

3.1.2 Layered Design

By integrating C#.Net and Flex together, Flex programs can operate in a browser, and the browser's plug-in FlashPlay is responsible for interpretative execution [7]. Flex is mainly in charge of customer display. The middle layer is separated into interface layer, business logic layer, web layer, and data layer. Figure 4 indicates the layered system architecture.

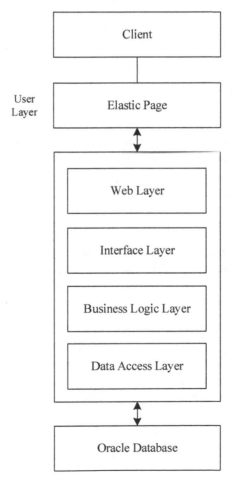

Fig. 4. Hierarchical system framework

User layer: Flex elements such as MXML and ActionScript are adopted as a service to provide users with a graphical interface [8];

Interface layer: Provide interface functions to facilitate the interaction between the user layer and the business logic layer;

Web layer: display several setting files applied in the communication mechanism;

Business logic layer: the intermediate connection between the data access layer and the interface layer, used to realize the data exchange, separate user operations from the database, including user class (BUserInfo.cs), role class (BUserRole.cs) and Permission class (BUserPrivilege.cs), etc., can realize business processes, such as adding, updating, deleting, etc.

e) Data access layer: Directly interact with the database for the underlying operations of the database, and realize the connection with the data and the interaction with the business logic layer.

3.2 Database Design

The massive data is a multi-disciplinary project, involving basic geographic data, marine environment data, RS image data, metadata and so on, and it requires all-around consideration of data sources. Thus, RBAC model is designed, which is made up of the following ten tables: table for user, role, user role, permission, role permission, permission menu, menu, list, database and data. In the data management system, it is a convenient method to use the above model as the basic infrastructure, which can dynamically assign and revoke authorization, and precisely control data access, data operation and operation modules. Thus, users can play and activate different roles simultaneously, and various permission types are available to access infrastructure managed resources.

4   Method Design

4.1 Identity Verification

There are four kinds of authentication for RBAC: user name and password, X.509 certificate, network address, and existing authentication token.

Password authentication, through a dedicated network service, checks the user name and password according to the central nice account database. User account information is kept in RBAC's own database.

Certificate authentication, if the user has X.509 certificate, it can be used on the standard client authentication mechanism of TLS/SSL protocol. The certificate data is then adopted to find the user name in the RBAC database.

Network address authentication, some clients can use the lookup table in RBAC database to verify their IP address. Generally, address authentication is only allowed on a very limited number of devices (e.g. control room console).

Using existing token to request a new token as long as the original token has not expired, the token will have a valid tag, and be published to the same location address. The validity of the new token will not exceed that of the original token.

User identification and authentication is adopted to identify the visitor's identity. It can identify whether each user is in the user set through the unique identifier (i.e. user

ID) in the user table; besides, it adopts the password mechanism, only the user entering the user name, the correct password, and the consistent verification code is allowed [9].

4.2 Verification Code

The system program will automatically generate pictures composed of a series of random numbers and letters mixed, these pictures deform the font and place them on a complex background. Actually, the user should enter the password and submit the user information through visual recognition, and then enter after successful verification.

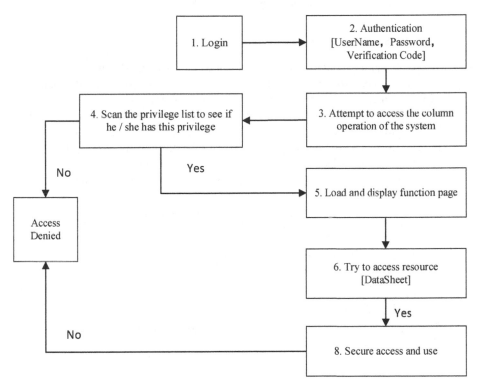

Fig. 5. Authorization process

4.3 AC Interface

For users, it is very significant to supervise authorization and control access scope. Users will build a session when logging into the system during which he/she can request activation of a subset of the roles he/she is entitled to play. The user obtains all permissions linked with the role activated. Figure 5 indicates the authorization processing flow.

4.4 Prevent Illegal Users from Logging in to the System

For the information system in the Web environment, it can be accessed through IP address or computer name. To prevent any illegal users, it can be solved by the AC page. When a link is opened, each function interface (adding a custom function) will judge the user's permissions. If the user is illegal, the system will reject this user and display a prompt and switch to the login page. Besides, the login page is also added to some pre-tested content, calling the code named "HasDangerousContents" of the BinJection class to confirm whether there are dangerous characters to protect the system from being similar to "SQL injection" Attack of the attack [10], which will add some operators to your legitimate input parameters, such as AND or OR.

4.5 Database Security: Oracle Parameters

The purpose of user data and resources separation kept in various databases is to reduce the data security risk. After judging the access legitimacy, the system will obtain the connection information to the data source so that resource operations can be performed. On the other hand, by using triggers, unique IDs can be specified, for example, role IDs must be automatically enabled for roles. Besides, the database operation SQL statement in this process uses OracleParameter. Writing is complicated to some extent, but it makes sense to avoid security risks brought by the code and can improve the performance of Oracle. For instance, here are some common programming statements practically:

```
string sql = "select * from dtName where field = '" +value + "'";
OracleParameter[] param = {
New OracleParameter("@tbName",OracleType.VarChar),
new OracleParameter("@field",OracleType.VarChar),
new OracleParameter("@Value",OracleType.VarChar)};
param[0].Value = dtName.ToUpper();
param[1].Value = field;
param[2].Value = Value;
string sqlStr = "select * from " + @dtName + "where " + @field + "='"
+ @Value + "' and IsValidate=1";
```

4.6 Database Security: Stored Procedures

Security database is a special part of the system, which has two main functions: audit rules and audit analysis. To meet higher security requirements, the system need to achieve access through views by executing stored procedures. Rather than using SQL statements directly in the application, calling stored procedures [11] has some advantages. First, several SQL statements can be put into a stored procedure and conducted in batch. Therefore, the network traffic can be reduced, and secondly, it is faster. Stored procedure needs to be analyzed and optimized for the first call. However, when the stored procedure is called again, it will be called directly from internal memory. Besides, oracle can be used to pass parameters rather than introducing specific values directly. An example is given below, showing the integration of stored procedures:

```
OracleParameter[] param = {
new OracleParameter("p_url",OracleType.VarChar),
new OracleParameter("p_name",OracleType.VarChar),
new OracleParameter("p_pass",OracleType.VarChar),};
param[0].Value = "210.37.45.87"; // parameter1
param[0].Direction = ParameterDirection.Input;
param[1].Value = "aud";// parameter2
param[1].Direction = ParameterDirection.Input;
param[2].Value = "a";// parameter3
param[2].Direction = ParameterDirection.Input;
OracleCommand cmd = new OracleCommand();
cmd.CommandText = storedProcName; //state the name of storage pro-
cedure
cmd.CommandType=CommandType.StoredProcedure;
```

5 Conclusion

This article focuses on the massive data's centralized management. Flex technology for user interface interaction has the characteristics of unified planning, overall layout and direct display. Its security model for reducing authorization management workload is absolutely effective. All the approaches used in this article mainly lie in the encapsulation of security policies and the applications flexibility. For complex data management systems, this method can also be used to obtain role access and data security in engineering security.

Acknowledgement. This paper is supported by the science and technology project of State Grid Corporation of China: "Research and Application of Key Technology of Data Sharing and Distribution Security for Data Center" (Grand No. 5700-202090192A-0-0-00).

References

1. An-Qi, Y., et al.: Hospital information system based on C/S structure automatic update practice. Smart Healthcare (2019)
2. Linan, Z.: Design and realization of surveying and mapping instrument information management system based on B/S. Geospatial Inform. (2019)
3. Power, D., Slaymaker, M., Simpson, A.: On formalizing and normalizing role-based access control systems. Computer J. **52**(3), 305–325 (2018)
4. Li, Q., Xu, M., Zhang, X.: Towards a group-based RBAC model and decentralized user-role administration. In: 2008 The 28th International Conference on Distributed Computing Systems Workshops. IEEE (2008)
5. Technology, Technology, Hefei. Model design of a network security system for project management systems based on the B/S architecture in ASP.NET platform. Comput. Sci., 35(2), 101–103 (2008)
6. Qian, H.: Server communication technology based on Flex. J. Guangdong Transport. Vocat. Tech. Coll., 2012(04):20–22+101

7. Zou, S., et al.: Peer-assisted video streaming with RTMFP flash player: a measurement study on PPTV. IEEE Trans. Circuits Syst. Video Technol. **28**(1), 158–170 (2018)
8. Jones, M.E.: Developing Flex 4 Components: Using ActionScript & MXML to Extend Flex and AIR Applications. Addison-Wesley Professional (2010)
9. Sun, B.: Research on identity tracing based on ABS fine-grained privacy isolation. Electron. Design Eng., 26(377(03)), 10–14 (2018)
10. Lian, K., et al.: Research on multi-level detection methods for SQL injection vulnerabilities. Comput. Sci. Explor. **05**(005), 474–480 (2011)
11. Zhang, W., Chang, H.: Model design of a network security system for project management systems based on the B/S architecture in ASP. NET Platform% design. Comput. Sci., 035(002), 101–103,108 (2008)

Research on Network Optimization and Network Security in Power Wireless Private Network

Jun-yao Zhang[✉], Shan-yu Bi, Liang-liang Gong, Wei-wei Kong, and Xiao-yuan Zhang

NARI Group Corporation/State Grid Electric Power Research Institute, Nanjing, China

Abstract. With the explosive growth of communication demand, all kinds of services require higher and higher wireless communication indicators, and the power wireless private network and 4G public network are not enough to support the massive connection, bandwidth access and low delay service requirements in the unit area, and can not support the development of the power internet of things. On the basis of this situation, this paper puts forward planning research of technologies in power system, analyzes the requirements of network in detail, and the coverage and capacity planning of network. As an important infrastructure to support the development of power system, the network will greatly promote the development of energy Internet strategy, and will greatly promote and upgrade the power services.

Keywords: TD-LTE · Network optimization · Network security · Wireless private network · Interferometric analysis · Coverage optimization

1 Introduction

After many years of construction, the State Grid has a good foundation in terms of site, communication network and so on [1–5], and has natural advantages in power access, which can provide strong basic resource support for 5G network. Aiming at this situation, this paper puts forward research on network planning in power system. The problem of optical fiber access or the high construction cost and long construction cycle of optical fiber will lead to the problem of service access. The wireless communication network is more suitable for the access of distributed terminals, especially to meet the communication needs of mobile terminals [6–10].

Coverage, capacity and quality of wireless communication network are the key factors. Network coverage, network capacity and network quality fundamentally reflect the service level of wireless network, and it is the part that needs to be improved in wireless network optimization. As we all know, network optimization is a complex, arduous and far-reaching work. As a new 4G technology, the content of TD-LTE network optimization has both similarities and differences with other standard systems.

© Springer Nature Singapore Pte Ltd. 2021
Y. Tian et al. (Eds.): ICBDS 2020, CCIS 1415, pp. 97–110, 2021.
https://doi.org/10.1007/978-981-16-3150-4_9

2 Analysis of Service Requirements

For wireless access networks, base stations are distributed and consist of BBU, RRU and antennas [9]. RRU and antenna are deployed in the power tower or the roof of its own property, and BBU of many stations are concentrated in the power communication room. Control services and other services of the power network are transmitted back to the core network through different physical ports of BBU and different wavelengths of transmission equipment.

As far as carrying network is concerned, the three-level structure of inter-provincial trunk line, provincial trunk line and metropolitan area network is adopted, in which the inter-provincial and provincial trunk lines adopt 100G OTN technology. The metropolitan area network is divided into core, convergence and access layers, in which the access layer uses 10G of equipment to network, and the convergence layer and core layer use 40G or 100G of equipment to network.

Core network, the use of regional and provincial deployment mode, in which control, signaling, management and other network elements in the company's six branches of the provincial company centralized deployment, user-face network elements in the provinces or prefectural companies deployment, and MEC equipment can be deployed according to needs of services.

As the technical means to support the operation and maintenance of the 5G network, the management support platform mainly realizes the functions of equipment management, business distribution, billing, user management, data statistics and analysis, and adopts the mode of centralized deployment.

For security protection, a unified, flexible and scalable network security architecture is built to meet the security requirements of different security levels for different applications [11]. A eSIM security chip is deployed on the terminal side to realize the security of terminal access. Wireless network and a host network itself do not perceive user data, through the air-port encryption, IPSec to achieve transmission security. The unified identity authentication management system is deployed on the core network side to realize the identity authentication of the whole chain. Deploy firewalls or security gateways on the network boundary side to ensure security on the Internet side. 5G network slicing software and hardware isolation to achieve security isolation between service streams.

3 Link Budget

The propagation model is used to predict the loss of radio waves on various complex propagation paths, which is the basis of mobile communication network. Whether the communication model is accurate or not is related to whether the district planning is reasonable and whether it can meet the needs of construction with more economical and reasonable investment [12].

The frequency range of communication mode in network is 0.5–6 Ghz, divided into two models, dense urban area, suburban area and rural area. The formula of propagation model in dense urban area is

$$P_L = 161.04 - 7.1 \lg w + 8.5 \lg h - (24.37 - 3.7h/h_{BS}^2) \lg h_{BS} + (43.32 - 3.1 \lg h_{BS})$$

$$(\lg d_{3D} - 3) + 20 \lg f_C - [3.2(\lg 17.625)^2 - 4.97] - 0.6(h_{UT} - 1.5)$$

For suburban and rural areas, the formula used for the propagation model is as follows

$$P_L = 161.04 - 7.1 \lg w + \lg h + 7.5 \lg h - (24.37 - 3.7h/h_{BS}^2) \lg h_{BS}$$
$$+ (43.32 - 3.1 \lg h_{BS})(\lg d_{3D} - 3) + 20 \lg f_C - [3.2(\lg 11.75h_{UT})^2 - 4.97]$$

PL is the propagation path loss in the formula, and the unit is the dB. h_{BS} is the actual height of the terminal equipment, and the unit is the meter [13]. f_C is central frequency, and the unit is GHz. d_{2D} is the ground horizontal distance between base station and terminal equipment, and the unit is the meter. d_{3D} is the space distance between base station and terminal equipment, and the unit is the meter. W is the width of the street, and the unit is the meter. h is the average height of the scene building, and the unit is the meter. The specific parameters are shown in Fig. 1.

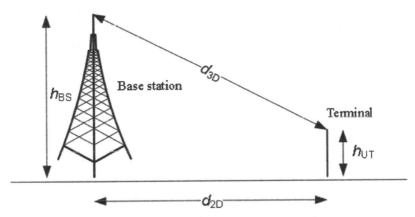

Fig. 1. Parameters of the propagation model

In the propagation model, the lower the frequency, the smaller the propagation loss, the farther the coverage distance, the stronger the diffraction ability, but the frequency resources in the low frequency band are tight and the system capacity is limited [14]. The higher the frequency, the greater the propagation loss, the closer the coverage, especially the worse the indoor coverage. The number of sites required for high frequency bands is much larger than that for low frequency bands. At the same time, the coverage is also affected by the height of building density, topography, vegetation distribution and so on. Appropriate increase in antenna height can reduce propagation loss. Through the analysis, the coverage radius of 5G in the 700 MHz frequency band of dense urban area, general urban area, suburb or rural area is shown in the following table (Table 1).

Table 1. Link budget

Parameter		Dense area		Urban area		Rural area	
		UL	DL	UL	DL	UL	DL
System	Rate of edge data	1M	10M	1M	10M	1M	10M
	Frequency (GHz)	0.7	0.7	0.7	0.7	0.7	0.7
	Bandwidth (MHz)	60	60	60	60	60	60
	Number of RB	21	63	21	63	21	63
	Bandwidth used (KHz)	7560	22680	7560	22680	7560	22680
Transmitter	Total transmit power (dBm)	23	53	23	53	23	53
	Single antenna transmission power (dBm)	23	50	23	50	23	50
	Actual transmit power (dBm)	14.13	63.90	14.13	63.90	14.13	63.90
	Multi-antenna gain (dB)	0	3	0	3	0	3
	RB required to allocate	21	63	21	63	21	63
	Height of transmitting antenna (hbs/m)	1.5	30	1.5	30	1.5	30
	Gain of transmitting antenna (dBi)	0	15	0	15	0	15
Receiver	SINR (dB)	−16	−16	−16	−16	−20	−20
	Noise coefficient of the receiver (dB)	2.3	7	2.3	7	2.3	7

(*continued*)

Table 1. (*continued*)

Parameter		Dense area		Urban area		Rural area	
		UL	DL	UL	DL	UL	DL
	Sensitivity of the receiver (dB)	−136.81	−109.34	−136.81	−109.34	−140.81	−113.34
	Height of receiving antenna (hut/m)	30	1.5	30	1.5	30	1.5
	Diversity gain of the receiver (dB)	3	0	3	0	3	0
	Gain of receiving antenna (dBi)	15	0	15	0	15	0
Other gains and margins	Edge coverage (%)	82.5	82.5	82.5	82.5	82.5	82.5
	Shadow fading standard deviation (dB)	8	8	6	6	4	4
	Shadow fading margin (dB)	7.48	7.48	5.61	5.61	3.74	3.74
	Penetration loss (dB)	15	15	10	10	7	7
	Human losses (dB)	0	0	0	0	0	0
	Interference allowance (dB)	1.5	1.5	1.5	1.5	1.5	1.5
	Feeder losses (dB)	0.5	0.5	0.5	0.5	0.5	0.5
	Switching Gain (dB)	0	0	0	0	0	0
	Fast fading margin (dB)	0	0	0	0	0	0

(*continued*)

Table 1. (*continued*)

Parameter		Dense area		Urban area		Rural area	
		UL	DL	UL	DL	UL	DL
Scene	The width of the street (W/m)	20	20	15	15	8	8
	Average height of buildings (h)	30	30	25	25	10	10
Maximum path loss (dB)		126.46	148.76	133.33	155.63	142.2	164.5
Coverage (m)		848	3181	1382	5187	3006	11282

4   Coverage Simulation

Adopt 700 MHz frequency band, select urban political and economic center area, rural area as simulation verification area [15] (Fig. 2).

Fig. 2. Schematic representation of simulation areas in dense urban areas

4.1   Dense Urban Areas

Using frequency band of 700 MHz and using network planning simulation software to carry out iterative simulation, 7 stations are planned, the radius of single station coverage is about 850 m, and the station distance between each other is about 1.4 km. The simulation results are shown below (Fig. 3).

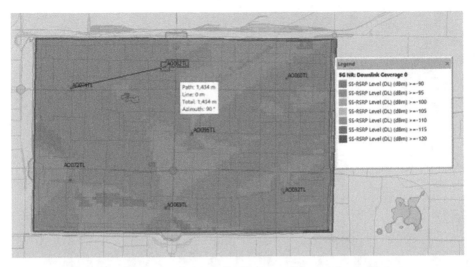

Fig. 3. Coverage simulation diagram of dense urban area

Statistics on signal coverage are shown in the table below (Table 2).

Table 2. Statistical table of signal coverage in dense urban areas

Name	Arae (km^2)	Percentage of coverage %
Coverage Forecast (700 M) Intensive Urban Areas	12.181	100
RSRP > = −90	0.013	0.107
RSRP > = −95	0.047	0.388
RSRP > = −100	8.515	70.372
RSRP > = −105	11.775	97.314
RSRP > = −110	12.1	100
RSRP) > = −115	12.1	100
RSRP > = −120	12.1	100

4.2 Urban Areas

The simulation area in the county is 10.14 km^2, as shown in Fig. 4.

By using the network planning simulation software, the schematic diagram of the simulation area in the general urban area adopts 700 MHz frequency band, and the iterative simulation is carried out. Four stations are planned, the station distance is about 1800 m, and the coverage radius of single station is about 1300 m. The simulation results are shown in Fig. 5.

Fig. 4. Schematic illustration of the simulation area in general urban area

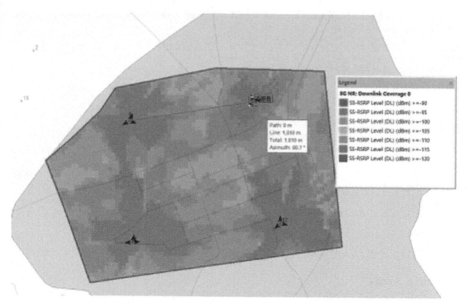

Fig. 5. Schematic illustration of simulated coverage in general urban areas

Statistics on signal coverage are shown in the table below (Table 3).

Table 3. Statistical table of signal coverage in general urban areas

Name	Arae (km^2)	Percentage of coverage %
Coverage Forecast (700 M)	10.165	100
RSRP > = −90	2.793	27.477
RSRP > = −95	5.685	55.927
RSRP > = −100	8.678	85.371
RSRP > = −105	10.05	98.869
RSRP > = −110	10.165	100
RSRP) > = −115	10.165	100
RSRP > = −120	10.165	100

4.3 Suburban and Rural Areas

The simulation area is 12.07 square kilometers, as shown in Fig. 6.

Fig. 6. Schematic representation of simulation areas in suburbs and rural areas

By using 700 m frequency band, the network planning simulation software is used to carry out iterative simulation, one station is planned, and the coverage radius of one station is about 3000 m. The simulation results are shown below (Fig. 7).

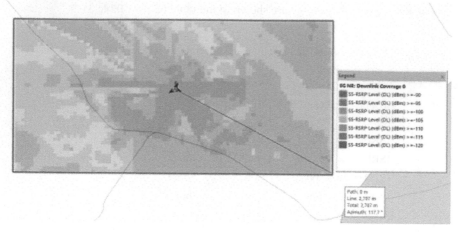

Fig. 7. Schematic diagram of coverage simulation in suburban and rural areas

Statistics on signal coverage are shown in the table below.

Name	Arae (km^2)	Percentage of coverage %
Coverage Forecast (700M)	12.073	100
RSRP > = −90	1.493	12.567
RSRP > = −95	6.367	53.594
RSRP > = −100	9.76	82.155
RSRP > = −105	10.953	92.197
RSRP > = −110	11.508	96.869
RSRP) > = −115	11.88	100
RSRP > = −120	11.88	100

Compared with the link budget, the coverage radius is basically the same as that of the link budget.

5   Capacity Planning

Based on experience, the simulation is divided into four different scenarios, core-intensive area, business-intensive area, business-based area and business-dispersing area. The simulation results of the business model in the core dense area are shown in the following table (Table 4).

Table 4. Service model simulation estimation in dense areas

Type of service	Name	Bandwidth (bps)	Terminal density (/km^2)	Prediction of integrated capacity (Mbps/km^2)
Basic service	Two shakes of electric power	2.4 k	71.04	0.01332
	Threeshakes of electric power	19.2 k	23.68	0.03552
	Electricity information collection	560 k	3000	65.625
	Load control instructions	2.5 k	23.68	0.004625
	Charging station - Data acquisition	4 k	1	0.0003125
	Distributed power	4 k	23.68	0.0074
	Remote metering	1.13 M	2	0.18078125
	Remote signalling	1.13 M	2	0.18078125
Activate service	Charging station - Image acquisition	1 M	1	0.08
	Charging station - Video capture	1 M	1	0.08
	Transmission line monitoring	1 Mbps	0.2	0.016
	Data collection	18.5 k	0.5	0.000722656
	Image acquisition	1 M	0.5	0.04
	Video capture	1 M	0.5	0.04
	Transmission and distribution operations	1 M	0.2	0.0016
	Manual inspection - Voice	64 k	0.1	0.0005
	Manual inspection - Video	1 M	0.1	0.008
	Manual inspection - Data	1 Ms	0.1	0.008

(*continued*)

Table 4. (*continued*)

Type of service	Name	Bandwidth (bps)	Terminal density (/km^2)	Prediction of integrated capacity (Mbps/km^2)
	Transmission and distribution machine inspection	1 M	1	0.08
	Power quality monitoring	1 M	20	1.6
	Smart home	1 M	2000	16
	Smart busines	1 M	0.2	0.016
	Mobile Office - Voice	64 k	100	0.05
	Mobile Office - Video	2 M	100	0.8
	Mobile Office - Data	1 M	100	0.8
	Video surveillance - Ultra Clea	20 M	48	7.68
	Smart jobs - Data	1 M	1	0.08
	Smart Jobs - Video	1 Mbps	1	0.08
	Smart jobs - Voice	64 k	1	0.0005
	Deepening application of intelligent meter	7 k	3000	0.01640625
	Distributed energy storage	1 M	100	0.08
	Intelligent distribution terminal	1 M	30	0.024
Total				11.7 MB/km^2

The service model estimates for the three regions are shown in the table below (Table 5).

Table 5. Service model measurement tables for various scenarios

Type of area	Capacity demand forecasting
Core dense areas	11.7 MB/km^2
Core dense areas	2.41 MB/km^2
Operational base are	0.1 MB/km^2
Decentralized area	0.01 Mbps/km

Under the definition of 3GPP, three different types of services will emerge in the next 5G in the future, that is eMBB, mMTC and uRLLC. eMBB service requires high rate, mMTC service requires high connection number and power consumption standby, and uRLLC service requires high delay and reliability.

The following is a simple calculation of the capacity of a single station and the whole network.

The system with 30 M bandwidth has 156 resource blocks, 30 kHz subcarriers 12 subcarriers, and the spectrum utilization is 93.6%.

Modulation mode is 256QAM, downlink support 4 streams, peak throughput of single cell is as follows

$$30 \times 8 \times (948/1024) \times (12/14) \times 4 = 0.75\,\text{Gbps}$$

Modulation mode is 256QAM, uplink support 2 stream, peak throughput of single cell is as follows

$$30 \times 8 \times (948/1024) \times (12/14) \times 2 = 0.375\,\text{Gbps}$$

From the above analysis, we can see that the current configuration of base station can meet the needs of the services.

6   Conclusion

Driven by the construction of power Internet of things, the services of power grid stock needs to be optimized and upgraded, the emerging services is booming, the requirement of the network security is higher and higher, and all kinds of services require higher and higher wireless communication index. Network with low delay, large connection and large bandwidth fundamentally meets all kinds of requirements and in the construction and development of the power Internet of things, and forms a new form of power network. This paper analyzes the requirements of network and the coverage and capacity planning of network in detail. As an important infrastructure to support the development of power system, the construction of network will greatly promote the development of energy Internet strategy, and will greatly promote and all links of service in power system.

References

1. Xia, X., Zhu, X., Mei, C., Li, W., Fang, H.: Research and practice on 5G slicing in power internet of things. Mobile Commun. **43**(1), 63–69 (2019)
2. You, X.H., Pan, Z.W., Gao, X.Q., et al.: The 5G mobile communication: the development trends and its emerging key techniques. Sci. Sinica **44**(5), 551 (2014)
3. Liu, G., Jiang, D.: 5G: vision and requirements for mobile communication system towards Year 2020. Chin. J. Eng. **2016**, 1–8 (2016)
4. Suo, H., Wan, J., Zou, C., Liu, J.: Security in the internet of things: a review. In: 2012 International Conference on Computer Science and Electronics Engineering, pp. 648–651. Hangzhou (2012). https://doi.org/10.1109/ICCSEE.2012.373.
5. Gao, F., Zeng, R., Qu, L., et al.: Research on identification of concept and characteristics of energy internet. Electric Power **2018**, 1–6 (2018)
6. Xu, X.: Time-sensitive network technology and its application in industrial network. Telecommun. Network Tech. **2018**(5), 1–5 (2018)
7. Craciunas, S.S., Oliver, R.S.: Combined task and network-level scheduling for distributed time-triggered systems. Real-Time Syst. **52**(2), 161–200 (2016)
8. Sun, G.: Research and Simulation of clock synchronization and scheduling algorithm in time-sensitive Networks, Beijing University of Posts and Telecommunications (2018)
9. Li, B., Zhou, J., Ren, X.: Research on key issues of TD-LTE network optimization. Telecom Eng. Tech. Standard. **1**, 57–61 (2015)
10. Bahnasse, A., Louhab, F.E., Oulahyane, H.A., et al.: Novel SDN architecture for smart MPLS Traffic Engineering-Diff Serv Aware management. Futur. Gener. Comput. Syst. **11**(2), 212–219 (2018)
11. Zheng, L., Tse, D.N.C.: Diversity and multiplexing: a fundamental tradeoff in multiple antenna channels. IEEE Trans. Inform. Theory (2003)
12. Panda, M.: Performance analysis of encryption algorithms for security. In: 2016 International Conference on Signal Processing, Communication, Power and Embedded System (SCOPES), pp. 278–284. Paralakhemundi (2016). https://doi.org/10.1109/SCOPES.2016.7955835.
13. Gupta, C.P., Sharma, I.: A fully homomorphic encryption scheme with symmetric keys with application to private data processing in clouds. In: 2013 Fourth International Conference on the Network of the Future (NoF), pp. 1–4. Pohang (2013). https://doi.org/10.1109/NOF.2013.6724526.
14. Wang, K.: The application of the internet of things in the 5G era in the power system. Telecom Power Technol. **35**(5), 187–188 (2018).
15. Ma, Z., Zhang, Z.Q., Ding, Z.G., et al.: Key techniques for 5G wireless communications: network architecture, physical layer, and MAC layer perspectives. Sci. China **58**(4), 41301–41321 (2015)

Research on Location Planning of Multi-station Integration Based on Particle Swarm Optimization

Xincong Li[✉], Mingze Zhang, Jun Wang, and Minhao Xia

State Grid Shanghai Economic Research Institute, Shanghai, China

Abstract. With the development of national energy strategy, the construction of the Energy Internet has become an important direction for the development of energy systems. The emerging field of multi-station integration has laid a good foundation for the construction of the Energy Internet. Based on the analysis of multi-station integration architecture, a mathematical model for location planning of multi-station integration was proposed. The model is based on the substation and integrates data center, charging station and photovoltaic power station. The particle swarm optimization (PSO) in the artificial intelligence algorithm was used to solve the model and determine the optimal site. Finally, a case was used to verify the correctness and effectiveness of the proposed model and method.

Keywords: Energy Internet · Multi-station Integration · Location Planning · Particle swarm optimization

1 Introduction

Multi-station integration is one of the important applications for the implementation of the Energy Internet. It converges substations, data center, charging stations and photovoltaic power stations to optimize the allocation of urban resources, improve data perception, analysis and computing efficiency, carry out local load consumption and other functions.

At present, the research on the location and planning of single station such as substations, data centers, and photovoltaic power stations is relatively mature. Reference [1] took the sum of the product of the distance from the substation to the load point and the power load of the load point as the objective function, and used the immune optimization algorithm to solve the substation location planning. Reference [2] proposed a solution based on modern heuristic search algorithm for the automatic location of cloud data center. Reference [3] proposed a two-level planning model for distribution network considering the investment income of energy storage stations. The upper-level planning model took the lowest cost of distribution network line construction as the optimization goal, and the lower-level planning model took the highest profit of the energy storage station as the optimization goal, and used genetic algorithms to study the location of energy storage stations. Reference [4] proposed a location model targeting the investment cost of charging station construction, and realized the optimization calculation

© Springer Nature Singapore Pte Ltd. 2021
Y. Tian et al. (Eds.): ICBDS 2020, CCIS 1415, pp. 111–121, 2021.
https://doi.org/10.1007/978-981-16-3150-4_10

of site, scale and service capacity through the global optimization capability of PSO to minimize the total cost; Reference [5] took the photovoltaic power station's voltage index, grid loss index, and harmonic index as the goal to achieve the best comprehensive effect, considered the upper limit of the node voltage harmonic content as constraints, the model is solved by a multi-objective optimization algorithm based on an improved genetic algorithm.

However, there is less research on the location planning of multi-station including substations, data centers, charging stations and data centers. In this paper, each single power station is taken into consideration, the mathematical model of each single power station is constructed with the goal of minimum load distance, and the multi-station location planning model is obtained after addition. And use PSO in the intelligent algorithm to solve the model and select the optimal site. Finally, a case was used to illustrate the accuracy and scientific of the proposed method.

2 Mathematical Model of Multi-station Location

2.1 Multi-station Integration Architecture

There are many types of power stations that can be included in multi-station. This paper mainly studies the collaborative planning between substation, data center, charging station and photovoltaic power station.

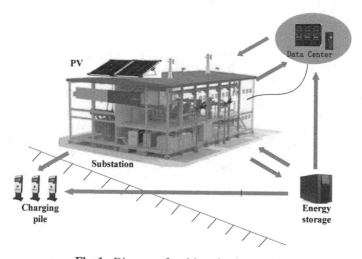

Fig. 1. Diagram of multi-station integration

It can be seen from Fig. 1 that the multi-station is based on the substation, integrating other station equipment to achieve the complementarity and coordination of each equipment, and then making full use of existing land resources to achieve the multi-station function in a single location. The substation provides power for charging piles, data centers, energy storage stations and surrounding users; the energy storage equipment serves as a backup power source for charging piles, substations, and data centers to improve power supply reliability; the data center provides data storage services for surrounding enterprises, municipalities, etc. Charging piles provide charging services for electric vehicles around the power station.

2.2 Mathematical Model of Location

Objective Function. The main content of this paper is to determine the site of the multi-station, and the location of the candidate site has the greatest impact on the line cost. There are not only regular electricity loads, but also other types of loads such as data center loads and charging station loads in multi-station load. In order to reduce power loss and line investment, and ensuring the stability of power supply, this paper takes load distance cost as the optimization goal, and uses a single-dimensional standard to measure multiple types of entities.

The cost calculation of the load distance $C_{l,i}$ between the load point l and the site i is shown in Eq. (1).

$$C_{l,i} = \alpha_l P_l \sqrt{(u_i - x_l)^2 + (v_i - y_l)^2} \tag{1}$$

Where α_l is the cost coefficient of the unit load distance from load point l to candidate site i; P_l is the power of load point l; (u_i, v_i) is the coordinate of candidate site i and (x_l, y_l) is the coordinate of load point l.

Due to the different functions and service entities of each single station in the multi-station, the cost coefficients of unit load distance from each type of load point to multi-station are different. The load distance cost of each single station is as follows:

Substation. The load distance cost coefficient and load distance cost between the sub-station load and multi-station are shown in Eq. (2)–(3), which are measured according to the line investment cost converted to unit capacity and unit distance.

$$\alpha_{substation} = u_{xl} \frac{r(1+r)^{z_1}}{(1+r)^{z_1} - 1} \tag{2}$$

$$C_{substation} = \alpha_{substation} \sum P_{substation} \sqrt{(u_i - x_s)^2 + (v_i - y_s)^2} \tag{3}$$

Where u_{xl} represents the line investment cost per unit capacity and unit distance; r represents the discount rate of funds; z_1 represents the service life of the line, and the line investment cost is converted to each year; $P_{substation}$ represents the substation load; (u_i, v_i) represents the coordinate of multi-station candidate site; (x_s, y_s) represents the coordinate of the load point of the substation.

Data Center. The load distance cost coefficient and load distance cost between data center load and multi-station are shown in Eq. (4)–(5), including the line investment cost coefficient converted to unit capacity and unit load distance.

$$\alpha_{data} = \varphi u_{xl} \frac{r(1+r)^{z_1}}{(1+r)^{z_1} - 1} \tag{4}$$

$$C_{data} = \alpha_{data} \sum P_{data} \sqrt{(u_i - x_d)^2 + (v_i - y_d)^2} \tag{5}$$

Where φ represents the power supply reliability correction factor. The data center has a large load scale and high reliability requirements, so double-circuit lines are used, and φ is 2; P_{data} represents the data center load; (u_d, v_d) represents the coordinates of data center load point.

Charging Station. The load distance cost coefficient and load distance cost between the charging load and multi-station are shown in Eqs. (6)–(7), based on the time cost converted to the unit capacity and unit distance electric vehicle charging demand to go to multi-station charging measure.

$$\alpha_{EV} = \frac{K_{time}}{P_{charge} v_{road}} \tag{6}$$

$$C_{EV} = \alpha_{EV} \sum P_{EV} \sqrt{(u_i - x_e)^2 + (v_i - y_e)^2} \tag{7}$$

Where K_{time} represents the time value coefficient of electric vehicle users per hour; v_{road} represents the average driving speed of electric vehicle users after considering the road conditions in the planning area; P_{charge} represents the single charging pile power of the charging station; P_{EV} represents the charging station load; (u_e, v_e) represents the coordinates of charging station load point.

Photovoltaic Station. The load distance cost coefficient and load distance cost between the photovoltaic power station load and multi-station are shown in Eq. (8)–(9). Photovoltaic loads mainly include rural road lights, park lights, and other loads that require less power supply reliability and consume less electricity. The cost coefficient of the load distance between the photovoltaic power station load and multi-station is measured according to the solar cell converted to unit capacity and the line investment cost per unit distance.

$$\alpha_{PV} = \left(\frac{u_{PV} V_{PV}}{R_{PV}}\right)\frac{r(1+r)^{z_2}}{r(1+r)^{z_2} - 1} + u_{xl}\frac{r(1+r)^{z_1}}{r(1+r)^{z_1} - 1} \tag{8}$$

$$C_{PV} = \alpha_{PV} \sum P_{PV} \sqrt{(u_i - x_p)^2 + (v_i - y_p)^2} \tag{9}$$

Where u_{PV} represents the investment cost of solar cells per unit capacity; V_{PV} represents the capacity of a solar cell; R_{PV} represents the service radius of the energy storage to the photovoltaic power station, z_2 represents the service life of the solar cell; P_{PV} represents the photovoltaic power plant load; (x_p, y_p) represents the coordinates of photovoltaic power plant load point.

Multi-station location planning is essentially a multi-objective collaborative optimization problem. The optimization objectives include substation, data center, charging station and photovoltaic power station. This paper takes the minimum load distance cost as the objective function, and uses a single-dimensional standard to measure multiple targets to be optimized, and solves the problem of diversification of multi-station service entities. The objective function of multi-station location is shown in Eq. (10):

$$\min C = C_{substation} + C_{data} + C_{EV} + C_{PV} \qquad (10)$$

Where $C_{substation}$ represents the cost of substation load distance; C_{data} represents the cost of data center load distance; C_{EV} represents the cost of charging station load distance; C_{PV} represents the cost of photovoltaic power station load distance.

Restrictions
Power Supply Radius of Substation.

$$l_{ik} = \sqrt{(u_i - x_k)^2 + (v_i - y_k)^2} \leq R_{substation} \qquad (11)$$

Where l_{ik} represents the straight-line distance from multi-station to the load of the substation; $R_{substation}$ represents the maximum power supply radius of the substation under the current voltage level.
    Charging Station Service Radius.

$$l_{ig} = \sqrt{(u_i - x_g)^2 + (v_i - y_g)^2} \leq R_{EV} \qquad (12)$$

Where l_{ig} represents the straight-line distance from multi-station to the charging load; R_{EV} represents the average service radius of the city's public charging network.

3 Solution of Multi-station Location Model

3.1 Particle Swarm Optimization (PSO)

PSO is a widely used artificial intelligence algorithm, which was proposed by Kennedy and Eberhart from the process of finding food by birds. The idea of the algorithm is to initialize the solution space of the optimization problem into a group of random vectors called particles. The properties of each particle include two: particle speed and particle position. The optimization process of the optimal solution set is a process in which particles continuously update their velocity and position through iteration. Assuming that the velocity and position of particle a in dimension b are v_{ab} and x_{ab}, respectively, the velocity of the particle is updated as shown in Eq. (13).

$$l_{ig} = \sqrt{(u_i - x_g)^2 + (v_i - y_g)^2} \leq R_{EV} \qquad (13)$$

Where v and x are respectively expressed as the velocity variable and position variable of the particle in the iterative process; the equation contains three weighting factors: inertia factor ω, particle swarm algorithm acceleration coefficient c_1 and c_2; r_1 and r_2

are random adjustment coefficients between 0 and 1, which are conducive to the random flight of particles to find more possible optimal solutions; pb and gb are individual optimal particles and global optimal particles.

The PSO update is shown in Eq. (14).

$$x_{ab}(k+1) = x_{ab}(k) + v_{ab}(k+1) \tag{14}$$

With the continuous update of particle speed and position, the PSO ends when the optimal solution meets the preset requirements or reaches the maximum number of iterations.

3.2 Solution Process of Location Model Based on PSO

The model proposed in this paper is to solve the problem of single-location within a certain range. Therefore, the location of multi-station is represented as a two-dimensional plane coordinate geographically, and the two coordinates of the location of multi-station are each as a variable. The search space of PSO is a two-dimensional space, and each point in the space represents a feasible position of multi-station. In the search process, the fitness value of the particle represents the load distance cost of multi-station planning. The current fitness value of the particle can be calculated by substituting the current position of the particle in the objective function. This fitness value is used to evaluate the degree of the solution, which is the quality of the multi-station position. The lower the fitness value, the lower the load distance cost and the better the multi-station location. In the search space, there is an optimal point. This point has the lowest fitness value and corresponds to the optimal position of multi-station. The ultimate goal is to let the particles find the best points through search. The specific process is as follows:

Step 1: Initialize the coordinates of multi-station in the planning area, and set various load power, coordinates, line costs, discount rates, service life and other parameters in the planning area;

Step 2: Calculate the fitness value of the initial value, and obtain the initial fitness value of each coordinate of the multi-station according to Eq. (10);

Step 3: Calculate the optimal fitness value of the individual and the overall optimal fitness value in the entire population.

Step 4: Update the particle velocity. According to Eq. (13) and (14), get the updated velocity and position of the particles.

Step 5: Determine whether the iteration is over, that is, whether the set convergence condition is met. If satisfied, the optimal result will be output, if not satisfied, go to step 2 and continue the iteration.

The iterative flowchart of PSO is shown in Fig. 2.

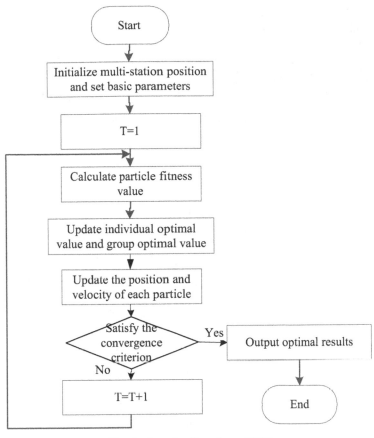

Fig. 2. Iterative flowchart of PSO

4 Case Study

This paper takes the development zone of a city as an example to verify the correctness and rationality of the method. The area spans 30 km from east to west and 25 km from north to south. According to local planning and development, it is planned to build a multi-station integrating substation, data center, charging station and photovoltaic power station. There are more regular electricity load and charging load in this area, as well as a certain amount of data center load and photovoltaic power station load.

4.1 Basic Parameters

In order to verify the feasibility and effectiveness of the PSO in multi-station location planning, the location coordinates and loads of various major loads in the area are collected. The distribution data is shown in Tables 1–4. The investment cost per unit length of the line is 200,000 yuan/km, the discount rate is 0.08, the line depreciation period is 16 years, the photovoltaic cell depreciation period is 10 years, the power supply reliability correction factor is 2, and the charging power of a single charging pile is 80 kW, which is expected to average Every day, 260 electric vehicles have a charging demand. The average speed of electric vehicles is 40 km/h, and the average time cost for each owner is 50 yuan/h. The investment cost of solar cells is 8 yuan/W, and the power generation of solar panels is 250 W/m^2.

Table 1. Regular electricity load distribution data

Number	Abscissa/km	Ordinate/km	Load/kW
1	1	20	617
2	24	9	127
3	20	17	363
4	7	15	617
5	10	19	577
6	23	14	4830
7	17	15	707
8	7	8	1300
9	1	10	3845
10	7	18	617
11	5	15	443
12	8	17	617
13	6	15	1243
14	7	16	517
15	8	18	880
16	2	16	450
17	5	14	1110
18	24	20	280

Table 2. Data center load distribution data

Number	Abscissa/km	Ordinate/km	Load/kW
1	14	17	3240
2	16	22	2407

Table 3. Charging load distribution data

Number	Abscissa/km	Ordinate/km	Load/kW
1	12	2	1237
2	21	11	637
3	22	12	1643
4	14	7	637
5	19	5	1510
6	21	4	1237
7	24	4	1063
8	25	2	710
18	26	4	830

Table 4. PV load distribution data

Number	Abscissa/km	Ordinate/km	Load/kW
1	13	4	22
2	26	7	27
3	30	8	30
18	21	5	33

4.2 Case Results and Analysis

The PSO is used to solve the multi-station location planning model, and the maximum number of iterations is set to 100. The optimization results are shown in Table 5, and the convergence situation is shown in Fig. 3. The distribution diagrams of various loads and optimal site locations are shown in Fig. 4.

Table 5. Optimal site result

Optimal site	Minimum cost/yuan
(15.814,15.353)	8604900

It can be seen from Fig. 3 that when the PSO is used to solve the multi-station location planning model, the convergence speed is very fast. The objective function tends to converge when the number of iterations reaches about 30 times and the optimal site location and the minimum load distance cost are obtained. It can be seen from Fig. 4 that the optimal site location is located at the center of all loads. It means that the sum of the distances from the site to each load is relatively small, and it is logical to find the minimum load distance cost at this point.

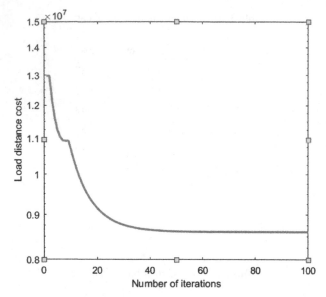

Fig. 3. Convergence curve of PSO

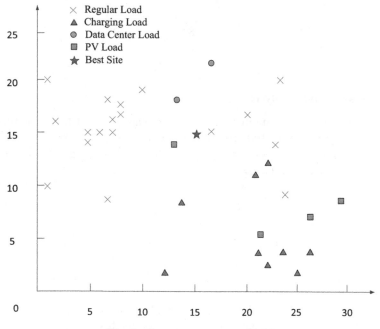

Fig. 4. Convergence curve of PSO

5 Conclusion

The multi-station mentioned in this article is the integration of four types of power stations: substation, data center, charging station and photovoltaic power station. First, this paper constructs a multi-station location model, and then applies the PSO to the multi-station location planning problem. Finally, selects the optimal site location with the load distance cost as the objective function. The main conclusions obtained from the study are as follows:

(1) This article integrates the multi-agent planning problem into a unified master plan. Taking the load distance cost as the objective function and builds a unified standard to measure multi-objective entities including substation, data center, charging station and photovoltaic power plant;
(2) When calculating the load distance, this paper considers the differences between substation, data center, charging station and photovoltaic power station, and sets different load distance cost coefficients.
(3) Using the PSO in artificial intelligence algorithm to calculate and analyze the location of multi-station, and select the optimal station location. In practical applications, the optimal candidate site can be compared with existing substations, and the most suitable substations for transformation can be screened out to provide reference for the implementation of multi-station projects.

References

1. Yonghui, L.: Substation location planning based on immune optimization algorithm. Autom. Instrum. **08**, 104–106 (2017)
2. Renming, Z., Bo, Z.: Research on cloud data center automatic location model based on modern heuristic search algorithm. Software Guide **12**(12), 44–46 (2013)
3. Jifeng, H., et al.: distribution network planning model considering investment income of energy storage station. Electr. Power Constr. **38**(06), 92–99 (2017)
4. Haiqing, C.: Study on Planning Model of Electric Vehicle Swapping Station Based on Microgrid. Shanghai Institute of applied technology (2015)
5. Ke, W.: Research on Evaluation Method of Photovoltaic Grid Connection Site Selection and Capacity Determination Scheme and Access Mode. Wuhan University (2018)
6. Zilong, C., Pin, W., Jian, S., Bo, Y.: Location planning model of electric vehicle public emergency charging station. Power Syst. Protect. Control **48**(16), 62–68 (2020)
7. Jiuxing, W., Jiumiao, C.: Study on site selection and planning of photovoltaic power station – taking Wuhu City as an example. J. Ludong Univ. (Nat. Sci. Ed.) **35**(01), 59-65+89 (2019)
8. Man, W., Wuyang, Z.: Location planning of mobile substation based on discrete particle swarm optimization. J. Electr. Power **33**(02), 134–139 (2018)
9. Wenjie, P., Zhe, W., Yanghong, T., Fangwei, L., Jian, Y.: Opportunity constrained planning of electric vehicle charging station with photovoltaic distributed generation distribution network. J. Power Syst. Autom. **29**(06), 45–52 (2017)
10. Xiaorong, L., Jie, W., Jianmin, D., Hua, M., Cheng, Y.: Site selection and sizing optimization of multi station integrated substation based on Voronoi diagram. Power Grid Clean Energy **36**(02), 44–54 (2020)
11. Xiao, Z.: Multi Objective Optimization of Substation Engineering Projects Based on Particle Swarm Optimization Algorithm. North China Electric Power University (2018)

Quick Response Code Based on Least Significant Bit

Zhuohao Weng[1], Jian Zhang[1], Cui Qin[1]([⊠]), and Yan Zhang[2]

[1] School of Information and Communication Engineering, Nanjing Institute of Technology, Nanjing 211167, China
qincui@njit.edu.cn
[2] Swissgrid Ltd., Short-term Network Modelling, Bleichemattstrasse 31, 5001 Aarau, Switzerland

Abstract. Quick response (QR) code design based on Least Significant Bit (LSB) image is studied. The basic principle of the research is to put the required information into the QR code first, and embed the QR code into the lowest bit of the pixels in the background image for hiding the information. If the picture information is necessary to read by obtaining the QR code picture, the lowest bit of the picture pixel is extracted through the program language, and the hidden information can be obtained by parsing the QR code picture. In this scheme, the information is put into the QR code picture, and the QR code is merged with the least significant bit of the picture. It is shown that cannot be recognized by the naked eye. This method can ensure the safety and security of the information during the transmission process. Accuracy, and greatly improve the visual aesthetics of the QR code.

Keywords: QR code · Disclosure of privacy · Least significant bit · Image pixels · Beauty

1 Introduction

At present, we are living in the Internet era, many life information has been data, network, in the process of information transmission, security and concealment is extremely important, however, at the same time, with the gradual rise of people's requirements for aesthetics, the aesthetics of the two-dimensional code has also become a major highlight in the process of information transmission. In this paper, the Least Significant Bit (LSB) algorithm will be used as the basic algorithm for designing image quick response (QR) codes, and the watermarking technology will be applied to the design of image QR codes [1–3]. The method ensures the correct identification and concealment of the QR codes, and at the same time, adds the aesthetics of the QR codes, making the QR codes both information transfer function and interesting.

QR Code is one kind of the 2D barcodes, which was invented by Japan company Denso in 1994 as a matrix 2D code, the original name of which means that the inventor hopes the content of the code to be deciphered quickly [4–6]. In addition to the advantages of other one-dimensional barcodes and other two-dimensional codes, such as large information capacity, high reliability and the ability to represent Chinese characters and images, it also has the features of effective representation of Chinese characters and high-speed all-round reading.

The QR code is a square pattern composed of two rectangles in black and white, in its four corners, three of which are printed with a special pattern, these three patterns are used as a positioning pattern. Thus, the QR code can be detected from any angle without accurately scan, then get the information in the QR code.

QR code as a two-dimensional barcode, can store more information than the ordinary barcode, can accommodate up to 7,089 bytes of numbers, 4,296 bytes of letters, if the binary number (8 Bit) can accommodate up to 2,953 bytes, the Chinese character capacity is 984 bytes (UTF-8), 1,800 bytes (BIG5) respectively. As the 2D code has a special identification pattern, there is no need to align the 2D code with the scanner in a straight line like the common barcode.

The standard QR code is composed of two parts: the coding area and the functional image as shown in Fig. 1. The coding area is the main part that carries the QR code data, which consists of format information, version information, error correction code and data code, and its specific value varies according to different factors such as version number, error correction level and input data. The function graphics are composed of calibration graphics, location graphics, position detection graphics and their delimiters, and the function of this part is to provide accurate and precise position for QR code identification.

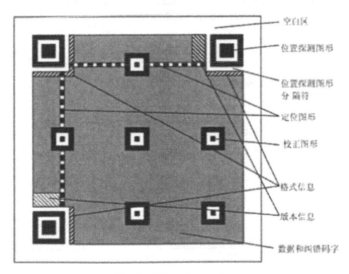

Fig. 1. QR code structure

LSB is the lowest valid bit in the binary array, that is, the 0th bit, also known as the rightmost bit [7, 8]. LSB algorithm is one of the traditional information hiding algorithm in the airspace algorithm, and the core idea of the algorithm is to embed the information to the information image of the lowest bit. In the pixel, due to the human eye's limit to the visual threshold, it is possible to hide the information without changing the appearance. For example, if information is embedded in the least important pixel of a 256-color bitmap with 8-bit depth, i.e. in the 0th bit, then the amount of information that can be hidden in the pixel is 1/8; if information is embedded in the lowest two bits, i.e. in the 0th and 1st bit, then the amount of information that can be embedded in the pixel is 1/4; if information is embedded in the lowest three bits, i.e. in the 0th, 1st and 2nd bit, then the amount of information that can be embedded in the pixel is 1/2. From the above example, we can know that the LSB algorithm can hide large amount of data and the information hiding method is simple and convenient, so the LSB algorithm is widely used. However, since the location of information embedding is the lowest effective bit of the image, there may be a disadvantage of poor robustness of the image algorithm, and the information may be destroyed by image denaturation, filtering and other operations in the process of sending, transmitting and receiving.

The LSB algorithm is a typical spatial domain information hiding algorithm proposed by L.F. Turner and R.G. van Schyndel. The color values of image pixels have 2^{24}. If you embed the hidden information into the lowest few pixels of the image, that is, changing only the lowest bit of the color component, the human eye will not be able to distinguish the color difference before and after the change. Information is embedded. If you want to hide information in 8-color, 16-color, 256-color and 24-bit true-color images, the LSB algorithm also applies. For example, for a 256-color image, after binarizing the image, if you want to store one pixel for each byte from the highest bit to the lowest bit of the image, a pixel can hide at least 1 bit of information, then without considering compression, a 640 * 480 pixel 256-color image can hide at least 307200 bits (38400 bytes) of information, which is shown if Fig. 2.

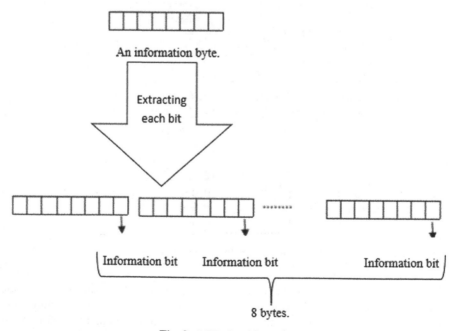

Fig. 2. LSB algorithm rules.

The traditional LSB algorithm is simple and has been well researched in information hiding technology. However, if it is applied to QR codes, such a traditional algorithm may not bring the best information hiding effect. Therefore, some scholars have proposed an improved LSB algorithm [9, 10].

The image pixels in png and bmp images are generally composed of three primary RGB colors, each color occupies 8bit, the value range is 0x00–0xFF. In order to hide the information, the information is embedded in the least important pixel. Because each pixel has three color components, each pixel can provide at least three replaceable lowest pixels. Since the RGB value of a random color increases or decreases within 1–3, it is difficult for the human eye to distinguish the change. The QR code can be transformed into a 256 gray scales image. From the highest bit to the lowest bit, every bit has different affection. Relatively, the higher the pixel bit, the greater the influence on the image.

When the lowest three pixels of a picture are embedded in a bar code, the human eye cannot distinguish the subtle color changes, but the bar code can still be identified and extracted. In the improved LSB algorithm, $A(i,j)_7$, $A(i,j)_6$, $A(i,j)_5$, $A(i,j)_4$, $A(i,j)_3$, $A(i,j)_2$, $A(i,j)_1$, $A(i,j)_0$ represents any one pixel bit of the bar code whose length and width are M and N pixels, and takes out the lowest 3 bits, $A_{(i,j)2}A_{(i,j)1}A_{(i,j)0}$. The data is embedded according to the following rules.

(1) $A_{(i,j)2} = A_{(i,j-1)1}$
(2) $A_{(i,j)1}$ Embed Bit
(3) $A_{(i,j)0} = A_{(i,j--1)1}$
(4) Embed in the first step $A_{(i,j)2}$
     (If j equals N, then j assigns a value of 1. Then if i equals N, i assigns a value of 1, i.e. $A_{(i,j)2} = A_{(1,1)1}$, otherwise i is assigned i + 1, i.e. $A_{(i,j)2} = A_{(i+1,1)1}$)
(5) Embed at step 3 $A_{(i,j)0}$, if j is equal to 1, then j assigns N, which, if i is equal to 1, obliges i to assign M, that is: $A_{(i,j)0} = A_{(M,N)1}$, otherwise i assigns i − 1, that is: $A_{(i,j)0} = A_{(i-1,N)1}$.

Here are the basic steps of the LSB algorithm.

First, converts decimal pixels that need to be loaded into hidden information into binary data.

Second, embed the hidden information in the lowest pixel of the QR code and replace the lowest bit of binary data obtained in step (1) with the lowest pixel of the QR code.

Third, when the substitution is complete, the resulting binary data containing the hidden information is converted to decimal pixel values to obtain an image containing the hidden information.

2 Test Results

LSB algorithm is to change the value of the pixels in the image, because only the lowest pixel is changed, so there will be no perceived distortion, that is, the human eye will not change the appearance and content of the picture. After inputting the content to generate the default size of 500 * 500 2D code, the image that needs to be embedded with the 2D code information will be cropped and compressed, and then parsed to binary data through the program code, at this time, the RGB component in the image pixels can be extracted, the lowest effective bit in the background image will be erased, and then each 2D code pixel and background pixel will be mixed, and the RBG component of the 2D code will be used instead of the image pixels. The RGB component of the QR code. Once the substitution is complete, the code converts the image that contains the QR code information into a pixel decimal image to get the QR code image with the hidden information.

Information extraction is mainly to separate the QR code image and background image, and by scanning can get the hidden information in the QR code image. First of all, the decimal pixel value image containing QR code information will be converted to binary data set, after parsing, the QR code image will be extracted from the image, because the lowest RGB bit is the QR code data, so just take a component can be identified, you can get the QR code image, the original background image and the information contained in the QR code image. The information embedding process and information extraction process are shown in Fig. 3 and Fig. 4.

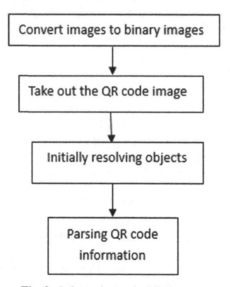

Fig. 3. Information embedding process

A QR code image with message "123" is shown in Fig. 5. After entering the background image, since the size of the QR code is set to 500 × 500, if the size of the background image does not match, the background image should be cropped to fit the size of the QR code, and the QR code pixels should replace the lowest pixels of the background image to achieve the purpose that the QR code can be hidden without changing the appearance of the background image. The QR code image with hidden message "123" is shown in Fig. 6.

Extracts background image pixels.
and get the pixel that generated the QR code.

Erase the lowest bit of background pixels

Place the QR code at the lowest background pixel.

Mix each background pixel and QR code pixel.

Fig. 4. Information extraction process

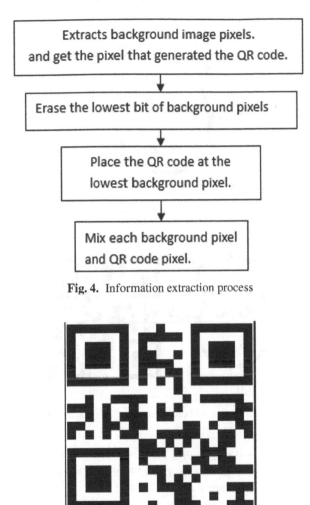

Fig. 5. QR code image with message "123".

The ten-bit pixel value image with a QR code is parsed to binary and the lowest pixel bit in the RGB component of the image is extracted to get the information in the QR code, which is shown in Fig. 7. The flowchart of program execution is shown in Fig. 8.

By comparing the background figure, we can see that based on the LSB algorithm, we can realize the function of adding information to the picture, which ensures the beauty and visibility of the picture without affecting the transmission of information and improves the concealment and security of the information.

The hidden information is correctly parsed and the algorithm is used to clearly separate the background image from the QR code image.

Multiple images have been selected to demonstrate the feasibility and accuracy of the system.

Fig. 6. QR code image with hidden message "123".

(a)   (b)

Fig. 7. Image information before parsing (a) and after parsing (b)

The original pictures are shown in Fig. 9, Fig. 11, Fig. 13. The Pictures after adding the information are shown in Fig. 10, Fig. 12 and Fig. 14. The SNRs of before and after the scenery embedded QR code are shown in Table 1.

SNR is the signal power ratio on the noise power, the unit is dB, the larger the value means that the picture distortion is smaller, the higher the picture quality, generally considered to be excellent SNR value of more than 60 dB picture quality. It can be seen from the above data, the use of LSB algorithm to embed information on the lowest pixel of the picture does not reduce the picture quality, and the information can be accurately transmitted and identified. At the same time, the aesthetics of the QR code image is ensured because the black and white rectangular module constitutes the QR code is hidden.

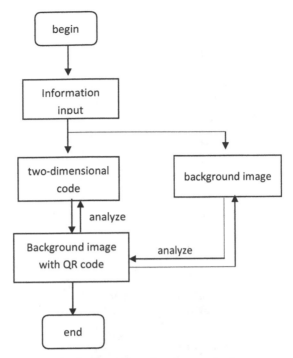

Fig. 8. Flowchart of program execution

Fig. 9. Original landscape map

From the above three examples, it can be seen that the software can insert hidden information for different types of images and at the same time hide the QR code image, without changing the visibility and aesthetics of the original image. And it can restore the original information without any damage, ensuring the accuracy of information transmission.

Fig. 10. QR code image with watermark message "landscape".

Fig. 11. Original portraits

Fig. 12. QR code image with watermark message "portrait"

Fig. 13. Original cartoon diagram

Fig. 14. QR code image with watermark message "cartoon diagram"

Table 1. The SNRs of before and after the scenery embedded QR code

Original picture	QR code image with watermark	SNR
Figure 9 Original Landscape Map	Figure 10 QR code image with watermark message "Landscape"	68.6640
Figure 11 Original portraits	Figure 12 QR code image with watermark message "portrait"	67.3856
Figure 13 Original cartoon diagram	Figure 14 QR code image with watermark message "cartoon diagram"	82.7119

3 Conclusion

In this paper, the information embedding technique for QR code is proposed, which verifies the feasibility of embedding information in the lowest bit of the image and tests the software performance on the improvement of LSB algorithm technique. The test results show that the encrypted image does not affect the quality of the image, and it is guaranteed that the embedded information does not change the graphic structure of the QR code, which is very beneficial for information concealment and improves the amount of information embedding; and the QR code image with stored information remains clear and blur-free after being restored, which shows that the algorithm can achieve lossless extraction and confirms the high retention of the algorithm for image processing.

At present is the era of rapid development of information communication, with the in-depth application of the two-dimensional code technology in daily life, people's demand for information security continues to increase, and the information hiding technology proposed in this paper greatly improves the security of the two-dimensional code information. In the naked eye only an ordinary picture contains a lot of information, which ensures the concealment of information, and at the same time, the QR code picture also has certain aesthetics.

Acknowledgments. This work was supported by the Natural Science Foundation of Jiangsu Province (BK20191012); Scientific Research Foundation of Nanjing Institute of Technology (JCYJ201822, CKJB201803 and CXY201932).

References

1. Zhu, B.W., Wan, W., Chen, Y.: Research on QR code digital watermarking algorithm based on LSB. J. Chengdu Inst. Inform. Eng. **6**, 20–26 (2012)
2. He, X.L., An, H., Zhang, W., Li, K., Yang, W.: QR barcode digital watermarking based on improved LSB algorithm. Comput. Inform. Technolo. **10**, 5–8 (2010)
3. Yu, C., Hu, W.: Past and present lives of QR codes. Confidential Sci. Technol. **12**, 6 (2017)
4. Chen, B., Yu, L.: Research on the application of information hiding technology in secure email. Comput. Eng. Appl. **24**, 91–92 (2001)
5. Zhu, Q., Liu, Y.: Expansion of the functions of QR code and print media. Media **07**, 66–68 (2007)
6. Huang, F.: LSB-based digital watermarking algorithm and MATLAB implementation. Mod. Mech. **02**, 70–72 (2008)
7. Li, H., Wang, C., Gao, Y.: Research and design of LSB-based image information hiding technology. Netw. Security Technol. Appl. **6**, 2 (2016)
8. Fei, L.: Implementation of digital watermark based on LSB algorithm. J. Anqing Normal College (Nat. Sci. Ed.) **03**, 67–72 (2011)
9. Zhou, Y., Zou, Z., Yang, Z.: Application of information hiding technology in computer network warfare. Naval Electron. Countermeas. **01**, 9–13 (2005)
10. Hao, L., Qiang, F.: Status and development of digital watermarking technology. Heilongjiang Sci. Technol. Inform. **31**, 57 (2008)

Event-Based H_∞ Control for Networked Control System with Saturation Constraints

Wenlin Zou[1(✉)], Lisheng Jia[2], and Liuwen Li[3]

[1] School of Information Engineering,
Nanjing Xiaozhuang University, Nanjing 210017, China
zouwenlin123@njxzc.edu.cn
[2] Shenxian Experimental Senior Middle School, Liaocheng 252400, China
[3] School of Computer Engineering, Jinling Institute of Technology,
Nanjing 211169, China

Abstract. The event-based H_∞ control problem is researched for networked control systems subject to saturation constraints. In consideration of event-triggered mechanism and saturation constraints concurrently, the networked control system is modeled as a nonlinear system. By using Lyapunov-functional method and the linear matrix inequality techniques, the mean square stable criteria and H_∞ controller has been got for the controlled system with suitable event-driven matrix. A numerical example is given to illustrate the feasibility of the control approach in the paper.

Keywords: Event-driven mechanism · Sensor saturation Networked control system

1 Introduction

Event-based mechanism has been widely studied recently for the advantages of reducing transmission frequency and saving limited communication resources. The event-driven communication mechanism does not transmit information according to a fixed time period, but decides whether to transmit sampled signals based on predefined trigger conditions. Different from the traditional time-triggered scheme, the experimental results in reference [1] show that the event-triggered scheme can greatly reduce the information transmission frequency on the premise of ensuring the control performance of the system. Event-triggered filtering and control problems have been widely studied in many types of networked control systems, such as linear control systems [2,3], Markov jumping systems [4], descriptor systems [5], T-S fuzzy systems [6], and multi-agent systems [8]. In the literature mentioned above, event-triggering mechanism can be divided into two types: one is

Supported by the Natural Science Foundation of Jiangsu Province of China (No. BK20150793), Natural Science Foundation of China (No. 61976118), and Doctoral/High-level Talents Research Foundation of Jinling Institute of Technology (No. jit-b-202043).

© Springer Nature Singapore Pte Ltd. 2021
Y. Tian et al. (Eds.): ICBDS 2020, CCIS 1415, pp. 133–141, 2021.
https://doi.org/10.1007/978-981-16-3150-4_12

the continuous event-triggering mechanism [2,3,7,9], and the other is the discrete event-triggering mechanism [4–6]. The continuous event trigger is accomplished by detecting whether the current state exceeds the pre-defined trigger threshold via additional hardware continuously supervising state of the system. Based on discrete event-triggering mechanism, the event generator only needs to use the monitoring and sampling signals at discrete moments. For most practical systems, it is easy to realize the joint design of controller and trigger parameters.

Because of technical, physical, or safety constraints, the output of the sensor or actuator may be saturated. Saturation will introduce nonlinear characteristics into the control system, which may seriously affect the performance of the control system. If the saturation constraints are not properly handled, it not only might degrade the filter or control performances but also results in undesirable oscillatory behavior and even instability [11]. Considering the theoretical and practical significance of actuator/sensor saturation, the control and filter problem of control systems subject to saturation constraints has been extensively studied in recent years [12,13]. For example, in [12], the robust sampled-data control problem has been studied for an automotive seat-suspension system with actuator saturations. It should be emphasized that in most relevant literatures, few existing results involve the control systems subject to both actuator and sensor saturations [10,14], although this phenomenon is very common in engineering applications.

In this paper, the main contributions can be summed up as follows: (1) a new model of nonlinear system is developed for the use of robust H_∞ control synthesis with simultaneous consideration of event-based mechanism and both sensor and random actuator saturations; (2) by way of Lyapunov-functional method and the LMI technique, the mean square stability criteria and H_∞ controller are obtained for the controlled system with suitable trigger parameter matrices.

2   System Description

Consider the linear networked control system as follows:

$$\begin{cases} \dot{x}(t) = Ax(t) + Bu(t) + G\omega(t) \\ z(t) = Cx(t) + Eu(t) + F\omega(t) \\ x(t_0) = x_0 \end{cases} \tag{1}$$

in which $u(t) \in \mathbb{R}^m$, $x(t) \in \mathbb{R}^n$, $z(t) \in \mathbb{R}^p$ and $\omega(t) \in \mathcal{L}_2[0,\infty)$ are the control input, state vector, control output and disturbance input, respectively. A, B, C, E, G and F are system parameter matrices, and $x_0 \in \mathbb{R}^n$ is the initial condition at initial time t_0.

In order to save the valuable bandwidth resources and reduce the signal transmission frequency in the control system, an event-triggering mechanism is introduced between the controller and the sensor. Considering the control system which has sensor saturation, we employ the trigger condition similar to [1]:

$$[\sigma_s(x(t_kh+jh)) - \sigma_s(x(t_kh))]^T \, \Omega \, [\sigma_s(x(t_kh+jh)) - \sigma_s(x(t_kh))]$$
$$\leq \rho\sigma_s^T(x(t_kh+jh)\Omega\sigma_s(x(t_kh+jh)) \tag{2}$$

where $\Omega > 0$ is a trigger matrix, $\rho \in (0,1)$ is a constant and $\sigma_s(\bullet)$ is the sensor saturation function. $jh, t_k h$ are the sampling instant and the trigger instant, respectively. The latest sampled signal $x(t_k h + jh)$ will be sent to the controller on condition that the condition (2) is violated. Denote $e_k(t) = \sigma_s(x(t_k h)) - \sigma_s(x(t_k h + jh)), t \in [t_k, t_{k+1})_{k=0}^\infty$, and $\eta(t) = t - t_k h - jh, l = 0, 1, 2, \cdots$. Suppose $\eta(t) \in [0, \eta_M)$, where η_M is a positive real number. According to the definition of $e_k(t)$, we can rewrite the trigger condition (2) as follows:

$$e_k^T(t)\Omega e_k(t) \le \rho \sigma_s^T(x(t - \eta(t)))\Omega \sigma_s(x(t - \eta(t))), \qquad (3)$$

We can express the controller as follows:

$$u(t) = K(\sigma_s(x(t - \eta(t))) + e_k(t)) \qquad (4)$$

If we consider random actuator saturation, the controller (4) can be rewritten as

$$\bar{u}(t) = \beta(t)u(t) + (1 - \beta(t))\sigma_u(u(t)) \qquad (5)$$

where $\sigma_a(\bullet)$ denotes the function of actuator saturation. $\beta(t)$ is a white sequence which obeys Bernoulli distribution, and its value is 0 or 1, and satisfies the statistical characteristics as follows:

$$Prob\{\beta(t) = 1\} = \beta_0, \ Prob\{\beta(t) = 0\} = 1 - \beta_0 \qquad (6)$$

$$\mathbb{E}\{\beta(t)\} = \beta_0, \quad \mathbb{E}\{(\beta(t) - \beta_0)^2\} = \beta_0(1 - \beta_0) \qquad (7)$$

In which $\beta_0 \in [0, 1]$ is a known constant. The stochastic variable $\beta(t)$ can be applied to describe the random actuator saturation. According to the formula (5), when $\beta(t) = 1$, the real actuator output is $\bar{u}(t) = u(t)$, which means that there is no actuator saturation. When $\beta(t) = 0$, the real actuator output is $\bar{u}(t) = \sigma_a(u(t))$, which shows that the actuator saturation comes up.

Referring to the method proposed in [15], we can the decompose the saturation functions $\sigma_s(x(t - \eta(t)))$ and $\sigma_a(u(t))$ as follows:

$$\sigma_s(x(t - \eta(t))) = x(t - \eta(t)) - \zeta(x(t - \eta(t))), \qquad (8)$$

$$\sigma_a(u(t)) = u(t) - \xi(u(t)), \qquad (9)$$

in which $\xi(u(t))$ and $\zeta(x(t - \eta(t)))$ are two nonlinearity functions. By using $\eta(t)$, $e_k(t)$, (8) and (9), the control system (1) can be rewritten as follows:

$$\begin{cases} \dot{x}(t) = Ax(t) + BKx(t - \eta(t)) + BKe_k(t) - BK\zeta(x(t - \eta(t)) \\ \qquad -(1 - \beta(t))B\xi(u(t)) + G\omega(t) \\ z(t) = Cx(t) + EKx(t - \eta(t)) + EKe_k(t) - EK\zeta(x(t - \eta(t)) \\ \qquad -(1 - \beta(t))E\xi(u(t)) + F\omega(t) \end{cases} \qquad (10)$$

3   Main Results

In the following, we firstly obtain a stable criterion for the control system (10).

Theorem 1. *For prescribed scalars* $\rho \in [0,1)$, $\varepsilon_1, \varepsilon_2, \beta_0 \in (0,1)$, $\gamma > 0$, $\eta_M > 0$ *and the controller* K, *the system (10) is mean square stable with the event-driven mechanism (2), if there exist positive definite matrices* P, Q, R, Ω, *and matrices* S, U *satisfying the following matrix inequalities:*

$$
\Sigma(s) \triangleq
\begin{bmatrix}
\Sigma_{11}+\Gamma+\Gamma^T & * & * & * & * & * & * & * & * & * \\
\Sigma_{21} & -\gamma^2 I & * & * & * & * & * & * & * & * \\
\mathcal{G}^s & 0 & -R & * & * & * & * & * & * & * \\
\sqrt{\eta_M}\mathcal{A} & \sqrt{\eta_M}G & 0 & -R^{-1} & * & * & * & * & * & * \\
\Sigma_{51} & 0 & 0 & 0 & -I & * & * & * & * & * \\
\Sigma_{61} & 0 & 0 & 0 & 0 & -I & * & * & * & * \\
\Sigma_{71} & 0 & 0 & 0 & 0 & 0 & -\Omega & * & * & * \\
\mathcal{B} & F & 0 & 0 & 0 & 0 & 0 & -I & * & * \\
\mathcal{C} & 0 & 0 & 0 & 0 & 0 & 0 & 0 & -R^{-1} & * \\
\mathcal{D} & 0 & 0 & 0 & 0 & 0 & 0 & 0 & 0 & -I
\end{bmatrix} < 0 \qquad s = 1,2. \quad (11)
$$

where

$$
\Sigma_{11} =
\begin{bmatrix}
PA + A^T P + Q & * & * & * & * & * \\
K^T B^T P & 0 & * & * & * & * \\
0 & 0 & -Q & * & * & * \\
K^T B^T P & 0 & 0 & -\Omega & * & * \\
-K^T B^T P & 0 & 0 & 0 & -I & * \\
-B^T P & 0 & 0 & 0 & 0 & -I
\end{bmatrix}
$$

$$
\Sigma_{21} = \begin{bmatrix} G^T P\, 0\, 0\, 0\, 0\, 0 \end{bmatrix}
$$
$$
\mathcal{G}^1 = \sqrt{\eta_M} S^T, \quad \mathcal{G}^2 = \sqrt{\eta_M} U^T
$$
$$
\Gamma = \begin{bmatrix} S\ U\ -S\ -U\ 0\ 0\ 0 \end{bmatrix}
$$
$$
\mathcal{A} = \begin{bmatrix} A\ BK\ 0\ BK\ -BK\ -(1-\beta_0)B \end{bmatrix}
$$
$$
\Sigma_{51} = \begin{bmatrix} 0\ \sqrt{\varepsilon_1} I_n\ 0\ 0\ 0\ 0 \end{bmatrix}
$$
$$
\Sigma_{61} = \begin{bmatrix} 0\ \sqrt{\varepsilon_2} K\ 0\ \sqrt{\varepsilon_2} K\ -\sqrt{\varepsilon_2} K\ 0 \end{bmatrix}
$$
$$
\Sigma_{71} = \begin{bmatrix} 0\ \sqrt{\rho}\Omega\ 0\ 0\ -\sqrt{\rho}\Omega\ 0 \end{bmatrix}
$$
$$
\mathcal{B} = \begin{bmatrix} C\ EK\ 0\ EK\ -EK\ -(1-\beta_0)E \end{bmatrix}
$$
$$
\mathcal{C} = \sqrt{\eta_M \beta_0 (1-\beta_0)} \begin{bmatrix} 0\ 0\ 0\ 0\ 0\ B \end{bmatrix}
$$

$$
\mathcal{D} = \sqrt{\beta_0(1-\beta_0)}\, 0\ 0\ 0\ 0\ 0\ E
$$

Proof. Define the Lyapunov-Krasovskii functional as follows:

$$
V(x_t) = x^T(t) P x(t) + \int_{t-\eta_M}^{t} x^T(s) Q x(s)\, ds + \int_{t-\eta_M}^{t} \int_{s}^{t} \dot{x}^T(v) R \dot{x}(v)\, dv\, ds \quad (12)
$$

in which P, Q and R are positive definite matrices. Calculating the infinitesimal operator of $V(x_t)$ and using free matrices approach, by using a similar proof method in [1], we can prove that the control system (10) is mean square stable. Because of page limitation, the proof procedure is omitted.

Based on analysis results in Theorem 1, A robust design method of the controller K and trigger parameter matrices is proposed.

Theorem 2. *For prescribed scalars $\rho \in [0,1)$, $\varepsilon_1, \varepsilon_2, \beta_0 \in (0,1)$, $\varepsilon_3, \varepsilon_4 > 0$, $\gamma > 0$, $\eta_M > 0$, the control system (10) is mean square stable, if there exist positive definite matrices X, $\tilde{Q}$, $\tilde{R}$, $\tilde{\Omega}$, and matrices $\tilde{U}$, $\tilde{S}$, Y, satisfying the following LMIs:*

$$\tilde{\Sigma}(s) \triangleq \begin{bmatrix} \tilde{\Sigma}_{11} + \tilde{\Gamma} + \tilde{\Gamma}^T & * & * & * & * & * & * & * & * & * \\ \tilde{\Sigma}_{21} & -\gamma^2 I & * & * & * & * & * & * & * & * \\ \tilde{\mathcal{G}}^s & 0 & -\tilde{R} & * & * & * & * & * & * & * \\ \sqrt{\eta_M}\tilde{A} & \sqrt{\eta_M}G & 0 & -2\varepsilon_3 X + \varepsilon_3^2\tilde{R} & * & * & * & * & * & * \\ \tilde{\Sigma}_{51} & 0 & 0 & 0 & -I & * & * & * & * & * \\ \tilde{\Sigma}_{61} & 0 & 0 & 0 & 0 & -I & * & * & * & * \\ \Sigma_{71} & 0 & 0 & 0 & 0 & 0 & -\tilde{\Omega} & * & * & * \\ \mathcal{B} & H & 0 & 0 & 0 & 0 & 0 & -I & * & * \\ \mathcal{C} & 0 & 0 & 0 & 0 & 0 & 0 & 0 & -2\varepsilon_4 X + \varepsilon_4^2\tilde{R} & * \\ \mathcal{E} & 0 & 0 & 0 & 0 & 0 & 0 & 0 & 0 & -I \end{bmatrix} < 0 \quad (13)$$

where

$$s = 1, 2.$$

$$\tilde{\Sigma}_{11} = \begin{bmatrix} AX + XA^T + \tilde{Q} & * & * & * & * & * \\ Y^T B^T & 0 & * & * & * & * \\ 0 & 0 & -\tilde{Q} & * & * & * \\ Y^T B^T & 0 & 0 & -\tilde{\Omega} & * & * \\ -Y^T B^T & 0 & 0 & 0 & -2\varepsilon X + \varepsilon^2 I & * \\ -B^T & 0 & 0 & 0 & 0 & -I \end{bmatrix}$$

$$\tilde{\Sigma}_{21} = \begin{bmatrix} G^T & 0 & 0 & 0 & 0 & 0 \end{bmatrix}$$

$$\tilde{\mathcal{G}}^1 = \sqrt{\eta_M}\tilde{S}^T, \quad \tilde{\mathcal{G}}^2 = \sqrt{\eta_M}\tilde{U}^T$$

$$\tilde{\Gamma} = \begin{bmatrix} \tilde{S} & \tilde{U} -\tilde{S} & -\tilde{U} & 0 & 0 & 0 \end{bmatrix}$$

$$\tilde{A} = \begin{bmatrix} AX & BY & 0 & BY & -BY & -B \end{bmatrix}$$

$$\tilde{\Sigma}_{51} = \begin{bmatrix} 0 & \sqrt{\varepsilon_1}I & 0 & 0 & 0 & 0 \end{bmatrix}$$

$$\tilde{\Sigma}_{61} = \begin{bmatrix} 0 & \sqrt{\varepsilon_2}Y & 0 & \sqrt{\varepsilon_2}Y & -\sqrt{\varepsilon_2}Y & 0 \end{bmatrix}$$

$$\tilde{\Sigma}_{71} = \begin{bmatrix} 0 & \sqrt{\rho}\tilde{\Omega} & 0 & 0 & -\sqrt{\rho}\tilde{\Omega} & 0 \end{bmatrix}$$

$$\tilde{\mathcal{B}} = \begin{bmatrix} CX & EY & 0 & EY & -EY & -E \end{bmatrix}$$

$$\mathcal{C} = \sqrt{\eta_M\beta_0(1-\beta_0)}\begin{bmatrix} 0 & 0 & 0 & 0 & 0 & BX \end{bmatrix}$$

$$\mathcal{D} = \sqrt{\beta_0(1-\beta_0)}\begin{bmatrix} 0 & 0 & 0 & 0 & 0 & E \end{bmatrix}$$

The controller of the system is $K = YX^{-1}$.

4   Illustrative Examples

Example 1. Consider the control system (1) with parameter matrices as follows:

$$\begin{cases} \dot{x}(t) = \begin{bmatrix} -2 & -0.1 \\ -0.1 & 0.01 \end{bmatrix} x(t) + \begin{bmatrix} 0.1 \\ 0.2 \end{bmatrix} \sigma_a(u(t)) + \begin{bmatrix} 1 \\ -1 \end{bmatrix} w(t) \\ z(t) = \begin{bmatrix} 0.5 & -0.1 \\ -0.8 & 0.1 \end{bmatrix} x(t) + \begin{bmatrix} -0.7 \\ 0.3 \end{bmatrix} \sigma_a(\bar{u}(t)) + \begin{bmatrix} -1 \\ 1 \end{bmatrix} w(t) \end{cases} \tag{14}$$

Suppose the external disturbance as

$$w(t) = \begin{cases} 0.4\mathrm{sgn}(\sin(t)), & if\ t \in [0, 15] \\ 0, & otherwise \end{cases}$$

Set $\varepsilon = 1$, $\varepsilon_1 = 0.1$, $\varepsilon_2 = 0.2$, $\rho = 0.03$, $\varepsilon_3 = \varepsilon_4 = 1$, $\beta_0 = 0.7$, $\gamma = 20$, and the sampling period $h = 0.05$. According to Theorem 2, the upper bound of η_M is 0.8523. Choosing $\eta_M = 0.7$, we can derive the trigger matrix Ω as

$$\Omega = \begin{bmatrix} 11.1874 & 0.1434 \\ 0.1434 & 0.9024 \end{bmatrix} \tag{15}$$

and the controller K of the system is

$$K = \begin{bmatrix} 0.1649 & -0.3794 \end{bmatrix} \tag{16}$$

When we choose the initial condition of the system as $x(0) = \begin{bmatrix} 1.2 & -0.7 \end{bmatrix}^T$, the state responses of the system, the output of the sensor with saturation constraints and the input of the system with random saturation are illustrated

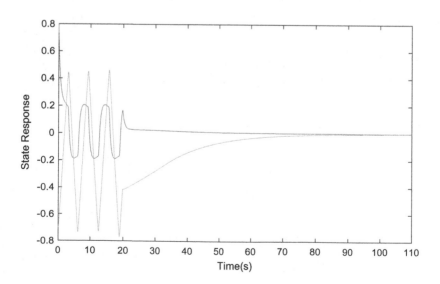

Fig. 1. The state of the system with the controller (16)

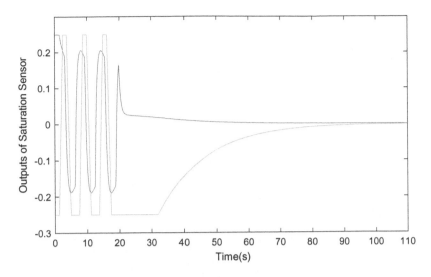

Fig. 2. The sensor outputs with the controller (16)

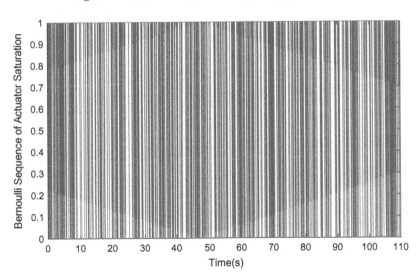

Fig. 3. The probability distribution of the randomly occurring actuator saturation

in Figs. 1, 2, and 4, respectively. The probability distribution of the randomly occurring actuator saturation is illustrated in Fig. 3. Figure 5 shows the signal release instants and event intervals. The transmitted signals only take 4.8% of all sampled signals.

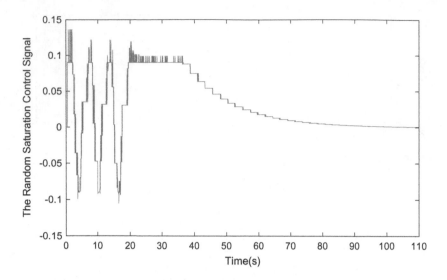

Fig. 4. The outputs of the random saturation actuator with the controller (16)

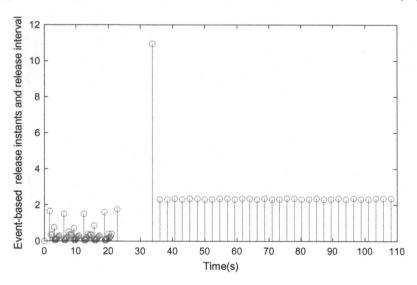

Fig. 5. The event-triggered instants and event-triggered interval with the controller (16)

5   Conclusion

This paper mainly researches the H_∞ control problem of networked control systems with event-driven mechanism and sensor and random actuator saturation. In order to overcome the adverse effects of sensor and random actuator saturations, a novel networked nonlinear control system model is established based on event-triggered mechanism. By using Lyapunov function method, stochastic analysis theory and linear matrix inequality technique, the stability criterion of the system is obtained and the co-design method of the controller and trigger parameter matrices is implemented simultaneously. A numerical example has been given to illustrate the feasibility of the proposed control technology.

References

1. Dong, Y., Tian, E., Han, Q.L.: A delay system method for designing event-triggered controllers of networked control systems. IEEE Trans. Autom. Control **58**(2), 475–481 (2013)
2. Donkers, M.: Output-based event-triggered control with guaranteed L_∞-gain and improved and decentralized event-triggering. IEEE Trans. Autom. Control **57**(6), 1362–1376 (2012)
3. Lunze, J., Lehmann, D.: A state-feedback approach to event-based control. Automatica **46**(1), 211–215 (2010)
4. Li, H., Zuo, Z., Wang, Y.: Event triggered control for Markovian jump systems with partially unknown transition probabilities and actuator saturation. J. Franklin Inst. **353**(8), 1848–1861 (2016)
5. Shi, P., Wang, H., Lim, C.C.: Network-based event-triggered control for singular systems with quantizations. IEEE Trans. Industr. Electron. **63**(2), 1230–1238 (2016)
6. Hu, S., et al.: Event-triggered controller design of nonlinear discrete-time networked control systems in T-S fuzzy model. Appl. Soft Comput. **30**, 400–411 (2015)
7. Wang, X., Lemmon, M.D.: Event-triggering in distributed networked control systems. IEEE Trans. Autom. Control **56**(3), 586–601 (2011)
8. Zhang, H., et al.: Finite-time distributed event-triggered consensus control for multi-agent systems. Inf. Sci. Int. J. 132–142 (2016)
9. Tabuada, P.: Event-triggered real-time scheduling of stabilizing control tasks. IEEE Trans. Autom. Control **52**(9), 1680–1685 (2007)
10. Wang, Z., et al.: Robust finite-horizon control for a class of stochastic nonlinear time-varying systems subject to sensor and actuator saturations. IEEE Trans. Autom. Control **55**(7), 1716–1722 (2010)
11. Dong, H., Wang, Z., Gao, H.: Fault detection for Markovian jump systems with sensor saturations and randomly varying nonlinearities. IEEE Trans. Circ. Syst. I Reg. Papers **59**(10), 2354–2362 (2012)
12. Zhou, G., et al.: Robust control of automotive active seat-suspension system subject to actuator saturation. J. Dyn. Syst. Meas. Control **136**(4), 041022 (2014)
13. Dong, H., et al.: Robust H filtering for Markovian jump systems with randomly occurring nonlinearities and sensor saturation: the finite-horizon case. IEEE Trans. Sig. Process. **59**(7), 3048–3057 (2011)
14. Zhu, Y., Zhang, L., Basin, M.V.: Nonstationary H_∞ dynamic output feedback control for discrete-time Markov jump linear systems with actuator and sensor saturations. Int. J. Robust Nonlinear Control **26** (2016)
15. Sun, L., Wang, Y., Feng, G.: Control design for a class of affine nonlinear descriptor systems with actuator saturation. IEEE Trans. Autom. Control **60**(8), 2195–2200 (2015)

Privacy Preserving Data Sharing in Online Social Networks

Randa Aljably[✉]

Shaqra University, Druma, Kingdom of Saudi Arabia
raljebly@su.edu.sa

Abstract. Social networks pervaded human lives in mostly each aspect. The vast amount of sensitive data that users produce and exchanged on these platforms call for intensive concern about information and privacy protection. Moreover, the users' statistical usage data collected for analysis is also subject to leakage and therefor require protection. Although there is an availability of privacy preserving methods, they are not scalable, or tend to underperform when it comes to data utility and efficiency. Thus, in this paper, we develop a novel approach for anonymizing users' statistical data. The data is collected from the user's behavior patterns in social networks. In particular, we collect specific points from the user's behavior patterns rather than the entire data stream to be fed into local differential privacy (LDP). After the statistical data has been anonymized, we reconstruct the original points using nonlinear techniques. The results from this approach provide significant accuracy when compared with the straightforward anonymization approach.

Keywords: Privacy preservation · Local deferential privacy · Data sharing · Online social networks

1 Introduction

With the rapid development of social networks, and the massive volume of data generated by users on these online platforms, there has been a growing concern over user privacy and data protection and an increasing demand for user's privacy preservation. To guarantee the users' continuous dedication to using online social networks (OSNs), it is essential to collect and distribute the user related data in a secure and trustworthy manner. However, this matter is challenged on two different levels, the first is that social networks collect users' data and metadata (user behavioral statistics), which is sensitive in nature [1]. Therefore, it is the responsibility of the social platform to protect the confidentiality of this collected data from in-depth mining of machine learning algorithms. This protection was proven not sufficient as in 2019, 267 million Facebook user's personal data such as user IDs, names and passwords were exposed [2].

The second level of challenge lays in the way social platforms willingly share some of the user's information with third parties for financial profits and statistical analysis as seen later in the motivational scenario. In order to preserve the privacy of shared information,

© Springer Nature Singapore Pte Ltd. 2021
Y. Tian et al. (Eds.): ICBDS 2020, CCIS 1415, pp. 142–152, 2021.
https://doi.org/10.1007/978-981-16-3150-4_13

social networks used several methods such as decentralized Online social networks (DOSNs) [3], blockchains [4], Graph modification techniques, Differential privacy [5], classification, clustering, k-anonymity, l-diversity [6, 7], k-degree anonymity, and t-closeness [7].

In this research we focus on differential privacy as it is considered a de facto standard for privacy preservation used in many applications [8]. It is also used under names such as centralized differential privacy to escape the distribution responsibility found in decentralized approaches and evade the challenge of continuous coordination to maintain a secure state of the system. Other research used local differential privacy to indicate the locality of application in the users' devices before data is transferred to the collecting servers.

Local differential privacy (LDP) is mainly applied by the users to their original data to perturb the data. There are several options for applying noise in LDP. The Laplace mechanism is the most famous for its utility advantages [9]. The anonymized version is later aggregated in a data collecting repository in the social network [1]. In this way, the users can control their privacy before their data is securely shared. LDP has proven to provide plausible deniability; Meaning that, it cannot be reversed nor can an adversary deduce the user's confidential information with the prior knowledge they have [10].

Based on the previous discussion, we developed an anonymization technique, that works under different levels of privacy protections. The technique is applicable to behavioral patterns and aggregated statistics extracted from user's social data, through means of leveraging local differential privacy to preserve the data privacy in the process of distribution. Our approach relies on LDP to support multilevel privacy guarantee mechanisms depending on the degree of trust between users and the social network platform. We also present a method to effectively reconstruct the original anonymized and distributed data. Experimental results with social network data sets demonstrate that the proposed approach achieve lower average error compared to the straightforward application of LDP.

Hence, in this paper, our contribution is to leverage an LDP to anonymize users' behavioral data collected from their social network's records, rather than the traditional relational data. In addition, we use a non-linear approach to reconstruct the original data while minimizing the reconstruction error as compared to the straightforward solution.

In Subsect. 1.1 we justify our selection for LDP using a motivational scenario, In Sect. 2 we introduces the preliminaries. Then, we introduce related works in Sect. 3. Section 4 shows the system model and the LDP based algorithm and demonstrates the experimental results in Sect. 6. Followed by the paper conclusion.

1.1 Motivational Scenario

It is no secret to anyone, that the availability, connectivity and the digital representation of social networks, come with a cost of data distribution and exposure. Sometimes even data that are not expected to be worthy. As illustrated in Fig. 1, social networks collect and store user's personal data which were willingly created and shared by the users themselves, and more importantly behavior statistics and metadata. This information is latter on distributed to multiple third parties to support the network's continuity and ensure targeted and non-targeted marketing profits in addition to other various purposes [3].

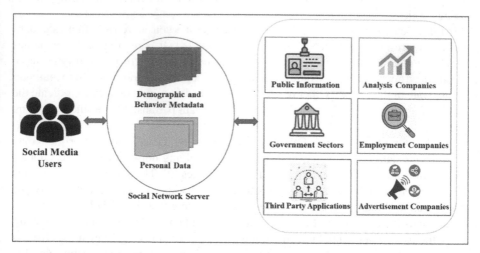

Fig. 1. Motivational scenario for privacy preservation

Privacy preservation does not only serve the purpose of protecting distributed data, but also promote privacy aware control over user's emotions, personality traits, behavioral pattern, and interests that could be obtained and targeted as a result of an analysis of the online social data and metadata [3].

2 Preliminaries

Deferential privacy (DP) is used to determine the amount of disclosed information to a third party. Conventionally, epsilon ϵ and delta δ are parameters used to control the level of privacy obtained by a privacy preservation algorithm $\mathcal{M}$. Each algorithm should satisfy the *(ϵ, δ) properties [11].

In local differential privacy, the random anonymization is performed by the social network instead of an aggregator. So, the server only keeps the anonymized results, which makes an adversary uncapable of determining with high confidence depending on a privacy level called the privacy budget ϵ whether a value held is x or $\dot{x}$. The privacy budget ϵ controls the tradeoff between privacy and utility in a reverse relationship (higher privacy budget yields lower privacy protection).The network anonymize the user's data using an algorithm $\mathcal{M}$, then the network can send the anonymized data to any aggregator or third party.

Average Error probability (δ) is the parameter of events that cause privacy loss. It is the probability of an adversary identifying the origin of a particular piece of data, this can occur $n \times \delta$ times, where n is the number of records. Therefore, the probability δ must be minimized in order to minimize this risk of privacy loss [11].

Definition 1 *(Local Differential Privacy)*. *Let* $\mathcal{M}$ *be a randomized function with domain* $\mathbb{X}$ *and range* $\mathbb{Y}$, *Such that* $\mathcal{M}$ *maps each element in* $\mathbb{X}$ to a probability distribution with sample space $\mathbb{Y}$. *For a non-negative* ϵ *the randomized mechanism* $\mathcal{M}$ *satisfies local differential privacy if:*

$$\left| ln\, \frac{\mathbb{P}_{\mathcal{M}}[Y \in S|x]}{\mathbb{P}_{\mathcal{M}}[Y \in S|\dot{x}]} \right| \le \epsilon, \forall x, \dot{x} \in \mathbb{X}, \forall S \subseteq \mathbb{Y}. \tag{1}$$

$\mathbb{P}_{\mathcal{M}}[\,.\,|\,.\,]$Means conditional probability distribution depend on [10].

Definition 2. *(Laplace mechanism). Given a function* $f : D \to \mathbb{R}$ *over a dataset* D, *the Laplace mechanism is defined as* [1]*:*

$$\hat{f}(D) = f(D) + Laplace\left(\frac{S}{\epsilon}\right). \tag{2}$$

3 Related Work

Differential privacy was handcrafted by Dwork et al. [1] and has been embraced as a de facto standard for preserving privacy in a variety of applications. The traditional differential privacy (DP) works in two phases, it collects the user's original data first, then releases the perturbed aggregated information to the public user. DP's main drawback is its assumption of trusted data curator. Unfortunately, that is not always the case in the real world.

Recently, LDP has begun to gain popularity as a reliable way of anonymizing large volumes of data and guaranteeing privacy preservation in the process of data collection and. In autonomous and self-driven vehicles, user's traffic information such as real time location, and route details become available to crowdsource application owners. The work in [9, 10] proposed an integrated LDP to facilitate crowdsourcing application. The anonymized data was then subject to machine learning models operated by intelligent traffic management systems. The model also participated in lowering the communication cost between vehicles and the cloud server.

Similar to autonomous vehicles, IoT platforms deal with multiple data contributors, to which it must perturb real world data before sharing with data collectors [12]. The data collectors, then could utilize the data, and the service provider could further process the contents to retain exclusive utility. Deferential privacy in such applications tackles many considerations namely privacy, data utility, bandwidth efficiency, payment, and rationality for data sharing. With the growing demand for healthcare environments where patients can be treated by multiple healthcare providers [13, 14], it becomes essential to preserve the sensitive health data from authorized access. Using multilevel privacy preserving data sharing, a data owner is able to safely share his health data with a collaborative health system under local different levels of privacy protections.

In social networks, Graphs are usually used to ensure privacy [5, 7], Anonymization in graphs is carried out in two models; cluster-based and graph modification. The first approach clusters the vertices and the edges into groups. Then replaces a subgraph with a super vertex. On the other hand, in graph modification, the topological structure [7] presented in the edges and vertices are modified via various randomization techniques in the graph. However, two issues arise from this graph anonymization, firstly the anonymization may affect the usability of the noised data, thus decreasing user experience [7]. Secondly, maintaining privacy in graphs with a structure that varies over time is very complicated, indicating that anonymization algorithm may not always perform well on different graphs.

Decentralized Online Social Networks (DOSNs) has been also used to preserve privacy in OSNs. The work in [3] argue that decentralization, need to be designed and carried out carefully and properly, otherwise it may cause more serious implications on users' privacy rather than solve them. Moreover, the research on (DOSNs) is not yet mature, as it needs more innovative technical solutions in the area of identity validation and prevention of fake accounts.

Recent research, tackled privacy at different levels of the OSN, rather than dealing with user's attributes at the user level, the approach [6] considers data privacy at the network level. Equi-cardinal clustering (ECC) achieves user similarity clustering (k-anonymity) when applied to nodes, edge and attribute privacy. k-anonymity is further enhanced with l-diversity through the assumption that at least k users in a particular network in addition to attributes in each cluster have at least l – distinct values.

Despite the long going research in privacy preservation methods, the current methods available suffer from issues such as efficiency, scalability, data utility, or continuous privacy. Hence the need for novel approaches to preserve privacy in big data. The work in [11] introduced optimal geometric transformations. The approach was an irreversible input perturbation mechanism which introduced a new privacy model, i.e. ϕ–separation. The separation parameter provides privacy guarantee against data reconstruction attacks. The approach applied random axis reflection, noise translation, and multidimensional concatenated sub plane rotation followed by randomized expansion and random tuple shuffling for further randomization.

Privacy preserving data mining (PPDM) approach [15] usually involves extracting the association rules from the database, data sanitization and data restoration. Key extraction is selected using Opposition Intensity-based Cuckoo Search Algorithm. PPDM presented an improvement in scalability and efficiency as opposed to classical privacy preservation techniques [16].

In some cases, it is crucial to provide privacy protection and prevent privacy leakage in the training phase of datasets.

Therefore, differential privacy may be applied with other mechanisms such as deep learning models [10]. It guarantees that the output of deep learning model does not show significant statistical differences when the model is trained on multiple datasets.

4   The System Model and LDP Algorithm

Local differential privacy has become the standard privacy protection model in the field of social networks applications. LDP anonymizes individual's data before leaving their devices and therefore woks independently from the assumption of a trusted data curator.

Figure 2 depicts the structure of our approach, where the users create their data and social information on the networks, the networks then applies privacy model to the data

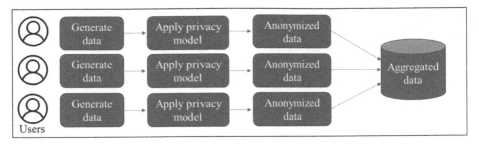

Fig. 2. Applying privacy models in OSNs

to create a non-traceable version which is saved on the servers. After wards if the data is to be shared with other parties, only the anonymized version will be released.

Amongst these privacy models is the standard LDP model, in which the steps are shown in Fig. 3. The first step is to recognize the eminent activities in each user's behavioral data stream, over the time period from which the data is collected. LDP attempts to single out these activities by calculating the first order derivative $d(x)$ between consecutive points. Thus, creating a list of points where $d(x) \neq 0$, consecutively called salient points (SPs).

The purpose of creating salient points is to represent the data stream as continuous data values, but such data in OSN is high in volume and cannot be redundantly processed. Therefore, calculating SPs, the points are separated into increasing and decreasing ($0 < d(x)$ or $d(x) > 0$) intervals over the time series [17]. The list is further shortened to include only the beginning and end of each interval, while the intermediate points are eliminated.

In LDP the multiple parameters impact the privacy of the released data, such as privacy budget, privacy error and sensitivity. The privacy budget is occasionally labeled as privacy level. And is calculated in two different ways. First is a uniform privacy level, where $\epsilon_i \leftarrow (Epsilon/n)$, where n is the length of the data stream, thereby, each privacy level will be the same between users.

The second way to calculate a pricy level is adapted from each users' data stream. It calculates a temporal scale

$$\mu_h = \left(\frac{|Current\ SP - Previous\ SP| + |Current\ SP - Next\ SP|}{2} \right)^{\alpha}, \tag{3}$$

Where *Epsilon*, α are predefined system parameters, then calculates a temporal sum as the sum of each temporal scale, the privacy level will be

$$\mu_{sum} = \sum_{1 \leq h \leq r} \mu_h, \tag{4}$$

$$\varepsilon_i = Epsilon \cdot \frac{Temporal\_scale(i)}{temporal\_sum}. \tag{5}$$

On the other hand, the sensitivity parameter Δf considers the maximum difference between the highest and lowest points in the user's behavioral data stream [17]. It reflects the impact that a single sample can make to the added Laplace noise in a worst case scenario. After calculating the privacy levels the Laplace noise is created according to formula 2, where each SP will yield a new point that is stored in the OSN platform.

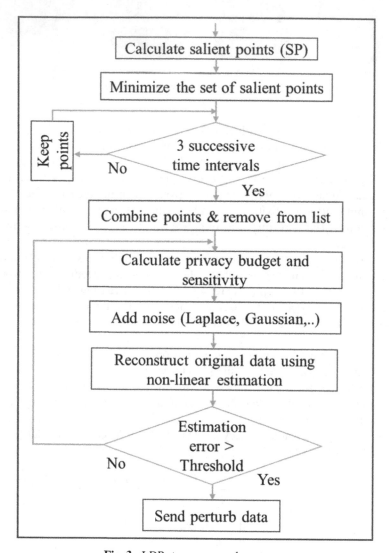

Fig. 3. LDP steps on user data stream

We attempt to reconstruct the original data using non-linear approach, using the logistic and symmetric functions $f(t), f'(t)$, where:

$$f(t) = \frac{L}{1 + e^{-\beta t}}, \; f'(t) = -\frac{L}{1 + e^{-\beta t}}. \tag{6}$$

In the previous formula L represents $2 \times |current\ SP - next\ SP|$, while the system parameter β is the steepness of the curve [13, 14], when the formula is applied,it yields four curves that could be used to reconstruct the segment between two pairs of SPs as shown in Fig. 4.

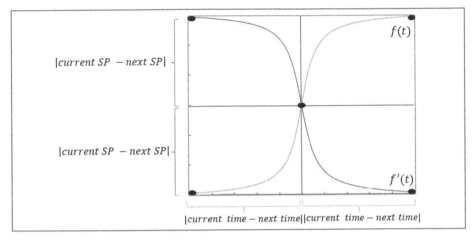

Fig. 4. Logistic and symmetric curves for current and next SP

The reconstructing curve selection depends on the time scale ratio and the value of the SP points as seen in Table 1.

Table 1. Selection of reconstructing curve segment

Condition	Curve user to reconstruct stream segment
Current SP > next SP and time scale ratio > 1	Top left curve
Current SP < next SP and time scale ratio > 1	Bottom left curve
Current SP > next SP and time scale ratio < 1	Bottom right curve
Current SP < next SP and time scale ratio < 1	Top right curve

5 Experimental Setup

We evaluate our approach on Twitter user data set, found at Data society: https://data.world/data-society/twitter-user-data. The dataset contains 20,000 rows, each with a user-name, a random tweet, account profile and image and location info. We extracted the number of tweets for each user for 10 days. Then we applied LDP using $\mu = 0, \beta = 1, \epsilon \in [0.5 - 2]$. After applying LDP with uniform and adaptive privacy levels to the extracted user activity streams, we attempted to construct the original data streams using non-linear functions, as demonstrated in Fig. 5. The adaptive non-linear reconstruction achieved closer match to the original data compared to the uniform non-linear reconstruction. This similarity is due to the selection of the privacy level which is adapted from each user's specific data stream.

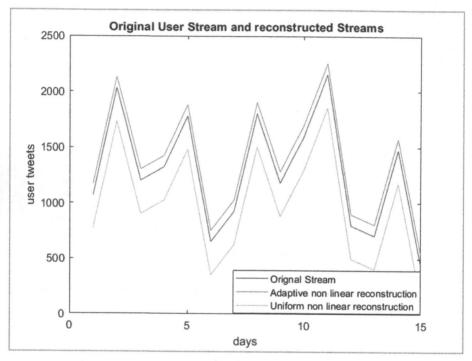

Fig. 5. Reconstructed data streams using non-linear estimation

We calculated the average reconstruction error after using non-linear estimation to obtain the original values according to the following equation:

$$Avg_{nl-est}(SP) = \frac{1}{w} \times \sum_{s_i' \in S} SP \qquad (7)$$

Knowing that w represents the number of users, while s_i' represents the set of sequences stored in the database. The estimated average error obtained in our method is displayed in Fig. 6 for 10 days and 20 days. When our approach is compared to the straightforward solution it shows that our approach was not badly affected by increasing the stream lengths, because it operated on a selected set of SPs instead of all the points in the stream as seen in the straightforward solution.

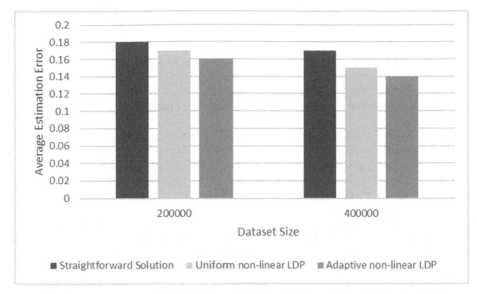

Fig. 6. Average Error in Straightforward solution, uniform LDP and adaptive LDP

6 Conclusion

Recently OSNs have gained worldwide popularity. Users create digital accounts to connect to others and share their information, without considering the security risks their information are targeted for.

As OSNs collect, analyze and republish user's information to other parties, it becomes necessary for users to confirm that their information is shared in the most secure and privacy protecting possible ways. Extensive research has been carried out to protect the data from privacy violations in social networks and propose appropriate security counter measure. In this paper we proposed taking advantage of local differential privacy to protect the privacy data of social nature. After the statistical data has been anonymized using LDP, we reconstructed the original points using nonlinear functions. The results from this approach improve the estimated average error when applied on multiple volumes of data when compared with the straightforward anonymization approach.

References

1. Yang, M., Lyu, L., Zhao, J., Zhu, T., Lam, K.Y.: Local differential privacy and its applications: a comprehensive survey. arXiv preprint arXiv:2008.03686 (2020)
2. Fisher, C.: Over 267 million Facebook users reportedly had data exposed online. Engadget, 19 December 2019. https://www.engadget.com/2019-12-19-facebook-data-exposed-online. html. Accessed 22 Dec 2019
3. Bahri, L., Carminati, B., Ferrari, E.: Decentralized privacy preserving services for online social networks. Online Soc. Netw. Media **6**, 18–25 (2018)
4. Chen, Y., Xie, H., Lv, K., Wei, S., Hu, C.: DEPLEST: a blockchain-based privacy-preserving distributed database toward user behaviors in social networks. Inf. Sci. **501**, 100–117 (2019)

5. Kiranmayi, M., Maheswari, N.: A review on privacy preservation of social networks using graphs. J. Appl. Secur. Res. 1–34 (2020)
6. Siddula, M., Li, Y., Cheng, X., Tian, Z., Cai, Z.: Anonymization in online social networks based on enhanced Equi-Cardinal clustering. IEEE Trans. Comput. Soc. Syst. 6(4), 809–820 (2019)
7. Zhang, C., Jiang, H., Cheng, X., Zhao, F., Cai, Z., Tian, Z.: Utility analysis on privacy-preservation algorithms for online social networks: an empirical study. Pers. Ubiquit. Comput. 1–17 (2019)
8. Dwork, C., Kenthapadi, K., McSherry, F., Mironov, I., Naor, M.: Our data, ourselves: privacy via distributed noise generation. In: Vaudenay, S. (ed.) EUROCRYPT 2006. LNCS, vol. 4004, pp. 486–503. Springer, Heidelberg (2006). https://doi.org/10.1007/11761679_29
9. Zhao, P., Zhang, G., Wan, S., Liu, G., Umer, T.: A survey of local differential privacy for securing internet of vehicles. J. Supercomput. 76(11), 8391–8412 (2019). https://doi.org/10.1007/s11227-019-03104-0
10. Zhao, J., Chen, Y., Zhang, W.: Differential privacy preservation in deep learning: challenges, opportunities and solutions. IEEE Access 7, 48901–48911 (2019)
11. Chamikara, M.A.P., Bertók, P., Liu, D., Camtepe, S., Khalil, I.: Efficient privacy preservation of big data for accurate data mining. Inf. Sci. 527, 420–443 (2020)
12. Zheng, X., Cai, Z.: Privacy-preserved data sharing towards multiple parties in industrial IoTs. IEEE J. Sel. Areas Commun. 38(5), 968–979 (2020)
13. Kim, J.W., Edemacu, K., Jang, B.: MPPDS: multilevel privacy-preserving data sharing in a collaborative eHealth system. IEEE Access 7, 109910–109923 (2019)
14. Kim, J.W., Lim, J.H., Moon, S.M., Yoo, H., Jang, B.: Privacy-preserving data collection scheme on smartwatch platform. In: 2019 IEEE International Conference on Consumer Electronics (ICCE), pp. 1–4. IEEE, January 2019
15. Shailaja, G.K., Rao, C.G.: Opposition intensity-based cuckoo search algorithm for data privacy preservation. J. Intell. Syst. 29(1), 1441–1452 (2019)
16. Almani, D.: Privacy preservation data mining and security. In: 2020 3rd International Conference on Computer Applications and Information Security (ICCAIS), pp. 1–6. IEEE, March 2020
17. Aljably, R., Tian, Y., Al-Rodhaan, M., Al-Dhelaan, A.: Anomaly detection over differential preserved privacy in online social networks. Plos ONE 14(4), e0215856 (2019)

Indoor and Outdoor Fusion Positioning and Security Technology Based on Beidou Satellite

Bing-sen Xia[1], Zhao-zheng Zhou[1], Zhang-huang Zhang[1], Yang Li[2], and Jia Yu[2(✉)]

[1] State Grid Fujian Economic Research Institue, Fuzhou, Fujian, China
[2] NARI Group Corporation, State Grid Electric Power Research Institute, Nanjing, China

Abstract. Location information service is especially important in complex environment. With the increasing demand of Beidou satellite navigation system in China, Beidou satellite navigation integrates with other GNSS positioning, navigation and timing technologies such as mobile base station, WLAN station and so on, and becomes an important means to solve the seamless positioning in and out of the room. A kind of indoor seamless fusion positioning technology which combines WiFi signal fingerprint matching and positioning technology with outdoor Beidou satellite high sensitivity receiving technology and anti-multipath technology is proposed in this paper. A dual-mode receiver with Beidou second generation receiving module and WiFi module was selected in the experiment. Beidou satellite positioning is used outdoors. When entering the room, the AP access point which is known to receive the position information is switched to the fingerprint matching algorithm to realize the indoor positioning. Simulation results show that the indoor and outdoor fusion positioning technology based on Beidou can realize seamless switching of indoor and outdoor positioning, and this indoor positioning algorithm based on WiFi can effectively improve the applicability and positioning accuracy of the positioning system.

Keywords: Indoor positioning · Seamless fusion · Beidou satellite · Location based services · Location fingerprinting

1 Introduction

Location-based service (Location Based Services, IBS) has become one of the hot issues in mobile computing research in recent years [1–3]. Especially in the complex indoor environment, the positioning accuracy and availability of location information service are more and more demanding [4]. At present, positioning technologies such as GPS, base stations have been widely used in people's lives [5]. When mobile devices are located outdoors, GPS can provide simple and effective solutions for such applications. However, these positioning technologies can not be used in indoor, mine and other closed complex environment, so the realization of indoor and outdoor seamless switching positioning technology is still a scientific problem to be solved [6, 7]. With the application and popularization of WiFi technology, WLAN local area network access points (access

© Springer Nature Singapore Pte Ltd. 2021
Y. Tian et al. (Eds.): ICBDS 2020, CCIS 1415, pp. 153–164, 2021.
https://doi.org/10.1007/978-981-16-3150-4_14

point, AP) have been widely deployed indoors, which makes many indoor environments can be covered by WiFi signals. Therefore, indoor positioning technology based on WiFi signal intensity (signal strength indication, RSSI) has been developed rapidly [8–10]. This paper combines the advantages of Beidou satellite navigation system and WiFi, adopts Beidou satellite navigation and positioning technology in outdoor environment, and automatically switches seamlessly to WiFi mode after entering the room to realize indoor positioning.

2 Positioning Technology Based on Signal Strength of WiFi

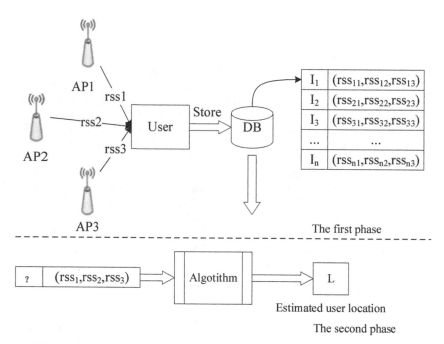

Fig. 1. Process of based on the WiFi signal fingerprint positioning technology

WiFi is a kind of wireless LAN [3], which belongs to short distance wireless technology used in office and home. At present WiFi technology has been widely used in indoor positioning, wireless communication, video surveillance and other fields. The initial purpose of deploying WiFi wireless router is not to realize positioning service, and WiFi the wireless router itself does not have positioning ability, it is arranged in a fixed position, so it has certain address fixation. WiFi positioning technology is used in the environment of deploying a large number of WiFi hotspots [11]. It is mainly divided into two kinds of methods, based on the wireless signal intensity propagation model and the location method based on the position fingerprint (location fingerprinting), which are used in the environment. WiFi based location fingerprint location method includes two stages, off-line sampling and on-line location. Firstly, a set of wireless signal access points is formed according to the distribution of indoor location area. The sampling point information is set up in the off-line sampling stage according to a certain interval distance in the indoor area to be located. The sampling point information includes the geographical coordinates of the point and the WiFi signal intensity vector value received at the point, forming the RSSI fingerprint database of all sampling points. At the location stage, the WiFi signal intensity of the points in the location area is obtained in real time, and the fingerprint library formed by the location matching algorithm and the line sampling stage is used to calculate the final location results . The process of positioning is shown in Fig. 1 [12, 13].

WiFi location technology is divided into location technology based on location fingerprint and location technology based on signal propagation model. The location technology based on the signal propagation model is to calculate the distance between the mobile terminal and the beacon node according to the signal intensity value received by the mobile terminal, and finally to establish the terminal position equation system. Finally, the corresponding positioning algorithm is used to solve the problem. The positioning principle is shown in the Fig. 2.

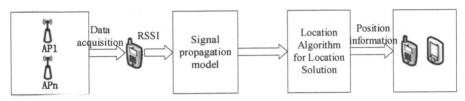

Fig. 2. The principle of WiFi positioning based on RSSI model

2.1 Propagation Model of WiFi Indoor Signal

A typical location method based on propagation model mainly includes logarithmic distance path loss model, free space loss model and Huawei indoor path loss model.

Logarithmic path loss model by changing path loss index to achieve the purpose of adjusting the path loss model. Its model expression is shown below [3].

$$PL(d) = PL(d_0) + 10n \log(\frac{d}{d_0}) \tag{1}$$

Among them, d is the reference distance, the general value is 1 m. $PL(d_0)$ is the path loss at the d of the reference distance, which can be calculated by the free space model or measured by the actual measurement. In practice, a Gaussian random variable should be added to the formula. Different buildings and different frequencies have different path loss indices. The range of path loss indices varies from 1.8 to 3.0 [3].

The loss model of free space requires short distance between receiver and transmitter, and high requirement for hardware conditions such as antenna. Assuming distance between the mobile terminal and the beacon node is d, the power of the mobile terminal to receive the beacon node is $P_{FSPL}(d)$, the expressions is as follows.

$$P_{FSPL}(d) = \frac{P_t G_t G_r \lambda^2}{(4\pi)^2 d^2 r}. \tag{2}$$

Among them, P_t is transmit power, G_t is the antenna gain of the transmitter, λ is the wavelength of the transmitted signal, r is a system loss parameter independent of the propagation environment. It is generally assumed that the hardware of the system has no loss $r = 1$. Assuming that the system loss is 1, the path loss in free space can be derived directly from the following formula [14]

$$PL_{FSPL}(d) = 10 \log(\frac{P_r}{P_t}) = 10 \log \frac{G_t G_r \lambda^2}{(4\pi)^2 d^2} \tag{3}$$

2.2 WiFi Indoor Positioning System

The main component of indoor positioning system is the location of people and objects in indoor environment. WiFi indoor positioning system is based on RSSI model. When positioning, the terminal dynamically scans the AP points in the room to complete the WiFi data acquisition, and processes the collected data accordingly. At the time of positioning, the distance from the terminal to the AP point is calculated by the signal propagation loss model, and the location algorithm is used to calculate the location. The block diagram of the positioning system is shown below [15].

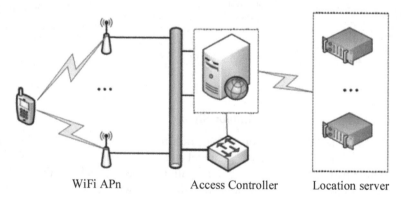

WiFi APn   Access Controller   Location server

Fig. 3. The framework schematic of Wi Fi positioning system (Color figure online)

2.3 Fusion Positioning System Based on Beidou and Indoor WiFi

The positioning range and accuracy of different positioning techniques are also different. Satellite navigation and positioning is mainly used in outdoor open and unobstructed areas [16]. When the receiver is located in the indoor or outdoor semi-closed area with buildings, the satellite signal will be greatly weakened by the influence of walls, buildings and other occlusions, which makes it difficult to apply satellite navigation and positioning to the semi-closed area. Indoor positioning technology can achieve accurate positioning in a certain space range, but with the expansion of positioning range, positioning accuracy

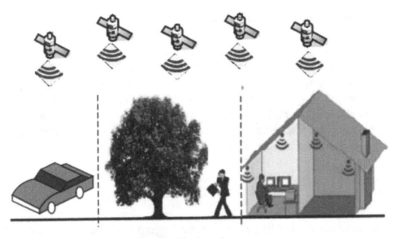

Fig. 4. The location scene

decreases or even can not be located [17]. As a result, Beidou positioning and wifi fusion positioning are adopted at the indoor and outdoor junction.

Beidou positioning is used when the Beidou satellite signal can only be received or the WiFi signal received is very weak [18]. Although sometimes the satellite signal can be received indoors, it is very weak, and sometimes the satellite signal can not be located. At this time, the location is carried out WiFi a separate location method. The area can be covered by Beidou and WiFi at the same time. In order to ensure that the terminal can be located accurately and continuously during the moving process, the Beidou and WiFi fusion positioning method is adopted in this area.

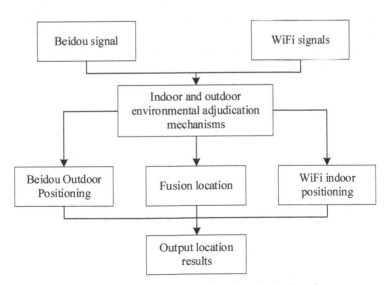

Fig. 5. Principle of indoor and outdoor fusion location

3 WiFi Fingerprint Matching Algorithm

The most commonly used WiFi fingerprint matching algorithm is k nearest neighbor in signal space (k-NNSS). The RSSI vector $v = [v_1, v_2, ..., v_n]$ is calculated at location, and calculate the fingerprint database generated in off-line sampling phase. The RSSI vector value formed in the fingerprint database records two parts of the data, one is the geographical coordinate value of the sampling point, the other is the RSSI value of the AP access point corresponding to the sampling point. Definition of RSSI distance between vectors as shown in formula 4 [19]

$$L_i = \|V, s_i\| = \sum_{k=1}^{n} \sqrt{(v_k - s_{i,k})^2} \tag{4}$$

Suppose there are n sampling points in the fingerprint library, there are n L_i values. k-NNSS nearest neighbor algorithm is to sort the L_i obtained, for the smallest L_i, the coordinates are $R = \{R_1, R_2, ..., R_k\}$, of which $R_i = \{x_i, y_i\}$, and then the mean coordinates of k sampling points are calculated by formula 5 [20]

$$R = \frac{1}{k} \sum_{i=1}^{k} R_j \tag{5}$$

Using $1/k$ as the coordinate weight coefficient in the k-NNSS algorithm, it is estimated that the coordinate value of the point to be located can meet the requirement of location in the open environment. But the precision of positioning can not be satisfied in complex indoor environment. The kWNN algorithm of weighted signal space is an improved location matching algorithm based on the original kNNSS algorithm. The weight coefficient in the localization algorithm is related to the distance. The closer the distance, the greater the influence on the location, the greater the value of weight, the greater the distance, the smaller the influence on the location, and the smaller the value of weight. Because the indoor environment is very complex, the signal intensity received at different locations is different, even if the signal intensity received at different times at the same location is different, so the range distance may be zero. The weight formula used in this paper is shown in formula 6

$$w_i = \frac{\frac{1}{(dist(V,S_i)+\varepsilon)}}{\sum_{j=1}^{k} \frac{1}{dist(V,S_j)+\varepsilon}} \tag{6}$$

Therefore, the positioning result of the point to be located is shown in formula 7

$$(\overline{x}, \overline{y}) = \sum_{i=1}^{k} w_i(x_i, y_i) \tag{7}$$

4   Simulation Experiment of Indoor Positioning Based on Weighted Signal Space kWNN Algorithm

The experimental environment is shown in Fig. 2, which is a more complex indoor office environment. The indoor environment includes a wide office and a copy room, as well as a small conference room and a corridor. The wide office is distributed in multi-compartment desks, with a corridor of about 1 m between desks and no restrictions on indoor mobility. The signals used in positioning are WiFi signals for daily data transmission, 26 effective AP are detected, and no new equipment is added (Fig. 6).

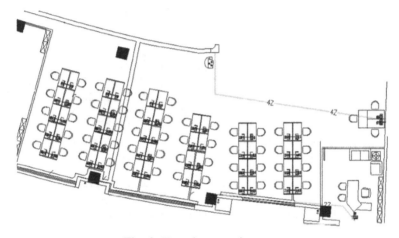

Fig. 6. Experiment environment

The experimental process includes two parts, offline processing and online positioning. According to the characteristics of indoor environment to be tested, a total of 60 sampling points were arranged in the office and corridor according to an average of 1.6 m each. The blue mark in Fig. 3 shows a mesh distribution of sampling points in rooms and corridors. During the sampling process, the average signal intensity is obtained 30 times for each sampling point, and the fingerprint library of signal intensity is formed,

Table 1. RSSI fingerprint database

	AP1	AP2	AP3	AP4	...	AP26
1	25.23	26.83	25.53	31.66	...	25.0
2	46.67	36.0	36.97	38.0	...	38.15
3	26.33	28.10	32.6	31.43	...	33.15
4	43.23	45.33	42.0	30.97	...	0
...	...	...	...	...	...	...
60	42.40	36.03	31.23	29.80	...	9.75

as shown in Table 1. At the same time, 15 test points are collected (shown in red mark in Fig. 3). These test points are not only distributed in office, but also in copy room and small conference room (Fig. 7).

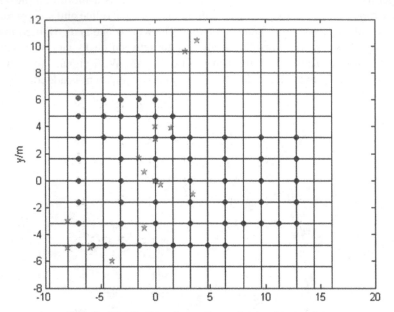

Fig. 7. Distribution of sampling points and test points

The selection of k in the weight signal space kWNN algorithm is very important to the positioning accuracy. The selection of k is small to a certain extent, the error of positioning will increase, and the selection of k will not only affect the calculation time of the algorithm, but also affect the accuracy of positioning. The values of k are 2, 3, 4, 5, 6, 7 in this paper, the influence of k value on positioning accuracy is tested respectively. As shown in Fig. 4, when the k is taken to 3 (black thickening curve in figure), the positioning accuracy is the most suitable (Fig. 8).

Synthesizing, according to the improved kwnn algorithm, the positioning accuracy of all test points is shown in Fig. 5 when k takes 3. The positioning accuracy of all test points is shown in Fig. 5. Some test points are obtained in the compartment of the indoor environment, and the positioning accuracy is controlled at about 3.5 m. Average error of all test points is 2.28 m, meet the requirement of indoor positioning accuracy (Fig. 9).

In order to verify the location performance of the fusion algorithm, 1000 random positions are randomly selected in the location area, and the results of the three positioning methods are simulated and compared. The results of the actual location are as shown in the diagram. In order to show the location result more clearly, every 10 random location points are set, and the root mean square error is counted. The root mean square error of fusion positioning is 1.963 m, which improves the accuracy of the other two positioning methods 1.288 m and 0.615 m respectively. The positioning accuracy is better than the other two positioning methods (Fig. 10).

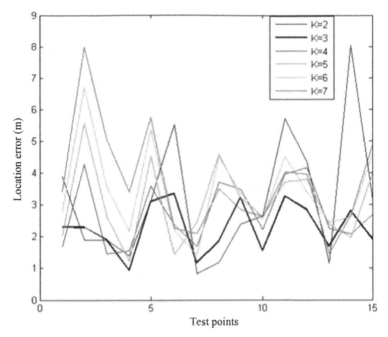

Fig. 8. Test point positioning accuracy of different k value

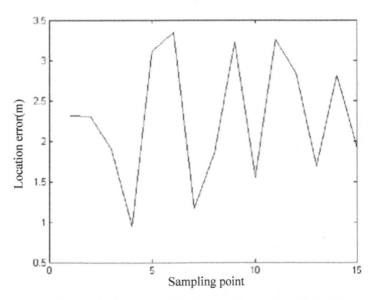

Fig. 9. Indoor single point positioning precision of kWNN algorithm

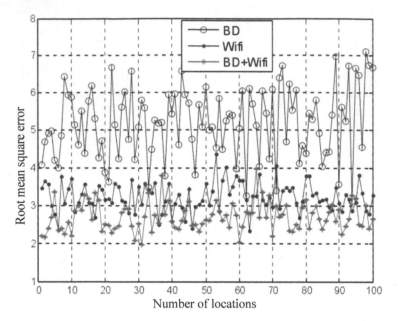

Fig. 10. Location results

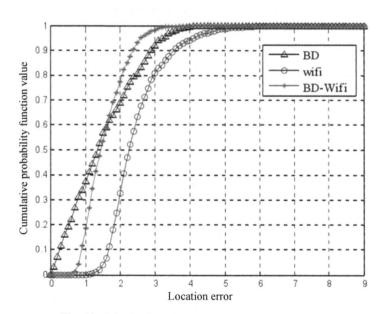

Fig. 11. Distribution of cumulative probability of error

In order to solve the problem of location error probability distribution under three positioning methods, 1000 Monte Carlo experiments were carried out, and the (cumulative distribution function of location error was carried out. The curve is shown below.

Fusion algorithm has better positioning accuracy, the accuracy of WiFi positioning is 3.88 m, the accuracy of Beidou positioning is 3.30 m. It can be seen that the accuracy and robustness of fusion localization algorithm are better than those of other algorithms (Fig. 11).

5 Conclusion

This article created a RSSI fingerprint library in kNNSS. The weight coefficient is added to the algorithm to form a new algorithm. By using MATLAB software to simulate the location algorithm, the simulation results show that the algorithm basically meets the location requirements. Fusion algorithm has better positioning accuracy. It can be seen that the accuracy and robustness of fusion localization algorithm are better than those of other algorithms. Seamless fusion positioning is a new and practical research field. In this paper, some of the problems are studied and excavated. On the basis of this paper, there is still a lot of research space for seamless fusion positioning, and the following directions can be further explored, including but not limited to the following two aspects. In this paper, the fusion determination is realized on the premise of covering, positioning accuracy and robustness. Next, the Beidou constellation and beacon can be studied in depth from the aspects of location algorithm and fusion.

Acknowledgments. The authors would like to thank the anonymous reviewers and editor for their comments that improved the quality of this paper. This work is supported by scientific project of State Grid Fujian Economic Research Institue under Grant NO. SGFJJ00GHJS2000044.

References

1. Rycroft, M.J.: Understanding GPS: principles and applications. J. Atmos. Solar-Terr. Phys. **59**(5), 598–599 (2006)
2. Deng, Z., Yu, Y., Yuan, X., Wan, N., Yang, L.: Situation and development tendency of indoor positioning. China Commun. **10**(3), 42–55 (2013)
3. Bahl, P., Padmanabhan, V.N.: RADAR: an in-building RF-based user location and tracking system. In: INFOCOM 2000. Nineteenth Joint Conference of the IEEE Computer and Communications Societies, vol. 2, pp. 775–784 (2000)
4. Shaukat, M., Chitre, M.: Adaptive behaviors in multi-agent source localization using passive sensing. Adapt. Behav. **24**(6), 446–463 (2016)
5. Patil, N.A., Munson, J., Wood, D., Cole, A.: Blue bot: asset tracking via robotic location crawling. Comput. Commun. **31**(6), 1067–1077 (2008)
6. Ni, L.M., Liu, Y., Lau, Y.C., Patil, A.P.: LANDMARC: indoor location sensing using active RFID. Wirel. Netw. **10**(6), 701–710 (2004)
7. Liebe, C.C., Murphy, N., Dorsky, L.: Three-axis sun sensor for attitude determination. IEEE Aerosp. Electron. Syst. Mag. **31**(6), 6–11 (2016)
8. Broumandan, A., Nielsen, J., Lachapelle, G.: Indoor GNSS signal acquisition performance using a synthetic antenna array. IEEE Trans. Aerosp. Electron. Syst. **47**(2), 1337–1350 (2011)
9. Jardak, N., Samama, N.: Indoor positioning based on GPS-repeaters: performance enhancement using an open code loop architecture. IEEE Trans. Aerosp. Electron. Syst. **45**(1), 347–359 (2009)

10. Alexandre, V.P., Samama, N.: Interference mitigation in a repeater and pseudolite indoor positioning system. IEEE J. Sel. Top. Sig. Process. **3**(5), 810–820 (2009)
11. Manandhar, D., Kawaguchi, S., Torimoto, H.: Results of IMES (indoor messaging system) implementation for seamless indoor navigation and social infrastructure platform. In: Proceedings of International Technical Meeting of the Satellite Division of the Institute of Navigation, vol. 7672, no. 6, pp. 1184–1191 (2010)
12. Mehmood, H., Tripathi, N.K., Tipdecho, T.: Seamless switching between GNSS and WLAN based indoor positioning system for ubiquitous positioning. Earth Sci. Inf. **8**(1), 221–231 (2014). https://doi.org/10.1007/s12145-014-0157-3
13. Cui, Q., Zhang, X.: Research analysis of wireless localization with insufficient resources for next-generation mobile communication networks. Int. J. Commun. Syst. **26**(9), 1206–1226 (2013)
14. Wei, K., Wu, L.: Mobile location with NLOS identification and mitigation based on modified Kalman filtering. Sensors **11**(2), 1641 (2011)
15. Guan, W., Deng, Z., Yu, Y., Ge, Y.: A NLOS mitigation method for CDMA 2000 mobile location. In: 2010 2nd IEEE International Conference on Network Infrastructure and Digital Content, Beijing, China, pp. 668–672 (2010)
16. Dammann, A., Raulefs, R., Zhang, S.: On prospects of positioning in 5G. In: 2015 IEEE International Conference on Communication Workshop (ICCW), London, England, pp. 1207–1213 (2015)
17. Lee, J.-E., Lee, S.: Indoor initial positioning using single clock pseudolite system. In: 2010 IEEE International Conference on Information and Communication Technology Convergence (ICT), pp. 575–578. IEEE (2010)
18. Ward, A., Jones, A., Hopper, A.: A new location technique for the active office. IEEE Pers. Commun. **4**(5), 42–47 (1997)
19. Xu, R., Chen, W., et al.: A new indoor positioning system architecture using GPS signals. Sensors **15**(5), 10074–10087 (2015)
20. Ma, B.-l., Yang, F.: The design and implementation of WiFi localization GIS for mine. J. Xian Univ. Sci. Technol. **32**(3), 301–305 (2012)
21. Guanglong, Y., Yongping, K., Zhiming, Z., et al.: Indoor positioning system design and implementation of based on multimode fingerprint matching. Comput. Eng. Des. **34**(5), 1896–1901 (2013)
22. Ouyang, R.W., Wong, A.K.: Indoor localization via discriminatively regularized least square classification. Int. J. Wirel. Inf. Netw. **18**(2), 52–72 (2011)
23. Tang Li, X., Yubin, Z.M., et al.: Research on K nearst neighbors algorithm under the indoor WLAN. Comput. Sci. B **36**(4), 54–55 (2009)

Research on Safety Protection Scheme of Distribution Network Automation

Xue Gao, Sai Liu, Jun Liu, and Jia Yu[✉]

NARI Group Corporation, State Grid Electric Power Research Institute, Nanjing, China

Abstract. In order to meet the requirements of automatic security protection in smart grid, a security protection scheme for distribution automation based on security encryption chip is proposed. Without affecting the normal operation of the distribution terminal, the characteristics of distribution automation are added, such as wide distribution range and outdoor operation. The LKT4305-GM security chip is used, the security operating system is adopted, the function of sm1, sm2, sm3, sm4 state secret algorithm and the PKI system are realized. PKI power dispatching digital certificate uses digital certificate authentication technology, and based on the encryption technology of national commercial cipher algorithm, it realizes the two-way identity authentication between distribution station and distribution terminal.

Keywords: Security protection · Two-way authentication · Encryption chip · National cryptographic algorithm · Distribution network automation

1 Introduction

Because there are a lot of distribution terminals in the distribution automation network, the security of the original distribution terminals is insufficient, which leads to the failure to ensure the security of the new terminals [1]. For the distribution master station, many distribution terminals are configured into the network, which makes the information processing speed of the distribution master station slow, and can not effectively identify and screen the loopholes in the massive information, which eventually leads to more and more serious security problems in the distribution network [2–4].

Nowadays, there are two kinds of communication modes between distribution terminal and distribution automation system [5]. Optical network is used, because it is in a closed environment, it is not easy to be monitored and has strong security [6]. However, for many terminals, the arrangement of optical fiber network is very heavy, and the physical circuit is easy to be damaged [7]. Because of the transmission distance is very long, the construction will become very difficult and expensive [8]. All along, the security measures of distribution network are weak, and the way of network attack is endless, which is a great threat to distribution network. Because of the versatility of the distribution terminal, the methods of attackers to destroy the security of the distribution network include forgery of terminal identity and replay attack, which seriously affect the reliability and security of the power supply [9]. Therefore, the common security scheme can no longer meet the security requirements of distribution automation business.

© Springer Nature Singapore Pte Ltd. 2021
Y. Tian et al. (Eds.): ICBDS 2020, CCIS 1415, pp. 165–176, 2021.
https://doi.org/10.1007/978-981-16-3150-4_15

2 Design of Safety Protection Schemes

Distribution network automation security protection system is applicable to the remote monitoring of medium and low voltage power network with 10 kV or less, as well as the security protection of distribution network automation system, including distribution master station, vertical communication, distribution terminal security protection measures [10]. Protection measures include security partition, horizontal isolation, physical security protection and so on [10].

(1) Design of the framework

The security protection system of distribution network automation mainly concludes three main parts, the security protection terminal of distribution automation, the security receiving area of distribution network and the security protection of distribution master station [11]. The distribution terminal digitally signs the data of each application the distribution terminal through the algorithm data access of the distribution terminal to the distribution master station, and realizes the protection of

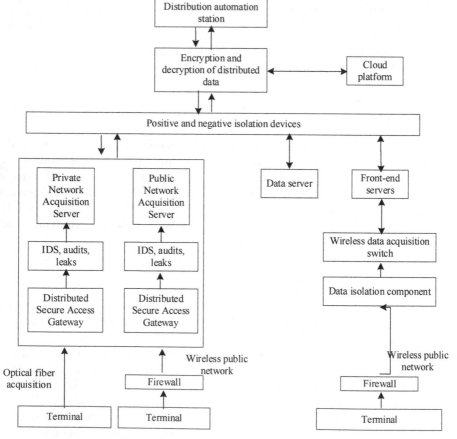

Fig. 1. Security protection scheme of system

identity authentication and message integrity. Through firewall, data gateway and other security measures, the service between distribution terminal and master station is connected to ensure the security of data. The authentication technology based on digital certificate and the encryption technology based on national commercial cipher algorithm.

The framework of the system is shown [11] (Fig. 1).

(2) Introduction of system

The authentication between distribution terminal and distribution master station adopts asymmetric encryption algorithm to ensure the security of data. In the security protection area and security access area of the dispatching automation system [12], the horizontal one-way security isolation equipment specific to the power supply is deployed. The data acquisition server is deployed in the secure access area. Operating system, dynamic password, hardware equipment, digital certificate and so on, special communication or wireless public network communication is used.

3 Data Classification Processing Based on Random Forests

Random forest is a simple but powerful machine learning algorithm [12], which is composed of multiple weak classifiers. The decision tree helps us to judge whether a certain decision is feasible through the intuitive use of probability analysis. Because this decision branch is drawn into a graph like the branch of a tree, it is called a decision tree. The decision tree is based on the entropy value and information gain in informatics theory. The entropy value represents the richness of information. The greater the entropy, the richer the information, while the information gain represents the difference between the information entropy. The formula for information gain is as follows.

$$G(D, X) = I(D) - I(D|X)$$

I(D) is the information entropy and I(D|X) is the conditional information entropy. The formulas are as follows:

$$I(D) = -\sum_{k=0}^{K} \frac{|C_k|}{|D|} log \frac{|C_k|}{|D|}$$

where C_k $(k = 0, 1)$ represents the number of samples belonging to a label category, D is the number of training sets.

$$I(D|X) = \sum_{i=1}^{n} \frac{|D_i|}{|D|} H(D_i) = -\sum_{i=1}^{n} \frac{|D_i|}{|D|} \sum_{k=1}^{K} \frac{|D_{ik}|}{|D_i|} log \frac{|D_{ik}|}{|D_i|}$$

The n is the type of feature, D_i is the number of the feature category, and D_{ik} is the number of label categories in the feature category k. Random forest is an integrated learning method composed of multiple decision trees. It synthesizes the classification results of multiple decision trees and obtains the final classification results according to the modes in the output categories of individual trees. Therefore, it is superior to the prediction results of any single classification.

Random forests require training sets to be random and feature random, and booststrap sampling is used to ensure that each decision tree has different training samples and features. In this way, multiple decision trees make sense. In the current machine learning algorithm, random forest has excellent accuracy and can run on big data set to process input samples with high dimensional characteristics, and at the same time overcome the disadvantage that decision tree is easy to overfit.

3.1 Data Collection and Disaggregation of Data Sets

First, we need to collect the sample data, then divide the data set into two parts [13], that is training set and test set, one part is used to train the random model, the other part is used to test the performance of the model, the ratio of the two is roughly 4:1. The data set comes from the terminal device of a distribution system and contains several features, and the label has two categories, that is confidential data and non-confidential data.

3.2 Data Preprocessing

Because the order of magnitude of each feature in the data set is different, in order to speed up the training speed of the algorithm and improve the accuracy of prediction, it is necessary to preprocess the data. There are generally two methods of preprocessing, normalization and standardization. Because the normalization operation is easy to be affected by the structure of the data, once the data set is unbalanced, it will cause a large error, so the data is processed by standardization.

The steps of standardization are as follows: first, the mathematical expectation $E(X_i)$ and standard deviation, S_i of each feature are obtained, and then the standard value is obtained according to the following formula

$$Z_{ij} = \frac{X_{ij} - E(X_i)}{S_i}$$

3.3 Optimization of Random Forest Model

First, the processed data is input into the random forest model for training. The random forest is composed of many decision trees, and the excessive number of decision trees will lead to a large load, affect the training speed, too little can not achieve good classification results. The depth of the decision tree is too large, which will lead to overfitting and too small will affect the accuracy of classification. Therefore, in order to make the random forest achieve better training effect, the model needs to be optimized. The optimization methods are as follows, the number of trees in the forest is set to 100, 250, 400, 600 and 800, the optional depth of the tree is 5, 10, 15, 20 and 25, and cross validation is added. The training set is divided into training set and verification set, that is, the data is divided into five parts, one of which is used as the verification set, and then after five tests, different verification sets are replaced each time, and the results of five groups of models are obtained. Take the average value as the final result, also known as 50% cross-validation. Through these settings, the random forest will calculate the classification effect under the above parameters, optimize the algorithm parameters, and output the best results.

3.4 Classification Results and Model Evaluation

Through the above treatment, we can get the optimal model of random forest. As shown in Fig. 2, it can be seen from the final results that the real value coincides with the predicted value, which indicates that the algorithm model has a good classification effect.

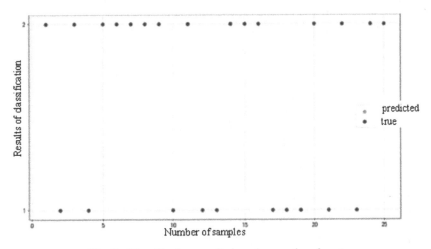

Fig. 2. Classification results based on random forest.

4 Symmetric Encryption Based on Neural Network

Neural network is developed by machine learning. It processes the input information of external environment by establishing axons and dendrites similar to brain neurons, imitating the behavior characteristics of human or animal neural networks. In this paper, the input data classified by the above classification is encrypted by using the private key, and then transmitted to the receiver in the form of ciphertext. The receiver decrypts and restores the plaintext information through the private key.

4.1 Mathematical Modeling Based on Neural Networks

With the construction of the power Internet of things, power equipment, vehicles, smart homes and various terminals are linked together, we have entered an era of interconnection of all things. In such an environment, a large amount of data information is generated every moment, and the transmission of data is happening all the time. However, for some confidential data, it will cause great problems to be directly exposed to the Internet. Therefore, the encrypted transmission of data has become particularly important. The emergence of artificial intelligence means that machines can also imitate human behavior characteristics and encrypt some data autonomously. As long as we input enough data information and learn and extract the data through neural network, the machine can also help us to encrypt the data. The basic unit of a neural network is a neuron, and a complete neural network consists of several neurons connected to each other. Simple neurons have only linear functions, that is, they can only process the input data linearly. Nonlinear functions can better help us learn the characteristics of various things, and it also makes all kinds of data more meaningful. The linear function carries on the ordinary weighting processing to the data, then carries on the nonlinear processing to the data through the activation function, then passes the data to the output layer step by step through the similar processing, and outputs the final result from the output layer. The structure of individual neurons is shown in the Fig. 3.

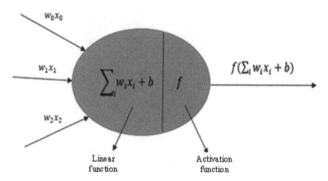

Fig. 3. Single neural network modeling

The output of a single neuron is

$$z = f\left(\sum_i w_i x_i + b\right)$$

where the w_i is the weight of each unit of the input layer to the output layer and the b is the bias unit.

The loss function represents the degree of differentiation between the real value and the predicted value. In other words, our goal is to make the value of the loss function close to zero. It is defined as follows

$$l(w, b) = \frac{1}{n} \sum_{i=1}^{n} (z^{(i)} - y^{(i)})^2$$

n is the number of input data, $z^{(i)}$ is the predicted value, and $y^{(i)}$ is the true value.

A complete neural network consists of multiple neurons connected by dendrites and axons. A single neuron does not help us to deal with the problem well, which is why we want to build a neural network. This paper uses a two-layer neural network to encrypt data that requires confidential transmission. The model contains an input layer containing M units, a hidden layer containing N units, and an output layer. As shown in Fig. 4:

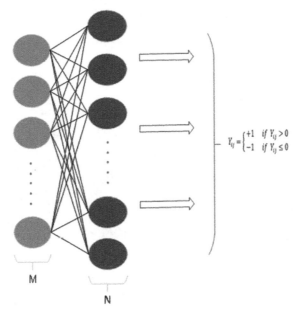

$$Y_{ij} = \begin{cases} +1 & if\ Y_{ij} > 0 \\ -1 & if\ Y_{ij} \le 0 \end{cases}$$

Fig. 4. Encryption algorithm modeling diagram of neural network

4.2 Symmetric Encryption Algorithm Based on Neural Network

In this paper, the random forest and neural network algorithm are used to encrypt the data of power system equipment, and all the data are classified data and non-confidential data by random forest algorithm. Non-confidential data can be transmitted directly in the form of plaintext in the network. Confidential data needs to be processed by encryption algorithm and transmitted in the form of ciphertext in the network. It greatly protects the privacy of users and terminals, reduces the risk of data leakage and tampering, and improves the security of data transmission. The classified data is input into the neural network model for training. Neural network training uses hebb learning rules, which change weights according to the activation levels between the various synapses of neurons. This learning rule is very similar to the process of observing and understanding unknown things in human or animal brains. Therefore, this method is also called correlation learning. The formula is as follows.

$$\Delta W = K_{ij}^T * f\left(K_i W_j\right)$$

Therefore, the weights are updated as follows

$$W_{ij} = W_{ij} + \Delta W$$

At the same time, the following assumptions are proposed. The flow chart of the symmetric encryption algorithm is as follows (Fig. 5).

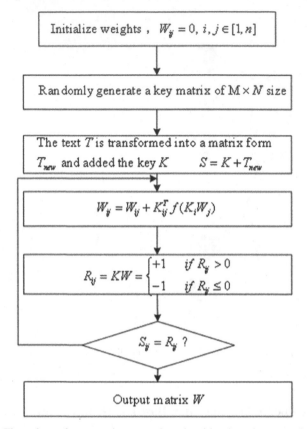

Fig. 5. Flow chart of symmetric encryption algorithm based on neural network

4.3 Design of Secure Encryption Device Based on Symmetric Encryption Algorithm

The general application of information and communication technology such as big data, cloud computing, Internet of things, mobile Internet and so on has made us enter a new power grid era. The general application of information and communication technology such as big data, cloud computing, Internet of things, mobile Internet and so on has made us enter a new era. The heterogeneous intelligent terminals of the new power network are diversified, the network security protection boundary is ubiquitous, and the service security access demand is diversified. At the same time, with the effective integration of the new generation of information technology such as Internet of things and Internet and smart grid, the traditional power grid is gradually transformed into the two-way interactive service mode of smart grid. By studying the encryption scheme of terminal equipment based on security chip, we can build a more secure smart grid system. According to the different requirements of practicality and industrialization, the implementation scheme of terminal equipment security encryption device based on security chip can be divided into two types, external module and embedded module. In order to satisfy the connection and modification of the existing terminal equipment, this paper proposes a design scheme of the distribution terminal device based on symmetric encryption algorithm. The whole module is shown in Fig. 6.

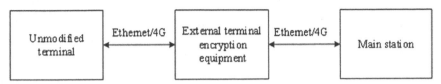

Fig. 6. Security external encryption module of distribution terminal based on symmetric encryption algorithm

According to the environment of distribution line, the security encryption device can communicate with the main station and terminal through industrial Ethernet and 4G. The security encryption device will be placed in the middle link of the main station and terminal. The device can not only parse and verify the ciphertext issued by the master station, but also decide whether to transmit the original data to the terminal according to the verification results, but also encrypt the data uploaded by the terminal and transmit the data to the master station in the form of ciphertext. Security encryption device has encryption and decryption unit, identity authentication unit, network communication unit and serial communication unit. A special encryption chip is embedded in the security encryption device, and the encryption algorithm and communication module are integrated to realize the encryption and decryption of the data and the transmission and communication of the external data. The encryption and decryption of data flow based on symmetric encryption algorithm is shown in Fig. 7.

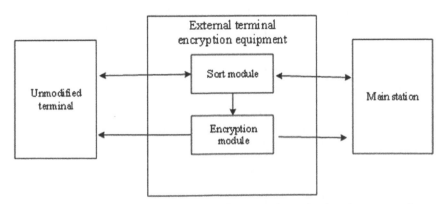

Fig. 7. Distribution terminal data transmission encryption/decryption based on symmetric encryption algorithm

The external module is used to realize the encrypted transmission of data. Firstly, the data is transported to the external terminal through the terminal unmodified equipment, and the plaintext data is classified by naive Bayes algorithm. The confidential data need to be encrypted by neural network encryption algorithm to meet the requirements of standard communication protocol and information security protection.

Results and Analysis

Since the key K is a matrix of $M \times N$ size, where $M = 2 * N$, $N = 4, 6, 8$ and so on, we randomly generate a key matrix K of size $8 * 4$

$$\begin{bmatrix} -1 & 0 & 1 & 0 \\ 1 & 0 & 1 & 0 \\ 1 & 0 & -1 & 0 \\ -1 & 0 & -1 & 0 \\ -1 & 0 & 1 & 0 \\ 1 & 0 & 1 & 0 \\ 1 & 0 & -1 & 0 \\ -1 & 0 & -1 & 0 \end{bmatrix}$$

Where $M = 8$, $N = 4$, therefore, the length of the text data that requires encryption is 16, and the text data t is:

1	-1	-1	1	1	1	-1	1	-1	-1	-1	1	1	-1	1	-1

A) encryption

The text data is transformed into a $M \times N$ matrix T_{new}, in which the odd number of the T_{new} is 0, the converted matrix is added to the key K, in other words, the text is embedded in the key matrix to obtain the S:

$$\begin{bmatrix} -1 & 1 & 1 & -1 \\ 1 & -1 & 1 & -1 \\ 1 & -1 & -1 & -1 \\ -1 & 1 & -1 & 1 \\ -1 & 1 & 1 & 1 \\ 1 & -1 & 1 & -1 \\ 1 & -1 & -1 & 1 \\ -1 & 1 & -1 & -1 \end{bmatrix}$$

Key k is input into the neural network model, and the final weight matrix W is obtained by iterative algorithm, which is the final ciphertext, as follows:

$$\begin{bmatrix} 8 & -4 & -2 & -4 \\ -4 & 8 & 2 & 0 \\ -2 & 2 & 8 & -2 \\ -4 & 0 & -2 & 8 \end{bmatrix}$$

B) decryption

The weight matrix W is transmitted to the receiving end of the data through the Internet, and the receiving terminals uses the key k to decrypt it. The decryption formula is as follows: $R = KW$, The calculation of R is as follows

$$
\begin{bmatrix}
-10 & 14 & 14 & -6 \\
14 & -10 & 6 & -14 \\
18 & -14 & -10 & -10 \\
-14 & 10 & -6 & 14 \\
18 & 14 & 10 & 10 \\
6 & 6 & 10 & -14 \\
10 & -14 & -14 & 6 \\
10 & 2 & 6 & -10
\end{bmatrix}
$$

The following activation rules are then applied:

$$
R_{i,j} = KW = \begin{cases} +1 & if\ R_{i,j} > 0 \\ -1 & if\ R_{i,j} \leq 0 \end{cases}
$$

We can get the final matrix as follows:

$$
\begin{bmatrix}
1 & 1 & 1 & -1 \\
1 & -1 & 1 & -1 \\
1 & -1 & -1 & -1 \\
-1 & 1 & -1 & 1 \\
-1 & 1 & 1 & 1 \\
1 & -1 & 1 & -1 \\
1 & -1 & -1 & 1 \\
-1 & 1 & -1 & -1
\end{bmatrix}
$$

The second and fourth columns are decrypted data, the nested data is taken out, and the plaintext information transmitted by the sender can be obtained in a certain order, as follows:

1	-1	-1	1	1	1	1	-1	1	-1	-1	-1	1	1	-1	1	-1

5 Conclusion

This paper presents a symmetric encryption algorithm based on neural network. By collecting the data that needs to be transmitted, the naive Bayes algorithm is used to divide the data into confidential data and non-confidential data. For confidential data, the neural network is used to convert the data into incomprehensible ciphertext information and then transmit it in the network, but only the terminal with the decryption key can decrypt the data. It greatly protects the privacy of users and avoids illegal copying, destroying, and tampering with data. It provides technical support for the safe transmission of data in power network.

Acknowledgments. The authors would like to thank the anonymous reviewers and editor for their comments that improved the quality of this paper. This work is supported by state grid scientific project under Grant NO. SGSHXT00JFJS1900093, the name of the project is research and demonstration application of key technologies for disaster recovery backup and service continuity management in the cloud environment.

References

1. Suo, H., Wan, J., Zou, C., Liu, J.: Security in the internet of things: a review. In: 2012 International Conference on Computer Science and Electronics Engineering, Hangzhou, pp. 648–651 (2012). https://doi.org/10.1109/ICCSEE.2012.373
2. Diffie, W., Hellman, M.: New directions in cryptography. IEEE Trans. Inf. Theory **22**(6), 644–654 (1976). https://doi.org/10.1109/TIT.1976.1055638
3. Yassein, M.B., Aljawarneh, S., Qawasmeh, E., Mardini, W., Khamayseh, Y.: Comprehensive study of symmetric key and asymmetric key encryption algorithms. In: 2017 International Conference on Engineering and Technology (ICET), Antalya, pp. 1–7 (2017). https://doi.org/10.1109/ICEngTechnol.2017.8308215
4. Noura, H.N., Chehab, A., Couturier, R.: Overview of efficient symmetric cryptography: dynamic vs static approaches. In: 2020 8th International Symposium on Digital Forensics and Security (ISDFS), Beirut, Lebanon, pp. 1–6 (2020). https://doi.org/10.1109/ISDFS49300.2020.9116441
5. Boicea, A., Radulescu, F., Truica, C., Costea, C.: Database encryption using asymmetric keys: a case study. In: 2017 21st International Conference on Control Systems and Computer Science (CSCS), Bucharest, pp. 317–323 (2017)doi: https://doi.org/10.1109/CSCS.2017.50
6. Chandra, S., Paira, S., Alam, S.S., Sanyal, G.: A comparative survey of symmetric and asymmetric key cryptography. In: 2014 International Conference on Electronics, Communication and Computational Engineering (ICECCE), Hosur, pp. 83–93 (2014). https://doi.org/10.1109/ICECCE.2014.7086640
7. Panda, M.: Performance analysis of encryption algorithms for security. In: 2016 International Conference on Signal Processing, Communication, Power and Embedded System (SCOPES), Paralakhemundi, pp. 278–284 (2016). https://doi.org/10.1109/SCOPES.2016.7955835
8. Gupta, C.P., Sharma, I.: A fully homomorphic encryption scheme with symmetric keys with application to private data processing in clouds. In: 2013 Fourth International Conference on the Network of the Future (NoF), Pohang, pp. 1–4 (2013). https://doi.org/10.1109/NOF.2013.6724526
9. Wang, G., Liu, C., Dong, Y., Han, P., Pan, H., Fang, B.: IDCrypt: a multi-user searchable symmetric encryption scheme for cloud applications. IEEE Access **6**, 2908–2921 (2018). https://doi.org/10.1109/ACCESS.2017.2786026
10. Jang, C., Lee, J., Yi, O.: Encryption scheme in portable electric vehicle charging infrastructure: encryption scheme using symmetric key. In: 2017 4th International Conference on Computer Applications and Information Processing Technology (CAIPT), Kuta Bali, pp. 1–5 (2017). https://doi.org/10.1109/CAIPT.2017.8320674
11. Sha, P., Zhu, Z.: The modification of RSA algorithm to adapt fully homomorphic encryption algorithm in cloud computing. In: 2016 4th International Conference on Cloud Computing and Intelligence Systems (CCIS), Beijing, pp. 388–392 (2016). https://doi.org/10.1109/CCIS.2016.7790289
12. Dhakar, R.S., Gupta, A.K., Sharma, P.: Modified RSA encryption algorithm (MREA). In: 2012 Second International Conference on Advanced Computing and Communication Technologies, Rohtak, Haryana, pp. 426–429 (2012). https://doi.org/10.1109/ACCT.2012.74

Research on Experimental Verification Scheme of 5G in Power System

Ningzhe Xing[1], Shen Jin[1], Wei Song[1], Yang Li[2], and Jia Yu[2(✉)]

[1] State Grid Jibei Information and Telecommunication Company, Xicheng, Beijing, China
[2] NARI Group Corporation State Grid Electric Power Research Institute, Nanjing, China

Abstract. This paper presents a new and higher requirement for the collection, bearing, analysis and application of the power base data in the power network, and puts forward a higher requirement for the communication technology. The development requirements of State Grid Corporation are also highly in line with the scenario of 5G application. In response to this situation, the network performance, application mode, network scheme and security policy of 5G wireless communication are tested. The test scheme includes the laboratory test and the outfield test, and the test scheme is given. The test scheme verifies the supporting ability of 5G technology in power system, and lays a foundation for the application of 5G technology in power system.

Keywords: 5G · Smart grid · The Internet of things in power system · Test protocol · Network performance

1 Introduction

Under the strategic objective of constructing "three-type and two-net", the construction of universal power Internet of things requires that all kinds of equipments be used in the whole access, the whole process on-line, the overall perception of grid information and equipment status, the overall realization of real-time and reliable control of power distribution equipment at the end of the grid, and finally realize the information exchange and sharing of energy production and consumption [1, 2]. In recent years, with the rapid development of new information and communication technologies such as cloud computing, Internet of things, big data, mobile interconnection and software definition networks, broadband wireless and so on, the company has actively promoted the construction of smart grid [3]. China Network Company closely follows the trend of new technology development, develops new technology to tackle key problems, and forms a large number of technical achievements and successful application [4, 5].

5G provides 10 times the user experience rate of 4G with a new network architecture, peaking at up to 20 Gbps [6]. The 5G technique is characterized by empty-port delays as low as 1 ms, 99.999% ultra-high reliability and 1million connection density per square kilometer [6]. China has become one of the leaders of 5G technology, and is the first echelon of 5G industry in the world. The three major basic telecommunications operators have built 5G networks in different cities, promoted by the Ministry of Industry

© Springer Nature Singapore Pte Ltd. 2021
Y. Tian et al. (Eds.): ICBDS 2020, CCIS 1415, pp. 177–193, 2021.
https://doi.org/10.1007/978-981-16-3150-4_16

and Information Technology and the NDRC. In June 2019, the Ministry of Industry and Information Technology issued a 5G licence, marking the official entry of China into the 5G commercial era [7]. Due to the different characteristics of the operators themselves, the 5G network construction differs in frequency resources, carrying network, coverage capacity, networking mode, investment scale and target users. At the same time, 5G can provide customized private network service for industry users to better meet the needs of business differentiation [8]. The development needs of the smart grid are highly compatible with the 5G, and have the innate resource advantages in the base station site, communication network and so on, and have the ability to participate in and lead the 5G industry application. Therefore, for the new technology, new business and new situation, it is urgent to test and verify the network performance, application mode, networking scheme and security strategy of the new 5G wireless communication technology more thoroughly and comprehensively. In this paper, the experimental verification scheme based on 5G is studied in power system.

2 Selection of Validation Environment

2.1 Laboratory Validation

For the 5G eMBB, uRLLC and mMTC application scenarios, we can select eight typical types of services, such as differential protection, distribution automation, precision load control, power information collection, distribution network condition monitoring, physical ID, intelligent inspection and video surveillance. Based on the analysis of network bandwidth, delay, transmission distance and terminal density, security and reliability, protocol interface and so on, an end-to-end network slicing scheme and typical application networking scheme are proposed and verified by laboratory [9].

Compared with 4G, 5G has a great improvement in peak rate [10], network delay and reliability. However, the actual network performance indexes under different network and slice schemes need to be verified. On the other hand, the coverage range of 5g base station is lower than that of 4G, and the actual coverage radius, the access rate and network delay of different signal intensity also need to be verified.

The slicing technology of 5G network enables the deployment of multiple separate differentiated networks on a unified infrastructure [11]. End-to-end slicing involves multiple network devices such as access networks, transmission networks and core networks. Therefore, it is necessary to verify the resource isolation and network security between different slices. Based on the different power application scenarios and business requirements, the function, performance and safety reliability of 5G network carrying many typical power services are verified.

2.2 Field Validation

Network performance verification, service carrying capacity verification and interference testing are carried out through the new 5G network. Network performance verification includes three aspects: network coverage verification, network performance verification and environmental adaptability verification [12], verify that whether the 5G network satisfies the coverage, bandwidth, delay, capacity, mobility, reliability and adaptability of the complex environment. Power service load-carrying verification includes service connection performance, service bandwidth capability, service delay and jitter, service stability and reliability, service quality assurance, etc.

Power service load-carrying verification includes service connection performance, service bandwidth capability, service delay and jitter, service stability and reliability, service quality assurance, etc., and verify that whether the 5G network environment meets the requirements of various functions, performance, security, reliability, etc. The types of power services include on-site video surveillance, distribution automation, electricity information collection, distribution network condition monitoring, physical ID, intelligent inspection, video surveillance and emergency communication. The interference test mainly analyzes the interference situation in the 3.5 GHz frequency, verifies the anti-interference ability of the 5G network and the radiation interference of the 5G to the electric power.

3 Application of Network Slice Technology in Power System

3.1 Characteristics of Power Service

At present, the power wireless private network mainly carries four categories of service, such as network control, information collection, video and mobile applications. Specific services include distribution automation, electricity information collection, distributed power supply, precision load control, video surveillance, mobile operations, etc. Overall, the current minimum delay for all types of power services is 10 ms, with a bandwidth of less than 4 Mbps for single services. In the future, with the development of energy Internet, in order to adapt to the new power grid mode with UHV as the backbone and coordinated development of power grid at all levels, the universal connection will become the basic form of power grid. Therefore, it is urgent to build a real-time, efficient, safe and reliable communication network to achieve accurate control of all kinds of loads. A new type of visualization, real-time and lean operation is introduced to realize the monitoring and inspection of important corridors in power grids at all levels. Therefore, in the future, the Internet of things and broadband services of power systems will coexist in large numbers, and present the characteristics of high-density, low-delay, high-reliability and high-security. The number of concurrent terminals will reach 100,000, the delay requirement is millisecond and the reliability requirement is 99.999%. Therefore, higher requirements are put forward for the service carrying capacity of the power wireless private network.

3.2 Adaptive Model of 5G and Multiple Power Services

Considering the requirements of bandwidth, real-time, reliability and large connection of all kinds of power services, this paper analyzes the compatibility of different business requirements with 5g application scenarios. The scenarios of 5G are divided into eMBB, uRLLC and mMTC. The adaptive models are shown in Fig. 3 for the eight typical types of services, such as differential protection, distribution automation, precision load control, power information acquisition, distribution network condition monitoring, physical ID, intelligent inspection and video surveillance (Fig. 1).

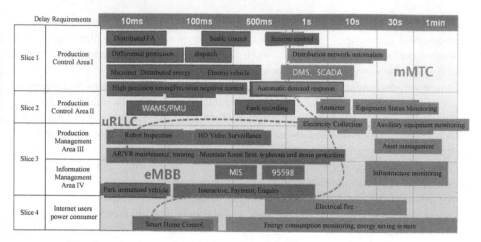

Fig. 1. Adaptive model of 5G and power multiple application scenarios

3.3 Customized Scheme for Power Network Slicing

Wireless network architecture based on 5G network slicing is divided into three layers. The underlying network is the physical infrastructure layer, which is the actual carrier of network data. The middle layer provides the whole virtual resource pool for the virtualized network resources, and realizes the centralized management and efficient allocation of resources. The upper layer is the user-oriented actual layer, different types of network services will form different network slicing. The realization of layer function and the interaction between each layer need to be managed and controlled by the SDN controller (Fig. 2).

In order to realize the effective control of the network nodes and the accurate forwarding of the network data by the SDN controller, the slicing table is introduced in the nodes RRH and BBU of the wireless access network with reference to the Openflow protocol. On the one hand, slicing table can effectively split the transmission of network data. On the other hand, the slicing table also contains various network parameters, which can realize the rapid configuration of the network. Moreover, the SDN controller will manipulate the slice table by slicing the message.

The slicing dynamic deployment system of power network consists of information collection module, virtualization module, resource management module, slicing network management module and SDN controller. The information collection module will run in the physical infrastructure layer. Virtualization module will realize the effective mapping of underlying network and virtual resource pool. The resource management module will effectively schedule and manage the virtual resources. The slice network management module will manage and maintain the final slice network. The SDN controller will achieve centralized control and coordinated management of each functional module (Fig. 4).

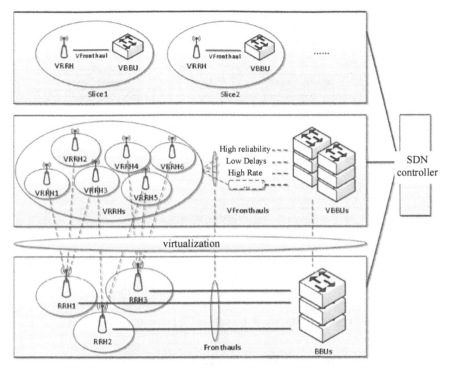

Fig. 2. Wireless network architecture based on 5G network slicing

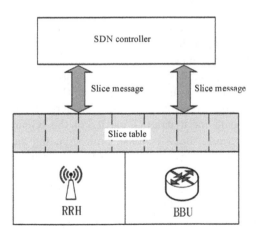

Fig. 3. Network slicing based on SDN controller

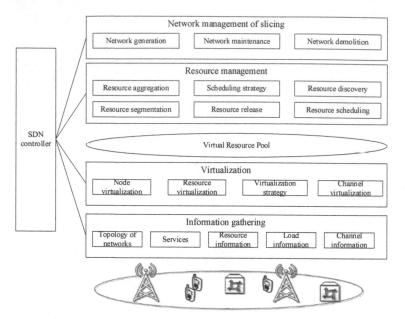

Fig. 4. Dynamic deployment system for 5G power network slicing

4   Validation in the Laboratory Environment

4.1   Environment of Validation

The 5G macro station and some indoor distribution systems were constructed, covering the indoor and outdoor areas of the laboratory. At the same time, the carrier network equipment is deployed in the computer room, and the core network equipment is deployed in the core computer room, which is sent back to the laboratory through special lines. The network topology is shown in the following figure (Fig. 5).

Two networking schemes, NSA and SA, are considered for network construction. In the NSA network scheme, the signaling is carried on the 4G network and the service is carried on the 5G network. In SA scheme, both signaling and service are carried on 5G network. The network access in NSA or SA of different services is carried out according to the coverage of indoor and outdoor. The terminals for electricity information collection, distribution network condition monitoring, video surveillance and intelligent inspection are connected to the outdoor macro station via the 5G CPE. The terminals of the differential protection, distribution automation, physical ID and precision load control is connected to the building through the 5G CPE.

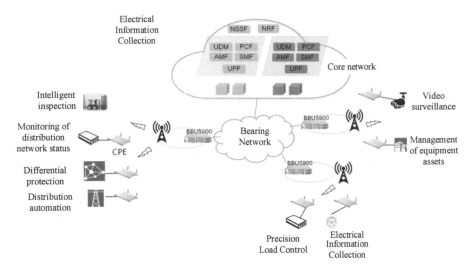

Fig. 5. Schematic diagram of 5G test networking in

4.2 Content of Validation

For the 5G application scenarios of eMBB, uRLLC and mMTC, this paper selects eight typical types of services, such as differential protection, distribution automation, precision load control, power information acquisition, distribution network condition monitoring, physical ID, intelligent inspection and video surveillance, and analyzes the service requirements from the aspects of network bandwidth, delay, transmission distance, terminal density and security reliability. In this paper, an end-to-end network slicing scheme and laboratory verification are proposed. Through carrying the electric power service in the laboratory test network, it is ensured that under the premise of satisfying the communication demand of the related business, the relevant test verification scheme is formulated to ensure the safe and orderly development of the electric power production business.

(1) It verifies the actual network performance, coverage range, access rate, network delay under different network and slicing schemes. Using slicing technology of 5G network, it is possible to deploy multiple separate differentiated networks on a unified infrastructure. End-to-end slicing involves multiple network devices such as access networks, bearer networks and core networks. It validates resource isolation and network security between different slices Table 1.
(2) For different power application scenarios and business requirements, it verifies the function, performance and safety reliability of various typical power services carried by 5g networks Table 2.

4.3 Scheme of Validation

(1) Verification of network performance.

Table 1. Verification of Network performance in laboratory

Verified items		Content of validation
Network performance of the laboratory	Basic business processes	Session management, contract management, policy control management, mobility management, QoS guarantee
	Peak rate	Single user up-and-down peak rate (different packet length), cell multi-user up-and-down peak rate
	Network delay	Single user up-down delay, multi-user up-down delay, jitter, etc.
	Network capacity	System throughput (different network locations), maximum cell users and concurrent users
	Time synchronization	Synchronization function and precision of Beidou clock
	Adaptation to the environment	The Influence of extreme environment and electromagnetic harassment on network performance
Outdoor coverage and network performance	Remote testing of single station	Verify the limit coverage distance for single station of the 5G network and measure the quality of wireless signal received by the wireless base station in the uplink and downlink respectively
	Outdoor coverage test	Verify that the 5G network is in the outdoor continuous coverage area and test the quality of the downlink signal and the uplink signal of the wireless base station in the coverage area
	Indoor coverage test	Verify the quality of the downlink signal and the uplink signal of the 5g network in the indoor coverage area

(*continued*)

Table 1. (*continued*)

Verified items		Content of validation
	Peak rate for single user	Verify that the peak rate (different packet lengths) for single-user of a 5G network in a scenario with continuous coverage and multi-cell networking
	Edge rate for single user	Verify that the edge rate (different packet lengths) for single-user of a 5G network in a scenario with continuous coverage and multi-cell networking
	Network delay	Delay of single user (different network locations), delay of multi-user, jitter, etc.
	Network capacity	System throughput (different network locations), cell number of concurrent users
	Mobility	Switching delay and success rate of terminal
	Long-term stability	Variation of long-term packet loss rate and network delay under heavy load
	Electromagnetic compatibility of high voltage and strong electricity	Verify whether the 5G network meets the requirements of the power industry for network coverage, business capability, long-term reliability and so on under the high voltage strong power scenario
Network slicing	Slice management of 5G	Slice deployment, slice monitoring, slice deletion
	Slice function of 5G	QoS configuration and performance of security isolation (frequency resource, core network, return network)
	Selection of 5G slice	Access mobility function (AMF) selection, AMF redirection, data transfer unit session, slice selection, slice reselection

(*continued*)

Table 1. (*continued*)

Verified items		Content of validation
Network security	Physical layer security	Protocol security of terminal, base station, core network side, port detection, vulnerability mining, log security, pseudo base station attack, etc.
	Network layer security	Access authentication, signaling integrity, user data encryption, network slicing resource isolation and key isolation, etc.
	Application layer security	Security risk of business data, impact of security protection on network performance, etc.

Table 2. Verification of service bearer in laboratory

Type of service	Verified items	Content of validation
Differential protection	Function	Sampling test of differential protection, time test of differential protection action
	Performance	End-to-end communication delay test, end-to-end multi-terminal communication delay test, CPE bandwidth test, CPE timing test
	Safety and reliability	Testing of communications reliability and operational security
Distribution automation	Function	Functional testing of Sanyo
	Performance	Test of telemetry response time, remote signal response time, remote control response time
	Safety and reliability	Correct rate of remote control, correct rate of remote communication, safety test of business
Precision load control	Function	Function Testing of remote control remote communication
	Performance	Remote signal response time test, remote control response time test, delay test

(*continued*)

Table 2. (*continued*)

Type of service	Verified items	Content of validation
	Safety and reliability	Testing of the correctness of telemetry data, testing of the correctness of remote communications, reliability testing of operations, security testing of operations
Electrical information collection	Function	Data survey, control operation, etc.
	Performance	Control operation response time, call and set response time test for regular data, call response time test for historical data
	Safety and reliability	Remote control accuracy of power information acquisition service, test success rate of remote one-time acquisition of power information acquisition service, test of business security
Monitoring of distribution network status	Function	Line load information, cable failure information, equipment status information query
	Performance	Query response time, telemetry response time
	Safety and reliability	Security testing of operations
Physical ID	Function	Import material group and equipment classification matching, code generation of physical id
	Performance	System login response time, asset list query response time, pass rate of mixed transaction
	Safety and reliability	Reliability testing, business security testing
Video surveillance	Function	Testing of Video Access, Video Replay, Video Control, Cloud Mirror Control, Video Wheel Patrol, Audio intercom, Video Storage
	Performance	Delay testing of video surveillance services and packet loss testing of services

(*continued*)

Table 2. (*continued*)

Type of service	Verified items	Content of validation
	Safety and reliability	Security testing of operations
Intelligent inspection	Function	Two-way audio and video management test, state real-time monitoring test, speech modification test, shared whiteboard function modification test, audio and video interactive organization modification test
	Performance	Response test of intelligent inspection task, capability test of intelligent inspection task, adaptability test of transmission and distribution machine inspection service
	Safety and reliability	accuracy test of algorithm, security test of business

Test the access rate, network delay, network flow, time synchronization, environment adaptability of 5G network through the comprehensive tester, road testing tool and test terminal. Verify the cellular, single-user uplink/downlink peak throughput performance of NSA/SA network, single-user up-and-down delay, multi-user up-and-down delay, jitter, etc., GPS/dipper clock synchronization function, synchronization accuracy, extreme environment, effect of electromagnetic disturbance on network performance (Fig. 7).

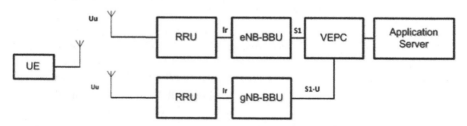

Fig. 6. The topology of the NSA networking test

(2) Coverage validation of indoor and outdoor.

Through the road testing tool and the test terminal, the indexes of single station coverage, outdoor network coverage, indoor traversal coverage, peak rate of single user, edge rate of single user and mobility are verified. It verifies the limit coverage distance of 5G network and measure the quality of wireless signal received by wireless base station in uplink and downlink respectively.

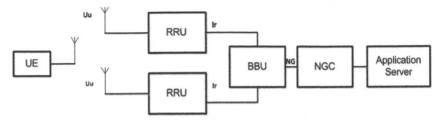

Fig. 7. The topology of the SA networking test

(3) Verification of network slicing.
It verifies slice deployment, selection, monitoring, deletion, etc. (Fig. 8).

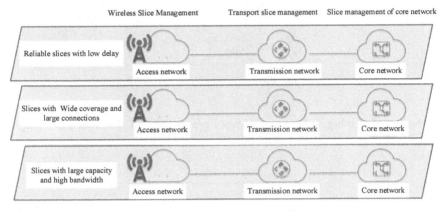

Fig. 8. Topology of network slices

(4) Business validation.
The network performance of 5G and the carrying capacity of power service are verified in the laboratory through the selected test instrument and communication terminal. The distribution network differential protection, distribution automation, precision load control, power information collection, distribution network state monitoring, physical id, intelligent inspection, high-definition video monitoring and other business indicators were tested. It verifies that whether the 5G network meets the network performance and security requirements of traditional and emerging power services (Fig. 9).

5   5G Verification Scheme in Field Environment

5.1   Verification Environment

Based on the coverage of 5G network, the key technologies and business applications of 5G load-carrying power distribution network control, acquisition and emergency communication support, 4k high-definition video interaction, hybrid reality, virtual reality

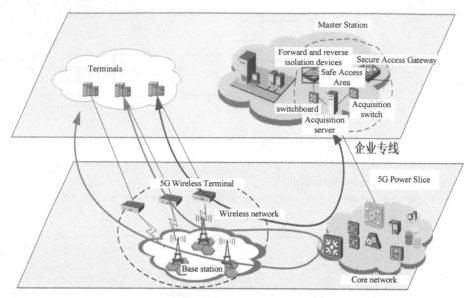

Fig. 9. Schematic diagram of service access in laboratory

intelligent patrol training and remote guidance are carried out. The schematic diagram of the network is shown in Fig. 6 (Fig. 10).

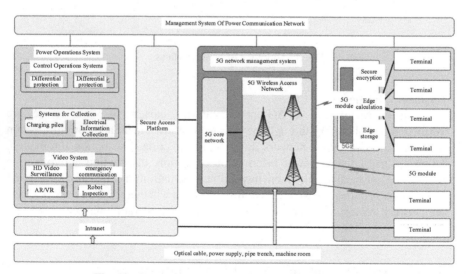

Fig. 10. Schematic diagram of 5G test networking in field

5.2 Content of validation

It carries out the test of acquisition and mobile application. Verification includes electrical information collection, electric vehicle charging station/pile, integrated monitoring of distribution stations, video surveillance, environmental monitoring of opening and closing stations, etc. In the process of emergency repair, it can realize the precise guidance of experts remotely, improve the efficiency of fault handling and reduce the duration of obstacles. It can realize the omni-directional operation guidance and intelligent maintenance of the work site, ensure that the field operation is accurate and timely, and reduce the probability of misoperation.

5.3 Scheme of validation

Based on the four network construction models of 5G in smart grid, the test verification is carried out.

(1) Mode 1

Using the slicing function of 5G network, a virtual 5G wireless private network is built for the grid. The company only needs to build a network slicing customization and management system to independently use the 5G network, and ensure the business isolation and network service quality. After the business data is connected to the core network through the link base station, then through its backbone network to the Internet of things platform, finally docking with the company Internet of things platform.

(2) Mode 2

Using the network slicing function of the 5G network of the operator, the Internet of things platform of the company is connected with the core network of the 5G network by special line. Power terminal accesses 5G network using the rights allocated by the operator. After the business data is connected to the core network through the link base station, then enters the company data communication network through the special line.

(3) Mode 3

In this mode, the company does not need to apply for exclusive frequency resources, and can use the spectrum and base station resources of the operator by co-construction and sharing with the operator. The base station of the operator is connected to the transmission network of the company, and the core network of the 230 MHz power wireless private network is upgraded to realize the unified management of the power wireless private network and the 5G base station. This mode is to some extent equivalent to the 5G NSA mode of public network.

(4) Mode 4

In this mode, the company does not need to apply for exclusive frequency resources, and can use the spectrum and base station resources of the operator by co-construction and sharing with the operator. The base station is connected to the transmission network of the company, and the construction of 5G network and application are realized through the self-built 5G core network and network management operation and maintenance system. This mode is to some extent equivalent to the 5G SA mode of public network (Fig. 11).

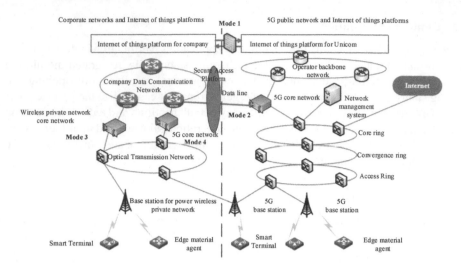

Fig. 11. Schematic diagram of four modes of network construction

6 Conclusion

The Internet of things puts forward new and higher requirements for collecting, carrying, analyzing and applying the basic data of electric power, and puts forward higher requirements for communication technology and method. The company's business development needs are also highly compatible with the 5G application scenario. In this paper, the network performance, application mode, network scheme and security strategy of 5G wireless communication technology are tested and verified. The test plan includes laboratory test and field test, and the test plan is given. The proposed test scheme verifies the support ability of 5G technology to power service and external service, and lays a foundation for the application of 5G technology in power grid.

Acknowledgments. The authors would like to thank the anonymous reviewers and editor for their comments that improved the quality of this paper. This work is supported by state grid scientific project of STATE GRID JIBEI INFORMATION & TELECOMMUNICATION COMPANY under Grant NO. 5700-202014175A-0-0-00, the name of the project is application research and verification of power 5G network innovation based on co-construction and sharing mode.

References

1. Wang, K.: The application of the internet of things in the 5G era in the power system. Telecom Power Technol. **35**(5), 187–188 (2018)
2. Xia, X., Zhu, X., Mei, C., Wei, L., Fang, H.: Research and practice on 5G slicing in power internet of things. Mobile Commun. **43**(1), 63–69 (2019)
3. You, X.H., Pan, Z.W., Gao, X.Q., et al.: The 5G mobile communication: the development trends and its emerging key techniques. Sci. Sin. **44**(5), 551 (2014)
4. Liu, G., Jiang, D.: 5G: vision and requirements for mobile communication system towards year 2020. Chin. J. Eng. **2016**, 1–8 (2016). https://doi.org/10.1155/2016/5974586

5. Ma, Z., Zhang, Z.Q., Ding, Z.G., et al.: Key techniques for 5G wireless communications: network architecture, physical layer, and MAC layer perspectives. Sci Chin. **58**(4), 41301–41321 (2015)
6. Qiu, J., Ding, G., Wu, Q., et al.: Hierarchical resource allocation framework for hyper-dense small cell networks. IEEE Access **4**(99), 8657–8669 (2017)
7. Yao, J.: Random access technology of electric dedicated LTE network based on power priority. Autom. Electr. Power Syst. **40**(10), 127–131 (2016)
8. Cao, J., Liu, J., Li, X.: A power wireless broadband technology scheme for smart power distribution and utilization network. Autom. Electr. Power Syst. **37**(11), 76–80 (2013)
9. Yu, J., Liu, J., Cai, S.: Performance siulation on TD-LTE electric power wireless private network. Guangdong Electr. Power. **30**(1), 39–45 (2017)
10. Yu, J., Liu, J., Cai, S.: Research on LTE wireless network planning in electric power system. Electr. Power Inf. Commun. Technol. **10**(2), 7–11 (2016)
11. Wu, J., Zhang, Y., Zukerman, M., et al.: Energy-efficient base-stations sleep-mode techniques in green cellular networks: a survey. IEEE Commun. Surv. Tutor. **17**(2), 803–826 (2015)
12. Li, W., Chen, B., Wu, Q., et al.: Applied research of TD-LTE power wireless broadband private network. Telecommun. Electr. Power Syst. **33**(241), 82 (2012)

Immune Network Based Anomaly Detection Algorithm

Xinlei Hu[✉], Zhengxia Wang, and Yunbing Hu

Chongqing College of Electronic Engineering, Chongqing 401331, China

Abstract. Inspired by immune network theory, this paper proposes an immune network-based anomaly detection algorithm (INADA), which effectively solves the problems of detection based on group theory. INADA is divided into three stages: In the immune network generation stage, mature detectors are generated through the negative selection algorithm. Each mature detector is not isolated. In the detector training phase, the mature detector is not only stimulated by the antigen during the life cycle, but also stimulated and suppressed by other detectors in the network. In the detection stage, the UCI standard data set is used as the test sample to determine whether all mature detectors in the immune network match the test sample. The result shows that the INADA algorithm has high detection rate and low false alarm rate.

Keywords: Artificial immune · Immune network · Mature detector · Anomaly detection

1 Introduction

Immune algorithm is divided into immune algorithm based on group theory and immune algorithm based on network. The immune algorithm based on group theory is inspired by the early mutation process of immune cells before they are released into the lymphatic system. There is no direct connection between the elements of the system, and the system elements directly interact with the system environment. If they are to be connected, they can only be indirectly connected [1]. At present, many researchers have proposed lots of immune algorithms based on group theory, which are widely used in network security, pattern recognition, intelligent optimization and other fields.

However, the anomaly detection algorithm based on group theory has the following problems:

1) In the anomaly detection algorithm based on the group theory, the criterion to decide whether the detector should clone proliferation is only by the ability of recognizing antigens. The stronger the recognition ability, the stronger the clone proliferation ability. When there are too many antigens, the detectors which recognize these antigens will increase exponentially in the system. Since each detector is independent and has no connection with each other, it is difficult for the system to find the redundant detectors. Moreover, the total number of detectors in the system is limited, and

© Springer Nature Singapore Pte Ltd. 2021
Y. Tian et al. (Eds.): ICBDS 2020, CCIS 1415, pp. 194–203, 2021.
https://doi.org/10.1007/978-981-16-3150-4_17

the number of detectors that recognize other antigens will be reduced accordingly, resulting in the possibility that the system cannot detect other antigens effectively. Therefore, the existing anomaly detection algorithms based on group theory are difficult to determine the most effective antibody for non-self antigen recognition, which directly affects the detection rate of the system.

2) The anomaly detection algorithm based on group theory only uses the generation and interaction mechanism of T cells in the biological immune system [2, 3], but ignores the mutual stimulation and suppression between T cells and the immunoregulation capability of the immune system. The immunoregulation capability plays an important role in the process of immune response. Lack of immunoregulation capability will destroy the stability of the system. That is, when there are too many detectors of a certain type in the system, the immune response will be too intense, which will increase the probability of detecting self-antigens and cause false alarm alert.

The network-based immune algorithm is inspired by immune network theory [1]. The immune network theory proposed by Jerne in 1974 [2] believes that part of the antibody molecules of immune cells can be recognized by other immune cells. When an immune cell recognizes an antigen or an immune cell, then it is activated. On the other hand, when immune cells are recognized by other immune cells, they will be suppressed. The immunoregulation capability of the immune network on the immune system is manifested in: on the one hand, when an antigen appears, it can promote the rapid response of the immune system to the antigen; on the other hand, when the antigen is eliminated, it can suppress the proliferation of immune cells and maintains the immune balance of the body.

Aiming at the problems of anomaly detection algorithm based on group theory, this paper is inspired by immune network theory and proposes an anomaly detection algorithm based on immune network (Immune Network based Anomaly Detection Algorithm, INADA). The INADA algorithm includes three stages: 1) Immune network generation stage: mature detectors are generated through a negative selection algorithm, each mature detector is not isolated, they form a dynamic balanced network structure through mutual recognition, mutual stimulation and mutual suppression; 2) Detector training stage: During the life cycle of a mature detector, it is not only stimulated by antigens, but also stimulated and suppressed by other detectors in the network. The higher the level of stimulation, the greater the chance of cloning and mutation of the mature detector. Add a new detector of clone mutation to the network and update the network structure. When reaching the life cycle, those mature detectors with low levels of stimulation, that is, mature detectors that have no effect or little effect on antigen classification, are eliminated. While those with high levels of stimulation are mature detectors that have a good classification of antigens, which are reserved by the network; 3) Detection stage: Determine whether all mature detectors in the immune network match the test sample. If some test sample is matched, it indicates an abnormality, otherwise it is normal.

2 Proposed Algorithm

Immune network theory is also called idiosyncratic network theory. According to the unique network theory, the immune system is defined as a network structure of antibodies that can recognize each other even without antigen stimulation. Define the part of an antibody that can be recognized by other antibodies, called idiotype (Id) epitope; on the other hand, the antibody that can recognize it and cause a reaction is called anti-idiotype (AId). AId can be recognized by other anti-anti-idiotypic (AAId) antibodies. Antibodies respond to recognition signals stimulated or inhibited by other antibodies. The stimulation response leads to cell activation, while the suppression response leads to antibody secretion. The process of stimulation-suppression is shown in Fig. 1.

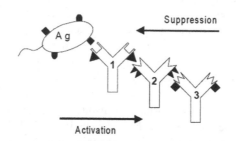

Fig. 1. The process of stimulation-suppression

Immune network theory is the theoretical basis of network-based immune algorithms, and has been widely used in pattern recognition, intelligent optimization [3–7] and other fields. Inspired by this, we build an immune network and use the mature detector set generated by the stimulation and suppression mechanism between the detectors in the network to achieve anomaly detection.

2.1 Basic Definition

Definition 1 *Antigen* represents all the sample from the feature space. There is

$$Ag = \{ag|ag = \langle x_1, x_2, \cdots, x_n \rangle, x_i \in [0, 1], i = 1, 2, \cdots, n\} \tag{1}$$

Where n is the data dimension and x_i is the *ith* normalized attribute.

Definition 2 *Self antigens(Self)* are defined as the normal sample from the antigen set. *Non-self antigens(Nonself)* are defined as the abnormal sample in the antigen set. There is

$$Self \cup Nonself = Ag, \, Self \cap Nonself = \varnothing \tag{2}$$

$$Self = \left\{ <c, r_s> | ab \in U, r_s \in R^+ \right\} \tag{3}$$

Where $c \in U$ is a n-dimension vector, represents normal sample, r_s is radius of self.

Definition 3 *Detector set(D)* simulates B cells in biological immune system for detecting antigens. There is

$$D = \left\{ <c, r_d> | ab \in U, r_d \in R^+ \right\} \tag{4}$$

$$f_{distance}(x, y) = \sqrt{\sum_{i=1}^{n} (x_i - y_i)^2}$$ (5)

Where c is the central vector of D, r_d is the detector radius, $f_{disance}(x,y)$ is the distance between antigens and detector or between detectors. When the distance between antigens and detector D less than r_d, the antigens will be identified as non-self elements.

2.2 Immune Network

The immune network is an incompletely connected weighted directed graph composed by mature detectors.

$$I = < D, E, W >$$ (6)

Among them, the node set D is the set of mature detectors; the edge set $E = \{e|e = \langle d_i, d_j \rangle, d \in D, i, j = 1, 2, \cdots, n\}$ represents the connection between the detectors; W is the weight set of E, $w_{ij} \in W$ represents the degree of stimulation of the detector d_j to the detector d_i, and w_{ji} represents the suppression of the detector d_j to the detector d_i degree.

The structure of the immune network I is shown in Fig. 2. In order to facilitate observation, only the weights between the detectors d1 and d2, and d1 and d8 are marked in the figure.

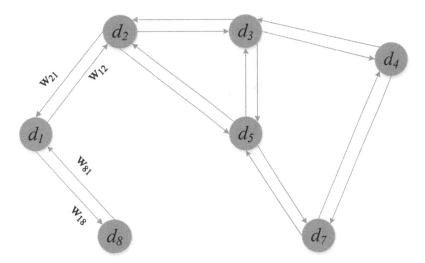

Fig. 2. The structure of immune network

3   Algorithm Detail

The INADA algorithm includes three stages: 1) Immune network generation stage: mature detectors are generated through a negative selection algorithm. Each mature detector is not isolated. They form a dynamically balanced network structure through mutual recognition, mutual stimulation and mutual suppression; 2) Detector training stage: During the life cycle of a mature detector, it is not only stimulated by antigens, but also stimulated and inhibited by other detectors in the network. The greater the level of excitation, the greater the chance of cloning and mutation of the mature detector. Add a new detector of clone mutation to the network and update the network structure. When reaching the life cycle, those mature detectors with low levels of stimulation, that is, mature detectors that have no effect or little effect on antigen classification, are eliminated, while those with high levels of stimulation are mature detectors that have a good classification of antigens. The detectors are reserved by the network; 3) Detection stage: Determine whether all mature detectors in the immune network match the test sample. If they are matched, it indicates an abnormality, otherwise it is normal.

The specific algorithm implementation of each stage is given below.

3.1   Immune Network Generation Phase

In this stage, the stimulation and suppression of the mature detector are calculated by affinity, and the mature detectors are connected according to the stimulation and

---

Procedure

Begin

    1. $I = \varnothing$, $D = \varnothing$;

    2. use NSA generate mature detectors

    3. For each d_i in D do

    4.   Begin

    5.   For each d_j in D do

    6.   Begin

    7.   CreateImmuneNetwork(d_i, d_i, I);

    8. $dis(d_i, d_j)$;

    9.   Edge(d_i, d_j);

    10. $w_{ij} = \dfrac{1}{dis(d_i, d_j)}$, $w_{ji} = dis(d_i, d_j)$;

    11.   End;

    12.   End;

End.

Fig. 3. Immune network generation algorithm

suppression to form a dynamic balanced network structure of mutual recognition, mutual stimulation and mutual suppression. The pseudocode of the algorithm is shown in Fig. 3.

3.2 Mature Detector Training Phase

In the mature detector training phase, the INADA algorithm calculates their stimulation levels based on the mutual stimulation and inhibition between mature detectors. Mature detectors compete with each other through their stimulation levels. Mature detectors with low stimulation levels. That is, mature detectors that have no effect or little effect on antigen classification are eliminated, while mature detectors with high levels of stimulation, that is, mature detectors with good antigen classification, are retained by the network. The higher the level of stimulation, the greater the probability of the cloning and mutation. Thereby increasing the diversity of mature detectors, effectively improving the algorithm's abnormal detection ability. The cloned and mutated mature detectors are then added to the network, and similar mature detectors are eliminated. The specific strategies adopted include:

(1) Competitive Strategy
    Maturity detectors compete with each other to obtain the right to evolve, and competition is measured by the level of stimulation. A certain number of mature detectors with a high level of stimulation have a higher probability of winning in the competition, so that subsequent operations such as clonal mutation can be performed. It can be seen that designing an appropriate competition strategy is the key to achieving excellent algorithm performance. Suppose a mature detector $d_i \in D$, the excitation level of d_i is represented by $L(d_i)$, N is the total number of detectors, and the probability of selection is represented by $P(d_i)$. There are:

$$P(d_i) = \frac{2\exp(-\frac{1}{L(d_i)}) - 1}{\sum\limits_{j}^{N} (2\exp(-\frac{1}{L(d_i)}) - 1)} \tag{7}$$

It can be seen from Eq. (7) that the greater the level of stimulation of the mature detector d_i, the greater the selection probability $P(d_i)$.

(2) Clone strategy
    The cloning strategy mimics the cell clone surge mechanism of the biological immune system. When antibodies detect non-self antigens, clone surges will occur. This strategy is to perform cloning operations on mature detectors in the network. At this time, instead of cloning each mature detector in the network, a mature detector with a higher level of stimulation is selected to perform the cloning operation. The higher the level of stimulation, the greater the number of clones. At the same time, in order to avoid an excessive increase in the number of similar mature detectors (similar stimulation levels), the number of clones is limited according to the concentration of mature detectors. The greater the concentration of the mature detector, the fewer the number of clones; the lower the concentration of the mature detector, the more the number of clones.

The concentration $C(d_i)$ of the mature detector d_i is defined as:

$$C(d_i) = \frac{\sum\limits_{k=1}^{m} d_k}{\sum\limits_{j=1}^{n} d_j} \qquad (8)$$

Where $\sum\limits_{k=1}^{m} d_k$ is the number of mature detectors with similar stimulation levels as d_i, and $\sum\limits_{j=1}^{n} d_j$ is the total number of mature detectors in the network.

The number of clones of the maturity detector di $Clone\_num(d_i)$ is defined as:

$$Clone\_num(d_i) = (1 - C(d_i))Level(d_i) \qquad (9)$$

In the formula, $Level(d_i)$ is the stimulated level of d_i, $C(d_i) \in [0, 1]$. It can be seen from Eq. (9) that the higher the level of stimulation of the mature detector, the greater the number of clones. As the concentration of the mature detector increases, the number of clones will decrease. At the same time, it also ensures the diversity of mature detectors.

(3) Mutation strategy

The mutation strategy simulates the high-frequency mutation mechanism of the biological immune system. The purpose of mutation is to produce mature detectors with higher affinity, thereby enhancing the diversity of the mature detector set. The traditional immune network algorithm aiNet [8] uses Gaussian mutation, and the mutation formula is $c' = c + \alpha N(0, 1)$, where $\alpha = (1/\beta)exp(-f^*)$, $N(0, 1)$ is a Gaussian random variable, the mean is 0, and the deviation is 1. β is user-defined control parameters, adjust the variation range. In this method, the setting of the value β affects the variation. A larger value will slow the algorithm's convergence speed; a smaller value is not conducive to the detector's mutation to the optimal detection capability.

Therefore, this paper improves the above method so that the β value can be dynamically adjusted with the number of iterations. Let t be the number of iterations, $\frac{1}{dis(d_i,d_j)}$ is the affinity between the detectors d_i and dj, the new mutation method is as follows:

$$d_i(t + 1) = d_i(t) + \alpha N(0, 1) \qquad (10)$$

$$\alpha = \frac{exp(-\frac{1}{dis(d_i,d_j)})}{\beta} \qquad (11)$$

$$\beta = \frac{1}{1 + exp(-t)} \qquad (12)$$

Combining Eqs. (10)–(12), it can be seen that in the initial stage of the algorithm, the value of β is larger, and $d_i(t + 1)$ is also larger, which helps to increase the diversity of mature detectors; when the algorithm is iterated for a certain number of times, the value gradually Decrease, $d_i(t + 1)$ gradually changes toward the optimal detector.

(4) Update strategy of immune network

This strategy simulates the immune network dynamic adjustment process. In the set of the clonal variant detectors and the original detectors, using the principle of antibody stimulation and suppression in the biological immune system, comparing the affinity between all detectors in the network, and eliminating the similar detection. If the mature detectors are in too low stimulation level and reach the life cycle of age, they are also be eliminated. Therefore, the reserved detectors are formed into a new immune network. This not only maintains the diversity of the mature detector set, but also reduces redundant detectors.

3.3 Detection Phase

In this stage, the set of mature detectors finally reserved in the immune network is used to determine whether the tested sample is abnormal or normal. If the sample to be tested matches the detector, the sample to be tested is considered to be abnormal, otherwise it is considered to be abnormal.

4 Experiment

In order to verify the effectiveness of the INADA algorithm, the DynamiCS proposed by Kim et al. [9, 10] was selected as the experimental comparison object, and the experiments were carried out on the Breast Cancer Wisconsin Original and Iris data sets [11]. These two data sets were It is widely used in immune-based abnormality detection research [9, 10, 12–14].

The data set (abbreviated as BCW) has 683 records, and each record contains 9 numeric attributes, divided into two categories: benign and malignant. 444 records are benign and 239 records are malignant. In order to use this data set, the data is preprocessed first, and the data is normalized to real-valued [0, 1] space. Among them, benign data are regarded as self-antigens, and malignant data are regarded as non-self-antigens.

Experiment with INADA algorithm and DynamiCS algorithm respectively, running key parameters and their values: self-radius $r_{self} = 0.01$, detection radius of mature detector $r_d = 1.5$, suppression threshold of mature detector $\theta = 2.2$, lifetime of mature detector $\lambda = 20$, the number of iterations is 100. Figure 4 shows the changes in the detection rate and false alarm rate of the INADA algorithm as the iterations changing; Fig. 5 shows the difference in the detection rate and false alarm rate of the DynamiCS algorithm as the iterations changing.

Comparing Fig. 4 and Fig. 5, it can be found that the detection rate and false alarm rate of the INADA algorithm on the BCW data set are significantly better than the DynamiCS algorithm. The detection rate of the DynamiCS algorithm after 80 generations is still low, and the INADA algorithm runs for 50 generations. Higher detection rate (Table 1).

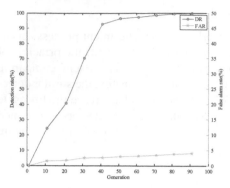
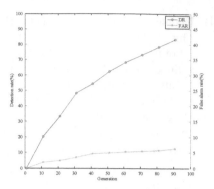

Fig. 4. INADA runs on BCW   **Fig. 5.** DynamiCS runs on BCW

Table 1. Comparison of INADA and DynamiCS on BCW data set

Algorithm	Iteration	DR(%)	FAR(%)
INADA	40	92.71	2.65
DynamiCS		54.34	4.65
INADA	60	97.4	3.15
DynamiCS		68.24	5.25
INADA	90	99.7	4.03
DynamiCS		83.31	6.32

5 Summary

Inspired by immune network theory, this paper proposes an immune network-based anomaly detection algorithm (INADA), which effectively solves the above problems and provides a new research method for the application of immunity in anomaly detection.

The implementation of the INADA algorithm is divided into three stages: In the immune network generation stage, mature detectors are generated through a negative selection algorithm. Each mature detector is not isolated. They form a dynamically balanced network through mutual recognition, mutual stimulation and mutual inhibition. Structure: In the detector training phase, the mature detector is not only stimulated by the antigen during the life cycle, but also stimulated and inhibited by other detectors in the network. The mutual stimulation and inhibition between mature detectors determines their level of stimulation. The higher the level of stimulation, the greater the chance of mature detectors' cloning and mutation. Add a new detector of clone mutation to the network and update the network structure. When reaching the life cycle, those mature detectors with low levels of stimulation, that is, mature detectors that have no effect or little effect on antigen classification, are eliminated, while those with high levels of stimulation are mature detectors that have a good classification of antigens. The detector is reserved by the network; in the detection stage, the UCI standard data set is used as the test sample to determine whether all mature detectors in the immune network match the test sample. If they are matched, it is abnormal, otherwise it is normal. The result shows that the INADA algorithm has high detection rate and low false alarm rate.

Acknowledgements. This work was supported by the National Natural Science Foundation of Chongqing, China (No. cstc2020jcyj-msxmX1022).

This work was supported by the Science Foundation of Chongqing Municipal Commission of Education (No. KJQN202003108).

Conflict of Interests. The authors declare that there is no conflict of interests regarding the publication of this article.

References

1. Dozier, G., Brown, D., Hou, H., et al.: Vulnerability analysis of immunity-based intrusion detection systems using genetic and evolutionary hackers. Appl. Soft Comput. **7**, 547–553 (2007)
2. Jerne, N.K.: Towards a network theory of the immune system. Ann. Immunol. (Paris) 373–389 (1974)
3. De Castro, L.N., Timmis, J.: An artificial immune network for multimodal function optimisation. In: Proceedings of IEEE World Congress on Evolutionary Computation, pp. 669–674 (2002)
4. Yue, X., Mo, H.W., Chi, Z.X.: Immune-inspired incremental feature selection technology to data stream. Appl. Soft Comput. **8**(2), 1041–1049 (2008)
5. Nasraoui, O., Gonzalez, F., Cardona, C., et al.: A scalable artificial immune system model fordynamic unsupervised learning. In: Proceedings of International Conference on Genetic and Evolutionary Computation, vol. 2723, pp. 219–230. Morgan Kaufmann, San Francisco (2003)
6. Zhong, Y., Zhang, L.: An adaptive artificial immune network for supervised classification of multi-hyperspectral remote sensing imagery. IEEE Trans. Geosci. Remote Sens. **50**(3) (2012)
7. Xu, Q., Wang, L., Si, J.: Predication based immune network for multimodal function optimization. Eng. Appl. Artif. Intell. **23**, 495–504 (2010)
8. Nunes de Casto, L., Von Zuben, F.J.: An evolutionary immune network for data clustering. In: Sixth Brazilian Symposium on Neural Networks. Proceedings, pp. 84–89 (2000)
9. Kim, J., Bentley, P.: Immune memory and gene library evolution in the dynamic clonal selection algorithm. Genet. Program Evolvable Mach. **5**(4), 361–391 (2004)
10. Kim, J., Bentley, P.J., Aickelin, U., et al.: Immune system approaches to intrusion detection–a review. Nat. Comput. **6**(4), 413–466 (2007)
11. Blake, C.L., Merz, C.J.: UCI repository of machine learning databases. The University of Cal-ifornia, Irvine. http://archive.ics.uci.edu/ml/datasets
12. Kim, J., Bentley, P.J.: Towards an artificial immune system for network intrusion detection: an investigation of dynamic clonal selection. In: Proceedings of the 2002 Congress on Evolutionary Computation, CEC 2002, pp. 1015–1020 (2002)
13. Stibor, T., Timmis, J., Eckert, C.: A comparative study of real-valued negative selection to statistical anomaly detection techniques. In: Jacob, C., Pilat, M.L., Bentley, P.J., Timmis, J.I. (eds.) ICARIS 2005. LNCS, vol. 3627, pp. 262–275. Springer, Heidelberg (2005). https://doi.org/10.1007/11536444_20
14. Harmer, P.K., Williams, P.D., Gunsch, G.H.: An artificial immune system architecture for computer security applications. IEEE Trans. Evol. Comput. **6**(3): 252–280 (2002)

Incremental Anonymous Privacy-Protecting Data Mining Method Based on Feature Correlation Algorithm

Yongliang Jia[1]([envelope]), Peng Tao[1], Dapeng Zhou[2], and Bing Li[1]

[1] State Grid Hebei Marketing Service Center, Shijiazhuang 050000, China
[2] Information and Communication Branch, State Grid Liaoning Electric Power Co., Ltd., Shengyang 110000, China

Abstract. With the arrival of the information age, privacy leaks have been getting increasingly serious. The commonly-used method for privacy protection is to introduce k-anonymity when data publishing. In this paper, how to employ k-anonymity in stream data sets is studied, and the relationship and the sensitivity matrix of the basic knowledge about Quasi identifier (QI) and sensitive attributes are established. RSLK-anonymity algorithm is proposed for solving the private information leakage during the streaming data publishing. The main idea is to anonymize the streaming data set on the basis of sliding window as well as relation and sensitive matrix, which can make anonymous streaming data effectively defense background knowledge attack and homogeneity attack while solving sensitive attribute diversity. Experimental results indicate that RSLK-anonymity algorithm is practical, effective and highly efficient.

Keywords: K-anonymity · Privacy protection · Sliding window · Algorithm of correlation feature

1 Introduction

In the field of conventional database, k-anonymity is a hot topic in protecting privacy, which was proposed by Samarati P and Sweeney L in 1998. In order to solve privacy leakage, k-anonymity model requires some unidentified individuals in the published data, which makes the attacker unable to differentiate the privacy of specific individuals and prevent individual privacy leakage. In recent years, k-anonymity has raised widespread concern in academia. Many scholars have studied privacy protection at different levels.

In many cases, transaction data presents the form of high-speed data stream [2, 3], such as wireless sensor networks. Therefore, it needs a solution that specifically considers the features of data flow. Data flow has the following features:

(1) The elements come online;
(2) The system cannot control the arrival sequence of data elements;
(3) Once the elements are seen or processed, it is not easy to retrieve or see them again, unless they are explicitly stored in memory.

© Springer Nature Singapore Pte Ltd. 2021
Y. Tian et al. (Eds.): ICBDS 2020, CCIS 1415, pp. 204–214, 2021.
https://doi.org/10.1007/978-981-16-3150-4_18

This paper adopts the data structure of rule tree [3, 4] to complete the data k-anonymization in sliding window, and creates the correlation features and sensitivity matrix of background knowledge about QI and sensitive attributes. To solve privacy leakage in data stream publishing, an improved RSLK anonymity algorithm is proposed to protect the privacy of anonymous data stream.

2 Related Work

Many researchers try to combine privacy protection and data stream management to achieve data stream privacy protection.

Li Jianzhong etc. put forward a new approach called SKY (Stream K-anonymity) to promote the k-anonymity of data streams continuously. It considers the k-anonymity of data streams to protect privacy [2]. In [3], how to protect the privacy of users on the sliding window of transaction data stream is studied. It is challenging since the sliding windows are updating frequently and quickly. Later, a novel method called SWAF (Sliding Window Anonymization Framework) was proposed which can promote k-anonymity on sliding windows. SWAF has the following three advantages:

(1) The processing time of each tuple of data stream is very short;
(2) The memory requirement is very small;
(3) Privacy protection and the anonymous sliding window practicability are considered.

In [4], Zhang Junwei etc. studied KIDS (K-anonymity Data Stream Based on Sliding Window), and adopted continuous k-anonymity on sliding window. KIDS can protect the data stream privacy well, and consider the data distribution density in data stream, thus greatly improving the practicability of data.

Cao Jianneng etc. proposed CASTLE (Continuous Anonymization of Stream Data Through Adaptive Clustercring), which is a cluster based scheme, which can anonymize the data stream in real time, and ensure the novelty of anonymous data by meeting the certain delay constraint [5, 6].

Sylvia L. Osborn and Hessam zakerzadeh proposed a cluster based k-anonymity algorithm, which is named as FAANST (Fast Anonymous Algorithm for Numerical Stream Data), which can anonymize numerical stream data very quickly. As is shown by research, extending FAANST to support data streams composed of classification and numerical values is very easy [7].

Yang Gaoming etc. proposed a new k-anonymity data publishing method based on weak clustering. The practicability has two advantages: first, the processing time of each data stream tuple is very short. Second, less memory is needed [8].

However, few research has considered the relationship between sensitive attributes based on data flow and QI, sensitive attributes of their own features, diversity features of sensitive attributes, etc. [9–12].

3 Problem Definition

3.1 Anonymous Stream Data on Sliding Window

Here are some definitions of the terms mentioned in this paper.

Definition 1. Data stream (DS) is an infinite time series, and its increment order is $DS\{s_1, p_1,... s_n, p_n,...\}$; where s_i is a tuple with sequence number p_i, and $p_i < p_j$ indicates that p_i arrives before p_j. Each S_i contains vectors of m values $(a_1, a_2,..., a_m)$, where a_i is derived from the finite field D_i [2].

Among many data stream mining research, to highlight the latest data stream and avoid storing potential infinite data stream in memory, researchers usually use sliding window method to process data. Sliding windows always keep the latest part of the data flow. As new tuples continue to enter from the data stream, the sliding window replaces the oldest tuple with a new one. The sliding window can be classified into two types, one is based on counting and the other is based on time. To make it simple, this paper describes our work with the sliding window based on counting.

Definition 2. Define $<s_n, p_n>$ to be the latest tuple from data stream s, and the sliding window SW_l to be a subset of DS $\{<s_n, p_n>, ... <s_{n-l}, p_{n-l}>\}$.

Definition 3. K anonymous data stream on sliding window. Suppose the sliding window $SW_l = \{<s_n, p_n>,... <s_{n-l}, p_{n-l}>\}$ and the QI attribute set Q, the data set $ASW_l = \{<g_n, p_n>,..., <g_{n-l}, p_{n-l}>\}$ is generated to make:

(1) ASW_l meets the k-anonymity of Q;
(2) $\forall I \in[n-l, n]$, $<g_i, p_i>$ is a tuple summary of $<s_i, p_i>$.

For the protocol of sliding window, when the sending window and receiving window sizes are fixed to 1, the protocol will degenerate into stop-and-wait protocol. According to that, the sender shall stop the follow-up action after sending a frame, and can continue to send the next frame only after the receiver has received the correct response. As the receiver shall determine whether the received frame is a newly sent or a resent frame, in each frame, the sender shall add a sequence number. Since the stop-and-wait protocol stipulates that a new frame can only be sent after one frame has been successfully sent, only one bit is enough to carry out numbering.

The following is the communication process when the 1-bit sliding window protocol is executed. In the triplet (i, j, k), i represents the number of the message sent by the sender (either A or B), j represents the number of the message received by the sender from the other party last time, and k represents the data. Figure 1 shows the execution of the sliding window protocol.

3.2   Correlation Feature and Sensitivity Matrix on the Basis of Background Knowledge

Domain experts, or direct analysis of basic data can provide background knowledge. which describes the impact of various sensitive attributes generated by QI attributes [9, 12].

The relationship and sensitivity matrix MIS is used to explain the impact level of sensitive attributes generated by QI attribute and sensitive attribute themselves:

- t_{ij}: The impact level of NO.j. OI sensitive attribute generated by NO.i.
- b_i: The weight of sensitivity attribute value of NO.i.

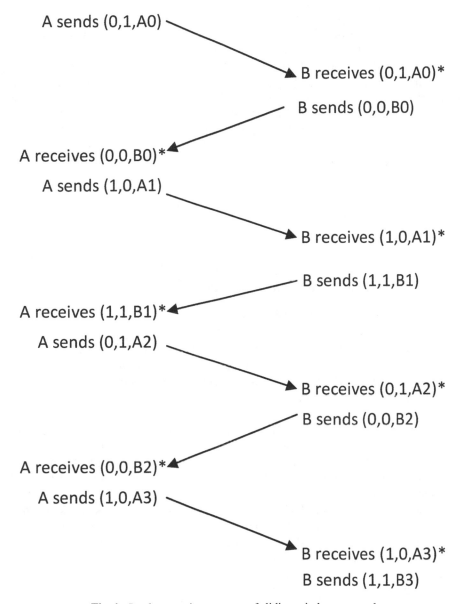

Fig. 1. Implementation process of sliding window protocol

There are $n + 1$ columns and m rows in the relationship and sensitivity matrix MIS, m is the quantity of sensitivity attribute, n is the QI attribute quantity, thus the sample matrix is:

$$M \mid S = (t_{ij} \mid b_i)_{m \times (n+1)} = \begin{matrix} QI_1 & QI_2 & QI_n & S \\ [\, t_{11} & t_{12} & t_{1n} & \mid b_1 \,] \\ t_{m1} & t_{m2} & t_{mn} & b_m \end{matrix}$$

The weight values of t_{ij} and b_i are determined by experts or experience values. For instance, the weight of QI in the aforementioned formula can be divided into five grades: 1, 0.8, 0.4, 0.1, 0, and the weight of S in the formula mentioned above is divided into five grades: 0.10, 0.30, 0.50, 0.80, 0.90. Taking diseases as an example, influenza is a common disease. Due to the features of local influenza, disease weight can be 0.11, ZIP weight can be 0.8, gender weight can be 0.2, etc. The obesity disease weight can be used as 0.12, and the weight of influenza and obesity can be used as 0.1, 0.01 and 0.02 to indicate disease. The respiratory disease weight is 0.31, the weight of AIDS, breast cancer and lung cancer are 0.93, 0.92 and 0.91. Different diseases shall not have the same disease weight values. Thus, the sensitivity matrix can be expressed as:

$$M\,|S = (t_{ij}|b_i)_{9\times(5+1)} = \begin{bmatrix} \text{race} & \text{occupation} & \text{Birth} & \text{Sex} & \text{ZIP} & \text{Disease} \\ 0 & 0 & 0 & 0.2 & 0.8 & 0.11 \\ 0 & 0.1 & 0.4 & 1 & 0 & 0.92 \\ 0 & 0.1 & 0.4 & 1 & 0 & 0.92 \end{bmatrix}$$

3.3 Overview of Feature Correlation Algorithm

3.3.1 Overview of Correlation Rule

Feature rule was proposed by Agrawal et al. in 1993, mainly to excavate the correlation between data. Suppose that the set of data items is A, the task set of database events is B, and each event I is the set of all A, then there is an identifier in the event of $I \subseteq A$, which is indicated by IAB. Suppose M is a subset of A, if I contains M, if and only if $M \subseteq I$. In this case, the correlation rule can be expressed as a form similar to $M \Longrightarrow N$, where $M \subset A, N \subset A$, and $M \cap N = \emptyset$.

The correlation rules of $M \Longrightarrow N$ can be quantified by the following two methods: support level (percentage of B contains both M and N at the same time, which is an evaluation of importance) and confidence level (percentage of B contains N while containing M, which is an evaluation of accuracy). Among them, the support level is s (M ∪ N), and the confidence level is C (N|M) = s (M ∪ N) * s (M).

A well-known story of correlation feature is "diapers and beer". This story shows that putting diapers and beer together will greatly increase the turnover of supermarkets. This is because men will buy beer for themselves when they buy diapers for their children after work, so putting diapers and beer together will increase the probability of purchasing. This is the reflection of the correlation feature. For example, taking diapers and beer as examples, the following table shows the categories of commodities, and the correlation rule is $X \Longrightarrow y$ (Table 1).

If the correlation rule is: {milk, diapers} $\Longrightarrow$ beer, then, the support level is:

$$s = \frac{\sigma(X \cup y)}{|T|} (s = P(X, y))$$

The confidence level is

$$c = \frac{\sigma(X \cup y)}{\sigma(X)} (c = P(y|X))$$

Table 1. Commodity list

No.	Category
1	Bread, milk
2	Bread, diapers, beer, eggs
3	Milk, diapers, beer, coke
4	Bread, milk, diapers, beer
5	Bread, milk, beer, coke

3.3.2 Feature Selection Algorithm Based on Correlation Rules

In recent years, feature selection algorithm has attracted widespread concern, especially in the field of pattern recognition and data mining. Many researchers have fully studied the feature algorithm, but the feature selection algorithm based on correlation rules is relatively rare. The research based on correlation rules can find the correlation between data items, and make full use of the association between attributes by selecting the best rules for the data.

The algorithm consists of three steps, including generating rule set, constructing attribute set and testing attribute set.

Step 1: Generate rule set: firstly, the training set is generated into a rule set, if necessary, the continuous attributes of non-class attributes are discretized, and then the rules selected from the rule set as class attributes are calculated to generate effective rule sets, and the support level and confidence level of the new rule set are calculated.

Step 2: Construct the attribute set. On the basis of the rule set generated in step 1, select the number of iterations to generate the attribute set.

Step 3: Test the attribute set. The generated attribute set needs to be evaluated to show the effectiveness of the feature selection algorithm based on correlation rules. The dataset is classified by the classifier, and the classification accuracy is given to evaluate the advantages and disadvantages of feature selection.

3.3.3 Rule Tree

Feature selection has always been a pattern recognition and an active research field in statistical and data mining aspects. The most important thought of feature selection is to select a subset of input variables through eliminating features with little or no prediction information. Feature selection can obviously enhance the comprehensibility of the classifier model, and usually establish a model that can be better extended to invisible points. In addition, under normal conditions, discovering the correct subset of prediction feature itself is a critical problem [13].

Rule tree is introduced in this paper. The domain general hierarchy is a tree. The root node of the tree is the value of D_n, and the leaf node is the set of values of D_1. The edge from v_i to v_j ($i < j$) indicates that v_j is a generalization of v_i, in which $v_i \in D_i$, $v_j \in D_j$.

3.4 Anonymization

Definition 4. RSLK anonymity. T $(a_1,\ldots, a_n)$ is a table if T satisfies K anonymous data stream on sliding window and the following conditions are satisfied:

(1) In FS (g), $\forall b_i < c$, all tuples in FS (g) are output directly. Otherwise, condition (2) and condition (3) must be met. Here, the threshold $c > 0$, b_i is the s column vector in the MIS, FS (g) is the buffer area of g, and $1 \le i \le |FS(g)|$, $|FS(g)| \ge k$.

(2) $L = \sum\limits_{j=1,\ldots,|FS(g)|} count(|b_i, b_j| > 0)$, $1 \le i \le |FS(g)|$, the count b_i, b_j is the s column vector in the MIS, L is the number of different sensitive attribute values, which represents the sensitive attribute diversity.

(3) If in the count matrix MIS, $P = count(|MAX_{i=1,\ldots}|FS(g)|t_{ik}| = 1) > 0$, when t_{ik} is generated, the generalized hierarchy is promoted to the parent node or suppressed directly under the premise of anonymity.

4 RSLK Anonymous Algorithm

RSLK Anonymous Algorithm is described in details as follows.

Input: Flow s, rule tree S-Tree, relationship and sensitivity level matrix MIS based on background knowledge, threshold value c, parameter k of k anonymity.

Output: Anonymous tuples.

1. While (true)
2. Read a new tuple t from S;
3. According to $P > 0$, search S-Tree from root to node g, which is the most specific node containing t;
4. If (g. disease $< C$, G is the work node, L > 0)
5. Anonymize tuple t with g and output it;
6. else
7. Insert t into the buffer area FS(g) of G;
8. if (L > 0 and FS (g) satisfies k-anonymity)
9. Anonymize and output FS(g)with g;
10. Mark g as work node;
11. end if
12. end if
13. end while

In RSLK-anonymity algorithm, the nodes of rule tree are divided into 2 categories as candidate node and work node [2]. Candidate nodes do not meet the requirements of K anonymity. The work node satisfies the k-anonymity features. Each candidate node g is allocated with a buffer FS (g) as a holding area.

While the new tuple t reaches sliding window, RSLK-anonymous algorithm searches the specialized tree to determine the most specific generalized node g containing t based on P > 0. If g is a work node, the tuple t is anonymized with g based on g.disease < c and L > 0, which ensures the diversity of "diseases" of sensitive attributes and outputs them immediately. Otherwise, g is a candidate node, and t is stored in FS (g) until FS (g) meet the requirements of k-anonymity of definition 2, then output all tuples in FS (g), and candidate node g will become a working node.

5 Experiment Result

This experiment is performed on a PC (Windows 10, Intel Core i5 2.4 GHz CPU)and 4 GB main memory. The algorithm is implemented in Visual C++ 6.0. Each experiment was tested 10 times, and the average value of ten experiments was obtained.

In the experiment, adult census data sets from UC Irvine machine learning repository are used [14, 15]. The database has been used by many researchers and has become a benchmark in the field of data privacy. The race, occupation, age, gender and ZIP of adults are regarded as quasi identifier (QI), and the "disease" column is added as the sensitive attribute composed of {influenza, lung cancer, shortness of breath, obesity, breast cancer, AIDS}.

10000 tuples were randomly selected from adults as sliding window, and disease values were randomly assigned to each tuple based on basic medical knowledge.

5.1 Effective Time

Figure 2 shows the advantages of RSLK anonymous algorithm. The algorithm makes data publishing available and efficient by using c (the weight of sensitive attributes). From the experimental diagram, we can see that the larger the value of c, the more effective the running time is. This is because c represents the weight of sensitive attributes, and the data is anonymous through tuples, which can ensure the effective output of data and efficient and useful.

5.2 Running Time

As shown in Fig. 3, the running time increases with tuples numbers in the sliding window, since more time is needed by the algorithm to calculate and search tuples in the rule tree satisfying the anonymity condition. Because the computation level of tuples satisfying the anonymity condition increases, the running time increases with the increase of k value.

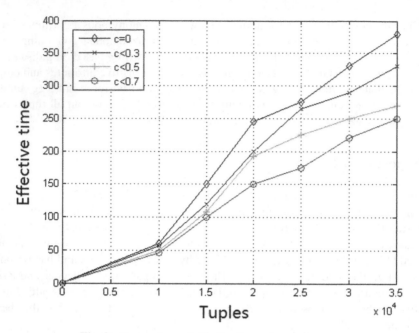

Fig. 2. Comparison of effective time when c changes

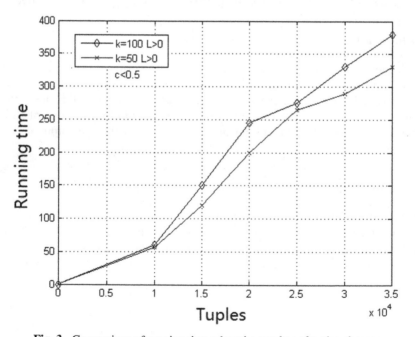

Fig. 3. Comparison of running time when the number of tuples changes

6 Conclusion

The main contribution of this paper is to put forward RSLK anonymity algorithm to avoid privacy leakage when stream data is published. The main thought is to anonymously process the background knowledge of stream data set in sliding window based on relation and sensitivity matrix. It can effectively defense the background knowledge attack and homogeneity attack in the process of stream data output, and solve the diversity of sensitive attributes. It's shown in the experimental results that RSLK algorithm is practical, effective and efficient, and its performance is better than that of k anonymous algorithm.

Acknowledgement. This paper is supported by the science and technology project of State Grid Corporation of China: "Research and Application of Key Technology of Data Sharing and Distribution Security for Data Center" (Grand No. 5700-202090192A-0-0-00).

References

1. Samarati, P., Sweeney, L.: Generalizing data to provide anonymity when disclosing information. In: Proceedings of the Seventeenth ACM SIGACT-SIGMOD-SIGART Symposium on Principles of Database Systems, p. 188 (1998)
2. Li, J., Ooi, B.C., Wang, W.: Anonymizing Streaming Data for Privacy Protection (2008)
3. Wang, W., Li, J.: Privacy protection on sliding window of data streams, Collaborative Computing: Networking, Applications and Worksharing, 12–15 November 2012, pp. 213–221 (2012)
4. Zhang, J., Jing, Y., Zhang, J., et al.: An improved RSLK-anonymity algorithm for privacy protection of data stream. Int. J. Adv. Comput. Technol. 4(9), 218–225 (2012)
5. Cao, J., Carminati, B., Ferrari, E., et al.: CASTLE: continuously anonymizing data streams. IEEE Trans. Dependable Secure Comput. 8(3), 337–352 (2011)
6. Cao, J., Carminati, B., Ferrari, E., et al.: CASTLE: A delay-constrained scheme for ks-anonymizing data streams. In: IEEE International Conference on Data Engineering. IEEE (2008)
7. Zakerzadeh, H., Osborn, S.L.: FAANST: fast anonymizing algorithm for numerical streaming DaTa. In: Garcia-Alfaro, J., Navarro-Arribas, G., Cavalli, A., Leneutre, J. (eds.) Data Privacy Management and Autonomous Spontaneous Security. Springer, Heidelberg (2011). https://doi.org/10.1007/978-3-642-19348-4_4
8. Yang, G., Yang, J., Zhang, J., et al.: Research on data streams publishing of privacy preserving. In: IEEE International Conference on Information Theory & Information Security. IEEE (2015)
9. Ren, X., Yang, et al.: Research on CBK (L, K)-anonymity algorithm. Int. J. Adv. Comput. Technol. (2011)
10. Machanavajjhala, A., Gehrke, J., Kifer, D., et al.: ℓ-diversity: Privacy beyond k-anonymity. In: Proceedings of the 22nd International Conference on Data Engineering, ICDE 2006, 3–8 April 2006, Atlanta, GA, USA. IEEE (2006)
11. Sun, X., Wang, H., Li, J., et al.: (p+, α)-sensitive k-anonymity: a new enhanced privacy protection model. In: IEEE International Conference on Computer & Information Technology. IEEE (2014)
12. Tai-Yong, L.I., Chang-Jie, T., Jiang, W.U., et al.: k-anonymity via twice clustering for privacy preservation. J. Jilin Univ. 27(02) (2009)

13. Chen, X., Wu, X., Wang, W., et al.: An improved initial cluster centers selection algorithm for K-means based on features correlative degree. Adv. Eng. Sci. **047**(001), 13–19 (2015)
14. Hong-Wei, L., Guo-Hua, L.: (L, K)-anonymity based on clustering. J. Yanshan Univ. (2007)
15. Chen, C.Y., Li, S.A., et al.: A clustering-based algorithm to extracting fuzzy rules for system modeling. Int. J. Adv. Comput. Technol. (2016)

The Privacy Data Protection Model Based on Random Projection Technology

Wen Shen[1,2(✉)], Qian Guo[1,2], Hui Zhu[3], Kejian Tang[4], Shaohui Zhan[4], and Zhiguo Hao[5]

[1] Global Energy Interconnection Research Institute Co., Ltd., Nanjing 210003, China
shenwen@geiri.sgcc.com.cn
[2] State Grid Key Laboratory of Information & Network Security, Nanjing 210003, China
[3] State Grid Financial Technology Group, Xiongan 071000, China
[4] State Grid Jiangxi Electric Power Co., Ltd., Nanchang 330000, China
[5] Xingtai Huancheng Power Supply Branch of State Grid Hebei Electric Power Co., Ltd., Xingtai 054000, China

Abstract. In general, as the technology developed, big data analysis provides opportunities to reduce the implementation time and budget. Compared with traditional methods, big data analysis has a greater advantage. It seeks to establish a privacy framework consistent with the factors and measures of mutual understanding in the context of random projection technology. Privacy concerns and perceived benefits have proven to greatly influence personal data protection. The success of stochastic projection techniques depends on voter privacy and personal data protection needs being met. It explores independent component analysis as a possible tool for breaking privacy with deterministic multiplicative perturbation-based models, for example: random orthogonal transformations and random rotations. An approach based on approximate random projection is then proposed that improves privacy protection while maintaining certain date statistical characteristics.

Keywords: Personal data protection · Privacy framework · Random projection technology

1 Introduction

Over the years, the way that ideal personal privacy data protection is used to vote on personal privacy data protection systems has undergone major changes. There are four properties: anonymity, speed, scalability and accuracy [1, 2]. Therefore, all personal privacy data protection involves some way to convert the intent of the voter, many of them multiple times, and errors will accumulate in each conversion step [3–5]. Paper privacy data protection or optical scanning has been used in personal privacy data protection for about two decades because the system requires voters to record privacy data protection on paper privacy data protection and then insert the privacy data protection into the scanner [6, 7]. People still face many challenges in computing devices and virtual world, which

© Springer Nature Singapore Pte Ltd. 2021
Y. Tian et al. (Eds.): ICBDS 2020, CCIS 1415, pp. 215–226, 2021.
https://doi.org/10.1007/978-981-16-3150-4_19

also requires them to understand and determine a series of new boundaries in order to negotiate privacy in the spaces. Facts have proved that the interaction perspective is particularly effective for theoretical and empirical research on privacy related to the daily use of information technology, especially privacy issues related to social media and rapidly changing technologies [8, 9]. Although this view has proved to be memorable, there are still unresolved questions about how to turn the results of this view into the practice of design [10].

For lots of data mining applications, involving medical, security, finance, behavior, and other sensitive data, privacy has become an increasingly important issue. This is particularly important in the applications of anti-terrorism and homeland defense. They may need to create configuration files, build social network models, and detect terrorist communications from privacy-sensitive data. For example, the analysis of clinical records and pharmacy transaction data for certain off-the-shelf drugs may be needed to detect bioterrorism. But combining various data sets owned by different parties may contravene privacy laws. Although WHO can publish data after the identifier (e.g., name, SSN, address, etc.) is removed, a reconstruction attack can be constructed to link multiple public data sets to identify the data. As such, it is not considered secure enough. Particular care should be taken to hide privacy-sensitive data while retaining the inherent statistical dependencies that are significant to data mining applications.

Practical solutions include guidelines for designing to avoid privacy intrusions (design for understanding privacy), privacy management mechanisms (privacy enhancement and disclosure control), privacy implications and assessment of information systems (privacy impact assessment), and interpersonal privacy practice assistance. With random projection technology, many studies have focused on practical solutions to provide appropriate mechanisms to strengthen privacy protection in certain situations, but there are few advantages of management. Most of the personal privacy data protection fraud may be Occurred due to external reports of technical issues. In fact, the theory does not necessarily have to remain the same in different situations or participants, and it is highly likely to consider similar relationships and interactions that may be interdependent and complementary, such as interrelated threads, in the wrong direction. Therefore, this paper studies the privacy framework in terms of management, technology, and law enforcement to support personal data protection in random projection technology.

2 Random Projection Technology

For decades, the Internet appeared in daily life for a variety of purposes, many scholars have studied the social psychology aspects of random projection technique (RPT). A concern is that due to the lack of non-verbal clues, immature etiquette and depersonalization process, RPT is an inappropriate way for people to share emotional content, not to mention the development of meaningful and lasting relationships to the social norms of decision-making influences. At the same time, others described RPT as a clue filtering theory, also known as streamlining clues. It believed that the social presence of computers was low because computers screened out significant aspects of communication that face-to-face participants were unwilling to communicate (sub-tone, Intensity, pressure, rhythm, volume), so that the conversation is in a social vacuum. The self-regulatory policies of various countries require consumers to take responsibility and take part in the privacy and security procedure and reflect their appropriate behavior. They support consumers trying to understand online security and privacy risks. These issues involve what is happening with personal data, which tools can be used to protect the data, and how to deal with them. Therefore, to make consumers aware of this or to learn such complex skills to adapt to changes in technology development, it will take lots of time and effort to educate. Therefore, electronic social support needs to make some changes in the provision of these functions. At the same time, Kosa mentioned that trust is positively related to privacy, while privacy is negatively related to trust.

The random projection technique performs the Charnes-Cooper transformation and takes its dual programming, while introducing the non-Archimedean infinitesimal ε, the evaluation model can be obtained.

$$
\begin{cases}
\min V_D = \left[\theta - \varepsilon \left(e^T s^- + e^T s^+ \right) \right] \\
s.t. \sum_{j=1}^{n} x_j \lambda_j + s^- = \theta x_0 \\
\sum_{j=1}^{n} x_j \lambda_j - s^+ = y_0 \\
\lambda_j \geq 0 (j = 1, 2, \cdots, n), s^+, s^- \geq 0
\end{cases}
\tag{1}
$$

$e^T = (1, 1, \cdots, 1)$ Is an m-dimensional vector with elements of $1, x_{ij}, y_{rj} > 0$ Is a p-dimensional vector with all elements 1. It is usually necessary to establish an evaluation model to better assess the technical effectiveness among different production departments. The model can be built as below:

$$
\begin{cases}
\min V_D = \left[\varphi - \varepsilon \left(e^T s^- + e^T s^+ \right) \right] \\
s.t. \sum_{j=1}^{n} x_j \lambda_j + s^- = \varphi x_0 \\
\sum_{j=1}^{n} x_j \lambda_j - s^+ = y_0 \\
\sum_{j=1}^{n} \lambda_j = 1 \\
\lambda_j \geq 0 (j = 1, 2, \cdots, n), s^+, s^- \geq 0
\end{cases}
\tag{2}
$$

The "projection" of the non-evaluated cases is analyzed and adjusted to obtain a (new) decision unit for the evaluated decision unit on the relatively valid side of the assessment. The formula is as below:

$$
\begin{cases}
x_0' = \theta^0 x_0 - x^{0-} \\
y_0' = y_0 + s^{0+}
\end{cases}
\tag{3}
$$

Among them, $\left(x_0', y_0'\right)$ It is the "projection" of (x0, y0) corresponding to the decision unit j0 on the evaluated relative effective surface.

According to Eq. (3), Adjustments can be obtained for the non-evaluation valid sectors, correcting for each input indicator while keeping the output volume constant.

3 Personal Privacy Data Protection Model

3.1 Secure Subspace Method

Based on random projection, the security subspace method proposes the concept of safe subspace. According to the privacy protection method, the leakage of the random projection matrix will cause the attacker to guess the original data, and then construct a random matrix that is not easy to launch. The constructed projection The transformation is also extremely safe. Through the low distortion embedding of the random projection itself, the original data spacing is effectively protected, and the internal machine data is effectively converted. After obtaining the random projection matrix, the attacker can reconstruct the original data according to the sample data, using the underdetermined blind source separation method and the maximum posterior probability estimation, because only the converted data, the attacker can only use the projection matrix probability distribution Random guessing cannot get all the relevant information about the original data. Therefore, the possibility that the attacker knows the random projection matrix determines the data security. The direct storage of the projection matrix and the generation of the projection matrix by the explicit random number generation method will cause the risk of leaking the projection matrix data. After the random number generation method is determined, the same random matrix can be generated by finding the seed. The safe subspace method does not need to store the speculation matrix, only the random seed is used to generate the hash function family.

This principle represents a set of values that guide and govern specific social behaviors. Therefore, the law builds an obligation in the personal cognition, which is in the cultural field of accepting these values. It believes that individual freedom is the reason for acting without external coercion through the process of socialization, although the importance of principles is often overlooked. At the same time, reducing interpersonal communication will reduce the ability of candidates and voters to communicate, forcing them to rely on mass media as the main means of disseminating political information on election campaigns. In other words, as the population of the personal privacy data protection zone increases, the successful communication of problematic positions in the campaign is likely to decrease. The gap between principle and practice exists largely because politics is not conducted in a vacuum. The conflict of rights is not abstract but occurs in the crucible of policy choices. Intentional pain is usually considered a moral error, so clear moral reasons are needed. In the absence of sufficient reasons to punish individuals found guilty, all actors in the criminal justice system should be morally responsible. It can be said that enforcement of regulations does not necessarily encourage penalty, but it can pay more attention on crime prevention or deterrence, through intervening before security crimes (through training and education programs), and providing incentives (incentives, supplementary measures), Use logos, loose inspection) to companies participating in the program. Therefore, by providing legal aid, incentives, and support to food operators, the role of regulatory agencies has evolved in the direction of common regulation.

3.2 Random Orthogonal Transformation

This chapter introduces the deterministic multiplication perturbation method adopting a random orthogonal matrix when calculating the inner product matrix. Generally, a random projection matrix is used to better protect data privacy.

Orthogonal transformation [11] is linear R: $IR^n \rightarrow IR^n$, It preserves the vectors length and the angle between them. Let data set X and Y belong to Alice and Bob respectively. X is an m1 × n matrix, and Y is m2 × n. They both have the same attributes. R is a n × n random orthogonal matrix. Now, perform the following linear transformation on the two datasets:

$$U = XR$$
$$V = YR$$
$$UU^T = XX^T \tag{4}$$
$$VV^T = YY^T$$
$$UV^T = XRR^T Y^T = XY^T$$

Therefore, if both Alice and Bob use a secret orthogonal matrix to transform their data, and only release the disturbed version to a third party. All paired angles/distances between the row vectors in the data $\begin{pmatrix} X \\ Y \end{pmatrix}$ will be calculated, where $\begin{pmatrix} X \\ Y \end{pmatrix}$ is the horizontal concatenation of X and Y. Then, it is not difficult to conduct distance-based privacy protection data mining applications in third parties to achieve evenly distributed (horizontally divided) data. In the same way, if we use $U = XR$ and $V = YR$ to transform the data, we will get $U^T V = X^T Y$. And from the data $(X : Y)$ all pairwise distances and similarities between the column vectors are completely retained in the perturbed data, among which $(X : Y)$ represents the vertical series connection of X and Y. Thus, third parties can analyze the data attributes correlation from heterogeneous distribution (vertical partition) without access to the original data.

Because only when the transformed data is published, an infinite number of inputs and transformation processes can be used for output simulation, without the observer knowing the true form of the original data. Thus, random orthogonal transformations seem to be a good method to protect data privacy while retaining their utility. But from the viewpoint of geometric, orthogonal transformation is a pure rotation when the orthogonal matrix determinant is 1, or a rotation inversion (rotation followed by flip) when the orthogonal matrix determinant is −1. So the original data can be re-identified via appropriate rotation. Figure 1(a) and 1(b) show how the random orthogonal transform works in 3D space. The data is not well covered up after conversion. In view of this, the security of similar methods of protecting data privacy through random rotation is also questionable. In addition, statistically, if all the original data vectors are independent without following a Gaussian distribution, independent component analysis (ICA) can be adopted to estimate their original form fairly accurately. In the next section, we

will briefly study the properties of ICA, and then put forward a multiplicative perturbation technique on the basis of random projection to increase the privacy level while
maintaining the data usefulness.

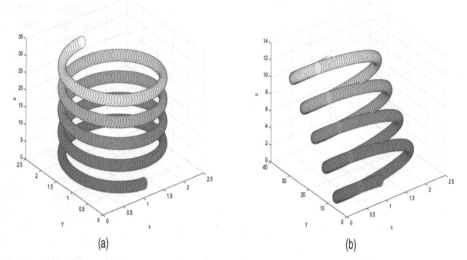

(a)   (b)

Fig. 1. (a) Sample data set. (b) Disturbance data after random orthogonal transformation.

4   Multiplicative Perturbation Technique Based on Random Projection

ICA [12] is a method to find independent hidden factors. These hidden factors are the
basis of linear or nonlinear mixing of some unknown variables, in which the mixed
system is also unknown. Assuming that these unknown variables are statistically independent and non-Gaussian, they can be defined as independent components (IC) of the
observed data. The IC can be discovered through ICA. The classic example of ICA is the
cocktail party problem (see Fig. 2). Suppose you are attending a cocktail party. Various
background sounds are mixed, such as other people's chats, music, TV news reports,
and even police sirens from passing ambulances, but you can still identify the neighbors'
discussion. It is not clear how the human brain separates different sound sources. But if
there are as many "ears" or receivers in the room as there are various sound sources at
the same time, ICA can do it. What the ear hears is a linear combination of two of the
four audio signals, i.e. four signals compressed into two.

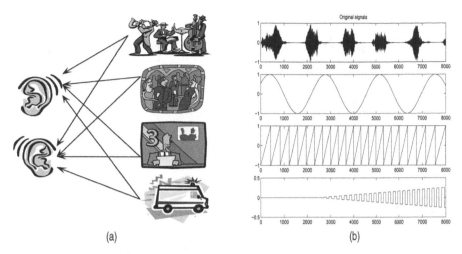

Fig. 2. Illustration of cocktail problem

4.1 ICA Model

The basic model of ICA can be built as below:

$$u(t) = Rx(t) \tag{5}$$

where $x(t) = (x1(t), x2(t), ..., xm(t))^T$ means collecting m-dimensional vector of m independent source signals $x_i(t), i = 1, 2, ..., m$, where t represents time dependence. Each signal $x_i(t)$ can be seen as the result of a random process with continuous values. R is an unknown mixed matrix with a constant k × m, which can be regarded as a hybrid system with k receivers. $u(t) = (u1(t), u2(t), ..., u_m(t))^T$ is the observed mixture. The purpose of ICA is designing a filter that can only recover the original signal from the observed mixture. For any diagonal matrix and permutation matrix P, because $u(t) = (u1(t), u2(t), ..., u_k(t))^T$ the recovered signal $x_i(t)$ can never have a completely unique representation. Therefore, the uniqueness of the recovered signal obtained by ICA can only be guaranteed after the ambiguity is replaced and scaled.

For example, consider four statistically independent audio signals, represented as a 4 × 8000 matrix X as displayed in Fig. 2(b). For simplicity, some signals are deterministic. But ICA usually uses a continuous value stochastic procedure. The linear mixture of these signals as displayed in Fig. 3(a) is produced by pre-multiplying a 4 × 4 non-singular random matrix by X. The ICA's goal is to restore the original signal only by the mixed signal. Figure 3(b) shows the estimated signal through ICA. The basic structure of the original signal has been well restored. But the order and amplitude of the restored signal are not necessarily the same as the original signal.

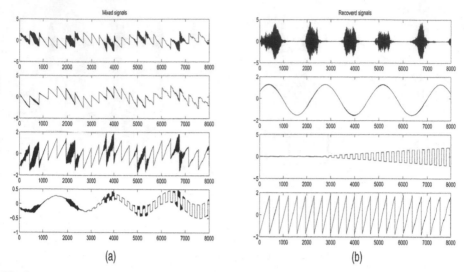

(a)   (b)

Fig. 3. (a) Use a square random matrix to linearly mix the original source signal. (b) Use ICA to restore the signal.

4.2 Decomposability

For k-dimensional input $u(t) = (u1(t), u2(t), ..., ul(t))^T$, Design a linear filter to obtain the recovered signal $y(t) = (y1(t), y2(t), ..., yl(t))^T$, which is

$$y(t) = Bu(t) \tag{6}$$

where B is the $l \times k$-dimensional separation matrix. By combining Eq. (5) and (6) together, you can get

$$y(t) = BRx(t) = Zx(t) \tag{7}$$

where $Z = BR$ is a $1 \times m$ matrix. Therefore, Each element of $y(t)$ is linear combination of $x_i(t)$, whose weight is determined by z_{ij}. When $k \geq m$ (i.e. the number of receivers is larger than or equal to the number of source signals), if the mixed matrix R has a complete column rank, there will always be a $l \times k$ separation matrix B such that $Z = BR = I$, where I is the identity matrix. Therefore, all signals will be restored up to scaling and displacement of ambiguities.

4.3 Multiplicative Disturbance Based on Random Projection

Generally speaking, the multiplicative perturbation technique based on random projection can ensure that the dimensionality and precise value of each element in the original data are kept secret. These properties are on the basis of the assumption that the data and random noise come from the continuous real domain, and all participants are semi-honest.

In this chapter, it is assumed that the adversary has a priori knowledge of different types of data and does not meet the basic assumptions of the technology. The more rigorous analysis on how much privacy the interference technology can retain is carried out.

Random projection means to project a set of data points from a high-dimensional space to a randomly selected low-dimensional subspace. The core idea of random projection comes from Johnson-Lindenstrauss Lemma [13]. This lemma indicates that any set of s points in m-dimensional Euclidean space can be embedded in $O(\frac{\log s}{\varepsilon^2})$ dimensional space. In this way, the paired distance of any two points is kept within an arbitrarily small factor. This means that the original data format can be changed by reducing the dimensionality of the data, while still maintaining its statistical properties. In this chapter, we will demonstrate how to use random matrices for this type of mapping. In order to better represent how the random projection method disturbs the data, we have performed row and column projections on the sample data given in Fig. 1(a). The results are displayed in Fig. 4(a) and 4(b). The original data structure has been greatly obscured. These attributes are very helpful for maintaining the utility of the data.

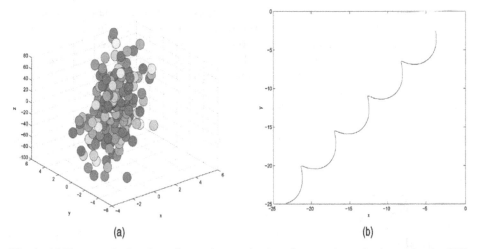

(a)   (b)

Fig. 4. (a) The perturbation data after random projection of rows reduces the data points by 50%. (b) Disturbance data after columnar random projection

5 Results and Analysis

5.1 The Influence of Safety Subspace on Inner Product and Euclidean Distance

The questionnaire consists of six parts, namely 11 multiple answer questions in demographics, 14, 15 and 13 questions of the three-part factor and one part of 15 result items, including Likert scale questions And comment section. In order to strengthen the reliability and effectiveness of the constructed instrument, the researchers evaluated each item in the questionnaire by two-stage pilot study, that is, pre-test (6 people) and post-test (44 people) that avoided time and budget Two stages. Convergence validity also shows

Table 1. Overview of latent variable quality

	AVE	Compound reliability	R square	Cronbachs Alpha	Community	Redundancy	LV Index value
LReg	0.530432	0.849415		0.778964	0.530432		4.951774
SNor	0.687876	0.815039		0.546706	0.687876		4.527046
TSol	0.520809	0.812888		0.694102	0.520809		4.944040
PBen	0.578391	0.872425	0.572917	0.816928	0.578391	0.046626	5.063385
PCon	0.586243	0.809292	0.489818	0.647314	0.586243	0.100488	4.932448
PDPro	0.554889	0.788709	0.469154	0.602740	0.554889	0.218820	5.016462

good results in the case where the AVE values of all constructs are greater than 0.50 and the minimum value of TSol is 0.521 (Table 1).

In this experiment, the arcane data set is selected. Because the matrix is randomly generated, the experiment is run about 10 times, and the average value of the error is selected. Under different projection dimensions, the relative error between the Euclidean distance and the inner product is shown in Fig. 1. The inner product and the Euclidean distance of the subspace is roughly equivalent to the Gaussian projection, and the larger the projection dimension, the closer the result is to the Gaussian projection, and the larger the projection dimension, the lower the relative error. If the projection dimension is 3000, then the relative error will be reduced by 0.2%. This fully shows that the safe subspace can ensure data availability within a reasonable and effective projection dimension (Fig. 5).

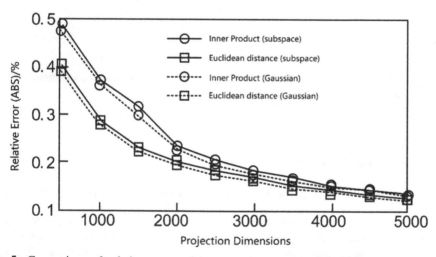

Fig. 5. Comparison of relative errors of inner product and Euclidean distance in different projection dimensions

5.2 Multiplicative Disturbance Analysis Based on Random Projection

Practically, considering the communication costs and security, a specific implementation of the random matrix R will always be adopted. Therefore, more about the distribution of $R^T R$ needs to be learned to quantify $R^T R$.

Suppose k × m items of random matrix R are selected from the Gaussian distribution whose mean value is zero and variance is σ_r^2. The statistical characteristics of the inner product estimation can be studied.

We select two randomly generated data sets from the uniform distribution of [0,1]. Each has 10,000 observations and 100 attributes. All attributes are normalized to be unified and the column inner products of the two data sets before and after row random projection are compared. Figure 6(a) shows the result, which describes that even at a data projection rate of 50% (when k = 5000), the inner product can still be well preserved after perturbation. The error is indeed close to the Gaussian distribution, with zero mean and variance that is slightly greater than 2/k. Figure 6(b) indicates the root mean square error (RMSE) of the estimated inner product matrix with respect to the dimension of the reduced subspace. As k increases, the error decreases exponentially, which represents that the higher the data dimensionality, the better the effect of this technique.

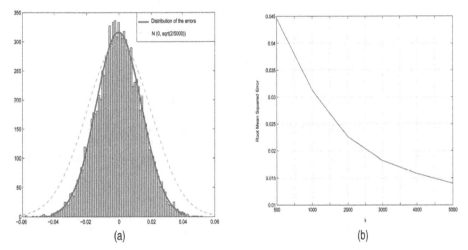

(a) (b)

Fig. 6. (a) The distribution of the error of the estimated inner product matrix on two distributed data sets; (b) The root mean square error (RMSE) of the estimated inner product matrix relative to the reduced subspace dimension

6 Conclusion

In the protection of personal privacy data, from a user's perspective through a survey, the legal framework is not enough to effectively regulate the development and use of voting machines, especially in terms of security, authentication processes and tabulation software. In addition, they also said that without a strong regulatory framework, suppliers have failed to update technology in accordance with modern security requirements, making voting machines vulnerable to internal and external security threats. In general, many studies have shown that information system project management still shows a high failure rate, which is mainly related to the uncertainty of legal concepts and the lack of focus on policies. Through recognizing the benefits of IT governance and investment are critical to competitive advantage and reduce the IT projects failure rate.

Acknowledgement. The work in this paper is supported by the science and technology project of State Grid Corporation of China: "Research on credit and digital finance supporting technology based on power big data" (Grand No.5700-202072180A-0-0-00).

References

1. Conti, A., Delbon, P., Laffranchi, L., Paganelli, C., De. Ferrari, F.: Hiv-positive status and preservation of privacy: a recent decision from the italian data protection authority on the procedure of gathering personal patient data in the dental office. J. Med. Ethics **38**(6), 386–388 (2012)
2. Ming, H., Guohua, C., Wenhui, L., et al.: Research on cloud data storage security and privacy protection strategies in the Internet of Things environment. Comput. Sci. **039**(005), 62–65 (2012)
3. Jiang, L., Guo, D.: Dynamic encrypted data sharing scheme based on conditional proxy broadcast re-encryption for cloud storage. IEEE Access 1 (2017)
4. Yahui, L., Tieying, Z., Xiaolong, J., et al.: Personal privacy protection in the era of big data. Comput. Res. Dev. **52**(1), 229–247 (2015)
5. Tchernykh, A., Babenko, M., Chervyakov, N., et al.: AC-RRNS: anti-collusion secured data sharing scheme for cloud storage. Int. J. Approx. Reason. 102, 60–73 (2018)
6. Halik, U., Smaczyński, M.: Geovisualisation of relief in a virtual reality system on the basis of low-level aerial imagery. Pure Appl. Geophys. **175**(9), 3209–3221 (2018)
7. Lan Lihui, J., Shiguang, J.H., et al.: A review of privacy protection research in data publishing. Comput. Appl. Res. **08**, 28–33 (2010)
8. Xinling, T., Zhixiao, H.: The paradox of "public data opening" and "personal privacy protection." News Univ. **6**, 55–61 (2014)
9. Liu, C., Ranjan, R., Yang, C., et al.: MuR-DPA: top-down levelled multi-replica merkle hash tree based secure public auditing for dynamic big data storage on cloud. IEEE Trans. Comput. **64**(9), 2609–2622 (2015)
10. Xuehui, W., Xin, Z.: Exploration on the integration and protection of public-private law of privacy rights—from the perspective of "big data era" personal information privacy. Hebei Law **5**, 63–71 (2015)
11. None: On the orthogonal transformation used for structural comparisons. Acta Crystallograph. Sec. A Found. Crystallography **45**(2), 208–210 (2010)
12. Comon, P.: Independent component analysis, a new concept?. Signal Process. **36**(3), 287–314 (1994)
13. Johnson, W.: Extensions of lipshitz mapping into hilbert space. Contemporary Math. p. 26 (1984)

Event-Driven H_∞ Control for Networked Control Systems with Random Actuator Nonlinearity

Liuwen Li[1], Wenlin Zou[2(✉)], and Haiqiang Liu[1]

[1] School of Computer Engineering, Jinling Institute of Technology, Nanjing 211169, China
[2] School of Information Engineering, Nanjing Xiaozhuang University, Nanjing 210017, China
zouwenlin123@njxzc.edu.cn

Abstract. The event-based H_∞ control problem of the networked control system is studied, which is under the constraint of stochastic actuators nonlinearity. Under event-triggered scheme and stochastic actuator nonlinearity restricted condition, a closed-loop system is constructed as a event-based nonlinear control system. Based on Lyapunov-Krasovskii function method and the stochastic analysis technology, H_∞ sufficient conditions have gained in the form of LMIs. The controller and the event-based weighted matrix are designed simultaneously. A simulation example is given to show the feasibility of the control method in this paper.

Keywords: Actuator nonlinearity · Event-driven · Networked control system

1 Introduction

Due to the advantages of reducing transmission frequency and saving limited network resources, event-driven mechanism has been widely studied recently. Different from the traditional time-triggered mechanism, the discrete event-triggered mechanism proposed in reference [1] can effectively reduce the transmission frequency of unnecessary signals and realize the joint design of event trigger and controller. As regards event-driven control, chaos synchronization, filtering or state estimation, many scholars at home and abroad have carried out in-depth research on various types of control systems, such as neutral systems, Markov systems [2], singular systems [3], fuzzy systems [4], neural networks, multi-agent systems [5].

Nonlinearity phenomena usually occur during the operation of actuators. For example, there is gap effect in gear coupling during transmission [6], dead zone effect in various amplifiers in high-speed motors and precision electronic circuits [7], dynamic friction when mechanical mechanisms are in contact with each other and move relatively [8], and complex hysteresis nonlinearity often exists in drivers composed of intelligent materials such as piezoelectric ceramics [9]. When the control signal passes through the nonlinear

Supported by Natural Science Foundation of China (No. 61976118), and Doctoral/High-level Talents Research Foundation of Jinling Institute of Technology (No. jit-b-202043).

link of the actuator, the output signal usually cannot be directly measured and has non-smooth characteristics, which will lead to fluctuations, oscillations and even instability of the controlled plant under the action of the control input with unknown variations [10], bringing great negative effects to the performance of the controlled system.

The main contributions of this paper can be summarized as the following aspects. (1) Under event-triggered mechanism and actuators stochastic nonlinearity restricted condition, a controlled system is modeled as a event-based control system with nonlinear items; (2) By using Lyapunov-Krasovskii function approach and the stochastic analysis technology, the controller and the event-driven weighted matrix can be co-designed.

2   System Description

Consider the linear networked control system as follows:

$$
\begin{cases}
\dot{x}(t) = Ax(t) + Bu(t) + G\omega(t) \\
z(t) = Cx(t) + Eu(t) + F\omega(t) \\
x(t_0) = x_0
\end{cases}
\tag{1}
$$

in which $u(t) \in \mathbb{R}^m$, $x(t) \in \mathbb{R}^n$, $z(t) \in \mathbb{R}^p$ and $\omega(t) \in \mathcal{L}_2[0, \infty)$ are the control input, state vector, control output and disturbance input, respectively. A, B, C, E, G and F are system parameter matrices, and $x_0 \in \mathbb{R}^n$ is the initial condition at initial time t_0.

We first consider H_∞ asymptotic stability under the disturbance attenuation index γ, and then study the controller design problem.

To reduce the frequency of information transmission, we introduce the event-driven mechanism to the control system. The event-driven mechanism is constructed between the controller and sensor. Predefine the following event-driven condition [1]:

$$
\|\Omega^{\frac{1}{2}} [(x(t_k h + lh)) - x(t_k h)]\|_2 \leq \rho \|\Omega^{\frac{1}{2}} x(t_k h + lh)\|_2
\tag{2}
$$

where Ω is a positive definite matrix, and $\rho \in (0, 1)$ is a constant. $lh, t_k h$ are the sampling instant and the trigger instant, respectively. The latest sampled signal $x(t_k h + lh)$ will be sent to the controller on condition that the condition (2) is violated. Denote $e_k(t) = x(t_k h) - x(t_k h + lh), t \in [t_k, t_{k+1})_{k=0}^\infty$, and $\tau(t) = t - t_k h - lh, l = 0, 1, 2, \cdots$. Suppose $\tau(t) \in [0, \tau_M)$, where τ_M is a positive numbers. The trigger condition (2) can be rewritten as follows:

$$
e_k^T(t)\Omega e_k(t) \leq \rho x^T(t - \tau(t)\Omega x(t - \tau(t))
\tag{3}
$$

The transmitted state signal of the system is as follows:

$$
\overline{x}(t) = x(t_k h) = x(t - \tau(t)) + e_k(t)
\tag{4}
$$

Design the controller as follows:

$$
u(t) = K\overline{x}(t) = Kx(t_k h) = K(x(t - \tau(t)) + e_k(t))
\tag{5}
$$

Random nonlinearity usually occurs in the process of actuator operation. When the control signal passes through the nonlinear link of the actuator, output signals are usually not directly measurable, and it will cause fluctuation and even instability of the controlled system under the action of unknown distortion control input.

Assumption 1. The nonlinear function $g(u(t))$ satisfies constraints as follows:

$$\|g(u(t))\|_2 \leq \|Wu(t)\|_2 \tag{6}$$

where W is that upper bound of a nonlinear function and is a constant matrix. Considering the random nonlinearity of the actuator, the control input (5) can be rewritten as

$$\widetilde{u}(t) = \alpha(t)u(t) + (1 - \alpha(t))g(u(t)) \tag{7}$$

where $\alpha(t)$ is a white sequence which obeys Bernoulli distribution, and its value is 0 or 1, and satisfies the following distribution characteristics:

$$P\{\alpha(t) = 1\} = \alpha_0, \ P\{\alpha(t) = 0\} = 1 - \alpha_0 \tag{8}$$

$$\mathbb{E}\{\alpha(t)\} = \alpha_0, \quad \mathbb{E}\{(\alpha(t) - \alpha_0)^2\} = \alpha_0(1 - \alpha_0) \tag{9}$$

According to (5) and (7), the system (1) can be rewritten as follows:

$$\begin{cases} \dot{x}(t) = Ax(t) + \alpha(t)BKx(t - \tau(t)) + \alpha(t)BKe_k(t) + (1 - \alpha(t))Bg(\widetilde{u}(t)) + G\omega(t) \\ z(t) = Cx(t) + \alpha(t)EKx(t - \tau(t)) + \alpha(t)EKe_k(t) + (1 - \alpha(t))Eg(\widetilde{u}(t)) + F\omega(t) \end{cases} \tag{10}$$

3 H_∞ Control Performance Analysis

Theorem 1. *For prescribed scalars $\rho \in [0, 1)$, $\gamma > 0$, $\tau_M > 0$ and the controller K, the system (10) with random actuator nonlinearity is mean square stable with the event-driven mechanism (2), if there exist positive definite matrices P, Q, R, Ω, and matrices S, U satisfying the following matrix inequalities:*

$$\Sigma(s) \overset{\Delta}{=} \begin{bmatrix} \Sigma_{11} + \Gamma + \Gamma^T & * & * & * & * & * & * & * \\ \Sigma_{21} & -\gamma^2 I & * & * & * & * & * & * \\ \mathcal{G}^s & 0 & -R & * & * & * & * & * \\ \mathcal{A}_1 & \sqrt{\tau_M}G & 0 & -R^{-1} & * & * & * & * \\ \mathcal{A}_2 & 0 & 0 & 0 & -R^{-1} & * & * & * \\ \Sigma_{61} & 0 & 0 & 0 & 0 & -I & * & * \\ \Sigma_{71} & 0 & 0 & 0 & 0 & 0 & -\Omega & * \\ \mathcal{B} & F & 0 & 0 & 0 & 0 & 0 & -I \end{bmatrix} < 0, \quad s = 1, 2 \tag{11}$$

where

$$\Sigma_{11} = \begin{bmatrix} PA + A^T P + Q & * & * & * & * \\ \alpha_0 K^T B^T P & 0 & * & * & * \\ 0 & 0 & -Q & * & * \\ \alpha_0 K^T B^T P & 0 & 0 & -\Omega & * \\ (1 - \alpha_0)B^T P & 0 & 0 & 0 & -I \end{bmatrix}$$

$$\Sigma_{21} = \begin{bmatrix} G^T P\, 0\, 0\, 0\, 0 \end{bmatrix}$$
$$G^1 = \sqrt{\tau_M} S^T, \quad G^2 = \sqrt{\tau_M} U^T$$
$$\Gamma = \begin{bmatrix} S\ U - S\ -U\ 0\ 0 \end{bmatrix}$$
$$\mathcal{A}_1 = \sqrt{\tau_M} \begin{bmatrix} A\ \alpha_0 BK\ 0\ \alpha_0 BK\ (1 - \alpha_0)B \end{bmatrix}$$
$$\mathcal{A}_2 = \sqrt{\tau_M \alpha_0 (1 - \alpha_0)} \begin{bmatrix} 0\ BK\ 0\ BK\ -B \end{bmatrix}$$
$$\Sigma_{61} = \begin{bmatrix} 0\ WK\ 0\ WK\ 0 \end{bmatrix}$$
$$\Sigma_{71} = \begin{bmatrix} 0\ \sqrt{\rho}\Omega\, 0\, 0\, 0 \end{bmatrix}$$
$$\mathcal{B} = \begin{bmatrix} C\ \alpha_0 EK\ 0\ \alpha_0 EK\ (1 - \alpha_0)E \end{bmatrix}$$

Proof. In order to prove that the system (11) is mean square asymptotically stable when $\omega(t) = 0$, choose the following Lyapunov-Krasovskii functional as

$$V(t) = x^T(t)Px(t) + \int_{t-\tau_M}^{t} x^T(s)Qx(s)ds + \int_{t-\tau_M}^{t} \int_{s}^{t} \dot{x}^T(v)R\dot{x}(v)dvds \qquad (12)$$

in which $P > 0$, $Q > 0$ and $R > 0$. Calculating the infinitesimal operator of $V(t)$ and calculating its expectation along the trajectory of system (10) as follows:

$$\mathbb{E}\{\mathcal{L}(V(t))\} = 2x^T(t)P[Ax(t) + \alpha_0 BKx(t - \tau(t)) + \alpha_0 BKe_k(t) \\
+ (1 - \alpha_0)Bg(\overline{u}(t))] + x^T(t)Qx(t) - x^T(t - \tau_M)Qx(t - \tau_M) \qquad (13) \\
+ \{\dot{x}^T(t)(\tau_M R)\dot{x}(t)\} - \int_{t-\tau_M}^{t} \dot{x}^T(s)R\dot{x}(s)ds + \Upsilon_1 + \Upsilon_2$$

where Υ_1 and Υ_2 are introduced by using free weight matrix method

$$\Upsilon_1 = 2\eta^T(t)S \left[x(t) - x(t - \tau(t)) - \int_{t-\tau(t)}^{t} \dot{x}(s)ds \right] = 0 \qquad (14)$$

$$\Upsilon_2 = 2\eta^T(t)U \left[x(t - \tau(t)) - x(t - \tau_M) - \int_{t-\tau_M}^{t-\tau(t)} \dot{x}(s)ds \right] = 0 \qquad (15)$$

Set

$$\eta^T(t) = \left[x^T(t)\ x^T(t - \tau(t))\ x^T(t - \tau_M)\ e_k^T(t)\ \xi^T(\overline{u}(t)) \right]$$

we can derive

$$- 2\eta^T(t)S \int_{t-\tau(t)}^{t} \dot{x}(s)ds \leq \tau(t)\eta^T(t)S R^{-1} S^T \eta(t) + \int_{t-\tau(t)}^{t} \dot{x}^T(s)R\dot{x}(s)ds \qquad (16)$$

$$-2\eta^T(t)U \int_{t-\tau_M}^{t-\tau(t)} \dot{x}(s)ds \leq (\tau_M - \tau(t))\eta^T(t)UR^{-1}U^T\eta(t) + \int_{t-\tau_M}^{t-\tau(t)} \dot{x}^T(s)R\dot{x}(s)ds \qquad (17)$$

By using (16–17), we can derive

$$- \int_{t-\tau_M}^{t} \dot{x}^T(s)R\dot{x}(s)ds \leq 2\eta^T(t)U\left[x(t - \tau(t)) - x(t - \tau_M)\right] \\
+ 2\eta^T(t)S\left[x(t) - x(t - \tau(t))\right] + \tau(t)\eta^T(t)S R^{-1} S^T \eta(t) \\
+ (\tau_M - \tau(t))\eta^T(t)UR^{-1}U^T\eta(t) \qquad (18)$$

Rewrite $\mathbb{E}\{\dot{x}^T(t)(\tau_M R)\dot{x}(t)\}$ as follows:

$$
\begin{aligned}
\mathbb{E}\{\dot{x}^T(t)(\tau_M R)\dot{x}(t)\} = &[Ax(t) + \alpha_0 BKx(t - \tau(t)) + \alpha_0 BKe_k(t) \\
&+ (1 - \alpha_0)Bg(\widetilde{u}(t))]^T(\tau_M R)[Ax(t) + \alpha_0 BKx(t - \tau(t)) + \alpha_0 BKe_k(t) \\
&+ (1 - \alpha_0)Bg(\widetilde{u}(t))] + \alpha_0(1 - \alpha_0)[BKx(t - \tau(t)) \\
&+ BKe_k(t) - Bg(\widetilde{u}(t))]^T(\tau_M R)[BKx(t - \tau(t)) \\
&+ BKe_k(t) - Bg(\widetilde{u}(t))]
\end{aligned} \tag{19}
$$

According to Assumption 1, the actuator nonlinear function satisfies the inequality as follows:

$$
\widetilde{u}^T(t)W^T W\widetilde{u}(t) - g^T(\widetilde{u}(t))g(\widetilde{u}(t)) \geq 0 \tag{20}
$$

In order to facilitate the use of the above nonlinear conditions, we can rewrite (20) as follows:

$$
\eta^T(t)\Theta^T \Theta\eta(t) - g^T(\widetilde{u}(t))g(\widetilde{u}(t)) \geq 0 \tag{21}
$$

in which $\Theta = [0 \quad WK \quad 0 \quad WK \quad 0]$.
Similarly, the event-triggered condition (3) as follows:

$$
\rho\eta^T(t)\Psi^T \Omega\Psi\eta(t) - e_k^T(t)\Omega e_k(t) \geq 0 \tag{22}
$$

where $\Psi = [0 \quad I \quad 0 \quad 0 \quad 0]$.
Substituting (18) and (19) into (13) and combining (21) and (22), we derive

$$
\begin{aligned}
\mathbb{E}\{\mathcal{L}(V(t))\} \leq &2x^T(t)P[Ax(t) + \alpha_0 BKx(t - \tau(t)) + \alpha_0 BKe_k(t) \\
&+ (1 - \alpha_0)Bg(\widetilde{u}(t))] + x^T(t)Qx(t) - x^T(t - \tau_M)Qx(t - \tau_M) \\
&+ [Ax(t) + \alpha_0 BKx(t - \tau(t)) + \alpha_0 BKe_k(t) \\
&+ (1 - \alpha_0)Bg(\widetilde{u}(t))]^T(\tau_M R)[Ax(t) + \alpha_0 BKx(t - \tau(t)) + \alpha_0 BKe_k(t) \\
&+ (1 - \alpha_0)Bg(\widetilde{u}(t))] + \alpha_0(1 - \alpha_0)[BKx(t - \tau(t)) \\
&+ BKe_k(t) - Bg(\widetilde{u}(t))]^T(\tau_M R)[BKx(t - \tau(t)) \\
&+ BKe_k(t) - Bg(\widetilde{u}(t))] + \tau(t)\eta^T(t)NR^{-1}N^T\eta(t) \\
&+ (\tau_M - \tau(t))\eta^T(t)MR^{-1}M^T\eta(t) + 2\eta^T(t)N[x(t) - x(t - \tau(t))] \\
&+ 2\eta^T(t)M[x(t - \tau(t)) - x(t - \tau_M)] + \rho\eta^T(t)\Psi^T \Omega\Psi\eta(t) \\
&- e_k^T(t)\Omega e_k(t) + \eta^T(t)\Theta^T G\Theta\eta(t) - g^T(\widetilde{u}(t))g(\widetilde{u}(t)) \\
= &\eta^T(t)\Xi\eta(t)
\end{aligned} \tag{23}
$$

where

$$
\begin{aligned}
\Xi = &\Sigma_{11} + \Gamma + \Gamma^T + \tau_M \mathcal{A}_1^T R\mathcal{A}_1 + \tau_M \alpha_0(1 - \alpha_0)\mathcal{A}_2^T R\mathcal{A}_2 + \tau(t)NR^{-1}N^T \\
&+ (\tau_M - \tau(t))MR^{-1}M^T + \Theta^T \Theta + \rho\Psi^T \Omega\Psi
\end{aligned} \tag{24}
$$

According to Schur complement, we have

$$\Pi(s) \triangleq \begin{bmatrix} \Sigma_{11} + \Gamma + \Gamma^T & * & * & * & * & * \\ \mathcal{G}^s & -R & * & * & * & * \\ \mathcal{A}_1 & 0 & -R^{-1} & * & * & * \\ \mathcal{A}_2 & 0 & 0 & -R^{-1} & * & * \\ \Sigma_{61} & 0 & 0 & 0 & -I & * \\ \Sigma_{71} & 0 & 0 & 0 & 0 & -\Omega \end{bmatrix} < 0, \quad s = 1, 2$$

we can obtain $\mathbb{E}\{\mathcal{L}(V(t))\} < 0$ and the control system (10) is mean square asymptotically stable.

Introduce the performance index as

$$J = \int_0^\infty \mathbb{E}\{z^T(t)z(t) - \gamma^2 \omega^T(t)\omega(t)\}dt \tag{25}$$

Under the zero initial condition, it can be derived that

$$\begin{aligned} J &= \int_0^\infty \mathbb{E}\{z^T(t)z(t) - \gamma^2 \omega^T(t)\omega(t) + \mathcal{L}(V(t))\}dt - \mathbb{E}\{\mathcal{L}(V(\infty))\} \\ &\leq \int_0^\infty \mathbb{E}\{z^T(t)z(t) - \gamma^2 \omega^T(t)\omega(t) + \mathcal{L}(V(t))\}dt \end{aligned} \tag{26}$$

If $\omega(t) \neq 0$, we can rewrite the inequality (23) as

$$\begin{aligned} \mathbb{E}\{\mathcal{L}(V(t))\} &\leq \eta^T(t)[\Sigma_{11} + \Gamma + \Gamma^T + \tau_M \alpha_0(1 - \alpha_0)\mathcal{A}_2{}^T R \mathcal{A}_2 + \tau(t)NR^{-1}N^T \\ &+ (\tau_M - \tau(t))MR^{-1}M^T + \Theta^T\Theta + \rho\Psi^T\Omega\Psi]\eta(t) \\ &+ 2x^T(t)PG\omega(t) + \begin{bmatrix} \eta(t) \\ \omega(t) \end{bmatrix}^T [\mathcal{A}_1 \quad \sqrt{\tau_M}G]^T R[\mathcal{A}_1 \quad \sqrt{\tau_M}G]\begin{bmatrix} \eta(t) \\ \omega(t) \end{bmatrix} \end{aligned}$$

and then

$$\begin{aligned} \mathbb{E}\{\mathcal{L}(V(t)) &+ z^T(t)z(t) - \gamma^2 \omega^T(t)\omega(t)\} \\ &\leq \eta^T(t)[\Sigma_{11} + \Gamma + \Gamma^T + \tau_M \alpha_0(1 - \alpha_0)\mathcal{A}_2{}^T R \mathcal{A}_2 + \tau(t)NR^{-1}N^T \\ &+ (\tau_M - \tau(t))MR^{-1}M^T + \Theta^T\Theta + \rho\Psi^T\Omega\Psi]\eta(t) \\ &+ 2x^T(t)PG\omega(t) + \begin{bmatrix} \eta(t) \\ \omega(t) \end{bmatrix}^T [\mathcal{A}_1 \quad \sqrt{\tau_M}G]^T R[\mathcal{A}_1 \quad \sqrt{\tau_M}G]\begin{bmatrix} \eta(t) \\ \omega(t) \end{bmatrix} \\ &+ \begin{bmatrix} \eta(t) \\ \omega(t) \end{bmatrix}^T [\mathcal{B} \quad H]^T[\mathcal{B} \quad H]\begin{bmatrix} \eta(t) \\ \omega(t) \end{bmatrix} - \gamma^2\omega^T(t)\omega(t) \end{aligned}$$

Based on Schur complement Lemma, from (11), we can get that $J < 0$. Therefore, we can obtain $\|z(t)\|_2 \leq \gamma\|\omega(t)\|_2$ for any nonzero $\omega(t) \in \mathcal{L}_2[0, +\infty)$. This completes the proof.

4 H_∞ Controller Design

Theorem 2. *For prescribed scalars $\rho \in [0, 1)$, $\tau_M > 0, \gamma > 0, \beta > 0$, the control system (10) is mean square stable, if there exist positive definite matrices X, $\tilde{Q}$, $\tilde{R}$, $\tilde{\Omega}$, and matrices $\tilde{S}$, $\tilde{U}$, Y, satisfying the following LMIs:*

$$\tilde{\Sigma}(s) \triangleq \begin{bmatrix} \tilde{\Sigma}_{11} + \tilde{\Gamma} + \tilde{\Gamma}^T & * & * & * & * & * & * & * \\ \tilde{\Sigma}_{21} & -\gamma^2 I & * & * & * & * & * & * \\ \tilde{\mathcal{G}}^s & 0 & -\tilde{R} & * & * & * & * & * \\ \tilde{\mathcal{A}}_1 & \sqrt{\tau_M}G & 0 & -2\beta X + \beta^2 \tilde{R} & * & * & * & * \\ \tilde{\mathcal{A}}_2 & 0 & 0 & 0 & -2\beta X + \beta^2 \tilde{R} & * & * & * \\ \tilde{\Sigma}_{61} & 0 & 0 & 0 & 0 & -I & * & * \\ \tilde{\Sigma}_{71} & 0 & 0 & 0 & 0 & 0 & -\tilde{\Omega} & * \\ \tilde{\mathcal{B}} & F & 0 & 0 & 0 & 0 & 0 & -I \end{bmatrix} < 0 \quad (27)$$

where $s = 1, 2$, and

$$\tilde{\Sigma}_{11} = \begin{bmatrix} AX + XA^T + \tilde{Q} & * & * & * & * \\ \alpha_0 Y^T B^T & 0 & * & * & * \\ 0 & 0 & -\tilde{Q} & * & * \\ \alpha_0 Y^T B^T & 0 & 0 & -\tilde{\Omega} & * \\ (1 - \alpha_0)B^T & 0 & 0 & 0 & -I \end{bmatrix}$$

$$\tilde{\Sigma}_{21} = \begin{bmatrix} G^T & 0 & 0 & 0 & 0 \end{bmatrix}$$
$$\tilde{\mathcal{G}}^1 = \sqrt{\tau_M}\tilde{S}^T, \quad \mathcal{G}^2 = \sqrt{\tau_M}\tilde{U}^T$$
$$\tilde{\Gamma} = \begin{bmatrix} \tilde{S} & \tilde{U} - \tilde{S} & -\tilde{U} & 0 & 0 \end{bmatrix}$$
$$\tilde{\mathcal{A}}_1 = \sqrt{\tau_M}\begin{bmatrix} AX & \alpha_0 BY & 0 & \alpha_0 BY & (1 - \alpha_0)B \end{bmatrix}$$
$$\tilde{\mathcal{A}}_2 = \sqrt{\tau_M \alpha_0 (1 - \alpha_0)}\begin{bmatrix} 0 & BY & 0 & BY & -B \end{bmatrix}$$
$$\tilde{\Sigma}_{61} = \begin{bmatrix} 0 & WY & 0 & WY & 0 \end{bmatrix}$$
$$\tilde{\Sigma}_{71} = \begin{bmatrix} 0 & \sqrt{\rho\tilde{\Omega}} & 0 & 0 & 0 \end{bmatrix}$$
$$\tilde{\mathcal{B}} = \begin{bmatrix} C & \alpha_0 EY & 0 & \alpha_0 EY & (1 - \alpha_0)E \end{bmatrix}$$

The controller of the system is $K = YX^{-1}$.

Proof. Setting $\mathcal{I} = diag\{I, I, I, I, I, I, I, I, P, P, I, I, I\}$, and pre-multiplying and post-multiplying (11) by $\mathcal{I}$, we can derive

$$\tilde{\Sigma}(s) \triangleq \begin{bmatrix} \Sigma_{11} + \Gamma + \Gamma^T & * & * & * & * & * & * & * \\ \Sigma_{21} & -\gamma^2 I & * & * & * & * & * & * \\ \mathcal{G}^s & 0 & -R & * & * & * & * & * \\ \tilde{\mathcal{A}}_1 & \sqrt{\tau_M}G & 0 & -PR^{-1}P & * & * & * & * \\ \tilde{\mathcal{A}}_2 & 0 & 0 & 0 & -PR^{-1}P & * & * & * \\ \Sigma_{61} & 0 & 0 & 0 & 0 & -I & * & * \\ \Sigma_{71} & 0 & 0 & 0 & 0 & 0 & -\Omega & * \\ \mathcal{B} & H & 0 & 0 & 0 & 0 & 0 & -I \end{bmatrix} < 0 \qquad (28)$$

where

$$\tilde{\mathcal{A}}_1 = \sqrt{\tau_M}\left[PA \ \alpha_0 PBK \ 0 \ \alpha_0 PBK \ (1-\alpha_0)PB \right]$$

$$\tilde{\mathcal{A}}_2 = \sqrt{\tau_M \alpha_0 (1-\alpha_0)}\left[0 \ PBK \ 0 \ PBK \ -PB \right]$$

We can easily obtain that

$$- PR^{-1}P \leq -2\beta P + \beta^2 R \qquad (29)$$

where $\beta > 0$ is a constant. By using the inequality (29), we can get the inequality from (28) as follows:

$$\hat{\Sigma}(s) \triangleq \begin{bmatrix} \Sigma_{11} + \Gamma + \Gamma^T & * & * & * & * & * & * & * \\ \Sigma_{21} & -\gamma^2 I & * & * & * & * & * & * \\ \mathcal{G}^s & 0 & -R & * & * & * & * & * \\ \tilde{\mathcal{A}}_1 & \sqrt{\tau_M}G & 0 & -2\beta P + \beta^2 R & * & * & * & * \\ \tilde{\mathcal{A}}_2 & 0 & 0 & 0 & -2\beta P + \beta^2 R & * & * & * \\ \Sigma_{61} & 0 & 0 & 0 & 0 & -I & * & * \\ \Sigma_{71} & 0 & 0 & 0 & 0 & 0 & -\Omega & * \\ \mathcal{B} & F & 0 & 0 & 0 & 0 & 0 & -I \end{bmatrix} < 0 \qquad (30)$$

Setting new matrix variables $\mathcal{K} = diag\{X, X, X, X, I, X, X, X, I, X, I\}$, $X = P^{-1}$, $\widetilde{Q} = XQX$, $\widetilde{R} = XRX$, $\widetilde{\Omega} = X\Omega X$, $Y = KX$, $\mathscr{X} = diag\{X, X, X, X, I\}$, $\widetilde{M} = \mathscr{X}M\mathscr{X}$, and $\widetilde{N} = \mathscr{X}N\mathscr{X}$, pre- and post-multiply (31) with $\mathcal{K}$. It is obvious that (27) implies the (11). The controller of the system can be determined by $K = YX^{-1}$. Thus the proof is completed.

5   Illustrative Examples

Example 1. Consider the control system (1) with parameter matrices as follows:

$$\begin{cases} \dot{x}(t) = \begin{bmatrix} -2 & -0.1 & 0 \\ -0.1 & 0 & 0.2 \\ 0 & -0.5 & 0 \end{bmatrix} x(t) + \begin{bmatrix} 0.1 & 0.5 \\ 0.02 & 0.6 \\ 0.1 & 0.8 \end{bmatrix} \widetilde{u}(t) + \begin{bmatrix} 1 \\ 1 \\ 1 \end{bmatrix} \omega(t) \\ z(t) = \begin{bmatrix} 0.5 & 0 & 0 \\ 0 & -0.8 & 0 \\ 0 & 0 & 0.6 \end{bmatrix} x(t) + \begin{bmatrix} -0.7 & 0.5 \\ 0.3 & 0.4 \\ 1 & 0.3 \end{bmatrix} \widetilde{u}(t) + \begin{bmatrix} 1 \\ 1 \\ 1 \end{bmatrix} \omega(t) \end{cases} \qquad (31)$$

Assume that the external interference is as follows:

$$\omega(t) = \begin{cases} 0.5\text{sgn}(\sin(t)), & t \in [0, 15] \\ 0, \end{cases}$$

The actuator nonlinear function is as follows:

$$g(u_1(t)) = 0.2tanh(u_1(t))$$
$$g(u_2(t)) = 0.1tanh(u_2(t))$$

Set the upper bound of transmission delay $\tau_M = 0.4$, H_∞ performance parameter $\gamma = 50$, matrix scaling parameters $\beta = 1$, event-triggered parameter $\rho = 0.02$, the probability parameter of actuator nonlinearity $\alpha_0 = 0.8$, and the upper bound matrix of actuator nonlinear function $W = diag\{0.2 \ 0.1\}$. According to Theorem 2, by solving the corresponding LMIs, the event-triggered matrix can be obtained as follows:

$$\Omega = \begin{bmatrix} 3.1796 & -0.0517 & -0.0545 \\ -0.0517 & 23.7421 & 7.1235 \\ -0.0545 & 7.1235 & 7.3254 \end{bmatrix} \tag{32}$$

The controller feedback gain K is

$$K = \begin{bmatrix} 0.1245 & 0.2351 & -0.1899 \\ -0.0321 & -0.9418 & -0.5324 \end{bmatrix} \tag{33}$$

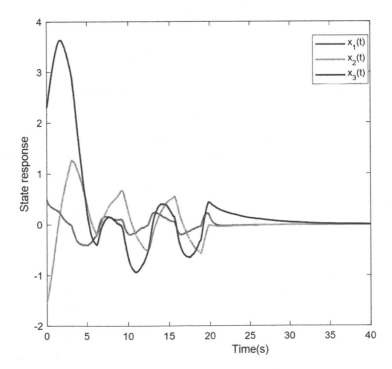

Fig. 1. The state responses under feedback gain (34)

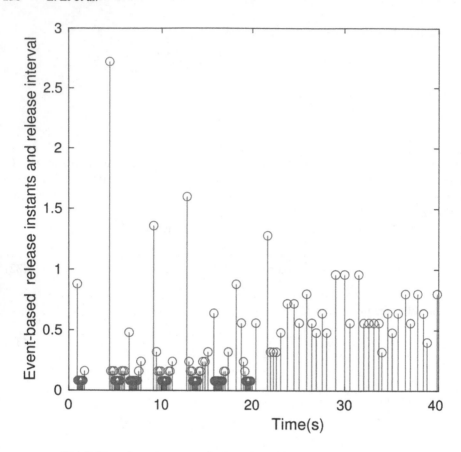

Fig. 2. The release instants and release interval with feedback gain (34)

When the initial condition and the sampling interval are chosen as $x(0) = [0.5 - 1.5\ 2.3]^T$, and $h = 0.08$, the state of the system $x(t)$ is illustrated in Fig. 1. The Fig. 2 shows the signal release instants and event intervals under the designed event-triggered mechanism. During the simulation duration 40 s, only 134 sample signals out of a total of $40/h = 500$ are transmitted to the controller, with takes 26.8% of all sampled signals.

6   Conclusion

This paper discusses the H_∞ control problem of networked control systems with event-driven mechanism and stochastic actuator nonlinearity. Based on Lyapunov function method, stochastic analysis theory and linear matrix inequality technique, the stability criterion of the system and the design method of the reliability controller are obtained. The main contributions of this paper include two aspects: (1) Random variables obeying Bayesian distribution are used to describe the random occurrence of actuator nonlinearity, and the event-triggered mechanism and stochastic actuator nonlinearity are jointly modeled and described to establish a new control system model. (2) A sufficient condition for mean square stability of the controlled system is given, and a specific controller design algorithm is given. Finally, a simulation example is given to verify the effectiveness of the algorithm in this paper.

References

1. Yue, D., Tian, E.G., Han, Q.L.: A delay system method for designing event-triggered controllers of networked control systems[J]. IEEE Trans. Autom. Control **58**(2), 475–481 (2013)
2. Shi, P., Wang, H.J., Lim, C.C.: Network-based event-triggered filtering for Markovian jump systems[J]. IEEE Trans. Industr. Electron. **63**(2), 1230–1238 (2016)
3. Wang, H.J., Ying, Y.J., Lu, R.Q., et al.: Network-based H-infinity control for singular systems with event-triggered sampling scheme. Inf. Sci. **329**(1), 540–551 (2016)
4. Hu, S.L., Yue, D., Peng, C., et al.: Event-triggered controller design of nonlinear discrete-time networked control systems in T-S fuzzy model. Appl. Soft Comput. **30**, 400–411 (2015)
5. Zhang, H.P., Yue, D., Yin, X.X., et al.: Finite-time distributed event-triggered consensus control for multi-agent systems. Inf. Sci. **339**, 132–142 (2016)
6. Rocca, E., Russo, R.: Theoretical and experimental investigation into the influence of the periodic backlash fluctuaions on the gear rattle. J. Sound Vib. **330**(20), 4738–4752 (2011)
7. Kim, W., Lee, C.W., Baek, J.S., et al.: Nonlinear controller with dead-zone and saturation for optical disk drive systems in the presence of extend shocks. IEEE Trans. Mechatron. **19**(4), 1458–1463 (2014)
8. Siyu, C., Jin, Y.T., Cai, W.L., et al.: Nonlinear dynamic characteristics of geared rotor bearing systems with dynamic backlash and friction. Mech. Mach. Theory **46**(4), 466–478 (2011)
9. Riccardi, L., Naso, D., Turchiano, B., et al.: Adaptive control of positioning systems with hysteresis based on magnetic shape memory alloys. IEEE Trans. Control Syst. Technol. **21**(6), 2011–2023 (2013)
10. Zhou, J., Wen, C.: Adaptive Backstepping Control of Uncertain Systems: Nonsmooth Nonlinearities, Interactions or Time-Variations. SPringer, London (2008)

Research on the Sensitive Data Protection Method Based on Game Theory Algorithm

Yunfeng Zou[1]([✉]), Pengfei Yu[2,3], Chao Shan[1], and Meng Wu[4]

[1] State Grid Jiangsu Marketing Service Center (Metrolgy Center), Nanjing 210000, China
[2] Global Energy Interconnection Research Institute Co., Ltd., Nanjing 210003, China
[3] State Grid Key Laboratory of Information & Network Security, Nanjing 210003, China
[4] AnHui Jiyuan Software Co., Ltd., Hefei 230000, China

Abstract. Due to the gradual application of 5G, Internet of things, the smart transportation and telemedicine, etc., the explosive growth of data volume brings challenges as well as opportunities. While the big data brings more economic benefits, the security issues have become more severe. In response to this problem, this paper proposes a privacy protection method for the big data oriented to user location. It firstly designs a big data system model for user location. Then a game theory based privacy protection algorithm for user location is proposed. The core idea of the algorithm is to allow users who generate virtual paths to obtain some certain benefits through the game method. Furthermore, this paper gives the detailed steps of the algorithm. Finally, the validity of the method is established via simulation and analysis.

Keywords: Large data · Privacy protection · User location · Gaming

1 Introduction

The rapid development of 5G, Internet of Things, artificial intelligence and other high-tech has brought great convenience to people's lives, but it is big data that supports these high-tech and the interaction between high-tech and human beings [1, 2]. Big data has aroused the interest of academia and industry since it was proposed. In the academic world, major universities and scientific research institutions have invested huge scientific research forces to study some of the challenges faced by existing technologies in processing big data and some new big data algorithms [3]. In the industrial sector, leading Internet companies represented by Alibaba, ByteDance, and Tencent have set up a big data research room to further enhance their influence in related fields [4]. It has to be said that while big data brings convenience to people's lives, it also brings huge economic benefits. However, if the value of the network is proportional to the amount of data, then the security threat it faces is the square level of the amount of data [5]. With the vigorous development of big data, data protection has become a key issue that has to be faced in the development of big data. If the big data server of an individual or a company is controlled by criminals, then in the world of the Internet, we are equivalent to running naked. Regarding the research related to big data privacy protection, the

© Springer Nature Singapore Pte Ltd. 2021
Y. Tian et al. (Eds.): ICBDS 2020, CCIS 1415, pp. 238–248, 2021.
https://doi.org/10.1007/978-981-16-3150-4_21

academic community can be traced back to 2008 when Nature released a special issue on big data "Big Data" [6, 7]. Materials and other aspects analyzed the convenience brought by big data to humans and the privacy leakage problems. Furthermore, Science also released a special issue "Dealing with data" in 2011, which is mainly based on the opportunities that big data brings to future development [8, 9].

With the continuous development of 5G, Internet of Things and smart terminals, the users of location-based services (LBSs) are showing an exponential growth trend [10], e.g. we usually use more navigation and location-related service recommendations. In LBS, the location server continuously records the user's location information, and then pushes personalized services based on their location. However, if the location server is untrusted or attacked, the personal information of the LBS user will be leaked, which brings great hidden dangers to the user's privacy.

In response to this problem, Elias et al. focused on the trajectory data representation suitable for the GeoSpark environment in the literature [11], and designed a real-time spatiotemporal data management method based on GeoSpark, and further applied k-nearest neighbor (k-NN) by using the index method.) Query to deepen the privacy protection of data. Verhelst et al. [12] focused on the analysis of personal privacy issues in large-scale surveillance metadata for large-scale video surveillance data in machine learning. M.A.P et al. proposed an efficient and scalable irreversible perturbation algorithm in literature [13]. The article protects the privacy of big data through optimal geometric transformation. Further articles used 9 data sets and 5 classification algorithms to test the efficiency, scalability, anti-attack and accuracy of PABIDOT. Wu Xiaoping first summarized the privacy risks of big data in literature [14], and then proposed a framework for location information privacy protection under big data. In reference to the two goals of data privacy and privacy query, Hu et al. proposed an overall and effective solution in literature [14], which specifically includes a secure traversal framework and an encryption scheme based on privacy homomorphism. Liu et al. proposed a false user location generation scheme in the literature [15]. Specifically, each user generates false location information through the location software on the terminal, and reports both the real location information and the false location information. To the location server, while protecting your own location, it also protects the location information of other users.

However, when performing location protection, it is obviously unreasonable for a user to undertake the generation of false location information. In response to this problem, the article proposes a game-based privacy protection algorithm for user location big data. The core idea of the algorithm is that all users in the system decide a user through a game to generate false path trajectory data, and then other users compensate the user by paying a certain fee.

2 Big Data Privacy Protection Method for User Location Information

2.1 System Model

A typical system model based on location-based services (LBSs) is shown in Fig. 1. Observing the picture, it is not difficult to find that the system is composed of satellites that provide positioning, LTE base stations for communications, user terminal mobile devices, users, and location servers. Specifically, first, users obtain their current location information from LTE base stations or satellites through their own handheld terminals (mobile phones, smart bracelets, etc.). Then, the smart terminal provides the location information to the location server (Baidu Maps, Meituan and other mobile apps). Finally, the location server will provide users with better location services. In this process, users generally hide their location information through random numbers or pseudonyms, but the location information data of users is very large. If the location server is untrustworthy, it is easy to infer very private information such as the user's identity, residence, and company through illegal means. In response to this problem, the article proposes a method for privacy protection of big data for user location information.

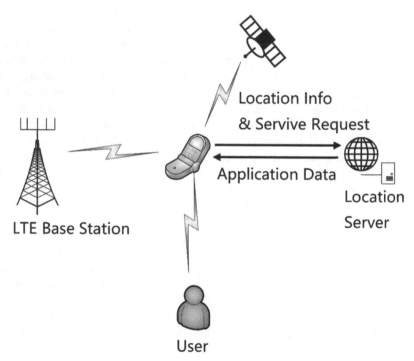

Fig. 1. System model based on location services

It is assumed that in an experimental area, the set of users with similar location trajectories is defined as $N = \{1, 2, \cdots, n\}$. The ith LBS user continuously provides its own location information to the location server, and its location information forms a track T_i. It is defined that $T = \{T_1, T_1, \cdots, T_n\}$ is the collection of track information formed by all LBS users. It needs to be explained that each T_i is a combination of two-dimensional space and one-dimensional time information, which means that $T_i = \{l_1, l_2, \cdots, l_m\}$, where $l_i = (x_i, y_i, t_i)$. (x_i, y_i) indicates the location information of the user, t_i indicates time information related to the current location.

In the system model based on location services shown in Fig. 1, it is generally considered that the location server is illegally hacked, i.e. it is untrustworthy. A common attack mode is inferential attack, that is, the attacker (Attacker) invades the location server, and then illegally obtains a large amount of user's location data, and then obtains illegal revenue through these location data. Specifically. First, Attacker obtains complete and large amounts of location information with pseudonyms from the location server. Then, attacker will further collect the user's auxiliary information. The so-called auxiliary information is some user location information with noise. It is useless to analyze a piece of auxiliary information separately, but after integrating a large amount of auxiliary information, inferential attacks can be launched. Auxiliary information is generally obtained through information disclosed by users on the Internet, such as location information when publishing on Weibo or WeChat.

This paper uses the concept of information entropy in information theory to quantitatively evaluate the degree of privacy of a LBS user. The higher the information entropy of user i, the better the privacy of the user, and vice versa. Its mathematical expression is as follows

$$H_i^O(T) = -\sum_{j=1}^{n} \Pr(T_j|S_i) \log_2 \Pr(T_j|S_i) \tag{1}$$

According to the previous research [14], under normal circumstances, only a pseudonym or random number method for a user cannot completely protect the user's location privacy. k anonymization is a common multi-user location privacy protection method, which can effectively improve the location privacy of each LBS user. The core idea of k anonymization is to ensure that for every user i there are $k-1$ similar trajectories. The premise of this method is that $k > n$. If $k \leq n$, it can't satisfy k Anonymization request. Therefore, in this case, a LBS is required to generate $k-1$ pieces of false track information. It is defined that the generated false position trajectory data of LBS user i is $\widehat{T}_i = \{\widehat{T}_{i,1}, \widehat{T}_{i,2}, \cdots, \widehat{T}_{i,k-1}\}$. Through k Anonymization, the anonymization of LBS users is improved from formula (1) to the following.

$$\begin{aligned} H_i(T, \widehat{T}_i) &= H_i^O(T) + H_i^K(\widehat{T}_i) \\ &= -\sum_{j=1}^{n} \Pr(T_j|S_i) \log_2 \Pr(T_j|S_i) \\ &\quad -\sum_{z=1}^{K-1} \Pr(\widehat{T}_{i,z}|S_i) \log_2 \Pr(\widehat{T}_{i,z}|S_i) \end{aligned} \tag{2}$$

Where $H_i^K(\widehat{T}_i)$ represents the increase in user privacy caused by k anonymization. $\widehat{T}_{i,z}$ represents the fake trajectory data generated by ith LBS user.

While k anonymization improves user privacy, it also brings a problem, that is, which user should be selected to generate $k-1$ pieces of false track information. User that generates $k-1$ pieces of false trajectory information will need a certain amount of power consumption and communication pressure. It means that the user's service quality may be reduced due to false information generation. Aiming at how to choose the user who generates false information and the compensation for the user to provide false information, this paper further proposes a game theory based privacy protection algorithm for user location. Through this algorithm, all users will actively participate in the false information generation activities designed by the paper. The generation of trajectory data further improves the privacy of all users' location information.

2.2 User Location Big Data Privacy Protection Algorithm Based on Game Theory

The game theory based privacy protection algorithm model for user location big data is shown in Fig. 2. According to Fig. 2, it is not difficult to find that each LBS user assumes both the buyer and seller identities. In other words, the article needs to be from the system n Select a winning LBS user from among the LBS users to generate $k - 1$ pieces of false position track data. At the same time, other LBS users who have not won as buyers need to pay a certain fee to the winning LBS users as compensation. The key steps of the auction are as follows.

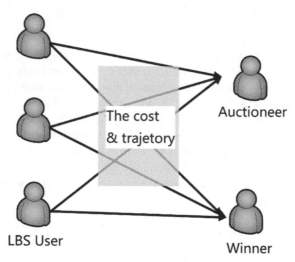

Fig. 2. Game theory based privacy protection algorithm model for user location big data

Firstly, every LBS user in the system evaluates the value of the generation of $k - 1$ pieces of false trajectory data. It is defined that the valuation of user $i \in N$ is c_i. The valuation of a user is confidential to other users, and a user will not know the valuation of other users until the auction is completed.

Secondly, every LBS user in the system makes a quote. It is defined that quote of user i is $b_i = (\hat{v}_i, \hat{T}_i)$, where $\hat{v}_i$ represents the desired price of user i to generate fake trajectory data $\hat{T}_i = \{\hat{T}_{i,1}, \hat{T}_{i,2}, \cdots, \hat{T}_{i,k-1}\}$ for himself. It is defined that $\mathbf{b} = (b_1, b_2, \cdots b_n)$ is a collection of quotes from all LBS users in the system. $\mathbf{b}_{-i}$ is the collection of prices except user i.

Furthermore, according to the auction rules, the auction will produce the winner's LBS user who is responsible for producing $k - 1$ pieces of false track data. Define the allocation function $f_i : \omega \rightarrow \{0, 1\}$ that determines whether user i is a winner. $w = w_1 \times w_2 \times \cdots \times w_n$ where w_i represent the collection of all quotes of each user i. If and only if $f_i = 1$, user i is the winner of the auction.

Finally, other LBS users who have not become the auction winner need to pay a certain fee for the winner LBS users. Define payment function $g_i : \omega \rightarrow \mathbf{R}$ that determines the price to be paid by user i. When $g_i > 0$, user i is the winner who is responsible for generating $k - 1$ pieces of false trajectory data. When $g_i < 0$, user i is not the winner of the auction. At this time, the user needs to pay the winner of $- g_i$.

The definition v^* indicates the final transaction price of this auction. T^* represents the false trajectory generated by the winner. The goal of this paper is mainly divided into two aspects. On the one hand, considering that all users except the winning user need to pay a certain fee, the smaller the final auction price, the better. On the other hand, the false trajectory generated by the winner represents the privacy degree of the user, so the greater the privacy degree of the user's location, the better. Combining the above two aspects, the objective function of this auction can be obtained as follows:

$$\min_{v^*, T^*} \frac{v^*}{\sum_{i=1}^{n} H_{i(T, T^*)}} \tag{3}$$

$$s.t.\ v^* \in \mathbf{R}^+$$

$$T^* \in \{\widehat{T}_1, \widehat{T}_2, \cdots, \widehat{T}_n\}$$

It should be noted that in order to maximize Eq. (3), all LBS users are required to report their real quotes. This is because, only when any LBS user has quoted their real price, can he get the most benefit for himself. Analyzing formula (3) further, it can be found that the purpose of this paper is not to let the winning LBS users get the most benefits, but to let all LBS users bear the cost of big data privacy protection together.

2.3 Algorithm Description

Based on the analysis in Sect. 2.2, it is not difficult to see that the game process can be divided into two steps. The first step is to decide the winner of the auction. Based on the previous analysis and formula (3), the distribution function of the winner of the game can be obtained as follows

$$f_i(\mathbf{b}) = \begin{cases} 1, & if \ \dfrac{\hat{v}_i}{\sum_{z=1}^{n} H_z(T_i, \widehat{T}_i)} \leq \min_{j \neq i}\{\dfrac{\hat{v}_i}{\sum_{z=1}^{n} H_z(T_i, \widehat{T}_i)}\} \\ 0, & if \ \dfrac{\hat{v}_i}{\sum_{z=1}^{n} H_z(T_i, \widehat{T}_i)} > \min_{j \neq i}\{\dfrac{\hat{v}_i}{\sum_{z=1}^{n} H_z(T_i, \widehat{T}_i)}\} \end{cases} \tag{4}$$

In formula (4), if $f_i(\mathbf{b}) = 1$, it represents that the user i is the winner of this game. Otherwise, $f_i(\mathbf{b}) = 0$ and user i is not the winner of this game who needs to pay a certain fee to the winner.

Table 1. Game-based privacy protection algorithm steps of user location information

Input: LBS user collection N . User's quote collection $\vec{b}$	
Output: the winner of the auction W . Other users' fees and revenue collection $\vec{g}$	
1.	For i=1 to n do:
2.	$s = 0$;
3.	For j =1 to n do:
4.	Compute $p = \Pr(T_j \vert S_i)$;
5.	$s = s - p \log_2 p$;
6.	End for
7.	For j = 1 to k-1 do:
8.	Compute $p = \Pr(\mathcal{F}_i \vert S_i)$;
9.	$s = s - p \log_2 p$;
10.	End for
11.	If $\dfrac{\bar{v}_i}{s} < \alpha$ then:
12.	$w = i$
13.	$\alpha = \dfrac{\bar{v}_i}{s}$
14.	End if
15.	End for
16.	For i = 1 to n do:
17.	$ESW_{-i}(b_i) = \mathbf{E}_{b_{-i}} \left[\sum\limits_{j \neq i}^{n} v_i f_j (b_i, b_{-i}) \right]$
18.	$g_i(b) = ESW_{-i}(b_i) - \left(\dfrac{1}{n-1} \sum\limits_{j \neq i}^{n} ESW_{-j}(b_j) \right)$
19.	End for
20.	Return W and $\vec{g}$

After deciding on the winner of the auction, the second critical step is to decide how much other users need to pay the winner. According to the Bayesian game principle [14], v_i follows a random distribution of probability, that is $v_i \sim D_i$. The average value of the fees that each LBS user needs to pay can be obtained as follows.

$$g_i(b) = ESW_{-i}(b_i) - (\frac{1}{n-1} \sum_{j \neq i}^{n} ESW_{-j}(b_j)) \tag{5}$$

where $ESW_{-i}(b_i) = \mathbf{E}_{b_{-i}}[\sum_{j \neq i}^{n} v_i f_j(b_i, b_{-i})]$.

If $g_i(b) > 0$, it represents that the user i is the winner of this game who receives fees paid by other users. On the contrary, if $g_i(b) < 0$, user i is not the winner of this game and needs to pay a certain fee to the winner of the auction. In summary, the steps of the game theory based privacy protection algorithm for user location information are shown in Table 1.

From Table 1, it can be seen that the first step of the code is 1–15, and the second step is 16–19. Further analysis can be easily obtained, the time complexity of the first part is $O(n(n + k))$. The time complexity of the second part is $O(n)$. Therefore, the overall time complexity of the algorithm proposed can be obtained as $O(n^2 + nk)$.

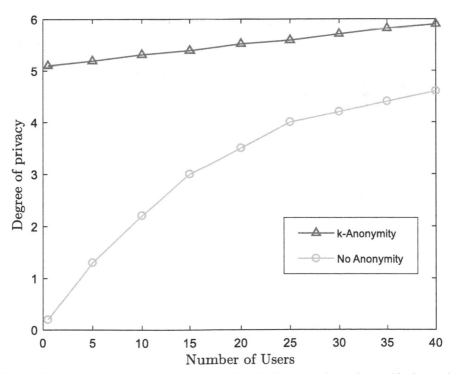

Fig. 3. With or without-k Comparison of privacy levels of user location trajectory big data under anonymization

3 Simulation and Result Analysis

The article uses MATLAB 2017a for simulation. MATLAB simulation software is a very efficient software for big data analysis. It integrates various functions (such as neural network algorithms, decision tree algorithms, random forest algorithms, etc.). The article performs Monte Carlo simulation, and the number of simulations is set to $Num = 10^6$. If not otherwise specified, the simulation parameters of the system studied in this article are as follows:$n \in \{1, 2, \cdots , 40\}$ LBS users, each user ismoves in the square of 1000×1000. The position of the LBS user is recorded once every minute, and the recording time is two hours, so the track length of any user is 120.

First, Fig. 3 shows the comparison of the degree of privacy of user location trajectory big data in the two cases of anonymization. It can be seen that the degree of privacy of k anonymization is higher than that under no anonymity. This simulation shows that k Anonymization is a good way to protect user privacy, and it also proves the correctness of the analysis.

Then, the influence of the number of false location trajectories on the privacy protection degree of user location big data is analyzed, and the simulation results are shown in Fig. 4. It can be found that as the number of false trajectories increases, the privacy of users continues to increase. It should be noted that when the number of false trajectories is constant, the privacy degree of the proposed algorithm tends to change smoothly.

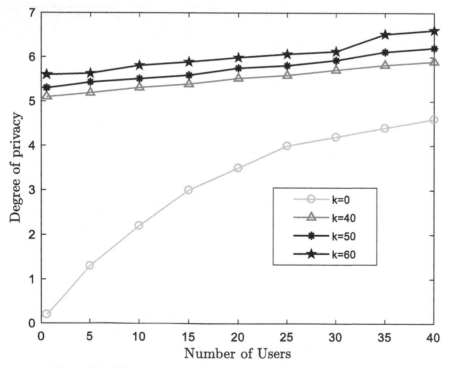

Fig. 4. The influence of the number of false trajectories on user privacy

Finally, the article analyzes the impact of the number of users without LBS on the cost and privacy. The simulation results are shown in Fig. 5. It can be found that as the number of users increases, the total cost privacy ratio shows a decreasing trend. This shows that in an environment with a relatively large user base, a small number of users can achieve high user track privacy, which is very instructive to reality.

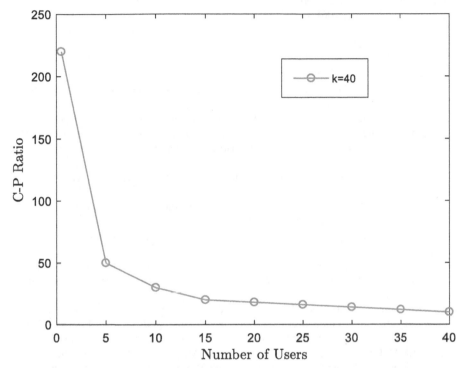

Fig. 5. The influence of the number of users without LBS on the cost and privacy

4 Conclusion

This paper proposes a big data privacy protection method for user location information. The article first introduces the big data privacy algorithm model for user location information. Then a game theory based privacy protection algorithm for user location big data is proposed. The details of the algorithm are further explained. Finally, simulations verify the correctness of the analysis.

Acknowledgement. This paper is supported by the science and technology project of State Grid Jiangsu Electric Power Co., Ltd.: "Research and application of key technology for power marketing sensitive data security protection" (Grand No. J2020007).

References

1. Yang, Y., Chen, H.: A review of research on privacy protection data mining technology. Microcomput. Appl. **36**(08), 41–44+54 (2020)
2. Zhang, L.: Research on location big data statistics division and release and privacy protection method. Lanzhou University of Technology (2020)
3. Lei, W.: Research on the information flow and privacy protection of digital library in the big data era. J. Lib. Sci. **41**(06), 119–122 (2019)
4. Yu, G.: Research on key technologies of big data access control. Inner Mongolia University of Science and Technology (2019)
5. Zhang, J.: Research on differential privacy clustering algorithm based on location big data. Guangdong University of Technology (2019)
6. Xu, W.: Research and implementation of privacy protection of medical data sharing based on blockchain. Xidian University (2019)
7. Engineering - Materials Engineering; Research Data from Hainan University Update Understanding of Materials Engineering (A Distributed Privacy Preservation Approach for Big Data in Public Health Emergencies Using Smart Contract and Sgx). Technology News Focus (2020)
8. Xinkangkang. Research on user privacy issues and countermeasures in the era of big data. Collect. Writ. (04), 77–79 (2020)
9. Xiaming, Z., Yan, Z.: Research on data privacy protection strategy in artificial intelligence applications. Artif. Intell. **04**, 76–84 (2020)
10. Lengauer, T.: Statistical data analysis in the era of big data. Chemie Ingenieur Technik **92**(7) (2020)
11. Dritsas, E., Kanavos, A., Trigka, M., Vonitsanos, G., Sioutas, S., Tsakalidis, A.: Trajectory clustering and k-NN for robust privacy preserving k-NN query processing in GeoSpark. Algorithms **13**(8) (2020)
12. Verhelst, H.M., Stannat, A.W., Mecacci, G.: Machine learning against terrorism: how big data collection and analysis influences the privacy-security dilemma. Sci. Eng. Ethics (2020)
13. Information Technology - Data Mining; Studies from Royal Melbourne Institute of Technology - RMIT University Add New Findings in the Area of Data Mining (Efficient Privacy Preservation of Big Data for Accurate Data Mining). Information Technology Newsweekly (2020)
14. Wu, X.: Research on privacy protection and its key technologies in big data environment. Nanjing University (2017)
15. Hu, H., Xu, J., Ren, C., et al.: Processing private queries over untrusted data cloud through privacy homomorphism. ICDE. IEEE (2011)
16. Liu, X., Liu, K., Guo, L., et al.: A game-theoretic approach for achieving k-anonymity in Location Based Services. Infocom, IEEE. IEEE (2013)

Research on Differential Protection and Security in Power System Under 5G Environment

Guo-feng Tong[1], Yuan-wen Jin[1(✉)], Kang-yi Li[1], and Jia Yu[2]

[1] State Grid Shaoxing Power Supply Company, Nanjing, China
[2] NARI Group Corporation, State Grid Electric Power Research Institute, Nanjing, China

Abstract. In the face of the differentiation of business requirements, the diversification of application scenarios and the challenge of isomerization of network equipment, the construction of universal Internet of things needs to introduce 5G technologies such as network slicing, edge computing, flexible return and low delay technology. Aiming at these problems, this paper studies the key technologies of 5G network with low delay and high reliability, and a mobile edge computing platform for distribution network differential protection is designed. Through the platform, the information flow does not need to return to the 5G core network, and can complete the information interaction and transmission at the edge of the network, which can meet the delay requirement of the distribution network. This scheme can replace optical fiber communication for real-time communication between distribution network differential protection devices, and provide a solution for low-delay and high reliability application scenarios of universal Internet of things access network.

Keywords: 5G · Network slicing · Edge calculation · Low-delay · Service bearing

1 Introduction

As a new generation of mobile communication technology after 2020, 5G is the development direction of wireless technology in the future [1–3]. 5G brings the user experience of ultra-high bandwidth, ultra-low delay and super-large-scale connectivity [4–6]. Network architecture which based on software definition, network function virtualization and other technologies can support the on-demand customization, high dynamic expansion and automated deployment of network resources. 5G supports end-to-end network slicing from access networks and core networks to bearer networks, thus creating customized services for power industry users [7, 8]. 5G can better adapt to the demand of the multi-scene and differentiated service of the future power, and promote the innovation of the application of the energy Internet [9, 10].

At present, the special optical cable is used in the differential protection, which has the problems of high laying cost and insufficient resources of underground pipe trenches [11]. If the differential protection and the existing distribution automation share optical cable, there is a problem of multiple fiber jump between the two ends of the

© Springer Nature Singapore Pte Ltd. 2021
Y. Tian et al. (Eds.): ICBDS 2020, CCIS 1415, pp. 249–260, 2021.
https://doi.org/10.1007/978-981-16-3150-4_22

station, resulting in lower reliability and other problems [12, 13]. Therefore, based on the technology of low delay and high reliability of 5G network, this paper presents the application of differential protection in 5G environment [14–16].

2 Research on Multi-access EdgeCompute

For the most demanding services in the Internet of things, we can reduce the transmission delay and signaling processing delay from the wireless side to the core side by deploying the mobile edge computing platform. In the distribution network differential protection scenario, the massive distribution terminal requires the smart grid communication with low delay, which must be inseparable from the application of 5G network slicing and edge computing technology [17]. Considering the limited caching and computing capabilities of distribution terminals, edge computing nodes can be deployed within the service distribution area to carry control, management and data functions associated with low latency. Based on the architecture design of MEC platform, the shunt mechanism of low delay service and the interface of MEC platform, the mobile edge computing platform with low delay and adaptive power service features is constructed.

2.1 Architecture Design of MEC Platform

In the design and implementation of the MEC platform architecture, the mobile edge computing platform architecture shown in Fig. 1 is used. There are three sets of reference points among system entities, namely, reference point (Mp) for mobile edge platform functionality, management-related reference point (Mm) and reference point (Mx) for connecting external entities [18].

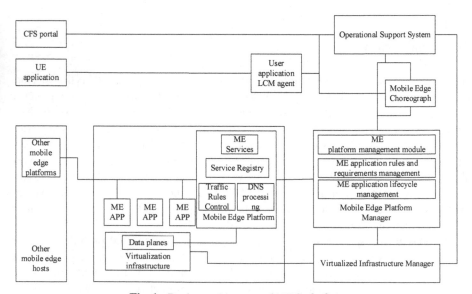

Fig. 1. Design architecture of MEC platform

According to architecture of MEC, the data is transmitted to the mobile edge computing platform through the Internet of things access network. The bottom layer of the platform uses GTP parsing encapsulation and TOF shunt technology to process the data. The data that needs to be processed by the core layer is transferred to internet via the core network. Data that needs to be locally processed on the mobile edge computing platform is forwarded to the virtual and application layers above the platform through the data plane development suite. The virtual layer of the platform abstracts resources such as the computing storage of the mobile edge computing server. A variety of related services with higher requirements for delay and reliability are assigned to network transport through virtualization management. Finally, they are connected to the application layer through the network edge service (NES) [19]. The application layer is composed of multiple virtual machines, and the Mp1 interface is used to obtain relevant data from each service of the virtual layer for processing. The virtual machine mainly implements some control management and other functions. The mobile edge computing platform manager is connected to the edge computing platform through the Mm5 interface, mainly responsible for database management and some information management, and connected to the cloud. The cloud receives the data from the mobile edge computing server and makes the control decision. It can update the upper application of the edge computing platform.

2.2 Diversion Mechanism of Low Delay Service

Aiming at the shunt mechanism of MEC service in low delay scenario, the TOF shunt of physical layer and the function design of Mp1 and Mm5 interface are further studied to realize the functions of life cycle management, service management and transmission control of low delay service. To implement the local shunt, the GTP parsing package is first required. The flow is shown in Fig. 2. Its functions are as follows.

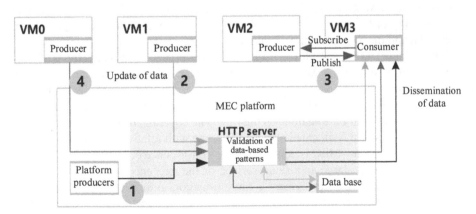

Fig. 2. Data stream for four types of service

(1) The IP data stream of low delay service is encapsulated into GTP data stream and forwarded to core network and base station.

(2) The GTP data stream forwarded by the base station is received and analyzed in real-time, and forwarded to the low-delay service application in the form of IP packet.

(3) The GTP data stream forwarded by the core network is received and parsed in real time, and forwarded to the low-time service application of the power Internet of things in the form of IP packet.

Type 1 of service: The host of the mobile edge platform generates service data, stores it in the platform database, and provides platform-related services.

Type 2 of service: Virtual machines for mobile edge applications generate and store service data and publish it via mobile edge platforms.

Type 3 of service: Virtual machines for mobile edge applications generate and store service data and receive subscriptions directly from other mobile edge applications.

Type 4 of service: Virtual machines for mobile edge applications generate service data, which are stored in the database of the mobile edge platform and provide related services by the platform.

In terms of deployment, the MEC server needs to have the ability to integrate deployment with existing return networks in different scenarios, depending on the different requirements of the Internet of things. There are three strategies for deploying MEC in the power Internet of things.

Edge level. MEC is deployed between base station and return network. This deployment is close to the base station and can be deployed in the site computer room or in the wireless access computer room with the Cloud-BBU pool. In this deployment mode, the number of base stations covered by MEC is small, the effect on transmission is small, and the delay of return link is the shortest, which is more suitable for local CASH and CDN services. At the same time, the coverage performance of this deployment mode is more relevant to the current proximal transport, and needs to be comprehensively evaluated for coverage requirements and transport status. In this kind of scenario, the network mode of MEC server is mostly L2 group network mode, so it is necessary to have the ability of Bypass to ensure that the service is not interrupted when the system is abnormal and the low delay of transmission is guaranteed.

Regional level. MEC is deployed between the convergence and access loops. At this point, we need to deploy the MEC in the UNI interface of the two linked transmission devices, and channel the base station traffic through the MEC. In this scenario, the coverage of the MEC can be a base station on one or more access rings and can be split selectively for different base stations on the ring. The coverage is large and the delay is low. This kind of scene is more suitable for the scene with relatively large area.

City level. When the MEC is deployed in the convergence core layer, this coverage is mainly aimed at the large-area shunt service or the existence of access to the ring island to be covered. This deployment is more time-consuming than the other two. In this scenario, the network mode of the MEC server is mostly L3 group network mode, so it is necessary to modify the transport configuration of the docking network element to ensure that the message can be sent to the MEC server, and to change the other transport path when the MEC server is not accessible.

2.3 Research on Channel Model

5G power communication system is composed of N antennas, and the channel model can be expressed as a whole under the assumption of NLOS. The channel model can be expressed as a whole [18]

$$G = HD^{1/2}$$

$D = \text{diag}\{\beta_1, \beta_2, \ldots, \beta_k\}$ is large scale propagation matrix. $\beta_k = \phi d_k^{-\alpha} \xi_k$. ϕ is a constant associated with antenna gain and carrier frequency. d is the distance between the same user side of the base station. ξ_k is a shadow fading variable in accordance with lognormal distribution. According to the fast fading matrix, CBS can be further divided into three types of channels, Rayleigh fading channel, correlation channel model, mutual coupling channel model and so on. 5G power communication model is based on the existing fast fading model of 3 GPP. The large scale parameters of the model are set first, and then the small scale parameters are generated according to the following steps.

1) Cluster delay characteristics under 3D model

First, the cluster delay is usually represented by exponential delay distribution, as follows

$$\tau'_n = -r_\tau \text{DSln}(X_n)$$

Among them, r_τ is the proportional coefficient of the demonstration distribution. $X_n \sim N(0, 1)$. If the delay distribution is uniform, the delay τ'_n is extracted from the corresponding range. The delay is normalized by subtracting the minimum delay value and the normalized delay is arranged in ascending order. Specifically, it states

$$\tau_n = \text{sort}\left(\tau'_n - \min\left(\tau'_n\right)\right)$$

There will be LOS in communication. According to the los situation, the delay should be extended to compensate for the influence of los leakage on the delay expansion. The scale constant determined by the Rice factor is

$$C_r = 0.7705 - 0.0433K + 0.0002K^2 + 0.000017K^3$$

K is the Rice factor measured by dB. The corresponding delay is expressed as

$$\tau_n^{LOS} = \tau_n/C_r$$

3 Application of Network Slice Technology in Power System

3.1 Characteristics of Power Service

At present, the power wireless private network mainly carries four categories of service, such as network control, information collection, video and mobile applications. Specific services include distribution automation, electricity information collection, distributed power supply, precision load control, video surveillance, mobile operations, etc. Overall, the current minimum delay for all types of power services is 10 ms, with a bandwidth of less than 4 Mbps for single services. In the future, with the development of energy Internet, in order to adapt to the new power grid mode with UHV as the backbone and coordinated development of power grid at all levels, the universal connection will become the basic form of power grid. Therefore, it is urgent to build a real-time, efficient, safe and reliable communication network to achieve accurate control of all kinds of loads. A new type of visualization, real-time and lean operation is introduced to realize the monitoring and inspection of important corridors in power grids at all levels. Therefore, in the future, the Internet of things and broadband services of power systems will coexist in large numbers, and present the characteristics of high-density, low-delay, high-reliability and high-security. The number of concurrent terminals will reach 100,000, the delay requirement is millisecond and the reliability requirement is 99.999%. Therefore, higher requirements are put forward for the service carrying capacity of the power wireless private network.

3.2   Adaptive Model of 5G and Multiple Power Services

Considering the requirements of bandwidth, real-time, reliability and large connection of all kinds of power services, this paper analyzes the compatibility of different business requirements with 5g application scenarios. The scenarios of 5G are divided into eMBB, uRLLC and mMTC. The adaptive models are shown in Fig. 3 for the eight typical types of services, such as differential protection, distribution automation, precision load control, power information acquisition, distribution network condition monitoring, physical ID, intelligent inspection and video surveillance.

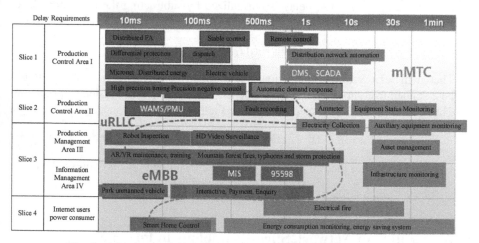

Fig. 3. Adaptive model of 5G and power multiple application scenarios

3.3   Customized Scheme for Power Network Slicing

Wireless network architecture based on 5G network slicing is divided into three layers. The underlying network is the physical infrastructure layer, which is the actual carrier of network data. The middle layer provides the whole virtual resource pool for the virtualized network resources, and realizes the centralized management and efficient allocation of resources. The upper layer is the user-oriented actual layer, different types of network services will form different network slicing. The realization of layer function and the interaction between each layer need to be managed and controlled by the SDN controller (Fig. 4).

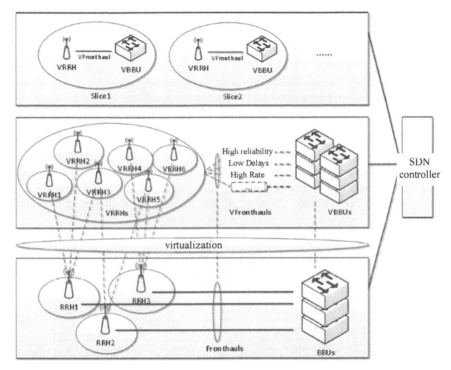

Fig. 4. Wireless network architecture based on 5G network slicing

In order to realize the effective control of the network nodes and the accurate forwarding of the network data by the SDN controller, the slicing table is introduced in the nodes RRH and BBU of the wireless access network with reference to the Openflow protocol. On the one hand, slicing table can effectively split the transmission of network data. On the other hand, the slicing table also contains various network parameters, which can realize the rapid configuration of the network. Moreover, the SDN controller will manipulate the slice table by slicing the message (Fig. 5).

The slicing dynamic deployment system of power network consists of information collection module, virtualization module, resource management module, slicing network management module and SDN controller. The information collection module will run in the physical infrastructure layer. Virtualization module will realize the effective mapping

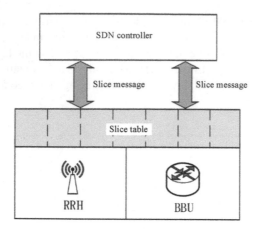

Fig. 5. Network slicing based on SDN controller

of underlying network and virtual resource pool. The resource management module will effectively schedule and manage the virtual resources. The slice network management module will manage and maintain the final slice network. The SDN controller will achieve centralized control and coordinated management of each functional module (Fig. 6).

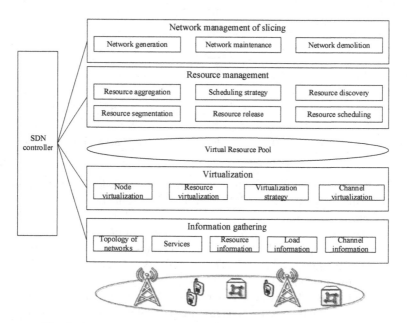

Fig. 6. Dynamic deployment system for 5G power network slicing

4 Application of Differential Protection Based on 5G

4.1 Characteristics of Differential Protection Services

With the development of strong smart grid and power Internet of things, the reliability of distribution network has been paid more and more attention. Service extends from high voltage to low voltage. However, the on-line rate of differential protection service is generally low, usually using the way of DTU to upload signals, there is no special protection channel. In order to realize the differential function of distribution network, optical fiber multiplexing is usually adopted. However, there are several problems with fiber multiplexing. The first is that the fiber channel is usually arranged according to the requirement of automation, and the loop is formed in series between the ring network and the station, so it is difficult to realize the point-to-point direct connection, which leads to the uncertainty of the delay. If the communication mode of special fiber is adopted completely, the price is high and the construction is difficult, some areas cannot be constructed at all. It is more economical to use wireless network, but the communication problem becomes the bottleneck to realize the function of differential protection, because the delay and jitter of 4G wireless network cannot meet the demand of differential protection service. With the commercial use of 5G networks, the low-delay and high-reliability characteristics of 5G networks have become an important and feasible means to realize the differential protection of distribution network. The core network sinking, data shunting and edge computing in MEC are the important technical supports for 5G low-delay and high-reliability performance.

The terminal communication at both ends of the line adopts a private protocol based on HDLC, point-to-point fiber communication. The protection signal is uploaded to the main station via a communication network. The current differential protection is formed by using the characteristic difference of the current waveform or the current phasor between the two ends of the protected line. A schematic diagram of the terminal layout and communication network is shown in Fig. 7.

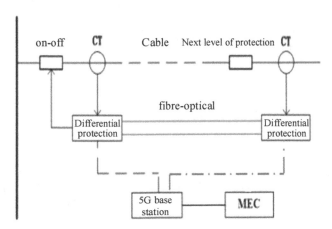

Fig. 7. Terminal layout and communication network diagram

Communication rate for differential protection services is 2048 kbit/s. The delay of the receiving route is the same as the delay of the sending route, jitter <20 us, the delay of receiving the letter is not more than 12 ms. Each terminal sends a private message to the opposite side, and the length of each frame is calculated at 512B.

4.2 Application of Differential Protection Service

The differential protection is formed by using the characteristic difference of the current waveform at the two ends of the protected line. The deployment diagram is shown in Fig. 8.

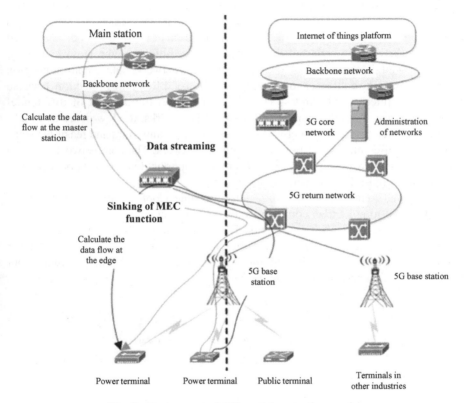

Fig. 8. Deployment of differential protection services

(1) Deployment of MEC

At present, the main purchaser of MEC equipment is the operator. Operators can deploy MEC anywhere between base station and core network according to the requirements. The data can enter the private user network directly via MEC on the base station side without passing through the operator's core network. The edge calculation is mainly to combine and analyze the data collected by the terminals of one or more base stations, and return the processing results directly to the terminal equipment for the next operation, thus satisfying the transmission of high reliability and low delay service. The last step is business optimization, the essence of optimization is the further sinking of CDN (Content Distribution Network).

(2) Programmes for carrying operations

There is no need to apply for exclusive frequency resources, and the spectrum and base stations of telecom operators are used together by means of co-construction and resource exchange with telecom operators. Power companies and telecom operators connect base stations through their respective transmission networks, and realize the construction and application of power 5G networks. The MEC platform is deployed near the edge of the substation. Based on the existing network of telecom operators, the 5G core network is no longer built, and the multi-access edge computing (MEC) function module can be independently deployed on the server, which can realize the functions of computing, storage and data processing. The telecom operator realizes the functions of managing and maintaining the users in the slice through the way of network slicing, similar to the virtual core network.

5   Conclusion

In this paper, the key technology of 5G network with low delay height is studied, and a mobile edge computing platform is designed. The exchange and transmission of information can be accomplished without returning to the 5G core network at the edge of the network, which can meet the delay requirement of the distribution network for the end-to-end communication. The 5G communication replaces the optical fiber communication and becomes the communication mode between the devices of differential protection, which provides the solution for the low-delay and high-reliability application scenarios of the power Internet of things network. The research results can also be extended to other scenarios with high reliability and low delay. The research results of this paper lay a theoretical foundation for the application of other power services in 5G scene.

References

1. Gao, X., Zhu, J., Chen, Y.: Research on multi-services bearing solution of LTE power wireless private network. Electric Power Inf. Commun. Technol. 12(12), 26–29 (2014)
2. Yu, J., Liu, J., Cai, S.: Research on LTE wireless network planning in electric power system. Electric Power Inf. Commun. Technol. 10(2), 7–11 (2016)
3. You, X.H., Pan, Z.W., Gao, X.Q., et al.: The 5G mobile communication: the development trends and its emerging key techniques. Sci. Sinica 44(5), 551 (2014)
4. Liu, G., Jiang, D.: 5G: vision and requirements for mobile communication system towards year 2020. Chin. J. Eng. 1–8 (2016)
5. Ma, Z., Zhang, Z.Q., Ding, Z.G., et al.: Key techniques for 5G wireless communications: network architecture, physical layer, and MAC layer perspectives. Sci. China 58(4), 41301–41321 (2015)
6. Qiu, J., Ding, G., Wu, Q., et al.: Hierarchical resource allocation framework for hyper-dense small cell networks. IEEE Access 4(99), 8657–8669 (2017)

7. Wang, K.: The application of the internet of things in the 5G era in the power system. Telecom Power Technol. **35**(5), 187–188 (2018)
8. Xia, X., Zhu, X., Mei, C., Li, W., Fang, H.: Research and practice on 5G slicing in power internet of things. Mobile Commun. **43**(1), 63–69 (2019)
9. Li, B., Zhou, J., Ren, X.: Research on key issues of TD-LTE network optimization. Telecom Eng. Tech. Stand. **1**, 57–61 (2015)
10. Fernekess, A., Klein, A., Wegmann, B., Dietrich, K., Litzka, M.: Load dependent interference margin for link budget calculations of OFDMA networks. IEEE Commun. Lett. **12**(5), 398–400 (2008)
11. Zheng, L., Tse, D.N.C.: Diversity and multiplexing: a fundamental tradeoff in multiple antenna channels. IEEE Trans. Inf. Theory **49**(5), 1073–1096 (2003)
12. Yao, J.: Random access technology of electric dedicated LTE network based on power priority. Autom. Electric Power Syst. **40**(10), 127–131 (2016)
13. Cao, J., Liu, J., Li, X.: A power wireless broadband technology scheme for smart power distribution and utilization network. Autom. Electric Power Syst. **37**(11), 76–80 (2013)
14. Chen, S., Qin, F., Hu, B., et al.: User-centric ultra-dense networks for 5G: challenges, methodologies, and directions. IEEE Wirel. Commun. **23**(2), 78–85 (2018)
15. Sun, J., Lin, C.: Research of smart distribution terminal communication technology based on TE-LTE. Telecommun. Electric Power Syst. **33**(7), 80–83 (2012)
16. Li, W., Wang, J., Shao, Q., Li, S.: Efficient resource allocation algorithms for energy efficiency maximization in ultra-dense network. In: GLOBECOM 2017–2017 IEEE Global Communications Conference, pp. 1–6 (2017)
17. Xie, J., Liu, J.: Optimization simulation of wireless network communication coverage. Comput. Simul. **33**(6), 271–275 (2015)
18. Hamidi, M.M., Edmonson, W.W., Afghah, F.: A non-vooperative game theoretic approach for power allocation in interstatellite communication. In: 2017 IEEE International Conference on Wireless for Space and Extreme Environments (WISEE), pp. 13–18 (2017)
19. Li, W., Chen, B., Wu, Q., et al.: Applied research of TD-LTE power wireless broadband private network. Telecommun. Electric Power Syst. **33**(241), 82–87 (2012)

Research on Intelligent Fault and Security Handling Based on IMS in Power System

Peng Jia[✉], Shao-peng Wanyan, and Xiao-yuan Zhang

NARI Group Corporation, State Grid Electric Power Research Institute, Nanjing, China

Abstract. The operation and maintenance pressure of IMS system is large, and the number of equipments to be maintained is large. It is urgent for advanced maintenance management methods and intelligent monitoring to be carried out. In view of this situation, the intelligent fault handling of IMS is analyzed in detail. Firstly, the overall architecture and deployment architecture of the integrated operation and maintenance platform are analyzed. On this basis, the network signaling monitoring and service monitoring based on IMS system are accomplished, and the intelligent fault handling function of IMS is realized. Through the construction of IMS intelligent fault handling platform, it will provide all-round support for the operation, maintenance and management of IMS system. It will bring remarkable economic, social and management benefits to the field of power communication network management, and make new and greater contribution to the safe and stable operation of power grid and the operation and management of the company.

Keywords: IMS · Fault handling · Operation · Functional design · Condition monitoring

1 Introduction

Softswitch and IMS (IP Multimedia Subsystem) are two kinds of next-generation network (NGN) switching technologies which have been developed in public network and private network after circuit switching [1]. As a new form of multimedia service, IMS system has more advanced technology network architecture, more open business development environment and more uniform standard protocol [2]. IMS shielded the difference of access layer, through the further separation of service and session control, it was oriented to the development of multimedia service and the integration of fixed mobile service platform [3]. IMS technology can meet the needs of newer and more diversified multimedia services and is regarded as the core technology of the next generation network [4]. With the development of power communication service, the integration of voice and data network is an inevitable trend. The wide application of multimedia and high bandwidth technology has changed the demand of network [5, 6].

With the continuous development of IP and other grouping technologies, the programmable switching equipment based on circuit switching technology is gradually facing the problem of technological evolution [7]. The State Grid Corporation's switching

© Springer Nature Singapore Pte Ltd. 2021
Y. Tian et al. (Eds.): ICBDS 2020, CCIS 1415, pp. 261–273, 2021.
https://doi.org/10.1007/978-981-16-3150-4_23

network is also facing the problem of network transformation at present, so it is necessary to design a switching network with advanced technology, rich business, controllable cost and convenient operation and maintenance as the direction of network evolution, so as to solve the challenge of the gradual shutdown of the current program-controlled switching equipment to the operation of the current network. The construction of the power company's IMS platform will greatly enhance the support capacity of voice and data [8]. However, the operation and maintenance pressure of IMS system is mainly concentrated in ICT company, the number of access equipment to be maintained will be greatly increased, and it is urgent for advanced maintenance management methods and intelligent monitoring to be carried out. At present, the operation and maintenance of IMS cannot fully meet the needs of management.

At present, the user data of IMS need to be configured in many network elements of IMS core system [9]. The operation is more complex, the maintenance is difficult and the configuration experience is poor, so it is difficult to deal with the large-scale configuration requirement by manual method only. And the access equipment of IMS system can only monitor the working status of the equipment through the network management of the manufacturer, and cannot be tested and monitored at the signaling level and the business level. It is difficult to effectively guarantee the availability of voice service by relying solely on the monitoring of the equipment level. It is necessary to establish the foreground interface specification of IMS, construct the foreground management and maintenance platform of IMS system, establish the fault monitoring of voice network and maintenance system at the signaling level, and protect the operation and maintenance management and intelligent monitoring of IMS voice exchange system. Based on these problems, this paper presents the research of intelligent fault handling of IMS.

2   Theoretical Research on Intelligent Fault Handling in IMS

With the development of IMS, the demand for the maintenance management, fault analysis and service quality assurance of IMS network is increasing gradually. In order to ensure the reliability and quality of IMS network, a lot of testing and verification process is needed. Network signaling monitoring is an important technology to ensure the high quality operation of IMS network. The network structure of IMS is shown in the following figure. The monitoring range of network signaling in the IMS includes the service layer, the control layer and the access layer [10] (Fig. 1).

The service layer includes devices such as SIPAS, IM-SSF/SCP, service capability engines and open gateways [11]. Operators use SIP AS to provide services directly to users. Operators provide third-party services through an open gateway with a service capability engine. Operators provide users with traditional smart services through IM-SSF and SCP. The control layer includes devices such as P/I/S-CSCF, HSS/SLF, IBCF, BGCF, MGCF, MRFC, MRFP, BGF, MGW and ENUM/DNS, completes user authentication, session control and routing, business triggers, and network interworking.

The access layer mainly realizes the service access of IMS users, realizes the interworking of user services under different network environments, ensures the security of softswitch network, supports QoS management, cooperates with user roaming management, media management and so on. The protocol for the communication between the three layers is shown in Fig. 2.

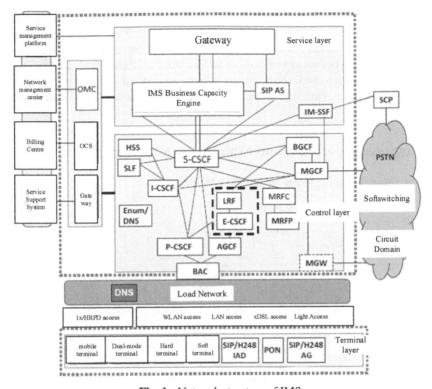

Fig. 1. Network structure of IMS

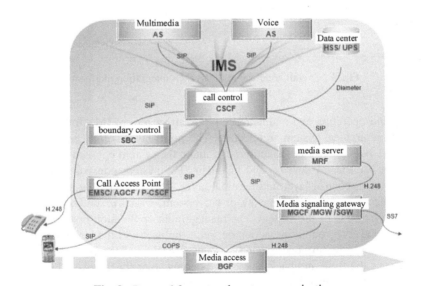

Fig. 2. Protocol for network metacommunication

SIP (Session Initiation Protocol) is a multimedia communication protocol developed by IETF (Internet Engineering Task Force). It is a text-based application layer control protocol for creating, modifying, and releasing sessions of one or more participants. SIP is widely used in the networks of CS (Circuit Switching), NGN (Next Generation Network) and IMS (Ip Multimedia Subsystem), which can support and apply to multimedia services such as voice, video and data, as well as features such as presentation, instant messaging.

3 Integrated Operation and Maintenance Platform for IMS

3.1 The Overall Architecture of the IMS Platform

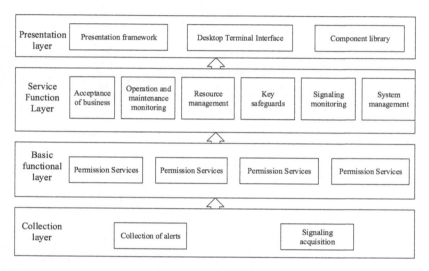

Fig. 3. Overall architecture of the IMS integration platform

The integrated operation and maintenance platform system of IMS follows the design concept of hierarchical system architecture. The multi-layer architecture can limit the dependencies between system functions and make the system coupled in a looser way, thus making it easier to develop and maintain. The system consists of management application layer, control layer and terminal layer. The management application layer is responsible for the main framework of the system, which is the basis for realizing the business function of the system. The management application layer is responsible for handling the foreground interaction between the user and the software, displaying information and providing background services. Because of the tight logic and interdependence of the front and back, this layer is convenient for the overall development of the system. The control layer will involve the IMS core network's network element equipment and the access network's equipment, reduces with the upper layer's dependence laziness, not only can guarantee the future equipment's access extensibility well, in the multiplexing also is the superiority obvious. Once a uniform interface has been defined, functional modules for business distribution and access equipment management can access the equipment of each manufacturer without repeated development for different types of device interfaces. The terminal layer is a managed access-side terminal device, and its deployment and replacement have no dependence on the upper layer and will not create a performance bottleneck for the system. The schematic diagram of the system is shown in Fig. 3.

3.2 Deployment Architecture of IMS Platform

The platform system of IMS is aimed at improving the efficiency of equipment management and maintenance. The responsibility for the operation and maintenance of IMS is consistent with the responsibility for the administration of the core network. An access network operations management system has been deployed in provincial companies. Units at all levels of the company are remotely connected to the company's system via web maintenance client. A schematic diagram of the deployment is shown in Fig. 4.

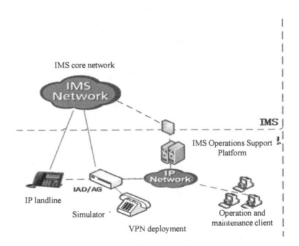

Fig. 4. Schematic diagram of the IMS platform

By integrating and integrating the business scope of fixed network and mobile network, IMS can be fully deployed, so that the user can access from any terminal anytime and anywhere, without being bound by fixed network and mobile network, and experience the same service. Moreover, based on the IMS, carried by the ip, the business on the Internet is collected into its own business system, which expands the scope of business and allows users to have more business experience. All in all, the goal of conference building based on IMS is the integration of multi-networks to achieve multi-business integration. IMS self-help conference business platform includes conference application server, resource processing server etc. The conference platform realizes the operation and management of the IMS multimedia conference by the national network company, and can also provide the functions of session control, resource management, authentication, routing, meeting notification and so on, and connect with the IMS core network through the IMS sip interface. Portal can provide users with self-service management functions such as conference management and venue control, provide users with direct access to web pages to participate in the meeting. A media resource service can reserve and allocate conference resources related to processing, as well as playing voice notification and receiving secondary dialing. H.323 gateway can realize the interworking between H.323 terminal and the original H.323 video conference system. Short message gateway and mail server mainly forward the notice of video conference; MGCF is responsible for interconnection with PSTN terminal and mobile terminal (Figs. 5 and 6).

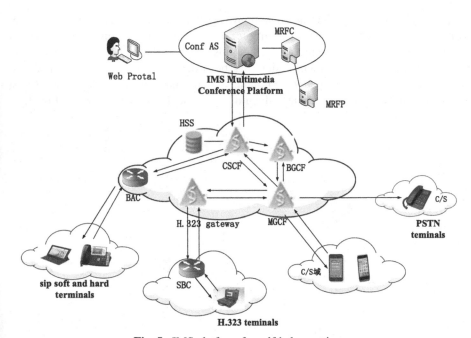

Fig. 5. IMS platform for self-help meetings

Information security protection includes production control area security protection and management information area security protection, as shown below [25]. Among them, the production control area and the management information area adopt the horizontal safety isolation device dedicated to electric power [26]. The management information is divided into information intranet and information extranet, and the information security isolation device is used between the information intranet and the information extranet. IMS administrative exchange network is deployed in the management information area, there is no business interaction with the production control area, and there is no need for special horizontal safety isolation device for electric power [27]. However, for IMS services across internal and external information networks, it is necessary to force the security isolation device to meet the requirements of information security.

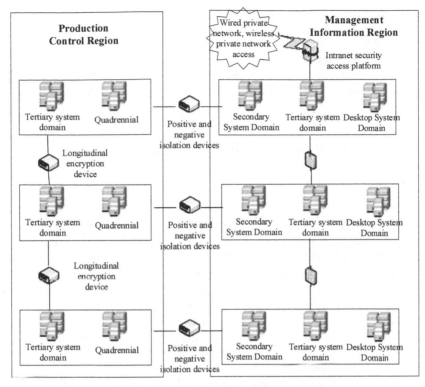

Fig. 6. Schematic diagram of security domain partition

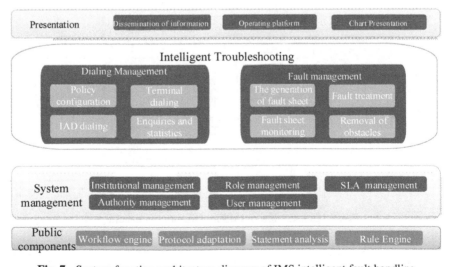

Fig. 7. System function architecture diagram of IMS intelligent fault handling

3.3 Function Design of Intelligent Fault Handling

In the functional architecture diagram of intelligent fault handling in IMS, intelligent fault handling includes dialing test management and fault management. Dialing management includes policy configuration, IAD dialing, terminal dialing and query statistics. Fault management includes fault sheet, fault sheet monitoring, fault handling and obstacle elimination (Fig. 7).

4 Realization of Intelligent Fault Handling

4.1 The Process of Fault Handling

The intelligent fault handling of IMS is mainly to find the related terminal fault automatically through the voice testing technology of the signaling layer. Then, the system analyzes the fault occurring, and gives the solution of the fault or the direct automatic processing according to the result of the analysis. There are three fault sources for intelligent fault handling of IMS, which are call center customer fault declaration, automatic analysis after alarm collection, and zero perception automatic dialing of key terminals. The overall flow of intelligent fault handling for IMS is shown in Fig. 8.

Step 1, for the alarm of core network, once the cause of failure is analyzed, the network administrator should be notified while generating the fault sheet.

Step 2, for the obstacle of the manual declaration, the verification dial test should be done after the fault is generated.

Step 3, after the fault processing is completed, it is necessary to do the dial test verification to make sure that there is no problem before it can be removed.

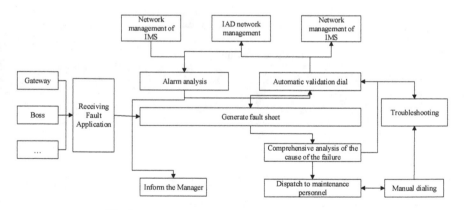

Fig. 8. General flow of IMS intelligent fault handling

4.2 Process of Fault Analysis for Core Network

The flow of fault analysis for the core network is as follows, as shown in Fig. 9.

Step 1, using SNMP protocol and U2000, the alarm information of equipment is collected.

Step 2, determine the alarm level after discovering the equipment alarm.

Step 3, the alarm is analyzed, the processing strategy is selected and displayed on the device topology if page presentation is required.

Step 4, if the fault cannot be dealt with, then generate a report card, transfer to manual processing, and then call multimedia is used to push the alarm message.

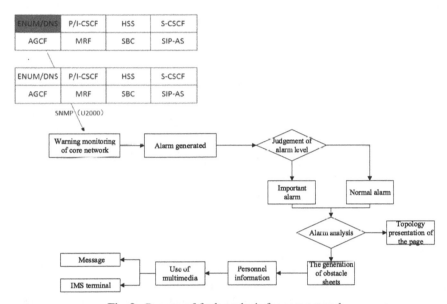

Fig. 9. Process of fault analysis for core network

4.3   Monitoring Process of IAD

The monitoring process for IAD is shown in Fig. 10.

Step 1, the system periodically monitors IAD through telnet.

Step 2, it is possible that the relationship between IAD and phone may vary, and the relationship between IAD and phone is collected periodically.

Step 3, if the monitored IAD is found to be faulty, check if the IAD in the same area is normal. At the same time, observe whether there is an alarm in the core network, if there is an alarm, generate a report card, and transfer to manual processing.

Step 4, if IAD is a single point of failure, it determines whether you can log on to the console or restart the device with a reboot command if the state is abnormal.

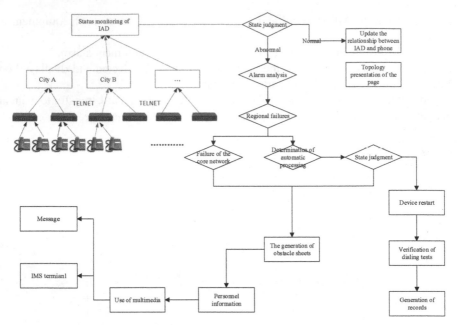

Fig. 10. Monitoring process for IAD

4.4   Process to Secure Key Users

The process of securing key users is shown in Fig. 11.

Step 1, first of all, to determine the level of terminal security, to determine whether it belongs to the first type of telephone, the second type of telephone or the three types of telephone. Power Grid Control Telephone, Uninterruptible Telephone and Distribution Network Emergency Repair Telephone belong to the first class telephone, the important user telephone belongs to the second class telephone, the common user telephone belongs to the third class telephone.

Step 2, Class I and Class II phones are detected more frequently, and Class I and Class II phones use a more active, real-time configuration.

Step 3, one or two types of telephone failures are production failures with the highest priority.

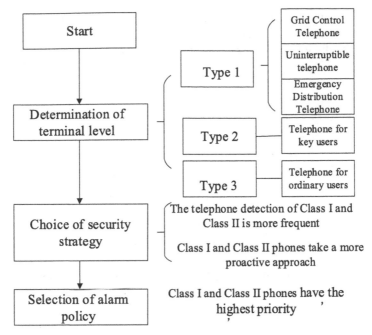

Fig. 11. Process to secure key users

4.5 Display of Intelligent Fault Handling in IMS

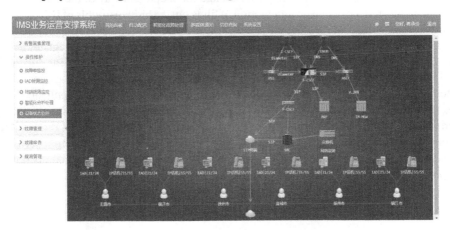

Fig. 12. Interface of intelligent fault handling for IMS

Figure 12 shows the interface of IMS intelligent fault handling. One function of the IMS operation support system is intelligent fault handling, including alarm collection management, operation and maintenance, fault management, five declarations and dialing management. The interface in Fig. 11 is device status monitoring in operation and maintenance.

Figure 13 shows the result of intelligent analysis in operation and maintenance, in the interface, the fault handling strategy of serial number 3 is that the call-turn number is incorrectly configured and the result is automatically fixed.

Fig. 13. Results of intelligent analysis and processing of IMS

5 Conclusion

This paper makes full use of the accumulated experience of electric power company, through constructing IMS platform, it can change the inefficient way of the current IMS system mainly rely on manual configuration. It finds out the hidden trouble of IMS system in time, and greatly improve the efficiency and level of communication operation and maintenance. Through the research of this paper, the monitoring of network signaling and service based on IMS system is completed, and the intelligent fault handling function of IMS is realized, which protects the operation and maintenance management and intelligent monitoring of IMS system. The further popularization and application of the results of this paper will provide strong support for the operation, maintenance and management of IMS system. The establishment of IMS platform brings remarkable economic, social and management benefits to the field of power communication network management, and makes new and greater contribution to the safe and stable operation of power grid and the management of company operation.

References

1. Liu, C., Zhang, Y.: Application of IMS technology in power communication administrative switching network. Inf. Commun. **7**(11), 175–176 (2016)
2. Peng, X.: Research of an interactive voice-video response system based on IMS. Comput. Technol. Dev. **9**(2), 207–210 (2011)
3. Wang, S.-G., Sun, Q.-B.: Uncertain QoS-aware skyline service selection based on cloud model. J. Softw. **23**(6), 1397–1412 (2017)
4. Gu, Y.: Research on the application of wavelet neural network in temperature control system. Adv. Mater. Res. **12**(5), 33–49 (2014)

5. Vidal, I., de la Oliva, A.: TRIM: an architecture for transparent IMS-based mobility. Comput. Netw. **55**(7), 1472–1486 (2017)
6. Thomas, M., Metcalf, L., Spring, J.: SiLK: a tool suite for unsampled network flow analysis at scale. In: IEEE International Congress on Big Data, pp. 184–191 (2014)
7. Zhu, X., Liao, J.: The IMS: IP multimedia concepts and services in the mobile domain. J. Assoc. Inf. Sci. Technol. **58**(11), 1705–1706 (2015)
8. Wang, Q., Sun, Y.: The next generation network of the soft exchange and IMS. Netw. Secur. Technol. Appl. **8**, 37–38 (2014)
9. Sun, J.: Network optimization design of NGN. Shanxi Electron. Technol. (6), 78–83 (2014)
10. Chen, R., Tang, H., Zhao, G.: Study and implementation of user agent for SIP protocol. Commun. Technol. (2), 163–165 (2010)
11. He, C., Yang, H., Lu, X.: Evolution scheme from soft switch to IMS in electric power communication. Electric Power Inf. Commun. Technol. **13**(11), 1–6 (2015)

Research on System Simulation and Data Analysis of Power Wireless Private Network

Weiwei Yan[✉] and Hui Chu

NARI Group Corporation, State Grid Electric Power Research Institute, Nanjing, China

Abstract. Aiming at the problems existing in the application of power wireless communication, in order to better serve the smart grid and carry out the application research of TD-LTE technology in the field of power communication, the simulation platform of power wireless private network is established. The perform of power wireless private network is simulated from two aspects, are link level simulation and system level simulation, and the influence of wireless parameters on the performance of wireless private network is analyzed. The establishment of the simulation platform provides technical support for the unified construction of power communication network, laying a solid foundation for the application of the power wireless special network, and laying a theoretical foundation for the later network planning.

Keywords: TD-LTE · Wireless private network · Coverage · Link level simulation · Throughput

1 Introduction

With the development of smart grid and the continuous progress of information construction, the requirements of power communication network for network bandwidth and delay is high [1–4]. At the same time, the number of terminals is large and the distribution is relatively scattered. Traditional communication methods, such as power carrier and 230 MHz digital radio station have been difficult to meet the communication needs of different regions and different kinds of service [5–7]. The construction cost of the optical fiber is high, the construction period is long, and all the terminals are difficult to cover [8, 9]. Therefore, it is the development trend of power grid to connect power terminal equipment to power communication network [10, 11].

At present, the construction of public power network mainly depends on leasing the data channel of public network to carry electric power service. However, due to the limitations of security, reliability and bandwidth flow, wireless public network is not suitable as the communication mode of power network, so it is very necessary to establish wireless private network. The new wireless communication technology has great advantages in transmission rate [12]. Driven by the construction of power Internet of things, the services of power grid stock needs to be optimized and upgraded, the

© Springer Nature Singapore Pte Ltd. 2021
Y. Tian et al. (Eds.): ICBDS 2020, CCIS 1415, pp. 274–284, 2021.
https://doi.org/10.1007/978-981-16-3150-4_24

emerging services is booming, the requirement of the network security is higher and higher, and all kinds of services require higher and higher wireless communication index.

At present, there are many literatures to simulate and analyze the performance of wireless network. However, based on the particularity of power system, there is a lack of establishment and analysis for power service and power wireless private network at present. Therefore, this paper establishes TD-LTE simulation platform in power wireless private network, and puts forward a performance simulation scheme of wireless private network.

2 Analysis of User Requirements in Power Network

The wireless special network can support the smart grid, support distribution automation, marketing load control, smart home, new energy grid-connected communication, operation inspection and repair monitoring and other smart grid services, to meet the requirement of reliability, security, real-time [13] (Tables 1 and 2).

Table 1. Demand analysis of power distribution automation services

	Department	Name of the service	Irish coefficient	Delay requirements	quantity demand
1	Operation monitoring	Distribution automation	1	<500 ms	1000
2	Distribution transportation inspection room	Robot inspection	1	<2 s	30
3		Environmental monitoring	1	<2 s	15
4		Three-dimensional emergency repair	0.3	<2 s	15
5		Field remote management and visualization	0.3	<2 s	15

Table 2. Demand analysis of smart grid extension service

	Department	Name of the service	Irish coefficient	Delay requirements	quantity demand
1	Transformation and transportation room	Digitization and informatization management of substation equipment	0.3	<2 s	15
2		Remote video monitoring and application of maintenance site	0.3	<2 s	15

(*continued*)

Table 2. (*continued*)

	Department	Name of the service	Irish coefficient	Delay requirements	quantity demand
3	Power transmission and inspection room	Intelligent monitoring of transmission line operation state	0.3	<2 s	10
4	Cable inspection room	Popularization and application of intelligent grounding box for power cable	1	<2 s	60
5	Sales department	Intelligent building construction	0.1	<2 s	10
6		Scenery storage microgrid	1	<2 s	15
7		Smart home	1	<2 s	1000
8		Demand response information platform	0.1	<2 s	15
9		Electricity information collection	0.1	<2 s	5000
10		Power management service platform	0.5	<2 s	150
11		Electric automobile charging pile	1	<2 s	30
12		Shore charging pile	1	<2 s	15
13		Electric load control	1	<2 s	100

3   Introduction of Simulation System

Dynamic simulation is to analyze network performance through the mobility of terminal in continuous time [15]. The process of dynamic simulation is from the beginning of the new terminal access network to the end of disconnection, so it is more reliable in the accuracy of simulation evaluation. Dynamic simulation takes into account many dynamic factors, such as user's moving speed and direction, real-time state of wireless propagation channel, multi-cell switching and multi-service switching, therefore, one of the main disadvantages of dynamic simulation compared with static simulation is that the simulation speed is slow and the time consuming is long.

3.1 Parameter Configuration of the System

Tables 3 gives the parameter configuration of simulation [14], as well as the comparison table between CQI and modulation mode. A total of 15 CQI values are used [16]. The parameter configuration of system simulation is given in Table 4.

Table 3. Parameters

Parameter	Value
Number of users	1
Bandwidth	1.4 MHz
Number of retransmissions	0和3
Type of channel	Flat rayleigh fading
Time-varying characteristics of channels	Block fading
Type of receiver	Soft sphere decoding
Length of simulation	5000subframes
Mode of transmission	Single input, single output, transmit diversity, space division reuse

Table 4. Parameters

Parameter	Value
Frequency	1785 MHz
Bandwidth	20M, 10M, 5M, 3M, 1.4M
Thermal noise spectral density	−174 dBm/Hz
Number of transmit antennas	1 or 2
Number of receiving antennas	1 or 2
Mode of transmission	Transmit diversity, space division reuse
Length of simulation	5000 subframes
Number of simulations	200 times per scene
Distance of base station	3000 m
The height of the base station	12 m, 25 m
Coupling loss between base stations	70 dB
Transmission power of base station	43/46/49 dBm
The location of the user	Random distribution, 20 users/sectors
The height of the user	1 m, 3 m

4 Link-Level Simulation

4.1 Topological Structure of the System

The system topology used in the simulation is shown in Fig. 1. Each sector has 20 users.

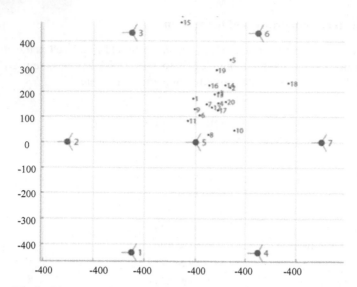

Fig. 1. System topology (7 base stations, 3 sections, 20 users/section)

4.2   Simulation of Channel Environment

The path loss is shown in Figs. 2, 3 and 4, as can be seen from the figures.

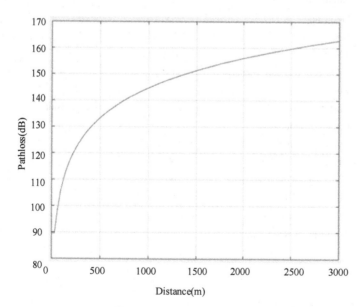

Fig. 2. Path loss (h = 12 m)

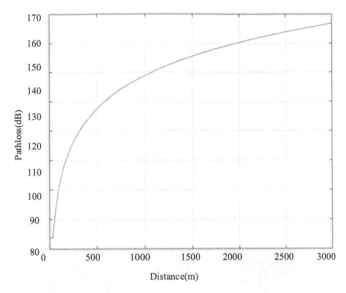

Fig. 3. Path loss (h = 15 m)

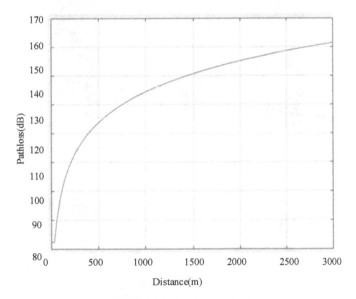

Fig. 4. Path loss (h = 25 m)

5 System-Level Simulation

Figures 5, 6, 7 and 8 shows the coverage maps when the height of the base station is 25 m and 12 m, respectively. The increasing the height of the base station can improve the coverage of the cell, but it can increase the interference. When the height of base station is 12 m, the quality of service (QoS) at the cell edge can not be guaranteed.

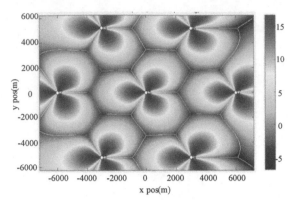

Fig. 5. Coverage (h = 25 m)

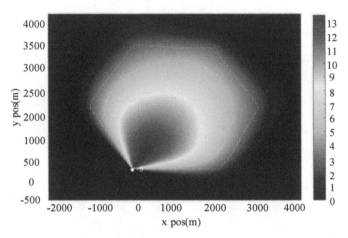

Fig. 6. Coverage (h = 25 m)

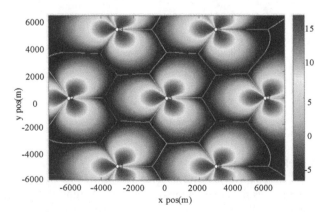

Fig. 7. Coverage (h = 12 m)

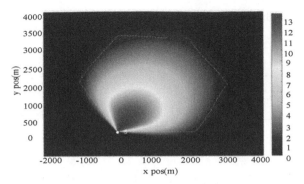

Fig. 8. Coverage (h = 12 m)

Figures 9 and 10 show the error block rate curves of users when the user height is 3 m and 1 m. It can be seen that when the user's height is 3 m, the highest throughput rate is slightly higher than the scene.

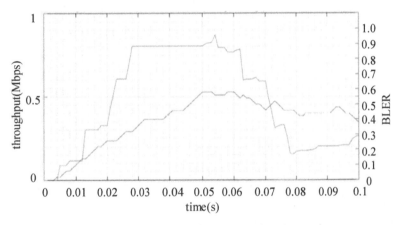

Fig. 9. BLER and Throughput (h = 1 m)

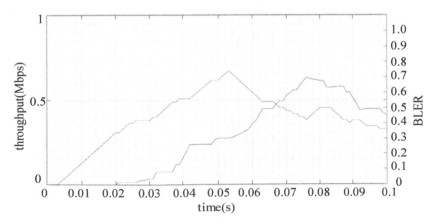

Fig. 10. BLER and Throughput (h = 3 m)

Figure 11 shows the variation of throughput with time.

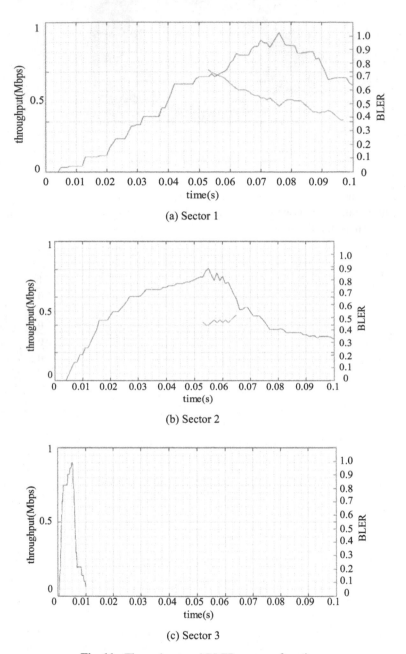

(a) Sector 1

(b) Sector 2

(c) Sector 3

Fig. 11. Throughput and BLER curves of sections

6   Conclusion

The performance simulation of the network is carried out based on the architecture of the TD-LTE power wireless private network. Through simulation, it can be concluded that different kinds of service can be supported by a variety of modulation and coding methods. With the adoption of COMP technology, based on the TD-LTE technology, the transmission of data can be supported under different transmission environments, the application requirement of the power wireless special network system can be met. Increasing the height of base station can improve the QoS and overall throughput, and adjusting the dip angle of antenna can improve the throughput. As an important infrastructure to support the development of power system, the construction of network will greatly promote the development of energy Internet strategy, and will greatly promote and all links of service in power system.

References

1. Sun, S., Chen, Y.: Research on business-oriented covering LTE power wireless private network. Electric Power Inf. Commun. Technol. **13**(4), 6–10 (2015)
2. You, X.H., Pan, Z.W., Gao, X.Q., et al.: The 5G mobile communication: the development trends and its emerging key techniques. Sci. Sinica **44**(5), 551 (2014)
3. Liu, G., Jiang, D.: 5G: vision and requirements for mobile communication system towards year 2020. Chin. J. Eng. 1–8 (2016)
4. Suo, H., Wan, J., Zou, C., Liu, J.: Security in the internet of things: a review. In: 2012 International Conference on Computer Science and Electronics Engineering, Hangzhou, pp. 648–651 (2012). https://doi.org/10.1109/ICCSEE.2012.373
5. Diffie, W., Hellman, M.: New directions in cryptography. IEEE Trans. Inf. Theory **22**(6), 644–654 (1976). https://doi.org/10.1109/TIT.1976.1055638
6. Yassein, M.B., Aljawarneh, S., Qawasmeh, E., Mardini, W., Khamayseh, Y.: Comprehensive study of symmetric key and asymmetric key encryption algorithms. In: 2017 International Conference on Engineering and Technology (ICET), Antalya, pp. 1–7 (2017). https://doi.org/10.1109/ICEngTechnol.2017.8308215
7. Noura, H.N., Chehab, A., Couturier, R.: Overview of efficient symmetric cryptography: dynamic vs static approaches. In: 2020 8th International Symposium on Digital Forensics and Security (ISDFS), Beirut, Lebanon, pp. 1–6 (2020). https://doi.org/10.1109/ISDFS49300.2020.9116441
8. Boicea, A., Radulescu, F., Truica, C., Costea, C.: Database encryption using asymmetric keys: a case study. In: 2017 21st International Conference on Control Systems and Computer Science (CSCS), Bucharest, pp. 317–323 (2017). https://doi.org/10.1109/CSCS.2017.50
9. Chandra, S., Paira, S., Alam, S.S., Sanyal, G.: A comparative survey of symmetric and asymmetric key cryptography. In: 2014 International Conference on Electronics, Communication and Computational Engineering (ICECCE), Hosur, pp. 83–93 (2014). https://doi.org/10.1109/ICECCE.2014.7086640
10. Panda, M.: Performance analysis of encryption algorithms for security. In: 2016 International Conference on Signal Processing, Communication, Power and Embedded System (SCOPES), Paralakhemundi, pp. 278–284 (2016). https://doi.org/10.1109/SCOPES.2016.7955835
11. Gupta, C.P., Sharma, I.: A fully homomorphic encryption scheme with symmetric keys with application to private data processing in clouds. In: 2013 Fourth International Conference on the Network of the Future (NoF), Pohang, pp. 1–4 (2013). https://doi.org/10.1109/NOF.2013.6724526

12. Wang, K.: The application of the internet of things in the 5G era in the power system. Telecom Power Technol. **35**(5), 187–188 (2018)
13. Ma, Z., Zhang, Z.Q., Ding, Z.G., et al.: Key techniques for 5G wireless communications: network architecture, physical layer, and MAC layer perspectives. Sci. China **58**(4), 41301–41321 (2015)

Research on Attitude Control System
of Four-Rotor Aircraft

Zhan Shi[1(✉)], Yonghui Liu[1], Fengxian Zhao[1], and Chenxu Liu[2]

[1] School of Computer Engineering, Nanjing Institute of Technology, Nanjing 211100, China
[2] Industrial Center, Nanjing Institute of Technology, Nanjing 211100, China

Abstract. With the characteristics of simple mechanical structure, light weight, and low R & D cost, the four-rotor aircraft is widely used in many fields at present. Aiming at attitude control accuracy and anti-jamming of the four-rotor aircraft, it has been one of the hot topics. In order to improve the attitude control accuracy of the four-rotor aircraft and the resistance of it to the external environment, this paper analyzes the dynamic model of the four-rotor aircraft in detail, optimizes the RBF neural network by improving the particle swarm algorithm, and uses the neural network to learn to achieve adaptive adjustment of control parameters in PID controller. Then, based on a three-dimensional scene, the simulation platform is built for simulation testing and result analysis in this paper. From experimental results, it shows that the designed control algorithm in this paper not only enhances the anti-jamming ability of the four-rotor aircraft, but also improves its control accuracy. It has a good application effect.

Keywords: Four-rotor aircraft · Particle swarm algorithm · RBF neural network · Simulation platform

1 Introduction

The four-rotor aircraft has the advantages of hovering in the air, vertical take-off and landing, accurate positioning operation and so on, which makes it widely used in many fields of military and civil use. The tasks it performs are becoming more and more complex and diversified, such as monitoring, rescue, power line inspection, and express delivery, which are multiple and dangerous.

The four-rotor aircraft is a kind of coaxial aircraft, which has the characteristics of strong coupling, nonlinear and under-actuated [1]. Although the four-rotor aircraft can achieve a series of operations, such as low speed and low altitude navigating, multi-attitude transformation, omnidirectional flight and precision hovering, the accuracy and anti-interference ability of attitude control in the course of flight are always difficult problems.

At present, many scholars have conducted research on the control of UAV and have achieved a lot of research results [2–7]. Lin Jiang [8] proposes a control method based on fuzzy single neuron, which greatly improves the dynamic performance of the system. Wei Yu [9] designed an anti-interference cascade attitude controller, which is superior

© Springer Nature Singapore Pte Ltd. 2021
Y. Tian et al. (Eds.): ICBDS 2020, CCIS 1415, pp. 285–296, 2021.
https://doi.org/10.1007/978-981-16-3150-4_25

to traditional PID cascade control in terms of anti-interference and robustness. Youyuan He [10] proposed a control algorithm based on backstepping sliding mode to improve the anti-interference ability of the system. Zhenyue Jia [11] uses an adaptive neural network to approximate nonlinear functions and achieves a good control effect. Fuzzy adaptive backstepping control law is used by Laihong Zhou [12], through fuzzy constraint compensation fuzzy control law, enhance the system's anti-interference ability.

Literature research and experimental results show that the nonlinear robust control of four-rotor aircraft can achieve better flight control effects, and the backstepping control method also has special advantages in attitude control. However, they are all based on a specific mathematical model to achieve control. The calculation involved in the process is large, and the real-time data processing requirements are high, so there are certain difficulties in realization. For this reason, we proposes an improved method of particle swarm optimization and uses this algorithm to further optimize the RBF neural network. Then use the learning of the neural network to adaptively adjust the control parameters of the PID controller to achieve the control of the four-rotor aircraft. Finally, a simulation platform based on 3D scenes was designed and constructed, and then dynamic modeling and flight simulation were carried out to verify the stability and effectiveness of the control method. The experimental results show that the radial basis function neural network controller optimized by particle swarm optimization has good control performance and strong anti-interference ability.

2   Dynamic Model of the Four-Rotor Aircraft

As shown in the following figure, the physical structure of the four-rotor aircraft is M1, M2, M3, M4 as the four rotors of the aircraft. For each rotor, its profile is asymmetric. If the rotor rotates, the air velocity on the upper surface will be faster than that on the lower surface, so the air pressure on the upper surface is less than the lower surface, and the pressure difference between the upper and lower surfaces forms a lift. Rotors M1 and M3 rotate counterclockwise, while rotors M2 and M4 rotate clockwise (Fig. 1).

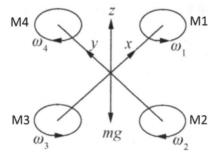

Fig. 1. Schematic view of four-rotor aircraft

In order to establish the mathematical model of the aircraft more accurately, the following assumptions are made: the mass distribution of the four-rotor aircraft is uniform and symmetric. The lift produced by the rotor is proportional to the square of the rotational speed. The influence of ground effects is ignored. At the same time, let Φ, θ, and ψ be the roll angle, pitch angle and yaw angle of the four-rotor respectively, then the geographic coordinate system can be obtained from its body coordinate system, and the conversion matrix [13] is:

$$\begin{bmatrix} \cos\psi\cos\theta & \cos\phi\sin\theta\sin\psi - \sin\psi\cos\phi & \cos\psi\sin\theta\cos\phi + \sin\psi\sin\phi \\ \sin\psi\cos\theta & \sin\psi\sin\theta\sin\phi + \cos\psi\cos\phi & \sin\psi\sin\theta\cos\phi - \sin\phi\cos\psi \\ -\sin\theta & \cos\theta\sin\phi & \cos\psi\cos\phi \end{bmatrix} \quad (1)$$

In addition, according to the Newton-Euler equation, the dynamic model of the four-rotor aircraft can be obtained by Hang LI [14]:

$$\begin{cases} \ddot{x} = \frac{u_1}{m}(\cos\phi\sin\theta\sin\psi - \sin\phi\cos\psi) \\ \ddot{y} = \frac{u_1}{m}(\cos\phi\sin\theta\sin\psi - \sin\phi\cos\psi) \\ \ddot{z} = \frac{u_1}{m}(\cos\phi\cos\theta) - g \\ \ddot{\phi} = \dot{\theta}\dot{\psi}(\frac{I_y - I_z}{I_x}) + \frac{l}{I_x}U_2 \\ \ddot{\theta} = \dot{\theta}\dot{\psi}(\frac{I_z - I_x}{I_y}) + \frac{l}{I_x}U_3 \\ \ddot{\psi} = \dot{\theta}\dot{\psi}(\frac{I_x - I_y}{I_z}) + \frac{l}{I_x}U_4 \end{cases} \quad (2)$$

M is the weight of the four-rotor aircraft, and x, y, z are the displacements of the four-rotor aircraft in the direction of the X, Y and Z directions, respectively. I_x, I_y, I_z are the moments of inertia of the four-rotor aircraft around the X axis, the Y axis and the Z axis, respectively. The U_1 is the lift of the four-rotor aircraft, the U_2 is the torque in the pitch direction of the four-rotor aircraft, the U_3 is the torque in the roll direction of the four-rotor aircraft, and the U_4 is the torque in the yaw direction of the four-rotor aircraft. l is the distance from the center of the four-rotor aircraft to each motor.

3 Algorithm Design Based on PSO-RBF

3.1 RBF Neural Network

RBF neural network is a feed forward neural network, and its network structure is shown in Fig. 2.

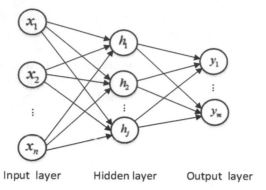

Fig. 2. RBF neural network structure

The RBF neural network in the figure above has n input layer neurons, j hidden layer neurons, and m output layer neurons. The commonly used radial basis function of the hidden layer is Gaussian function, the general form is:

$$h_i(x) = \exp(\frac{\|x - c_i\|^2}{2b_i^2}), b > 0 \tag{3}$$

In this formula, $i = 1, 2, ..., j$, The input vectors are $x = (x_1, x_2, \cdots, x_n)^T$, c_i and b_i are the center point and base width of the i-th hidden layer neuron, respectively. At this time, the output of the neural network is:

$$y(k) = \sum_{i=1}^{n} {}^{k}_{j=1} w_{ik} h_j(x), k = 1, 2, 3, \cdots, K \tag{4}$$

3.2 Particle Swarm Algorithm

In 1955, Eberhart and Kennedy proposed a swarm intelligence algorithm called particle swarm algorithm (PSO) [15]. Compared with other intelligent optimization algorithms, PSO algorithm has the advantages of fewer control variables, fast convergence speed and simple implementation [16]. In the PSO algorithm, a possible solution of the actual problem corresponds to a particle, and the particle's objective function determines its fitness. For each particle, iterate through p_{best} and g_{best} to update its own speed and position to achieve objective optimization.

Suppose there are N particles in a D dimensional search space, and the position and velocity of each particle are expressed as $X_i = [x_{i1}, x_{i2}, \cdots, x_{id}]$ and $V_i = [v_{i1}, v_{i2}, \cdots, v_{id}]$. The position and velocity of the particles will be adjusted according to the following formula:

$$\begin{cases} v_{id}(t + 1) = wv_i(t) + c_1k_1(p_{best}(t) - x_i(t)) + c_2k_2(g_{best}(t) - x_i(t)) \\ x_i(t + 1) = x_i(t + 1) + v_i(t) \end{cases} \tag{5}$$

W is the inertial weights; c_1 and c_2 are learning factors; k_1 and k_2 are random numbers between 0 and 1.

3.3 Improved PSO Algorithm

Since the standard PSO algorithm has the disadvantage of easily falling into the local optimal solution prematurely, many studies have explored how to improve the PSO algorithm. Generally speaking, if you want to improve the global search ability of the algorithm, you need to increase the value of the inertia weight w; if you want to improve the local search ability of the algorithm, you need to reduce the value of the inertia weight w. As for the PSO algorithm, it should have a larger search space in the early stage, and it should have a strong local search ability in the later stage. Therefore, Dong Hu [17] proposed an inertial weight adjustment strategy:

$$w = w_{max} - \frac{t}{t_{max}}(w_{max} - w_{min}) \tag{6}$$

w_{max} is the initial inertia weight, t is the current iteration number, t_{max} is the maximum iteration number, and w_{min} is the final inertia weight. Literature [18] introduced the sine function to adjust the inertia weight, as shown in the following formula.

$$w = w_{max}(1 - \sin k) + rand * w_{min} * \sin k \tag{7}$$

In this formula $k = \frac{\pi t}{2t_{max}}$, $w_{max} = 0.9$, $w_{min} = 0.4$. This method makes the rate of change of inertia weight nonlinear and satisfies the change from large to small. However, the inertial weight change rate is too fast in the early stage of the change, which makes the global search ability of the initial particle algorithm worse, so that the global optimal solution cannot be found, which leads to the later local optimal solution.

Therefore, we introduce a new inertia weight adjustment formula, which can realize that the inertia weight decreases slowly in the initial stage, and its decrease rate is accelerated in the later stage, which greatly reduces the possibility of the algorithm falling into the local optimal solution. Enhanced the local search capability of the algorithm. The adjusted inertia weight formula is:

$$w = w_{max}(1 - \frac{t^2}{t_{max}^2}) + rand * w_{min} * \frac{t^2}{t_{max}^2} \tag{8}$$

The actual change process of the adjusted inertia weight formula is shown in Fig. 3. It can be seen from the figure that the change rate of the inertia weight curve is slow in the initial stage, so its global search ability is stronger; in the later period, the change rate of the curve is accelerated, so its local search ability becomes stronger, which is more conducive to seeking the global optimum solution.

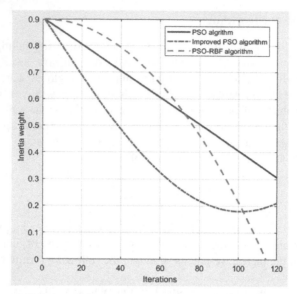

Fig. 3. Comparison of inertia weight change curve between the algorithm in this paper and other PSO algorithms

3.4 PSO-RBF Algorithm Design

On the basis of the above-mentioned improved PSO algorithm, the corresponding basis function center, width and connection weight of the RBF neural network are further determined to realize the optimization of the RBF neural network. The specific steps are shown in Fig. 4 below.

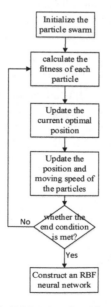

Fig. 4. PSO-RBF algorithm flow

In Fig. 4, the specific steps are as follows.

(1) Initialize the particle swarm, each particle is composed of the parameters of the RBF neural network.
(2) Take the mean square error of the actual output and the expected output as the fitness evaluation function, which is used to calculate the fitness of the current iterations of each particle. The fitness function is as follows:

$$f = \frac{1}{N} \sum_{i=1}^{n} {}_{k=1}^{N} (y_k - \hat{y}_k)^2 \qquad (9)$$

Among them, N is the number of training samples; y_k is the expected output; $\hat{y}_k$ is the actual output. The smaller the fitness, the closer the particle position is to the optimal position.
(3) Update the current optimal position and the global optimal position of the individual particles.
(4) Update the position and moving speed of the particles.
(5) Judge whether the end condition is met, if it is met, go to the next step, otherwise, return to step (2) and continue the iteration.
(6) Construct an RBF neural network based on the particles at the global optimal position.

4 Construction and Simulation of the Control System of the Four-Rotor Aircraft

4.1 Construction Based on PSO-RBF Controller

At present, the classic PID (proportional-integral-differential) controller generally adopts the deviation method to design the feedback quantity, does not rely on various specific mathematical models of the controlled object, and its structure is simple, so it is a frequently used control method, it also has a good performance in the control system of the quadrotor. This paper designs a PID controller based on PSO-RBF, as shown in Fig. 5, in accordance with the requirements of the four-rotor aircraft in terms of control accuracy and anti-interference ability.

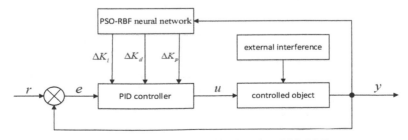

Fig. 5. Structure of controller based on PSO-RBF

In Fig. 5, e is the control error, ΔK_p, ΔK_i, ΔK_d are the output of PSO-RBF neural network, which is used to adjust the PID parameters. The PSO-RBF neural network adjusts the PID parameters through the error function of the system. Here we use incremental PID, taking the four-rotor aircraft's altitude error $e(k)$ as example.

$$e(k) = y(k) - y_m \tag{10}$$

The inputs of P, I, and D are:

$$\begin{cases} x_h(1) = e(k) - e(k-1) \\ x_h(2) = e(k) \\ x_h(3) = e(k) - e(k-1) \end{cases} \tag{11}$$

The objective function of RBF is $J = \frac{1}{2}e(k)^2$.
Then which can be obtained by gradient descent algorithm is:

$$\begin{cases} \Delta K_i = -\eta_i \frac{\partial J}{\partial k_i} = \eta_i e(k) \frac{\partial y(k)}{\partial u(k)} x_h(1) \\ \Delta K_d = -\eta_d \frac{\partial J}{\partial k_d} = \eta_d e(k) \frac{\partial y(k)}{\partial u(k)} x_h(2) \\ \Delta K_p = -\eta_p \frac{\partial J}{\partial k_p} = \eta_p e(k) \frac{\partial y(k)}{\partial u(k)} x_h(3) \end{cases} \tag{12}$$

Among them, η is the learning rate, and $\frac{\partial y}{\partial u(k)}$ is the Jacobian matrix, that is, the sensitivity information of the output of the object to the change of the control input, which is processed as follows:

$$\frac{\partial y}{\partial u(k)} \approx \frac{\partial y_m(k)}{\partial u(k)} = \sum_{i=1}^{m} w_i h_i(x) \frac{c_{ij} - \Delta u(k)}{b_i^2} \tag{13}$$

4.2   Simulation and Result Analysis

In order to more realistically simulate the flight control situation of the four-rotor aircraft in the actual environment, the simulation platform is constructed by using Matlab and the three-dimensional engine Unity to construct the simulation platform. The structure is shown in Fig. 6 below.

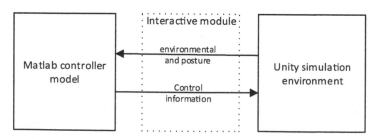

Fig. 6.   Structure of simulation platform

The simulation platform consists of three parts: the controller model under Matlab, the environment under Unity, the foue-rotor aircraft model and the interaction module between Matlab and Unity. Among them, the controller model mainly realizes the controller based on PSO-RBF. The controller can use the interaction module to obtain the environment information in Unity and the flight attitude information of the four-rotor aircraft, and then adjust the parameters to generate control information, and further use the interaction Module to control the flight of the four-rotor aircraft in Unity.

The following Fig. 7 shows the operation effect of the four-rotor aircraft flight in the Unity simulation environment. The model uses the interactive module in Fig. 6 to interact with the controller model in the Matlab for attitude, control and other information.

Fig. 7. Four-rotor aircraft flight on simulation platform

For the validity of the algorithm, the corresponding controller model is established in the MATLAB platform and verified. Set the desired position of the aircraft to a [1 1 1], and the initial values of the PID controller are Kp = 0.03, Ki = 0.03, Kd = 0.03. The actual control effect is shown in Fig. 8 below.

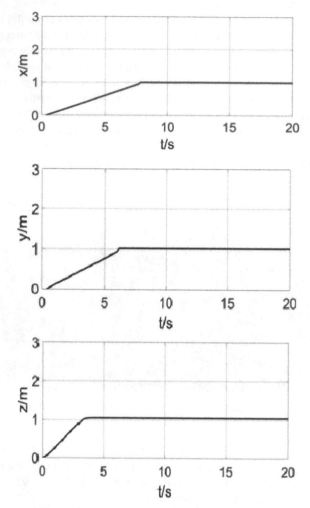

Fig. 8. Position response of the four-rotor aircraft

Add a disturbance signal of size 2 at 0.1 s, as shown in Fig. 9. It can be seen from the diagram that when the four-rotor aircraft is disturbed by the outside world, it can quickly recover to its original position.

For the change of PID value, as shown in Fig. 10. It can be seen that when the four-rotor model is disturbed, the RBD neural network can adjust the PID parameters in time, thereby improving the anti-interference ability of the four-rotor UAV.

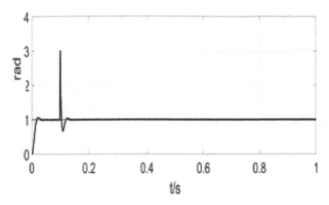

Fig. 9. Step response of pitch angle added disturbance signal

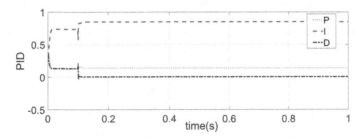

Fig. 10. Change of PID value

5 Conclusion

This paper aims at the problems of low control accuracy and poor anti-interference ability of the four-rotor aircraft. Based on the in-depth analysis of its controller, the RBF neural network is optimized by improving the PSO algorithm, and then the control parameters of the PID controller are adjusted adaptively by using the learning of the neural network to achieve the control of the four-rotor aircraft. Finally, the simulation platform based on 3D scene is designed and constructed, and the control effect and anti-interference performance are verified by the simulation platform. Experimental results show that the control method has good control performance and strong anti-interference ability.

Acknowledgments. This work is supported by the Natural Science Foundation of the Jiangsu Youth of China under grant BK20181019 and Science Foundation of Nanjing Institute of Technology under grant YKJ201723.

References

1. Zhang, L., Li, H.: Attitude control of four-rotor aircraft via fuzzy PID. Comput. Simul. **31**(08), 73–77 (2014)

2. lai Guo, C., Ren, H., Xing, Y., Lang, J., Xiong, L.: The research of four rotor aircraft based on STM32. In: IEEE 3rd Information Technology, Networking, Electronic and Automation Control Conference (ITNEC) (2019)
3. Hongpeng, T., Weibo: Stability control of flight attitude angle for four rotor aircraft. In: IEEE 9th International Conference on Software Engineering and Service Science (ICSESS) (2018)
4. Pang, J.: Research on adaptive control of four-rotor aircraft posture stability. In: IEEE International Conference on Mechatronics and Automation (ICMA) (2019)
5. Harrington, P., Chen, T., Ng, W.P.: Establishing the flightpath of a quadcopter drone from the relative angular velocity of the four rotors. In: 11th International Symposium on Communication Systems, Networks & Digital Signal Processing (CSNDSP) (2018)
6. Nakamura, Y., Watanabe, K., Nagai, I.: Notice of removal: position control for a VTOL-type UAV by tilting some of four rotors. In: 54th Annual Conference of the Society of Instrument and Control Engineers of Japan (SICE) (2015)
7. Chen, B., Li, S., Tang, Z.: Kinodynamic planning algorithm based on vector field for quadrotors. Appl. Res. Comput. 38(1) (2020)
8. Jiang, L., Leng, X., Luo, X., Xia, X.: Quadrotor control based on fuzzy - single neuron PID controller. Comput. Simul. 36(10), 39–43 (2019)
9. Yu, W., Bu, X.: Design of MFAC anti-interference cascade attitude controller for quad-rotor aircrafts. J. Electron. Meas. Instrum. 33(07), 166–172 (2019)
10. He, Y., Li, G., Wang, H.: Design of an adaptive backstepping sliding mode attitude controller for quadrotor helicopters. J. HangZhou Dianzi Univ. (Nat. Sci.) 39(02), 57–63 (2019)
11. Jia, Z., Wang, L., Jianqiao, Y., Ai, X.: Distributed adaptive neural networks leader-following formation control for quadrotors with directed switching topologies. ISA Trans. 93, 93–107 (2019)
12. Zhou, L., Zhang, J., Dou, J., Wen, B.: A fuzzy adaptive backstepping control based on mass observer for trajectory tracking of a quadrotor UAV. Int. J. Adapt. Control Signal Process. 32(12), 1675–1693 (2018). https://doi.org/10.1002/acs.2937
13. Chen, H., Zhang, D., Sheng, X., Wang, K.: Modeling and attitude control simulation for four-rotor aircraft in hover. Comput. Simul. 30(11), 41–45 (2013)
14. Li, H., Wang, Y.: Optimization of PID control in four rotor aircraft. Appl. Electron. Tech. 43(02), 73–76 (2017)
15. Ye, W., Feng, W., Fan, S.: A novel multi-swarm particle swarm optimization with dynamic learning strategy. Appl. Soft Comput. 61, 832–843 (2017). https://doi.org/10.1016/j.asoc.2017.08.051
16. Zhu, X., Han, Z.: Research on LS-SVM wind speed prediction method based on PSO. Proc. Chin. Soc. Electr. Eng. 36(23), 6337–6342+6598 (2016)
17. Hu, D., Gui, X., Jiang, H., Wu, H.: Modeling and calculating of auxiliary power unit based on newly improved particle swarm optimization. Comput. Simul. 37(01), 35–39 (2020)
18. Nan, J., Wang, X.: Particle swarm optimization algorithm with improved inertia weight. J. Xi'an Polytech. Univ. 31(06), 835–840 (2017)

Big Data

A Method for Image Big Data Utilization: Automated Progress Monitoring Based on Image Data for Large Construction Site

Chengtao Li[1(✉)], Li Chen[1], Jiafeng Wang[2], and Tianjian Xia[3]

[1] School of Economics and Management, Nanjing Institute of Technology,
Nanjing 211167, China
lichengtao@njit.edu.cn
[2] Land Surveying, Planning and Design Institute of Shaanxi Provincial Land
Engineering Construction Group Co., Ltd., Xi'an 710075, China
[3] Department of Electronic Engineering and Computer Science, Syracuse University,
Syracuse, NY 13210, USA
txia09@syr.edu

Abstract. Construction progress monitoring is very necessary for project management. At present, the commonly used manual inspection method is tedious and error prone. In recent years, image data analysis methods based on artificial intelligence and computer vision are emerging in the research of construction progress automated monitoring. In this paper, for large-scale residential projects, point clouds are generated and the UAV aerial photographs of the construction site are reconstructed. Based on the extracted area of individual buildings, the statistical peak value of point cloud elevation is used to identify the elevation of the main construction working face, and compared with the design elevation. The progress monitoring results in floor level are automatically obtained. In this paper, less than 300 copies of UAV aerial photos for each batch are used to conduct 3D reconstruction for the a large-scale project site (about $500\,\mathrm{m} * 400\,\mathrm{m}$) and identify the construction progress. The experimental results show that the identified floors under construction are consistent with the reality progress, which verifies the effectiveness of the proposed method. The method in this paper can be a important reference for the automated progress monitoring of other types of large construction sites as well.

Keywords: Image big data · Large-scale construction site · Automated progress monitoring · 3D reconstruction · Structure-from-motion

1 Introduction

Construction progress monitoring is very necessary for project management. At present, the most widely used manual inspection method is tedious and error prone. With the popularity of mobile phones, unmanned aerial vehicles (UAVs) and other camera devices, the acquisition of site images is becoming more and

© Springer Nature Singapore Pte Ltd. 2021
Y. Tian et al. (Eds.): ICBDS 2020, CCIS 1415, pp. 299–313, 2021.
https://doi.org/10.1007/978-981-16-3150-4_26

more convenient. In the field of project management, there are a lot of big data image application scenarios. In such circumstances of massive image data, manual browsing and interpretation can not fully and effectively realize its value. In view of this situation, in recent years, image data analysis methods based on artificial intelligence and computer vision are emerging in the research of automated monitoring of construction progress. In these studies, using the image data of the construction site, combined with the advanced engineering information technology such as building information modeling (BIM) and geographic information system (GIS), the automated monitoring of construction progress has been deeply studied, and a lot of beneficial results have been achieved. From the current literature, in the practice of image-based progress monitoring, an individual building is the most common monitoring object, while the research on automated monitoring of progress which practice in large-scale construction sites is rare.

Large scale construction site has the characteristics of large space scale (hundreds of meters) and the surrounding environment of each individual building is not stable. Considering the problems of image acquisition, spatial reference, analytical accuracy and calculation time, it is necessary to take reasonable methods and verify them according to the characteristics of large-scale construction projects. In this paper, for large-scale residential projects, UAV is used to obtain images, and 3D reconstruction of the construction site is carried out to generate point clouds. After the point clouds of individual buildings are extracted from the image area of an individual building, the elevation of the main construction working face is identified by the statistical peak value of the elevation distribution of the edge of point cloud elevation data, and compared with the designed floor elevation, the floor is automatically obtained from progress monitoring results.

2   Research Status and Progress

2.1   Progress Recognition Method Based on Image

The automated progress monitoring method improves the efficiency of construction site progress monitoring and accuracy of engineering data collection. The existing automated acquisition methods of construction progress include laser scanning, time-lapsed images, image-based 3D reconstruction and so on. With the decrease of image acquisition cost and the development of computer vision technology, the research and application of image-based construction progress automated monitoring method came out constantly. The existing image-based methods are mainly based on the technology of multi-view geometry [9], which in some field is referred as "Structure from Motion (SfM)" or "photogrammetry" [12]. The technology of multi-view geometry is mainly used to reconstruct the 3D construction scene using the 2D site photos, and the 3D point cloud or 3D mesh can be obtained as the as-built 3D model. The next step is to compare the as-built 3D model with the as-planned model of the building (especially BIM model). Finally implementing the visualization of the progress. Golparvar-Fard et al. used the SfM-MVS method to monitor the progress of a dining hall and a residence hall, and combined with BIM model to express the monitoring results in three dimensions [6]. In the introduction of Golparvar-Fard and others paper, daily and unordered construction pictures are used for site image recognition, and the point cloud is compared with BIM model of buildings. At the same time, probabilistic model is introduced to judge whether the components are completed or not, so as to obtain the construction progress at the component level [7]. Han et al. used the corresponding relationship between BIM model and image to calculate the imaging area of the component on the image, and used support vector machine (SVM) to identify the appearance features of the component image. The paper also reasons the construction stage of the component [8]. Braun et al. solved the problem of component occlusion by considering the precedence relationship in construction, and pointed out that there are "articulation point" nodes in the network. Those "articulation point" components can represent the components of the preceding nodes. For the building in the papers case, taking the slab of each floor as an articulation point in the procedure: when a floor component is observed, it can be considered that the main components of each floor below it have been completed [3]. Bognot et al. used CAD drawings to generate the 3D design model of the structure, and used UAVs to reconstruct the environment photos of the building to generate the 3D point cloud of the as-built building, and identify the construction progress by comparing the as-planned 3D model with the point cloud [2]. In addition, in terms of indoor construction progress monitoring, although the development of automated method confronts many obstacles, some scholars solved it by using indoor images to monitor the progress of indoor construction [2, 4].

Moreover, it should be pointed out that UAV is more and more widely used in image acquisition. UAVs are widely used in the construction field due to its good mobility and monitoring view, as well as the gradually reduced use cost [11]. Research shows that, while satisfying the technical requirements of image overlap and other technical requirements, 3D reconstruction using consumer UAV aerial photographs can achieve centimeter level accuracy in project [13]. The popularity of UAV brings potential opportunities for large-scale construction site monitoring.

2.2   The Work of This Paper

From the current research progress, (1) in the case of automated monitoring of construction progress by using images, most of the monitoring objects are individual buildings. There are few cases of using image-based method to monitor the progress of large-scale construction sites; (2) it is reasonable to monitor the progress of residential buildings in floor levels [3]. In the practice of project management, for the development of large-scale construction projects, the construction progress is described by the floor as the basic unit. This kind of project is the concerned object of the government supervision department, enterprise operation, engineering, cost and other departments. It is reasonable and practical to take the floor as the progress monitoring unit. (3) With the board vision of UAV, the panorama of the construction site can be easily obtained from multiple views, and the accuracy of 3D reconstruction can be guaranteed. Therefore, this paper intends to study the method for processing the UAV images and extracting the main construction progress information. In addition, considering the relatively simple structural form of residential buildings, the traditional design methods are often adopted, so there is no such existed BIM model. This paper will make use of some critical design information, such as the elevation information of each floor, and the feature information of 3D point cloud generated by UAV aerial photographs, so as to realize the automated construction progress monitoring of large-scale projects with the floor as the description unit.

3   Automated Monitoring Method of Individual Building Progress in Large-Scale Level Construction Site

3.1   Design Information Extraction

According to the information factors, it is necessary to know the image area of each individual building and the elevation information of each floor for monitoring the construction progress of each individual building. In the plot plan of the residential area, we can obtain the accurate design position of each unit, as well as the elevation of the ± 0.000; from the individual drawing, we can obtain the height of each floor relative to the ± 0.000 level.

In order to extract the point cloud of the individual building from the 3D point cloud of the residential area, the bounding box of each image area can be specified; more precisely, the building geometric area information can be rasterized, and the position of the individual building can be rasterized into a binary image under the condition that the coordinates is consistent. At this time, it is necessary to specify a certain point (x_0, y_0) in the real world as the coordinate origin of the raster image, and a raster unit spacing represent the actual lengths dx and dy.

For floor elevation, strictly speaking, the estimated height of each floor stab in construction stage is inconsistent with the height of building floor including decoration layer and heat insulation layer. However, considering the accuracy of 3D reconstruction of a large-scale project scene, these differences can be ignored. We can extract the height of each floor according to the construction drawing, and after overlapping of the elevation at the ± 0.000, we can get the design elevation of each floor, which is the reference for the subsequent progress monitoring. For the design elevation of the ith floor of the jth building, it is recorded as $\overline{H}_{ij}$.

3.2   3D Reconstruction of Construction Site Scene

Image Acquisition
The analysis of insufficient photo quality and high image overlapping can be extremely hard. If the photo collection is controllable, it is better to pay attention to the angle and quantity of photo collection to meet the requirements of overlap degree and improve the modeling accuracy; when it is safe, try to select a better shooting angle; while ensuring the overlap of photos is sufficient, reduce the number of photos. As the number of images increases, the number of pairing problems increases. Reducing the number of pictures collected can save field time and reduce the calculation works.

3D Reconstruction

3D reconstruction is a method to recover the scene information of 3D Euclidean space through the image information of 2D projection [9]. In this paper, the SfM method is used to conduct the 3D reconstruction. The common SfM method of 3D reconstruction is a multi-step method, which is divided into two steps: sparse reconstruction and dense reconstruction. This method first calculates the image posture (sparse reconstruction), and then calculates the 3D coordinates of dense points in the image (dense reconstruction) according to the stereo vision algorithm. In building monitoring, two-step method is widely used. In sparse reconstruction, the feature points of series of images are extracted first, and then matching with other feature points to form tie points. There are several kinds of feature points, and SIFT [10] is a common one. In calculation, since the characters of feature points can be retrieved and the geometric constraints of image can be detected, random sample consensus (RANSAC) algorithm can be used to realize automated matching of connection points [5]. After getting a series of connection points, the camera parameters can be adjusted to locate and orient the photos, and the inside and outside orientation elements of the camera can be obtained. For 3D reconstruction of large scenes, bundle adjustment method is generally used to correct the results [14]. For dense reconstruction, the associated image pairs are rotated to find possible matching points.

3D Model Registration

When the camera position can be accurately obtained (such as the UAV equipped with RTK), the location information of the camera station can be used as the location information to avoid manual operation. When 3D reconstruction is operated on a group of pictures without location information, either specifying image control points or manually register point cloud with the as-planned model will work. We can also match the reconstructed 3D model with the reference instead. In this paper, a measurement result will be used as the benchmark, and the other measurement results will be registered with the 3D model as same as the reference model through iterative closest point (ICP) algorithm [1]. In this case, the premise of automatic registration is that construction site appearance in 2 batches should not differ remarkably, otherwise it is necessary to specify the area with unchanged appearance to realize the registration.

3.3 The Extraction of the Point Cloud and Progress Identification

In this paper, the progress is identified by automatically extracting the as-built status information and comparing the design information. The steps are as follows:

(3.1) According to the image area of individual buildings, the point cloud of the jth individual building is extracted from the site point cloud, the total number of points falling into the image area of the jth individual building is N_j, the set of points in a point cloud is denoted as $\{P_j(x_k, y_k, z_k)\}(k = 1, 2, \ldots, N_j)$, where$z_k$ is the elevation coordinate, for $z_k(k = 1, 2, \ldots, N_j)$ the statistics were made by elevation segment, count the number of points in each segment. Take the midpoint of the elevation segment with the most points, i.e. "statistical peak value of point cloud distribution along the elevation" as the working face elevation, it is denoted as $\widehat{H}_j$;

(3.2) Compare $\widehat{H}_j$ with $\overline{H}_{ij}$, the i which makes $|\widehat{H}_j - \overline{H}_{ij}|$ minimum is denoted as $\hat{i}$, it is the estimation of the jth individual building construction progress floor number in the monitoring data, as shown in the formula below:

$$\hat{i} : \min_{\hat{i}} |\widehat{H}_j - \overline{H}_{ij}| \tag{1}$$

In order to observe the accuracy of the estimated value, we can check elevation error ϵ_j, the difference between $\widehat{H}_j$ and $\overline{H}_{i_R,j}$ (where i_R means the real construction progress floor):

$$\epsilon_j = \widehat{H}_j - \overline{H}_{i_R,j} \tag{2}$$

In order to illustrate the recognition algorithm better, an example is given: Take No. 30 building as an example, the elevation of the ±0.000 level is 7.65 m, the floor height is 3 m, and the total number of floors is 26, and then the design elevation of each floor should be $\overline{H}_{i,30} = 7.65 + 3i$ m $(i = 1, 2, \ldots, 26)$. The elevation values of each point in the point cloud of No. 30 building are counted in a histogram, and the histogram group distance is taken as 0.2 m. The histogram distribution is shown in the following Fig. 1:

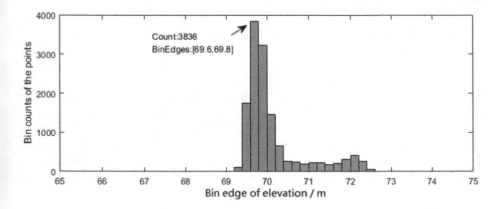

Fig. 1. Elevation point distribution of No. 30 building

As shown in the above figure, the maximum histogram frequency of each bin is 3836, and the group boundary is 69.6–69.8 m, then the estimated elevation of the working face under construction is: $\widehat{H}_{30} = (69.6 - 69.8)/2 = 69.7$ m, and the difference between $\widehat{H}_{30}$ and the design elevation of the 21st floor $\overline{H}_{21,30} = 70.65$ m and is the smallest, then the estimated construction progress floor number $\hat{i} = 21(floor)$, and $\epsilon_{30} = 69.7 - (7.65 + 3*21) = -0.95$ m (it takes $\hat{i} = 21$ as i_R here).

4   Case Study and Method Validation

4.1   Site Scale and Building Positioning

In order to verify the method, this paper takes a residential area under construction as the research object to carry out the progress monitoring experiment. The length of the construction site is about 500–600 m, and the width is about 400 m. See the plot plan of the site in Fig. 2, and the detailed size including the center line of the surrounding roads is shown in Fig. 3. The monitoring range is defined according to four cardinal directions, and due to the inclination of the residential area, the horizontal scale of the monitoring area reaches 736 m * 658 m (see Fig. 3). The residential area contains 30 high-rise individual buildings. The total number of floors of each individual building is from 21 to 26, and the design height is within 100 m.

According to the plot plan, the following position information can be obtained: the location information in the horizontal plane is the location and exterior contour position of each individual building; the vertical position information is the ±0.000 elevation of each building, ranging from 7.65 m to 8.15 m. In order to facilitate the processing of 3D reconstruction, we raster the image area information to get the binary image as shown in Fig. 3 (the position of solid filling is the image area of individual building). In addition, according to the ±0.000 elevation and

Fig. 2. Plot plan of some construction site

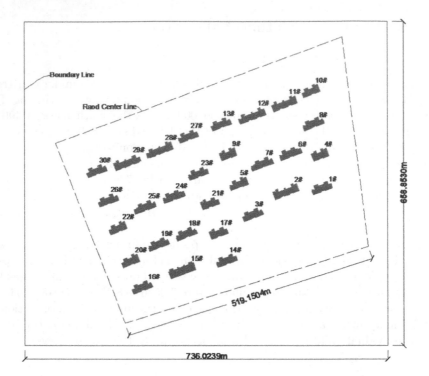

Fig. 3. Rasterized plot plan of the individual buildings. The location information of each building is extracted and rasterized. In this example, each pixel represents a length of 0.2 m (rounded up if less than 0.2 m). According to the length and width of the site area in this example, the location map is rasterized to 3295 pixels × 3681 pixels.

floor elevation of each individual building specified in the plot plan, it is converted into the elevation list of each floor, namely $\overline{H}_{ij}$ (design elevation of the ith floor of building j).

4.2   Image Acquisition

The monitoring pictures of the construction site are obtained by the DJI Phantom 4 Pro UAV. This case analyzes the two site monitoring picture groups, the two monitoring time is September 16th, 2020 and October 5th, 2020. In order to record the whole scene of the construction site, 237 and 294 UAV aerial photographs were taken respectively. The shutter mode of aerial camera was global mechanical shutter. The pixel value of single image was 5274 * 3628, and the nominal focal length was 24 mm (Table 1).

Table 1. Comparison of two batches

Batch	Time	Image number	Positioning mode
Batch 0916	September 16th	237	Positioning based on batch 1005 model
Batch 1005	October 5th	294	Positioning based on photo control point

There is no strict flight path planning for UAV in this case, the mode of tilt photography and ring shot are adopted. Part of the aerial photo thumbnails of the construction site are shown in Fig. 4, and the schematic diagram of the aerial photo posture monitored in the 2 batches in the scene model is shown in Fig. 5.

Fig. 4. Aerial photos of construction site

(a) Batch0916   (b) Batch1005

Fig. 5. 3D reconstruction model and POS of the cameras

4.3   3D Reconstruction and Point Cloud Generation

3D Reconstruction

In this paper, sparse reconstruction and then dense reconstruction are adopted to realize the 3D reconstruction of construction site scene. This case uses the CON-TEXT CAPTURE CENTER software package to carry out the automated 3D reconstruction. In order to obtain the highest resolution accuracy, the resolution of the original photo is maintained (20 million pixels for a single photo) when the aerial triangulation posture is performed in sparse reconstruction step. In dense reconstruction for the 3D modeling, in order to reduce the hardware cost and shorten the calculation time, the monitoring pictures are down-sampled by 60% (the resolution is reduced by 60%, the number of pixels of a single photo is reduced to about 7 million).

In this case, batch 1005 is the benchmark batch used to conduct model positioning, while batch 0916 is the general batch (no photo control point). When the 3D reconstruction is carried out in batch 1005, several coordinate-known points are selected as image control points (Some road signs are selected as control points, as shown in Fig. 6). In combination with the information of plot plan, the coordinates of these control points are easy to obtain. For the aerial images of batch 0916, in order to present the automated analysis process during general monitoring, the batch does not specify control points, but obtains the 3D point cloud and then registers with the point cloud of batch 1005 as the benchmark. The point cloud after batch 0916 registration was calculated by ICP algorithm based on batch in October. The registration area should be the same shape area in two batches. Considering that the period between the two monitoring batches in this case is short, the shape of the whole construction site is not changed much, so ICP registration is directly carried out by all the point clouds, instead of dividing the point cloud into the construction in progress and the built-up area.

(a) Image control point distribution

(b) Detail of some control point

Fig. 6. Schematic diagram of image control point

After 3D reconstruction, the obtained 3D model is shown in Fig. 5 above, and the 3D graph of point cloud of batch 1005 and the horizontal projection of point cloud in two batches are shown in Fig. 7. The hardware configuration of this case: CPU: Intel core i5-8400 CPU 2.80 GHz; Memory: 24.0 GB, DDR4, 2666 MHz; Video card: NVIDIA Geforce GTX 1060, 6 GB. Under this hardware condition, the analysis time of single batch is less than 2 h.

Point Cloud Down Sampling

The number of points in the point clouds of batch 0916 and batch 1005 are 253462786 and 157160270 respectively. The amount of data is huge, and the operation takes up a large amount of memory, and the calculation efficiency is low. In order to reduce the hardware cost and improve the efficiency of the subsequent calculation, the point clouds of the two batches were down sampled by 1/1000, and the counts of points of the two batches were 253463 and 157160, respectively. The point cloud computing involved in the following paper takes the down sampling point cloud as the operation object.

(a) 3D point cloud for batch 1005

(b) point cloud projecting for batch 0916

(c) point cloud projecting for batch 1005

Fig. 7. Point cloud obtained by 3D reconstruction using aerial photos of construction site

Because the colors are distinguished according to the height, the point cloud level map can reflect the construction progress of each individual building, and the image itself can play a certain reference role for project management. In order to get the project progress of each individual building with "floor" as the unit, the floor number under construction will be extracted in the following part of this paper.

4.4   Extract the Construction Floor Number of Each Batch

Using this method, the point cloud image of construction scene is extracted according to the horizontal area of each individual building. The corresponding relationship between the horizontal projection of point cloud and each individual building is shown in Fig. 8. It can be seen from the figure that the position of 3D reconstruction point cloud is consistent with that of individual building in design information. This is the basis of the method in this paper.

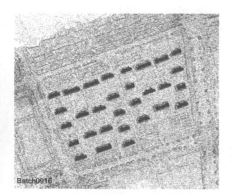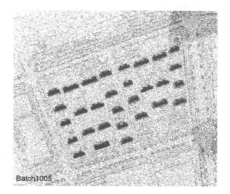

Fig. 8. The relationship between horizontal projection of point cloud and the location of individual buildings (the orange solid block is an individual building). (Color figure online)

The progress and real value of the identified individual building are shown in Fig. 9. It can be seen that the identified construction floor number is completely consistent with the actual situation. Figure 9 also shows the elevation error distribution ϵ_j In the process of extracting the construction floor number, when the elevation segment is 0.3 m, the distribution range is 0.4 m to −0.9 m. For large construction sites, the accuracy is within the acceptable range and will not affect the

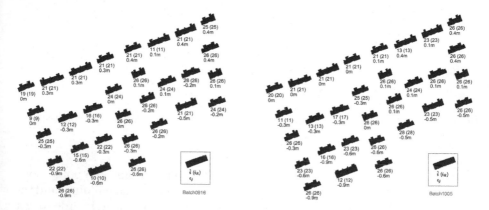

Fig. 9. Construction floor number and elevation error distribution of each individual building

identification results. The results in Fig. 9 show the effectiveness of the proposed method.

The first digit in the first line is the identified construction floor number, the number in brackets is the real construction floor number, and the second line is the difference between the elevation value recognized by working face and the design elevation of corresponding floor.

The total floor numbers and the identified construction floor numbers in two batches of each individual building are shown in Fig. 10, and the construction progress of each batch and difference between batches can be seen. In the actual project management, these progress results can be easily combined with construction records, project payment, progress evaluation, construction resource allocation and other works.

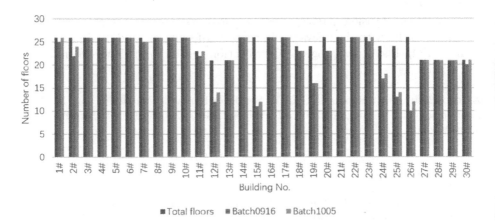

Fig. 10. Total floor number of each individual building and construction progress chart of each batch

5   Conclusion and Prospect

In this paper, the method of extracting individual building point cloud and identifying the progress of the building is built by using the basic design information such as image area of the building and floor design elevation. The method of using the image data of residential construction site for progress monitoring is recommended, and the experimental research is carried out. The experimental results show that: (1) the data volume is in the level of hundreds of aerial photos, and can effectively meet the needs of 3D reconstruction of large scale residential areas. Due to the small number of images, the analysis of a single batch of images can be completed within 2 h, and its efficiency can meet the needs of the project; (2) the experimental results also show that in the main construction stage, the monitoring batch interval is short and the shape change is small, the point cloud can be globally registered by ICP algorithm, and the accuracy can meet the requirements of construction progress monitoring in the unit of floor; (3) through the statistical peak value of individual building point cloud elevation can accurately extract the construction progress floor number of the building.

In addition, there are many aspects that can be further improved:

1. The 3D point cloud generated by this method has rich shape and texture features locally. On the basis of existing image data, combined with intelligent algorithm, it is possible to further identify the construction progress status in higher fineness level.
2. When using the aircraft, the route planning can be further optimized for the purpose of monitoring, and the automated cruise can be realized, and the balance between the number of photos and the amount of information can be achieved better.
3. Support the decision-making of various projects, connect the progress monitoring results with the relevant engineering information, and realize the automated pipeline of the progress identification results to its downstream applications.

Acknowledgment. Supports from the Scientific Research Foundation for the High-level Personnel of Nanjing Institute of Technology (Grant No. YKJ201983) are gratefully acknowledged.

References

1. Besl, P.J., McKay, N.D.: A method for registration of 3-D shapes. IEEE Trans. Pattern Anal. Mach. Intell. **14**(2), 239–256 (1992)
2. Bognot, J.R., Candido, C.G., Blanco, A.C., Montelibano, J.R.Y.: Building construction progress monitoring using unmanned aerial system (UAS), low-cost photogrammetry, and geographic information system (GIS). ISPRS Ann. Photogram. Remote Sens. Spatial Inf. Sci. **IV-2**(2), 41–47 (2018)
3. Braun, A., Tuttas, S., Borrmann, A., Stilla, U.: A concept for automated construction progress monitoring using BIM-based geometric constraints and photogrammetric point clouds. J. Inf. Technol. Constr. **20**(5), 68–79 (2015)
4. Deng, H., Hong, H., Luo, D., Deng, Y., Cheng, S.: Automatic indoor construction process monitoring for tiles based on BIM and computer vision. J. Constr. Eng. Manag. **146**(1), 04019095 (2020)
5. Fischler, M.A., Bolles, R.C.: Random sample consensus: a paradigm for model fitting with applications to image analysis and automated cartography. Commun. ACM **24**(6), 381–395 (1981)
6. Golparvar-Fard, M., Peña-Mora, F., Savarese, S.: Application of D4AR - A 4-dimensional augmented reality model for automating construction progress monitoring data collection, processing and communication. J. Inf. Technol. Constr. **14**(1), 129–153 (2009)
7. Golparvar-Fard, M., Peña-Mora, F., Savarese, S.: Automated progress monitoring using unordered daily construction photographs and IFC-based building information models. J. Comput. Civ. Eng. **29**(1), 04014025 (2015)

8. Han, K.K., Golparvar-Fard, M.: Appearance-based material classification for monitoring of operation-level construction progress using 4D BIM and site photologs. Autom. Constr. **53**(1), 44–57 (2015)

9. Hartley, R., Zisserman, A.: Multiple View Geometry in Computer Vision. Cambridge University Press, Cambridge (2004). ISBN 0521540518

10. Lowe, D.G.: Distinctive image features from scale-invariant keypoints. Int. J. Comput. Vision **60**(2), 91–110 (2004)

11. Tatum, M.C., Liu, J.: Unmanned aircraft system applications in construction. Procedia Eng. **196**(1), 167–175 (2017)

12. Westoby, M.J., Brasington, J., Glasser, N.F., Hambrey, M.J., Reynolds, J.M.: Structure-from-motion photogrammetry: a low-cost, effective tool for geoscience applications. Geomorphology **179**, 300–314 (2012)

13. Zhang, C., et al.: Topographic data accuracy verification of small consumer UAV. J. Remote Sens. **22**(1), 185–195 (2018)

14. Zhu, S., et al.: Very large-scale global SfM by distributed motion averaging. In: 2018 IEEE/CVF Conference on Computer Vision and Pattern Recognition, vol. 1, no. 1, pp. 4568–4577 (2018)

Big Data from Collection to Use in Competitive Games—A Study Case on Badminton

Guanzhe Zhao[1], Zaichao Duan[1], Chengbo Zhang[2], Zilong Jin[2,3(✉)],
and Benjamin Kwapong Osibo[4]

[1] HuiHua College of Hebei Normal University, Shijiazhuang, China
[2] School of Computer and Software, Nanjing University of Information
Science and Technology, Nanjing, China
zljin@nuist.edu.cn
[3] Jiangsu Collaborative Innovation Center of Atmospheric Environment and Equipment
Technology (CICAEET), Nanjing University of Information Science and Technology,
Nanjing, China
[4] School of Computer Science, Nanjing University of Information Science and Technology,
Nanjing, China

Abstract. Big data technologies have been widely applied and accepted in a variety of areas e.g. industries, social networking, and finance industry. Big data technologies are also used in sports, especially competitive sports. However, the data mining and utilization are far from enough in terms of extent and extent and fine details. In this research, the author focused on the collection and application of big data in competitive sports and carried out statistical work and analysis after turning the features of opponent's plays into mathematical variables. Multiple orders and multiple dimensions data are collected so as to provide adequate information support to our players to better meet challenges in the competition. In this article, badminton game, the fastest racket sport in the world, was taken as an example to demonstrate that it was of critical importance for players to be acquainted with and make predictions of opponents' routine tactics.

Keywords: Big data · Competitive sports · Badminton

1 Introduction

Big data marks the beginning of a major transformation [1]. Big data technologies are making the world more intuitive and clearer: on one hand, big data enables enterprises to faster understand market changes, seize each client's characteristics more precisely and better provide individualized services; on the other hand, with big data, enterprises are able to provide services to individuals in a faster, more appropriate and more satisfying manner. In other words, big data technologies will enable direct fast acquaintance and infatuation of two appropriate strangers.

Nowadays, big data technologies have been increasingly used in the field of sports and competitive sports in particularly, such as NBA [2], UEFA Champions League [3], etc. However, these applications are for guidance purposes at a macro and strategic level [4, 5]. There are also researches which used big data for analysis of professional athletes and their action characteristics and effects [6], and for comparison with the actions with junior athletes, so as to identify the difference of actions between them. In this way, the training effect of junior athletes is improved through constant practice and comparison.

However, as often as not, competitive sports are a process of restriction and counter-restriction. When it comes to a specific fight, the competition between the offensive and defensive is not merely about basic skills and macro strategies. Instead, the judgment and decision-making in an instant moment may decide the final result. This moment of confrontation is full of breakthrough and restriction and involves the process of design and identification of tricks. If an athlete intends to gain advantage of initiative in the match, the athlete must fast make predictive response. This drive of the response comes from inference of the actions of opponents as well as from physiological conditioned reflex. Misjudgment or slipping into the opponents' trap due to conditioned reflex will immediately result in a passive situation or failure. Acquaintance with the opponents' routine tactics will help identify the trap and make correct and effective actions.

The real revolution is not in the machines that calculate data but in data itself and how we use it [1]. There is still much space for research of collection, analysis and application of big data of the instant moment of confrontation among individual athletes in terms of professionalism. Although action made by an athlete at a specific moment is random, depending on individual habit and capacity, etc., the selection of actions follows certain laws. Therefore, it often seen in the matches that some professional athletes are able to show their own unique skills in a fierce confrontation frequently. In this work, the research was carried out by taking badminton sports as a specific case with individual athletes as the research objects. The author committed to research and collection of characteristics of actions which will induce competitors to make actions during the process of confrontation. These characteristics are referred to as the information which involves fake actions, traps, and deception as well as the final true actions. The author carried out statistical work and analysis of the information and offered guidance on its application to training, capacity test and selection of athletes in real scenarios.

2   Data Collection from Badminton Match

Badminton is a racket sport for two or four people, and has five events: men's and women's singles, men's and women's doubles, and mixed doubles, each requiring specific preparation in terms of technique, power, and consciousness. This sport is one of the most popular sports in the world, with 200 million enthusiasts.

Competitive badminton is ranked as the world's fastest racket sport. As high-tech materials are being constantly used in manufacturing of Badminton racket and strings, the record of badminton speed get broken ever and again. According to Guinness World Records, the newest officially recognized badminton speed was 426 km/h [7]. For professional players, a hit speed of over 300 km/h occurs frequently. Therefore, it's absolutely too late to make a response for the purpose of receiving the badminton after the hit by the opponent. Instead, pre-judgment must be made for receiving the badminton based on the position of the opponent's player, predicted position of badminton when it is hit, the position of the player to receive the badminton, the habit of the opponent's player in hit the badminton at such position, etc.

In a high-level badminton game where two sides are well-matched, every score is not won easily through several hits but through a process with multiple rounds of restrictions and counter-restrictions, as well as offensive and defensive actions. In the whole of the process, the side which makes an effective and correct judgment of an action will have the chance to win a score. Contrarily, if one side is trapped by the opponent, the side will fall into a passive situation. Where the players of both sides are equally competitive in terms of physical quality and basic skills, the key factor that determines the score is the acquaintance with and correct judgment of the routine tactics of the opponent.

2.1   1st Order Data – Only Considering the Real Hit Path

Taking women's single for example, female athletes are restricted by a series of factors e.g. height, movement speed and hit strength. During confrontation, direct violent offensive is relatively rare. In most cases, effective offensive is performed targeting at the empty or unprotected area through disrupting the opponent's movement. With effective disruption, a player is able to identify the opponent's weakness and cause the opponent shuttle among the positions at which she is weak to hit the badminton. Furthermore, the opponent will suffer physical exhaustion after shuttling among distant strike positions, resulting in poorer strike quality. The process of disruption involves not only direct strike but also fake actions and other means. In real professional games, fake actions will achieve better effect in this regard.

In this research, the author started with the analysis of the real strike actions of a player who makes offensive attacking. Taking the common athletes who hold racket with right hand for example, the author first collected the data of strike made by a player at the left rear court. This hit point is called "dead point" by badminton players, because it is difficult for any player who holds racket with right hand to control the strike (including path and strength) at this position due to the structure of human body. Therefore, players will frequently strike the badminton to this position deliberately to restrict the attacking by the opponent. Any player with a better control of the strike at this position will gain more initiatives. Once a player has any inherent drawbacks at this hit point, the opponent will inevitably make attacking by seizing this weakness. If a professional athlete is able to deal with the strike at this position appropriately, the player will avoid being trapped in a passive situation and even seize the opportunity to make initiative actions.

In dealing with the strike at this position, professional players usually adopts 6 means as shown in Fig. 1: Straight High Clear, Cross-Court High Clear, Straight Drop, Cross-Court Drop, Straight Smash and Cross-Court Smash. No player will intentionally hit the badminton to the middle court or other areas, because this will give the opponent a perfect opportunity to make a deadly strike in a comfortable way.

In this research, the sample data was from the women's singles final of All England Open Badminton Championships in 2020 [8]. The players were Tai Tzu Ying from Taipei, China and CHEN Yufei from mainland of China. Finally, Tai Tzu Ying beat CHEN Yufei by 2-0 (21-9, 21-15) and won the game. The author first collected the strike data of Tai Tzu Ying at the "dead point" in this game to analyze her strike habits and hit quality at this point and hoped that such data would be applied to simulation

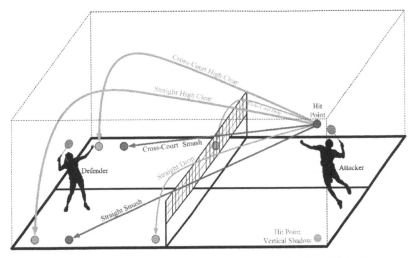

Fig. 1. Routine tactics of badminton players at the "Dead Point"

training, sports capacity testing and selection of players. The fields of its application will be specifically discussed in the following chapters. By watching the videos of the game, the author recorded the strike means, badminton movement and the final effect of 62 times of strike by Tai Tzu Ying at the left rear position. The data was summarized in the following table and shows that Straight Drop and Cross-Court Drop were given most, but have no idea about the effect.

Table 1. Real strike paths of Tai Tzu Ying's hits at the "Dead Point"

Hit path	Probability
Straight high clear	19%
Cross-court high clear	18%
Straight drop	23%
Cross-court drop	27%
Straight smash	11%
Cross-court smash	2%

2.2 2nd Order Data – Considering the Predict Path and Real Path

From the data in Table 1 above, the characteristics of strike by at "dead point" can be analyzed. It can be seen that Cross-Court Drop were applied most frequently and the Cross-Court Smash were rarely adopted. Such extraction and analysis of data may be adequate for junior players, but it is far from enough for a world-class fake action master like Tai Tzu Ying. Anyone who has watched Tai Tzu Ying's game knows that she is most

adjust the center of body weight. When a player tries to receive the badminton which is in the opposite direction of the center of body weight, it is difficult for the player to apply adequate force to the strike the badminton even if the hit point is quite close to the body. Professional players will try to disturb the opponent's control of the center of body weight as much as possible and then smash the badminton in an opposite direction, causing greater difficulties to the opponent in receiving the badminton. With regard to application of specific statistics, the center of body weight of a defensive player is divided into 9 parts with different values.

(3) Considering the Continuous Smashing Times

The fastest and most effective way of striking a badminton is powerful smashing which requires physical strength. However, even if given the opportunities of continuous smashing, professional players will not hastily make smashes. First, it consumes too much physical strength. Second, in defending the same type of continuous striking, the opponent will easily establish adequate defense habits. When given the opportunities of continuous smashing, some professional players will smash the badminton several times relentlessly; some will change routine tactics of attacks after 2 or 3 attempts; some will strike the badminton in other means with fake actions when the first opportunity of smashing appears. These choices are seemingly ruleless, but in fact, there is certain regularity for an individual player. Take CHEN Yufei for example, her attacking capacity is strong, but she did poorly in concealment of fake actions, and adopts direct attack at most times. Tai Tzu Ying, however, makes fake actions in a rather confusing and effective manner and is more willing to choose energy-saving fake actions to disrupt the defensive pace of opponent, thus seeking the attack opportunities. With regard to the parameters of continuous smashing, they can be set to 0, 1, 2, 3, 4, 5 times and above, with 7 specific values available for carrying out the analysis.

(4) Considering Preparing Duration

It's critically important for a player to get fully prepared in receiving the badminton. Badminton players shall well adjust their body gesture, so that they can apply the force in a fastest manner. The player shall also fully observe the actions of opponents and make pre-judgment of the strike path of the opponent. The player shall observe and consider the position of the opponent at the court and determine the subsequent strike path. All these preparations require preparing duration. The shorter the duration, the more favorable situation for the offensive player. In the games, it is often seen that when a player intentionally uses high clear, the greater intention is to extend the preparation duration. With regard to preparation duration, 4 values are set for analysis: extremely short, short, common, long.

2.5 Higher Dimensions Data – Considering the Specific Situations

In addition to the order-based linear influential multiple orders parameters prior to striking, there are more dimensions parameters which affect the choice of strike at each special time.

(1) Considering Physical Strength

As the physical consumption of a badminton player is huge, strong physical strength is required to support high quality strike. When the physical strength is reduced, the strike path and effect will change dramatically. The player may perform a drop hit instead of smash, so as to save physical strength. More mistakes may occur due to improper action caused by reduction of physical strength. A player who is well acquainted with physical conditions will make most appropriate hit when physical strength is reduced. Herein, physical strength is divided into 5 levels (from high to low) with 5 different values for this parameter.

(2) Considering Psychological State

It is undeniable that the psychological diathesis of players differs from one to another. When a player is ahead in scores, the player is more relaxed in dealing with hits in "advantageous situation", with more variety of strike path and higher quality hit. However, when a player is behind in scores, the player is more nervous in dealing with hit in "disadvantageous situation", resulting in hasty strike and higher rate of mistakes. There is a great correlation between mental state and psychological diathesis of players but a scientific and detailed division is not available. With regard to this dimension, 3 levels were set with different values: relaxed, stable, hasty.

(3) Considering Scores

In a game, a badminton player may constantly change the means of striking to make opponent difficult to adapt to the hits. There is a great connection between the option of means of striking and the stages of the game. At the early, middle, and late stage of each round in the game, both sides demonstrate respective characteristics during confrontation. As often as not, the two sides will make attempts to understand the opponent's playing condition by adopting a variety of means of striking. At the middle stage, the players will mainly target at the opponent's weakness and adopt combined attacks to restrict the opponent's hits. In dealing with key hits, reserved players will seek stability and won't make offensive attack before obvious opportunity appears; radical players may be more courageous to make offensive attack at first. With regard to this dimension, 3 levels of parameters are set for competition over key hits at the early, middle and late stage.

In addition to foregoing multiple orders and multiple dimensions parameters, there are also more parameters which may affect options of players and can be further discussed in the future researches. Up to now, the data of mere single strikes by players at "dead points" has reached Predict Path (6) × Real Path (6) × Opponent's Position (9) × Body Weight (9) × Continuous Smashing Times (7) × Preparing Duration (4) × Physical Strength (5) × Psychological State (3) × Scores (3) $\approx 3.7 \times 10^6$, such a large cumulative product already.

3 Data Analysis

With regard to the foregoing collected data, it is weighted based on common hits and key hits, etc., so as to enable correct analysis of effectiveness of a strike made by a player. Thought the analysis of multiple orders data, the internal correlation of continuous hits is identified. Through analysis of multiple dimensions data, the characteristics of strikes by players in different situations are reflected truly. The final data is given the human-based realness.

3.1 Analysis of Hits at a Specific Point

The author hoped to correctly analyze the probability of selection of different means of striking at a specific moment with foregoing collected data of multiple orders and multiple dimensions. In this way, the characteristics of strikes at different points can be identified: the advantageous points for the opponent to make strike; the disadvantageous points for the opponent to make strike; the points where the opponent is most capable at making traps with fake actions. By study Tai Tzu Ying's hit routine in the "Dead Point", we can easily find that she is so good at the Cross Court Drop path, especially made a fake Straight High Clear trap before the real hit (Fig. 2).

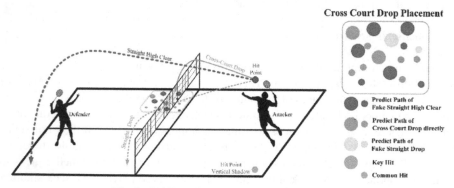

Fig. 2. Tai Tzu Ying's Cross-Court Drop effects

3.2 Analysis of Tactics that Leads to Initiative Situation

It's repeatedly stressed that the result of a badminton game is not determined by some single hits. Instead, it is an interlocking competition process. After start of the game, it's hard to tell which side is in a positive situation and which side is in a passive situation until after several rounds of strikes. For professional players, the thinking in the program of hit the badminton is like that is playing chess. They gradually gain the positive situation through one movement at a time and then seek opportunities to give a deadly hit to the opponent. Such continuous actions with clear purposes are referred to as a specific tactics. Each player may be adept at several routines for scoring. Without adequate understanding of the opponent's routines, a player may be easily led to failure by the opponent. The following 3 figures gives the steps how did Tai Tzu Ying win Chen Yu Fei three times. The same key hits are the fake drop strikes suddenly turn to real high clear given by Tai Tzu Ying in front of net. That leads Chen Yu Fei so difficult to hit return with high quality and lose the point finally. Tai designs this kind of tricks so expertly in the game (Fig. 3).

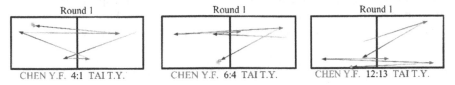

Fig. 3. One way of Tai Tzu Ying's to gain initiative

3.3 Analysis of Decisions that Results in Passive Situation

In a badminton game, loss of scores is also a result of multiple continuous strikes. Normally, a short player may easily make mistakes when being caused to make continuous long-distance movement; a tall player may be more passive in re-adjusting the center of body weight to fast receive the badminton in a opposite direction if deceived by fake actions; an play who is in favor of offensive attack may feel exhausted and anxious if attacks are successfully defended by the opponent; a player who is competent at defense may lose patience after when failed to wait for the all-out offensive attack of the opponent. Due to the factors of individual physical conditions, characteristics of strikes and psychological diathesis, etc., each player may be not willing to encounter certain continuous tactics. The following 3 figures gives the steps how did Tai Tzu Ying lost to Chen Yu Fei three times. The same key decisions are the direct drop instead of high clear given by Tai Tzu Ying in front of net. Chen Yu Fei was fully prepared to handle that kind of hit and gain the scores easily (Fig. 4).

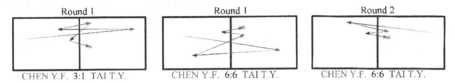

Fig. 4. The same decisions that lead Tai Tzu Ying to passive situation

4 Applications

After obtainment of adequate and approximately real data analysis result, such analysis result can be applied to the sports in practice. It will serve the training for players, more truthfully reflect their competition skills and aid coaches in selecting most appropriate players.

4.1 Training

Nowadays, many intelligent devices have been applied to badminton training. For example, on YouTube [9], Intanon demonstrated a touch lamp training device for testing of reaction speed. A lamp is placed at every corner of the court and only one lamp will be light up at one time. The player has to fast strike the lit lamp, so as to carry out training of paces in a simulated environment. However, she did not reveal the regularity or basis of light-up of lamps. Hopefully, the analysis in this research may be applied to the program of light-up of lamps, so that the paces in the coming games may be simulated in a more real way and that the players will get acquainted with the pace in the next game.

4.2 Identification of Opponent's Routine Tactics

Junior players only focus on the instant moment of a strike, but experienced players and coaches are able to develop a deeper understanding of the competition process. They are able to fast predict the subsequence three strikes based on the analysis of previous three strikes during each performance of strike. The analysis data herein will help players at different levels identify the continuous process of scoring of the opponent faster and clearer. In this way, they will find solutions and break the opponent's pre-designed steps of offensive attacks, thus lifting themselves out of restrictions.

4.3 Identification of Opponent's Tricks

Professional badminton players make many fake actions and all achieve high success rate with their unique tricks. Real data analysis will help players to identify the opponent's fake actions more correctly. With targeted training, players will get acquainted with the opponent's tricks, overcome physiological conditioned reflex, and identify the real strike path of the opponent.

4.4 Improvement of Drawbacks

After reaching a bottleneck, some players may find it's hard to make further improvement and breakthrough. At this time, the analysis data herein will help them identify their own weakness and strength of strike in a deeper and all-round way. By overcoming weakness through new training and designing more appropriate strategies to reduce the influence of weakness and exert strength and advantages, players will be able to gain more initiatives in the games.

4.5 Capacity Test

Some departments carry out division of a great number of junior athletes. The means of division may be based on their physical tests or real field observations. However, the physical test is often hard to reflect the competitive level of badminton players. The evaluation and analysis based on field observations are often too subjective, especially when the game between non-top players are easily interfered by human factors. Therefore, it's hoped that our analysis data of real competitions will better help different institutions perform fair and objective evaluation of players.

4.6   Selection of Players for the Next Competition

In some team badminton competitions, it is a huge challenge for coaches to select a player for the competition. Especially when coaches clearly know which player of the other side will be present, all hope to select a player from their team who is able to restrict the opponent mostly and most adapt to the opponent's tactics. With our analysis data, the real completion between the players may be simulated in a more real way and coaches may select the players based on the simulation result.

5   Difficulties and Solutions for the Further Study

If the data from a real competition is as comprehensive and correct as those set in the research, the analyzed data will be quite close to the real situation when applied to simulation. The author believes that by introduction of more accurate parameter analysis, the research will be infinitely close to the actual situations. However, at the same time, it's also undeniable that a number of difficulties shall be overcome in the future.

5.1   Accurate Appraisal by Professionals

Currently, some researchers have committed to automatic judgment of actions of badminton players. For example, the recognizing badminton action from depth map sequences acquired by Microsoft Kinect sensor [10]. Some researchers study the actions of players through the badminton games on the YouTube [11]. However, badminton sport involves many tiny actions and a number of fake actions cannot be automatically identified by machine currently. Therefore, more professional algorithms and machines are needed to identify these tiny actions, thus providing more accurate data support for the future researches.

5.2   Fast Updating and Computing

All professional players are constantly changing their means of playing, based on coaches' training methods at different stages, growth of individual capacity and the latest state of the player. It's often seen that after some period of closed training, some players demonstrated dramatic abrupt change in the means of playing which make opponents feel difficult to adapt themselves to it. Therefore, faster and stronger computing capacity is required, so that the latest competition data will play its role.

5.3   More Realistic Simulation

The data herein can be easily used in training similar to four-point (the four corners at the badminton court) movement. For example, the training means demonstrated by Intanon on YouTube [9]. Moreover, more stereoscopic and multi-point simulation applications are required. Based on the data of opponents, the parameters of the player's own actions and state shall be better applied to simulated confrontation in real time during training. While the trainee is considering the simulated opponent, the simulated opponent is also studying the trainee like a real person.

6 Conclusions

In this research, with the analysis of real cases of badminton game, the author proved that there were some laws in competitive sports and tried to establish multiple orders and multiple dimensions statistical analysis model. The author hopes that by applying the model to real situations, it will provide more real simulation for scientific trainings of players, provide more objective data for accurate evaluation of player's capacity and aid coaches in selection of the most appropriate players. The author also hopes that such researches and application will be extended to more competitive sports i.e. tennis, football, and basketball. People will gain easier and deeper understanding of competitive sport and feel the professional in-depth splendor of competitive sports.

References

1. Mayer-Schönberger, V., Cukier, K.: Big data: A revolution that will transform how we live, work, and think. Houghton Mifflin Harcourt (2013)
2. Li, L., Zhao, Y., Nagarajan, R.: Optimising NBA player signing strategies based on practical constraints and statistics analytics. Int. J. Big Data Intell. 6(3–4), 188–201 (2019)
3. Whitaker, G.A., Silva, R., Edwards, D.: Visualizing a team's goal chances in soccer from attacking events: a Bayesian inference approach. Big Data 6(4), 271–290 (2018)
4. Ren, J., Chen, C.-G.: Application of big data's association rules in the analysis of sports competition tactics. In: Zhang, Y.-D., Wang, S.-H., Liu, S. (eds.) ICMTEL 2020. LNICSSITE, vol. 326, pp. 236–246. Springer, Cham (2020). https://doi.org/10.1007/978-3-030-51100-5_21
5. Dick, U., Brefeld, U.: Learning to rate player positioning in soccer. Big data 7(1), 71–82 (2019)
6. Bačić, B., Hume, P.A.: Computational intelligence for qualitative coaching diagnostics: automated assessment of tennis swings to improve performance and safety. Big Data 6(4), 291–304 (2018)
7. https://www.guinnessworldrecords.com/world-records/fastest-badminton-hit-in-competition-(male)
8. https://www.youtube.com/watch?v=QD7ZxoVp8xw
9. https://www.youtube.com/watch?v=sxAGh2N7Ce0
10. Ting, H.Y., Sim, K.S., Abas, F.S.: Automatic badminton action recognition using RGB-D sensor. Advanced Materials Research. Trans Tech Publications Ltd, vol. 1042, pp. 89–93 (2014)
11. Ikizler-Cinbis, N., Sclaroff, S.: Object, scene and actions: combining multiple features for human action recognition. In: Daniilidis, K., Maragos, P., Paragios, N. (eds.) ECCV 2010. LNCS, vol. 6311, pp. 494–507. Springer, Heidelberg (2010). https://doi.org/10.1007/978-3-642-15549-9_36

The Interactive Query Method with Clustering and Differential Privacy Protection Model Under Big Data Environment

Huanyu Fan[✉], Yunan Zhu, and Chao Shan

State Grid, Jiangsu Marketing Service Center (Metrology Center), Nanjing 210000, China

Abstract. To enhance the privacy protection as well as to improve data availability, a differential privacy data protection approach is proposed. Through big data cross-platform query, differential privacy method is performed on the results of ICMD (insensitive clustering method for mixed data) based on the insensitive clustering algorithm. The combination of clustering and differential privacy achieves the distinction of query sensitivity from a single record to a group of records. In addition, to meet the requirements of maintaining differential privacy for mixed data, this paper uses different methods to calculate the distance and centroid of classification and numerical attributes. Finally, the experiment shows the validity of the method, which reduces the risk of information loss and leakage.

Keywords: Mixed data · Differential privacy · Clustering · Interactive query

1 Introduction

As the development of the Internet, the number of users on social networks has increased rapidly. User data and information are hugely attractive. Data mining can get huge value from it. At the same time, user privacy is also at risk of leakage [1]. Therefore, efforts should be made to protect user privacy. Users privacy protection and user data availability guarantee have become the hot topic in information sharing.

Privacy protection data release (PPDP) should consider the balance between two aspects: (1) Protect sensitive data greatly to eliminate worries about data sharing; (2) Reduce information loss of insensitive information to ensure maximum data availability [2].

k-anonymity and its extended method are very important for the protection of the user information privacy. In order to protect the privacy of users, k-anonymity needs to have at least k records in the group to ensure that the quasi-identifier cannot be distinguished, so that the attacker cannot identify the owner of the private information [3]. However, obtaining an accurate k anonymous table is an NP problem. Analyzing the influence of k value selection on privacy protection and data quality, reference [4] gives an algorithm to achieve diversity by controlling the size of the sensitive value in the equivalent class. After data mining, the attacker can obtain a large amount of background knowledge, k-anonymity and its extended model are however difficult to

© Springer Nature Singapore Pte Ltd. 2021
Y. Tian et al. (Eds.): ICBDS 2020, CCIS 1415, pp. 327–336, 2021.
https://doi.org/10.1007/978-981-16-3150-4_28

resist background knowledge attacks and similar attacks. Therefore, privacy protection methods under big data environment are very popular [5]. Dwork proposed a differential privacy protection model in [6] and gave a strict privacy proof, which overcomes the disadvantage of being unable to resist arbitrary background knowledge attacks. However, the differential privacy model also sacrifices the big data availability.

2 Relevant Work and Background

2.1 Relevant Research

With the development of big data and data mining technology, the research of data privacy protection has become more and more important. Clustering algorithms play an significant role in data mining and grouping, and have become the focus of privacy protection research. The purpose of clustering is dividing the records into several groups so that the similarity between groups is the largest while the similarity within a group is the smallest. The k-anonymity algorithm is a grouping algorithm where the data records number in each group is k at least. The MDAV (Maximum Distance to Average Vector) algorithm is suitable for numerical attribute data sets [7]. Torra proposed a micro-aggregation algorithm for classified data based on k mode [8]. They only deal with numeric or categorical attribute data.

The k prototype implements the cluster analysis on mixed data by integrating the k-means algorithm and the k-mode [9]. However, the algorithm parameters are difficult to determine, and the k-prototype cannot objectively reflect the difference between the record and the class center.

This paper puts forward an approach for calculating the distance and centroid of mixed attribute data, and proposes the anonymous insensitive clustering method for mixed data (ICMD).

2.2 Differential Privacy Protection Background

Differential privacy is to achieve privacy protection by adding noise to the original data set or statistical results. This method that provides a strict and strong privacy protection proof can ensure that a single record changed in the data set will not affect the statistical results while the practicability of the data set is guaranteed. In addition, the model can resist arbitrary background knowledge attacks [10].

Definition 1. Assuming that data sets D and D' can be obtained by modifying a single record from one another. Range (A) is the range of function A. Then, for output S of A on D, D' (S ∈ Range(A)), there is

$$Pr[A(D) = S] \le e^{\varepsilon} \times Pr[A(D') = S] \tag{1}$$

That is to say, A meets differential privacy of ε. And ε is called the privacy protection budget. The smaller it is, the better the privacy protection and the larger the noise is.

Differential privacy has the characteristics of sequence combination and parallel combination [11], and can be obtained through introducing Laplace noise.

Definition 2. For query function f and algorithm A

$$A(D) = f(D) + Lap(\frac{\Delta f}{\varepsilon})$$ (2)

It means that A still satisfies the differential privacy of ε. Δf Represents the sensitivity of the query function, which indicates the maximum distance in the neighboring data set.

2.3 Distance and Centroid Calculation of Mixed Data

Most existing data sets have two attributes (categorical attributes and numeric attributes). For different attribute data, there are different distance calculation and centroid solving methods. A single method usually leads to information loss, centroid deviation or various other problems. Therefore, this paper proposes a mixed data distance calculation and centroid solving method for the clustering differential privacy protection model. Suppose that X and Y are records in data set D, and each data set contains p classification attributes and q attributes.

Definition 3 (distance of classification attributes) Data set D contains p classification attributes, and record X and Y in D as classification attributes. The distance between X and Y can be achieved as follows:

$$d(X, Y)_C = \sum_{j=1}^{p} \delta(x_j, y_j)$$ (3)

$$\delta(x_j, y_j) = \begin{cases} 0 \ (x_j = y_j) \\ 1 \ (x_j \neq y_j) \end{cases}$$ (4)

It is known that each distance of the classification attribute is contained in [0, 1]. For numerical attributes, if Hamming distance is used to calculate the distance, the distance of the category attributes will be destroyed. Therefore, this paper defines the distance of numerical attributes as Definition 4.

Definition 4 (distance of numerical attributes). Record X and Y in D, and X_q is value of the qth dimension of X. The numerical attributes could be standardized by the formula below.

$$d(X^q)_n = \frac{X^q - X^q_{min}}{X^q_{max} - X^q_{min}}$$ (5)

Then distance of X, Y is:

$$d(X, Y)_n = \sum_{j=1}^{q} (d(X^j)_n - d(Y^j)_n)$$ (6)

Definition 5 (distance of mixed data). By adding the distance of category attribute and numerical attribute, the distance of X, Y (D(X, Y)) can be obtained as:

$$D(X, Y) = d(X, Y)_C + d(X, Y)_n$$ (7)

The mean and generalized values are used to replace the original numerical and categorical data in the equivalence class so as to avoid one-sidedness and errors caused by using a single method to cluster numerical and categorical data while retaining more semantics.

3   Research on Big Data Interactive Query Model with Differential Privacy Data

This paper suggests a mixed data clustering approach that satisfies the k-anonymity mechanism. Then noise is introduced to the clustered data set to achieve differential privacy. The cluster operation reduces the sensitivity of the query function and increases data availability by adding small noise to achieve the same privacy protection effect.

3.1   Distance and Centroid Calculation of Mixed Data

According to the proposed distance and centroid calculation method of mixed data, CMD (clustering method for mixed data) is proposed, which satisfies the k anonymity mechanism, as shown in Fig. 1.

Algorithm 1 Clustering method for mixed data ($CMD(D,k)$)
let D be the original data set
let k be the minimal cluster size
input: D 、 k
output: data set D' which satisfies the k- anonymous mechanism
step:

1. Calculate cluster centers using the method in literature [15] and let:
  $\bar{x}$ ←average record of D
  r ←most distant record to $\bar{x}$ in D
  s ←most distant record to r in D

2. Form a cluster with r and its k closest records   Form a cluster with s and its k closest records   Add clusters to the data set D' Remove the clustered records from D
3. For the remaining m records, repeat the steps 1 and 2. if $m \geq 2k$ Form a cluster and add it to D' ,if $m \in [k, 2k-1]$ Add remaining records to nearest cluster, if $m < k$
4. Replace the value of each attribute with the mean and generalization values
5. Return D'

Fig. 1. Clustering method for mixed data

3.2 Improved Clustering Query Method to Maintain Differential Privacy

Differential privacy and clustering algorithms provide different information disclosure protections. The use of clustering algorithms can reduce the noise required for differential privacy and achieve sensitivity distinction of query functions. Meanwhile, differential privacy can resist any background knowledge attack. This combination can achieve better privacy protection and data availability.

Let M be the clustering method and f be the query function. To decrease the sensitivity, M should satisfy that the cluster center is basically stable for the data sets D and D' (D is the original data set, and D' is the data set different from D in a single record). M is called the insensitive clustering method, and the definition of insensitive clustering is given in [12].

In order to make the clustering method CMD an insensitive clustering and to maintain differential privacy, the distance function D needs to be changed to a total order function [12]. For mixed data, a distance function satisfying the total order relationship could be constructed as below.

Let D contain n-dimensional attributes (p-dimensional classification attributes and q-dimensional numerical attributes), and X and Y are records in D. Let Z be the cluster center of D, X_b is the farthest one from Z, and X_t is the farthest one from X_b. We call $[X_b, X_t]$ the boundary of D.

$$D(X, Y) = \sqrt{\sum_{i=1}^{n} \frac{(dist(x^i, y^i))^2}{(dist(x_b^i, y_t^i))^2}} \qquad (8)$$

$D(X, Y)$ is a total order function, where

$$dist(x^i, y^i) = \begin{cases} \delta(x^i, y^i), \ x^i, y^i \ \text{are classification attributes} \\ |x^i - y^i|, \ x^i, y^i \ \text{are numerical attributes} \end{cases}, \qquad (9)$$

In order to better introduce the total order function into clustering, this paper proposes a sensitive CMD to satisfy differential privacy, as shown in Fig. 2.

3.3 Interactive Query of Big Data

For structured data, Oracle, SQL Server, MySQL, DB2 and other relational databases are undoubtedly the most popular and classic systems. In 1970, Codd [13] first put forward a new relational model, thus starting to research on relational methods and theories. After decades of development, relational databases have been widely applied in different business application and information management systems [14]. They are the capable tool for data warehouse storage and analysis. As the information technology varies, the relational databases architecture has been continuously enhanced from centralized databases, distributed databases to parallel databases while the storage capacity has grown from GB to TB. Nowadays, parallel databases on the basis of massively parallel processing (MPP) [15] architecture could administer hundreds of terabytes of data. This database is made up of lots of loosely coupled processing units. And each unit has its

Algorithm 2 Insensitive CMD($ICMD(D,k)$)

let D be the original data set
let k be the minimal cluster size
input: D ، k
output: data set D' which maintains differential privacy
step:
1. $[X_b, X_t]$ ←the bounds of the original data set
2. Form a cluster with X_b and its k closest records
   Form a cluster with X_t and its k closest records
   Add clusters to the data set D'
   Remove the clustered records from D
3. For the remaining m records, repeat the steps 2, if $m \geq 2k$
   Form a cluster and add it to D', if $m \in [k, 2k-1]$
   Add remaining records to nearest cluster, if $m < k$
4. Replace the value of each attribute with the mean and generalization values
5. Return D'

Fig. 2. Insensitive CMD (ICMD)

own dedicated storage and computing resources, such as CPU, memory, cache, hard disk and OS.

MapReduce is a programming framework put forward by Google. It is a classical big data processing technology [16]. Because of its high throughput and super-large-scale node scheduling ability, MapReduce plays an important role in processing massive unstructured data [17]. Each calculation demand will start a job in the MapReduce framework. To fulfill this work, the MapReduce framework shall conduct two tasks: mapping and reduction. First, it separates the input data set into independent blocks and then distributes them to multiple nodes. The job administrator initializes several mapping tasks, each of which deals with a data block and achieves an intermediate file after calculating. After that, the output files of the map task would be sorted by the MapReduce framework sorts and several reduction tasks would be initialized. These tasks integrate the sorted results into the ultimate output file. The framework is in charge of scheduling and monitoring tasks and restarting failed ones.

It is necessary for big data applications to access data sets on various platforms even across domains. For structured data, the time cost of data extraction and loading cannot satisfy the real-time requirements. As displayed in Fig. 3, multiple platforms involve interconnection through LAN or Internet, thus forming a distributed heterogeneous network architecture, in which the data source is dynamic, autonomous and heterogeneous.

This article implements a cross-platform query interface, the client can use this interface to directly perform online join queries between discrete deployments or by other relational databases (such as Oracle and MySQL). There are three main components in the cross-platform query interface, which are SQL interface, cross-platform module and global table. The SQL interface offers users with a command shell and transfers query

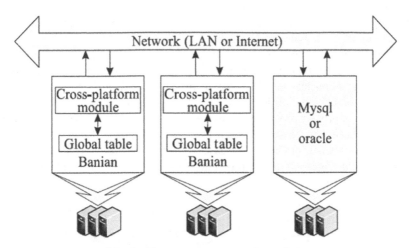

Fig. 3. Heterogeneous network topology

commands to the cross-platform module. If the command includes multiple data sets on various platforms, the cross-platform module will query the global table and obtains location data (data structure). Then, it separates the command based on the variable tagname of location and sends the sub-command as the master device to the slave platform, and receives the result thereafter.

4   Experiment

We use the same method as the k-anonymity evaluation to evaluate the combined scheme proposed in this article, including two aspects: information loss (affecting data availability) and information disclosure (representing the degree of privacy protection).

Information loss refers to the discrepancy between the anonymous and original data set, usually measured by SSE (Sum of Squared Error). SSE stands for the sum of squares of the attributes of all records in the anonymous and original data set.

Information disclosure is measured by the probability of successful record matching from anonymous data set to original data set, which is called RL (record links).

4.1   Experimental Data

The experimental data is the Adult data set of UCTs (http://archive.ics.uci.edu/ml/dat asets/Adult), which is usually used to evaluate privacy protection methods. The data set contains 6 numeric attributes and 8 category attributes. The data set contains 48,842 data records, and 30,000 data records that do not contain null values are selected for experiment.

4.2   Experimental Results and Analysis

To better illustrate the effectiveness of our approach, we use CMD and standard differential privacy as a baseline and compare ICMD with them. The privacy budget is usually

0.01, 0.1, 1, 10, and the k value is 2-500. The experimental results can be obtained by the above method, as shown from Fig. 2, 3, 4 and Fig. 5.

We know from Fig. 2 and Fig. 3 that the insensitive clustering algorithm ICMD has greater information loss than the original clustering algorithm CMD, and it also reduces the risk of information leakage. Differential privacy based on ICMD can effectively reduce the risk of information leakage. The smaller the protection budget, the more obvious the role of privacy protection, which also causes greater information loss. From Fig. 4, it shows that as k increases, when k is less than the standard differential privacy, the information loss of ICMD gradually decreases. From Fig. 5, we can learn that ICMD has less information leakage, and its data protection effect is better than standard differential privacy (Figs. 6 and 7).

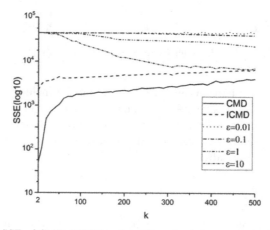

Fig. 4. SSE of CMD, ICMD under different privacy protection budgets.

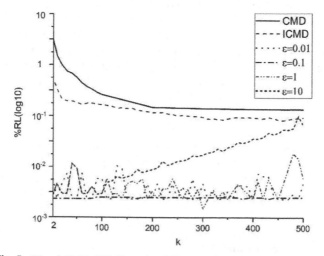

Fig. 5. RL of CMD, ICMD under different privacy protection budgets

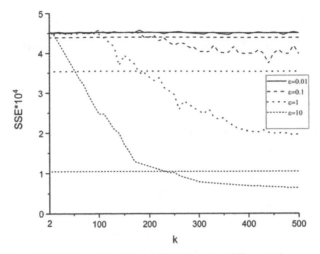

Fig. 6. SSE and standard ε differential privacy of ICMD under different privacy protection budgets

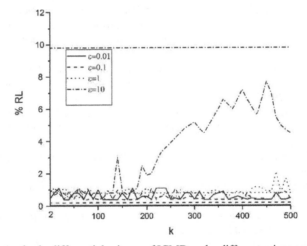

Fig. 7. RL and standard ε differential privacy of ICMD under different privacy protection budgets

5 Conclusion

This paper put forward a data query approach (ICMD) that integrates clustering and differential privacy. This method performs differential privacy after anonymous clustering, which reduces the risk of information leakage and increases data availability. First, a hybrid data clustering algorithm is proposed. Secondly, in order to effectively implement differential privacy, the total order distance function is introduced into CMD, and an insensitive clustering algorithm (ICMD) is proposed. Finally, the result of ICMD is used as the input of differential privacy to achieve better data release privacy protection effect. Through big data cross-platform query, experiments have proved the effectiveness of this method.

Acknowledgement. This paper is supported by the science and technology project of State Grid Corporation of China: "Research and Application of Key Technology of Data Sharing and Distribution Security for Data Center" (Grand No. 5700-202090192A-0-0-00).

References

1. Cao, C.-P., Zhang, X.: Research of anonymity model for privacy-preserving in social network. J. Chinese Comput. Syst. **37**(8), 1821–1825 (2016). (in Chinese)
2. Xiao-qian, L.I.U., Qian-mu, L.I.: Differentially private data release based on clustering anonymization. J. Commun. **37**(5), 125–129 (2016). in Chinese
3. Latanya, S.: k-anonymity: a model for protecting privacy. Int. J. Uncertain. Fuzz. Knowl. Syst. **10**(5), 557–570 (2002)
4. Han, J., Cen, T., Yu, J.: l-MDAV algorithm to realize l-diversity of sensitive attributes. In: Proceedings of the 27th China Control Conference (2008)
5. Li, H.-c., Wu, X.-p., Chen, Y.: k-means clustering method preserving differential privacy in Map Reduce framework. J. Commun. **37**(2), 124–130 (2016). (in Chinese)
6. Dwork, C.: Differential Privacy. Automata, Languages and Programming, pp. 1–12 (2006)
7. Engineering - Materials Engineering; Research Data from Hainan University Update Understanding of Materials Engineering (A Distributed Privacy Preservation Approach for Big Data In Public Health Emergencies Using Smart Contract and Sgx). Technology News Focus (2020)
8. Hundepool, A., Van de Wetering, A., Ramaswamy, R., et al.: μ-ARGUS version 4.1 software and user's manual Statistics Netherlands, Voorburg NL [EB/OL]. http: //neon.vb.cbs.nl/ casc. Accessed 14 Feb 2007
9. Torra, V.: Microaggregation for categorical variables: a median based approach. In: Privacy in Statistical Databases: CASC Project International Workshop, PSD 2004, Barcelona, Spain, 9–11 June (2004)
10. Zhao, X., L, J.: A weighted clustering algorithm for mixed data attributes based on information entropy. Comput. Res. Dev. **5**, 1018–1028 (2016)
11. Luo, F.: Research on the anonymous model and algorithm of multi-sensitive attribute microdata privacy protection. Zhejiang Normal University (2013)
12. Feng, X., Yu, H.: Research on density-insensitive nearest neighbor propagation clustering algorithm. Comput. Eng. **038**(002), 159–162 (2012)
13. Codd, E.F.: A relational model of data for large shared data banks. Commun. ACM **13**(6), 377–387 (1970)
14. Mi, W., Jianya, G.: Research and implementation of remote sensing image database management system based on extended relational database. Survey. Map. Inf. Eng. **05**, 1–3 (2002). in Chinese
15. Antova, L., El-Helw, A., Soliman, M.A., et al.: Optimizing queries over partitioned tables in MPP systems. 373–384 (2014)
16. Song, J., Sun, Z., Mao, K., et al.: MapReduce big data processing platform and algorithm research progress. J. Softw. (3), 514–543 (2017). (in Chinese)
17. You, M., Zhongzhi, L., Depei, Q.: Differentiating data collection for cloud environment monitoring. China Commun. **011**(004), 13–24 (2014)

Research on Spatio-Temporal Characteristics of Distribution Network Voltage Based on Big Data

Xin He[⊠], Zhentao Han, Nan Zhang, Yixin Hou, and Yutong Liu

Economic Research Institute of State Grid Liaoning Electric Power Co., Ltd., Shenyang, China

Abstract. The evaluation of the power supply voltage qualification rate of the distribution network adopts classification, sampling, and weighting to calculate the regional voltage qualification rate. There are problems such as point-to-surface, local and time-period characteristics. Integrate multi-source data such as power distribution SCADA system, marketing system, and geographic information system. It proposes the hierarchical aggregation of households-substations-lines-stations to analyze the spatial characteristics of the distribution network voltage; based on high-frequency sampling information, it is proposed to calculate the voltage qualification rate of feeders and substations in different periods, and to identify the warning period and analyze the time characteristics of local voltage. It can also realize the fine characterization of the spatiotemporal characteristics of the power supply voltage qualification rate of the distribution network. Data calculations of a distribution network in Guangxi show that the proposed voltage temporal and spatial characteristics analysis method can accurately reflect the voltage details of the distribution network, sort the unqualified rates of feeders and substation power supply voltages, and identify intermittent low voltages.

Keywords: Qualified rate of voltage · Spatiotemporal characteristics · Multi-source data fusion

1 Introduction

The power supply voltage qualification rate is an important indicator to measure the quality of power supply, which is the percentage of the cumulative time of the actual operating voltage deviation within the limit range and the total voltage monitoring time. Distribution network users have many power supply voltage levels and different voltage deviation requirements. In order to facilitate the assessment and management of the regional power supply voltage qualification rate, electric power companies divide users into four categories, *A*, *B*, *C*, and *D*. They are classified and assessed, and obtain the comprehensive qualification rate index of regional voltage through weighted summary.

The calculation method for the voltage qualification rate of four types of monitoring points is: Various voltage qualification rates (%) = (The sum of the voltage qualification

© Springer Nature Singapore Pte Ltd. 2021
Y. Tian et al. (Eds.): ICBDS 2020, CCIS 1415, pp. 337–352, 2021.
https://doi.org/10.1007/978-981-16-3150-4_29

3   Analysis of Distribution Network Voltage Spatial Characteristics

The popularization of smart meters has realized the low interval and full coverage of user voltage data collection by the distribution network, and provided basic data for finely characterizing the qualification rate of power supply voltage. With the development of computer and communication technology and the widespread application of intelligent terminals in the distribution network, the integration and interaction of system data such as geographic information systems, user acquisition systems, and production management systems provide platform data for transparent operation of the distribution network.

Use the data of voltage acquisition devices such as smart meters to calculate the voltage deviation of users, and through weighted aggregation, realize the hierarchical evaluation of the power supply voltage qualification rate of distribution transformers, feeders, and substations. Change the traditional voltage qualification rate sampling and wide-area evaluation to provide technical support for follow-up governance and governance effect evaluation. The specific evaluation structure and evaluation process are shown in Fig. 2 and Fig. 3.

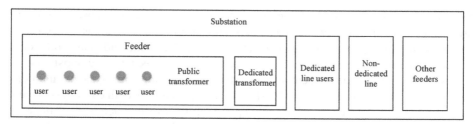

Fig. 2.   Structure for evaluating voltage space characteristics of distribution network.

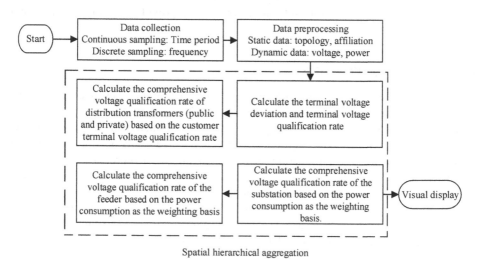

Fig. 3.   Distribution network voltage space hierarchical aggregation process.

3.1 User Voltage Qualification Rate

With the massive installation of smart meters and the development of communication and computer technology, real-time and quasi-real-time collection of electricity consumption information has been achieved in most areas. Based on the voltage collection data of the smart meter, calculate the user voltage deviation, the calculation formula is:

$$\Delta u_i = \frac{u_i - u_N}{u_N} \tag{2}$$

In the formula, u_i is the measured voltage at the user terminal; u_N is the nominal voltage at the user terminal.

For discrete sampling equipment, the calculation formula of the customer terminal voltage qualification rate is

$$C_T = \left(1 - \frac{N_T}{N}\right) \times 100\% \tag{3}$$

In the formula, C_T represents the user voltage qualification rate within T monitoring time; N_T represents the number of user voltage over-limit times within T time, and N represents the total number of voltage sampling times within T time.

For continuous sampling equipment, the formula for calculating the customer-side voltage qualification rate is:

$$C_T = \left(1 - \frac{T_t}{T}\right) \times 100\% \tag{4}$$

In the formula, T_t represents the user voltage limit time during the monitoring time, and T represents the total monitoring time.

3.2 Comprehensive Voltage Qualification Rate of Distribution Transformer

The statistics of the qualified rate of distribution transformer voltage should be based on users. Distribution transformers include public and special transformers. Public transformers include multiple users. Because voltage collection points and allowable ranges of voltage deviation are different, they need to be discussed separately.

1) Public transformer station area

There are a large number of users in the public transformer station area. Traditionally, the evaluation is mainly carried out by sampling at two points at the beginning and the end. Due to the large difference in user distribution, the voltage at the beginning and end of the distribution transformer cannot accurately reflect the comprehensive voltage qualification rate of users in the station area. The comprehensive voltage qualification rate of the distribution transformer is proposed, and the calculation formula is:

$$T_T = \frac{\sum\limits_{h=1}^{m} C_{Th}}{m} \times 100\% \tag{5}$$

In the formula, T_T represents the comprehensive voltage qualification rate of the public transformer station area during the T monitoring period; C_{Th} represents the voltage qualification rate of the h-th user during the T monitoring period, and m represents the total number of users in the station area.

The comprehensive voltage qualification rate of the common transformer is a characteristic quantity that includes the voltage characteristics of all users under it, and provides a unique parameter for subsequent calculations.

2) Dedicated transformer station area

There is only one user in the dedicated transformer station area, and its voltage qualification rate calculation formula is the same as the user voltage qualification rate.

3.3 Feeder Comprehensive Voltage Qualification Rate

There are multiple public transformers and dedicated transformers under the feeder, and the comprehensive voltage qualification rate of each transformer has been unique after the aforementioned calculation. Due to the large difference in the capacity of each transformer in the feeder, the calculation of the feeder voltage qualification rate needs to be weighted according to the power consumption of each transformer. The calculation formula is:

$$F_T = \sum_{j=1}^{n} \left(\frac{E_{Tj}}{\sum_{j=1}^{n} E_{Tj}} T_{Tj} \right) \times 100\% \tag{6}$$

In the formula, F_T represents the comprehensive voltage qualification rate of the feeder during the T monitoring time; T_{Tj} represents the voltage qualification rate of the j-th distribution transformer during the T monitoring time; E_{Tj} represents the power consumption of the j-th distribution transformer during the T monitoring time, and n represents the total number of distribution transformers in the feeder.

The above-mentioned calculation of the comprehensive voltage qualification rate of the feeder is unique, which is convenient for comparing the voltage qualification rate indexes of different feeders.

3.4 Comprehensive Voltage Qualification Rate of Substation

The substation has multiple power supply modes such as feeders and dedicated lines. The calculation method of the comprehensive voltage qualification rate is the same as the comprehensive voltage qualification rate of the feeder, and the power weighted calculation is adopted for each line.

$$S_T = \sum_{j=1}^{l} \left(\frac{E_{Tj}}{\sum_{j=1}^{l} E_{Tj}} F_{Tj} \right) \times 100\% \tag{7}$$

In the formula, S_T represents the comprehensive voltage qualification rate of the substation during the T monitoring time; F_{Tj} represents the voltage qualification rate of the j-th line within the T monitoring time; E_{Tj} represents the power consumption of the j-th line within the sampling time T, and l represents the total number of lines in the substation.

The analysis of the distribution network voltage space characteristics based on the household-substation-line-station hierarchical aggregation has changed the traditional wide-area evaluation mode of voltage qualification rate, and can sort the comprehensive voltage qualification rate of substations, lines, and substations in layers, reflecting the severity of voltage deviations in different substations, feeders, etc., and prompt warnings in time to provide technical support for subsequent treatment.

4 Analysis of Voltage-Time Characteristics of Distribution Network

The analysis of the voltage spatial characteristics of the distribution network has realized the detailed evaluation from the wide-area evaluation to the partial evaluation. The traditional voltage qualification rate evaluation time domain selects a long time range such as month and quarter. The long-term evaluation overwhelms some important user power information. The subordinate users of the transformer and the feeder may have similar power consumption characteristics. The voltage limit is more serious. Most of the existing sampling equipment supports real-time sampling or short-term sampling, and the sampling interval of smart meters has been 15 min or less. Identifying these time periods and discovering the time-to-period law of users' power consumption is conducive to scheduling optimization operations or technological transformation. The specific evaluation process is shown in Fig. 4.

4.1 Calculation of Voltage Failure Rate by Time Period

With 1 h as the statistical interval, the voltage qualification rate of each period of the station change and feeder is calculated every day, and the proportion of voltage failures in each period of the day is calculated. Taking the station area transformer as an example, according to the aforementioned formula (5), the time interval is set to 1 h, and the comprehensive voltage qualification rate T_k for each period of 24 h a day is calculated. On this basis, calculate the proportion of the voltage failure rate in each period, as shown in formula (8):

$$T_k\% = \frac{1 - T_k}{\sum\limits_{k=1}^{24} (1 - T_k)} \times 100\% \tag{8}$$

In the formula, k is the number of periods; $T_k\%$ represents the proportion of the voltage failure rate in each period, such as $T_1\%$ represents the proportion of the voltage failure rate in the 0–1 point period; T_k represents the comprehensive voltage qualification rate of the station area in each period.

If $T_k\%$ exceeds the warning threshold, the period of the day will be set as a warning period for subsequent periodical voltage failure identification.

(2) Determination of the optimal number of clusters K

In order to evaluate whether the clustering results meet the conditions of intra-class aggregation and inter-class separation, this study proposes a more effective evaluation method, which is to construct an evaluation function to evaluate the effectiveness of clustering by using the degree of intra-class difference and the degree of inter-class difference.

Assuming that a set of data set $X = \{x_1, x_2, ..., x_N\}$ is given, it is required to divide this data set into k clusters $(C_1, C_2, ..., C_k)$, and the final cluster center of each cluster is $(m_1, m_2, ..., m_k)$.

The degree of intra-class difference is used to measure the compactness of clusters. It is expressed by the average value of the distance between each data object in the class and the cluster center of the class it belongs to, which is defined as:

$$D_{in} = \frac{\sum_{i=1,j=1}^{i=k,j=k} \sqrt{(x_j - m_i)^2}}{N} \tag{10}$$

The degree of difference between clusters is used to measure the degree of separation between different clusters, expressed by the minimum distance between cluster centers, which is defined as:

$$Dout = \min_{2 \leq k \leq k_{max}} d(m_i, m_j) \tag{11}$$

In the formula, N is the number of data objects; m_i is the cluster center of class c_j; x_j is the data object in class c_j; $d(m_i, m_j)$ is the Euclidean distance between class c_i and class c_j.

Based on D_{in} and D_{out}, this research proposes a new cluster validity evaluation function:

$$V(k) = \frac{Dout - Din}{Dout + Din} \tag{12}$$

It can be seen from the evaluation function that the value range of the function is $[-1, 1]$. The closer $V(k)$ is to 1, it means that the intra-class difference of the data object can be ignored relative to the inter-class difference, and the better the clustering effect; If $V(k)$ is closer to -1, it means that the degree of difference between classes of the data object can be ignored relative to the degree of difference within classes, and the worse the clustering effect. In order to make the clusters gather as much as possible, and separate the clusters as much as possible; when $V(k)$ is the largest, the clustering result is the best, and the corresponding k is the optimal number of clusters K.

4.3 Recognition of Interval Voltage Unqualified Based on Improved K-means Clustering Algorithm

On the basis of the calculation of the above-mentioned time-division voltage qualification rate, the warning period is identified. If the repetition rate of the warning period exceeds the set repetition rate threshold within a period of time (such as one week), then the period is marked as periodical voltage failure. This identification method can automatically discover the time-period characteristics of voltage in time, and give full play to the advantages of big data in the distribution network.

Among them, the setting of the repetition rate threshold of the warning period can be modified according to actual needs. For example, this paper calculates and collects the unqualified voltage data of a certain public transformer station area for one week according to the formula proposed above, and uses the K-means clustering algorithm to reflect the regularity of the unqualified period.

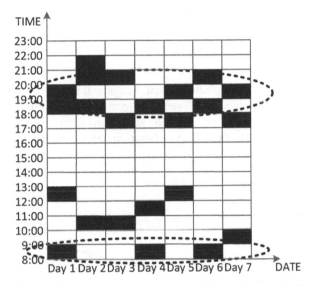

Fig. 6. Clustering results during unqualified voltage period.

Collect the unqualified rate of voltage in a public transformer station area in a certain area, use a black square to indicate that the voltage is unqualified, and an ellipse drawn with a dotted line to indicate the unqualified period clustered by the K-means clustering algorithm. The result is shown in Fig. 6. It can be seen from the figure that 8:00–9:00 and 18:00–21:00 of this week are the unqualified voltage periods obtained by cluster analysis.

5   Case Analysis

5.1   Comparison of K-means Clustering Algorithm Before and After Improvement

Comparing the improved K-means clustering algorithm with the traditional method, it can be seen from Fig. 7 that the improved K-means clustering algorithm has better convergence characteristics for the objective function. Before the improvement, the

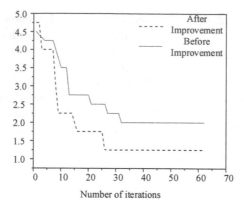

Fig. 7. Iteration speed comparison chart.

algorithm runs more than 30 iterations to reach the optimal solution, while the improved algorithm only needs 25 iterations. Moreover, the improved algorithm has faster convergence for the objective function. Under the same number of iterations, the improved algorithm reduces the value of the objective function faster, which is more conducive to finding the optimal solution.

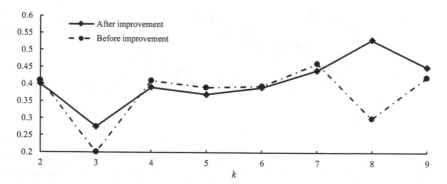

Fig. 8. Curve of clustering evaluation function before and after improvement.

In order to facilitate comparison, the cluster effectiveness evaluation function proposed in this paper is used to compare the two clustering algorithms before and after the improvement. Evaluate and get the line chart shown in Fig. 8. It can be seen from the evaluation function line graph shown in Fig. 8 that the evaluation function value of the clustering algorithm before the improvement is generally lower than the evaluation function value after the improvement, and the clustering result is affected by the initial cluster center, and the randomness is strong. The evaluation function value of the improved clustering algorithm shows a trend of increasing first and then decreasing, reaching the maximum when k = 8, and the clustering result is the best.

6   Analysis of Distribution Network Voltage Spatial Characteristics

Based on the user voltage data of the 10 kV two small 907 lines of Luhe Power Supply Station in February 2018, calculate the comprehensive voltage qualification rate of all distribution transformers according to the aforementioned formula (5). The total length of the known line is 47.149 km, and the total number of operating transformers is 45, of which 34 are public transformers with a total capacity of 5950 kVA; 11 are special transformers with a total capacity of 1075 kVA. The calculation method of the comprehensive voltage qualification rate of the special transformer in the article is the same as the calculation result of the data collected by the export terminal of the special transformer, so it is not analyzed here. Table 1 only lists the communal transformers where the comprehensive voltage qualification rate of the public transformer station area of the line is lower than 98.6% (based on the measurement data of high and low voltage users (station area) judgment criteria).

Table 1. Qualified rate of public transformer voltage at the end of two small 907 lines.

Serial number	Station area name	Pass rate of terminal alternating voltage	Comprehensive voltage qualification rate of station area
1	Public transformer NO. 1	91.00	89.93
2	Public transformer NO. 2	90.60	90.09
3	Public transformer NO. 3	92.00	91.55
4	Public transformer NO. 4	96.40	96.03
5	Public transformer NO. 5	96.70	96.42
6	Public transformer NO. 6	97.40	97.18
7	Public transformer NO. 7	97.70	97.51

In the table, the comprehensive voltage qualification rate of the common transformer station area is sorted from low to high. At the end of the power supply line, No. 2 public transformer terminal has the lowest passing voltage qualification rate, which conforms to the voltage drop distribution characteristics.Comparing the calculation results of the comprehensive voltage qualification rate of the public transformer station area, it is found that NO. 1 public transformer with the same long power supply line has the lowest comprehensive voltage qualification rate. Query the topological map of NO. 1 public transformer and analyze the related user information list. It can be seen that 140 users are scattered, and the power supply radius of 1.5 km results in the comprehensive voltage qualification rate of the station area being lower than the comprehensive voltage qualified for the public transformer NO. 2. Therefore, the public transformer NO. 1 should give priority to low-voltage management.

6.1 Recognition of Voltage Period Characteristics of Distribution Network

Power users under the same distribution transformer have similar power consumption characteristics, and there is a certain regularity in the period of voltage fluctuations. Taking a single station area as an example, calculate the comprehensive voltage qualification rate T_k and the voltage unqualified rate $T_k\%$ of the station area 24 h a day according to formula (5) and formula (8), and identify the voltage unqualified period of the station area.

Figure 9 shows the public transformers on Guhe Street in the urban power supply station of the Dahua Bureau. From March 3 to 10, 2019, all the time periods where the voltage failure rate is greater than one twelfth (the warning time threshold has been set to twelve points 1), the figure shows the percentage value by the shade of the color block. For example, the warning period on the 3rd day is 10–11, 15–17, 20–21. The preset repetition rate threshold is 50%, and voltage unqualified identification is performed for all warning periods from 3 to 10. During the cumulative date, the period in which the repetition rate of the warning period exceeds the threshold is the periodical voltage failure. In Fig. 9, the repetition rate of the warning period from 15–16 o'clock is 100%, and the repetition rate of the warning period from 16–17 o'clock is 75%. The above two periods are all intermittent voltage failures.

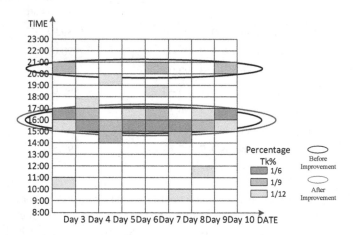

Fig. 9. Statistics of unqualified period of voltage in public transformer station area.

Analyzing the electricity consumption information of users associated with the public transformer on Guhe Street, it was found that between 15–17 o'clock, the agricultural technology extension station of Guhe Township led the villagers to practice agricultural technology, which caused the voltage qualification rate to be low during this period. The identification method can identify the characteristics of the voltage period except for the morning and evening peak hours, and discover the time period regularity of the user's power consumption, which is conducive to scheduling and optimizing operation.

Table 2. The partition scheme before and after the algorithm improvement and the calculation result of V(k).

	Division of voltage failure period	*Dout*	*Din*	*V(k)*
Before improvement	15:00–17:00 20:00–21:00	9.309	4.054	0.393
After improvement	15:00–17:00	6.955	2.010	0.552

Table 2 can be summarized from Fig. 9. The voltage unqualified period after the cluster analysis before the improvement is divided into 15:00–17:00 and 20:00–21:00, and the time period after the improvement is 15:00–17: 00, and the evaluation function values corresponding to the two schemes are calculated according to formula 12. It can be seen that the improved scheme has a higher evaluation value. Obviously, the improved algorithm has better accuracy, which shows the value of the improved algorithm in this paper.

This article proposes a refined evaluation method for low-voltage distribution network considering the spatial characteristics. Compared with the traditional extraction method, the method in the article is more accurate and can accurately locate the low-voltage area and time period. It has the following advantages:

(1) Integrate multi-source data such as power distribution SCADA system, marketing system, geographic information system, and divide the data into static data related to topology and affiliation and dynamic collection data related to real-time changes in voltage and electricity, providing a basis for subsequent evaluation data.
(2) Make full use of multi-source data to accurately evaluate the overall or partial refined voltage levels of the station-line-substation-household multi-level, and analyze the spatial characteristics of the distribution network voltage.
(3) Based on the calculation of the qualified rate of the substation transformer and feeder voltage in different periods, find out the warning period, and identify the periodical voltage unqualified, and realize the fine characterization of the voltage time characteristics of the distribution network.

The calculation example shows that the analysis of the temporal and spatial characteristics of the distribution network voltage can sort the overall or partial voltage qualification rate, identify the time-period law of users' electricity consumption. Provide technical support for follow-up governance and governance effect evaluation.

References

1. Li, D., Chen, W., Ma, M., Yang, Y., Xiong, N., Tan, T.: Voltage management business oriented index system of voltage qualification rate. Electr. Meas. Instr. **53**(19), 55–61 (2016)
2. Ma, J., Liu, X.: Conditional characteristic evaluation based on G_2-entropy weight method for low-voltage distribution network. Electric Power Autom. Equip. **37**(01), 41–46 (2017)

but detrimental to function. The model we propose will include dynamic changes due to the addition of new attributes and the collection of new data.

What data do we need to protect? For example, in the medical virtual database, "address", "age" and "occupation" are personal fundamental data, while "hepatitis", "depression", "AIDS" and "thyroid (function)" are their medical data, and the data protected is the unique "uid" (AIDS, suicide, etc.). The model proposed in this text (called an association network) consists of two parts. One is on the basis of a probability causal network model, and the other explained functional dependencies or similarity relationships.

Before introducing those two components, the Bayesian theory is introduced first of all. With the renaissance of Bayesian methods in decision support systems (Shachter 1986; Pearl 1988; Shafer and Pearl 1990; Andreassen et al., 1991b), the construction of effective belief correction methods in causal probability networks (Pearl 1988; Lauritzen and Spiegelhalter 1988; Andersen da 1989; Jensen et al. 1990; Shenoy and Shafer 1990), the knowledge acquisition process under the Bayesian paradigm has become more and more significant. When constructing a causal probability network model, a variety of sources can be used, from ignorance of the subjective assessment of experts to sophisticated scientific theories and statistical models on the basis of large databases. Usually, the model is a combination of various contributions from different epistemological features.

Occasionally, the recovery model is incomplete (for example, ignorance forces a 'guess' on some distributions), or the model must change with the context, and the context cannot be specified in advance. While under some circumstances the domain drifts over time-the model is required to drift with it, or the model is very simple, but it does not accurately reflect the real world.

All these problems require the system to modify the model based on actual experience, a process we call "dynamic adaptation", and systems that perform automatic adaptation are called adaptive systems. In this paper we have chosen to distinguish between adaptation and training. Training is used to describe activities, or incubate large databases to create models..

3.1 Probabilistic Causal Network Model

In order to make better classification choices, people often evaluate cases based on the possibility generated by the causal relationship model of the category. For example, as shown in Fig. 2 below.

c: Probability of occurrence of feature C.
m: When C exists, the successful operational probability of mechanism connecting C and E (i.e. C leads to the occurrence of E).
b: When C does not occur, the occurrence possibility of E.
Necessity: $b = 0$, that is, if E occurs, it must be caused by C, otherwise C does not occur.
Sufficiency: $m = 1$, that is, if C occurs, E must exist, otherwise E does not necessarily occur.

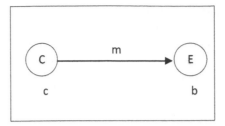

Fig. 2. Causality model

Therefore, in the causality model, deterministic causality is often a restrictive case. In the theory of causality model, although the value is close to sufficiency and necessity, the possibility of violating causality relationship is relatively low.

3.2 Similar Attributes Identification

To avoid inference attacks, certain data (for example: names) should be automatically removed from the database. Simply removing this kind of attribute is not sufficient, though. Other data (for example: a person's address) may disclose the same information in essence. Thus, these data shall also be invisible to ordinary users. Think of the natural relationship between two attributes and their attribute values in the database. If the relationship is "close" to the double shot, then the attributes are considered similar. If "uid" corresponds to the "address" value, then "address" is the same as "uid" is the same. But the mapping between the two is almost bijective, so they are similar (only three addresses correspond to more than one uid, in these cases they correspond to two uids). Intuitively, the smaller the frequency distribution displayed in the table, the greater the similarity between the candidate and target attributes.

Based on the information-theoretic rules, it is possible to determine the criteria for confirming which attributes are akin to the target ones.

Definition 1 (Dispersion V):

$$Vi = - \sum_{j=1}^{N} \Pr(tj|ci) \log(\Pr(tj|ci)); \; V = \left(\sum_{i=1}^{M} Vi\right) \Big/ M \qquad (1)$$

Among them, N represents the attribute values number of the target attribute T (with value tj) and M represents that of the object attribute C (with value ci). Vi represents the i-th attribute value dispersion of C, and V represents the total dispersion after normalization, and a low V score is a selection criterion for similar items. $\Pr(tj|ci) = nij/ni$, where nij represents the frequency count in row i and column j, and ni represents the sum of row i. Observe that the dispersion is measured from 0 to logn. when just one entry with a non-zero value exists in each row, the minimum value will appear. When the mass ni is equally allocated over all attribute values of T, the maximum value appears. Given T = "uid", the V score of C = "address" is 3/17 = 0.18. Pay attention that if the V score of C is no more than 1, for some i, there is a Vi score of C is 0. The value of the attribute corresponding to a low score can be modified.

An object attribute can be a mixture of multiple attributes. For example, each item in Table 1 can be uniquely identified by the mixture of "address" and "mental depression". Figure 1 indicates this kind of mixture. In reality, combining multiple attributes with a higher V-score will result in a lower V-score. With the Index V-score, search and evaluate possible combinations of different attributes until you reach a bijection with the target attribute or the desired V-score. Store the attribute or combine it with a low V-score.

Table 1. Medical records released to ordinary users

Hepatitis	Mental depression	AIDS	Thyroid
n	n	?	n
y	d	?	1
?	d	?	1
y	?	?	1
y	d	?	n
n	n	?	n
y	n	?	n
y	d	?	1
y	d	?	1
n	n	?	n
y	n	?	n
n	n	?	n
y	d	?	1
n	d	?	1
n	n	?	n
n	d	?	1
y	d	?	n
n	d	?	1
y	n	?	n

3.3 Calculation of Probability Effects

The analysis of probability dependence is on the basis of Bayesian network representation. As described earlier, the joint of "address" and "mental depression" will result in the "uid" identification. Figure 2 illustrates the connected network.In particular, in case of a potential connection between "uid" and "AIDS", the information must be reduced to "mental depression" (as it helps both networks). In addition to protecting sensitive information, blocking and aggregation strategies are used (Fig. 4).

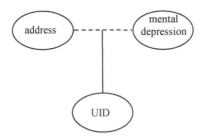

Fig. 3. Example of attribute combination (the nodes represent attributes; the dotted line represents combination; the straight line represents similar relationship)

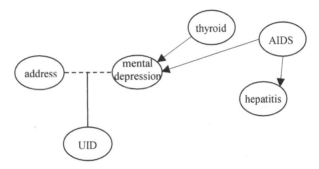

Fig. 4. The architecture of the connected network

4   Data Privacy Protection System

4.1   Narrowing the Range

In order to objectively and quantitatively describe user tolerance for potential errors caused by database modifications, we call this the database quality index (QI), which is formed in the phase of data collection. The analysis in this paper expresses it as the sample probability logarithm (based on 2). Definition 2 (QI)

$$QI = \log(\Pr(D|m))   \tag{2}$$

Where D represents the data set and m represents the model. If m is a BNM Bn, QI will be $\log \Pr(D|Bn)$. The QI is considered to be the lower tolerance level limit, and in this case the validity of the inferences drawn from the adjusted database is uncertain. The working range is described according to the change rate γ.

Definition 3 (Reduction ratio)

$$\gamma \equiv |QI\_(original) - QI\_(modified)| / |QI\_(original)| \tag{3}$$

4.2   Blocking

The chunking method is performed by replacing some attribute values of certain data items with question marks. Blocking is performed by selecting a set of attribute values

of examples for each group. This large-scale biometric database also requires training algorithms, because recent algorithms are based on learning. Building such a large
database requires a lot of work to find a large number of volunteers and keep them
cooperating with the process of building the database. Transferring the database to other
organizations means less responsibility for database protection, and the possibility of
individual data leakage is greater. Figure 6 is a schematic representation of the database
capture and biometric authentication system evaluation.

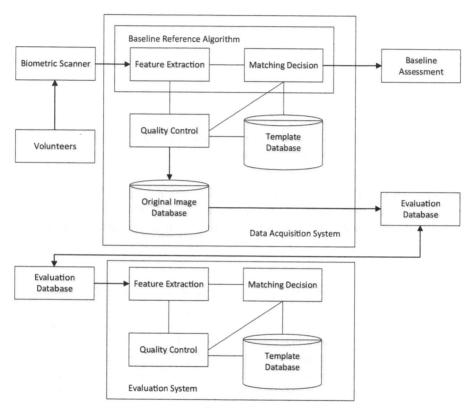

Fig. 6. Schematic diagram of database collection and biometric authentication system evaluation

5.2 Effectiveness Assessment

According to the blocking result, the target probabilities tend to be uniformly distributed.
The entropy measure of T and $Pr(T|Dm, Bn)$ has an increase in single weight w.r.t.
blocking. This attribute, namely uniformity, provides the greatest entropy, while speci-
ficity gives the smallest entropy. Through cross-validation of Dm, the effectiveness of
the modifications in our framework can be evaluated. Among them, the effectiveness is
measured according to the error rate $Ucf(e, s)$, which means that the chance of e error
in the s test data is cf in confidence. For example, using 3 misclassified test data and 7

test data, when cf $= 10\%$, Ucf $(3, 7)$ is 0.43. In conclusion, the higher the error rate is, the more unreliable the network model will be, thus reducing inference.

6 Conclusion

This paper presents a framework based on the Oracle database that provides some assistance in the formal analysis of database inference problems. This architecture is on the basis of association networks and consists of similarity metrics and BNMs. The results show that privacy protection needs extensive evaluation and data relationships analysis. Two processing layers are required in this paper. Firstly, the similarity analysis is conducted to check the similar attributes. Secondly, the probability dependence analysis on the basis of attributes is carried out. Blocking and aggregation are adopted to prevent inference, and associative networks are used to analyze inference. The probability dependence structure, classification structure and similarity measures build a system for database privacy protection.

Acknowledgement. This thesis is derived from the National Grid Corporation's Science and Technology Tackle Project. "Research and Application of Key Technology of Data Sharing and Distribution Security for Data Center" (Grand No. 5700-202090192A-0-0-00).

References

1. Xiong, P., Zhu, T., Jin, D.: Differential private data publishing algorithm for building decision tree. Appl. Res. Comput. **31**(10), 3108–3112 (2014)
2. Sun, Z., Sun, F.: Constructing the privacy protection system of users' big data based on institutional trust. Res. Libr. Sci. **436**(17), 98–100 (2018)
3. Huang, R., Wen, F.: The construction of policy problems of opening and sharing government data in China. Libr. Inf. Serv. **61**(20), 26–36 (2017)
4. Zhu, D., Li, X.B., Wu, S.: Identity disclosure protection: a data reconstruction approach for privacy-preserving data mining. Decis. Support Syst. **48**(1), 133–140 (2019)
5. Kasai, H., Uchida, W., Kurakake, S.: A service provisioning system for distributed personalization with private data protection. J. Syst. Softw. **80**(12), 2025–2038 (2017)
6. Kumar, S., Mahulikar, S.P.: Design of thermal protection system for reusable hypersonic vehicle using inverse approach. J. Spacecraft Rock. **54**(2), 436–446 (2017)
7. Chern, J., Liu, C.: Morakot post-disaster reconstruction management using public and private resources for disaster prevention and relief efforts. J. Chinese Inst. Eng. **37**(5), 621–634 (2014)
8. Bai, C., Lu, J., Tao, Z.: Property rights protection and access to bank loans: evidence from private enterprises in China. Econ. Trans. **14**(4), 611–628 (2016)
9. Chang, L., Moskowitz, I.S.: An integrated framework for database privacy protection. In: Thuraisingham, B., van de Riet, R., Dittrich, K.R., Tari, Z. (eds.) Data and Application Security. IFIP International Federation for Information Processing, vol 73. Springer, Boston (2002). https://doi.org/10.1007/0-306-47008-X_15

Enterprise Credit Decisions Using Logistic Regression and Particle Swarm Optimization Based on Massive Data Records

Caixin Kang[1]($\boxtimes$), Mingrui Wan[1], Murong Du[2], and Daokang Zhang[1]

[1] School of Computer Science, Sichuan University, Chengdu 610207, China
[2] School of Chemistry, Sichuan University, Chengdu 610207, China

Abstract. In the current big data environment, in order to improve the low efficiency of banks' credit decision-making to enterprises, and easy to make mistakes in decision-making, this paper proposes an algorithm based on logistic regression and particle swarm optimization to model the loan default rate of small, medium and micro enterprises, solves the problem of bank lending strategy, and has a certain range of popularization when dealing with big data. Using six important indicators including gross profit rate, business stability, customer concentration, customer stability, capital flow time distribution standard deviation and credit rating, this paper establishes an evaluation system, summarizes and quantifies the characteristics of big data information from different angles. Using logistic regression algorithm to further establish the default rate calculation model based on the sales invoice data of enterprises with credit records. According to the training set and test set, the model is used to predict, and cross validation is carried out to calculate the average default situation prediction results. Then, using the predicted default rate combined with the statistical data of the relationship between the annual interest rate of bank loans and the customer churn rate, the particle swarm optimization algorithm is used for multiple optimization calculation to obtain the optimal value of the bank's profit expectation, and then determine the bank's lending strategy for small and medium-sized enterprises.

Keywords: Particle swarm optimization algorithm · Logistic regression algorithm · Big data · Enterprise credit decision

1 Introduction

Small and medium-sized enterprises often lack of mortgage assets. In order to support small and medium-sized enterprises, banks usually judge the strength and reputation of their enterprises according to the credit policy and big data information such as the influence of upstream and downstream enterprises of small and medium-sized enterprises and transaction bill information, so as to evaluate the credit risk, and finally integrate the information to determine whether to lend or not, and determine the loan amount and profit Credit strategy including rate and term. Weiss et al. [2] studied the credit decision-making problem of enterprises, taking the uncertainty of loan return and information asymmetry

© Springer Nature Singapore Pte Ltd. 2021
Y. Tian et al. (Eds.): ICBDS 2020, CCIS 1415, pp. 364–376, 2021.
https://doi.org/10.1007/978-981-16-3150-4_31

as the starting point, and pointed out that with the increase of the actual loan interest rate of each risk type investor, the default of loan contract also increased. When the lender does not have the complete information of the investor's risk type, Credit contract may lead to adverse selection and moral hazard. Bester [3] studied that when the lender simultaneously uses loan interest rate and collateral requirements as incentive means for investors, there may be a loan contract that enables the lender to screen out the harmful risks. Jin Wu et al. [4] Based on the concept of second-order stochastic advantage of risk description, Considering that there are two different types of loan enterprises with high and low risk in society, This paper discusses the problems of adverse selection, credit rationing, moral hazard and the economic significance of introducing guarantors in China's credit market. Fu Qiang et al. [7] embedded the interest protection multiple and inventory turnover rate into the logistic model to judge enterprise credit. Among them, the greater the security multiple of information, the stronger the enterprise's ability to pay debts, the greater the inventory turnover rate, which represents the operation of enterprises The better the situation is, the greater the factor of the combination of the two, the better the credit of the enterprise.

At present, there are two defects in the credit strategy of SMEs under incomplete information.

1) In the big data environment, many data can not be considered, or it is difficult to make correct decisions
2) Under incomplete information, the credit decision model is established from the perspective of maximizing the expected return

This paper proposes a method based on logistic regression and particle swarm optimization algorithm to establish enterprise credit decision-making model to deal with massive data records. Firstly, the data is cleaned and six important indexes are calculated, including gross profit rate, business stability, customer concentration, customer stability, standard deviation of capital flow time distribution and credit rating To credit score. After using the logistic model, we can make full use of the empirical data to solve the problem There is a certain customer churn rate in the process. The maximum profit expected value of the bank can be calculated. If the bank's profit is at the maximum value, whether the bank will grant loans to each enterprise is calculated. If the loan is decided, the loan strategy for the enterprise is obtained.

2   Logistic Regression Algorithm

2.1   Mapping

Logistic regression algorithm is a kind of generalized linear regression, which is used to deal with the regression problem in which the dependent variable is classified variable. It is generally used to solve the binary classification problem and to judge the probability of classification of sample events [5].

If the index input value is mapped to the [0, 1] interval, a predicted value can be obtained in linear regression, and the predicted value can be further mapped into the

sigmoid function. Sigmoid function, namely logistic function, can map real numbers into [0, 1] interval as activation function, which is a kind of S-type saturation function.
The formula of sigmoid function is as follows:

$$g(x) = \frac{1}{1 + e^{-z}} \tag{1}$$

According to the sigmoid function, the prediction function is obtained:

$$h_\theta(x) = g\left(\theta^T x\right) \tag{2}$$

Among them,

$$\theta_0 + \theta_1 x_1 + \cdots + \theta_n x_n = \sum_{i=1}^{n} \theta_i x_i = \theta^T x \tag{3}$$

2.2   Transformed into a Logarithmic Likelihood Function

Whether an enterprise defaults is a two category task, the equation is obtained:

$$P(y = 1|x; \theta) = h_\theta(x) \tag{4}$$

$$P(y = 0|x; \theta) = 1 - h_\theta(x) \tag{5}$$

The function is integrated into likelihood function:

$$P(y|x; \theta) = (h_\theta(x))^y (1 - h_\theta(x))^{1-y} \tag{6}$$

The likelihood function $L(\theta)$ is obtained by multiplying all the sample functions, and the likelihood function is converted into a logarithmic likelihood function:

$$l(\theta) = \log L(\theta) = \sum_{i=1}^{m} (y_i \log h_\theta(x_i) + (1 - y_i) \log(1 - h_\theta(x_i))) \tag{7}$$

2.3   Optimization Problem Solving

It is required to obtain the solution of default rate model. According to the above formula, the logarithmic likelihood function obtained is an ascending function, and a variable is introduced to make it a descending function. In other words, the smaller the function value is, the better the solution of the model is, the better the model is, that is, it can better predict the situation of enterprise default.

The following formula can be obtained by calculating the partial derivative of the function:

$$\frac{\delta}{\delta \theta_j} J(\theta) = \frac{1}{m} \sum_{i=1}^{m} (h_\theta(x) - y_i) x_i^j \tag{8}$$

The parameter update function is obtained and a multi class softmax is obtained

$$\left(x^{(i)}\right) = \frac{1}{\sum_{j=1}^{k} e^{\theta_j^T x^{(i)}}} A(k) \tag{9}$$

Among them,

$$A^T(k) = \left(e^{\theta_1^T x^{(i)}}, e^{\theta_2^T x^{(i)}}, \dots, e^{\theta_k^T x^{(i)}}\right) \tag{10}$$

3   The Processing Method of This Paper

See Fig. 1.

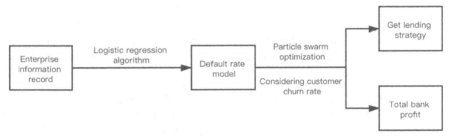

Fig. 1. Architecture of the proposed algorithm

3.1   Selection of Evaluation Indexes

After knowing the purchase and sales invoice data, credit rating, upstream and downstream company status and contract situation of each enterprise in recent years, the credit of small and medium-sized enterprises is graded. The credit status is reflected by the enterprise tax situation, annual sales return rate and repayment records, which has certain reliability and comprehensiveness. First of all, we clean the data to exclude the impact of void invoice data on the results; secondly, we analyze the credit rating of enterprises with existing credit records, loan default and recent sales invoice records. Based on the principles of systematization, typicality, comprehensiveness, conciseness and scientificalness, we summarize the gross profit rate and the experience. The five important indicators are business stability, customer stability, customer concentration and standard deviation of capital flow time distribution, and the given credit rating is transformed into credit score, which makes full use of the known data from the perspectives of enterprise profitability, risk response ability, customer cooperation stability, dependence on core customers and time distribution. The operation status of enterprises is quantified [1].

3.2 Quantitative Calculation of Evaluation Indexes

Gross Profit Margin. Gross profit rate is an index reflecting the profitability of an enterprise, which can directly reflect the strength of the enterprise's service profitability. The calculation formula is as follows:

$$X_g = \frac{p}{g} \times 100\% \tag{11}$$

Among them, p refers to the gross profit obtained by the enterprise, i.e. the difference between sales revenue and sales cost, and g refers to the enterprise's operating income, that is, the sum of main business income and other operating income.

Business Stability. The stability of business situation measures the stability of the business situation in the face of risks, which can be quantified by the sum of the number of upstream and downstream purchasing channels and sales channels. The calculation formula is as follows:

$$S = N_s + N_r \tag{12}$$

Among them, N_s is the number of purchasers that the enterprise has cooperated with in a period of time, and N_r is the number of retailers that the enterprise has cooperated with in a period of time.

Customer Stability. Customer stability reflects the stability of cooperative relationship by measuring the number of repeated cooperative customers, and further reflects the reputation of enterprises. The more repeated cooperation between customers, the more stable the cooperative relationship is and the higher the stability of customers. The calculation formula is as follows:

$$S_c = \frac{N_{rp}}{N} \tag{13}$$

Among them, N_{rp} is the number of repeated cooperative customers of the enterprise in that year, and N is the number of cooperative customers of the enterprise in that year.

Customer Concentration. Customer concentration reflects the number of core customers and the degree of dependence of multi-core customers. The calculation formula is as follows:

$$R_c = \frac{I_t}{I} \tag{14}$$

Among them, I_t refers to the total purchase amount of the top five customers and I represents the total purchase amount of the current year.

Standard Deviation of Time Distribution of Capital Flow. The standard deviation of time distribution of capital flow reflects the stability of transaction in time dimension. The calculation method is as follows: calculate the average number of economic activities in each month except the economic activities corresponding to the invalid invoice, and further calculate the standard deviation of the number of economic activities in each month.

3.3   Construction of Evaluation Index System

The decision of banks to make loans to enterprises and determine the lending strategy is complex, involving many business data and various considerations, and the relationship between each evaluation index is organic. Therefore, the enterprise reputation evaluation system as shown in the figure below is established to comprehensively and thoroughly evaluate the enterprise reputation and loan repayment ability from two aspects of enterprise strength and enterprise stability, as well as from different angles including enterprise profitability and risk response ability, and combined with the consideration of enterprise reputation rating, so as to facilitate the quantification and comprehensive utilization of evaluation indicators (Fig. 2).

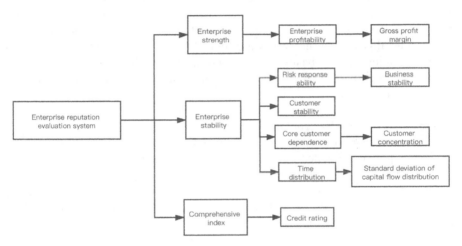

Fig. 2.   Credit evaluation system

3.4   Establishment of Evaluation Model Based on Logistic Regression Algorithm

From the reasons of the current loan pricing characteristics, we can see that the credit risk index evaluation affects the loan pricing. Therefore, after defining and calculating the above indicators, through the introduction of logistic regression algorithm, a calculation model of default rate in accordance with the sample situation is established, and the default rate data that fits well with the existing data is calculated, which is used as the credit risk evaluation index to determine the loan pricing and loan interest rate.

Using logistic regression model, this paper establishes the default rate model. The default rate refers to the possibility that the borrower can not repay the principal and interest of the loan or perform the relevant obligations according to the contract requirements in a certain period of time in the future. This index has a certain timeliness and reflects the possibility of customer default in the coming year.

3.5 Particle Swarm Optimization Algorithm for Optimal Numerical Solution

Introducing Particle Swarm Optimization Algorithm
Combined with the default rate P_w obtained before, we can get the expectation of bank profit:

$$E = \sum_1^i \{(1 - p_l)[(1 - p_w)x_i e_i - p_w e_i]\} \tag{15}$$

Where, E is the profit expectation and e_i is the corresponding loan.

It can be seen that this is an optimization problem of high-dimensional equation, and there is no accurate solution for this kind of problem at present, but the optimal numerical solution can be approximately found by using particle swarm optimization algorithm to further obtain the maximum profit of the bank. Particle swarm optimization (PSO) is a population intelligent algorithm, which is designed by simulating the behavior strategy of birds' predation, and can be used to solve optimization problems such as solving the maximum value of function, solving equations, fitting multivariate functions and fitting differential equations [6].

Mechanism of Particle Swarm Optimization
Particle Initialization. In particle swarm optimization algorithm, the solution of each optimization problem is called a "particle", all particles move in a solution space, and each particle has only two attributes: velocity and position. The velocity and position of each particle are initialized, and the fitness value of each particle is determined by fitness function, and then the bank profit here is calculated [8]. The formula of particle position velocity is as follows:

$$x_i = (x_{i1}, x_{i2}, \ldots, x_{id}) \tag{16}$$

$$v_i = (v_{i1}, v_{i2}, \ldots, v_{id}) \tag{17}$$

Seeking the Best Fitness Value of Individual. For each particle i, the fitness value of its current position is compared with that of the historical best position *pbest*, that is, the expected optimal value of bank profit of each particle. If the fitness value of current position is higher, the fitness value of current position is used to update the fitness value of historical optimal position, that is, higher bank profit value.

Seeking the Best Fitness of Population. For each particle i, the fitness value of its current position is compared with that of the global optimal position *gbest*. If the fitness value of the current position is higher, the fitness value of the global optimal position is updated with the fitness value of the current position, that is, it finds the highest expected value of bank profit among all particles.

Update Values. Update the velocity and position of each particle according to the formula. The specific formula is as follows:

The D-dimensional position updating formula of particles i is as follows:

$$x_{id}^k = x_{id}^{k-1} + v_{id}^{k-1} \tag{18}$$

The D-dimensional velocity updating formula of particles i is as follows:

$$v_{id}^k = w v_{id}^{k-1} + c_1 r_1 \left(pbest_{id} - x_{id}^{k-1} \right) + c_2 r_2 \left(qbest_d - x_{id}^{k-1} \right) \tag{19}$$

Where, x_{id}^k represents the d-dimensional vector of the position vector of the particle i in the kth iteration, v_{id}^k represents the d-dimensional vector of the velocity vector of the particle i in the kth iteration, c_1, c_2 represents the acceleration constant, and is used to adjust the maximum learning step size; r_1, r_2 is two random parameters in the range of [0, 1] to increase the random search. w represents the inertia factor, generally taken as 0.4–0.9.

Judge Whether the Algorithm is Finished and Output the Result. If the end condition is satisfied, the algorithm ends and the optimal solution is output; if the end condition is not satisfied, the algorithm returns to step 2, and the particle continues to search for the expected optimal value of bank profit.

Using the particle swarm optimization algorithm to decide the loan decision, the particle swarm optimization algorithm can find the optimal solution at a faster speed, and can well solve the problem of bank credit strategy function optimal solution. When searching for the optimal solution of credit policy, particle swarm optimization can adjust its current state by making full use of its own experience and group experience, and can make full and effective use of the information recorded by big data enterprises, so as to obtain relatively optimal results.

4   Experimental Results

The data set from 2020 National Undergraduate Mathematical Modeling Contest and 123 open data sets of credit record enterprises are divided into training group and test group. The ratio of sample size is 4:1, the loan line is set of 100000 yuan to 1 million yuan, the annual interest rate is 4%–15%, and the loan period is 1 year. The default rate model was established by using logistic regression, the estimated cut-off value was 0.50, and the step-in rate was set as 0.05; in particle swarm optimization algorithm, the initial population size was set as sizepop = 200, and the spatial dimension dim = 30, The maximum number of iterations is ger = 500, inertia weight c1 = 0.8, self-learning factor c2 = 0.5, group learning factor c3 = 0.5.

4.1   Establishing Default Rate Model by Logistic Regression

According to logistic regression algorithm, the default rate calculation model is established. The training group data is used to build and estimate the model, and the test group data is used to test the fitting of the model to the actual results. The ratio of sample size between training group and test group was controlled at about 4:1.

Compared with the real value, the correct rate of default prediction results obtained by test group data is 98.1%, as shown in Table 1. The results of the five important indicators were analyzed by SPSS software and the real situation. The analysis results are shown in Table 2.

Table 1. Forecast results of enterprise default.

	Forecast	Default = yes		Correct percentage
Actual measurement		0.00	1.00	
Default = yes	0.00	83	0	100
	1.00	2	18	90
Overall percentage				98.1

Table 2. Significance analysis.

	B	Standard error	Wald	Free degree	Significance	Exp (B)
Customer concentration	−.108	.378	.082	1	.775	.897
Net interest rate	2.343	3.171	.546	1	.460	10.413
Credit rating	−45.71	1575.779	.001	1	.977	.000
Customer stability	−2.100	3.467	.367	1	.545	.122
Standard deviation	−.011	.031	.125	1	.724	.989
Constant	88.031	3151.502	.001	1	.978	1.704E + 38

The default rate model is obtained:

$$P_W = \frac{1}{1 + e^{-z}} \tag{20}$$

$$z = 88.031 + 2.343x_g - 0.011s - 2.1s_C - 0.108R_C - 45.710x_5 \tag{21}$$

Among them, x_g represents gross profit margin, S represents standard deviation of monthly distribution of capital flow time, s_c represents customer stability, R_c represents customer concentration, and x_5 represents credit rating.

It can be seen that the model and the actual results fit well, the accuracy is high, and there is no significant difference between the model and the actual situation.

4.2   Particle Swarm Optimization

Combined with the default rate P_w obtained before, we can get the expectation of bank profit:

$$E = \sum_{1}^{i}\left\{(1 - p_l)\left[(1 - p_w)x_ie_i - p_we_i\right]\right\} \tag{22}$$

Where, E is the profit expectation and e_i is the corresponding loan, the constraints of the formula are as follows:

$$\begin{cases} 1 \leq e_i \leq 100 \\ 0.04 \leq x_i \leq 0.15 \\ \sum_{1}^{i} e_i \leq K \end{cases} \tag{23}$$

Through SPSS, the function of A, B, C rating churn rate on interest rate is obtained by linear regression between additional customer churn rate and interest rate.

$$P_l(A) = 7.524x - 0.098 \tag{24}$$

$$P_1(B) = 7.351x - 0.118 \tag{25}$$

$$P_1(C) = 7.468x - 0.138 \tag{26}$$

Where x is the interest rate;

The convergence curve obtained by the particle swarm optimization algorithm is shown in the Fig. 3:

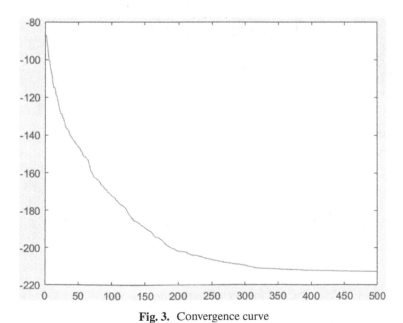

Fig. 3. Convergence curve

By using particle swarm optimization algorithm, we simulate the loan allocation strategies of banks under different fixed amounts, and the maximum profits are about 1.646 million yuan and 1.694.92 million yuan respectively, and the loan strategies of banks to each company are obtained. The specific credit strategies are shown in Fig. 4, Fig. 5 and Fig. 6, and the results are quite good.

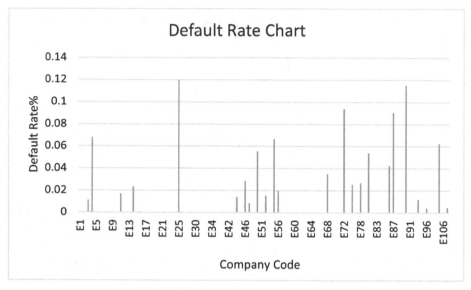

Fig. 4. Default rate forecast chart

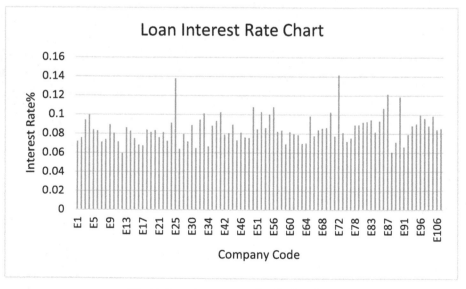

Fig. 5. Loan interest rate distribution chart

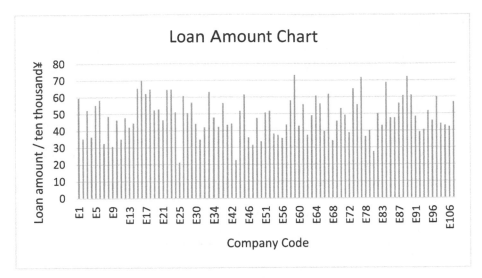

Fig. 6. Loan amount forecast chart

5 Conclusion

Based on logistic regression algorithm and particle swarm optimization, this paper establishes a mathematical model for the loan default rate of small, medium and micro enterprises, and explores the problem of bank lending strategy under the environment of big data, which has a certain range of generalization when dealing with big data. Through processing the open data set, the evaluation system is established by using six important indicators, including gross profit rate, business stability, customer concentration, customer stability, standard deviation of capital flow time distribution, and credit rating. The data characteristics are summarized and quantified from different angles. The logistic regression algorithm is used to analyze the sales invoice data of enterprises with credit records The default rate calculation model is established, which is in line with the characteristics of small and medium-sized enterprises lacking data and financial indicators not meeting the normal distribution. The data are divided into training set and test set. The model is used for prediction and cross validation. The prediction result of average default situation is calculated, and the accuracy rate reaches 98.1%. Then, using the predicted default rate combined with the statistical data of the relationship between the annual interest rate of bank loans and the customer churn rate in the data set, the particle swarm optimization algorithm is used for multiple optimization calculation, which can find the optimal solution at a faster speed and complete the full and effective use of the data, so as to obtain the optimal value of the bank's profit expectation, and then determine the bank's lending to small and medium-sized enterprises Strategy, got good results.

References

1. Weng, K.: Research on credit risk and pricing strategy of SMEs. Fuzhou University 2017)
2. Stiglitz, J., Weiss, A.: Credit rationing in markets with imperfect information. Am. Econ. Rev. **71**(3), 393–410 (1981)
3. Bester, H.: Screening vs. Rationing in credit markets with imperfect information. Am. Econ. Rev. **75**(4), 850–855 (2004)
4. Jin, W., Wang, H.C., Dong, X.H.: On banks' credit decision mechanism (1) - the case of credit market with imperfect competition. J. Syst. Eng. **11**(2), 52–58 (1996)
5. Dong, X.: Research on logistic regression algorithm and its GPU parallel implementation. Harbin Institute of technology (2016)
6. Rui, G.: Improved particle swarm optimization and its application in discrete problems. Jilin University (2005)
7. Fu, W., Li, Y.: Credit risk evaluation of listed companies based on logistic. East China Econ. Manag. **9**, 95–98 (2005)
8. CSDN. https://blog.csdn.net/xiaofalu/article/details/100576488

A Novel Artificial Immune Model on Hadoop for Anomaly Detection

Xinlei Hu$^{(\boxtimes)}$, Zhengxia Wang, and Yunbing Hu

Chongqing College of Electronic Engineering, Chongqing 401331, China

Abstract. The artificial immune system is an important algorithm for anomaly detection problems. But two major problems of the AIS algorithm are low efficiency of detector generation and excessive number of detectors. In this paper, we propose an improved AIS on Hadoop called AIMAD, which is with antibody suppression. In AIMAD, candidate detectors are generated randomly parallelly in Mapper Jobs, candidate detectors must go through self tolerance. Detectors not only match with self-cell for self tolerance, but also recognize other detectors. In Reducer phase, when a detector is recognized by other detectors, this detector is suppressed. Eliminating those suppressed detectors will significantly reduce detector redundancy in the non-self space. After Reducer phase, candidates detectors will be evolved into mature detectors. The dynamic evolution of the mature detector makes these detectors detect unknown network abnormal behavior or variants of known network abnormal behavior. The theory analysis shows that AIMAD effectively reduces the number of detectors and improves the efficiency of detector generation. Experimental results show that proposed algorithm outperforms other classic algorithms such as RNSA and V-detector. Under three UCI standard datasets, the proposed algorithm can get the highest detection rate, the lowest false alarm rate and the highest time efficiency.

Keywords: Artificial immune · Antibody suppression · Hadoop · Anomaly detection

1 Introduction

The biological immune system has the characteristics of tolerance, self-learning, distribution, robustness and adaptability, immune feedback, and self-organization. It can identify and eliminate pathogens (including viruses, bacteria, parasites, etc.) that invade biological organisms. Thereby protecting the health of biological organisms [1]. Anomaly detection and the problems faced by the biological immune system are surprisingly similar, both of which need to maintain the stability and availability of the system in a dynamically changing environment, and exclude invading foreign objects [2, 3]. Inspired by the characteristics of the biological immune system, many researchers at home and abroad have proposed a series of immune-based network anomaly detection models.

© Springer Nature Singapore Pte Ltd. 2021
Y. Tian et al. (Eds.): ICBDS 2020, CCIS 1415, pp. 377–390, 2021.
https://doi.org/10.1007/978-981-16-3150-4_32

The most representative immune anomaly detection model is the ARTIS [4] model proposed by Forrest et al. It has the characteristics of self-learning, distributed, diversity and adaptability. The main design ideas of various immune-based anomaly detection models and algorithms [5] that were subsequently proposed are derived from ARTIS [4], such as LYSIS proposed by Hofmeyr et al. [6], MAIDS proposed by Dasgupta et al. [7], CDIS proposed by Harmer et al. [8], DynamiCS proposed by Kim et al. [9, 10].

Various detection models based on ARTIS model have the problem of low generation efficiency of mature detectors. Because the ARTIS model uses the classic negative selection algorithm proposed by Forrest to randomly generate candidate detectors, as the coverage of the non-self space by the detector increases, the probability of overlap between the detectors also increases. If the overlap coverage space is too large, a large number of detectors are needed to cover the non-self space, which leads to a large set of mature detectors. Gonzalez F found during the experiment that when the non-self space coverage of the detector reaches 95%, tens of thousands of mature detectors need to be generated, and it takes a huge amount of time. The generation efficiency of mature detectors is too low, which leads to this algorithm can not be widely used in practice [14, 15].

Hadoop is a distributed system infrastructure developed by the Apache Foundation. [16] It is a parallel architecture. The MapReduce distributed computing model in Hadoop decomposes the work tasks of the application into many small work task pieces, each task works in parallel, and finally all tasks will be merged to get the desired result. This parallel feature of Hadoop improves the speed of data processing effectively.

To improve the efficiency of detectors generation, we introduce a novel artificial immune model on Hadoop for anomaly detection (AIMAD). In each Map job, randomly generates the center point of the candidate detector. If the generated candidate detector does not recognize the self, the self tolerance is passed. At this time, the detector radius is dynamically determined by the distance between the candidate detector and the nearest neighbor. Since each Map job runs in parallel, it reduces the generation time of candidate detectors and improves the generation efficiency. The Reducer function is used to eliminate the redundant candidate detectors. These candidate detectors not only recognize self/non-self cell, but also recognize other detectors. When a candidate detector is recognized by other detectors, this detector is suppressed. Eliminating suppressed candidate detectors not only reduces redundant detectors in the non-self space, and improves the time efficiency and efficiency of detectors generation, but also reduces the number of candidate detectors.

2   A Novel Artificial Immune Model on Hadoop for Anomaly Detection

In order to solve these problems, we propose a novel artificial immune model on Hadoop for anomaly detection. The details of AIMAD are presented in this section.

2.1   The Candidate Detector Generation Phase

The detector generation phase can be divided into two parts. The first part, generates candidate detector randomly. The second part eliminates the redundant candidate detectors through mutual suppression.

To improve the efficiency of detectors generation, we implement our detection model on Hadoop platform. We use Mapper function to implement the first part. In each Map job, randomly generates the center point of the candidate detector. If the generated candidate detector does not recognize the self, the self tolerance is passed. At this time, the detector radius is dynamically determined by the distance between the candidate detector and the nearest neighbor. Since each Map job runs in parallel, it means that multiple candidate detectors are generated in parallel at the same time and go through self-tolerance, which reduces the generation time of candidate detectors and improves the generation efficiency.

In the second part, the Reducer function is used to eliminate the redundant candidate detectors. These candidate detectors not only recognize self/non-self cell, but also recognize other detectors. When a candidate detector is recognized by other detectors, this detector is suppressed. The closer the candidate detectors are, the stronger the suppression is. Eliminating suppressed candidate detectors not only reduces redundant detectors in the non-self space, and improves the time efficiency and efficiency of detectors generation, but also reduces the number of candidate detectors.

Finally, the termination condition of AIMAD is met when the expected non-self coverage is reached. Figure 1 shows the MapReduce Process and Fig. 2 shows the flowchart of the candidate detector generation phase of AIMAD.

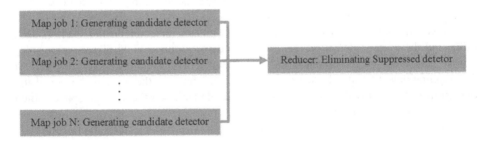

Fig. 1. The MapReduce Process

2.1.1   The Strategies of Antibody Suppression

In the detector generation stage, redundant detectors will not be able to expand the non-self space covered by the detector set. Because the candidate detectors are randomly generated, some detectors will recognize each other. And these mutual recognition detectors almost cover the same non-self space. If these overlap areas are too large, the overlap area is equivalent to one of them. These redundant detectors will not be able to expand the non-self space covered by the detector set.

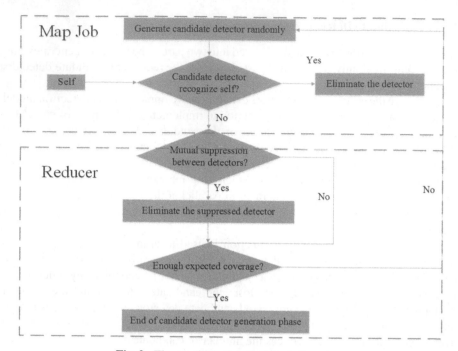

Fig. 2. The candidate detector generation phase

Therefore, in order to improve detection performance and detection efficiency, the generated detector set should be as small as possible, and the non-self space covered by the detector set should be as large as possible.

However, when the detection areas of each mature detector do not overlap each other and the average detection area of the detector group is maximized, many holes will be generated and performance will be reduced. Therefore, there should be a certain overlapping detection area between the detectors. However, the more the space of the detection area overlaps, the more detectors are needed to cover the non-self space, which will reduce the detection efficiency.

So in our algorithm, if there is a connection between the detectors, the holes can be reduced. The algorithm uses the suppression threshold to adjust the overlap range of the detector to improve the non-self space coverage of the detector.

In the process of mutual recognition of the detectors, the suppression threshold can determine whether the detector is suppressed by other detectors. If this detector is suppressed by other detectors, the detector can be eliminated to reduce the redundancy of the detector group and expand the non-self space covered by the detector group. Therefore, even if the detectors recognize each other, the non-self space covered by the detectors is not exactly the same.

However, the value of the suppression threshold must be reasonable. If it is too small, the detectors will not be able to cover enough non-self space, which will affect the detection rate of the system. On the contrary, the detectors still contains redundancy, which will also affect the detection rate of the system.

A reasonable suppression threshold among detectors can take fewer detector set to cover larger non-self space. In this paper, we determine the suppression threshold based on different data sets through a lot of simulation experiments in the Sect. 3.

The pseudo-code of Detector-Suppress is shown in Fig. 3.

Detector-Suppress(d, D)

d: the new candidate detector md_j: mature detector   D: mature detector set   r: radius of d

rd_j: radius of md_j N: the size of mature detector set

step 1: Sort the detectors in mature detector set from largest to smallest by size of radius.

step 2: Calculate the Euclidean distance $dis\left(d,md_j\right)$ in turn between d and md_j, where $1<j<N$. If

$r>rd_j$, and $dis\left(d,md_j\right)<\theta$, then d suppress md_j, replace md_j with d, sort d in D according r, goto step 4, otherwise, goto step 5.

step 3: To any detector md_j in D, $dis\left(d,md_j\right)>r+rd_j$, put d into D.

step 4: For each detector in D, calculate the Euclidean distance $dis\left(md_j,md_k\right)$, where $1<j<N$, $j<k<N$.

If $dis\left(md_j,md_k\right)<\theta$, then md_j suppress md_k, eliminate detector md_k.

step 5: stop the suppression process.

Fig. 3. The pseudo-code of Detector-Suppress

In the Detector-Suppress algorithm, a detector with a larger radius can cover more non-self space, that is, it has a greater probability of suppressing other detectors. In step 1, in order to reduce the execution time of the algorithm, we sort the candidate detectors according to the radius in advance.

Step 2 Calculates the distance between candidate detector md_i and d. In order to ensure that a smaller set of detectors covers a larger non-self space, the detector with a large radius suppresses the detector with a small radius. θ is the suppression threshold. The smaller the value of threshold θ, the stronger the suppression between detectors. When radius of d is much larger than detector md_j and satisfies (1), d suppress md_j, eliminate md_j and put d into the mature detector set.

$$dis(d, md_j) < \theta \tag{1}$$

Step 3 adds candidate detectors that are not recognized by any existing detectors to the detector set.

When a new candidate detector d is added to the detector set, the degree of suppression among the detectors in the detector set will change. Step 4 calculates the degree of suppression between the detector set, and remove the suppressed detectors.

2.2 Mature Detector Dynamical Evolution

All candidate detectors will be evolved into mature detectors. The dynamic evolution stage of the maturity detector simulates the memory process of immune cells in the biological immune system. The detector not only recognizes the antigen but also other detectors, and produces stimulation and suppression during the recognition process. The detector obtains the right to clone proliferation through competition. The stronger the stimulus, the higher the probability of clone proliferation, and the higher the efficiency of detecting abnormal behaviors in the known network. At the same time, the inhibitory effect maintains the diversity of the population and effectively controls the stability of the model. The mutated mature detector is used to detect unknown network abnormal behavior or variants of known network abnormal behavior.

$$T(t) = \begin{cases} \emptyset, & t = 0 \\ T(t-1) \cup T_{new}(t) \cup T_{clone}(t) - T_{suppression}(t) - T_{dead}(t), & t \geq 1 \end{cases} \tag{2}$$

$$T_{new}(t) = \{d \mid d \in I(t), \ d.age = 0, \ d.level = 0\} \tag{3}$$

$$T_{clone}(t) = \bigcup_{x \in T_{select}(t)} \bigcup_{i=1}^{\lceil (1-C(d_i)) \bullet d_i.level \rceil} \{d_i'\}, d_i'.age = 0 \tag{5.11}$$

$$T_{select}(t) = \{d \mid d \in T(t-1), \ P(d.\,level) > \eta, d.age = 0\} \tag{4}$$

$$T_{suppression}(t) = \{d \mid d \in T_{clone}(t) \wedge \exists td \in T(t-1), \ f_{suppression}(d, td) = 0\} \tag{5}$$

$$T_{dead}(t) = \{d \mid d \in T(t) \wedge d.age > \lambda\} \tag{6}$$

Among them, $T(t)$ and $T(t-1)$ represent the set of mature detectors at time t and $t-1$ respectively; $T_{new}(t)$ represent the newly generated mature detector at time t; $T_{dead}(t)$ represent the mature detector that died due to the life cycle exceeding the threshold at time t; $T_{select}(t)$ represent the set of mature detectors at time t win the competition and prepare to clone and multiply the mature detector. $P(d.level)$ is the probability of the detector winning, η is the expected probability. $T_{clone}(t)$ represents the mature detector in the pair at time t that clones proliferation and undergoes high-frequency mutation. $T_{suppression}(t)$ Represents the suppressed mature detector that s eliminated by the detector suppression mechanism.

2.3 The Detection Phase

Test data and mature detectors are used to detect normality or abnormality in the detection phase of AIMAD. If the Euclidean distance between a test data t and any mature detector d is less than radius of mature detector d, that is $dis(d, t) < r_d$, it means mature detector d recognizes test data t and we classify t as abnormal. Otherwise we classify t as normal.

Figure 4 shows the flowchart of the detection phase of AIMAD.

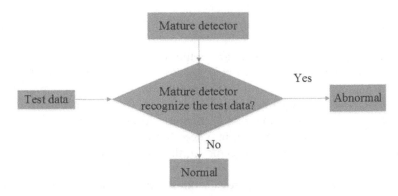

Fig. 4. The detection phase of AIMAD

3 Experiment

This section verifies the detection performance and effective of the AIMAD algorithm through experiments. The experimental data adopts UCI classic data set [11]: including Iris, Breast Cancer Wisconsin (BCW) and Abalone. The above data set has been widely used in the research of detector performance testing and detector generation efficiency analysis [12, 13].

In the experiment, the detection rate DR (detection rate) and false alarm rate FAR (false alarm rate) are the key criteria for evaluating the performance of the detector. The definitions of DR and FAR are as follows:

$$DR = \frac{TP}{TP + FN} \tag{7}$$

$$FAR = \frac{FP}{FP + TN} \tag{8}$$

Among them, TP represents the number of non-self correctly identified by the detector, FN represents the number of self-identified as non-self incorrectly by the detector, FP represents the number of self-identified by the detector incorrectly as non-self, and TN represents the number of self-identified correctly by the detector.

In experiments, MATLAB application is utilized to acquire results and perform analysis, the estimated coverage P_{exp} is 90%–99%, the self radius r_s is 0.1.

The suppression threshold θ is a key parameter that controls the degree of suppression of the detector. It has a great influence on the efficiency of detector generation, the number of detectors and the detection rate. In order to ensure the feasibility of the AIMAD algorithm, this section determines the value of the suppression threshold through experimental analysis.

Taking the BCW data set as an example, the relationship between the suppression threshold θ and the number of detectors is shown in Fig. 8. It can be seen from Fig. 5 that the number of detectors increases with the value of threshold θ. The probability of overlapping coverage between detectors also increases with the increase of the value of threshold θ. However, detectors with overlapping coverage cannot increase the non-self space covered by the detector set. In order to fully cover the non-self space while ensuring the minimum size of the detector set, the redundant detectors in the detector set must be reduced.

The relationship between the suppression threshold θ and the detection rate is shown in Fig. 6 . It can be seen from Fig. 6 that the smaller the value of threshold θ, the lower the detection rate. When the suppression threshold reaches a certain value, the increase in the detection rate slows down. As the suppression threshold increases, the degree of suppression between detectors gradually weakens, and the proportion of newly added detectors that overlap and cover non-self space increases, so the detection rate cannot be effectively improved.

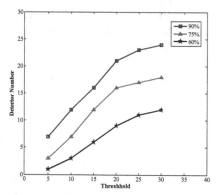

Fig. 5. The relationship between θ and number of detectors.

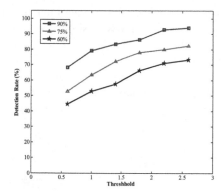

Fig. 6. The relationship between θ and detection rate.

From the perspective of detector generation efficiency, the smaller the value of the suppression threshold, the smaller the size of the detector set; from the analysis of the detection performance of the detector, the larger the value of the suppression threshold θ, the higher the detection rate. But when the suppression threshold reaches a certain value, the increase in the detection rate slows down. Therefore, the appropriate value of the suppression threshold is 1.75 through experiments.

Similarly, based on dataset Iris and Abalone, the parameter θ is 0.6 and 1.5 respectively.

The experimental parameters are shown in Table 1.

Table 1. Experimental parameters.

Parameter	Value
Expected coverage	90%–99%
Self radius	0.1
Suppression threshold	BCW:1.75 Iris:0.6 Abalone:1.5

There are three groups of experiments, first group uses AIMAD algorithm, second group uses RNSA algorithm [11], third group uses V-detector algorithm [12]. Each group experiment is repeated 20 times, it has the same experimental parameters and steps. The experimental steps are shown in Fig. 7. We program these three algorithms with MATLAB programming language and run them in the MATLAB application.

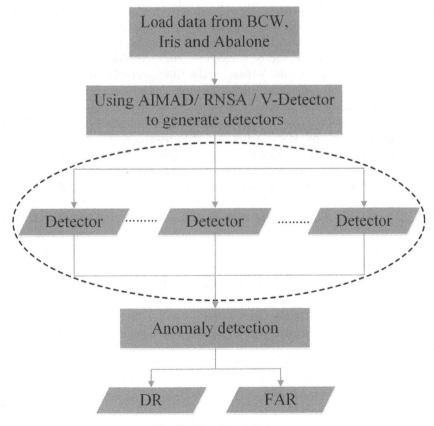

Fig. 7. Experimental steps.

In step 1, load data from every different datasets. All the data in three datasets are normalized into real-valued space [0, 1] during preprocess. The data attributes are shown in Table 2. BCW includes 683 records, 330 self data and 110 non-self data used for training, 114 self data and 129 non-self data used for testing. Iris includes 150 records, 25 self data and 60 non-self data used for training, 25 self data and 40 non-self data used for testing. Abalone includes 4177 records, 900 self data and 1150 non-self data used for training, 628 self data and 1499 non-self data used for testing.

Table 2. Data attributes

Data set	Records number	Dimension	Data type	Self number	Non-self number
BCW	683	9	Integer	Benign: 444	Malicious: 239
Iris	150	4	Real	Setosa: 50	Other: 100
Abalone	4177	8	Real, integer	Male: 1528	Other: 2649

In step 2, we respectively run AIMAD, RNSA and V-detector algorithm to generate detector set. In the RNSA proposed in [12], termination condition is the predefined detector quality. To compare the performance of algorithms under the same condition, in our experiment, RNSA is modified: the detector generation process will be terminated when the expected non-self coverage is reached. Then we code and run the modified RNSA. Also, we code and run the V-detector algorithm according to theory in [13]. In this step, we acquire the number of detectors and the time efficiency.

In step 3, in order to acquire detection rate and false alarm rate, we use the detector set to recognize test data loaded in step 1 as normality or abnormality. The detector set is generated respectively by AIMAD, RNSA and V-detector.

In order to verify the performance of detectors generated by AIMAD, we compare our work with other classic real-valued negative selection algorithms, which are RNSA and V-detector. The mean experimental results are shown in Figs. 8, 9, 10, 11, 12 and 13.

As shown in Figs. 8–9, under the expected coverage 99%, the DR of AIMAD on dataset BCW is 96.86%, which is higher than that of RNSA and V-detector by 21.07% and 1.20% respectively. The FAR of AIMAD is 5.68%, which is lower than that of RNSA and V-detector by 78.15% and 70.95% respectively.

As shown in Figs. 10–11, under the expected coverage 99%, the DR of AIMAD on dataset Iris is as the same as RNSA and V-detector. The FAR of AIMAD is 12.20%, which is lower than that of RNSA and V-detector by 72.47% and 53.88% respectively.

As shown in Figs. 12–13, under the expected coverage 99%, the DR of AIMAD on dataset Abalone is 85.99%, which is higher than that of RNSA and V-detector by 23.92% and 10.41% respectively. The FAR of AIMAD is 10.23%, which is lower than that of RNSA and V-detector by 56.52% and 37.16% respectively.

Thus, we compare AIMAD with RNSA and V-detector, AIMAD effectively reduces the false alarm rate while ensuring the detection rate.

In order to verify the efficiency of AIMAD, we compare our work with RNSA and V-detector. The mean experimental results are shown in Figs. 14, 15, 16, 17, 18 and 19.

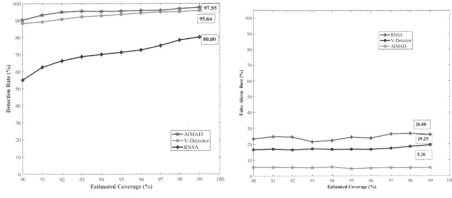

Fig. 8. DR of AIMAD, RNSA and V-detector on dataset BCW

Fig. 9. FAR of AIMAD, RNSA and V-detector on dataset BCW

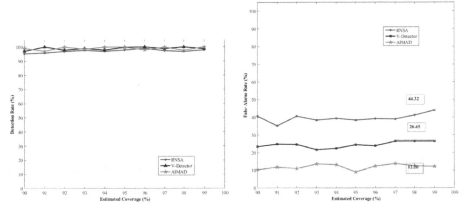

Fig. 10. DR of AIMAD, RNSA and V-detector on dataset Iris

Fig. 11. FAR of AIMAD, RNSA and V-detector on dataset Iris

As shown in Figs. 14, 15 and 16, under the expected coverage 99%, the number of detectors of AIMAD is lower than that of RNSA by 99.78%, 98.34% and 98.93% respectively. The number of detectors of AIMAD is lower than that of V-detector by 93.21%, 95.61% and 80.92% respectively.

As shown in Figs. 17, 18 and 19, under the expected coverage 99%, the time efficiency of AIMAD is higher than that of RNSA by 99.75%, 99.78% and 99.04% respectively. The time efficiency of AIMAD is higher than that of V-detector by 86.67%, 91.50% and 95.57% respectively.

Thus, under the same expected coverage, different dimensions and scales of training datasets, the efficiency of AIMAD improved significantly more than RNSA and V-detector. The efficiency of AIMAD algorithm will not be reduced significantly as the data dimension increasing.

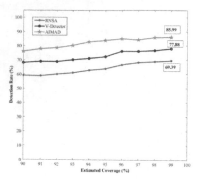

Fig. 12. DR of AIMAD, RNSA and V-detector on dataset Abalone

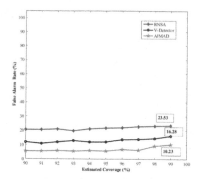

Fig. 13. FAR of AIMAD, RNSA and V-detector on dataset Abalone

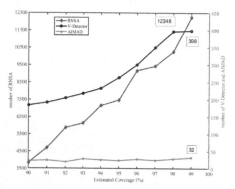

Fig. 14. The number of detectors of AIMAD, RNSA and V-detector on data set BCW.

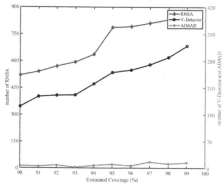

Fig. 15. The number of detectors of AIMAD RNSA and V-detector on data set Iris.

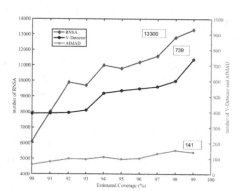

Fig. 16. The number of detectors of AIMAD RNSA and V-detector on data set Abalone RNSA and V-detector on data set Abalone

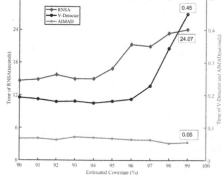

Fig. 17. The time efficiency of AIMAD, RNSA and V-detector on data set Iris

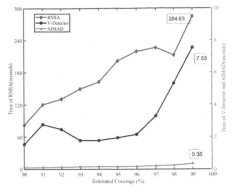

Fig. 18. The time efficiency of AIMAD RNSA and V-detector on data set BCW.

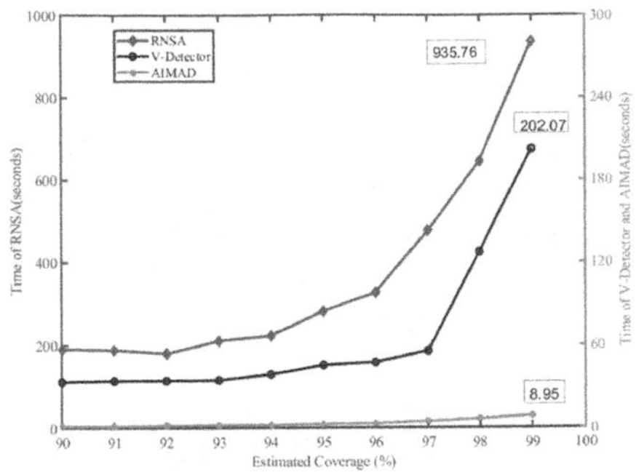

Fig. 19. The time efficiency of AIMAD, RNSA and V-detector on data set Abalone.

4 Summary

This paper first points out the problems of low generation efficiency and low detection performance of mature detectors that are common in existing anomaly detection models based on the immune group theory. In response to these problems, a network anomaly detection model based on antibody stimulation and inhibition is proposed. The mathematical definitions of antigens and detectors are given, and the dynamic evolution process of the model and the specific detector inhibition and detector competition mechanisms are described. Introducing an antibody suppression mechanism in the process of generating mature detectors and eliminating these similar candidate detectors can not only reduce redundant detectors in the non-self space, but also improve the generation efficiency of mature detectors; Mutual stimulation and inhibition make the detectors competitive, which can not only stimulate the clonal proliferation of the detector, eliminate invalid detectors, retain excellent detectors, promote the efficient response of the detector to non-self antigens, and effectively improve the detection rate of the model; It can restrict a certain type of excessive detectors, thereby controlling the stability of the model, and effectively reducing the false alarm rate of the model. Finally, the experimental comparison shows that compared with the typical immune-based anomaly detection model, the model proposed in this paper has higher generation efficiency and detection rate of mature detectors and lower false alarm rate.

Acknowledgements. This work was supported by the National Natural Science Foundation of Chongqing, China (No. cstc2020jcyj-msxmX1022).

This work was supported by the Science Foundation of Chongqing Municipal Commission of Education (No. KJQN202003108).

Conflict of Interests. The authors declare that there is no conflict of interests regarding the publication of this article.

References

1. Li, T.: An immune based dynamic intrusion detection model. Chin. Sci. Bull. **50**(22), 2650–2657 (2005)
2. Twycross, J., Aickelin, U.: Towards a conceptual framework for innate immunity. In: Jacob, C., Pilat, M.L., Bentley, P.J., Timmis, J.I. (eds.) ICARIS 2005. LNCS, vol. 3627, pp. 112–125. Springer, Heidelberg (2005). https://doi.org/10.1007/11536444_9
3. Dozier, G., Brown, D., Hou, H., et al.: Vulnerability analysis of immunity-based intrusion detection systems using genetic and evolutionary hackers. Appl. Soft Comput. **7**, 547–553 (2007)
4. Forrest, S., Dasgupta, D.: Artificial Immune System in Industrial Applications A. In: Proceedings of the IPMM (1999)
5. Richard, E.O.: Computational immunology and anomaly detection. Inf. Secur. Tech. Reprot **12**, 188–191 (2007)
6. Hofmeyr, S.A., Forrest, S.: Architecture for an artificial immune system. Evol. Comput. **7**(1), 45–68 (2000)
7. Dasgupta, D.: Immunity-based intrusion detection system: a general framework. In: The 22nd National Information Systems Security Conference, pp. 147–160 (1999)
8. Harmer, P.K., Williams, P.D., Gunsch, G.H., Lamont, G.B.: An artificial immune system architecture for computer security applications. IEEE Trans. Evol. Comput. **6**(3), 252–280 (2002)
9. Kim, J., Bentley, P.: Immune memory and gene library evolution in the dynamic clonal selection algorithm. Genet. Program Evolvable Mach. **5**(4), 361–391 (2004)
10. Kim, J., Bentley, P.J., Aickelin, U., et al.: Immune system approaches to intrusion detection–a review. Nat. Comput. **6**(4), 413–466 (2007)
11. Blake, C.L., Merz, C.J.: UCI repository of machine learning databases. The University of California, Irvine. http://archive.ics.uci.edu/ml/datasets
12. Gonzalez, F., Dasgupta, D.: Anomaly detection using real-valued negative selection. Genet. Program. Evolvable Mach. **4**, 383–403 (2003)
13. Zhou, J., Dasgupta, D.: V-detector: an efficient negative selection algorithm with "probably adequate" detector coverage. Inf. Sci. **19**(9), 1390–1406 (2009)
14. Stibor, T., Timmis, J., Eckert, C.: On the appropriateness of negative selection defined over Hamming shape-space as a network intrusion detection system. In: Proceedings of IEEE Evolutionary Computation, pp. 995–1002. IEEE Computer Society Press, Edinburgh (2005)
15. Li, T.: Computer Immunology (in Chinese), pp. 55–56. Publishing House of Electronics Industry, Beijing (2004)
16. Apache Hadoop project. http://hadoop.apache.org

Research on Accurate Location of Line Loss Anomaly in Substation Area Based on Data Driven

Zuobin Liang[1(✉)], Zhaojun Lu[2], Fei Yuan[1], Qing Wang[1], Guangfeng Zhao[2], Han Zhang[1], and Wei Zhang[1]

[1] State Grid Shandong Electric Power Company,
Tai'an Power Supply Company, Tai'an 271000, China
[2] Department of Development and Planning, State Grid Shandong Electric Power Company,
Jinan 250001, China

Abstract. We proposed a data mining-based method for precise positioning method of users associated with abnormal line loss. First, we based on the gap statistical algorithm (GSA) to determine the optimal number of clusters, using improved dichotomous K-means++ clustering to construct the line loss standard library and anomaly library. Secondly, we calculated the Spearman correlation coefficient (SCC) and Discrete Fréchet Distance (DFD) of the power consumption and line loss of each user during the abnormal time period. Based on the joint research of SCC and DFD, we constructed a new comprehensive evaluation index. By using TOPSIS algorithm, the descending order of the index value help us realize the precise positioning of all abnormal users. The example uses actual on-spot data in a certain area for verification and analysis, and the results show that the proposed method has better performance in clustering effectiveness, time consumption for calculation and identification accuracy.

Keywords: Data mining · Improved dichotomous K-means++ clustering · Spearman correlation coefficient · Discrete Fréchet distance · TOPSIS algorithm · Precise positioning

1 Introduction

With the implementation of the strategic decision of efficient development and utilization of national energy resources, energy conservation has gradually become an important means to alleviate the contradiction of energy supply. The electric power industry is one of the important fields in the energy conservation progress. As electric power is a firm support for economic and social development, reducing the loss of electric energy in

Project Supported by Science and Technology Project of State Grid Shandong Electric Power Company "Research on the key technology of intelligent judgment and precise positioning of abnormal line loss rate in the same period based on the fusion of multisource data and Internet of things" (5206091900C7).

transmission, distribution and sales is one of the important tasks of power supply industry [1]. Line loss is a comprehensive technical and economic index of power grid operation and management, which reflects the level of planning, design, production technology and operation management of a power grid [2]. Line loss analysis and management is the core work of power supply enterprises. In recent years, due to the reform of electricity market and the development of the energy Internet, the State Grid Corporation has stated explicitly that it will spare no effort to promote the high-quality development of the power Internet of Things [3], which involves data fusion, data mining, artificial intelligence and many other advanced technologies. According to the demand of line loss analysis, the collection, analysis and calculation of big data are realized from multi-system-mixed data such as power grid Supervisory Control And Data Acquisition (SCADA), power Production Management System (PMS) and user information acquisition system 3. The introduction of modern intelligent algorithm improves the accuracy of line loss calculation [5]. At present, problems such as abnormal line loss and power theft in the power supply area are still common, and most of the identification of abnormality mainly relies on manual work. Therefore, the work of abnormal line loss identification and precise positioning of associated users in the power supply area still needs to be improved currently.

At present, domestic and foreign researchers have done a lot on the abnormal line loss and precise positioning. Literature [6] proposed a comprehensive evaluation method of power information system based on curve similarity and correlation analysis, which realized intelligent identification and pre-warning analysis of power theft. Literature [7] proposed a variety of methods based on distance and spectral analysis to compare the similarity between line loss curve and user load curve. Literature [8] proposed the use of Pearson correlation coefficient algorithm to search for abnormal power meters, which avoided the blindness and uncertainty of qualitative analysis. However, on the one hand, most of the existing literatures only consider the application of data mining method to analyze the causes of user-side anomalies, and do not involve the mapping relationship between the line loss anomalies and the user load of the distribution network side. Therefore, there are still some limitations in practical engineering. On the other hand, with the continuous development of smart power grid, the monitoring terminal user load data is becoming more and more complex, which is gradually difficult for the traditional data analysis algorithm to meet the requirements of data processing, which requires further discussion and research.

To sum up, we proposes a precise positioning technology of associated users with abnormal line losses based on the combination of clustering algorithm and similarity measurement, aiming at the difficulty of precise positioning of associated users with abnormal line losses. Firstly, the optimal clustering number is determined based on GSA and we adopted the improved dichotomous K-means++ clustering algorithm to construct the standard and exception library of line loss of the power supply area. Secondly, we calculated the SCC and DFD of each user's power and line loss in the abnormal time period. Based on the joint study and judgment of SCC and DFD, we used TOPSIS algorithm to construct a new comprehensive evaluation index, and by selecting abnormal users in the descending order of the index value, the precise positioning of abnormal users is finally realized. The effectiveness of the proposed method is verified by an empirical analysis of user and line loss data of a certain power supply area.

2 The Architecture of Precise Positioning of Abnormal Line Loss Associated User

In the scenario described in this paper, we deeply researched the power supply area causing line loss anomalies and all users who belongs to it. Based on data mining theory and combined with various machine learning algorithms, we further realized intelligent identification and precise positioning of line loss anomalies. The scenario and architecture described in this paper are shown in Fig. 1, including partitioning exception library, joint judgment and intelligent identification. Combined with Fig. 1, the main flow of the precise positioning of the associated users with abnormal line loss based on data mining is as follows:

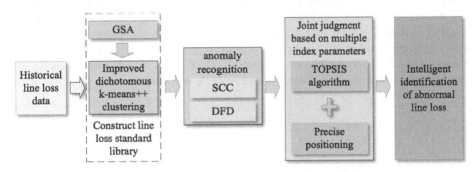

Fig. 1. Data mining-based precise positioning architecture for users associated with abnormal line loss

3 Line Loss Exception Library Generating Based on the Improved Dichotomous K-means++ Clustering

Due to the complex and irregular grid data sources [9], analyzing the internal correlation and similarity among data becomes the first task to solve the problem. In this paper, the clustering algorithm will be utilized to study the data characteristics of line losses in different periods. However, the initial clustering number of traditional clustering methods such as K-means, FCM and others is a super parameter, which needs to be determined artificially, which brings certain randomness. Moreover, the traditional clustering algorithm can only converge to the local optimal solution, which is vulnerable to the influence of noise data. In order to solve the algorithm defect caused by the initial centroid selection of traditional clustering algorithm, a method based on GSA algorithm was proposed to determine the optimal number of clustering, and an improved dichotomous K-means++ clustering method was utilized to generate line loss anomaly library of the power supply area.

3.1 Improved Dichotomous K-means++ Clustering a Subsection Sample

Dichotomous K-Means++ algorithm originates and evolves from traditional K-means algorithm. In order to optimize the method for selecting the initial centroid, Arthur, David, and Sergei Vassilvitskii [10] developed the K-Means++ initialization scheme in 2007, so that the initial centroid is far away from each other. As a result, a more reliable result than random initialization is generated. However, the influence of the initial centroid selection on the final clustering effect still cannot be well weakened. Based on this, we proposed a dichotomous K-means++ clustering method, and k-means++ was utilized multiple times to divide the data in the class into two parts. The minimum result of the sum of squares in the cluster was selected for the next clustering. Cycle continued and iterations repeated until the set clustering number was obtained.

3.2 Selection of Clustering Number Based on GSA Algorithm

GSA algorithm is a data mining algorithm to enhance clustering effect, which can estimate the optimal number of clustering data sets [11]. GSA algorithm is often used to identify bad data of power system, and effects remarkably in the scenario with low set value of cluster number. A set of data collections is set up as $V = \{x_1, x_2, \cdots, x_n\}$, which is divided into K clusters after clustering $(C_1, C_2, \cdots, C_n)$. For any class C_i, we calculate the sum of squares of the distance between all samples in the class and their centroid, and the formula is as follows:

$$S_i = \sum_{x_i \in C_i} (x_i - c_i)^2 \tag{1}$$

Where c_i is the centroid of the cluster C_i.
The clustering dispersion of K clusters is defined as:

$$W(K) = \sum_{i=1}^{K} S_i \tag{2}$$

The main idea of GSA algorithm is to calculate the natural logarithm of the corresponding clustering dispersion for the set number of clustering K each time, and then compare it with the threshold value to determine the optimal number of clustering. The data distribution after the natural logarithm process tends to be more linearized, making it more convenient to determine the gap value of the clustering dispersion and threshold $Gap(K)$. The gap value is defined as follows:

$$Gap(K) = E \ln[W_r(K)] - \ln[W(K)] \tag{3}$$

Where, r is the selected reference data set, and E is the mathematical expectation of the reference data set.

With the escalation of K value, K is considered as the best clustering number when a relatively large $Gap(K)$ value appears for the first time and the variation trend tends to be stable.

3.3 Generation of Line Loss Exception Library

In order to realize the automatic identification of line loss anomaly, it is necessary to first find the normal value range of the line loss, and then extract the standard pattern of line loss under different power supply area by clustering algorithm, which is finally took as the standard for line loss anomaly identification.

The generation diagram of the line loss exception library is shown in Fig. 2 below. First, an improved dichotomous K-means++ clustering algorithm based on GSA is adopted to select cluster A which contains the largest number of cases as the standard library of line loss, and the rest of the data is preliminarily divided into anomaly library B and C. Second, we determined the abnormal time period T corresponding to line losses in B and C. According to the experience of operation and maintenance staff and expert suggestions, generally speaking, T is required to meet continuity, which means it needs to be composed of several consecutive dates. Finally, we selected the line losses corresponding to continuous abnormal periods as the abnormal library, which can save the working intensity of operation and maintenance personnel and improve the economic efficiency of power grid.

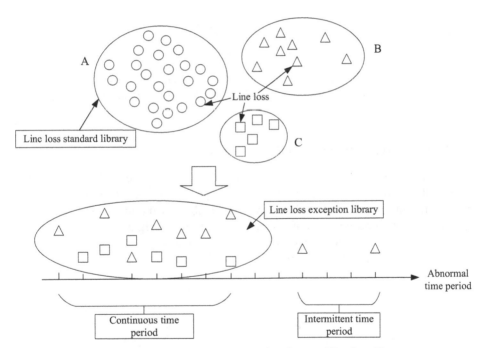

Fig. 2. Schematic diagram of generating abnormal line loss library

4   Joint Research and Judgment Based on Multi-indicator Parameters

4.1   Szpilman Correlation Coefficient (SCC)

SCC is a non-parametric index to measure the dependence of two variables, and the monotone equation is used to evaluate the correlation of two statistical variables [12]. On the one hand, this test does not require the premise that the sample follows a normal distribution, but only needs to determine the level of variables at each point to obtain. On the other hand, in this article, variables (line loss and the user power consumption) are in different dimensions. If we use covariance or Pearson correlation coefficient to calculate the similarity, we need to remove the dimension and then start the analysis. However, the SCC algorithm itself is a process of removing dimension. Therefore, it is more appropriate to calculate and analyze the relational degree of line loss and abnormal user power consumption with the SCC.

Confirm the level of each variable on the data sequence and calculate the level difference between the two groups of data. The specific formula of SCC is as follows:

$$r_{xy} = 1 - \frac{6 \sum_{i=1}^{N} d_i^2}{N(N^2 - 1)} \tag{4}$$

Where, N is the sample size, and d_i is the level difference of user power and line loss between data X and Y in abnormal time period T; greater the absolute value of r_{xy}, stronger the correlation is.

4.2   Discrete Fraser Distance (DFD)

FD was proposed by French mathematician Maurice Rene Frechet in 1906 as a way to describe the spatial similarity of path. This description also takes factors of path spatial distance into account, which has good applicability for the judgment of similarity between two curves on the two-dimensional plane. The most original and intuitive explanation of FD is the dog's leash distance. As it is shown in Fig. 3, the owner's path is A and the dog's path is B. FD describes the shortest rope length required for each of the two paths.

Suppose that two-tuples $(\mathbb{S}, d)$ is a metric space, where d is the metric function of $\mathbb{S}$. Suppose A and B are two continuous curves acting on the unit interval of $\mathbb{S}$, i.e., A: $[0,1] \rightarrow \mathbb{S}$, B: $[0,1] \rightarrow \mathbb{S}$, and suppose α and β are two re-parameterized functions of the unit interval, i.e., α: $[0, 1] \rightarrow \mathbb{S}$, β:$[0,1] \rightarrow \mathbb{S}$, then the FD expression of curve A and curve B is defined as:

$$F(A, B) = \inf_{\alpha, \beta} \max_{t \in [0,1]} \{d(A(\alpha(t)), B(\beta(t)))\} \tag{5}$$

Since the user's power consumption and line loss are equal time series and meet the discrete distribution, DFD is used to judge the similarity between the curve of each user's power consumption and line loss in the abnormal library. Suppose the power sequence

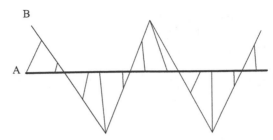

Fig. 3. Schematic diagram of intuitive understanding of FD

distribution of the user is $X(t) = \{x(1), x(2), \cdots, x(N)\}$, the line loss sequence distribution is $Y(t) = \{y(1), y(2), \cdots, y(N)\}$, and then the corresponding point pair sequence distribution is $\{(x(1), y(1)), (x(2), y(2)), \cdots, (x(m), y(m))\}$, so the DFD expression is:

$$F(A, B) = \lim_{m \to \infty, \max|t_{k+1}-t_k| \to 0} F_m(A, B)$$

$$= \lim_{m \to \infty, \max|t_{k+1}-t_k| \to 0} \inf_{\alpha, \beta} \max_{t \in [0,1]} \{d(A(\alpha(t)), B(\beta(t)))\} \tag{6}$$

Where, t_k is the kth time node. In the discrete case, the solution of DFD is not the true value, but the limit value that tends to infinity.

4.3 Construction of Joint Judgment Indexes

It can be seen from 3.1 and 3.2 that SCC and DFD describe the correlation between users and line losses from the perspectives of numerical and shape similarity respectively. However, these two indexes have their own advantages and disadvantages. Therefore, this paper considers constructing a new index set P, including the dimensions of these two indexes, and the specific representation is as follows:

$$P = \{F(SCC, DFD)\} \tag{7}$$

Where $F(SCC, DFD)$ is the function of SCC and DFD.

Since SCC ranges from -1 to 1, the greater the value, the higher the degree of similarity, and the greater the DFD, the lower the degree of similarity. Therefore, SCC and DFD changes oppositely, which is adverse to calculation. Therefore, homomorphism should be done, and the specific formula is as follows:

$$P_i = F_i(|r_{xy}|, e^{-F(A,B)}) \tag{8}$$

Obtaining the absolute value for SCC and $e^{-F(A,B)}$ value for DFD makes both of the result value within $0 \sim 1$ after the change of form, which also satisfies the relationship that the larger the DFD is, the smaller the similarity is.

The problem of this paper is that users need to be judged and made decisions, and abnormal users can be confirmed by the final comprehensive evaluation index. TOPSIS algorithm is a common intra-group comprehensive evaluation method, which is often utilized to solve multi-attribute decision-making problems, and its results can accurately reflect the difference between various evaluation schemes. Therefore, TOPSIS method is adopted in this paper to fuse SCC and DFD to confirm abnormal users in the platform. The specific steps are as follows:

Step1: According to Eqs. (5) and (6), the initial decision matrix is constructed as $\mathbf{A} = (a_{ij})_{N \times 2}$

$$\mathbf{A} = \begin{bmatrix} SCC_1 & DFD_1 \\ SCC_2 & DFD_2 \\ \vdots & \vdots \\ SCC_N & DFD_N \end{bmatrix} \tag{9}$$

Step2: Homogenize and normalize the index attribute SCC and DFD respectively to generate a new normalized decision matrix. $\mathbf{B} = (b_{ij})_{N \times 2}$

$$\mathbf{B} = \begin{bmatrix} k_1 SCC_1 & k_2 e^{-DFD_1} \\ k_1 SCC_2 & k_2 e^{-DFD_1} \\ \vdots & \vdots \\ k_1 SCC_N & k_2 e^{-DFD_1} \end{bmatrix} \tag{10}$$

Where $k_j = \begin{cases} \sqrt{\sum\limits_{i=1}^{N} a_{ij}^2}, j = 1 \\ \sqrt{\sum\limits_{i=1}^{N} (e^{-a_{ij}})^2}, j = 2 \end{cases}$

Step3: determine the ideal optimal solution $\mathbf{s}^+$ and the worst solution $\mathbf{s}^-$.

$$\mathbf{s}^+ = [\max\{b_{i1}|1 \le i \le N\}, \max\{b_{i2}|1 \le i \le N\}] \tag{11}$$

$$\mathbf{s}^- = [\min\{b_{i1}|1 \le i \le N\}, \min\{b_{i2}|1 \le i \le N\}] \tag{12}$$

Step4: calculate the row vectors in the normalized decision matrix B and the L^2 Norm of the optimal and worst solutions (i.e. Euclidean distance) d_i^+ and d_i^-.

$$d_i^+ = \left\| \mathbf{s}^+ - b_i \right\|_2 \tag{13}$$

$$d_i^- = \left\| \mathbf{s}^- - b_i \right\|_2 \tag{14}$$

Step5: calculate the comprehensive evaluation index S_i of each user based on L^2 norm, and rank S_i according to the size, and finally output the evaluation result of TOPSIS of each user sample.

$$S_i = \frac{d_i^-}{d_i^+ + d_i^-} \tag{15}$$

Where S_i is the comprehensive evaluation index of abnormal judgment of the ith user.

According to the final value of the comprehensive evaluation index of abnormal judgment S_i, the suspect coefficient of abnormal users is confirmed, so as to accurately locate abnormal users.

5   Example Simulation and Analysis

5.1   Case Background Introduction

The experiment was carried out on Tensorflow, which is Google's open source framework for deep learning. The open source Python-based machine learning toolkit Scikit-Learn was utilized. The machine used in the experiment included CPU: Intel(R) Core(TM) I7-8565U 1.8 ghz, 8 G RAM, and Python 3.7 software. Taking the historical user data of a certain public substation as the sample, the daily load data of all users and the line loss variation rule from January 1, 2019 to July 7, 2019 are recorded from the collection system. The original data set contains a total of 154 user load records and 188 daily line loss records.

5.2   Analysis of Example Results

The normalized line loss data of the station area was studied. First, the decision was made based on GSA algorithm. Second, the optimal clustering number of line loss data set is determined. Finally, the improved dichotomous K-means++ clustering analysis method is adopted to divide the exception library and standard library of line loss. The clustering number was initialized, and the clustering dispersion W(K), its natural logarithm ln[W(K)] and Gap value Gap(K) were calculated according to Eq. (2) and (3), respectively. The calculated results are shown in Table 1 below.

Table 1. When $K \geq 1$, the calculation results of W(K), ln[W(K)] and Gap(K)

K	W(K)	ln[W(K)]	Eln[W_r(K)]	Gap(K)
1	1.3025	0.2643	0.3965	0.1322
2	0.3645	−1.0092	−0.7584	0.2508
3	0.0221	−3.8121	−3.3609	0.4512
4	0.0115	−4.4654	−4.1504	0.315
5	0.0074	−4.9063	−4.6149	0.2914
6	0.0046	−5.3817	−5.1281	0.2536

Figure 4 is the graph of the number of cluster classes K and Gap(K). As can be seen from the Gap(K) curve in Fig. 4, when Gap(3) > Gap(1) and Gap(3) > Gap(2), i.e., K = 3, Gap(K) first appears maximum value. When $K \geq 4$, the change of Gap(K) gradually tends to be stable, so the optimal clustering number is 3 in this paper.

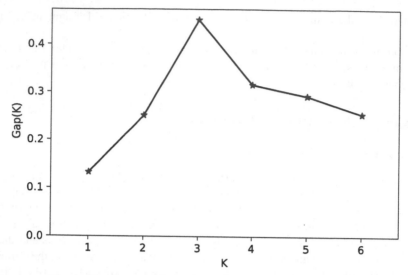

Fig. 4. The curve graph of the number of clusters K and Gap(K)

Based on the optimal clustering number, the clustering analysis of the line loss samples was operated, the clustering results are shown in Fig. 5. It can be seen from Fig. 5 that the purple area has the largest number of line loss cases, so it is judged as the standard library, while the yellow and green areas are not in the standard library, and then it is judged as abnormal.

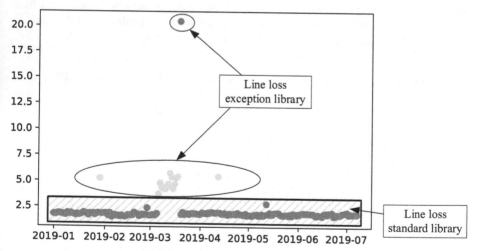

Fig. 5. Line loss clustering result graph.

Table 2 and Table 3 show the clustering results of data implemented by IBM SPSS Statistics software. It can be clearly seen from the table that when the cluster number is set to the optimal cluster number 3, the final cluster center and the number of cases in each cluster is completely consistent with the situation in Fig. 5.

Table 2. Final cluster class center

Cluster class	1	2	3
Center	0.167	0.018	1

Table 3. Number of cases in each cluster class

Cluster class	1	2	3
Number of cases	15	172	1

From Table 2 and 3 and Fig. 5, it can be seen that the cluster class with the largest number of cases is cluster class 2, with 172 sample data. The cluster center of cluster 2 was determined to be 0.018, and the maximum upper limit distance r_{upper} and the maximum lower limit distance r_{low} from the samples in the cluster to the cluster center was calculated, which constitute the standard library of historical line loss, and it is not difficult to figure out r_{upper} is equal to 0.051 and r_{low} is equal to 0.018, and the standard library is composed of the true value collected by the system before normalization, so it should be [0.6, 3]. The generation rules of the line loss exception library are completely consistent with the standard library. It can be seen from Fig. 5 that the historical line loss exception library is composed of two parts: one is a cluster class with 0.167 as the cluster center and the number of cases is 15. The other part is a cluster with 1 as the cluster center and the number of cases is 1. Since T specified in this paper must be a continuous time interval, we ignores the period with small line loss fluctuation and a cycle of 1 to 2 days, so the abnormal time can be preliminarily judged as March 6 to March 19.

Different from the standard library constructed in this paper, Fig. 6 is a diagram of the normal interval of line loss under the national standard. It can be clearly seen from Fig. 6 that if we utilize the computable accurate rate of average daily line loss to assess, the line loss of the normal power supply area (power distribution room) range from 0% to 8%. At this point, compared to the standard library of line loss above, some other line loss data was included. However, according to the on-site checking, we found several suspected point exists abnormal electricity consumption, so the construction of standard library of line loss and abnormal library conforms to the requirement of engineering application, which save the operational cost and improve the accuracy of the identification of abnormality.

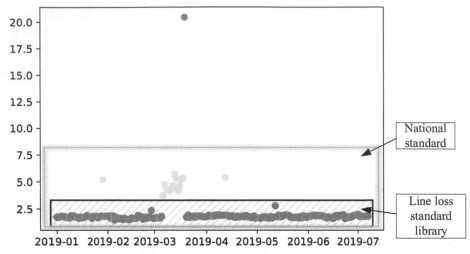

Fig. 6. Schematic diagram of normal range of line loss under national standard

We calculated the corresponding user's power consumption and line loss of SCC and DFD within the abnormal time period T respectively, to determine the threshold value of SCC $\alpha = 0.6$, and the standard is: when $\alpha \geq 0.6$ we take strong correlation, when $\alpha \leq 0.6$ we take weak correlation. In the progress of considering both shape and numerical similarity, DFD calculates the distance between two discretized curves and tends to be unstable on the abnormal data set, while SCC mainly considers the similarity degree of numerical values and has strong robustness, thus forming complementary advantages. This paper proposes a joint judgment based on SCC and DFD, and uses TOPSIS method to realize the accurate positioning of the associated users with abnormal line loss.

According to Eqs. (4) and (6), we respectively calculated the SCC and DFD of each user's power consumption and abnormal line loss. Users whose SCC is larger than the threshold value of 0.6 are selected and arranged in descending order according to the power consumption. The calculation results are shown in Table 4.

Table 4. Calculation results of SCC and DFD

User ID	SCC	DFD
5xxxxxx158	0.7675	1.1836
5xxxxxx813	0.7617	1.0997
7xxxxxx016	0.6052	1.4834
5xxxxxx803	0.6198	2.3217
5xxxxxx740	0.6629	2.6044

Based on the above calculation results, we obtained the normalized decision matrix is as follows:

$$B = \begin{bmatrix} 0.52454 & 0.58796 \\ 0.41122 & 0.63942 \\ 0.41361 & 0.43566 \\ 0.42359 & 0.1884 \\ 0.45305 & 0.142 \end{bmatrix}$$

Since the indicators in the normalized decision matrix after the forward and standardized processing are extremely large data, we only need to take the maximum value of each column to constitute the ideal optimal vector, and take the minimum value of each column to constitutes the ideal worst vector, namely

$$s^+ = [0.52454, 0.63942]$$

$$s^- = [0.41122, 0.142]$$

According to Steps 4 and 5 of TOPSIS method in 3.3, L^2, d_i^+, d_i^- and S_i of 5 users suspected of abnormal power consumption and ideal optimal and worst vectors in Table 4 can be obtained. The specific results are shown in Table 5:

Table 5. d^+, d^- and S_i obtained based on the initial decision matrix.

The user id	SCC	e^{-DFD}	d^+	d^-	S_i	Rank
5xxxxxx158	0.7675	0.30617	0.05146	0.46012	0.89941	1
5xxxxxx813	0.7617	0.33297	0.11331	0.49741	0.61446	2
7xxxxxx016	0.6052	0.22687	0.23199	0.29366	0.55866	3
5xxxxxx803	0.6198	0.09811	0.46218	0.04801	0.09411	4
5xxxxxx740	0.6629	0.07395	0.50252	0.04183	0.07684	5

It can be seen from Table 5 that the historical power consumption of the user numbered 5XXXXXX158 in the power supply area is the largest, and its comprehensive evaluation index Si = 0.89941 is the maximum value, which can be considered as the most suspected abnormal electricity consumption. At the same time, a line chart can also be utilized to verify the correlation between the user's power consumption and the line loss, as is shown in Fig. 7. The power loss in this power supply area is nearly identical to the change of 5XXXXXX158 users' power consumption, which means the power loss in this area changes with the change of 5xxxxxx158 users' power consumption, and it also verifies that the calculation results of SCC and DFD are completely correct.

As can be seen from Table 5, if only SCC is adopted for anomaly identification, users with user numbers of 5xxxxxx158 and 5xxxxxx813 are both suspected of abnormal power consumption, so accurate judgment cannot be made. It should be confirmed through on-site checking. If only DFD is adopted for anomaly identification, the user with user number 5xxxxxx813 is judged as an abnormal user, but it is not consistent with the actual situation. Therefore, we proposed a joint research and judgment based on SCC and DFD. Compared with the traditional similarity measurement algorithm, TOPSIS method can better realize the precise positioning of users associated with abnormal line loss in the power supply area.

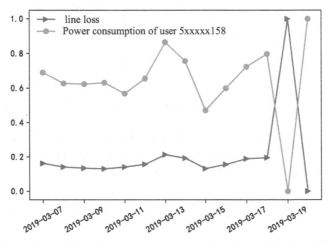

Fig. 7. Line loss and line chart of user power consumption change No. 5xxxx158 in abnormal time period

6   Conclusion

(1) In this paper, we proposed an improved binary K-means++ clustering algorithm based on GSA to construct the line loss standard library. This algorithm effectively ameliorates the problem which traditional clustering algorithm has in the selection of optimal clustering number, and improves the convergence and efficiency of clustering.

(2) The standard library of line loss constructed in this paper is more detailed than the standard set by the state, which can better describe the characteristics of the power supply area and realize the accurate identification of line loss rate anomaly.

(3) The comprehensive evaluation index based on SCC and DFD constructed in this paper can accurately analyze the correlation between users and abnormal line loss rate, and realize the precise positioning of users associated with abnormal line loss rate.

References

1. Acharjee, P.: Improvement of the line losses, weaker buses and saddle-node-bifurcation points using reconfigurations of the identified suitable lines. Int. J. Power Energy Convers. **10**(3), 423–430 (2019)
2. Meerimatha, G., Loveswara Rao, B.: Novel reconfiguration approach to reduce line losses of the photovoltaic array under various shading conditions. Energy **196**(10),125–129 (2020)
3. Acharjee, P.: Improvement of the line losses, weaker buses and saddle-node-bifurcation points using reconfigurations of the identified suitable lines. Int. J. Power Energy Convers. **10**(3), 674–681 (2019)
4. Rakesh, N., Senthil Kumar, S., Madhusudanan, G.: Mitigation of power mismatch losses and wiring line losses of partially shaded solar PV array using improvised magic technique. IET Renew. Power Gener. **13**(9), 379–385 (2019)
5. Yao, M., Zhu, Y., Li, J., et al.: Research on predicting line loss rate in low voltage distribution network based on gradient boosting decision tree. Energies **12**(13), 12–19 (2019)
6. Yi, K., Wang, W., Bai, R., et al.: A line loss calculation method for arbitrary partition of power grid based on measurement resource and matpower. IOP Conf. Ser. Mater. Sci. Eng. **533**(1), 272–276 (2019)
7. Li, N., Ning, L., Wei, Z., et al.: Research on key techniques for negative line loss rectification of interprovincial transmission lines. IOP Conf. Ser. Earth Environ. Sci. **558**(5), 677–682 (2020)
8. Adewuyi, O.B., Shigenobu, R., Senjyu, T., et al.: Multiobjective mix generation planning considering utility-scale solar PV system and voltage stability: Nigerian case study. Electric Power Syst. Res. **168**(4), 375–380 (2019)
9. Kłopotek, M.A.: .An aposteriorical clusterability criterion for k-means++ and simplicity of clustering. SN Comput. Sci. **1**(01), 254–260 (2020)
10. Mousavinasr, S., Gonçalves, C.R., Dorea, C.C.Y.: Convergence to Frechet distribution via Mallows distance. Stat. Probab. Lett. **16**(03), 423–426 (2020)
11. Yang, F., Liu, J., Li, S.Q.: Construction and application of theoretical line loss calculation platform for 220 kV and above power grid in Shanghai. IOP Conf. Ser. Mater. Sci. Eng. **199**(1), 99–103 (2017)
12. Liu, Y., Song, W., Li, N., et al.: A decentralized optimal load current sharing method for power line loss minimization in MT-HVDC systems. J. Power Electron. **16**(6), 223–228 (2016)

A Reactive Power Reserve Prediction Method for EV Charging Piles Based on Big Data and Optimized Neural Network

Yibin Guan[1], Wenlong Wu[2(✉)], Jianhua Chen[3], Xiaochun Xu[4], Kanglin Cai[1], and Wenhui Yuan[2]

[1] State Grid Jiangsu Electric Power Company, Nanjing 210024, China
[2] Nanjing Institute of Technology, Nanjing 211167, Jiangsu, China
[3] Nan Jing Nan Rui Group Co. Ltd., Nanjing 211100, China
[4] State Grid Huaian Power Company, Huaian 223001, Jiangsu Province, China

Abstract. A reactive power reserve prediction method for ev charging piles based on big data and optimized neural network is proposed. Firstly analyzes the big data environment on the influence of the reactive power reserve prediction method, put forward the electric vehicle charging pile, the concept of dynamic reactive power reserve, studied the factors impact on reactive power reserve, established the pulsating current and direct current (dc) reactive power reserve capacity correction of electric vehicle charging pile analysis, the mathematical model and particle swarm optimization neural network model is established, and put forward the reactive power reserve prediction scheme based on big data analysis. Finally, the proposed method is verified with grid data and compared with the predicted results of traditional artificial neural network. The results show that this method has high precision and can effectively reduce the time required for prediction, and improve the stability of the voltage of the power grid.

Keywords: Power big data · Power grid security · Particle swarm optimization · Neural network · Reactive power reserve · EV charging pile · Flexible load

1 Introduction

With the progress of current technology, the application of big data and big data in power grid has been greatly developed. The power consumption of users, measurement of smart electricity meters, management of power generation, transmission and distribution equipment and other relevant information are the main sources for generating large amounts of data in power grid [1]. Properly handling a large amount of data in the power grid is conducive to the correct operation of the power grid and the efficient operation of the equipment therein [2]. In addition, meteorological systems and traffic analysis related

Project name: Science and Technology Project of State Grid Corporation.
Project code: 5108-202018028A-0-0-00.

© Springer Nature Singapore Pte Ltd. 2021
Y. Tian et al. (Eds.): ICBDS 2020, CCIS 1415, pp. 406–419, 2021.
https://doi.org/10.1007/978-981-16-3150-4_34

to the operation of reactive power sources are also increasingly closely related to reactive power reserve. Big data technology has brought new opportunities and challenges to the calculation of reactive power reserves in the power grid [3].

Sufficient reactive power is the basic condition to ensure the voltage level. In the process of transmitting power resources in large quantities across a range, sufficient reactive power reserve is needed to maintain the stability of voltage [4]. Quantitative reactive power reserve can avoid voltage instability, Angle instability and voltage anomaly [5]. In recent years, with the continuous development of the power market and the gradual increase of the load, the voltage stability problem has attracted more and more attention, and the reactive power reserve prediction problem has become a hot spot.

In recent years, a great deal of research has been done on the stability of power grid. The methods to judge the stability of power network can be roughly divided into the following methods. The first one is the phasor measurement Angle. In literature [6], a robust state estimation method based on this is proposed, which can monitor the power system in real time under different working conditions. The second is to judge the state of the power grid based on big data. In literature [7], big data power generation prediction technology is used to establish an energy Internet, so as to coordinate and manage renewable energy and traditional energy more effectively. In literature [8], a new data mining technology and a core vector machine are combined to solve the problem of big data in the measurement unit, and an application framework is established for training and testing, so as to finally achieve the role of transient stability assessment of power system. The third is from the perspective of intelligent system. In literature [9], hierarchical intelligent system is used to evaluate the short-term voltage stability of power system. This method improves the efficiency of assessment and the richness of knowledge. However, these methods have some defects. The dynamic reactive power reserve used in this paper can effectively reflect the stability of the system voltage, and it has its advantages in intuitiveness and calculation.

In the aspect of artificial neural network, although there are few researches on reactive power reserve prediction, there are many related researches on power grid load prediction. In literature [10], a short-term power load prediction model based on deep residual network is proposed. This model uses a variety of neural networks to form a base block and integrates knowledge and understanding to improve the generalization ability of the model. In literature [11], short-term load forecasting for a single power customer improves load forecasting. Considering its high volatility and uncertainty, a framework of opportunity long-term and short-term memory recursive neural network is established. In literature [12], overfitting when learning uncertainty is not avoided, layers are added to the neural network to limit the prediction performance, and a deep recursive neural network based on pools is established. In the renewable energy grid, neural network algorithm is also widely used. In literature [13], AutoEncoder and LSTM neural network are used to predict the power of renewable energy power plants, thus reducing operating costs. In literature [14], the prediction interval is the preferred result of prediction. The multi-object genetic algorithm and neural network algorithm are considered and compared to evaluate the prediction interval of time series prediction, and it is found that the two have complementary advantages. In these papers, it is concluded that neural network forecasting has its advantages in load forecasting. In this paper, particle swarm optimization (PSO) neural network is used to predict reactive power reserve.

Nowadays, with the rapid development of ev charging pile technology, its influence on power grid cannot be ignored. Ev charging piles can participate in the system's reactive power optimization operation by providing reactive power reserve. In this paper, from the perspective of power grid big data and power grid security, combined with the big data technology, the optimized neural network is used to realize the prediction of reactive power reserve of ev charging piles. Because the current training algorithm for reactive power reserve prediction is not mature enough. A hybrid algorithm is also proposed to predict reactive power reserve of ev charging piles more quickly.

2 EV Charging Pile Dynamic Reactive Power Reserve

2.1 Reactive Power Source of Electric Vehicle Charging Pile

Evs charging piles with vehicle-to-grid (V2G) response ability can serve as reactive power sources to provide reactive power compensation for the power grid. When the charging pile plays its reactive compensation ability as a reactive power source, the remaining capacity of the charging pile can be fully utilized without causing additional loss to the power supply. As a power electronic converter, the reactive power regulation ability of EV charging piles is smooth and flexible, which can play a strong regulating ability in the balance of power grid voltage. The use of electric vehicles to supplement or replace the existing reactive power compensation devices can reduce the investment of related equipment, and to a certain extent, also improve the efficiency of the grid, improve the economy.

But the maximum reactive power an electric car can provide is limited by a number of factors. The direct current capacity of ev charging pile itself also needs some reactive power to maintain the stability of its own voltage. The capacity of DC capacity and rated current will affect the maximum reactive power it can provide, that is, it will affect the reactive reserve of electric vehicles as reactive power source.

2.2 The Definition of Reactive Power Reserve

System reactive power reserve can be divided into static reactive power reserve and dynamic reactive power reserve. Static reactive reserve is mainly provided by devices such as shunt capacitors, which lack the ability to flexibly adjust reactive power output in response to voltage changes. Dynamic reactive power reserve plays a more important role in the maintenance of system failure process and system voltage after fault removal. In the case of different faults, the dynamic reactive power reserve corresponding to the system can also make more flexible response.

Dynamic reactive power reserve generally refers to the difference between the maximum reactive power that can be output by charging pile of EV and the current steady-state reactive power output, the formula is shown below

$$Q_{res} = Q_{\max} - Q_0 \tag{1}$$

Where Q_{res} represents the dynamic reactive power reserve of ev charging piles, Q_{max} represents the maximum reactive power output of ev charging pile, Q represents the current steady-state reactive power output of ev charging pile.

However, in the actual operation, due to the capacity of ev charging pile itself, capacity of DC bus capacitance, ev topology and other factors, the actual reactive power reserve that can be used by EV charging pile cannot be calculated according to the theoretically output maximum reactive power. Moreover, the charging pile of EV needs to perform its own function of charging the battery well, and the technical reactive power limit of the reactive power source is often impossible to reach. Therefore, formula (1) is modified in this paper, and the maximum reactive power output of the dynamic reactive power source of ev charging pile in actual operation can be achieved under the current consideration of many factors as its maximum reactive power output, and the difference between its current reactive power output and its dynamic reactive power reserve, the formula is shown below

$$Q_{res} = Q_{0max} - Q_0 \tag{2}$$

Where Q_{res} represents dynamic reactive power reserve of charging piles for electric vehicles, Q_{0max} represents the maximum reactive power output of electric vehicle charging pile dynamic reactive power source can be achieved at present, Q represents the current steady-state reactive power output of ev charging pile.

2.3 Basic Model of Reactive Power Reserve of Charging Piles for Electric Vehicles

The one-way topological charging pile based on PFC can theoretically output reactive power, but the reactive power is limited and will greatly reduce its own power factor. Therefore, the charging pile of PFC one-way topology is not suitable for reactive power compensation. The bidirectional four-quadrant topology is not only more widely used, but also more suitable for the improvement of reactive power compensation ability. Therefore, based on the bidirectional four-quadrant topology reactive power analysis method, the reactive power mathematical model of EV charging pile is established.

The power flowing into the charging pile can be divided into average power and fluctuating power, among which the fluctuating power flowing between the charging pile and the power grid is temporarily stored in the DIRECT current capacity of the CHARGING pile of ev. Therefore, the energy stored in the direct current capacity of the charging pile can be obtained by pulsation integral, which can be expressed as:

$$E = \frac{1}{\omega}\sqrt{S^2 + \left(\omega L_c \cdot \frac{S^2}{V_s^2}\right)^2 - 2\omega L_c \cdot \frac{S^2}{V_s^2} \cdot Q_s} \tag{3}$$

Where ω represents the angular frequency, L_c represents the inductive impedance between the charging pile and the grid, S represents apparent power of charging pile, V_s represents the grid voltage, Q_s represents reactive power injected into the grid by charging piles of electric vehicles.

According to Eq. (2), when the charging pile outputs reactive power during active power charging, the pulsation energy value in the charging pile will increase, which will lead to the increase of second harmonic pulsation current and pulsation voltage, and ultimately affect the dc capacity in the circuit. Namely. The pulsation current and direct current capacity of the charging pile should be satisfied when the charging pile performs reactive compensation.

Where in, the charging pile pulsation current can be expressed as

$$I_c \approx \frac{S\left(1 - \frac{\omega L_c}{V_s^2} \cdot Q_s\right)}{\sqrt{2}V_{dc}} \tag{4}$$

Where V_{dc} represents Dc voltage.

Considering the charging pile pulsation current maximum value is $\frac{S_{max}}{\sqrt{2}V_{dc}}$, after transformation, the current maximum reactive power output of ev charging pile can be expressed as

$$\begin{cases} q_{max} = \sqrt{(S^2 - p^2)} & q \geq 0 \\ \left(p^2 + q_{max}^2\right) \cdot \left(1 - \frac{\omega L_c}{V_s^2} \cdot q_{max}\right)^2 = S_{max}^2 \left(p^2 + q_{max}^2\right) \cdot \left(1 - \frac{\omega L_c}{V_s^2} \cdot q_{max}\right)^2 = S_{max}^2 & q \leq 0 \end{cases} \tag{5}$$

Where p represents the active power injected into the power grid by charging piles of electric vehicles, q_{max} represents the maximum reactive power that ev charging piles can inject into the grid, S represents apparent power of charging pile, S_{max} represents maximum apparent power of charging pile, V_s represents the grid voltage.

According to Eq. (5), the maximum reactive power that can be injected into the grid by the current EV charging pile can be obtained, and then reactive power reserve of ev charging pile can be calculated according to Eq. (2).

$$q_{res} = q_{max} - q_0 \tag{6}$$

Where q_{res} represents dynamic reactive power reserve of charging piles for electric vehicles, q_{max} represents the maximum reactive power output of electric vehicle charging pile dynamic reactive power source can be achieved at present, q_0 represents the current steady-state reactive power output of ev charging pile.

3   Particle Swarm Algorithm

3.1   Basic Concepts of Particle Swarm Optimization

Particle swarm optimization (PSO) is an evolutionary algorithm. Starting from random solutions, it iteratively searches for the optimal solution and evaluates the quality of the solution through fitness. In the process, it constantly judges and moves to find the global optimal solution by following the currently searched optimal value [15]. The basic idea of particle swarm optimization is to assume that the potential solution of each optimization problem is a particle in the search space [16]. All particles have a fitness value, which is determined by the corresponding fitness function, and each particle itself has a "velocity" to determine where they update after each iteration. In addition to speed, in each iteration, each particle also needs to judge its updated position through two extreme values, one is the optimal solution that the particle itself can find, and the other is the optimal solution that the whole population can currently find, which is called the global extreme value [25].

3.2 The Basic Model of Particle Swarm Optimization

The flow chart of the basic model of particle swarm optimization is shown in Fig. 1. In an N-dimensional target space, A particles gather into A community, where the position of the ith particle is:

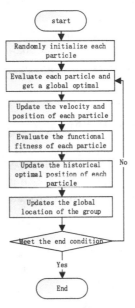

Fig. 1. Particle swarm optimization

$$X_i = (x_{i1}, \cdots, x_{iN}) \tag{7}$$

The velocity of the ith particle:

$$V_i = (v_{i1}, \cdots, v_{iN}) \tag{8}$$

The individual extreme value of the ith particle is:

$$p_{best} = (p_{i1}, \cdots, p_{iN}) \tag{9}$$

The historical optimal value searched for the whole particle swarm is:

$$g_{best} = (p_{g1}, \cdots, p_{gN}) \tag{10}$$

The formula used by particles to judge and update their own velocity is:

$$v_{in} = \omega v_{in} + c_1 r_1 (p_{in} - x_{in}) + c_2 r_2 (p_{gn} - x_n) \tag{11}$$

The formula used by particles to judge and update their positions is:

$$x_{in} = x_{in} + v_{in} \tag{12}$$

Where C_1, C_2 represents learning factor, r_1, r_2 represents the uniform random number within the range of [0, 1].

The specific flow of particle swarm optimization algorithm is shown in Fig. 1.

4 BP Neural Network Algorithm

4.1 Basic Concept of BP Neural Network

Neural network is a nonlinear system composed of a large number of interconnected nodes. Neural network algorithm establishes the theoretical model of neuron by studying the structure of biological neural network. Propagation (BP) neural network has been very mature in network theory, etc., and the method mainly USES back-propagation algorithm for training, so it has strong nonlinear analysis capability. This method has strong learning ability, and can approximate any function by training large amount of data.

4.2 Basic Model of BP Neural Network

The Bp neural algorithm model is usually composed of input layer, hidden layer and output layer. The BP neural network model with a hidden layer in this paper is shown in Fig. 2. The Bp neural network algorithm is a multi-layer network with one-way propagation, which can be divided into two propagation modes: forward propagation and back propagation.

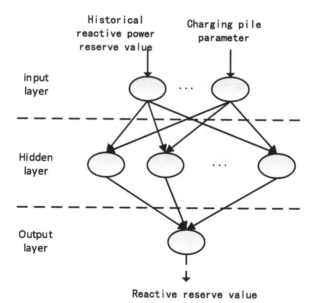

Fig. 2. BP neural network algorithm

The number of ganglion points in the hidden layer is determined by empirical formula, which is:

$$H = \sqrt{M + N} + P \tag{13}$$

Where H represents the number of nodes in the hidden layer, M represents the number of nodes in the input layer, N represents number of nodes in the output layer, P represents constant, $P \in [1, 10]$.

Where, the forward propagation is calculated according to Eq. (14) to calculate the network output, and the training error of the sample is calculated according to Eq. (15). The number of nodes in the input layer is I, the number of neurons in the hidden layer is J, and the number of nodes in the output layer is 1. Formula for:

$$y = \psi \left(\sum_{j=1}^{J} \omega_j v_j^J \right) \tag{14}$$

$$e(n) = d(n) - y(n) \tag{15}$$

Where y represents actual output value, $\psi(x)$ represents output function, J represents number of neurons in the hidden layer, ω_j represents the Jth neuron in the hidden layer represents the weight, V_j^J represents the output of the excitation function represented by the Jth neuron in the hidden layer, e(n) represents the error signal of the output layer neuron, d(n) represents desired output.

In the back propagation, the weights of each layer should be updated continuously according to the error. After one iteration, the weights between nodes in the hidden layer and any nodes in the output layer are shown in Eq. (16).

$$\omega_j(n+1) = \omega_j(n) + \Delta \omega_j(n) \tag{16}$$

Where $\omega_j(n)$ represents In the Nth iteration, the weight between the node in the hidden layer and the Jth node in the output layer, n represents the number of iterations, $\Delta\omega_j(n)$ is the correction quantity of $\omega_j(n)$ after the Nth iteration.

$$\omega_{mi}(n+1) = \omega_{mi}(n) + \Delta \omega_{mi}(n) \tag{17}$$

Where $\omega_{mi}(n)$ represents in the Nth iteration, the weight between the ith node in the hidden layer and the m node in the input layer, $\Delta\omega_{mi}(n)$ is the correction quantity of $\omega_{mi}(n)$ after the Nth iteration.

An iterative process is completed by using the BP neural network algorithm of Formula (13–17), which is called a one-time learning process.

5 Flexible Load Reactive Power Reserve Prediction Based on Big Data Analysis

5.1 Data Processing

The reactive power reserve of electric vehicles is affected by many factors, such as local weather, season, type of date, local economic level and so on. There are many limitations in the charging process, such as energy constraints of charging station, transformer capacity constraints, line load capacity constraints, etc. Here, charging parameters set to meet users' travel needs and energy constraints of the battery are mainly considered. As for these factors affecting reactive power reserve of EV charging piles, considering their differences to some extent, these data need to be standardized in advance.

5.2 Specific Steps

Using particle swarm optimization to optimize BP neural network, the specific steps are as follows:

Step1: Initialize the neural network and particle swarm optimization algorithm, and set corresponding parameters. In the particle swarm, the population size, iteration times, learning factors, inertial weights, position and velocity limits were determined, and the particle dimension was set according to the number of nodes in the neural network. In the part of neural network, the structure of neural network, learning rate, target accuracy and training times are determined.

Step2: Randomly generate particle swarm optimization as the initial value of neural network weights according to particle parameters, and the formula is:

$$n = M \times H + H \times N + H + N \tag{18}$$

Where n represents the dimension of the particle, M represents the number of nodes in the input layer, H represents the number of nodes in the hidden layer, N represents the number of nodes in the output layer.

Step3: calculate the fitness of each particle, assign a value to bp neural network according to the value of each particle dimension, and then train bp neural network with training samples. After reaching the accuracy, input the value of sample g, and the output value is the fitness of this particle. The calculation formula is as follows:

$$fitness = \frac{1}{S} \sum_{k=1}^{S} Y_n(k) \tag{19}$$

Where fitness represents the fitness of the particle, S represents the number of samples, $Y_n(k)$ represents the actual output of node N in the Kth sample.

Step4: Determine the individual optimal value and population optimal value of the population according to the corresponding fitness size of each particle, and update.

Step5: judge whether the current iteration number reaches the maximum iteration number or the accuracy meets the corresponding requirements. If the current iteration number reaches the maximum iteration number or the accuracy meets the corresponding requirements, enter Step7; otherwise, enter Step6.

Step6: Update the position and velocity of the particle according to Formula (11–12), and enter Step2.

Step7: Update the weights of the neural network according to the final optimal value.

Step8: Train the neural network with training data and update the weights of the neural network.

Step9: determine whether the number of iterations has been reached; if so, enter step10; otherwise, enter step 8.

Step10: Get the final neural network model and output the model.

The flow chart of neural network optimization implementation is shown in Fig. 3.

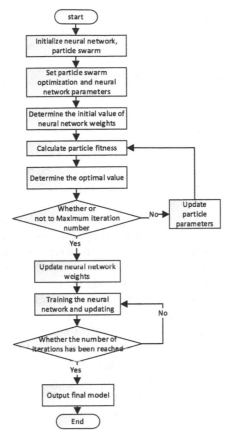

Fig. 3. Flow chart of neural network optimization implementation

5.3 Parameter Settings

In this paper, particle swarm optimization is used to optimize the neural network model. Before using the neural network, the parameters in the BP neural network model are used to determine the dimension of particle swarm, and particle swarm optimization is carried out in advance. According to Eq. (18), the dimension of particle swarm is obtained.

The prediction performance index is the average relative error. Formula for:

$$error = \frac{1}{n} \sum_{i=1}^{n} \left| \frac{y_{yi} - y_i}{y_i} \right| \times 100\% \tag{20}$$

Where error represents relative error of prediction, n represents predicted sample size, y_{yi} represents predictive value, y_i represents the actual value.

6   The Example Analysis

In order to verify the effectiveness of the optimization neural network algorithm mentioned in this paper, it will be compared with the traditional BP neural network, and the same data will be used for training, and the reactive power reserve situation in the same period will be predicted, so as to judge the advantages and disadvantages of the models.

6.1   Neural Network Training

In the part of particle swarm, the population size was set as 100, the number of evolution was set as 200, and the learning factor was set as 1.35. The position and velocity of the particles are iterated according to Eq. (11–12). The value range of inertia parameter is [0.5, 1].

In the neural network part, the input layer has a total of 8 nodes, including reactive power reserve values at 5 time points and three impact factors (weather, date and vehicle travel status). The output layer contains 1 node, which represents reactive power reserve prediction. The number of nodes in the hidden layer is determined according to Eq. (13), and then the optimal number of nodes in the hidden layer is determined by comparing the results in the experiment. The training times of neural network were 100, the training target accuracy was 0.001, and the learning rate was 0.05.

The model was trained in the MatlabR2020a platform, and the reactive power reserve data of the first 49 days were used to train each network model, and the reactive power reserve value of the 50th day was predicted. Figure 4 is the comparison diagram between the predicted value obtained by THE PSO-BP model and the actual value, and Fig. 5 is the comparison diagram between the predicted value obtained by the BP model and the actual value. Figure 6 shows the error comparison of the two models.

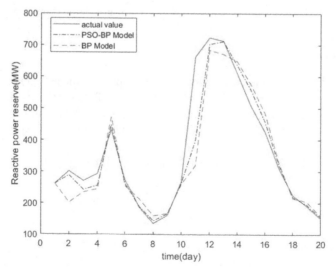

Fig. 4. Comparison of PSO-BP model with BP model and actual value

6.2 Example Results

The optimal neural network prediction model was used to predict the 20-day reactive power reserve value. The prediction results and errors were shown in Table 1, and the detailed comparison of the two prediction results was shown in Table 2.

Table 1. Prediction results and errors

Time/day	Forecast/MW	Actual value/MW	Error/MW	Relative error
1	262.5162	262	0.516187	0.00197
2	289.3998	302	−12.6002	−0.04172
3	243.7101	271	−27.2899	−0.1007
4	256.3864	293	−36.6136	−0.12496
5	447.819	432	15.81903	0.036618
6	261.6251	272	10.3749	−0.03814
7	189.9854	187	2.985355	0.015964
8	144.2664	136	8.266404	0.060782
9	166.1855	162	4.185507	0.025836
10	263.2393	268	−4.76065	−0.01776

Table 2. Comparison of prediction results

Model	Mean relative error	The training steps
Basic BP neural network	−0.02129	195
Improved neural network	−0.0169	6

6.3 Analysis of Example Results

According to Table 1 and Table 2, it can be analyzed that the optimized neural network model is superior to the traditional BP neural network in reactive power reserve prediction, which is mainly shown as follows:

The first aspect is relative accuracy. According to the average relative error in Table 2, it can be found that the optimized neural network has the highest average relative error level.

The second aspect is the iteration speed. According to the training steps in Table 2, it can be seen that the number of iterations of optimized neural network is far less than that of traditional neural network, and the training time required is greatly reduced.

It can be seen that the artificial neural network algorithm optimized by particle swarm optimization can effectively reduce the calculation time and improve the accuracy of reactive power reserve prediction results under the premise of keeping the accuracy within a certain range. The empirical results show that this method can solve the problem of reactive power reserve calculation well.

In this paper, the algorithm effect is verified through the comparison of algorithm models. After multiple verification, the prediction of reactive power reserve of ev charging piles based on big data and optimized neural network has the advantages of high prediction accuracy and fast prediction speed.

7 Conclusion

The voltage quality problem is affected by many factors. Only through analysis and calculation based on big data technology can the voltage problem of power grid be solved better. Through the research and implementation of the reactive power reserve prediction method for ev charging piles based on big data and optimized neural network, this paper successfully quantifies the stability of the power grid, which is conducive to the judgment of the current state of the power grid and the prevention and treatment of power grid faults.

References

1. Jiang, H., Wang, K., Wang, Y., Gao, M., Zhang, Y.: Energy big data: a survey. IEEE Access **4**, 3844–3861 (2016)
2. Yu, X., Xue, Y.: Smart grids: a cyber-physical systems perspective. Proc. IEEE **104**(5), 1058–1070 (2016)
3. Hu, J., Vasilakos, A.V.: Energy big data analytics and security: challenges and opportunities. IEEE Trans. Smart Grid **7**(5), 2423–2436 (2016)
4. Leonardi, B., Ajjarapu, V.: An approach for real time voltage stability margin control via reactive power reserve sensitivities. IEEE Trans. Power Syst. **28**(2), 615–628 (2013)
5. Capitanescu, F.: Assessing reactive power reserves with respect to operating constraints and voltage stability. IEEE Trans. Power Syst. **26**(4), 2224–2234 (2011)
6. Zhao, J., Zhang, G., Das, K., et al.: Power system real-time monitoring by using PMU-based robust state estimation method. IEEE Trans. Smart Grid **7**(1), 300–309 (2016)
7. Zhou, Z., et al.: Game-theoretical energy management for energy Internet with big data-based renewable power forecasting. IEEE Access **5**, 5731–5746 (2017)
8. Wang, B., Fang, B., Wang, Y., et al.: Power system transient stability assessment based on big data and the core vector machine. IEEE Trans. Smart Grid **7**(5), 2561–2570 (2016)
9. Xu, Y., Zhang, R., Zhao, J., Dong, Z.Y., Wang, D., Yang, H., et al.: Assessing short-term voltage stability of electric power systems by a hierarchical intelligent system. IEEE Trans. Neural Netw. Learn. Syst. **27**(8), 1686–1696 (2016)
10. Chen, K., et al.: Short-term load forecasting with deep residual networks. IEEE Trans. Smart Grid **10**, 3943–3952 (2018)
11. Kong, W., Dong, Z.Y., Jia, Y., Hill, D.J., Xu, Y., Zhang, Y.: Short-term residential load forecasting based on LSTM recurrent neural network. IEEE Trans. Smart Grid **10**, 841–851 (2017)
12. Shi, H., Xu, M., Li, R.: Deep learning for household load forecasting-a novel pooling deep RNN. IEEE Trans. Smart Grid **9**, 5271–5280 (2017)

13. Gensler, A., Henze, J., Sick, B., et al.: Deep learning for solar power forecasting-an approach using AutoEncoder and LSTM neural networks. In: 2016 IEEE International Conference on Systems Man and Cybernetics (SMC), pp. 002858–002865 (2016)
14. Ak, R., Fink, O., Zio, E.: Two machine learning approaches for short-term wind speed time-series prediction. IEEE Trans. Neural Netw. 27(8), 1734–1747 (2016)
15. Ramdan, B.A.K.: A novel MPPT algorithm based on particle swarm optimization for photovoltaic systems. IEEE Trans. Sustain. Energy Year 8(2), 468–476 (2017)
16. Li, J., Zhang, J., Jiang, C., Zhou, M.C.: Composite particle swarm optimizer with historical memory for function optimization. IEEE Trans. Cybern. 45(10), 2350–2363 (2015)

Research on Scattered Point Cloud Coordinate Reduction and Hole Repair Technology Based on Big Data Model

Liu Lei, Zhu Hao[(✉)], and Weiye Xu

School of Information and Communication Engineering, Nanjing Institute of Technology, Nanjing 211167, Jiangsu, China
zhuhao@njit.edu.cn

Abstract. For the point cloud simplification and hole repair in the process of scattered point cloud processing, a fast de-noising method for scattered point cloud data based on spherical model is designed. This paper introduces the method of establishing sphere model and including the scattered point cloud model of 3D objects in the sphere model, the coding sequence of the vertebral body region in the sphere and the distribution strategy of each coordinate point are discussed, the different distribution of point clouds in each cone region and the algorithm of data reduction and denoising are studied, this paper presents a method to transform 3D scattered point cloud model from spherical coordinates to rectangular coordinates. A hole repair algorithm based on improved radial basis function model is designed. The method of hole boundary extraction is introduced, the steps of fitting surface with radial basis function model are given. Experimental simulation and analysis show that, the method proposed in this paper can simplify scattered point cloud and repair holes, and the algorithm is simple, Low requirement for hardware system, It is more suitable for embedded system to calculate.

Keywords: Scattered point cloud · Fast streamlining · Radial basis function · Hole repair

1 Introduction

In reverse engineering, point cloud preprocessing is an important work in 3D reconstruction. In the process of target detection, massive point cloud data are usually obtained. Too much point cloud data becomes the burden of data calculation and storage, and not all points are useful for subsequent modeling. Therefore, under the premise of ensuring the data accuracy, effectively simplifying the point cloud data is an important content of point cloud preprocessing, and also the focus of the early steps of reverse engineering [1]. Because the cloud is usually divided into two kinds of cloud filtering methods, the cloud points are divided into two categories according to the cloud filtering technology. Common filtering algorithms include Gaussian filtering, Wiener filtering, Kalman filtering, etc. [2]. For scattered point clouds, there is no topological relationship between points, so it is impossible to construct filtering algorithm. The usual method is to establish the

Y. Tian et al. (Eds.): ICBDS 2020, CCIS 1415, pp. 420–432, 2021.
https://doi.org/10.1007/978-981-16-3150-4_35

topological relationship between point clouds and then filter. At present, for massive scattered point cloud models, simplification and denoising are usually treated as two different tasks, and the algorithm complexity is high, and the requirements for hardware system are high. Therefore, it is of great value to study the fast reduction method of scattered point cloud. The original point cloud data obtained from the measurement often has data missing, and the typical case is the generation of holes. Due to the damage of some parts of the measured sample, the missing measurement of the contact part between the fixture and the sample, the occlusion of line of sight in optical measurement and the lack of post-processing, the original point cloud data obtained from the measurement are often missing, and then holes are produced. The existence of these holes will affect the appearance of the model to a certain extent, and also interfere with the line of sight effect of subsequent image reverse engineering, and have different degrees of influence in many subsequent processing such as reverse modeling, rapid prototyping manufacturing and finite element analysis [3]. Therefore, for the point cloud data with holes, hole repair is needed to ensure the integrity of model data, and surface reconstruction is carried out on this basis. For scattered point cloud data, if mesh repair is needed, triangulation is needed, which will waste a lot of time on the establishment of triangular mesh [4]. If the surface is directly fitted by scattered point clouds, how to ensure the reliability of surface fitting, especially for complex surfaces, becomes a problem that must be solved by the algorithm.

2 Reduction and Denoising of Scattered Point Clouds

2.1 The Establishment of Ball Mould

Firstly, a sphere model is needed to include the scattered point cloud model of 3D objects in the sphere model. The sphere can be regarded as a series of pentahedrons with its vertex as its center and its bottom as its surface. When the base is small enough, the pentahedron can be approximately a pyramid. In this way, each coordinate point is dispersed in a cone area. The mathematical definition of the above construction method is as follows: the 3D scattered point cloud model is transformed from rectangular coordinate form (x, y, z) to spherical coordinate form (r, α, β). The transformation method is shown in formula 1–3:

$$r = \sqrt{x^2 + y^2 + z^2} \tag{1}$$

$$\alpha = \alpha \, tan\frac{y}{x} \tag{2}$$

$$\beta = \beta \, cos\frac{z}{r} \tag{3}$$

Taking the origin of Cartesian coordinate system $(0, 0, 0)$ as the center of the sphere, the maximum R is taken as the radius of all the points in the 3D scattered point cloud model, and the sphere Q is established, then the 3D scattered point cloud model is included in Q;

Among them, $\alpha \in [0°, 360°)$, $\beta \in [-180°, 180°)$, α and β changes divide the sphere into several vertebral regions with the center of the sphere as the apex. For example, when α and β increase $\Delta\alpha$ and $\Delta\beta$ respectively, the enveloped region OD1D2D3D4 is shown in Fig. 1.

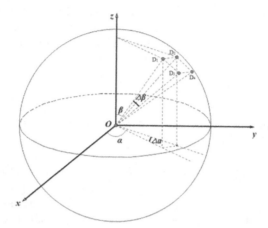

Fig. 1. The enveloped region OD1D2D3D4.

In the figure, if $\Delta\alpha = \Delta\beta = 1°$, the sphere can be divided into $180 \times 360 = 64800$ regions. Obviously, the target objects in the sphere are also divided into 64800 regions. Reducing the value of $\Delta\alpha$ and $\Delta\beta$ can increase the number of regions and improve the accuracy of discrimination, but increase the calculation time. Because the 3D object scattered point cloud model is also in the sphere, it is also segmented accordingly, and each coordinate point of the 3D object scattered point cloud model is scattered in a cone area.

2.2 Coding Sequence of Vertebral Region

In order to process the data of each vertebral body in sequence, it is necessary to code and sort the vertebral bodies. Starting from $\alpha = \alpha_0 = 0°$ and $\beta = \beta_0 = 0°$, the values of α and β are increased in turn, and the steps are $\Delta\alpha$ and $\Delta\beta$. At the same time, the 64800 intervals of the sphere are coded and sorted so that $\alpha_i = \alpha_{i-1} + \Delta\alpha$, $\beta_i = \beta_{i-1} + \Delta\beta$, then the coding and sorting method is as follows:

Φ_1: from α_0, β_0, to α_1, β_1, that is $\Phi_1 \in (0° ,0°) \sim (1° ,1°)$
Φ_2: from α_1, β_0, to α_2, β_1, that is $\Phi_2 \in (1° ,0°) \sim (2° ,1°)$
Φ_3: from α_2, β_0, to α_3, β_1, that is $\Phi_3 \in (2° ,0°) \sim (3° ,1°)$
......

Φ_{360}: from α_{359}, β_0, to α_0, β_1, that is $\Phi_{360} \in (359° ,0°) \sim (0° ,1°)$
Φ_{361}: from α_0, β_1, to α_1, β_2, that is $\Phi_{361} \in (0° ,1°) \sim (1° ,2°)$
Φ_{362}: from α_1, β_1, to α_2, β_2, that is $\Phi_{362} \in (1° ,1°) \sim (2° ,2°)$
......

Φ_{64800}: from α_{359}, β_{179}, to α_0, β_{179}, that is $\Phi_{64800} \in (359° ,179°) \sim (0° ,180°)$

The point cloud in each cone region is defined as a point cloud set Φ, which can realize the reduction and denoising of scattered point cloud data;

2.3 Fast Reduction Denoising Algorithm Based on Sphere Module

For each vertebral body, the idea of fast reduction and denoising algorithm is: if all the points r value in the cone area is similar, the surface of the object in the cone area is considered to be a smooth plane, and a feature point is set to replace all the original points in the cone area to realize the reduction of cloud Φ at the point; If the r values of the points in the cone area are not similar, the points with the maximum and minimum r values in the cone area are removed, and then the comparison is made. If the r values of the remaining points are similar, it indicates that there are noise points in the removed two points. The set of the remaining points is treated as a smooth plane, and a feature point is set to replace all the original points in the cone area, so as to realize the point aggregation of Φ Simplification; If the remaining point r value is not similar, the slope angle (i.e. the surface of the object is a slope or the surface curvature is larger) is found on the surface of the object corresponding to the cone area, and all points are reserved.

The implementation of the algorithm includes the following two steps.

Step1: Based on the coding and sorting results of vertebral body, n points on the target object in the i-th region are defined as point clouds Φ_i: $\{D_{i,j}, (j = 0, 1 \ldots N - 1)\}$. Where, $D_{i,j}, (j = 0, 1 \ldots N - 1)$ is N points in Φi; Let's call the r values of these N points $r_{i,1}, r_{i,2} \ldots r_{i,N-1}$, the N points are sorted from large to small according to r value, and the maximum value is $r_{i,max}$, and the minimum value is $r_{i,min}$; Let the range $R_{i,1} = r_{i,max} - r_{i,min}$, and record the median as $R_{i,0}$; As shown in Fig. 2;

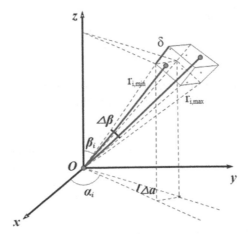

Fig. 2. Diagram of internal coordinate points of vertebral body

Step 2: Set threshold $\delta = 10^{-3}R_{i,0}$, adjust the delta value to adjust the noise tolerance, the smaller the δ, the smaller the tolerance, On this basis, the size of $R_{i,1}$ was determined:

If $R_{i,1} <= \delta$, then the set of points in Φ_i is a smooth surface of the original object, In this case, the feature point S_i is defined to replace all the original points in the region to represent the surface of the object in the region, The coordinates l_i, θ_i and φ_i of the characteristic point S_i are defined as follows:

$$l_i = \frac{(r_{i,1} + r_{i,2} + \cdots + r_{i,N-1})}{N} \tag{4}$$

$$\theta_i = \alpha + \frac{\Delta\alpha}{2} \tag{5}$$

$$\varphi_i = \beta + \frac{\Delta\beta}{2} \tag{6}$$

As shown in Fig. 3.

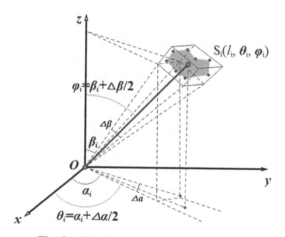

Fig. 3. All points inside the vertebral body

If $R1 > 10^{-3} R_0$, it means that there are noise points in this area or slope angle exists on the surface of the object composed of points in this area, the judgment method is as follows:

Delete a point with the largest r value and a point with the smallest r value among the N points in Φ_i, then, we can find the range $R_{i,2}$ for the remaining points;

If $R_{i,2} <= \delta$, then it means that the points in Φ_i are a smooth surface of the original object. There is one or two noise points in the deleted two points, The noise situation is shown in Fig. 4. At this time, the characteristic point S_i is defined to replace all the original points in the region to represent the surface of the object in this region. The definitions of the coordinates l_i, θ_i and φ_i of the characteristic points S_i are shown in Eqs. 5 to 8.

If $R_{i,2} > \delta$, then the surface of the object composed of points in this area has slope angle, and all points are reserved. The situation of slope angle is shown in Fig. 5.

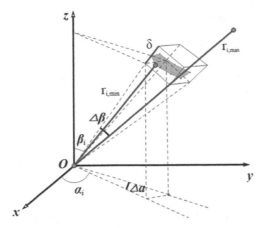

Fig. 4. Characteristic point in vertebral body

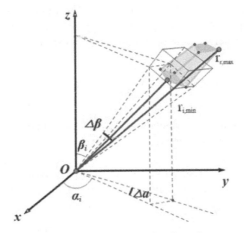

Fig. 5. There is slope break angle

After all the vertebral body regions are processed, the three-dimensional target scattered point cloud model is transformed from spherical coordinates to rectangular coordinates, and the three-dimensional target scattered point cloud model is transformed from spherical coordinates to rectangular coordinates:

$$x = r cos\alpha \tag{7}$$

$$y = r sin\beta cos\alpha \tag{8}$$

$$z = r cos\beta \tag{9}$$

3 Hole Repair of Scattered Point Cloud

3.1 Radial Basis Function Model

Suppose that the data point set $\{X_i\} \subset R$ and their corresponding function value set $\{f_i\}$ $\subset R$, in a three-dimensional space, a point $X = (x, y, z)$. The mapping $R^3 \rightarrow R$ is the radial basis function.

$$s(X_i) = f_i, \quad i = 1, \ldots, N \tag{10}$$

The radial basis function makes the surface smoothest and guarantees the minimum energy E. E is defined as follows

$$E = \int_{R^3} f_{xx}^2(X) + f_{yy}^2(X) + f_{zz}^2(X) + 2f_{xy}^2(X) + 2f_{yz}^2(X) + 2f_{zx}^2(X) \tag{11}$$

The energy functional is obtained in the second-order case, and the corresponding formula can be obtained in the higher-order case. The radial basis function (RBF) is evolved to solve the problem of minimum energy of Eq. 11 under the constraint of Eq. 10 by using variational technique, and the general explanation is as follows

$$s(X) = p(X) + \sum_{i=1}^{N} \lambda_i \phi(|X - X_i|) \tag{12}$$

Where p is a polynomial of low degree and λ_i is a combination coefficient. $p(X)$ and $\varphi(x)$ need to be customized. In general, we can let $\varphi(x) = |x|$, $p(X)$ be a polynomial of order one or $\varphi(x) = |x|3$.

According to the characteristics of scattered point cloud data, $\varphi(x) = |x|$ is selected as the interpolation basis function. The linear system can be obtained by synthesizing formula 10, 12 and 13:

$$\begin{bmatrix} \phi(|X_1 - X_1|) & \cdots & \phi(|X_1 - X_N|) & x_1 & y_1 & z_1 & 1 \\ \vdots & \vdots & \vdots & \vdots & \vdots & \vdots & \vdots \\ \phi(|X_N - X_1|) & \cdots & \phi(|X_N - X_N|) & x_N & y_N & z_N & 1 \\ x_1 & \cdots & x_N & 0 & 0 & 0 & 0 \\ y_1 & \cdots & y_N & 0 & 0 & 0 & 0 \\ z_1 & \cdots & z_N & 0 & 0 & 0 & 0 \\ 1 & \cdots & 1 & 0 & 0 & 0 & 0 \end{bmatrix} \begin{bmatrix} \lambda_1 \\ \vdots \\ \lambda_N \\ c_1 \\ c_2 \\ c_3 \\ c_4 \end{bmatrix} = \begin{bmatrix} f_1 \\ \vdots \\ f_N \\ 0 \\ 0 \\ 0 \\ 0 \end{bmatrix} \tag{14}$$

It can be abbreviated as:

$$\begin{bmatrix} A & P \\ P^T & 0 \end{bmatrix} \begin{bmatrix} \lambda \\ c \end{bmatrix} = \begin{bmatrix} f \\ 0 \end{bmatrix} \tag{15}$$

Among

$$A_{ji} = \phi(|X_j - X_i|) \tag{16}$$

$$P = \begin{bmatrix} x_1 & y_1 & z_1 & 1 \\ x_2 & y_2 & z_2 & 1 \\ \cdots\cdots\cdots\cdots \\ x_N & y_N & z_N & 1 \end{bmatrix} \tag{17}$$

$$p = c_1 x + c_2 y + c_3 z + c_4$$

In the process of matrix evaluation, in order to avoid the occurrence of trivial solutions, this paper takes a small distance along the normal direction of the point as the correlation coefficient. The combination coefficient and polynomial coefficient of the radial basis function can be obtained by solving formula 14.

3.2 Algorithm Flow

3.2.1 Hole Boundary Point Extraction

Firstly, the K-Neighborhood points of each data point in the point cloud should be calculated to extract the hole boundary, and the internal and external boundary feature points should be determined according to the distribution uniformity of these K-Neighborhood points. Then, by estimating the direction of the boundary edge, the feature points are connected to make them become boundary lines.

The algorithm consists of the following two steps:

The first step is to detect the boundary points. The precondition of hole repairing is to judge the boundary point. Many algorithms need user interaction to manually select the boundary of holes. However, the manual selection method is not suitable for the case of large number of holes in point cloud data. Therefore, this paper proposes a point cloud boundary point detection algorithm based on k-d tree. Let $p(xp, yp, zp)$ be a point in the target point cloud, $q_i (i = 1, 2, \ldots, m)$ is the point set of M sampling points. Ω is the least square surface of q_i, p' and q_i' correspond to the projection points of p and q_i on Ω, C is the unit circle of Ω centered on p' in the plane, q_i'' is the mapping point of q_i' on C. The points of q_i'' are arranged in clockwise or anticlockwise order. Each two adjacent points form an angle θ_i with point p. if the critical value of the included angle is ψ, then when θ_i is greater than ψ, point p is the boundary point,

The specific algorithm of boundary point detection is as follows:

Input: the initial set P of point cloud stored in k-d tree structure.
Output: boundary point set Q.
Step1: Select an initial point P in the k-d tree.
Step2: The point p is used to search for qi', and the corresponding least square plane Ω is obtained from qi.
Step3: Find p' and q_i'', and get the vector $vi = q_i' - p'$.
Step4: Calculate the value of θ_i at one time, that is, the angle between vi and $vi + 1$ vector.
Step5: Set a critical value ψ. If there is a value greater than ψ in θ_i then point p belongs to the boundary point, and qi is selected as the corresponding point of θ_i; If there are no boundary points in θ_i, the points in qi will be jumped out first to speed up the search. At the same time, a random point will be selected from the points close to qi.

Step6: Determine whether it is the last point in the k-d tree. If yes, the program ends; if not, enter the Step2 loop to execute the program.

The critical value ψ is usually determined by the number of m. if m points are evenly distributed on the unit circle, then the ideal angle difference $\omega = 2\pi/m$, and ψ is generally taken as 4ω (20 in this paper). The specific value should be determined according to the distribution density of point cloud and the complexity of holes, and according to the normal vector change of point cloud near the hole.

The second step is to connect the boundary points obtained in the first step into boundary lines. After the hole boundary points are detected, these boundary points need to be sorted first, and then the boundary points are connected to the boundary line in order. For a given boundary point, finding the next sequential boundary point can be divided into two cases: (1) When the distance between the surrounding boundary point and the known distance is large, the nearest point to the point is selected as the connection point; (2) when the distance between the surrounding boundary point and the point is very small, it is necessary to introduce the trend deviation for auxiliary judgment and select the next connection point. When the distance between point P and point q and p' is not much different, the direction of vector $p1p2$ and vector $p2p$ should be calculated first, and then the direction of vector pq and vector p'' should be calculated. Then, the vector point p' with smaller deflection angle should be selected as the next connection point of p. The measurement standard of this connection direction is called vector deflection angle θ. The calculation process of vector deflection angle is shown in Eq. 18:

$$\theta = ar\cos\left(\frac{\overrightarrow{p_1p_2} \cdot \overrightarrow{p_1p}}{|\overrightarrow{p_1p_2}| \cdot |\overrightarrow{p_1p}|}\right) \tag{18}$$

3.2.2 Neighborhood Selection and Point Column Parameterization

Before the surface fitting of the basis function, it is necessary to select the neighborhood of the detected hole boundary and parameterize the point column. For the points on the boundary line, the neighborhood radius points are selected according to their normal vector changes and the radius of the surface as weights, and then the points within the radius points are selected as the sample points for subsequent surface fitting. After selecting the corresponding boundary neighborhood, the incomplete surface can be fitted by the corresponding sampling points in the neighborhood.

The basic steps of neighborhood selection are as follows:

Step1: According to the principal component analysis method, the boundary line of the hole is divided into several sections, so that each section of the boundary line is basically kept in a straight line. According to the length of the boundary line as the initial radius r, the midpoint of the boundary line is selected as the standard point p_0, and the two ends of the line are taken as the comparison points p_1 and p_2.

Step2: According to the normal vector v_p of the point obtained in the first step, the angle difference between the normal vector of the standard point and the comparison point $\nabla\theta = vp0 - vp1$. If $\nabla\theta > \pi/4$, the radius r is the result and the algorithm stops;

If $\nabla\theta \leq \pi/4$, the radius will be expanded to 3/2 times of the original, and a new comparison point will be selected to start the first step of cycle, but the number of cycles will not exceed 4.

Step3: Adjust the radius r, judge on the k-d tree and search with p_0 as the starting point. Complete the search of a boundary line segment and enter the next line segment.

Step4: The sampling points collected from each segment are combined into a sample space, which is used as the initial data for surface fitting of basis function.

In order to meet the needs of surface fitting calculation and feature design of radial basis function surface, it is also necessary to parameterize the point column. The realization method is to find the maximum projection plane of the point series and project the point series onto the quadric surface to obtain the corresponding parameter values.

Basic steps of point column parameterization:

Step1: The quadric surface is fitted. The specific method is to calculate the coefficients of Eq. 19 of quadric surface according to the space point sequence of given points, so as to minimize the sum of squares of distances between quadric surfaces, i.e. Eq. 20.

$$f(x, y, z) = ax^2 + by^2 + cz^2 + 2exy + 2fyz + 2gzx + 2lx + 2my + 2nz + d = 0 \tag{19}$$

$$E = \min\left(\sum_{i=1}^{n} [f(x_i, y_i, z_i)^2]\right) = \min\sum_{i=1}^{n} e_i^2 \tag{20}$$

Step2: After solving the equation of quadric surface, it is necessary to determine the quadric surface. The specific method is to rewrite the equation in step1 into matrix form. Through rotation translation transformation, the standard equation in local coordinate system can be obtained and then judged.

Step3: Parameter value. After getting the local coordinate system, the point column Q is transformed into the local coordinate, and parameterized according to the type of quadric surface.

3.2.3 Fitting Incomplete Surface with Radial Basis Function

According to the point sequence Q obtained in the above steps, the corresponding radial basis function surface is defined as

$$\begin{cases} S(u, v) = \sum_{j=1}^{n} a_j\varphi_j(u, v) + a_0 \\ \sum_{i=1}^{n} a_j = 0 \end{cases} \tag{21}$$

And $(u, v) \in [0, 1] \times [0, 1]$.

Where $\varphi_j(u, v)$ is the radial basis function and a_j is the undetermined coefficient, a_j is the undetermined coefficient, and (U, V) is the point column parameter value obtained in the previous step, K is a submatrix composed of $K_{ij} = \varphi j(u, v)$. Because the samples involved in the calculation have been screened in the second step, the number is controlled and the solving speed is guaranteed.

The commonly used radial basis functions are MQ basis function, RMQ basis function and SOG basis function.

$$\phi_j(u, v) = 1/\sqrt{(u - u_i)^2 + (v - v_i)^2 + r^2} \tag{22}$$

Where r is a parameter and the value range is 0 to 1. After the parameters of the radial basis function are obtained, the incomplete surface of the hole can be generated. The fitted surface includes the original point cloud and also covers the range of holes.

3.2.4   Extraction and Adjustment of Filling Points

After the surface fitting, appropriate points should be selected as filling points in the corresponding hole range. First, the range of holes should be judged according to the boundary line. When selecting the filling point, it is usually selected according to a certain step size. Then, the selected point is fitted with the surrounding points, and the coordinates of the points are adjusted so that the newly generated points can be smoothed and over smooth with the surrounding points.

The method of filling is to project the polygon of the hole formed by closing the boundary line of the hole onto the feature surface to obtain the maximum and minimum u_{max}, u_{min}, v_{max}, v_{min} of the projected hole in the u, v directions. The distance between parallel lines $d = (T/3n)^{1/2}$, T is the area surrounded by the vertices of the hole polygon, and n is the number of vertices of the hole polygon.

For the adjustment of filling points, the least square plane Ω of the boundary points of the incomplete matrix needs to be calculated first, and then the filling points are projected onto the double plane. At the same time, the normal vectors of boundary points and filling points are calculated. The difference value of normal vectors is investigated. If the difference is large, the filling points are adjusted.

4   Experiment and Analysis

In this paper, strawberry point cloud model is used to verify the reduction and denoising effect of the algorithm. In this algorithm, the reduction degree can be adjusted by changing the $\Delta\alpha$ and $\Delta\beta$ of spherical coordinates. The reduction effect is shown in Fig. 6.

The hole repair model is a portrait model. Figure 7 intercepts the original scattered point cloud data of the hole repair on the nose part of the model. The left side is the original point cloud, and the right side is the repaired point cloud. The filling points after hole repair can be clearly reflected in the figure.

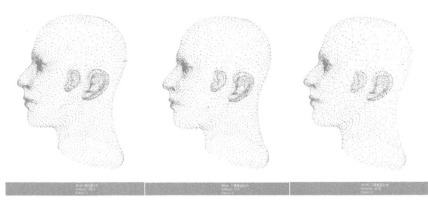

Fig. 6. Model simplification effect

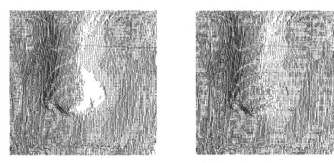

Fig. 7. Comparison of the nose part of the portrait model before and after the hole repair

5   Summary

Scattered point cloud processing is an important work in reverse engineering. The current simplification and denoising algorithms are usually complex to pursue the accuracy. The traditional point cloud repair needs triangulation, which will waste a lot of time on the establishment of triangular mesh. In this paper, a fast denoising and simplification algorithm for scattered point cloud is proposed based on spherical coordinate system. An improved radial machine hole repair algorithm is designed to repair the defects in scattered point cloud. In this paper, the algorithm has low computational complexity and high speed, which can be used in the machining occasions with low hardware configuration and low precision requirements.

References

1. Chmelar, P., Rejfek, L., Tan, N., Ha, D.-H.: Advanced methods for point cloud processing and simplification. Appl. Sci. **10**(10) (2020)
2. Zhang, K., Qiao, S., Wang, X., Yang, Y., Zhang, Y.: Feature-preserved point cloud simplification based on natural quadric shape models. Appl. Sci. **9**(10) (2019)

3. Zhu, Z., Gan, S., Wang, J., Qian, N.: Novel airborne 3D laser point cloud hole repair algorithm considering topographic features. J. Geodesy Geoinf. Sci. **3**(03), 29–38 (2020)
4. Liu, Y., Wang, M., Zhang, H., Li, C., Liu, Y.: Strategy of classification and repairing for hole of incomplete point clouds based on fuzzy inference. J. Comput. Theor. Nanosci. **13**(11) (2016)

Survey on Computation Offloading Schemes in Resource-Constrained Mobile Edge Computing

Huiting Sun$^{(\boxtimes)}$, Yanfang Fan, Shuang Yuan, and Ying Cai

School of Computer, Beijing Information Science and Technology University, Beijing, China
sunhuiting@bistu.edu.cn

Abstract. Mobile edge computing (MEC) is a new paradigm that has recently received a lot of attention. It extends computing power to the network edge, where tasks are not transmitted over long distances, thus reducing the risk of sensitive information leakage and theft. By offloading tasks to MEC servers, user equipments (UEs) can not only address its own lack of computing resources, but also reduce time and energy consumption. However, compared to the increasing computing requirements of UEs, the limited resources and heavy burden of MEC servers are becoming more and more obvious. Therefore, it will be a great challenge to design a proper computation offloading scheme to meet the requirements of UEs in resource-constrained MEC. In this paper, we analyze main computation offloading schemes. We divide computation offloading scenarios into two types. One is a single-server scenario, the other is a collaborative scenario with cloud, edge server, vehicle, etc. Challenges and conclusions have also been suggested in this paper.

Keywords: Computation offloading · Mobile edge computing · Collaborative computing

1 Introduction

In recent years, with the popularization of user equipments (UEs) such as smart phones, laptops, smart vehicles, many new computation-intensive and time-sensitive applications have emerged, such as image recognition [1], augmented reality [2], and autonomous driving [3]. However, the computing power and battery energy of UEs are constrained and often difficult to meet the computation requirements of applications. The traditional solution is to offload these tasks to the cloud center, however, this will increase the risk of leaking user privacy data [4]. And the long-distance transmission between UEs and cloud center may cause high delay, which is detrimental to the user's experience. In addition, some applications that require high bandwidth can cause network congestion [5]. To meet the above challenges, the concept of Mobile Edge Computing (MEC) is proposed [6].

MEC enables the cloud center to provide computation, communication, and storage capabilities closer to UEs by moving it down to the wireless network edge [7]. It provides

© Springer Nature Singapore Pte Ltd. 2021
Y. Tian et al. (Eds.): ICBDS 2020, CCIS 1415, pp. 433–444, 2021.
https://doi.org/10.1007/978-981-16-3150-4_36

better structured support for data security and privacy protection [10]. Meanwhile, completing computation offloading within the wireless access network not only significantly reduces network delay, but also saves bandwidth to the core network and reduces the risk of network congestion. However, MEC servers' resources are limited, especially in workload-intensive networks, and the mismatch between computing resources and computing requirements is even more obvious [8]. Therefore, it is unreasonable to blindly offload all tasks to one MEC server. For users, additional costs may be generated, such as energy consumption for data transmission and time consumption for remote execution; for MEC servers, it can be a waste of resources and an additional burden. Therefore, it is necessary to control the offloading tasks of UEs to make efficient use of limited resources. In addition, cloud servers, edge servers and UEs can be joined to enhance the computing power of MEC servers. In this paper, we summarize and analyze computation offloading schemes from the perspective of limited MEC server's resources. We hope that this research can stimulate more discussions and provide useful references for further research.

The rest of this paper is organized as follows. First, we introduce the related concepts in Sect. 2. Second, we analyze, classify and summarize existing works in Sect. 3. Finally, open challenges and conclusion are discussed in Sect. 4 and Sects. 5.

2 Introduction to Computation Offloading in MEC

2.1 Computation Offloading Concept and Process

Computation offloading means that UEs transmit computing tasks to computing nodes for saving energy or reducing time consumption [9]. The process can be divided into the following five steps:

1) Node discovery: UEs discover available computing nodes for subsequent offloading tasks.
2) Task partitioning: UEs divide a task into offloading and non-offloading parts, and the offloading parts can be further divided into more fine-grained parts, i.e., partitioning needs to consider the execution order and dependencies between subtasks.
3) Task upload: UEs send tasks to computing nodes.
4) Task execution: Computing nodes execute tasks for UEs.
5) Result return: Computing nodes return results to UEs.

The process of computation offloading is influenced by different factors [11], such as user habits, radio channel communication, quality of the backhaul connection, performance of the UEs and server availability. Therefore, the key to computation offloading is to specify the appropriate offloading policy.

2.2 Computation Offloading Policy

A key part of computation offloading is computation offloading policy, i.e., deciding whether to offload each task or not and how to allocate resources [12]. There are 3 types:

1) Full local process: The whole tasks are processed by UEs locally. It means no tasks are offloaded to severs, for example, due to unavailability of the MEC computing resources or if the offloading simply does not pay off [13].
2) Full offloading: The whole tasks are offloaded and processed by computing nodes. It is suitable for tasks with high integrity requirements or relatively simple tasks [13].
3) Partial offloading: One part of the task is processed locally and the other part is offloaded to computing nodes. It is suitable for data partitioning models where tasks are bit-by-bit independent and can be arbitrarily divided into groups that are executed by different entities in MEC [13]. Also, there may be dependent relationships between different subtasks, for example, the output of subtask A and B is the input of subtask C.

2.3 Computation Offloading Goals

Computation offloading is usually measured in terms of time, energy or cost consumption [14]. Its goals can be divided into 3 types:

1) Minimizing offloading delay: The delay generated by task offloading directly affects the quality of service of UEs, so the goal of minimizing offloading delay is an important direction for its optimization [15]. If the task is executed directly locally, then the delay is the time consumed to execute the task; if the task is offloaded, then the delay mainly consists of transmission time, execution time and waiting time.
2) Minimizing energy consumption: If the energy consumption is too high, it will lead to the rapid battery exhaustion of UEs, so the selection of a suitable energy optimization model with the goal of reducing energy consumption of UEs is also a major optimization direction [15]. If the task is executed directly locally, the energy consumption is the energy consumed to execute the task; if the task is offloaded, the energy consumption is mainly transmission energy.
3) Minimizing cost or maximizing profit: Computing nodes and UEs are different participants, so a charging mechanism can be designed to encourage computing nodes to serve UEs, i.e., there is a trade-off between the cost paid by UEs and the profit obtained by computing nodes. If the task is executed locally, then there is no offloading cost; if the task is offloaded, the offloading goal can be to minimize UEs' cost or maximize computing nodes' profit [16].

3   MEC Computation Offloading Schemes

Some literatures have addressed the problem of limited computing resources in MEC. According to whether new computing resources are introduced or not, the offloading schemes can be divided into 2 types [17]:

1) Single-server computing scenario, which uses rational resource allocation to fully utilize limited resources.
2) Collaborative computing scenario, which introduces new computing nodes to extend the computing resources of MEC servers.

Minimizing Cost or Maximizing Profit. Yuan et al. considered the CPU, memory, and bandwidth resource constraints of the edge computing layer, as well as the maximum energy, maximum number of available servers, and task queue stability of cloud servers [36]. They proposed a profit-maximizing collaborative computation offloading algorithm to optimize offloading between cloud and edge computing layer, as well as resource allocation for time-sensitive tasks at the edge computing layer. Ma et al. studied the resource provisioning problem by studying fault-tolerant and time-sensitive dynamic requests [37]. To minimize system cost when dealing with highly fluctuating requests or time-sensitive dominant requests, all delay-tolerant requests can be offloaded directly to remote clouds.

Edge Server Collaboration. Due to the randomness of task arrival, the computing tasks of different MEC servers are unevenly distributed in time and space. In this case, one server may have many tasks but insufficient computing resources, while the other server may be the opposite. Thus, tasks can be completed through collaborative computing among edge servers. We will analyze the current offloading schemes from the perspective of optimization goals.

Minimizing Offloading Delay. The authors in [38] proposed a framework to divide a task into subtasks and offload them to multiple MEC servers by taking both delay and reliability into account. They designed three algorithms based on heuristic search, reformulation linearization technique and semi-definite relaxation, respectively. Simulation results showed that among the three algorithms, the heuristic algorithm can achieve the best performance. Zhu et al. considered the interdependence of tasks [39]. They used three-dimensional decisions (matrices) to represent the order of offloading, and the problem was solved by an optimization solver, i.e., Gurobi. Simulation results showed that the proposed scheme can effectively reduce delay.

Minimizing Energy Consumption. In [40], the authors proposed a joint computing and communication collaboration method, which can enable neighboring MEC servers to share computing and communication resources, i.e., a server with insufficient computing resources can offload some tasks to a neighboring server with sufficient computing resources to make use of its idle CPU power, and in return, it can share some communication resources to relieve another server's communication load. Simulation results showed that the proposed algorithm based on convex optimization can significantly reduce energy consumption.

Trade-Off Between Energy Consumption and Offloading Delay. Fan et al. proposed a collaboration scheme based on the interior point algorithm to offload extra tasks of the MEC server to other MEC servers connected to it [41]. Simulation results showed that the proposed scheme can effectively reduce time and energy consumption.

Minimizing Cost or Maximizing Profit. Yang et al. proposed a location-based offloading scheme that offloaded computing tasks to the MEC server closest to UEs according to moving direction, and then the edge server decided whether to offload part tasks to the neighboring server to reduce pressure [42]. Simulation results showed that the proposed algorithm based on convex optimization algorithm can effectively reduce system cost.

UEs Collaboration. With the rapid development of social economy and the process of industrialization, UEs will be equipped with more powerful computers, larger capacity data storage units and more advanced communication modules. There are several literatures seeking task collaboration among peer devices by utilizing the rich computing resources distributed on UEs. It can also dramatically improve computation offloading performance. We will analyze the current offloading schemes from the perspective of optimization goals.

Minimizing Offloading Delay. Zhang et al. studied the impact of high mobility of vehicles and the ad hoc nature of networking on computation offloading [43]. They proposed a matching-based algorithm to select the appropriate collaborative vehicle or MEC server. Simulation results showed that this scheme can effectively reduce delay. Qiao et al. studied task offloading for immersive applications that would have considerable similar or identical computation-intensive tasks on vehicles driving in adjacent areas [44]. They proposed to offload such tasks to mobile vehicular cloud of adjacent area vehicles to remove redundant tasks in advance in a collaborative manner. Simulation results showed that the proposed scheme can reduce perception reaction time while ensuring the application-level driving experiences. Xie et al. used game theory to select appropriate vehicles to form a vehicle coalition [45]. They proposed to use Q-learning algorithm to determine the offloading decision, if the edge server has greater time and energy consumption, the task will be offloaded to the vehicle coalition, otherwise offloaded to the edge server. Simulation results showed that the proposed scheme can achieve better performance with average processing delay. Hong et al. designed a D2D-assisted offloading algorithm based on a Time Division Multiple Access (TDMA) system [46]. They proposed a benchmark scheme with fixed computation frequency and a greedy task assignment based heuristic algorithm to reduce delay.

Minimizing Energy Consumption. In [47], the authors studied the allocation of joint radio and computing resources for D2D-assisted MEC system in two phases. In the first phase, a low-complexity algorithm was developed to maximize the number of executed tasks; In the second phase, a complementary algorithm was proposed to minimize the total energy consumption while maintaining the maximum number of executed tasks. Simulation results showed that in dense users' scenarios, D2D-assisted MEC system had higher task execution rates and significantly lower energy consumption per executed task than traditional MEC system.

Trade-Off Between Energy Consumption and Offloading Delay. Diao et al. studied the MEC system based on D2D assisted and non-orthogonal multiple access (NOMA) [48]. They proposed an adaptive computing resource allocation algorithm, a power allocation algorithm based on the particle swarm optimization, and a matching channel allocation algorithm based on the pareto improvement and swapping operations. Simulation results showed that the proposed solution can effectively reduce the weighted sum of the time and energy consumption of all users. Seng et al. propose a blockchain-based decentralized computation offloading orchestration platform, which searched for available edge servers and D2D devices by paying computing and radio resources [49]. They developed a modified GS-based user matching algorithm to find the matching relationship between users and service providers. Simulation results showed that the algorithm provided significant improvements in both time and energy consumption.

Minimizing Cost or Maximizing Profit. In [50], edge servers and collaborative vehicles were managed by a VEC operator which can purchase physical resources (e.g., spectrum and backhaul) from realistic entities to provide payable services for users. They proposed Q-learning based DRL method to find computing nodes that maximize system profit. Simulation results showed that the proposed scheme can achieve better performance than that of the pure edge server or collaborative vehicle methods. The collaborative vehicles studied by Huang et al. were parked vehicles with available computing capability [51]. They used Stackelberg strategy method to solve the resource allocation problem. Simulation results showed that the proposed scheme can increase network capacity and reduce user cost.

3.3 Summary

According to the analyses and conclusions of the existing work, we can know that the problem of limited resources of MEC servers can mainly be solved by optimizing resource allocation and introducing collaboration computing nodes. Note that these two approaches are not completely separate. When faced with different computing tasks with different granularities and QoS requirements, it is obviously not enough to rely only on lightweight edge servers, and resource allocation also need to be considered in collaboration scenarios.

4 Open Challenges

Computation offloading is still an immature technology and there are many challenges in the practical implementation of MEC. In this section, we identify and discuss some key open research challenges as follows:

1) Mobility management: The high mobility of UEs leads to frequent handovers among the small-coverage edge servers, which is highly complicated and unreliable. Strict mobility management solutions are required to allow users to seamlessly access edge servers to ensure service continuity [11].
2) Security: Edge computing faces more complex network environments due to its distributed deployment, and security solutions for cloud computing may not be suitable for edge computing [52]. In addition to identity authentication and privacy protection, the interaction between heterogeneous edge nodes and the migration of services across edge nodes may also pose challenges to their security and privacy.
3) Task dependency: Some tasks can be partitioned into subtasks, and dependencies among these subtasks need to be considered simultaneously, such as line, tree, and mesh. However, most of the existing literatures only assume the dependencies between the subtasks and cannot reflect the real relationships among actual tasks. In addition, the existing algorithms for processing dependent task offloading are very complex, and it is still necessary to design a feasible low-complexity algorithm.

4) Interference management: If many UEs' tasks are offloaded to the MEC server at the same time, serious interference problems will occur. The essence of interference is the conflicting use of resources, and the unsatisfactory allocation of network resources is the root cause of interference [15]. Therefore, how to make a reasonable resource allocation based on the MEC network environment and the UEs' offloading request is one of the ways to solve the interference problem.

5) Incentive mechanism: UEs that provide services may be potentially malicious or selfish [53], a reasonably standardized incentive mechanism needs to be designed to increase UEs' willingness to participate.

5 Conclusion

In MEC, servers are deployed at the edge of the mobile network to support UEs with constrained hardware resources to perform computation-intensive and time-sensitive computing tasks, thus energy and time consumption can be reduced. However, the limited computing resources of MEC servers are a great challenge for the increasing computing demands of UEs. We first introduce computation offloading from different aspects, including concept, policy and goals. Next, classifying the existing work according to whether to introduce new computing nodes or not. Finally, we further explore the existing challenges. We hope it will inspire researchers working on edge computing.

Acknowledgement. This work was supported by the National Natural Science Foundation of China (No. 61672106), the Natural Science Foundation of Beijing (No. L192023), Foundation of Beijing Information Science and Technology University (2025028) and Graduate Science and Technology Innovation Project of Beijing Information Science and Technology University.

References

1. Soyata, T., Muraleedharan, R., Funai, C.: Cloud-vision: real-time face recognition using a mobile-cloudlet-cloud acceleration architecture. In: Proceedings of Computers & Communications, pp. 59–66. IEEE (2012)

2. Chen, Z., Klatzky, R., Siewiorek, D.: An empirical study of latency in an emerging class of edge computing applications for wearable cognitive assistance. In: Proceedings of the Second ACM/IEEE Symposium ACM, pp. 1–14 (2017)

3. Tian, D., Zhou, J., Sheng, Z.: Self-organized relay selection for cooperative transmission in vehicular ad-hoc networks. IEEE Trans. Veh. Technol. 66(10), 9534–9549 (2017)

4. Dinh, H.T., Lee, C., Niyato, D.: A survey of mobile cloud computing: architecture, applications, and approaches. Wirel. Commun. Mob. Comput. 13(18), 1587–1611 (2013)

5. Pan, J., McElhannon, J.: Future edge cloud and edge computing for internet of things applications. IEEE Internet Things J. 5(1), 439–449 (2018)

6. Hu, Y., Patel, M., Sabella, D.: Mobile edge computing—a key technology towards 5G. ETSI White Paper, vol. 11, no. 11, pp. 1–16 (2015)

7. Taleb, T., Samdanis, K., Mada, B.: On multi-access edge computing: a survey of the emerging 5G network edge cloud architecture and orchestration. IEEE Commun. Surv. Tutor. 19(3), 1657–1681 (2017)

51. Huang, X., Yu, R., Liu, J.: Parked vehicle edge computing: exploiting opportunistic resources for distributed mobile applications. IEEE Access **6**, 66649–66663 (2018)
52. Stojmenovic, I., Wen, S.: The fog computing paradigm: scenarios and security issues. In: 2014 Federated Conference on Computer Science and Information Systems, Warsaw, Warsaw, Poland, pp. 1–8 (2014)
53. Chen, X., Jiao, L., Li, W.: Efficient multi-user computation offloading for mobile-edge cloud computing. IEEE/ACM Trans. Netw. **24**(5), 2795–2808 (2016)

Blockchain and Internet of Things

Discussion on the Influence of 5G and Blockchain Technology on Digital Virtual Assets

YaNan Li, Hui Pang(✉), Zhixin Liu, and ShiJie Li

Hebei University of Architecture, Zhangjiakou 075000, Hebei, China

Abstract. In recent years, digital virtual assets such as virtual currency, digital copyright, equipment and game currency in electronic games have been inseparable from people's lives. However, for the protection of digital virtual assets, relevant research at home and abroad is in the preliminary stage of exploration. Digital copyright confirmation, secure transactions and traceability of digital virtual assets are also facing severe challenges. 5G network has the characteristics of high speed, ubiquitous network, low power consumption, and low latency. It aims to realize the interconnection of everything. Blockchain technology has the characteristics of decentralization, non-tampering, de-trust, and openness, and aims to realize mutual trust of everything. Blockchain can assist 5G network to ensure data security, privacy, and trust. 5G network can also make up for the deficiencies of blockchain technology. Cross fusion of 5G network and blockchain technology can optimize business models and improve network information security. This paper discusses the influence of 5G network and blockchain technology on digital virtual assets in depth.

Keywords: Digital virtual assets · 5G · Blockchain · Cross fusion

1 Introduction

Digital virtual assets refer to digital and non-materialized network assets, including virtual currency [1, 2], digital copyright [3, 4], and equipment and game currency in online games [5]. These virtual assets can be converted into real assets [6, 7] under certain conditions. At present, a variety of virtual assets are defined as citizens' legal property by law [8, 9]. However, digital virtual assets, with the characteristics of virtualization, networking and openness, are easy to be attacked, so they are particularly difficult to protect.

As the latest mobile communication network, 5G network has the following characteristics. (1) High speed. Compared with the widely used 4G network, 5G network can reach 10 GB/s at the fastest, which is several hundred times of 4G network, so the transmission rate has been greatly improved. People's sense of experience will also be greatly improved with the increase of transmission rate. For some new applications, such

Y. Tian et al. (Eds.): ICBDS 2020, CCIS 1415, pp. 447–457, 2021.
https://doi.org/10.1007/978-981-16-3150-4_37

as AR/VR, Internet of Vehicles, etc., it is not restricted. (2) Ubiquitous network. As the name implies, the ubiquitous network requires a wide range of networks, because only by realizing the comprehensive coverage of the network can it be possible to mine and realize richer services. Ubiquitous networks mainly include deep coverage and extensive coverage. For example, the network of each room in the house is different. The network in the bathroom may be a little bit worse, and some elevators and underground garages are not connected to the Internet. The advent of 5G can cover all the bad parts of the network. Extensive coverage refers to the need for extensive coverage in all parts of society, such as places with few people, mountains or grasslands, where network coverage is rarely carried out. If full coverage is carried out later, it will be useful for monitoring air quality, environment, and earthquakes. Mudslides and so on. (3) Low power consumption. 5G networks are designed to realize the interconnection of everything and have high requirements for power consumption. If 5G can reduce power consumption, it will be of great value for promoting the popularization of Internet of Things (IoT) applications. (4) Low latency. The normal communication between people can accept a delay of 140 ms, but for some 5G application scenarios, such as unmanned driving, industrial automation, etc., this delay is far from adequate. The lowest latency of 5G can reach 1 ms, or even lower. (5) Internet of Everything. At present, the devices that need to use the network are not limited to mobile phones and computers. There are also various devices that can be worn, shared cars, and smart home appliances. If networked, these devices can be managed uniformly and in real time.

On November 1, 2008, Satoshi Nakamoto published the paper *Bitcoin: A Peer-to-Peer Electronic Cash System* [10], and blockchain technology was born. Since blockchain technology has its own security properties, it can be applied to many industry problems, but there are also technical shortcomings. The emergence of 5G can just make up for these shortcomings. Blockchain technology can also provide a lot of support for 5G network in terms of ensuring data privacy, trust, and security. Therefore, 5G network and blockchain technology can be cross-integrated and mutually empowered.

The 5G+ blockchain model makes a great contribution to the security management of digital virtual assets, and can realize the security and control of the platform. The security of digital virtual assets includes identity authentication, registration, and secure storage. It is necessary to trace the source of digital virtual assets and establish a secure transaction mechanism for digital virtual assets.

2   Blockchain Technology

In July 2016, Gartner released the 2016 emerging technology maturity curve, as shown in Fig. 1. Blockchain technology is considered to be a bright new star, and it is now in a period of expansion. It is expected that it will fully land in the next 5–10 years and become the mainstream technology of society.

Fig. 1. 2016 emerging technology maturity curve

2.1 The Concept of Blockchain Technology

In essence, blockchain technology is a database, only decentralized and able to record previous transactions. It uses programming technology to realize all valuable information to itself, such as marriage certificate, ownership and birth certificate, etc. Of course, this information needs to be represented by code. The blockchain is divided into many blocks, and each block is actually a ledger. From the perspective of logical value, blockchain technology coincides with the thinking of the ancients. In ancient China, due to the low level of productivity, it was necessary to rely on neighbors to trust each other, exchange goods and consume on the spot, which was very similar to the core of blockchain technology. Therefore, blockchain technology is not so much to establish a new trust model, as it is to complete the previous mutual trust.

2.2 Characteristics of Blockchain Technology

As shown in Fig. 2, blockchain technology mainly includes the following four characteristics.

Decentralization. The Internet, which is familiar to the public, is centralized, but in this case, if the central node is attacked, the entire system will be severely damaged. Since the hidden dangers of centralization are relatively large, the researchers changed their minds and used decentralization to solve the problem, so blockchain technology appeared. Blockchain technology is different from the past. Using distributed recording, storage and peer-to-peer communication, it distributes permissions equally to each node on the chain and maintains a shared platform in a decentralized manner. In this mode, if someone attacks the platform or wants to manipulate the platform maliciously, it is impossible to happen. No matter which node is attacked, the operation of the whole system will not be affected.

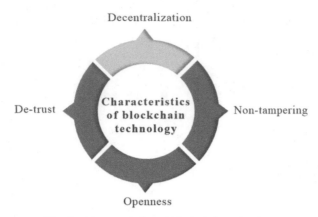

Fig. 2. Characteristics of blockchain technology

De-trust. In the well-known Internet, all transactions must first be trusted, or must be guaranteed by a reliable and credible third party. However, blockchain technology introduces a consensus algorithm, and the transaction rules of the entire system are open and transparent. Any transactions between nodes must be conducted in accordance with the rules of the consensus algorithm, and both parties must also conduct transactions within the specified time and scope. In this way, a certain node cannot deceive another node, so both parties to the transaction do not need any trust, nor need a third party to intervene.

Non-tampering. Blockchain technology uses a hash algorithm. For original data such as text, pictures, music, video, etc., it can be corresponded to specific numbers to form a hash value. If any of these nodes are tampered with, the hash value changes so that it can be easily identified. Therefore, as long as the original data is verified and then added to the blockchain for storage, tampering with one node has no impact on the whole system. There is another possibility that someone has manipulated more than 51% of the nodes, which will affect the entire system, but if a lot of human and financial resources are spent to attack more than 51% of the nodes, the benefits that can be brought are far less than the cost already spent. So the attacker will not do such a thankless thing. It can be seen that the security and stability of blockchain technology are particularly high.

Openness. Openness mainly includes the following three points. (1) The openness of accounts. The distributed accounting method has resulted in every historical record being made public, and everyone can verify the relevant historical records. (2) The openness of the organizational structure: In the blockchain system, the economic logic at the bottom of the company is open, which can also be called an open source economy. (3) Ecological openness: The bottom layer includes open accounts and an open organizational structure, and building an open ecology is the ultimate goal of the blockchain, which can make the efficiency of value transfer higher and higher and the cost lower and lower.

2.3   Smart Contract Based on Blockchain Technology

A smart contract is triggered by a Bitcoin transaction on the blockchain. It is a set of codes stored on the blockchain. This set of codes can read and write data in the blockchain [11], and can automatically execute what has been written for the contract content Good procedure. Networked digital virtual assets are the primary condition for the execution of smart contracts. The smart contract does not require third party intervention. When the conditions in the computer language are met, the program will automatically execute and produce results. The most common vending machine in life is based on smart contracts. Merchants sell goods through vending machines. Buyers select the goods to be purchased and put in the corresponding currency to trigger the built-in program of the vending machine and provide corresponding goods. If the buyer's currency does not match the product information or if the buyer inputs counterfeit currency, the vending machine will automatically refuse to provide the product.

3   Cross Fusion of 5G Network and Blockchain Technology

Blockchain technology and 5G network have obvious advantages, but there are also shortcomings. Combining the two can greatly promote digital virtual assets.

3.1   The Role of Blockchain Technology in Promoting 5G Network

The 5G network has high speed, low latency, and wide coverage, but data security, lack of trust in virtual asset transactions, and privacy protection are problems that must be solved by 5G network, and blockchain technology can just solve these problems.

Blockchain Technology Can Ensure Data Security and Privacy Protection in 5G Network Application Scenarios. The high-speed characteristics and massive connections of 5G network determine that computing and storage will be undertaken by edge computing nodes and smart terminals, which have higher requirements for data security and privacy protection capabilities. Blockchain technology has the characteristics of decentralization, non-tampering and de-trust, so it is naturally suitable for data security and privacy protection. Blockchain technology is a representative technology of cryptography application. It can reconstruct the security boundary of the network, establish a trust domain between various network devices, and enable each network device to achieve mutual trust, interconnection, and security. In addition, with the decentralized feature, there is no need to worry about the phenomenon of central equipment being attacked or tampered with, and there will be no theft of information by the administrator of the central database.

Blockchain Technology Can Help 5G Network to Carry Out Network Construction Faster. In network construction, first of all, the utilization of spectrum resources can be improved. Secondly, intelligent contract can automatically execute the protocol and rules between points, which can make network resources available in real time. Users can also cash in their idle traffic through smart contract technology, which can promote 5G development.

Mobile edge computing is based on the advancement of 5G network, which can aggregate various idle resources through blockchain technology to build a powerful resource pool. The resources distributed on each node can also be optimally deployed, which can improve efficiency, save costs. Blockchain technology is traceable to transaction records and cannot be tampered with, so as to ensure the fairness and justice of transactions, so that users can actively participate, and the application scenarios of mobile edge computing will also be widely deployed.

Blockchain Technology Can Help 5G Network Realize Point-to-Point Value Exchange. Application scenarios such as unmanned driving and smart cities are the key deployment targets in the 5G network operation process. Adding blockchain technology to these application scenarios does not need to be certified by a central organization, and each node directly performs identity authentication and distribution on the chain. In this way, point-to-point value circulation can be realized, the transaction efficiency of terminal equipment has been greatly improved, and transaction costs can be reduced.

3.2 The Role of 5G Network in Promoting Blockchain Technology

Blockchain technology itself is built on the network infrastructure, but after so many years of development, it has not been popularized or implemented. In the final analysis, the front-end technology like 5G network is not mature.

5G Network Can Improve the Transaction Rate and Network Stability of Blockchain Technology. As we all know, the transmission rate of the 5G network is much higher than 4G, and the data transmission rate is as high as 10 GB per second, which can make the transaction of blockchain technology faster. The 5G network delay is also lower. The delay refers to the time interval between data transmission and reception. Of course, the delay is lower and it is more capable of real-time communication. Blockchain is a distributed point-to-point communication, which results in changes on any node and real-time updates on other nodes, so real-time synchronization of data is very important for blockchain. In addition, the high rate of the 5G network can just meet the huge IoT transmission needs, and the low latency can also improve the computational efficiency of the consensus algorithm. The 5G network can also increase nodes, so that the blocking time of the blockchain will be shorter, and the scalability of blockchain technology will also be promoted.

5G Network Can Provide More Data on the Chain for Blockchain Technology. The 5G network aims to realize the interconnection of everything, and there will be more data on the chain. Relying on the high-speed transmission of 5G, blockchain technology can provide more stable services for the traceability of commodities and distributed point-to-point transactions.

4   Digital Virtual Assets

4.1   The Development of Digital Virtual Asset Protection

In 1998, the United States took the lead in the world in promulgating the Digital Millennium Copyright Act (DMCA) [12, 13], which made detailed provisions on the protection of digital copyright. In 2014, the US State of California legislated digital virtual currency as legal currency in California, and the US Internal Revenue Service also announced the legalization of encrypted digital assets in the same year [14]. In February 2015, the European Central Bank released the *Virtual Currency System*, which showed that it had confirmed the legitimate use of virtual currency [15].

According to a 2015 iResearch report [16], the loss of online literature piracy in China's publishing industry was as high as 10 billion yuan, while the loss of digital media such as digital images, music and video has reached an inestimable level. In 2016, large virtual currency transactions [17] such as Silk Road, MT.Gox and Bitstamp were all attacked by malicious attacks, resulting in hundreds of millions of dollars of bitcoins being stolen by hackers. Similar incidents emerge one after another, which has dealt a severe blow to digital virtual assets.

In recent years, the research on the protection of digital virtual assets has drawn close attention from the international academic frontier [18–20]. The protection of digital virtual assets first attracted the attention of the United States in 2013, and the United States raised it to the level of national strategy. In 2018, Ziegeldorf team of RWTH Aachen University in Germany proposed a new bitcoin efficient decentralized hybrid algorithm [21], which combines the anonymity and non-deniability of threshold cryptography to greatly improve the ability to resist malicious attacks.

During China's "Twelfth Five-Year Plan" period, the development of digital virtual assets is relatively rapid, which have become an important wealth of society. In 2015, the "13th Five-Year Financial Plan" was released to showcase the research results of digital currency. In general, there is no systematic research on the protection of digital virtual assets in the world, and it is still in the preliminary stage of exploration.

4.2   Characteristics of Digital Virtual Assets

Virtuality. Unlike traditional assets, digital virtual assets are invisible and intangible. In reality, users only have the right to use them, and ownership does not belong to individuals.

Limited Space. The value of digital virtual assets is limited to the virtual architecture built by operators. If you change a server or change an environment, these digital virtual assets have no value.

Limited Time. If the operator shuts down, the server is attacked, or the player voluntarily gives up, the digital virtual assets owned by the player will also lose value.

Limited Number. The number of digital virtual assets in online games is not unlimited. Pets, characters, props, etc. are all programs written by game developers, and they are all limited in number.

Transactional. After the two parties of the transaction reach an agreement, the operator can change the relevant parameters of the game account, and the digital virtual assets can be traded, transferred, and given away.

Quantifiable. Digital virtual assets have standards provided by operators, and many offline transactions have their own standards. Many private websites provide exchange rates between virtual currencies and real currencies.

5   The Effect of 5G+ Blockchain on Digital Virtual Assets

5.1   5G+ Blockchain Endows Digital Virtual Assets with New Features

As shown in Fig. 3, it is new features of digital virtual assets endowed by 5G+ blockchain technology.

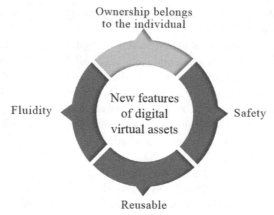

Fig. 3. New features of digital virtual assets endowed by 5G+ blockchain technology

Ownership Belongs to the Individual. Take electronic games as an example. In the past, the characters, skins, and props purchased by players in the game were all called virtual items, but in electronic games based on blockchain technology, players called them digital virtual assets. The difference between the two lies in the ownership. In traditional games, although these skins, props, etc., are bound to the player's account, these data are stored on the game manufacturer's server. If someone read the terms of use of the game carefully, he will find that game players only have the right to use these virtual items, not ownership, and ownership still belongs to the game manufacturer. If one day the game manufacturer announces that the game will be removed from the shelves, the player's virtual items cannot be returned. However, in electronic games based on blockchain technology, the ownership belongs to the player. Even if the game is removed, it will not affect the items owned by the player. These data will always be stored on the blockchain, and the 5G network will ensure that the huge data are all on the chain.

Fluidity. Traditional games have relatively closed environments, and player transactions can only be done inside the game. There are also many game developers who do not allow players to trade in order to avoid the chaos caused by player transactions and the cost of their own operations. But players can also trade by buying and selling game accounts. Based on the peer-to-peer transaction of blockchain technology, players can also conduct transactions outside the game, just as simple as our usual mobile phone transfers, transferring virtual assets from one blockchain address to another. And as long as the players reach a consensus, transactions can also be conducted between different games. The high-speed characteristics of 5G networks can also ensure fast and accurate virtual asset transactions.

In traditional games, if the player wants to abandon the game, all the virtual assets in the game must be discarded. However, in the blockchain-based electronic game, the player can sell the digital virtual assets to other players before giving up. This will not cause a lot of losses, even some limited assets, players can also receive more benefits. However, this also affects the profitability of game manufacturers in a certain sense. But in this mode, game manufacturers can also earn a lot of income by charging transaction fees.

Safety. Compared with distributed servers, hackers are more willing to attack centralized servers, so traditional digital virtual assets cannot be fully secured. In addition, some accounts, virtual equipment purchased at a high price, and rare items obtained through hard work are often hacked and resold to other players, so the scarcity of digital virtual assets will also decrease.

It can be seen from Bitcoin that blockchain technology can ensure the safe transactions and safe storage of digital virtual assets. In the distributed ledger of blockchain technology, each node will have a "ledger" of digital virtual assets, which records every transaction and ownership of digital virtual assets. If hackers want to maliciously tamper with the data, they must attack 51% at the same time. In theory, the network node cannot be completed. Even if it can be completed, the cost will be far greater than the benefits that can be obtained, and the gain will not be worth the loss.

Reusable. After the digital virtual assets are fully chained using the 5G network, because the data is linked to each user's blockchain address, the developer can obtain the player's data and use it for secondary use. Such a game can easily produce a derivative game, thereby generating a game ecology. Players' equipment can be used in different games, and different games can also be traded, so that players have different games Experience.

5.2 Application of 5G+ Blockchain in Confirmation of Digital Copyright

Starting from the date of completion of the work, digital copyright automatically belongs to the completion of the work, without the need for certification by other institutions. But authors can use their real name, pseudonym, or anonymity in digital copyright. In the process of dissemination of the work, if a third party wants to obtain the digital copyright authorization from the anonymous author, it will be difficult to find the author, and the third party may give up using the digital copyright, or it may directly infringe the copyright without the author's permission. Although the country has established a corresponding registration system, individuals and small businesses may not be able to bear the registration fee of up to thousands of dollars, and the need to register the true information of the copyright owner hinders the registration of anonymous authors.

5G and blockchain technology can start from the author's creation, stamp the updated data at each stage, and form a blockchain in the order of time to ensure the integrity and non-tampering of the data. Often the author is the first person to access the file. Stamping can confirm the author's identity, and the identity corresponds to a specific network ip and public key. Third parties who want to be authorized can contact the file through the network ip and public key. This can also hide the true identity of anonymous authors. In addition, the cost of each registration is minimal, as low as 0.4 yuan, which can be completed in an instant and is more acceptable to the author.

5.3 Application of 5G+ Blockchain Technology in the Secure Transaction of Digital Virtual Assets

Digital virtual assets can take advantage of the non-tamperable feature of blockchain technology to generate a confirmation certificate for each transaction. Before the buyer and seller make a transaction, firstly confirm whether the digital virtual assets issued by the seller are legal and the ownership belongs to the seller, and each node of the blockchain needs to synchronize the right certificate. If it is found that the seller is not authorized and it is a malicious pirate, it will be detected that it does not match the confirmation certificate, so the buyer can seek legal protection for protection. In this model, sellers do not have to worry about theft of digital virtual assets, and buyers can also find genuine virtual assets.

Digital virtual assets can be combined with adaptive digital watermarking algorithms to add digital watermarks to every asset. If you want to trace the source of the data of digital virtual assets, you only need to extract the digital watermark. Based on the classifier model, it is possible to perform abnormal classification detection on the transaction records of digital virtual assets. And then the group intelligent algorithm is utilized to realize the tracking of abnormal transactions of digital virtual assets such as virtual currency, digital copyright and online games.

6   Concluding Remarks

At present, the protection of digital virtual assets such as virtual currency, digital copyright, and online games is a key issue to be solved urgently. The cross integration of 5G network and blockchain technology can give digital virtual assets some new characteristics, including ownership of individuals, liquidity, security and reusability. In addition, 5G+ blockchain technology can also help digital copyright confirmation, secure transactions and traceability of digital virtual assets.

References

1. Guo, J., Chow, A.: Virtual money systems: a phenomenal analysis. In: Proceedings of the 2008 10th IEEE Conference on E-Commerce Technology and the Fifth IEEE Conference on Enterprise Computing, E-Commerce and E-Services, pp. 267–272. IEEE, Washington (2008)

2. Bek-Thomsen, J., Jacobsen, S.G., Christiansen, C.O.: Virtual money. Scand. J. Soc. Theory **15**(1), 1–5 (2014)
3. IEEE Spectrum Staff: Talking about digital copyright. IEEE Spectr. **38**(6), 9 (2002)
4. Voyatzis, G., Pitas, I.: Protecting digital image copyrights: a framework. IEEE Comput. Graphics Appl. **19**(1), 18–24 (1999)
5. Castronova, E.: On virtual economies [EB/OL] (14 October 2002). https://papers.ssrn.com/sol3/papers.cfm?abstract_id=338500. Accessed 09 June 2018
6. Eyal, I.: Blockchain technology: transforming libertarian cryptocurrency dreams to finance and banking realities. Computer **50**(9), 38–49 (2017)
7. Wang, C.: Liquidity and market efficiency in cryptocurrencies. Econ. Lett. **168**, 21–24 (2018)
8. Phillip, A., Chan, J.S.K., Peiris, S.: A new look at cryptocurrencies. Econ. Lett. **163**, 6–9 (2018)
9. Urquhart, A.: Price clustering in Bitcoin. Econ. Lett. **159**, 145–148 (2017)
10. Jagdeep, S.: Syscoin: a peer-to-peer electronic cash system with blockchain-based services for e-business. In: Proceedings of 2017 26th International Conference on Computer Communication and Networks (ICCCN). IEEE Press, Piscataway (2017)
11. Gideon Greenspan: Beware of the impossible smart contract, blockchain news (12 April 2016). http://www.the-blockchain.com/2016/04/12/beware-of-the-impossible-smart-contr-act/
12. The Digital Millennium Copyright Act of 1998-U.S. Copyright Office Summary [EB/OL]. (19 December 1998). http://www.copyright.gov/legislation/dmca.pdf. Accessed 09 June 2018
13. Rockman, H.B.: The Digital Millennium Copyright Act of 1998(DMCA)—An Overview, pp. 405–418. Intellectual Property Law for Engineers and Scientists. Wiley, Hoboken (2004)
14. Assembly Bill No. 129 [EB/OL] (28 June 2014). http://leginfo.legislature.ca.gov/faces/billNavClient.xhtml?bill_id=201320140AB129. Accessed 09 June 2018
15. Mikolajewicz-Wozniak, A., Scheibe, A.: Virtual currency schemes—the future of financial services. Foresight **17**(4), 365–377 (2015)
16. Karame, G.O., Androulaki, E., Capkun, S.: Two Bitcoins at the price of one? Double-spending attacks on fast payments in Bitcoin. In: Proceedings of the 2012 ACM Conference on Computer and Communication Security, pp. 906–917. ACM, Raleigh (2012)
17. Kaushal, P.K., Bagga, A., Sobti, R.: Evolution of Bitcoin and security risk in Bitcoin wallets. In: Proceedings of the 2007 IEEE International Conference on Computer, Communications and Electronics, pp. 172–177. IEEE, Jaipur (2017)
18. Zhang, D., Liu, Z.: A four stages protocol designed to protect copyright in digital museum. In: Proceedings of the 2010 Second International Workshop on Education Technology and Computer Science, pp. 327–330. IEEE, Wuhan (2010)
19. Webster, J., Romanik, M., Webster, C.: Protecting digital assets: legal protections do not equal practical security. IT Prof. **17**(6), 56–59 (2015)
20. Liu, X.L., Lin, C.C., Yuan, S.M.: Blind dual watermarking for color images' authentication and copyright protection. IEEE Trans. Circuits Syst. Video Technol. **28**(5), 1047–1055 (2016)
21. Ziegeldorf, J.H., Matzutt, R., Henze, M., et al.: Secure and anonymous decentralized Bitcoin mixing. Futur. Gener. Comput. Syst. **80**, 448–466 (2018)

Research on Power Universal Service Access Gateway Based on Blockchain

Shao-peng Wanyan$^{(\boxtimes)}$, Peng Jia, and Xiao-yuan Zhang

NARI Group Corporation, State Grid Electric Power Research Institute, Nanjing, China

Abstract. With the development of power Internet of things and energy Internet, the traditional centralized access authentication method of power Internet of things terminal is difficult to meet the application needs. At present, the centralized access authentication mode has brought great computing and communication pressure to the authentication center, especially large-scale concurrent access and mobile access have a serious impact on the authentication efficiency of the system. Based on the decentralized technology of block chain and the characteristics of power communication network, a distributed authentication scheme suitable for power Internet of things is proposed. The power ubiquitous service access gateway based on block chain is developed, and the terminal test is carried out in wired environment and wireless environment. The gateway can realize the terminal access authentication of the typical ubiquitous power Internet of things system, such as distribution automation, new energy and so on. It has the characteristics of good universality and convenient configuration, and can significantly improve the security of the terminal system without affecting the original system topology.

Keywords: Block chain · Distributed authentication · Power Internet of Things · Gateway · Terminal test

1 Introduction

With the increase of the demand of the intelligent service of the power grid and the universal access of the energy Internet, a large number of intelligent terminal devices have been connected [1, 2]. New changes have taken place in information acquisition methods, storage patterns, transmission channels and processing methods. Therefore, the information and communication technology to support the power grid business capacity put forward higher requirements [3, 4]. The growth of power communication network coverage and access services has resulted in an explosion of terminal types and number of terminals. In particular, the large-scale construction of the Internet of things will greatly accelerate this trend [5]. The ubiquitous power communication network is a multi-service integrated carrying network, and the service does not need to pay attention to the composition of the communication network. Because the network handles the massive traffic efficiently, the network resources has obtained the full play. Because of the huge number of terminals, there are a large number of different types of terminals to exit and access the network every day [6]. Access and terminal access must be plug-and-play

© Springer Nature Singapore Pte Ltd. 2021
Y. Tian et al. (Eds.): ICBDS 2020, CCIS 1415, pp. 458–470, 2021.
https://doi.org/10.1007/978-981-16-3150-4_38

flexible access without cumbersome access processes. The network coverage becomes bigger, and the type and number of terminals increase, which makes the network more vulnerable to attack, and puts forward higher requirements for the security authentication of terminals [7, 8].

The current power communication network is a typical convergent network with almost no data interaction between terminals and terminals [9, 10]. Terminal authentication relies on centralized proxy communication patterns and servers. All devices are verified and connected through a cloud server with strong operating and storage capabilities. With the construction of the energy Internet, such a centralized network faces challenge [11, 12]. First of all, the demand for direct communication between a large number of terminals is becoming more and more prominent due to the construction of the energy Internet and the access of services. The traditional convergent networks should be transformed into interconnected networks [13, 14]. Secondly, as the base of the Internet of energy interconnection, the Internet of things will bring a surge in the number of terminals. Centralized access that relies too much on authentication centers cannot meet the demands of the growing Internet of things ecosystem in terms of effectiveness and security [15].

The key to the above problem lies in the existence of the central node [16]. Decentralization is an important way to solve these problems because it is unable to deal with mass data processing, storage, forwarding, reliability and security risks [17]. For the application of power industry, the above problems can be solved by using blockchain technology [18]. In order to avoid the centralized processing of a large number of transaction information between devices, it can provide a flexible and credible access to protect the privacy and anonymity of users. However, from the existing applications, there are still some problems to be solved in the application of blockchain technology in power systems. In this paper, a distributed authentication scheme for power internet of things is proposed, and a blockchain-based universal access gateway is developed.

2 Distributed Authentication Based on Block Chain

2.1 Features of Power Communication Networks

In the energy Internet environment, there will be different characteristics, different needs of the Internet of things nodes together to apply for access. As shown in Fig. 1, the access scenario is characterized as follows.

Substations where communication sites are physically dispersed and where communication is required. The number of sensors in the substation is large, and there are many kinds of access services for each node equipment.

2.2 Model and Process of Distributed Authentication

The traditional access authentication model is shown in Fig. 2. All nodes with access to the network must be authenticated by a unified authentication center. When the number of nodes is large, the load of CA will be too large [19], which is not suitable for scenarios of a large number of nodes in power communication network.

Block chain-based access authentication includes the following steps.

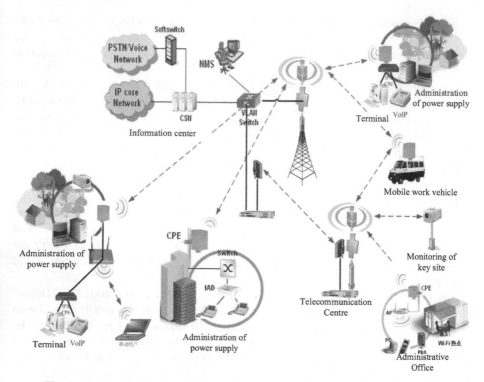

Fig. 1. Schematic diagram of ubiquitous access in power communication network

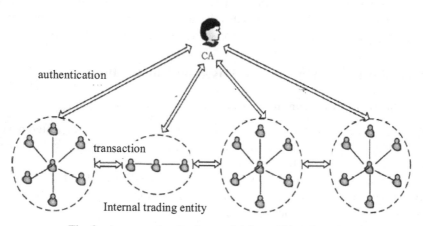

Fig. 2. Access authentication model for traditional services

Step 1. Make sure that each node uses a timestamp to form a block chain. Make sure each node determines the unique public key and the corresponding private key by firmware at the time of shipment.

Step 2. It establishes a consensus mechanism through the PBFT voting mechanism.

Step 3. It defines the virtual currency and establishes the incentive and punishment mechanism. When the node provides the authentication service, the node acquires a specified number of virtual currencies. When a node applies for a authentication service, it needs to consume a virtual currency.

Step 4. All nodes can download account information. Encryption algorithm ensures that privacy information is not leaked during authentication.

Based on the above steps, the power communication network is established to access the private block chain data structure and intelligent contract. The new equipment is uniquely identified when assembled by the factory, and transfer to a common blockchain after installation deployment. In this block chain, you can interact with other devices autonomously and cooperate with the authentication process without the participation of the certification center. The authentication model is shown in Fig. 3.

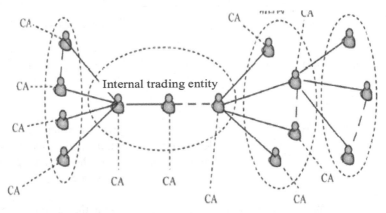

Fig. 3. Schematic of the distributed authentication

Each node in the system has the characteristics of high autonomy, and the nodes are free to connect with each other to form a new connecting unit. Any node may become a stage center but does not have a mandatory central control function. The influence between nodes will form a nonlinear causality through the network. It lets the device know the functions of other devices and the instructions and permissions of different users around these devices.

The first step for an IoT terminal to access authentication is to send an authentication request [10]. The main node requests the packet according to the authentication result, and then retrieves the appropriate node in the access authentication block chain. Appropriate nodes must meet legitimacy and authentication, as well as functional requirements. Legitimacy means that the node has been successfully connected to the system, authentication means that the node belongs to the same business, and functional requirements mean that it has sufficient processing power to run the algorithm. Finally, the request is sent to the authentication group by multicast. The entire access authentication process is shown in Fig. 4.

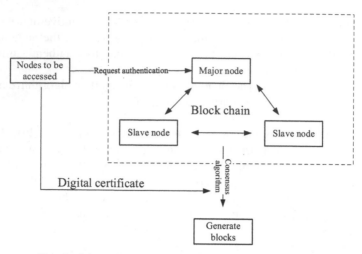

Fig. 4. Schematic diagram of access authentication process

The whole authentication process can be divided into request and confirmation phases.

(1) Phase of the request

The power terminal initiates the authentication application, in which the registration information of the terminal is included. After receiving the authentication application, the main node confirms the terminal signature with the terminal public key, and finally forms the authentication protocol request message.

(2) Phase of the confirmation

After the main node receives the authentication application, the authentication block chain is retrieved and then integrated matching is carried out. It is mainly based on the type of node, the running state, the type of business and so on. Finally, the most satisfied node is selected to form the authentication group G = {P1, P2,..., Pt}. It sends authentication protocol request message in G. The node completes the authentication through the consensus algorithm, generates the block, finally the terminal receives the confirmation information.

The consensus algorithm consists of request, preparation, preparation and submission, as shown in Fig. 5.

(1) Phase of startup preparation

Primary node randomly selected $t - 1$ elements, let $a_1, \ldots, a_{t-1} \in Z_p^*$,

$$f(x) = R + a_1x + a_2x^2 + \ldots + a_{t-1}x^{t-1} \tag{1}$$

$$y_i = f(x_i), 1 \le i \le n$$

Assign y_i to slave node i.

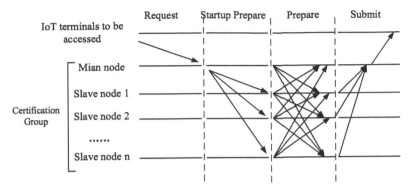

Fig. 5. Interactive process of access authentication based on consensus algorithm

(2) Phase of preparation

When the node receives the request, the recovery algorithm is adopted. The secret share held by the exchange of nodes in G, so we can get t point pairs, $(x_1, y_1), \ldots, (x_t, y_t)$. So the certificate information for the terminal is as follows.

$$R = \sum_{j=i}^{t} y_j \prod_{1<l<t, l\neq j} \frac{x_l}{x_l - x_j} \tag{2}$$

(3) Phase of submission

It submits the authentication results to the main node. The main node completes the authentication of the terminal according to the result of authentication.

3 Design of Service Access Gateway for Electric Communication Network

3.1 Hardware of Gateway System

The system hardware consists of a blockchain authentication server, a programmable switch and a configuration terminal.

(1) Authentication server

The server uses an industrial control computer with an X86 architecture, 8G memory, CentOS 7 operating system, gigabit Ethernet port.

(2) Three layer switch

Switches with remote configuration can receive control instructions from the authentication server. It establishes a connection link when the instruction is passed. When the instruction is blocked, cut off the network access to the corresponding interface.

(3) Certified terminals

The performance of certified terminals is shown in the table below (Table 1).

Table 1. Table of performance parameters for authentication terminals

Parameters of certified terminal	Performance
CPU	Broadcom BCM2837B0 A53 (ARMv8) 64 位 @ 1.4 GHz
GPU	Broadcom Videocore-IV
Internal memory	1 GB LPDDR2 SDRAM
Network	Gigabit Ethernet, 2.4 GHz and 5 GHz Dual - frequency Wi-Fi
Bluetooth	Bluetooth 4.2, Low-power Bluetooth (BLE)
Storage	Micro-SD
GPIO	40 pin GPIO dual row pin
Other interfaces	HDMI, 3.5 mm Analog Audio Video jack, 4x USB 2.0, Ethernet, Camera Serial Interface (CSI), Display Serial Interface (DSI)
Size	82 mm * 56 mm * 19.5 mm, 50 g

3.2 Software of Gateway System

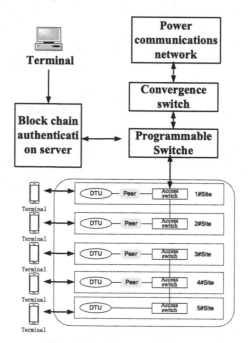

Fig. 6. Deployment of software

Fig. 7. The main interface of the software system (Color figure online)

Access to the home page, system configuration and system management via the navigation bar on the left of the interface. The state of all terminals can be seen in the main interface. The state is divided into three categories, red means denial of access, blue means access, and gray means the device is not online. When in blue, the corresponding device can access the system, otherwise it cannot access the system. The on-off of the device can be controlled manually, showing red or blue (Figs. 6 and 7).

4   Testing and Analysis of Gateway

4.1   Scenario for Testing

The test scenario is a distribution automation system. Distribution automation system is a typical scenario of power Internet of things application. The distribution terminal is mainly connected to the distribution automation system by means of optical fiber and wireless network. Due to the relatively weak security measures and enhanced means of hacking, the distribution automation system is vulnerable to network attacks from public networks or private networks, and then affect the distribution system to the user's safe and reliable power supply. At the same time, the current international security situation has undergone new changes, the attackers have circuitous attacks on the main station by misreporting the fault information at the distribution terminal, thus creating a wider security threat. In order to ensure the safe and stable operation of the power grid, it is very important for the safety protection of the distribution automation system.

4.2   System Topology for Gateway Deployment

The system topology is shown in the following figure. The authentication server verifies the access request of the terminal equipment by connecting the convergent switch to the power communication network. Demonstration verification system is divided into 2 pieces. DTU in slice 1 interworking with convergent switch in layer 2 via access switch, terminals in slice 2 interworking with convergent switches via 4G network. Before the terminal can access the backbone communication network, it needs to be authenticated by the block chain authentication server and obtain the communication token, otherwise it will not be possible to establish the network layer (three layers) communication link (Figs. 8 and 9).

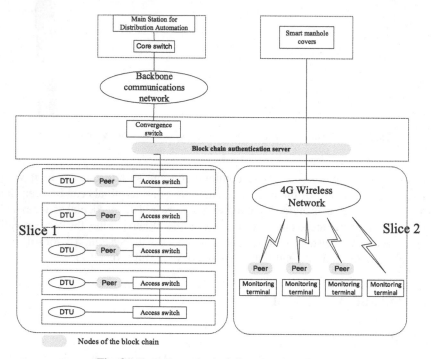

Fig. 8. General topological diagram of the system

4.3   Terminal Testing Under Wired Communication

This test scene is the monitoring service of the distribution automation terminal. The system uploads the monitored data to the monitoring center server via a three-tier switch via the Ethernet interface, and then the server acquires the data. If the authentication does not pass, the server sends blocking instructions to disconnect the bridge of the authentication terminal and realize the blocking function of the illegal terminal. In this field test, the blockchain authentication server is deployed in the computer room to communicate with the authentication terminal through the three-layer switch.

The IP address distribution table for the terminal is as follows (Table 2).

The deployment of the blockchain authentication server in the computer room is shown below (Fig. 10).

The test results are shown in the table below.

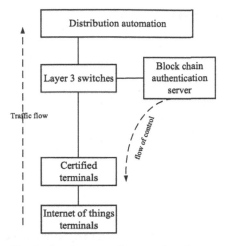

Fig. 9. Deployment diagram of equipment

Table 2. Address assignment for terminals

Terminal for testing	Parameters of gateway
Server: 10.10.0.2/29	10.10.0.1
Terminal 1: 0.10.0.18/29	10.10.0.9
Terminal 2: 10.10.0.18/29	10.10.0.17
Terminal 3: 10.10.0.26/29	10.10.0.25
Terminal 4: 10.10.0.34/29	10.10.0.33

Fig. 10. On-site deployment diagram of servers and gateways

Table 3. Test results of terminal access (wire communication)

	Access status	Address	Time
1	On	1# Station	2019 09 09 10:17:21
2	On	2# Station	2019 09 09 10:17:46
3	Off	3# Station	2019 09 09 10:19:25
4	On	4# Station	2019 09 09 10:26:13

As you can see from Table 3, four sites can be authenticated by block chain. The authenticated terminal can access to the network, has no impact on the service, and the uncertified terminal cannot access the network. In the table, the terminal showing the on status is authenticated and therefore accessible to the network. Terminals showing off status are not authenticated and therefore cannot access the network.

5 Conclusion

In this paper, a distributed authentication scheme for power Internet of things is proposed, and a blockchain-based gateway is developed. The gateway can realize the terminal access authentication of distribution automation, new energy and so on. It has the characteristics of good universality and convenient configuration, and can improve the security of the terminal system without affecting the original system topology. This paper makes an in-depth research on the power communication network technology based on information communication, introduces the blockchain technology, and extends the technology across fields. Through the necessary research and development, the technology is applied to all kinds of power service access application scenarios to improve the data transmission performance of the power communication network, and to solve the bottleneck problem of the network performance of the power communication. The next step is to continue to explore the unique advantages of blockchain in information security, combining with the specific application scenarios of the Internet of things, and to study the method of realizing high-efficiency access and fine-grained access control based on blockchain technology.

Acknowledgments. The authors would like to thank the anonymous reviewers and editor for their comments that improved the quality of this paper. This work was supported by science & research project of SGCC. (Research and application of terminal layer architecture and edge eIoT agent technologies in full service ubiquitous SG-eIoT. Project No. 5700-201958240A-0-0-00.)

References

1. He, P., Yu, G., Zhang, Y., Bao, Y.: Survey on blockchain technology and its application prospect. Comput. Sci. **44**(4), 1–7 (2017)
2. Xiao, Z., Chen, N., Wei, J., Zhang, W.: A high performance management schema of metadata clustering for large-scale data storage systems. J. Comput. Res. Dev. **52**(4), 929–942 (2015)
3. Sun, Y., Yu, Y., Li, X., Zhang, K., Qian, H., Zhou, Y.: Batch verifiable computation with public verifiability for outsourcing polynomials and matrix computations. In: Liu, J.K., Steinfeld, R. (eds.) ACISP 2016. LNCS, vol. 9722, pp. 293–309. Springer, Cham (2016). https://doi.org/10.1007/978-3-319-40253-6_18
4. Lou, J., Zhang, Q., Qi, Z., Lei, K.: A blockchain-based key management scheme for named data networking. In: 2018 1st IEEE International Conference on Hot Information-Centric Networking (HotICN), Shenzhen, China, pp. 141–146 (2018)
5. Samaniego, M., Deters, R.: Blockchain as a service for IoT. In: 2016 IEEE International Conference on Internet of Things (iThings) and IEEE Green Computing and Communications (GreenCom) and IEEE Cyber, Physical and Social Computing (CPSCom) and IEEE Smart Data (SmartData), Chengdu, pp. 433–436 (2016)
6. Kan, L., Wei, Y., Hafiz Muhammad, A., Siyuan, W., Linchao, G., Kai, H.: A multiple blockchains architecture on inter-blockchain communication. In: 2018 IEEE International Conference on Software Quality, Reliability and Security Companion (QRS-C), Lisbon, Portugal, pp. 139–145 (2018)
7. Li, H., Tian, H., Zhang, F., He, J.: Blockchain-based searchable symmetric encryption scheme. Comput. Electr. Eng. **73–78**, 32–45 (2019)
8. Andoni, M., et al.: Blockchain technology in the energy sector: a systematic review of challenges and opportunities. Renew. Sustain. Energy Rev. **100–105**, 143–174 (2019)
9. Ji, B., Mo, J., Wang, J.: Study on communication reliability of weakly centralized electricity mutual transaction based on blockchain technology. Guangdong Electr. Power **32**(1), 85–92 (2019)
10. Yuan, Y., Ni, X., Zeng, S., Wang, F.: Blockchain consensus algorithms: the state of the art and future trends. Acta Automatica Sinica **44**(11), 2011–2022 (2018)
11. Yihua, D., James, W., Pradip, K., et al.: Scalable practical byzantine fault tolerance with short-lived signature schemes. In: Proceedings of the 28th Annual International Conference on Computer Science and Software Engineering, CASCON 2018, pp. 245–256 (2018)
12. Min, X.P., Li, Q.Z., Kong, L.J., et al.: Permissioned blockchain dynamic consensus mechanism based multi-centers. Chin. J. Comput. **41**(5), 1005–1020 (2018)
13. Luu, L., Narayanan, V., Zheng, C., et al.: A secure sharding protocol for open blockchains. In: Proceedings of the 2016 ACM SIGSAC Conference on Computer and Communications Security, CCS 2016, pp. 17–30 (2016)
14. Castro, M., Liskov, B.: Practical byzantine fault tolerance and proactive recovery. ACM Trans. Comput. Syst. Assoc. Comput. Mach. **20**(4), 398–461 (1999)
15. Pan, C., Liu, Z., Liu, Z., Long, Y.: Research on scalability of blockchain technology: problems and methods. J. Comput. Res. Dev. **5**(10), 2099–2110 (2018)
16. Zhang, J.-Y., Wang, Z.-Q., Xu, Z.-L.: A regulatable digital currency model based on blockchain. J. Comput. Res. Dev. **55**(10), 127–140 (2018)
17. Guo, J.-W., Chu, J.-J., Cai, P., Zhou, M.-Q., Zhou, A.-Y.: Low-overhead paxos replication. Data Sci. Eng. **2**(2), 169–177 (2017)
18. Wang, J., Li, L., Yan, Y., Zhao, W., Xu, Y.: Security incidents and solutions of blockchain technology application. Comput. Sci. **45**(z1), 352–355,382 (2018)

19. Xu, Z.-H., Han, S.-Y., Chen, L.: CUB, a consensus unit-based storage scheme for blockchain system. In: Proceedings of IEEE 34th International Conference on Data Engineering, Paris, France, pp. 173–184 (2018)
20. Li, Y., Zheng, K., Yan, Y., et al.: EtherQL: a query layer for blockchain system. In: Proceedings of International Conference on Database Systems for Advanced Applications. Suzhou, China, pp. 556–567 (2017)

Application of Whole-Service Ubiquitous Internet of Things in Power System

Weiwei Yan[✉] and Hui Chu

NARI Group Corporation, State Grid Electric Power Research Institute, Nanjing, China

Abstract. The Internet of Things is the key technology to promote the operation efficiency of the power grid in the future, aiming at the problem of many kinds of terminals in the Internet of things, data model and interface protocol are not unified, and lack of unified management terminal equipment management platform, etc., based on the architecture of the Internet of things and the technology of the internet of things, the typical application scenarios under the structure of the internet of things are analyzed, and the feasibility of typical application scenarios of the internet of things is verified. Whole-service ubiquitous internet of things will be the bridge of the application and social application of the power grid, the application of the whole-service ubiquitous Internet of things in the power system has laid a theoretical foundation for the application of the internet of things in the power system.

Keywords: Internet of Things · Smart grid · Marginal material federation agency · Wireless communication · Application scene

1 Introduction

With the continuous development of new ICT technologies such as big cloud moving intelligence, the rapid growth of Internet of things industry is in the period of strategic opportunity before the big explosion. Since 2015, China has paid more attention to scientific and technological innovation, especially the role of Internet technology in enhancing the capabilities of various industries. The National Development and Reform Commission issued guidance on promoting the development of "Internet" smart energy in 2016. Industrial Internet, industrial Internet of things and other concepts are essentially consistent, all for the optimal allocation of industrial elements to promote continuous innovation.

The Internet of things is the key technology to promote the efficiency of grid operation in the future. At present, there are many kinds of terminals in the Internet of things, the data model and interface protocol are not unified, and the lack of a unified management terminal equipment management platform, resulting in terminal communication cannot authenticate authorization, data cannot be integrated and shared, and the application scenarios across business areas are not rich enough. Therefore, it is urgent to build a unified management equipment management platform, and adapt the edge of different terminals to the agent and combine some scenarios to carry out pilot demonstration and

© Springer Nature Singapore Pte Ltd. 2021
Y. Tian et al. (Eds.): ICBDS 2020, CCIS 1415, pp. 471–482, 2021.
https://doi.org/10.1007/978-981-16-3150-4_39

verification work. This paper analyzes in detail the general framework of the Internet of things and the application mode of the Internet of things technology in all aspects of the power system.

2 Architecture of the Internet of Things

2.1 Overall Structure

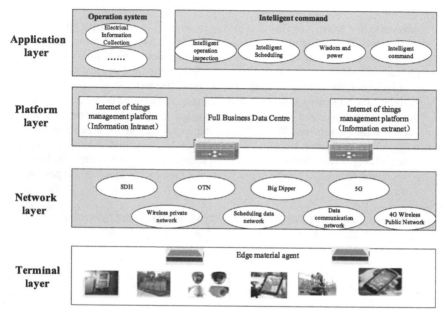

Fig. 1. Power Internet of things architecture

According to the top-level design of the Internet of things, combined with business requirements, the Internet of things architecture is shown in Fig. 1.

Terminal Layer. Through the adaptation of the underlying network protocol, the agent can shield the difference of the underlying network and access various types of terminals. It realizes the primary leveling of terminal ubiquitous interconnection, and supports the sharing of terminals by different business systems.

Network Layer. Different kinds of terminals are connected through the agent, and the data converge to the Internet of things platform, and then provide to different systems. Different kinds of service are carried on a logical network, how to ensure that different kinds of service are isolated from each other, and different kinds of service can configure the network resources, we need to use the virtualization technology of the network. Through network virtualization technology, the network can be divided into multiple virtual network tunnels according to different types. Different virtual network tunnels are isolated from each other and do not affect each other, which can improve the utilization of network resources and the reliability of service.

Platform Layer. The Internet of things platform is composed of the Internet of things management center and the capability opening center, which supports the terminal and network management. The WMC is mainly responsible for resource allocation, data gathering and the provision of basic service components. Capacity Open Center runs on the full business cloud, provides public components and open interfaces, and supports unified and efficient Internet of things application delivery.

Service Layer. Based on the whole business data center for data fusion and value mining, data sharing can be realized among service systems.

2.2 Technical Framework

(1) Internet of things platform

IoT platforms include the IoT Management Centre and the Capacity Open Centre. The main functions of the platform are connection management, network management, equipment management, user management, application enabling, business service and operation monitoring. The technical framework of the IoT platform is shown in Fig. 2.

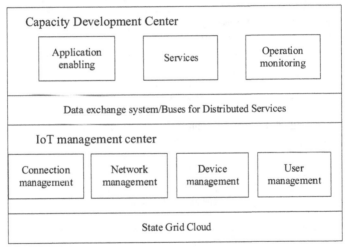

Fig. 2. Schematic diagram of the Internet of things

(2) Edge material agent

The edge material agent mainly realizes the unified access of local communication, the edge computation, the remote communication and so on. The Edge Agent provides standard communication protocol and standardized communication interfaces to support flexible access of multiple service terminals. The control module implements virtualization and flexible allocation of underlying physical resources. The security module mainly provides security in four aspects, integrated data, operation, network and equipment. The agent has the capability of edge computing to support multi-source data fusion computing, protocol parsing and behavioral analysis. The functional architecture of the edge material agent is shown in Fig. 3 (Fig. 4).

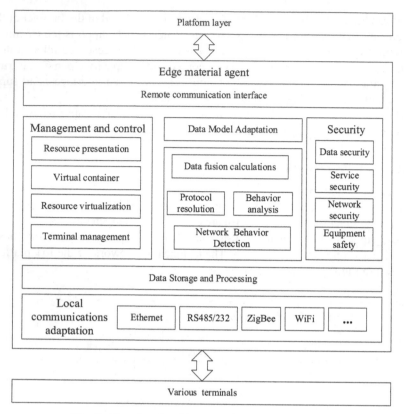

Fig. 3. Functional architecture of edge material agent

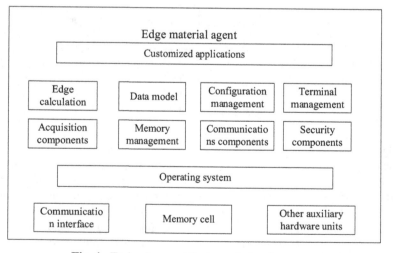

Fig. 4. Technology architecture of edge facts agent

3 Key Technology

3.1 Multiple Types of Terminal Communications

The communication module of the edge Agent supports the adaptation of multiple communication protocols, including those hosted in wired and wireless communication networks. Specific functions include the following.

(1) Access to different types of terminals through various physical interfaces;
(2) Interconnect with different protocols through built-in communication plug-ins of communication modules;
(3) The transformation of network layer communication protocol and the mapping of terminal address are accomplished by communication module.

3.2 Communication Technology of LTE Wireless Communication Private Network

The wireless communication of 230 MHz belongs to the ultrashort wave wireless communication, which is carried out by using the ultrashort wave electromagnetic wave in the band of 223–231 MHz. Ultrashort wave communication can only be transmitted in a straight line because of the large absorption of the ground and the inability of the ionosphere to reflect. The ultrashort wave communication is also called the sight distance communication, the transmission distance is about 50 km, the long distance transmission needs the relay station segment transmission, namely the relay communication. In order to meet the needs of the construction of power load management system, in 1991, the state explicitly allocated 15 dual frequency points and 10 single frequency points in the 223–231 MHz band to the special power.

3.3 Real-Time Video Conference Technology Based on Internet of Things

Videoconferencing technology realizes real-time voice and video communication based on web page. The essence of technology is to integrate voice/video capture needed for real-time communication applications into web browsers through processing modules, network transport and session control. The conference mainly includes voice module, video module and transmission module.

Voice engine is a series of audio multimedia processing framework, including from the audio acquisition card to the network transmission end of the entire solution.

The video engine contains a series of video processing framework, which realizes the solution of the whole process from video acquisition by camera to video information network transmission to video display.

3.4 Characteristics of Power Service

At present, the power wireless private network mainly carries four categories of service, such as network control, information collection, video and mobile applications. Specific services include distribution automation, electricity information collection, distributed power supply, precision load control, video surveillance, mobile operations, etc. Overall, the current minimum delay for all types of power services is 10 ms, with a bandwidth of less than 4 Mbps for single services. In the future, with the development of energy Internet, in order to adapt to the new power grid mode with UHV as the backbone and coordinated development of power grid at all levels, the universal connection will become the basic form of power grid. Therefore, it is urgent to build a real-time, efficient, safe and reliable communication network to achieve accurate control of all kinds of loads. A new type of visualization, real-time and lean operation is introduced to realize the monitoring and inspection of important corridors in power grids at all levels. Therefore, in the future, the Internet of things and broadband services of power systems will coexist in large numbers, and present the characteristics of high-density, low-delay, high-reliability and high-security. The number of concurrent terminals will reach 100,000, the delay requirement is millisecond and the reliability requirement is 99.999%. Therefore, higher requirements are put forward for the service carrying capacity of the power wireless private network.

3.5 Customized Scheme for Power Network Slicing

Wireless network architecture based on 5G network slicing is divided into three layers. The underlying network is the physical infrastructure layer, which is the actual carrier of network data. The middle layer provides the whole virtual resource pool for the

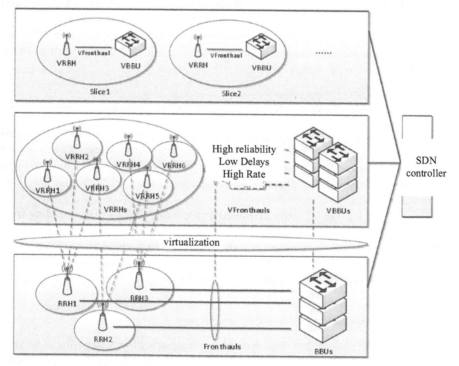

Fig. 5. Wireless network architecture based on 5G network slicing

virtualized network resources, and realizes the centralized management and efficient allocation of resources. The upper layer is the user-oriented actual layer, different types of network services will form different network slicing. The realization of layer function and the interaction between each layer need to be managed and controlled by the SDN controller (Fig. 5).

4 Typical Service Scenarios

4.1 Electrical Information Collection

Without changing the normal operation of the existing system, the parallel bypass is connected to the edge agent through the interface such as 485 of the cable. The terminal is connected to the Internet of things management platform via 230 MHz wireless private network. At the same time, the edge connection agent parses the national network standard protocol in the front end, and stores, adds the edge calculation function, carries on the edge calculation processing to the user data of the station area (Fig. 6).

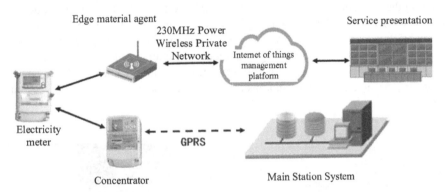

Fig. 6. The scene of electricity consumption information collection

4.2 Wisdom Inspection

Based on the Internet of things, through intelligent inspection robot, intelligent perception, state acquisition and other devices, the comprehensive acquisition and real-time monitoring of the operation state of equipment such as substation are realized. Using the information of video image, environment factor, real-time state, equipment history information and so on, data mining and intelligent algorithm are used to realize the comprehensive evaluation of the health state of power equipment. Combining with 3D GIS to realize visual display, it can effectively support the safe operation and high efficiency operation inspection of power equipment (Fig. 7).

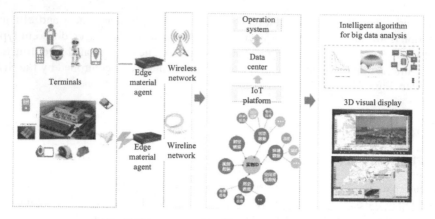

Fig. 7. The scene of intelligent inspection scene

4.3 Emergency Protection

Based on the Internet of things and Beidou's GPS system, a high-precision space-time location service is constructed, which provides real-time location for people, vehicles, venues and materials. Based on the key information of the data center, the dynamic demonstration of the integration of regional security resources is formed. It can ensure the transmission and on-line interaction of the real-time information between the command center and the field personnel, and ensure the power supply security in the core area (Fig. 8).

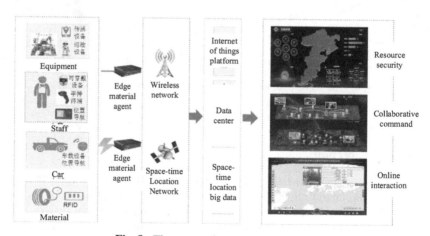

Fig. 8. The scene of emergency guarantee

4.4 Intelligent Warehousing

Relying on the edge of the agent, the platform connects RFID. RFID is attached to the surface of the item. The information of material flow can be stored in RFID at the front end and packaged and uploaded to the platform. Compared with the two-dimensional code operation, this method can greatly reduce the platform's communication burden. Through the mastery of upstream and downstream data, the scientific and efficient storage operation plan is formulated to improve the fine management level of warehousing management and meet the management requirements of the whole life cycle of materials. This scheme further improves the management of logistics process, tracking and monitoring the whole process of transportation and distribution, and improves the lean management level of material distribution (Fig. 9).

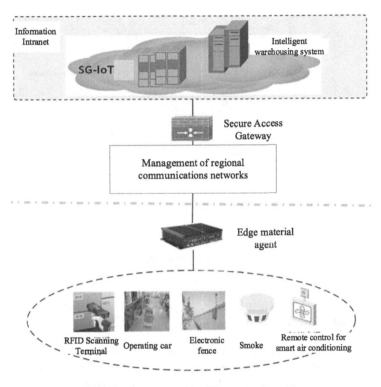

Fig. 9. The scene of intelligent warehousing

4.5 Integrated Monitoring of Ring Cabinets

The ring cabinet is equipped with intelligent electronic door lock, which realizes the opening of the door lock through the mobile operation terminal, and effectively reduces the tediousness of the mechanical key management. By collecting the monitoring data of the environment condition of the ring net cabinet, the environment in the cabinet body is monitored synthetically, and the temperature and humidity anomaly and noise anomaly are analyzed and alerted in time. The edge agent collects the data of the battery condition monitoring, realizes the comprehensive monitoring of the battery, and provides the effective support for the battery operation and maintenance management. The remote sensing and remote information of DTU are connected by the edge agent. The edge agent uploads the collected data to the application system for comprehensive monitoring and analysis. The integrated monitoring function and system framework of the ring cabinet are shown in Fig. 10.

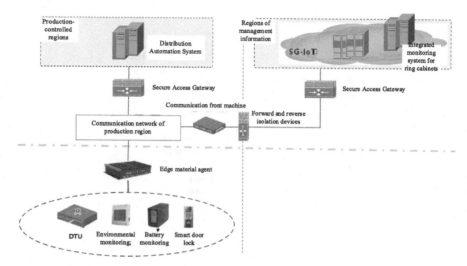

Fig. 10. The scene of comprehensive monitoring of ring network cabinet

4.6 Distributed Photovoltaic Monitoring

The status information of the photovoltaic station is collected by the agent of the edge connection, including voltage, current, active power, reactive power, switching state, electric quantity, etc. And upload this information to the distributed photovoltaic monitoring system, so as to realize the centralized monitoring of photovoltaic stations.

The distributed photovoltaic monitoring system combines the running state of the grid and the running state of the photovoltaic station to formulate the grid-connected strategy of the photovoltaic station, so as to promote the coordinated interaction between the grid and the distributed energy.

The distributed photovoltaic monitoring system makes a comprehensive analysis of the operation of photovoltaic stations, including grid-connected, off-grid, power supply quality, power supply reliability and so on. The functional implementation and system architecture of distributed photovoltaic monitoring are shown in Fig. 11.

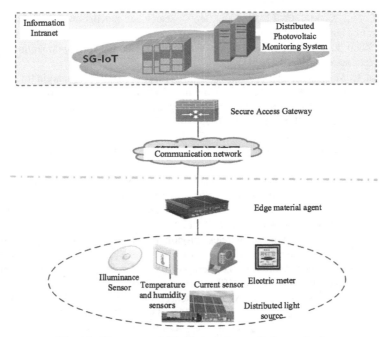

Fig. 11. The scene of distributed photovoltaic monitoring

5 Conclusion

Universal Internet of things is an important material basis for the construction of world-class energy Internet enterprises. The Internet of things is the second network of companies with the characteristics of intelligence, diversity and ecology. Based on the architecture and the technology of Internet of things, this paper analyzes the typical application scenarios under the Internet of things structure. This paper analyzes the feasibility of the typical application scenarios of the Internet of things. Through the integration construction of the two networks, the power flow and data flow can penetrate into the whole process of energy production, transmission and consumption. Universal Internet of things becomes a bridge for grid and social applications. Internet of things platform becomes the core competitive product of the company. This paper lays a theoretical foundation for the application of Internet of things in power system.

References

1. Gao, X., Zhu, J., Chen, Y.: Research on multi-services bearing solution of LTE power wireless private network. Electr. Power Inf. Commun. Technol. **12**(12), 26–29 (2014)
2. Yu, J., Liu, J., Cai, S.: Research on LTE wireless network planning in electric power system. Electr. Power Inf. Commun. Technol. **10**(2), 7–11 (2016)
3. Wang, K.: The application of the Internet of Things in the 5G era in the power system. Telecom Power Technol. **35**(5), 187–188 (2018)

4. Xia, X., Zhu, X., Mei, C., Li, W., Fang, H.: Research and practice on 5G slicing in power Internet of Things. Mob. Commun. **43**(1), 63–69 (2019)
5. Li, B., Zhou, J., Ren, X.: Research on key issues of TD-LTE network optimization. Telecom Eng. Tech. Stand. **1**, 57–61 (2015)
6. Andreas, F., Anja, K., Bernhard, W., et al.: Load dependent interference margin for link budget calculations of OFDM networks. IEEE Commun. Lett. **12**, 398–400 (2008)
7. Zheng, L., Tse, D.N.C.: Diversity and multiplexing: a fundamental tradeoff in multiple antenna channels. IEEE Trans. Inf. Theory **49**, 1073–1096 (2003)
8. Ma, Z., Zhang, Z.Q., Ding, Z.G., et al.: Key techniques for 5G wireless communications: network architecture, physical layer, and MAC layer perspectives. Sci. China **58**(4), 41301–41321 (2015)
9. Qiu, J., Ding, G., Wu, Q., et al.: Hierarchical resource allocation framework for hyper-dense small cell networks. IEEE Access **4**(99), 8657–8669 (2017)
10. Yao, J.: Random access technology of electric dedicated LTE network based on power priority. Autom. Electr. Power Syst. **40**(10), 127–131 (2016)
11. Cao, J., Liu, J., Li, X.: A power wireless broadband technology scheme for smart power distribution and utilization network. Autom. Electr. Power Syst. **37**(11), 76–80 (2013)
12. Wu, J., Zhang, Y., Zukerman, M., et al.: Energy-efficient base-stations sleep-mode techniques in green cellular networks: a survey. IEEE Commun. Surv. Tutor. **17**(2), 803–826 (2015)
13. Li, W., Chen, B., Wu, Q., et al.: Applied research of TD-LTE power wireless broadband private network. Telecommun. Electr. Power Syst. **33**(241), 82–87 (2012)
14. You, X.H., Pan, Z.W., Gao, X.Q., et al.: The 5G mobile communication: the development trends and its emerging key techniques. Sci. Sinica **44**(5), 551 (2014)
15. Liu, G., Jiang, D.: 5G: vision and requirements for mobile communication system towards year 2020. Chin. J. Eng. **2016**, 1–8 (2016)

Artificial Intelligence/Machine Learning Security

Learning Depth from Light Field via Deep Convolutional Neural Network

Lei Han$^{(\boxtimes)}$, Xiaohua Huang, Zhan Shi, and Shengnan Zheng

School of Computer Engineering, Nanjing Institute of Technology, Nanjing 211167, China
hanl@njit.edu.cn

Abstract. Depth estimation based on light field imaging is a new way of depth estimation. The abundant data of light field paves the way for deep learning methods to play a role. In recent years, deep convolutional neural network (CNN) has shown great advantages in extracting image texture features. Inspired by this, we design a deep CNN with EPI synthetic images as input for depth estimation, which is called EENet. Under the constrains of epipolar geometry, pixels corresponding to a common object point are distributed in a straight line in the epipolar plane image (EPI), and the EPI synthetic image is easier to extract features by convolution kernel. Our EENet has the structure characteristics of multi-stream inputs and skip connections. Specifically, the horizontal EPI synthetic image, the vertical EPI synthetic image and the central view image are first generated from the light field, and input into the three streams of EENet respectively. Next, the U-shaped neural network is designed to predict the depth information, that is, the convolution and pooling blocks are used to encode the features, while the deconvolution layer and convolution layer are combined to decode features and recover the depth information. Furthermore, we employ skip connections between the encoding layers and the decoding layers to fuse the shallow location features and deep semantic features. Our EENet is trained and tested on the light field benchmark, and has obtained good experimental results.

Keywords: Depth estimation · Deep learning · Convolutional neural network

1 Introduction

Estimating depth information is a crucial work in computer vision [1]. Many important tasks in computer vision have proven to improve performance by using the depth information, including 3D reconstruction, semantic segmentation, scene understanding, object detection and so on [2].

Recently, some new depth estimation methods using light field have emerged. Light field camera can record the position and direction of light at the same time, and this new imaging mode can capture more information about the angle and direction of light than the common methods based on stereo image or multi view [1]. The plenoptic cameras such as Lytro and Raytrix facilitate the acquirement and application of light field data. Sub-aperture images, refocusing images and epipolar plane images (EPIs) can be generated by light-field data computing. Based on these derived images, different

© Springer Nature Singapore Pte Ltd. 2021
Y. Tian et al. (Eds.): ICBDS 2020, CCIS 1415, pp. 485–496, 2021.
https://doi.org/10.1007/978-981-16-3150-4_40

depth estimation methods emerge, among which the depth estimation from EPIs is more popular.

EPIs show a very clear linear texture: each scene point captured by light-field camera exhibit a linear trace in an EPI, whose slope is relation to the distance between the scene and the light-field camera [3]. Among the methods represented by reference [3], the slope of straight line is detected by establishing feature metric such as color variance, 4D gradient or structure tensor, and then the depth map is obtained by using optimization technology. The accuracy of these methods depends on the feature description and measurement, but it is difficult to model the occlusion, noise and homogeneous region, so the improvement of algorithm performance is restricted. In addition, these methods are not practical due to the large amount of calculation. Although some depth estimation methods have been proposed to accelerate processing, these methods sacrifice accuracy while improving speed.

With the rise of deep neural network, Reference [4] and other literatures integrate feature extraction and optimization into a unified framework of convolutional neural network, and achieved good results. Deep learning research shows that deep convolution neural network is good at texture feature extraction. However, the current depth estimation methods based on deep CNN take the sub-aperture image stack in different directions as the input, and do not directly apply the rich texture of EPIs. In addition, most of the network models have complex structure and longer computational time. Taking EPINet [4] as an example, it has good performance on HCI benchmark. However, the resolution of the depth map obtained by the network is lower than that of the central sub-aperture image, and it is not completely pixel by pixel prediction.

In this paper, we focus on designing a lightweight and practical neural network to extract depth from light field. Similar to EPINet [4], our method also employ the geometry of EPI as multiple steam structure. Furthermore, we utilize EPI synthetic images instead of stacked sub-aperture images as multi-stream input. In order to couple structural and semantic information, we add some skip connections from shallow neural layers to deep neural layers.

The structure of the paper is as follows. Section 2 reports related studies on depth estimation using EPIs generated by light-field data. Section 3 describes our methodology including geometry pattern analysis, the network architecture and loss function. Section 4 shows the experiments performance and discussions. Finally, Sect. 5 is the conclusion of this paper.

2 Related Work

In this part, we briefly review the current methods, putting emphasis on the light-field depth estimation methods using EPIs. This research field is roughly divided into two directions, namely, EPI analysis methods and deep learning based methods.

EPI analysis based methods predict the slope of the lines on EPIs to compute depth information from light field. One idea is to try all the different directions, in other word, the direction the straight line on EPI with the least color change will be the best possibility to give the correct depth value. Based on this prior knowledge, there are several methods using different methods to measure color difference. Kim et al. [3] used an Epanechenikov kernel to propose a modified Parzen window to measure the direction of a line. Tao et al. [5] used the standard deviation to measure correspondence cue, then combined correspondence cues with defocus cues to calculate depth. Since each EPI data has similar gradient pattern, for just one optimal value, it is not necessary to try all directions. According to this nature, Mun et al. [6] efficiently reduced the number of angular candidates for cost computation. In reference [7], only 8 sub-apeture images were selected to calculate stereo disparity, and the final disparity map was generated by fusing stereo and defocus cues. Mishiba [8] proposed a new strategy for the offline viewpoint and cost volume to reduce computational time. Other EPI analysis methods employ gradient or structural tensor. For examples, Wanner and Goldluecke [9] applied the 2D structure tensor to evaluate the orientation of every block in the EPIs. Jeon [10] used phase-shift theory and optimization technology to estimate the depth of light field, this method was an indirect application of EPI imaging geometry and had achieved good results. Above methods adapt global optimization schemes to minimize the match-cost function. So computational complexity of those methods is heavy. Neri et al. [11] made a local estimation based on the maximization of the total log likelihood density distributed along the lines in EPI. Using epipolar geometry, Lourenco [12] first detected enlarged silhouettes, then devised a structural rendering method to calculate the depth map. Li [13] proposed a new tensor method, called as Kullback-Leibler Divergence (KLD), to analyze the histogram distributions of the EPI's window. Then, according to the variation scale of the tensor, the depths calculated by the vertical tensor and by the horizontal tensor are fused to obtain a high-quality depth map. Through EPI analysis, Schilling et al. [14] integrated occlusion processing into depth model to maximize the use of the available data, and obtain general accuracy and quality of object borders.

In recent years, depth estimation method based on deep learning has gradually emerged and become a kind of popular method. Heber et al. [15] explored a CNN to predict the 2D hyperplane orientation in the 4D light-field domain, where the hyperplane orientation was corresponding to the 3D scene depth. However, Heber's CNN was not an end-to-end depth prediction network, and the training process is more complicated. Guo et al. [16] also decomposed the complex task into several sub tasks and realizes one sub task with one sub network. An integrated network was designed to accurately estimate the depth of occlusion area. Johansen et al. [17] proposed a method to learn the central sub-aperture structure, and used this structural information to build a light-field dictionary, in which atom groups correspond to unique disparity. In 2017, Heber et al. [18] proposed a U-shaped regression network, which consists of two symmetrical parts, encoding part and decoding part. This network takes EPI volumes as input, and learns 3D filters to estimate disparity map. The network has a large amount of computation and a long operation time. To enhance reliability of depth predictions, Shin et al. [4] designed a multi-steam network which encoded each EPI separately. However, the output resolution of this network is smaller than that of sub-aperture image. Recently, Shi et al. [19] estimates parallax from an agile part of dense and sparse light-field images through finely adjusted flownet 2.0 and a refined network, and have been achieved good results.

3 Methodology

Utilizing the texture features of EPI synthetic image, we design a deep CNN to estimate depth with light field data. In this part, we first describe the geometry principle and state the overall design ideas and outline the network architecture, followed by two structural details of our network, namely multi-stream inputs and skip connection.

3.1 Geometric Pattern of Depth Information

Different from traditional cameras, light-field camera add microlens array between the main lens and the sensor. Images captured by light-field cameras have many angular resolutions in both vertical and horizontal directions, and the number of angular resolutions is much more than that of stereo cameras. Complex imaging geometry and abundant light-field data lay the foundation for light-field depth estimation.

There are many ways to represent light field, among which the two-plane parametrization (2PP) is very intuitive and commonly used. 2PP representation is to consider light field as a set of pinhole views from several view points parallel to a common image plane. In this way, a 4D light field is defined as the set of rays in a ray space $\Re$, passing through two planes Π and Ω, as shown in Fig. 1, Π presents the viewpoint plane which includes the points described by the coordinates (s, t), and Ω denotes the common image plane given by the coordinates (u, v). Therefore, each ray can be uniquely identified by its intersection (u, v) and (s, t) with two planes respectively. A 4D light field can be formulated as a map:

$$L : \Omega \times \Pi \to \mathbb{R}, (u, v, s, t) \mapsto L(u, v, s, t) \tag{1}$$

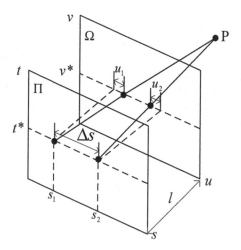

Fig. 1. Light field presentation in 2PP

An EPI can be regarded as 2D slice of 4D light field. If we fix the coordinate V to V^* in the image plane Ω and t to t^* in the viewpoint plane, then we get a slice $S_{v*,t*}$ of the light field. This slice is an EPI in horizontal direction, denotes as

$$S_{v*,t*} : (u, s) \rightarrow L(u, v*, s, t*) \tag{2}$$

Figure 2 shows an example of a typical EPI image. The top row is the central sub-aperture image of the scene, and the second row is the EPI image corresponding to the position of the red dotted line in the central sub-aperture image. Width of the EPI is same with that of sub-aperture image, and the height of EPI is affected by the number of angular views of light field. In addition, total number of EPI data has same number with sub-aperture image height H. As shown in Fig. 2, the EPI image has a linear texture structure. Next, we will analyze the relationship between this texture structure and scene depth.

Fig. 2. Example of EPI (Color figure online)

Let us consider the geometry of the map expression (2). As shown in Fig. 1, For the ray set emitted from a point P(X,Y,Z), if we fix the coordinates v* and t* and only change the coordinates u and s, it is equivalent to take a slice of the ray set. According to the properties of similar triangles, we have the formula (3).

$$\frac{\Delta s}{\Delta u} = -\frac{Z}{l} \tag{3}$$

In formula (3), Z represents the depth of the point P, l denotes the distance between two planes Π and Ω, Δs and Δu mean the coordinate changes of image plane and viewpoint plane respectively.

Under the assumption of Lambert surface, the pixels corresponding to the same object point have the same gray level. These approximate pixels are arranged in a straight line, when the 4D light field is transformed into 2D EPI. And formula (3) shows that the slope of this line is proportional to the depth of its corresponding point. Therefore, the linear texture can be used as the geometric basis for depth estimation.

3.2 Network General Framework

We formulate depth estimation from light field as a spatially dense prediction task, and design a deep convolution neural network to predict the depth of each pixel in the central sub-aperture image.

In general, the proposed model (EENet) can be regarded as a modified U-shaped network with multi-stream inputs and some skip connections shown in Fig. 3. In essence, our model is a two-stage network. The first stage conducts a encoding job, and the second stage performs an decoding work.

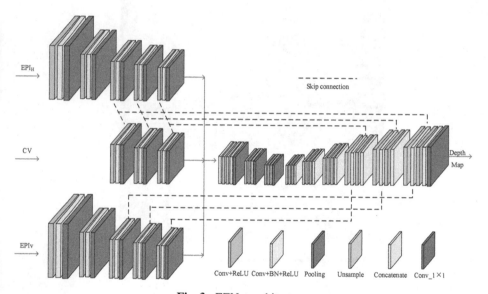

Fig. 3. EENet architecture.

In downsampling stage, a multi-stream architecture is utilized to extract the geometry information of light field. The main idea behind the multi-steam architecture is to receive different inputs from light-field data. Three streams, EPIh, CV and EPIv, are designed with the respective input of the horizontal EPI synthetical image, the center view, and the vertical EPI synthetical image. Different from EPInet [4], EPIh and EPIv are fed with EPI synthetical images rather than the stack of image in one direction. Some convolutional neural network (CNN) blocks are used to encode features in each stream. Then the outputs of these streams are concatenated for further encoding features.

In upsampling stage, the deconvolution layers are used to improve the resolution of feature map. Besides, we concatenate some layer outputs in the encoding stage to the same resolution feature maps in decoding stage, in order to fuse the lower texture features and the upper semantic information. Finally, we use 1×1 convolution layer to obtain the disparity map.

3.3 Multi-stream Architecture

As shown in Fig. 3, our model has three feature extraction streams: EPIh, CV and EPIv, which are fed with horizontal EPI synthetical image, central view image and vertical EPI synthetical image respectively.

Now we discuss the size of those input image in the three streams. Suppose the dimensions of light field are $(N_{ar}, N_{ac}, N_{sr}, N_{sc}, N_{ch})$, where N_{ar}, N_{ac} are angular resolution in row and in column direction, respectively, N_{sr}, N_{sc} indicate space resolution in row and column direction, and N_{ch} represents the number of channels in light field image. For example, the light field image captured by Lytro camera has the dimension of (9, 9, 381, 381, 3). The horizontal EPI from the light field has the dimension of $((N_{ac} \times N_{sr}), N_{sc}, N_{ch})$, the dimension of vertical EPI is $(N_{sr}, (N_{ar} \times N_{sc}), N_{ch})$, and the size of center view image is (N_{sr}, N_{sc}, N_{ch}). The subgraphs (a), (b) and (c) of Fig. 4 show examples of the above three kinds of image respectively.

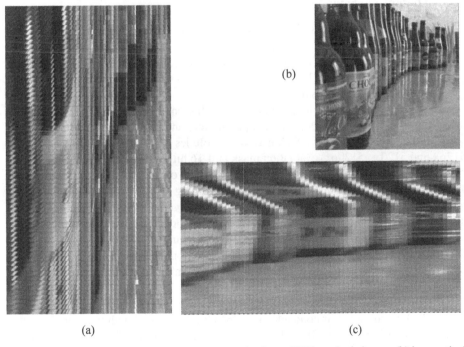

(b)

(a)   (c)

Fig. 4. Examples of input images. (a) Illustrates a horizontal EPI synthetic image, (b) is a vertical EPI synthetic image, and (c) shows a center view image.

3.4 Skip Connection

It has been found that, different from the upper neurons, the receptive field of the shallow neuron is smaller. Therefore, the shallow feature map contains less semantic information, but there are much the image details preserved [20]. Since both accurate location information and precise category prediction are necessary for depth estimation, fusing shallow and high-level feature maps is a good way to improve the accuracy of depth estimation. Therefore, the proposed model (EENet) utilizes skip connections to retain shallow detailed information from the encoder directly.

Skip connections is used to connect neurons in non-adjacent layers to realize information fusion. As shown in the Fig. 3, dotted lines indicate skip connections. With those skip connections in a concatenation fashion, local features can be transferred directly from a block of the encoder to the corresponding block of the decoder. Here, we should pay attention to the problem that our cascade is a stacking operation, and we must ensure that the feature maps of the cascade has the same resolution.

4 Experimental Results

4.1 Experimental Setup

Our model training is carried out on HCI Benchmark, and the evaluation is conducted on HCI Benchmark [21].

There are 28 scenes in HCI benchmark. The angular resolution of each scene is 9×9, and the spatial resolution is 512×512. Those scenes are created by the tool of Blender, specially, the stratified scenes are created by the internal renderer and the photorealistic scenes are created by the Cycles renderer. For each scene, HCI provides 8-bit light-field data ($9 \times 9 \times 512 \times 512 \times 3$), camera parameters and disparity range. For stratified scene and training scene, the benchmark also includes two kinds of resolution ($512 \times 512\text{px}$ and $5120 \times 5120\text{px}$) evaluation mask and 16 bit ground truth disparity map.

We use 16 scenes in the additional module of HCI dataset for network training, and 12 scenes in the modules of structured, test and training for network evaluation. In order to ensure that the training images are sufficient, we augment light-field data by rotating $45°$, $90°$ and $135°$. For the sake of reducing the memory consumption, the input of the network is a sub image with only 64×64 resolution randomly selected from the 512×512 resolution image during training the network. Through above measures, the number of training images is up to one million times of the number of scenes, which ensures the samples diversity for network input.

The proposed network model is implemented using Keras with Tensorflow as the backend. Our experiment is conducted on hardware configured with two intel I7 CPUs, 32 GB memory, and two NVIDIA RTX2060 GPU graphics cards.

4.2 Evaluation Metrics

Depth estimation belongs to the problem of pixel by pixel regression. In our experiment, MSE (mean square error) is selected as the evaluation metrics of algorithm performance analysis. MSE is described in reference [21] and are used by most of the current relevant methods. For the sake of clarity, we report it as follows.

We denote the estimated disparity map, the ground-truth and an evlution mask as d, gt and M, respectively, MSE is formulated as

$$MSE_M = \frac{\sum_{x \in M}(d(x) - gt(x))^2}{|M|} \times 100.$$

4.3 Comparison to State-of-the-Art

In this section, the performance of the proposed model is evaluated using synthetic light field datasets. We compared our model (EENet) with the following state-of-the-art models: EPInet [4], FDE [8], LF [10] and EPI1 [17].

As shown in Fig. 5, the estimation results of five methods are given in three scenes of backgammon, pyramids and stripes. The results of each method are arranged in a row; each scene occupies three columns: the first column represents the disparity map estimated by the corresponding method, the second column represents the difference between the estimated result and the ground truth, and the third column refers to the difference between the estimated result and the median value of the five methods. It can be seen from the Fig. 5 that the effect of LF method is not ideal in pyramids and stripes scenes, and other methods have achieved reasonable experimental results. The resolution of EPINet's disparity map is lower than that of sub-aperture image, so the error of disparity map boundary is large.

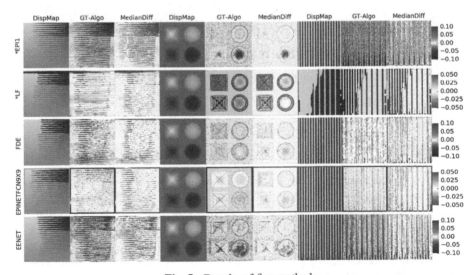

Fig. 5. Results of five methods

Figure 6 shows the MSE index scores of each method in some sample scenes. In the figure, each row corresponds to a scene, namely, cotton, dino and sideboard; each column corresponds to a method, namely EPI1, LF, FDE, EPINet and EENet; each image shows the difference between the estimated result and the ground true, and the number above each image is the score of MSE index. According to the MSE index score, the performances of EENet and EPINet are basically the same, which are obviously better than the other three methods. The MSE of FDE is larger than that of EENet, but in the same order of magnitude, the MSE of EPI1 and LF is almost one order of magnitude higher than that of EENet. Compared with EPINet, our EENet has less parameters and less computational time. Therefore, this paper achieves a reasonable depth estimation effect with relatively light calculation.

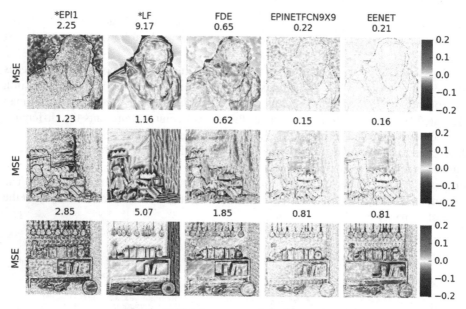

Fig. 6. MSE index scores of the five methods

5   Conclusions

Using epipolar geometry and deep learning technology, we propose a neural network (EENet) for estimating the depth from light field. EEnet network uses multistream input to receive three kinds of images with different texture features: horizontal EPI synthetic image, central view image and vertical EPI synthetic image. The two kind of EPI synthetic images have more abundant texture, while central view image contains position information, which is suitable for feature extraction by convolution neural network. EENet consists of two stages: encoding and decoding. Skip connections are added between equal resolution layers in the two stages to fuse the shallow location and deep semantic information. Our EENet achieves reasonable depth estimation with less computational cost.

Acknowledgment. This work has been supported by Natural Science Foundation of Nanjing Institute of Technology (Grant Nos. CKJB201804, ZKJ201906), National Natural Science Foundation of China (Grant No. 62076122) the Jiangsu Specially-Appointed Professor Program, the Talent Startup project of NJIT (No. YKJ201982), Science and Technology Innovation Project of Nanjing for Oversea Scientist.

References

1. Liu, F., Hou, G., Sun, Z., et al.: High quality depth map estimation of object surface from light-field image. Neurocomputing **252**(252), 3–16 (2017)
2. Liu, F., Shen, C., Lin, G., et al.: Learning depth from single monocular images using deep convolutional neural fields. IEEE Trans. Pattern Anal. Mach. Intell. **38**(10), 2024–2039 (2015)
3. Kim, C., Zimmer, H., Pritch, Y., et al.: Scene reconstruction from high spatio-angular resolution light fields. ACM Trans. Graph. **32**(4), 73:1–73:12 (2013)
4. Shin, C., Jeon, H.G., Yoon, Y., et al.: Epinet: a fully-convolutional neural network using epipolar geometry for depth from light field images. In: Proceedings of the IEEE Conference on Computer Vision and Pattern Recognition, pp. 4748–4757 (2018)
5. Tao, M.W., Hadap, S., Malik, J., et al.: Depth from combining defocus and correspondence using light-field cameras. In: Proceedings of the IEEE International Conference on Computer Vision, pp. 673–680 (2013)
6. Mun, J.H., Ho, Y.S.: Occlusion aware reduced angular candidates based light field depth estimation from an epipolar plane image. Electron. Imaging **2018**(13), 390-1–390-6 (2018)
7. Han, Q., Jung, C.: Guided filtering based data fusion for light field depth estimation with L0 gradient minimization. J. Vis. Commun. Image Represent. **55**, 449–456 (2018)
8. Mishiba, K.: Fast depth estimation for light field cameras. IEEE Trans. Image Process. **29**, 4232–4242 (2020)
9. Wanner, S., Goldluecke, B.: Globally consistent depth labeling of 4D light fields. In: 2012 IEEE Conference on Computer Vision and Pattern Recognition, pp. 41–48. IEEE (2012)
10. Jeon, H.G., Park, J., Choe, G., et al.: Accurate depth map estimation from a lenslet light field camera. In: Proceedings of the IEEE Conference on Computer Vision and Pattern Recognition, pp. 1547–1555 (2015)
11. Neri, A., Carli, M., Battisti, F.: A maximum likelihood approach for depth field estimation based on epipolar plane images. IEEE Trans. Image Process. **28**(2), 827–840 (2018)
12. Lourenco, R., Assuncao, P., Tavora, L.M., et al.: Silhouette enhancement in light field disparity estimation using the structure tensor. In: International Conference on Image Processing, pp. 2580–2584 (2018)
13. Li, J., Jin, X.: EPI-neighborhood distribution based light field depth estimation. In: ICASSP 2020–2020 IEEE International Conference on Acoustics, Speech and Signal Processing (ICASSP), pp. 2003–2007. IEEE (2020)
14. Schilling, H., Diebold, M., Rother, C., et al.: Trust your model: light field depth estimation with inline occlusion handling. In: Computer Vision Pattern Recognition, pp. 4530–4538 (2018)
15. Heber, S., Pock, T.: Convolutional networks for shape from light field. In: Computer Vision and Pattern Recognition, pp. 3746–3754 (2016)
16. Guo, C., Jin, J., Hou, J., et al.: Accurate light field depth estimation via an occlusion-aware network. In: 2020 IEEE International Conference on Multimedia and Expo (ICME), pp. 1–6. IEEE (2020)

17. Johannsen, O., Sulc, A., Goldluecke, B.: What sparse light field coding reveals about scene structure. In: Proceedings of the IEEE Conference on Computer Vision and Pattern Recognition, pp. 3262–3270 (2016)
18. Heber, S., Yu, W., Pock, T.: Neural EPI-volume networks for shape from light field. In: Proceedings of the IEEE International Conference on Computer Vision, pp. 2252–2260 (2017)
19. Shi, J., Jiang, X., Guillemot, C.: A framework for learning depth from a flexible subset of dense and sparse light field views. IEEE Trans. Image Process. 28(12), 5867–5880 (2019)
20. Long, J., Shelhamer, E., Darrell, T., et al.: Fully convolutional networks for semantic segmentation. In: Computer Vision and Pattern Recognition, pp. 3431–3440 (2015)
21. Honauer, K., Johannsen, O., Kondermann, D., Goldluecke, B.: A dataset and evaluation methodology for depth estimation on 4D light fields. In: Lai, S.-H., Lepetit, V., Nishino, Ko., Sato, Y. (eds.) ACCV 2016. LNCS, vol. 10113, pp. 19–34. Springer, Cham (2017). https://doi.org/10.1007/978-3-319-54187-7_2

Cycle-Derain: Enhanced CycleGAN for Single Image Deraining

Yuting Guo[1], Zifan Ma[2], Zhiying Song[3], Ruocong Tang[4(✉)], and Linfeng Liu[4]

[1] School of Science, Nanjing University of Posts and Telecommunications, Nanjing 210023, China
[2] School of Electronic and Optical Engineering and School of Microelectronics, Nanjing University of Posts and Telecommunications, Nanjing 210023, China
[3] School of Communication and Information Engineering, Nanjing University of Posts and Telecommunications, Nanjing 210023, China
[4] School of Computer Science and Technology, Nanjing University of Posts and Telecommunications, Nanjing 210023, China

Abstract. As the basis of image processing, Single Image Deraining (SID) has always been a significant and challenging theme. On the one hand, due to lack of enough real rainy images and corresponding clean images, most derain networks train in the synthetic datasets, which makes the outputs unsatisfactory in real environment. On the other hand, heavy rainfall is accompanied by fog. Traditional networks for deraining is used to remove the rain streaks in the rain image. The processed image may still have the problem of blurring. In this paper, we comprehensively consider the problems existing in SID, propose a Cycle-Derain network based on unsupervised attention mechanism. Specifically, this network makes full use of generative adversarial networks with two mappings and cycle consistency loss to train the unpaired rainy images and clean images. Besides, it introduces unsupervised attention mechanism and uses the loop-search positioning algorithm to make the network better deal with the details of rain and fog in images. Many experiments based on public datasets show that Cycle-Derain network is very competitive with other rain-removing networks, especially in the restoration of real rainy images.

Keywords: Image deraining · Generative adversarial network · Attention mechanism

1 Introduction

The images captured in rainy circumstances generally undergo some degradations, due to the rain streaks and rain drops, which affects the subsequent processing of image seriously. Single Image Deraining (SID) is still a vital issue currently. As an example, Fig. 1 indicates that rain-free images are much clearer than the rainy images, and more valuable information can be obtained from the rain-free images.

© Springer Nature Singapore Pte Ltd. 2021
Y. Tian et al. (Eds.): ICBDS 2020, CCIS 1415, pp. 497–509, 2021.
https://doi.org/10.1007/978-981-16-3150-4_41

Real rainy image   *Image after derain*   *Real rainy image*   *Image after derain*

Fig. 1. Real rainy images vs. images after derain.

Most single image deraining approaches tend to divide the rainy image into rain layer and background layer, and then find the maping relations between rainy images and rain layer to derain the images. However, considering that the rain can also produce some fog in real applications [1, 2], and thus we take each rainy image as the combination of rain layer, fog layer and background, which yields the following formula:

$$Z = B + R + F \tag{1}$$

where Z denotes a rainy image, B denotes background layer, R denotes the rain layer and F denotes the fog layer. The layered diagram example is given in Fig. 2. Especially, we apply Cycle-Derain to realize the transformation of images, and exact the rain layer from rainy images. Besides, the separation of fog layer is processed by an unsupervised attention-guided mechanism.

To remove the rain streaks and restore the details of a clear background, we study an image derain technology based on an attention-guided mechanism of GAN (Generative Adversarial Network) [3–5], and then a Nash equilibrium is expected to be achieved, for obtaining high-quality image outputs. Most existing approaches train the paired images from artificial datasets in a supervised manner, and numerous paired images are always required, which is actually a strict precondition. To this end, we propose a loop-search positioning algorithm based on CycleGAN and attention-guided mechanism, which can train unpaired images and achieve ideal results, while this algorithm reduces the computation complexity of removing the fog layer, and exact a clear background. Our contributions are summarized as follows:

(i) An unsupervised network termed Cycle-Derain is constructed, to realize the translation from source domain to target domain, and then back to source domain. The overall correspondence of these images is achieved through restricting the cycle consistency loss.

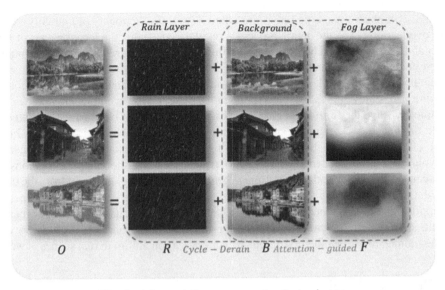

Fig. 2. A layered diagram example of rainy image.

(ii)   An attention-guided is adopted in an unsupervised way, and pixels are endowed with weights to carry out an element-wise product on each RGB channel. Thus, the fog layer in rainy images is positioned, and then the rainy images can be defogged.

(iii) A loop-search positioning algorithm is specially desgined, to deal with the background and the foreground, respectively, and then the situation that whether the fog layer has been removed is iteratively judged. If not, the foreground will be substituted into the loop. The loop-search positioning algorithm can reduce the computation and avoid the redundant processing of fog-free image areas.

2   Related Work

2.1   GAN and CycleGAN

Most trainings of generative adversarial nets require large amounts of paired data, which is expensive to abtain in practice. CycleGAN [6–8] emerged in response to the difficulty of style migration of unpaired images. Zhu JY et al. [9, 10] introduced cycle consistency loss on the basis of GAN counter loss, and realized style migration on unpaired images through two-way transformation from target domain to source domain and from source domain to target domain. The experimental results show that the CycleGAN network usually gets good results in image translation tasks involving color and texture changes, while making some mistakes in geometric changes.

2.2   Single Image Deraining (SID)

Since there is few effective approaches for detecting and remove rain streaks from the rainy image, the area of single image deraining draws the attention of many scholars.

Then discriminative sparse coding is presented. Under the dictionary of mutually exclusive overlearning [11], the derain process is regularized, so that the local patches of rain layer and background can be used for sparse modeling in the learning dictionary, and the sparse coding learned from the dictionary has a clear distinction between the rain removal image layer and the rain layer. Finally, a variational model was used to simultaneously monitor and remove the rain streaks in the input images. However, this method can not completely solve the fuzziness in the low channel, and can not be separated effectively when the image background is similar to the rain and the rain drop is enlarged. Fu X et al. [12, 13] presented "DerainNet" for single image deraining. Through the use of convolutional neural network on the high-frequency details, the mapping relationship between the rain image and the clear image detail layer is directly explored from the data, and the image processing domain knowledge is used to modify the objective function to improve the performance of deraining. Due to the lack of datasets, the experimental results show that this method is not ideal for processing of rain and fog, furthermore due to the training on the synthetic datasets, its generalization ability in real scenes is weak.

3   Problem Model

3.1   Network Architecture

The original supervised attention derain learns the mapping relations by using paired examples [14]. However, in the deraining task of real applications, a training set of aligned image pairs are not available. We explore the unsupervised Cycle-Derain using unpaired data which also can yield ideal recovery results. Furthermore, the integrated attention networks further strengthen the defogging effect and provides a better image-to-image translation.

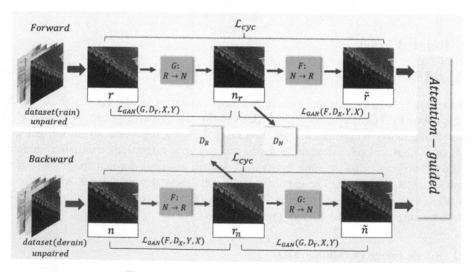

Fig. 3. Network architecture of Cycle-Derain.

The network pipeline of our proposed Cycle-Derain is shown in Fig. 3, which is a derivative of CycleGAN. Cycle-Derain can be divided into a forward and a backward branch: (i) with regard to the forward branch: the cycle-consistency from rainy to rainy is expressed as $r \rightarrow n_r \rightarrow \tilde{r}$, where the input rainy image r is used to generate the rain-free image n_r and then obtain the reconstructed rain image $\tilde{r}$ by a generator. (ii) with regard to the backward branch, the cycle-consistency from rain-free to rain-free is expressed as $n \rightarrow r_n \rightarrow \tilde{n}$, where the input rain-free image n is used to generate the rainy image r_n and then obtain the reconstructed rain image $\tilde{n}$ by a generator.

In addition, we introduce an attention network to extract the fog from rainy images. Three generators $G(R - N)$, $F(N - R)$ and $G(S - T)$ can generate the rain-free images, rainy images and fog-free images, respectively. Three discriminators Dn, Dr and Ds aim to distinguish real images from translated images that are generated by the aforementioned generators. This process can be defined as:

$$m_r = Cycle - Dearin\,(r) \tag{2}$$

where m_r is the output image processed by Cycle-Derain.

Generators. We introduce the five generators **GGr, GFr, GFn, GGn, G_{S-T}** into our method, where **GGr** uses rainy images **r** to generate the rain-free images **nr**, **GFr** uses rain-free images nr to generate the rainy images **$\tilde{r}$**, **GFn** uses rain-free images n to generate the rainy images **rn**, and **GGn** uses rainy images to generate the rain-free images **$\tilde{n}$**. **r** and **$\tilde{r}$**, **n** and **$\tilde{n}$** must satisfy the cycle consistency, i.e., we have that:

$$\begin{cases} r \rightarrow G_{Gr}(r) \rightarrow G_{Fr}(G_{Gr}(r)) \approx r \\ n \rightarrow G_{Fn}(n) \rightarrow G_{Gn}(\overset{\cdot}{G}_{Fn}(n)) \approx n \end{cases} \tag{3}$$

G_{S-T} uses images in source domain S to generate the images in target domain T. We define the translation as:

$$\begin{cases} n_r = G_{Gr}(r) \\ \tilde{r} = G_{Fr}(n_r) \\ r_n = G_{Fn}(n) \\ \tilde{n} = G_{Gn}(r_n) \\ t = G_{s-t}(s) \end{cases} \tag{4}$$

Discriminators. We introduce five adversarial discriminators D_{Gr}, D_{Fr}, D_{Fn}, D_{Gn}, D_{s-t} into our method. D_{Gr}, D_{Fn} and D_{s-t} are type-I discriminators to distinguish rainy images, rain-free images and fog-free images from the real images, respectively. To obtain more realistic generated images, the adversarial losses $min_G max_{D_Y} \mathcal{L}_{GAN}(G, D_Y, X, Y)$, $min_F max_{D_X} \mathcal{L}_{GAN}(F, D_X, Y, X)$ and $min_G max_{D_X} \mathcal{L}_{GAN}(G, D_S, S, T)$ are considered:

$$\mathcal{L}_{GAN}(G, D_Y, X, Y) = E_{y \sim p_{data}(y)}\big[logD_Y(y)\big] + E_{x \sim p_{data}(x)}[\log(1 - D_Y(G(x)))] \tag{5}$$

where x and y are training samples given by the two domain X and Y, we set the data contribution as $x \sim p_{data}(x)$ and $y \sim p_{data}(y)$.G tries to make the generated images $G(x)$

be similar to the images in domain Y. G aims to minimize the objective while D tries to maximize it.

However, the adversarial losses is highly under-constrained, because a network is possible to map the same images to any random images in the target domain, which implies that the generated images probably do not match the target images. Therefore, we introduce type-II discriminators D_{Fr} and D_{Gn} to guarantee that the learned mapping functions are cycle-consistent, i.e., with regard to each input image x the translation network should be able to bring it back to the original image. The difference between input images and output images is measured by a cycle consistency loss:

$$\mathcal{L}_{cyc}(G, F) = E_{x \sim p_{data}(x)}[||F(G(x)) - x||] + E_{y \sim p_{data}(y)}[||G(F(y)) - y||] \quad (6)$$

Our model includes two mappings, $G(F(y)) : R \rightarrow N$ and $F(G(x)) : N \rightarrow R$. In (6), $F(G(x))$ and $G(F(y))$ are reconstructed images. R denotes the rain domain, and N denotes the rain-free domain. Hence, two kinds of cycle consistency losses are applied: forward cycle consistent loss and backward cycle consistent loss, which are written as:

$$\begin{cases} r \rightarrow G(r) \rightarrow F(G(r)) \approx r \\ n \rightarrow F(n) \rightarrow G(F(n)) \approx n \end{cases} \quad (7)$$

In addition, the appearance of rain inevitably brings some fog which causes an adverse effect on the visual quality. However, neither type-I nor type-II discriminator can distinguish the fog domain. Therefore, an attention network is required to locate and process the fog layer.

3.2 Attention Mechanism

The images captured in heavy rain always include fog layers, and the adverse effect must be considered. In Cycle-Derain, an unsupervised attention mechanism without alerting the background [15, 16] has been taken to address this issue.

The attention network denoted by As, which selects area to translate. Attention map s_a is induced from S and reflects the weight of each pixel. After feeding the input processed rain-free image to the generator $G_{S \rightarrow T}$, the element-wise product is operated between s_a and $G_{S \rightarrow T}(s)$, and then the preliminary defogging layer s_f can be obtained as:

$$s_f = s_a \odot G_{S \rightarrow T}(s) \quad (8)$$

The background image s_b can be created as:

$$s_b = (1 - s_a) \odot s \quad (9)$$

By adding the masked output of $G_{S \to T}$, into the background, the defogged image is expressed as:

$$s' = s_f + s_b = s_a \odot G_{S \to T}(s) + (1 - s_a) \odot G_{S \to T}(s) \qquad (10)$$

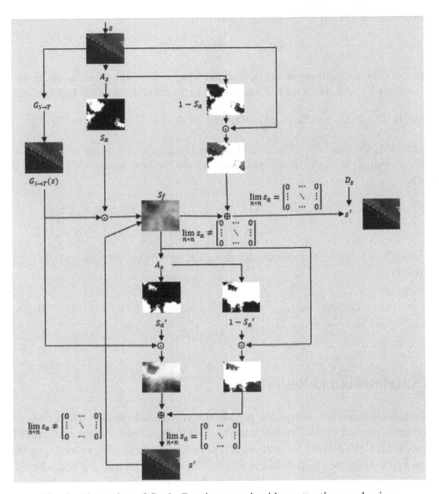

Fig. 4. Illustration of Cycle-Derain network with an attention mechanism.

As shown in Fig. 4, the rain-fog features are extracted by two convolution layers, sigmoid function and LeakyReLu activation function, then we can conduct subsequent processing.

After positioning the fog layer, we obtain s_a and use loop-search positioning algorithm to remove the fog layer. The flow chart of loop-search positioning algorithm is illustrated below. If the attention map s_a converges towards zero, indicating that the fog layer has already been removed, and the images s' is output; otherwise, s is updated by s_f, i.e., s_f is input into the attention network, and the above stages will be repeated until attention map s_a is close to zero.

We incent this behavior by a $L(s_a)$ loss:

$$L(s_a) = min||s_a - 0||^2 \tag{11}$$

where min denotes the minimizing operation of $||s_a - 0||^2$. In addition, we involve the discriminator D_s, and obtain the adversarial loss to make the final image be more realistic:

$$L_{GAN}(G, D_s, S, T) = E_{t \sim PT(t)}[logD_T(t)] + E_{s \sim PS(s)}[log(1 - D_T(G(s')))] \tag{12}$$

Generally, the final loss function of Cycle-Derain can be constituted by combining adversarial, cycle-consistency and $L(s_a)$ losses for both source domain and target domain:

$$L(G, F, D_X, D_Y, D_S, s_a) = L_{GAN}(G, D_X, S, T) + L_{GAN}(G, D_Y, S, T) \\ + L_{GAN}(G, D_s, S, T) + \lambda_1 L_{cyc}(G, F) + \lambda_2 L(s_a) \tag{13}$$

Through solving the minimax optimization problem, we can get the optimal parameters of $L()$:

$$G^*, F^*, D_X^*, D_Y^*, D_S^* = arg \min_{G,F,s_a} \left(arg \max_{D_X,D_Y,D_S} L(G, F, D_X, D_Y, D_S, s_a) \right) \tag{14}$$

4   Experiments and Results

The network architecture adopts our proposed Cycle-Derain model. The image data is trained unsupervised by the Pytorch framework in Python environment, with a NVIDIA GeForce GTX 1050 Ti GPU. We gather numerous datasets, including rainy-foggy images and background images with different styles. The original images are first filtered, and the patch-level discriminator architecture enables Cycle-Derain can work on images with arbitrary size and resolution ratios in a fully convolutional manner.

4.1   Baselines

We first compare DiscoGAN [17] and CycleGAN, which use the similar architectures in image processing, but they are with quite different losses: DiscoGAN adopts a standard GAN loss, while CycleGAN adopts a least-squared GAN loss. In addition, DualGAN employing Wasserstein GAN loss is similar to CycleGAN in term of loss measurement, and the attention module proposed by Wang et al. [18] is also compared by integrating it to the first layer of generators.

4.2 Datasets

Besides gathering considerable rainy images and rain-free images, we add the fog layer in some rainy images to construct the dataset of rainy-foggy images termed Cycle-Derain dataset. The Cycle-Derain dataset includes objects with different backgrounds and different proportions, making the transformation between images become more comprehensive. Additionally, we first input the paired images into Cycle-Derain for training, and then after obtaining the network parameters we input the unpaired images instead, therefore, the training time is largely reduced.

4.3 Network Architecture

With regard to the generators, two stride-2 convolutions are involved, along with other stride-1 convolutions. The images input into the convolution are with the size of 256 × 256 × 3 and must be normalized. Then, these images are processed by the ReLU activity function., Especially, the inverse convolution is carried out by nine residual blocks. Finally, the convolution with Tanh activity function is employed. The output images are with the same size with the input images.

With regard to the discriminators, stride-2 convolutions are involved. The specific contents contain convolution of input images with the scale of 256 × 256 × 3, the rain-fog features are extracted by Leaky RrLU activity function [19], convolution, instance normalization and employed Leaky RrLU activity function again. By repeating the above steps, the output images are with the size of 16 × 16 × 3.

4.4 Training Details

Cycle-Derain uses two loss functions to make the training stable. For adversarial loss, in order to reduce the model oscillation, we train the generator to minimize the value of $E_{x \sim p_{data}(x)}[(D(G(x)) - 1)^2]$, while the discriminator is trained to minimize the value of $E_{y \sim p_{data}(y)}[(D(y) - 1)^2] + E_{x \sim p_{data}(x)}[(D(G(x)))^2]$, and thus the authenticity of images is increased and the correspondence between different styles is improved. For cycle consistency loss, in order to make the input images match with the generated images, we ensure their styles be consistent with each other, through training the generator to minimize the value of $E_{x \sim p_{data}(x)}[||F(G(x)) - x||]$ and $E_{y \sim p_{data}(y)}[||G(F(y)) - y||]$.

4.5 Experimental Results

By observing the learned attention maps, it can be found that Cycle-Derain is able to learn about the relational image regions, and ignore the background. When the input images does not include any elements of the source domain, Cycle-Derain will not pay attention to these images, and the image will remain the unedited status and avoid the image distortions. Among the baseline approaches, DiscoGAN separates the background from foreground content, which causes the cycle consistency loss be with the same weights to the adversarial loss, while the background changes greatly. Compared with DiscoGAN,

DualGAN can achieve more ideal outputs. The UNIT algorithm is based on the assumption that the latent space between source domain and target domains is allowed to be shared, however, this assumption is unrealistic, and the image quality cannot be improved by combing the residual attention module into the image translation framework. Under such cases, the results are prone to be confused by the unrelated background, leading to some errors in handling the texture of output images. By learning attention maps, Cycle-Derain reduces the excessive processing of background and restores the input images successfully. In short, Cycle-Derain performs better than others when the image dataset includes the images with different sizes and different backgrounds. 1,096 images in Cycle-Derain dataset are applied to conduct 400 epochs training, and then the loss function results of the first 100 epochs are visually presented, as depicted in Fig. 5. In the beginning, the cycle consistency loss is quite large, and then it is rapidly reduced after 73 epochs. The generators and discriminators are trained as expected, i.e., the value of G becomes smaller with the increase of D.

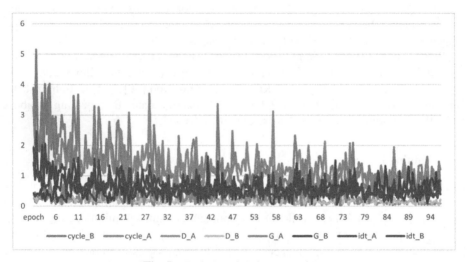

Fig. 5. Cycle-Derain's loss over time.

By training Cycle-Derain for 100, 200, 300 and 400 epochs, the obtained images at different translation stages are illustrated in Fig. 6. Table 1 indicates that, after training for 400 epochs the deraining effect of Cycle-Derain is preferable as shown in Fig. 7.

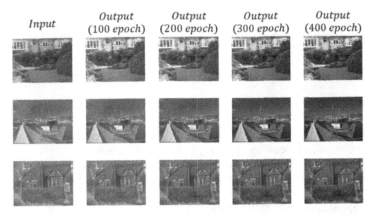

Fig. 6. Images translation trained 100, 200, 300, 400 epochs by Cycle-Derain.

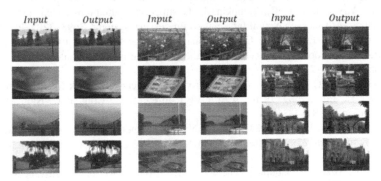

Fig. 7. Images translation trained 400 epochs by Cycle-Derain.

Table 1. Image quality comparison between original images and deraining images.

METRICS	Cycle-Derain	None
PSNR	31.49	19.6
SSIM	0.936	0.58

5 Conclusion

Single image deraining has become a core issue in the filed of computer vision processing, due to the fact that the paired image datasets are not available in real applications. To this end, we construct the Cycle-Derain model to process rainy images in an unsupervised manner. Additionally, most existing approaches have ignored the fog layer in the rainy images, and they always process the rainy images by using physical models, making the network model become much complex. Therefore, a loop -search positioning algorithm is proposed to deal with background and foreground, and the removal of fog layer is iteratively judged.

Acknowledgements. This research is supported by National Natural Science Foundation of China under Grant Nos. 61872191, 61872193, 61972210; Six Talents Peak Project of Jiangsu Province under Grant No. 2019-XYDXX-247.

References

1. Goodfellow, I., Pouget-Abadie, J., Mirza, M.: Generative adversarial nets. In: Advances in Neural Information Processing Systems, pp. 2672–2680 (2014)
2. Fu, X., Huang, J., Ding, X.: Clearing the skies: A deep network architecture for single-image rain removal. IEEE Trans. Image Process. **26**(6), 2944–2956 (2017)
3. Wei, W., Meng, D., Zhao, Q., et al. Semi-supervised CNN for single image rain removal. arXiv preprint arXiv:1807.11078 (2018)
4. Wei, Y., Zhang, Z., Fan, J.: DerainCycleGAN: An Attention-guided Unsupervised Benchmark for Single Image Deraining and Rainmaking. arXiv preprint arXiv:1912.07015 (2019)
5. Mejjati, Y.A., Richardt, C., Tompkin, J.: Unsupervised attention-guided image-to-image translation. Advances in Neural Information Processing Systems, 3693–3703 (2018)
6. Zhu, J.Y., Park, T., Isola, P.: Unpaired image-to-image translation using cycle-consistent adversarial networks. In: Proceedings of the IEEE International Conference on Computer Vision, pp. 2223–2232 (2017)
7. Wang, H., Xie, Q., Zhao, Q.: A model-driven deep neural network for single image rain removal. In: Proceedings of the IEEE/CVF Conference on Computer Vision and Pattern Recognition, pp. 3103–3112 (2020)
8. Shen, Y., Feng, Y., Deng, S.: MBA-RainGAN: Multi-branch Attention Generative Adversarial Network for Mixture of Rain Removal from Single Images. arXiv preprint arXiv:2005.10582 (2020)
9. Liu, M.Y., Tuzel, O.: Coupled generative adversarial networks. In: Advances in Neural Information Processing Systems, pp. 469–477 (2016)
10. Deng, L.J., Huang, T.Z., Zhao, X.L.: A directional global sparse model for single image rain removal. Appl. Math. Model. **59**, 662–679 (2018)
11. Engin, D., Genç, A., Ekenel, H.: Cycle-Dehaze: enhanced CycleGAN for single image dehazing. In: CVPR Workshops: NTIRE (2018)
12. Wang, H., Li, M., Wu, Y., Zhao, Q., Meng, D.: A Survey on Rain Removal from Video and Single Image. arXiv preprint arXiv:1909.08326 (2019)
13. Wang, T., Yang, X., Xu, K.: Spatial attentive single-image deraining with a high-quality real rain dataset. In: Proceedings of the IEEE Conference on Computer Vision and Pattern Recognition, pp. 12270–12279 (2019)
14. Wei, Y., Zhang, Z., Zhang, H.: Semi-DerainGAN: A New Semi-Supervised Single Image Deraining Network. arXiv preprint arXiv:2001.08388 (2020)
15. Yang, W., Tan, R.T., Feng, J.: Deep joint rain detection and removal from a single image. In: Proceedings of the IEEE Conference on Computer Vision and Pattern Recognition, pp. 1357–1366 (2017)
16. Jiang, K., Wang, Z., Yi, P.: Multi-scale progressive fusion network for single image deraining. In: Proceedings of the IEEE/CVF Conference on Computer Vision and Pattern Recognition, pp. 8346–8355 (2020)
17. Luo, Y., Xu, Y., Ji, H.: Removing rain from a single image via discriminative sparse coding. In: Proceedings of the IEEE International Conference on Computer Vision, pp. 3397–3405 (2015)

18. Ren, D., Zuo, W., Hu, Q.: Progressive image deraining networks: a better and simpler baseline. In: Proceedings of the IEEE Conference on Computer Vision and Pattern Recognition, pp. 3937–3946 (2019)
19. Wei, W., Meng, D., Zhao, Q.: Semi-supervised transfer learning for image rain removal. In: Proceedings of the IEEE Conference on Computer Vision and Pattern Recognition, pp. 3877–3886 (2019)

Sensitive Data Recognition and Filtering Model of Webpage Content Based on Decision Tree Algorithm

Sheng Ye[1], Yong Cheng[2], Yonggang Yang[2], and Qian Guo[3,4(✉)]

[1] State Grid ZheJiang Electric Power Company Ltd, Hangzhou 310000, China
[2] State Grid ShanXi Electric Power Company, Xi'an 710000, China
[3] Global Energy Interconnection Research Institute Co., Ltd, Nanjing 210000, China
guoqian@geiri.sgcc.com.cn
[4] State Grid Key Laboratory of Information & Network Security, Nanjing 210003, China

Abstract. In recent years, privacy-protecting data mining has attracted widespread concern because it is necessary to provide protection for the privacy level of sensitive and confidential data from unauthorized attacks. The purpose of this study is to develop a privacy-protecting anonymity algorithm using decision tree classification. This paper focuses on k-anonymity technology, which can prevent identity leakage. K-anonymity technology adopts generalization and suppression methods to achieve data anonymity. Then, the privacy level and mining quality of anonymous data sets will be tested by using decision tree classification, and then compared with other data mining technologies (logistic regression and support vector machine). As is shown in the research, compared with other data mining technologies, privacy level and data quality provide better results.

Keywords: K-anonymity · Privacy protection · Decision tree classification · Data mining

1 Introduction

In this era of digitalization, data mining is developing at a high speed. With the development of technology, it has many advantages, which makes our life much easier. Because devices can help human daily work and store data, and many sensitive data are included in the device or cloud, so it needs protection. Thus, it is necessary to provide protection for the data privacy to prevent the sensitive data abuse by irresponsible people [1].

Data mining is very important since it can extract or excavate information from a great mass of data. Because there is a mass of data in the database, it is very significant to analyze extracting data. With the sharing of data, the stored data is likely to be threatened. Therefore, many researchers have developed privacy-protecting data mining (PPDM) to get rid of these threats.

The security of sensitive data needs to be protected. Because PPDM is still in its infancy, it is regarded as one of the important research fields to be developed. PPDM is a process of extracting data from large databases, and it can protect sensitive data. PPDM

© Springer Nature Singapore Pte Ltd. 2021
Y. Tian et al. (Eds.): ICBDS 2020, CCIS 1415, pp. 510–521, 2021.
https://doi.org/10.1007/978-981-16-3150-4_42

hides sensitive data without sacrificing data availability. Researchers have developed various PPDM technologies, and the number is expected to grow to a considerable quantity due to its broad prospects and potential.

This paper's purposes are as below:

(1) To develop a k-anonymity algorithm as data anonymization to protect data privacy;
(2) To implement decision tree classification algorithm for data mining on health data sets;
(3) To evaluate and benchmark the use of quantitative measures in privacy level and mining quality.

This paper's organizational structure is as below: The first section describes the research background in detail, which brings about the need to provide protection for the security of sensitive data; the second section summarizes the related research work of sensitive data protection; the third section describes the identification and filtering methods of sensitive data based on decision tree based on sensitive data protection, data mining, privacy protection and mining quality. The fourth section gives the simulation experiment, and the experimental results and analysis effectively prove the effectiveness of the scheme, and compared with other data mining technology, privacy level and data quality provide better results.

2 Related Work

Researchers have come up with many methods to protect sensitive data. Among these methods, there are two models which are most important: k-anonymity and differential privacy. By clustering or generalization, K anonymity makes no less than k records with the same quasi identifier (QI). If there are K records with the same QI in the dataset, there is only 1/K probability for the attacker to surmise the correct one. Its implementation is easy and its leakage risk can be measured, which accounts for its widespread applications. But, since the attacker's background knowledge is increasing, the privacy protection effect is becoming worse and worse. To offer more sensitive data protection approaches, differential privacy has been adopted to sensitive data protection. Even if all the information has been got by the attacker except the protected information, he cannot always obtain sensitive information. However, the implementation cost of differential privacy program is very high, and as the increase of protection intensity, data availability will be seriously destroyed. Data availability will be severely compromised.

At present, for the identification and filtering of sensitive data, researchers have put forward three areas of work that seem to have different objectives. These three areas are privacy policy, statistical privacy and privacy in cryptography. Access control model is a privacy protection method, which belongs to the privacy policy. Privacy is protected by complete homomorphic encryption solution. The method proposed hereby belongs to the second field. K anonymity was put forward by Samarati and Sweeney in [6]. At least k have the same QI, which can prevent the leakage of QI, but cannot protect sensitive properties. For example, over k elements in an anonymous peer category have the same QI, however, sensitive attributes have the same value, for example "cancer".

The attacker can still know that the user in the anonymous category is a cancer patient. L-diversity overcomes this disadvantage. It not only requires that at least k records in the equivalent category with the same QI, but also the sensitive data has no less than 1 different values. t-closeness requires that the sensitive attributes distribution in anonymous datasets shall be close enough to the sensitive attributes distribution in the whole dataset. Both diversity and compact density can restrict the leakage of sensitive attributes. In addition, k-anonymity can be realized by generalization and suppression, but the author does not give an effective method to find equivalent classes. Subsequently, researchers also come up with micro aggregation method, but if the data set is large, the calculation cost will be high.

3   Recognition and Filtering Method of Sensitive Data Based on Decision Tree

3.1   Privacy Protection

The first stage is that the dataset must be anonymized at the very beginning [3]. The anonymous process is accomplished by using the ARX anonymous tool. ARX has four advantages:

(1)   It implements a variety of privacy methods in an efficient way;
(2)   It supports cross platform graphical interfaces;
(3)   It provides a programmable API interface;
(4)   Document support.

Through using this tool, the attributes selected for the anonymization process are age, people and classes who are not pregnant. Generalization technology is applied during anonymization, in which the attributes of the selected dataset are generalized so that the anonymity of the data can be generated [4].

Samarati and Sweeney proposed k-anonymous in [6], and the implementation method is list in [2, 5]. A brief introduction to its definition, implementation and improvement process is as following.

1.   Definition One (k-anonymity [5])

Suppose T (A1; A2; An) be a table and a QI, where QI is its associated quasi identifier. Suppose T meets the K anonymity of QI, and only if every value sequence in T [QI] appears at least k times in T [QI]. K anonymous property ensures that identity leakage is prevented. However, it cannot protect data from sensitive attribute leakage. For instance, if a sensitive attribute has the same value, we know the sensitive value element of that person in the anonymous group, although we don't know QI. To resist homogeneity attack and background knowledge attack, machanavajjhala put forward L-diversity model.

2. Definition Two (L diversity)

If the sensitive attribute has no less than L different values, the QI group satisfies L diversity. If each cluster of the table meets the diversity requirements, the modified table also meets the diversity requirements.

L-diversity improves the k-anonymous security, but there are still some shortcomings. If the sensitive information distribution in each anonymous group is very different from that of the whole data set, it may still cause the leakage of private information. For example, if the probability of a disease somewhere is 0.01, while in an anonymous group the probability is 0.5, although the anonymous group follows L diversity, we can still get the following data: someone in the anonymous group is more likely to have the disease. In order to overcome this shortcoming, we propose that the distance between the sensitive information distribution in the anonymous group and the whole data set distribution should not exceed t. The definition is as follows.

3. Definition Three (t-Closeness)

If the distance between the sensitive attributes distribution in this class and the attributes distribution in the whole table is not greater than the threshold t. If all equivalence classes have t-Closeness, the table is considered to have t-Closeness.

For example, ten records are in an anonymous class. If the attacker obtains the QI of user A. He knows that user A's records are in an anonymous set. The attacker wants to know which specific record belongs to user A. The only thing he needs to do is test these ten records.

Sharing K records with the same QI is not our ultimate objective, but our goal is that K records cannot be distinguished. If K records are indistinguishable, the value of their identification is not important. On the basis of this, we have come up with random k-anonymity as below.

4. Definition Four (random K anonymity)

q is a random query on dataset D, and the probability of q (D) generated by e1, e2, or ek 'is equal, where ei ∈ D; k' > k. For q, D meets random k-anonymity. Compared with definition one, K records may have different QIs, which means that there is own unique identifier for each record. The only demand is that each record corresponding to the query result has an equal probability of each other. The QI must have the same value. Definition One is only one of the ways to realize definition Four. In other words, definition Four is an extension of definition One.

3.2 Data Mining

The second stage is the process of data mining. The typical data mining architecture have the following main system components.The second stage is the process of data mining. The typical data mining architecture have the following main system components.

1. Database, or other data repository

It is a database or set of databases, data warehouses, spreadsheets, or other types of data repositories. Data cleaning and integration techniques can be conducted.

2. Database or data warehouse server

The component is in charge of obtaining relevant data according to the user's data mining demand.

3. Knowledge base

This is domain knowledge employed to guide the search or evaluate the result pattern. It includes a conceptual hierarchy for organizing properties or property values into different abstraction levels.

4. Data mining engine

It is an important part of data mining system. It contains a set of functional modules for performing tasks such as feature, association analysis, classification, evolution and deviation analysis.

5. Pattern evaluation module

It usually uses interest measure and interacts with data mining module to focus search on interesting patterns. It can access the interest threshold kept in the knowledge base.

6. GUI (Graphic User Interface)

It interacts between data mining system and users, and allows users to provide information to help centralized search by specifying data mining queries or tasks, and to conduct exploratory data mining on the basis of intermediate data mining results to interact with the system. The component also enables users to browse database and data warehouse patterns or data structures, evaluate mining patterns, and visualize patterns in different types.

This data mining technology is introduced by Quinlan in his C4.5 book, and the formula used is J48 formula [5]. The data mining process is completed by using WEKA tool [6]. The tool is very suitable for the data mining process. The following figure shows the process of data mining.

In this study, the data mining used is decision tree classification. The decision tree algorithm is an algorithm to achieve classification by means of the branches of the tree. Figure 2 shows a diagram example of the decision tree, in which the internal nodes of the tree represent the judgment of an attribute, the branches of the node are the judgment results, and the leaf node represents a class. Figure 2 shows the decision on whether a

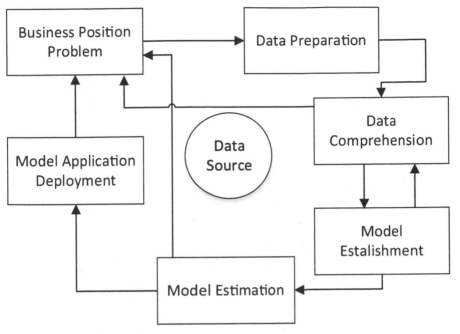

Fig. 1. Flow of data mining

user will buy a computer, which is displayed in the form of a decision tree. Through the decision tree, new records can be classified. Starting from the age of the root node, if the person is middle-aged, the decision to buy a computer will be given directly. If the person is a teenager, it is necessary to judge whether the user is a student. If the person is old, the user needs to be classified to judge its credit rating, and query the leaf node directly, so as to determine the category of records.

Compared with Bayes and neural network algorithms, the decision tree algorithm can express the decision results in a more intuitive way, and has a higher accuracy.

Without considering the relationship between classification and attribute, the information gain is taken as the index to measure ID3 algorithm. In practical application, there is a close relationship between them. An improved algorithm to overcome this shortcoming is proposed [2]. The related definitions are as follows: sample dataset S, classification attribute C has m different values $\{C1, C2,..., Cm\}$, the data set of S is divided into m subsets Si $(I = 1, 2,..., m)$, description attribute A has v different values $\{A1, A2,..., Av\}$, and description attribute A set S is divided into v subsets Sj $(J = 1, 2... v)$. The connection between attribute A and classification attribute C is defined as

$$F_A = \sum_{j=1}^{v} \frac{|S_j|}{|S|} \cdot W_j$$

The number of samples with j value of attribute A is $|Sj|$, the total number of samples is $|S|$ and the probability sum of classification results is Wj. Under the condition that the value of attribute A is Aj, it is about a subset of samples.

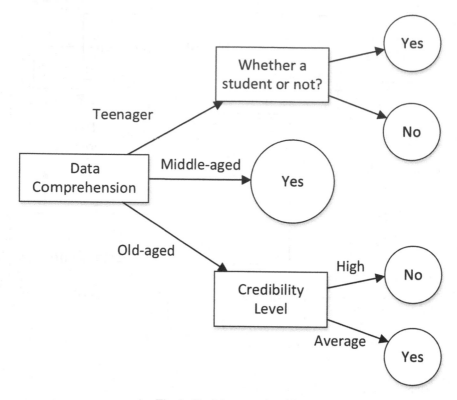

Fig. 2. Decision tree algorithm

The value of Wj is calculated as follows: the number of values of attribute A is Aj is t, there are t samples {m1, m2,..., mt}, the class label attribute value Ci of any sample Mj (j = 1, 2... T), the t samples obtained under the condition that the value of attribute A is Aj, the probability that the value of class label attribute in t samples is Ci is |Cij |/t. |Cij | is the number of samples with the value of classification attribute Ci among t samples. In the case that the classification attribute value of other description attribute values in sample mj is Ci, the probability in sample mj can be calculated by the same method, and each description attribute value in the sample is independent. According to the conjecture of sample mj, the attribute value Ci is classified, the probability value Pj is equal to the product of the data subset of probability obtained by each description attribute in the sample mj according to its own value. The condition of classification attribute value is Ci. Under the condition that the value of attribute A of attribute B corresponds to the data subset, the sum of the probabilities of correctly introducing the classified attribute value into the data subset is

$$W_j = \sum_{j=1}^{t} P_j$$

Using conditional probability to calculate the close correlation between attribute and decision attribute as weight and information gain, split attribute is selected. If an attribute has the maximum value of $Ma = Gain$ (id). F_A, it is selected as the segmentation attribute. For example, there are a lot of value attribute IDS, which can obtain a large amount of information. However, it is meaningless to use the method proposed in this paper to calculate the correlation between description attributes. The value ID and classification attributes are small, so $M_{id} = Gain$ (id). The value of F_A is small, so please avoid selecting attributes such as attribute id (attribute value is large but not important one) as decision tree model of decision node.

3.3 Privacy Level and Mining Quality

The last stage is based on the quantification of privacy level and mining quality. The quality used to quantify is accuracy. As the computer data storage capacity improves, a variety of new data mining algorithms were put forward. In the face of the urgent requirements of privacy protection in data mining, conventional privacy protection methods can not meet the requirements, because when they protect sensitive information, they can not access the knowledge in the data. Privacy preserving data mining mainly considers two problems. First, how to ensure that the ID number, name, address and other information will not be disclosed during the data application process. Whether sensitive original data is modified from the original database or deleted from the original database. The purpose is to protect individuals from privacy. Next is how to make more favorable data application. The sensitive knowledge extracted from database by service data mining algorithm may damage data privacy, so sensitive rules should be deleted. Using data mining technology to mine useful sensitive information from the database may destroy some data, so as to modify the original data in a certain way, and develop the related data mining algorithm. Now, privacy protection technique in database application mainly focuses on data mining and anonymity.

The research of privacy protection depends on the practical application of different privacy protection requirements. General privacy protection methods focus on data protection at a lower level of privacy. These methods implement privacy protection by introducing statistical model and probability model. Privacy protection in data mining is often used to realize privacy protection through different data features in advanced data. Privacy protection on the basis of data publishing aims to offer a universal privacy protection method for many applications.

There are many data mining methods for privacy protection. We classify privacy protection methods on the basis of the following aspects, for example: data distribution, data distortion, data mining algorithm, data or rule hiding and privacy protection.

Data distribution. Now, several algorithms conduct privacy preserving data mining on centralized data, while others conduct on distributed data, which is composed of vertical partition data. Different databases are recorded in different sites in horizontal partition data. In vertical partition data, each database records attribute values in different sites.

Data distortion. It modifies the original database records before publishing to protect privacy. It includes perturbation, blocking, aggregation or merging, switching and sampling. All complete the granular transformation of attribute values by changing attributes.

Data mining algorithm. Privacy preserving data mining algorithms include classification mining, association rule mining, clustering and Bayesian network.

Data or rule hiding. It refers to hiding the original data or the rules of the original data. Because the original data hiding rules are very complicated, some people put forward a heuristic method to solve this problem.

Privacy protection. To protect privacy, data needs to be carefully modified to get high data utility. (1) The data is modified on the basis of adaptive heuristic method, and only the selected values are modified, not all the values, which makes the information loss of the data minimum. (2) Encryption technology, for example: secure multiparty computing. If each site only knows its input, and knows nothing about other sites, the calculation is secure. (3) The data reconstruction appraoch can reconstruct the distribution of original data from random data.

Research on privacy protection methods focuses on data distortion, data encryption and data publishing, for instance: privacy protection classification mining algorithm, privacy protection association rule mining, distributed privacy protection collaborative recommendation, data publishing and so on. Many algorithms have been developed on the basis of encryption methods, for example: mining association rules in horizontal and vertical segmentation data, classification mining, clustering mining and decision tree mining.

The accuracy of anonymous data sets is measured by using examples of correct classification [7]. In Sect. 4.1 and 4.2, the quantization quality using decision tree algorithm and K anonymity is given in details.

4 Experiment

4.1 Experiment Result

The process of data anonymization is the first stage of the operational framework in this study. In this stage, pima Indian diabetes dataset was used as data input and k-anonymity technology was used for anonymization. ARX is an effective anonymization framework of open source data, which is realized in Java.

At this stage, it is necessary to identify the quasi identifier of the dataset in order to select the attributes suitable for anonymization. In this study, the attributes were age, number of pregnancies and class. In order to apply anonymization, the anonymity technique of each attribute is applied to each attribute.

The quantification of accuracy is a measure of the accuracy of anonymous data sets compared with the original data sets. The higher the precision value, the closer the anonymous dataset is to the original data. The accuracy of anonymous datasets is of great importance because it shows the value of dataset availability.

Based on WEKA, J48 decision tree classifier (DTC) has some parameters that need to be set in order to calculate the accuracy of data. The most important parameter values in precision determination are the minimum number of objects and the confidence level [8]. The minimum number of objects is set to 2 to 40, increasing by 2 each time. The confidence level is set from 0.1 to 1.0 by increasing 0.1 each time. Tables 1 and 2 show the accuracy of anonymous datasets in detail.

Table 1. Accuracy of DTC data mining based on minimum number of objects

Confidence level	Minimum number of objects	Accuracy
1	2	82.4219
1	4	80.3382
1	6	79.4269
1	8	78.5152
1	10	77.8645
1	12	78.6854
1	14	78.125
1	16	77.9944
1	18	77.3437
1	20	77.3437

Table 2. Hiding failure of anonymous dataset

K	Anonymous dataset	Original dataset	Hiding failure
10	85.60811	98.04067	87.31898
20	85.03044	98.04067	86.72976
30	86.00767	98.04067	87.72652
40	85.58478	98.04067	87.29518
50	86.04389	98.04067	87.76347

According to the HF of the dataset, the results show that the anonymous dataset is slightly better than the HF (hiding failure), which is about 86% to 87%. Although the hiding failure rate is very high, from the perspective of hiding failure, it will still increase, but it does not rise much. Therefore, it can be concluded that the privacy level of data sets can be improved by using k-anonymity technology.

This experiment is carried out on a PC running Windows 10 with Intel Core i5 2.4 GHz CPU and 4 GB main memory. The algorithm is implemented in Visual C++ 6.0. Each experiment was tested 10 times, and the average value of ten experiments was obtained.

In the experiment, adult census data sets from UC Irvine machine learning repository are used [14–15]. The database has been used by many researchers and has become a benchmark in the field of data privacy. The race, occupation, age, gender and ZIP of adults are regarded as quasi identifier (QI), and the "disease" column is added as the sensitive attribute, which is composed of {influenza, lung cancer, shortness of breath, obesity, breast cancer, AIDS}.

10000 tuples were randomly selected from adults as sliding window, and disease values were randomly assigned to each tuple based on basic medical knowledge.

4.2 Experiment Analysis

In this section, it compares with other data mining technologies to analyze the accuracy. In addition, other mining technologies, such as support vector machine (SVM) [9] and logistic regression (LR) [10], are tested on anonymous data sets to test their accuracy. Therefore, Table 3 below shows the comparison of LR, SVM and DTC (Decision tree Classifier).

Table 3. Comparison of LR, SVM and DTC

Data mining technology	Accuracy
DTC	82.4219%
LR	77.9948%
SVM	75.7813%

Table 4. Comparison with other methods

Method	Accuracy
This paper	82.4219%
Shafiq(2016)	82.1615%
Zhan (2016)	77.3438%

Last but not the least, the comparison with other PPDM works is discussed. Other works of PPDM include privacy-protecting data mining based on random substitution and decision tree classification (Shafiq, 2016) [11] and privacy-protecting data mining based on RSA encryption and decision tree classification (Zhan, 2014) [12]. Compared with other work, the research in this paper is a higher accuracy value after mining decision tree classification data. Table 4 shows the comparison results.

5   Conclusion

Based on this experiment, it can be concluded that privacy protecting technology, especially k-anonymity technology, provides better results for PPDM. It has been proved that the privacy of data can provide better results when the percentage of hiding faults is low. Anonymization can also be used to reduce the possibility of sensitive data leakage. The data mining process in this research also produced better results in terms of mining quality.

Acknowledgement. This paper is supported by the science and technology project of State Grid Corporation of China: "Research and Application of Key Technology of Data Sharing and Distribution Security for Data Center" (Grand No. 5700-202090192A-0–0-00).

References

1. Xu, N., Wang, H., Cen, L., et al.: Discussing the recognition method of sensitive data. Comput. Inf. Technol. **027**(002), 14–15, 59 (2019)
2. Huang, A., Chen, X.: An improved ID3 algorithm of decision trees . Comput. Eng. Sci. **31**(6), 109–111 (2009)
3. Song, F., Ma, T., Tian, Y., et al.: A new method of privacy protection: random k-anonymous. IEEE Access **7**, 75434–75445 (2019)
4. Prasser, F., Kohlmayer, F.: Putting statistical disclosure control into practice: the ARX data anonymization tool. In: Gkoulalas-Divanis, A., Loukides, G. (eds.) Medical Data Privacy Handbook, pp. 111–148. Springer, Cham (2015). https://doi.org/10.1007/978-3-319-23633-9_6
5. Heckerman, D.: Bayesian networks for data mining. data mining and knowledge discovery. Data Mining Knowl. Discov. 1(1), 79–119 (1997)
6. Holmes, G., Donkin, A., Witten, I.H . WEKA: a machine learning workbench. In: Proceedings of ANZIIS 1994 - Australian New Zealnd Intelligent Information Systems Conference, pp. 357–361 (1994)
7. Aggarwal, C.C., Yu, P.S.: A general survey of privacy-preserving data mining models and algorithms. J. Vasc. Surg. **8**(1), 64–70 (2008)
8. Milman, Y.: Minimum number of operations needed to identify an object in an array. J. Biotechnol. **85**(2):103–13 (1968)
9. Chauhan, V.K., Dahiya, K., Sharma, A.: Problem formulations and solvers in linear SVM: a review. Artif. Intell. Rev. (2018)
10. Song, L., Ma, C., Duan, G., et al.: Privacy-preserving logistic regression on vertically partitioned data . J. Comput. Res. Dev. **56**(10), 2243–2249 (2019)
11. Vaidya, J., Shafiq, B., Fan, W., et al.: A random decision tree framework for privacy-preserving data mining. IEEE Trans. Depend. Secure Comput. **11**(5), 399–411 (2014)
12. Zhan, J.: Using homomorphic encryption for privacy-preserving collaborative decision tree classiffication. In: 2007 IEEE Symposium on Computational Intelligence and Data Mining, pp. 637–645 (2007)

Hard Disk Failure Prediction via Transfer Learning

Rui Zhao[1,2], Donghai Guan[1,2]([✉]), Yuanfeng Jin[3], Hui Xiao[1,2], Weiwei Yuan[1,2], Yaofeng Tu[1], and Asad Masood Khattak[4]

[1] Nanjing University of Aeronautics and Astronautics, Nanjing, China
{zrui821,dhguan,xiaohui822,yuanweiwei}@nuaa.edu.cn
[2] Collaborative Innovation Center of Novel Software Technology and Industrialization, Nanjing, China
[3] Yanbian University, Yanbian, China
yfkim@ybu.edu.cn
[4] Zayed University, Abu Dhabi, UAE
Asad.Khattak@zu.ac.ae

Abstract. Due to the large-scale growth of data, the storage scale of data centers is getting larger and larger. Hard disk is the main storage medium, once a failure occurs, it will bring huge losses to users and enterprises. In order to improve the reliability of storage systems, many machine learning methods have been widely employed to predict hard disk failure in the past few decades. However, due to the large number of different models of hard disks in the heterogeneous disk system, traditional machine learning methods cannot build a general model. Inspired by a DANN based unsupervised domain adaptation approach for image classification, in this paper, we propose the DFPTL (Disk Failure Prediction via Transfer Learning) approach, which introduce the DANN approach to predict failure in heterogeneous disk systems by reducing the distribution differences between different models of disk datasets. This approach only needs unlabeled data (the target domain) of a specific disk model and the labeled data (the source domain) collected from a different disk model from the same manufacturer. Experimental results on real-world datasets demonstrate that DFPTL can achieve adaptation effect in the presence of domain shifts and outperform traditional machine learning algorithms.

Keywords: Disk failure · Transfer learning · Heterogeneous disk systems

1 Introduction

The development of the Internet has brought about an explosive growth in the amount of data, and the reliability of hard disks as the common and primary storage devices is crucial. Because of the complex structure and huge volume of the storage system, hard disk failures become the norm. However, due to the physical characteristics of the hard disk, once the hard disk fails, it will often cause a relatively large accident, and at the slightest degree, the data service provided by the data center is unavailable, and at the worst, it may cause permanent loss of the stored data, causing huge losses to users and

© Springer Nature Singapore Pte Ltd. 2021
Y. Tian et al. (Eds.): ICBDS 2020, CCIS 1415, pp. 522–536, 2021.
https://doi.org/10.1007/978-981-16-3150-4_43

enterprises. Microsoft has made statistics on hardware failures in data center [1]. Of these replacements failures, a majority (78%) were for hard disks, followed by a few (5%) due to raid controller and even fewer (3%) due to memory. In a year, approximately 2.7% of hard drives in the data center have been replaced. Furthermore, the hard disk as hardware, the longer it is used, the greater the probability of failure. Therefore, in order to improve the reliability of the storage system, some fault tolerance mechanisms have been adopted, which are mainly divided into passive fault tolerance and active fault tolerance. Compared with the passive fault tolerance mechanism of copying and erasing code, the advantage of active fault tolerance is that it can predict hard disk failure in advance. So that users have sufficient time to take protective measures, which can greatly reduce the loss of enterprises and users.

The original active fault tolerance mechanism of hard disks was implemented by the Self-Monitoring, Analysis and Reporting Technology (SMART) technology [2] built into the hard disk by hard disk manufacturers. Through SMART technology, individual hard disk can be monitored, and the collected information of each state attribute inside the hard disk is compared with the predefined fault threshold, if any attribute value exceeds its threshold, it will raise an alarm. However, this threshold-based detection method can only achieve a failure detection rate of 3%–10% at most (that is, it can predict 3%–10% of failed hard drives) with 0.1% false alarm rate [3, 4]. In order to solve the problem of low accuracy of hard disk failure prediction, many supervised machine learning methods are widely used [5–12]. These methods formulate the hard disk failure prediction problem as a binary classification problem. Specifically, these approaches take SMART attributes as input, and each hard disk is classified either as health or failure by the trained classifier. But these methods usually assume that training data and test data have the same distribution. The real storage systems consist of a large number of different models of hard disks, which are called heterogeneous disk systems [13, 14]. The distributions of hard drives SMART attributes from different models are different, so if the model trained with data from one model of hard drive is directly applied to predict another different model of hard drive, the results are usually inaccurate.

In order to eliminate the training–testing mismatch in heterogeneous disk systems, we utilize deep transfer learning technology to build an accurate and effective hard disk failure prediction model. Our work is inspired by a DANN based unsupervised domain adaptation approach for image classification [15]. This approach conducts domain adaptation based on the idea of adversary. Specifically, the classifier, the feature extractor, and the domain discriminator are learned at the same time. By minimizing the classifier error and maximizing the discriminator error, the learned feature representation has cross-domain invariance. Then in this feature representation space, the discriminative model learned from source domain features can also be applied to target domain features. In addition, this approach only needs the labeled training data from the source domain and unlabeled data from the target domain. In this study, we introduce the DANN approach to predict failure in heterogeneous disk systems by reducing the distribution differences between different models of hard disk datasets. However, applying DANN to predict disk failure is not straightforward and trivial. A critical challenge is one SMART record of the hard disk is collected at a specific time point, so it is one-dimensional, which is different from two-dimensional image features. To tackle this challenge, in this paper, we study how to construct the original 1D SMART data into 2D. The constructed 2D SMART attributes can directly deploy the deep transfer learning algorithm of DANN. We call the proposed approach DFPTL (Disk Failure Prediction via Transfer Learning).

We have conducted experiments on public datasets to verify the effectiveness of our method. The experimental results show that DFPTL achieves better performance than traditional unsupervised and supervised approaches when performing disk failure prediction on target dataset using the model learned from source dataset. The main contributions of our paper are summarized as follows:

- To the best of our knowledge, we pioneer the use of the transfer learning method based on unsupervised domain adaptation to predict disk failure, which can transfer knowledge of labeled disk data in the source domain to predict disk failure in the target domain.
- To deploy the deep transfer learning algorithm of DANN, we reconstruct the original 1D SMART data into 2D SMART data.
- We evaluate our approach on real-world datasets, and the experimental results demonstrate the effectiveness of the method.

The remainder of this paper is structured as follows: We first survey the related work in Sect. 2. Section 3 describes the details of the proposed method. Section 4 discusses experimental settings and results. Finally, conclusions are drawn in Sect. 5.

2 Related Work

Nowadays, most manufacturers equip hard disks with SMART technology to monitor and analyze the health status of the hard disk. A SMART record of the hard disk contains at most 30 meaningful attributes, describing the operating status of the hard disk from various aspects. Each SMART attribute contains four values, Raw value, Normalized Value, Threshold Value and Worst Value.

- ID: The unique identifier assigned to the SMART attribute.
- Raw: Measured value of each attribute when the hard disk is running, such as Celsius degree, Power-On Hours, etc.
- Normalized: Calculated by a specific algorithm built into the hard disk using its raw value.
- Threshold: The reliable attribute value specified by the hard disk manufacturer is calculated by a specific formula. If an attribute value is lower than the corresponding threshold, it means that the hard disk will become unreliable.
- Worst: The largest abnormal value that has ever occurred in the operation of the hard disk.

Because the raw value and normalized value can best reflect the current health status of the hard disk, in our paper, we use them as the characteristic value for building the hard disk failure prediction model.

There have proposed many machine learning algorithms for disk failure prediction models based on SMART data. Hughes et al. [16] proposed two statistical hypothesis test methods to improve performance of the detection method based on the SMART threshold. They used Wilcoxon rank-sum test and OR-ed single variate test and achieved 60% failure detection rate (FDR) and 0.5% false alarm rate (FAR). Hamerly et al. [17] studied two Bayesian methods named Naive Bayes clusters trained using expectation-maximization (NBEM) and naive Bayes classifier, and conducted experiment on a dataset from Quantum Inc., which contains 1927 hard disks, but only 9 failed hard disks. Experimental results show that under the condition of a FAR of 1%, the FDR of naive Bayes classifier can reach 55%, and the FDR of NBEM is 35–45%. Wang et al. [18] proposed a disk failure prediction model based on Mahalanobis Distance (MD), which converts multivariate SMART data into a single variable representing the health degree of disks. The health degree represents the change in the health of the hard disk. Finally, a specific health degree is used to analyze the abnormal changes of the hard disk's health state. When there are enough abnormal changes in a certain period of time, it means that the hard disk is about to fail. They achieved a 68% FDR with 0% FAR. Zhao Y et al. [9] proposed to employ Hidden Semi-Markov Models (HSMMs) and Hidden Markov Models (HMMs) to predict disk failure. They believe that there is a connection between the continuously collected SMART attribute values and the hard disk health status. The proposed model uses the connection of the same SMART attribute at different time points to represent the health status of the hard disk, which has the advantage that it does not require expensive parameter searching. Experimental results show that when using the best SMART attributes, HSMMs can achieve a failure detection rate of 30% and a false alarm rate of 0%, while HMMs model achieves a failure detection rate of 46% and a false alarm rate of 0%.

With the development of neural network technology, researchers have gradually turned their attention to the field of neural networks. A neural network includes an input layer, several hidden layers, and an output layer. Neuron nodes of different levels are connected by specific network weight values. The neural network-based hard disk failure prediction method uses historical hard disk SMART data as the input of the input layer to adjust and optimize the network weights of nodes at different layers in the network, and complete the training of the neural network model; when performing hard disk failure prediction, the real-time hard disk SMART data is input and processed by the entire neural network model to obtain the predicted hard disk operating state. Zhu et al. [11] implemented a backward propagation (BP) neural network model and an improved support vector machine (SVM) model. Both models were tested on a dataset from Baidu Inc., including 22962 good drives and 433 failed drives, and achieved much higher prediction accuracy compared with previous studies. Because SMART attributes gradually deteriorates over time, the methods mentioned above do not take into account time series characteristics. Xu et al. [19] introduced a new method based on Recurrent Neural Network (RNN) to assess the health of hard drives, making full use of the timing of SMART data. Experiments results show that this method can not only reasonably explain the health status of the hard disk, but also achieve better prediction results. But the standard RNN algorithm has the problem of gradient explosion or gradient disappearance. When the number of neurons in the loop layer is large, the early input historical data will be invalid due to the disappearance of the gradient. Lima et al. [33] made improvements on this basis and proposed a variant algorithm of recurrent neural network LSTM (Long Short-Term Memory) for long-term prediction of hard disk failures. Compared with the traditional recurrent neural network algorithm, this algorithm can achieve similar results in short-term prediction, and has a significant improvement effect in long-term prediction.

The above methods are all supervised algorithms, based on sufficient labeled data, and only train a model using SMART data from one disk model is not applicable to other different models even from the same manufacturer. When existing data set that are relevant but not identical to the target domain are available, transfer learning becomes an effective solution. Transfer learning has a wide range of applications, including but not limited to computer vision [20], text classification [21], behavior recognition [22], medical health [23] and so on. In recent years, transfer learning has been applied to the field of hard disk failure prediction. Botezatu et al. [10] adopted an instance-based transfer learning method to eliminate the sample selection bias between source data and target data, so as to apply a model trained on a specific hard drive model to a new one from the same manufacturer. Its main idea is to train a classifier to indicate the probability that a hard disk belongs to a certain model, and then utilize the classifier to sample the labeled hard disk model to make it obey the same distribution as the target hard disk dataset. Pereira et al. [13] proposed a new source building method called clustering-based information source and groups them according to their similarity to build a novel information source for transfer learning. Zhang et al. [24] explored an iterative transfer learning approach to solve the failure prediction problem of minority disks lacking sufficient training data. Specifically, the weights of instances are adjusted in each iteration, and larger weights are assigned to the instances of the majority disks that are similar to the instances of the minority disks, otherwise, smaller weights are assigned. They also proposed a method to select appropriate disk models based on the KLD value. These instance-based transfer learning methods mainly reduce the differences in the distribution of the source domain and the target domain in two ways: by adjusting the weight of the source domain instance and selecting the source domain instance according to the similarity with the target domain instance, they make it possible to transfer health status information from one disk model with enough data available to another disk model with insufficient data. Different from these methods, the transfer learning component in our method is a feature-based transfer learning method that learns a common feature representation space on the source domain and the target domain to realize shared-classifier.

3 Proposed Approach

In this section, we will introduce the details of our proposed approach, called DFPTL (Disk Failure Prediction via Transfer Learning), which use transfer learning technology for disk failure prediction. Figure 1 shows the overall workflow of DFPTL.

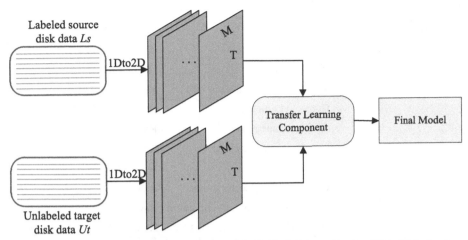

Fig. 1. The overall workflow of DFPTL. For each individual disk, we first use 1D to 2D technology to construct SMART records from two different domains L_s and U_t as 2D-SMART attributes of size M * T, then input them into the transfer learning component to train the base model.

There are two sets of input data. The unlabeled disk data U_t to be predicted serves as the target domain, and the labeled disk data L_s from the same manufacturer but different model as the target domain hard disk serves as the source domain. Every disk is classified either as "health" or "failure". DFPTL comprises three main components: (1) data processing, (2) Construction of 2D-SMART attributes, (3) transfer learning. We will describe more details about each component in the following sections.

3.1 Data Processing

In our disk dataset, each sample contains up to 30 SMART attributes, but some attributes are useless for failure prediction since they keep unchanged during operation, so we get rid of these attributes, while some attributes change significantly over time, and the values on healthy and failed hard disks are obviously different, so we keep these attributes. We select 15 attributes using principal component analysis (PCA), the selected SMART attributes are shown in Table 1.

Table 1. The 15 selected SMART attributes.

Smart ID	SMART attribute name	Attribute type
1	Raw read error rate	Normalized
3	Spin-up time	Normalized
5	Reallocated sectors count	Raw
7	Seek error rate	Normalized

(continued)

Table 1. (*continued*)

Smart ID	SMART attribute name	Attribute type
9	Power-on hours	Normalized
187	Reported uncorrectable errors	Raw
188	Command timeout	Raw
190	Airflow temperature	Raw
193	Load/unload cycle count	Raw
194	Temperature	Normalized
197	Current pending sector count	Raw
198	Offline uncorrectable sector count	Raw
240	Head flying hours	Raw
241	Total LBAs written	Raw
242	Total LBAs read	Raw

The 15 attributes above have different value intervals. The large difference in the value interval makes the model difficult or even unable to converge. Therefore, normalization is very necessary. We use min-max scaling [5, 12] to normalize the range of selected SMART attributes.

$$x_{norm} = \frac{x_i - x_{min}}{x_{max} - x_{min}} \tag{1}$$

Where x_i is the original value of i-th SMART attribute, x_{max} and x_{min} are the maximum and minimum value of the attribute, respectively. After normalization, all attribute values are mapped to the range [0, 1].

3.2 Construction of 2D-SMART Attributes

The DANN algorithm [15] was first proposed for image classification and achieved good performance in experiments. Correspondingly, the feature extractor in the DANN model architecture is composed of convolutional neural networks (CNN) to automatically extract image features. After the steps in Sect. 3.1, the feature of each sample is one-dimensional, referred to as 1D-SMART attribute. In order to support the deployment of DANN for transfer learning, the 1D-SMART attribute needs to be transformed into a two-dimensional feature similar to an image. In [25], in order to use the GAN-based model for disk failure prediction, Jiang et al. convert 1D-SMART attributes into 2D attributes chunks, this technology is called 1Dto2D. Inspired by [25], we employ 1Dto2D to reconstruct the 1D-SMART attributes into 2D-SMART attributes, which is regarded as the input of the feature extractor. As shown in Fig. 2, 1D-SMART attribute represents a SMART record of a hard disk, including M SMART attributes after feature selection. Then stack continual 1D-SMART attributes and segment data with time window of size T. The 2D-SMART attributes constructed in this way is conducive to deploying the deep transfer learning algorithm of DANN, and can take advantage of the automatic feature extraction of the CNN-based feature extractor.

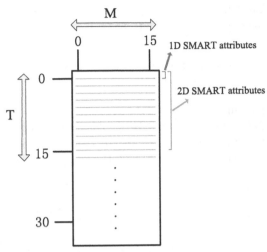

Fig. 2. Construction of 2D-SMART attributes. Each row of records (blue lines) represents selected 15 SMART attributes of a hard disk, and then stack the continuous SMART attributes. Because SMART attributes are collected on a daily basis, T represents hard disk data for T consecutive days. We call the constructed SMART attributes of size M * T as 2D-SMART attributes.

3.3 Transfer Learning Component

The main idea of transfer learning is to transfer related but different domain knowledge to complete or improve the learning effect of the target domain, which is suitable for situation where the source domain and target domain have different distributions. According to the analysis of [10, 24], we know that different models of hard drives exhibit different SMART value distributions, even from the same manufacturer, we refer to this phenomenon as covariate shift [27]. Therefore, the failure prediction model trained on disk data of one model can't be directly transferred to other models of hard disks, otherwise the prediction results will be inaccurate. The solution is to use the transfer learning algorithm to train the model with a large amount of labeled SMART data from source domain and a large amount of unlabeled SMART data from target domain. Inspired by the DANN based unsupervised domain adaptation approach for image classification [15], we adopt DANN to predict disk failure.

Figure 3 shows how to use the DANN approach in disk failure prediction. For the unlabeled disk data U_t in the target domain that needs to be predicted, and the labeled disk data L_s of other models in the source domain, first of all, we adopt the 1Dto2D method to construct each 1D-SMART attribute of U_t and L_s into image-like 2D-SMART attributes, which is then used as the input of the DANN-based transfer learning model. The network architecture is based on a standard feedforward neural network, which consists of three parts: a deep feature extractor G_f used to extract features, generally composed of convolutional layers and pooling layers; A label predictor G_y, which consists of fully connected layers and a logistic classifier, has an output of 0 (health) or 1 (failure); As well as a domain classifier G_d, which forms the adversarial network framework with G_f, is composed of fully connected layers and a cross-entropy classifier. We denote the source domain with 1 and the target domain with 0. The loss function of DANN is defined as:

$$E(\theta_f, \theta_y, \theta_d) = \sum_{i=1..N} L_y^i(\theta_f, \theta_y) - \lambda \sum_{i=1..N} L_d^i(\theta_f, \theta_d) \qquad (2)$$
$$d_i = [0, 1]$$

Where θ_f, θ_y, θ_d are the parameters of the network G_f, G_y, G_d respectively. For the i-th training sample, L_y^i and L_d^i represent label prediction loss and domain classification loss respectively. The parameter λ is introduced to trade off two losses during learning. Then we utilize the standard stochastic gradient (SGD) approach to seek the optimized parameters.

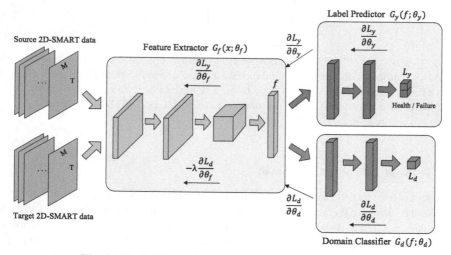

Fig. 3. The DANN approach used for disk failure prediction

4   Experimental Results

4.1   Dataset

We used BackBlaze's public dataset to evaluate our proposed method. From the datasets, we select disk data of different models from two manufacturers. Seagate's ST4000DM000 as the source domain dataset and Seagate's ST12000NM0007 as the target domain dataset respectively. And two models of hard drives from HGST manufacturer, HDS722020ALA330 and HDS5C3030ALA630 as source domain dataset and target domain dataset, respectively. Each hard disk is classified either as "health" or "failure", and each hard disk has many SMART records. Table 2 lists the selected datasets. In order to alleviate the problem that there are much more health disk samples than failure disk samples, we under-sample the health samples to balance the dataset [30]. We have chosen a 1:5 ratio of failure disks to health disks.

Table 2. The selected disk models

Manufacturer	Disk model	Health	Failure
Seagate	ST4000DM000	8230	1646
	ST12000NM0007	7650	1530
HGST	HDS722020ALA330	4580	229
	HDS5C3030ALA630	4020	134

4.2 Evaluation Metric

We evaluate the effectiveness of our proposed approach using Precision, Recall, F1-Score and AUC metrics, which have been widely used to evaluate the capability of a classification model in machine learning [29]. Precision is defined as the proportion of predicted failed disks that are predicted accurately:

$$\text{Precision} = \frac{\text{TP}}{\text{TP} + \text{FP}} \tag{3}$$

Recall represents the proportion of true failed disks that are correctly predicted as failed:

$$\text{Recall} = \frac{\text{TP}}{\text{TP} + \text{FN}} \tag{4}$$

Where TP, FP and FN denote true positive, false positive and false negative, respectively. F1-Score is the balance between Precision and Recall. The higher the F1-Score, the better the model:

$$\text{F1} - \text{Score} = \frac{2 * \text{Precision} * \text{Recall}}{\text{Precision} + \text{Recall}} \tag{5}$$

AUC represents the Area Under the Curve-Receiver Operating Characteristic (AUC-ROC) curve, it considers the classifier's ability to classify positive and negative samples at the same time. In the case of imbalanced classes, it can still make a reasonable evaluation of the classifier.

4.3 Results

The Effectiveness of Transfer Learning Component. In order to evaluate the effectiveness of the transfer learning component in our method, the transfer learning model trained with the labeled disk data of the source domain and the unlabeled disk data of the target domain will be compared with the SOURCE-ONLY model, which is trained without consideration for target-domain data (no domain classifier branch included into the network). In addition, The TRAIN-ON-TARGET model serves as an upper performance bound, which is trained and tested on the target domain, assuming labels are available.

Table 3. Experimental results of different methods.

Disk model	Methods	Precision	Recall	F1-Score	AUC
ST-A → ST-B	DFPTL	0.4309	0.8030	**0.5608**	**0.8332**
	SOURCE-ONLY	0.2204 0.2204	0.9303	0.3564	0.7533
	TRAIN-ON-TARGET	0.8011	0.8909	0.8436	0.8816
HDS-A → HDS-B	DFPTL	0.6923	0.6338	**0.6618**	**0.8101**
	SOURCE-ONLY	0.4742	0.6479	0.5476	0.8066
	TRAIN-ON-TARGET	0.8425	0.7571	0.7975	0.8471

Table 3 shows the Precision, Recall, F1-Score and AUC for disk failure prediction for different source and target domains. The experiments are conducted on two pairs of datasets, including ST-A → ST-B, and HDS-A → HDS-B. ST-A and ST-B represent hard drive models ST4000DM000 and ST12000NM0007 from the Seagate manufacturer, respectively. HDS-A and HDS-B represent hard drive models HDS722020ALA330 and HDS5C3030ALA630 from the HGST manufacturer, respectively. The right side of the arrow denotes the unlabeled disk dataset to be predicted and the left side of the arrow denotes the labeled auxiliary disk dataset.

As we can see, our DFPTL shows higher F1-Score and AUC than SOURCE-ONLY. The reason is that when the SMART attributes distributions of the source domain disk dataset and the target domain disk dataset are different, if the model trained with the disk dataset of the source domain directly predicts the disk failure of the target domain, the result is often inaccurate. The SOURCE-ONLY model only capture the feature distribution of hard disk data in the source domain, and the trained label predictor can only classify the source domain hard disk. Our DFPTL's transfer learning component can map the features of the two domains to the common feature space through the adversarial network framework, reducing the difference in the distribution of SMART attributes, so that the classifier trained based on the labeled data of the source domain can be applied to the target domain. The experimental results verify the effectiveness of the transfer learning component.

The Effectiveness of 1Dto2D. In this section, we evaluate the effectiveness of proposed 1Dto2D approach. We use sliding windows with lengths of 1, 5, 10, and 15 to segment continual 1D-SMART attributes stacked along with time, respectively. Note that each hard drive collects one SMART record a day, so $T = 1$ represents the 1D-SMART attribute of a certain day, $T = 5$ represents the SMART records collected for 5 consecutive days, the size of the corresponding 2D-SMART attribute is 15 * 5, and so on, for $T = 10$, 15, the size of corresponding 2D-SMART attribute are 15 * 10, 15 * 15, respectively. Figure 4 and Fig. 5 represent the prediction results on two target domains, respectively. We calculate the F1-Score of the model of different percentage of labeled data. Therefore, the horizontal axis represents the percentage of labeled data in the target domain. As shown in these figures, when $T = 1$, the prediction effect of the trained model was the worst, because 1D-SMART is not converted to 2D-SMART attributes, and the advantages of CNN's automatic feature extraction cannot be utilized well. The performance of the model at $T = 5$, 10, 15 is better than that at $T = 1$, indicating the effectiveness of 1Dto2D approach. Besides, we observe that when $T = 15$, the model achieved the highest F1-Score. Therefore, we set $T = 15$ in the experiments in this paper.

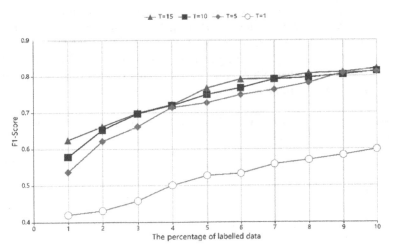

Fig. 4. F1-Scores under different time range T on dataset ST-B.

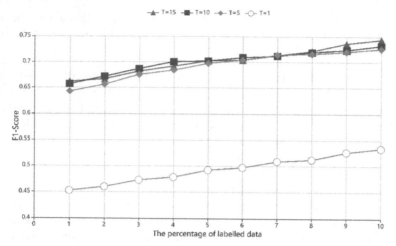

Fig. 5. F1-Scores under different time range T on dataset HDS-B

5 Conclusion

In this paper, we propose an approach called DFPTL for disk failure prediction, which can address the training–testing mismatch problem in heterogeneous disk system. Transfer learning can eliminate the differences of data distribution between the source and the target domains. Moreover, to deploy DANN-based deep transfer learning approach, we stack continuous hard disk SMART data into 2D image-like SMART data. The use of CNN gets rid of manually extracting features. Experimental results with real-world datasets have confirmed that DFPTL can achieve higher detection accuracy, compared to traditional machine learning methods.

Acknowledgements. This research is supported by the key research and development program of Jiangsu province(BE2019012).

References

1. Vishwanath, K.V., Nagappan, N.: Characterizing cloud computing hardware reliability. In: Proceedings of the 1st ACM symposium on Cloud computing, pp. 193–204 (2010)
2. Allen, B.: Monitoring hard disks with smart. Linux J. **117**, 74–77 (2004)
3. Eckart, B., Chen, X., He X., et al.: Failure prediction models for proactive fault tolerance within storage systems. In: 2008 IEEE International Symposium on Modeling, Analysis and Simulation of Computers and Telecommunication Systems, pp. 1–8. IEEE (2008)
4. Murray, J.F., Hughes, G.F., Kreutz-Delgado, K.: Machine learning methods for predicting failures in hard drives: a multiple-instance application. J. Mach. Learn. Res. **6**(May), 783–816 (2005)
5. Xiao, J., Xiong, Z., Wu, S., et al.: Disk failure prediction in data centers via online learning. In: Proceedings of the 47th International Conference on Parallel Processing, pp. 1–10 (2018)

6. Li, J., Ji, X., Jia, Y., et al.: Hard drive failure prediction using classification and regression trees. In: 2014 44th Annual IEEE/IFIP International Conference on Dependable Systems and Networks, pp. 383–394. IEEE (2014)
7. Murray, J.F., Hughes, G.F., Kreutz-Delgado, K.: Hard drive failure prediction using non-parametric statistical methods. In: Proceedings of ICANN/ICONIP (2003)
8. Yang, W., Hu, D., Liu, Y., et al.: Hard drive failure prediction using big data. In: 2015 IEEE 34th Symposium on Reliable Distributed Systems Workshop (SRDSW), pp. 13–18. IEEE (2015)
9. Zhao, Y., Liu, X., Gan, S., et al.: Predicting disk failures with HMM-and HSMM-based approaches. In: Industrial Conference on Data Mining, pp. 390–404. Springer, Berlin, Heidelberg (2010). https://doi.org/10.1007/978-3-642-14400-4_30
10. Botezatu, M.M., Giurgiu, I., Bogojeska, J., et al.: Predicting disk replacement towards reliable data centers. In: Proceedings of the 22nd ACM SIGKDD International Conference on Knowledge Discovery and Data Mining, pp. 39–48 (2016)
11. Zhu, B., Wang, G., Liu, X., et al.: Proactive drive failure prediction for large scale storage systems. In: 2013 IEEE 29th symposium on mass storage systems and technologies (MSST), pp. 1–5. IEEE (2013)
12. Xu, Y., Sui, K., Yao, R., et al.: Improving service availability of cloud systems by predicting disk error. In: 2018 {USENIX} Annual Technical Conference ({USENIX} {ATC} 18), pp. 481–494 (2018)
13. Pereira, F.L.F., dos Santos Lima, F D., de Moura Leite, L G., et al.: Transfer learning for Bayesian networks with application on hard disk drives failure prediction. In: 2017 Brazilian Conference on Intelligent Systems (BRACIS), pp. 228–233. IEEE (2017)
14. Jiang, W., Hu, C., Zhou, Y., et al.: Are disks the dominant contributor for storage failures? a comprehensive study of storage subsystem failure characteristics. ACM Trans. Storage (TOS). 4(3), 1–25 (2008)
15. Ganin, Y., Lempitsky, V.: Unsupervised domain adaptation by backpropagation. In: International conference on machine learning, pp. 1180–1189 (2015)
16. Hughes, G.F., Murray, J.F., Kreutz-Delgado, K., et al.: Improved disk-drive failure warnings. IEEE Trans. Reliab. 51(3), 350–357 (2002)
17. Hamerly, G., Elkan, C.: Bayesian approaches to failure prediction for disk drives. ICML 1, 202–209 (2001)
18. Wang, Y., Ma, E.W.M., Chow, T.W.S., et al.: A two-step parametric method for failure prediction in hard disk drives. IEEE Trans. Ind. Inf. 10(1), 419–430 (2013)
19. Xu, C., Wang, G., Liu, X., et al.: Health status assessment and failure prediction for hard drives with recurrent neural networks. IEEE Trans. Comput. 65(11), 3502–3508 (2016)
20. Zhu, Y., Zhuang, F., Wang, J., et al.: Multi-representation adaptation network for cross-domain image classification. Neural Netw. 119, 214–221 (2019)
21. Prettenhofer, P., Stein, B.: Cross-language text classification using structural correspondence learning. In: Proceedings of the 48th annual meeting of the association for computational linguistics, pp. 1118–1127 (2010)
22. Wang, J., Zheng, V.W., Chen, Y., et al.: Deep transfer learning for cross-domain activity recognition. In: proceedings of the 3rd International Conference on Crowd Science and Engineering, pp. 1–8 (2018)
23. Kermany, D.S., Goldbaum, M., Cai, W., et al.: Identifying medical diagnoses and treatable diseases by image-based deep learning. Cell 172(5), 1122–1131 (2018)
24. Zhang, J., Zhou, K., Huang, P., et al.: Transfer learning based failure prediction for minority disks in large data centers of heterogeneous disk systems. In: Proceedings of the 48th International Conference on Parallel Processing, pp.1–10 (2019)

25. Jiang, T., Zeng, J., Zhou, K., et al.: Lifelong disk failure prediction via GAN-Based anomaly detection. In: 2019 IEEE 37th International Conference on Computer Design (ICCD), pp. 199–207. IEEE (2019)

26. Zhang, X., Kim, J., Lin, Q., et al.: Cross-dataset time series anomaly detection for cloud systems. In: 2019 {USENIX} Annual Technical Conference ({USENIX}{ATC} 19), pp. 1063–1076 (2019)

27. Shimodaira, H.: Improving predictive inference under covariate shift by weighting the log-likelihood function. J. Stat. Plan. Infer. **90**(2), 227–244 (2000)

28. Yang, Y., Loog, M.: Active learning using uncertainty information. In: 2016 23rd International Conference on Pattern Recognition (ICPR), pp. 2646–2651. IEEE (2016)

29. Powers, D.M.: Evaluation: from precision, recall and F-measure to ROC, informedness, markedness and correlation (2011)

30. He, H., Garcia, E.A.: Learning from imbalanced data. IEEE Trans. Knowl. Data Eng. **21**(9), 1263–1284 (2009)

31. Liu, F.T., Ting, K.M., Zhou, Z.H.: Isolation forest. In: 2008 Eighth IEEE International Conference on Data Mining, pp. 413–422. IEEE (2008)

32. Breunig, M.M., Kriegel, H.P., Ng, R.T., et al.: LOF: identifying density-based local outliers. In: Proceedings of the 2000 ACM SIGMOD International Conference on Management of Data, pp. 93–104 (2000)

33. dos Santos Lima, F.D., Amaral, G.M.R., de Moura Leite, L.G., et al.: Predicting failures in hard drives with lstm networks. In: 2017 Brazilian Conference on Intelligent Systems (BRACIS), pp. 222–227. IEEE (2017)

Design and Application of CMAC Neural Network Based on Software Hardening Technology

Hao Zhu[1,2]([✉]), Mulan Wang[2], and Weiye Xu[3]

[1] School of Information and Communication,
Nanjing Institute of Technology, Nanjing 211167, China
zhuhao@njit.edu.cn
[2] Jiangsu Key Laboratory of Advanced Numerical Control Technology, Nanjing 211167, China
[3] Department of Informatics, University of Leicester, Leicester L1 7RH, UK

Abstract. The thought of designing CMAC (Cerebellar Model Articulation Controller) hardware control chip which bases on software hardening technology is put forward according to the working theories and inner structure characteristics of CMAC neural network. The method of software hardening based on FPGA (Field Programmable Gate Array) is discussed in detail. The corresponding simulation waveforms are given. The CMAC compound control strategy used in PMSLM (Permanent Magnet Synchronous Linear Motor) is designed. As the test object, IC22-050A2P1 PMLSM made by Kollmorgen is used in the actual application of hardening CMAC control chip to verify the correctness of the program.

Keywords: CMAC neural network · Software hardening · PMSLM

1 Introduction

CMAC is a table look-up adaptive neural network, which is constructed by J. S. albus in 1975, which imitates the basic principle of cerebellar control of limb movement. CMAC network is essentially a local approximation neural network. Compared with other neural networks, CMAC neural network has better nonlinear approximation ability and is more suitable for nonlinear real-time control in complex environment [1]. CMAC has a series of advantages. For example, the local learning makes the weight of each correction less, the learning speed is faster, and it is more suitable for real-time control. It has the ability of local generalization. Similar inputs produce similar outputs, and distant inputs produce independent outputs. It has continuous (Analog) input and output capability, which is closer to the control system. The basic structure of CMAC network is to divide the system input space into many blocks, each block specifies an actual memory location. The information learned by each block is distributed and stored in the position of adjacent blocks. The number of storage units is usually much less than the maximum possible input space for the problem to be considered. Therefore, the implementation of many to one mapping, that is, multiple blocks are mapped to the same memory address [2]. It

© Springer Nature Singapore Pte Ltd. 2021
Y. Tian et al. (Eds.): ICBDS 2020, CCIS 1415, pp. 537–548, 2021.
https://doi.org/10.1007/978-981-16-3150-4_44

can be seen that CMAC can be described according to the input spatial relationship and the output space. This feature is in good agreement with the internal characteristics of FPGA commonly used in the field of electronic system design. FPGA is composed of a large number of ram look-up tables. By loading programming data into the RAM unit, the logical function of the logical unit and the connection mode between the modules are determined by the value stored in the RAM unit [3]. Therefore, its basic feature is to use ram look-up table to realize combinatorial logic. Each lookup table is connected to the input of a D trigger and drives I/O. Multiple ram look-up tables (I/O units) ultimately determine the function of FPGA. According to the characteristics of the neural network control chip, the neural network control chip is developed based on the neural network. This hardware control chip has the advantages of high speed, good stability and strong adaptability.

2   Working Principle of CMAC Neural Network

2.1   CMAC Network Structure

The topology of CMAC with n-dimensional input and r-dimension output is shown in Fig. 1.

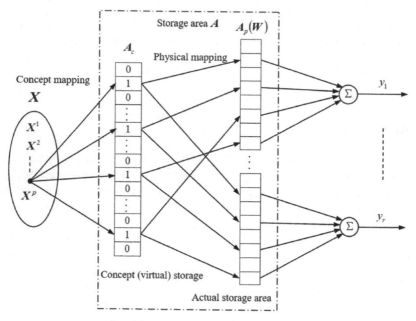

Fig. 1. Topological structure of CMAC.

The n-dimensional input state space in the graph is represented by X. Where $X^p = [x_1^p, x_2^p, \ldots\ldots, x_n^p]^T$, p is the sample number. The r-dimensional output vector of the system is represented by $[y_1, y_2, \ldots\ldots, y_r]$. $Y = [y_1, y_2, \ldots\ldots, y_r]^T = F(x_1^p, x_2^p, \ldots\ldots,$

$x_n{}^P$). The CMAC network represented by the virtual frame in the figure is essentially a storage area. It includes virtual storage area A_c and physical storage area $A_p(W)$. The working process of CMAC is: a state sample vector X^P is given in the input space. Activate the C elements in A_c successively so that they are 1 at the same time, while most other elements are 0. The network output y_j ($j = 1, 2, ..., r$) is obtained by summing the weights of C active units in A_c in $A_p(W)$. The actual response value is then compared with the expected output value. According to the error value and learning algorithm, the weight content of these activated memory cells is modified. This cycle until the corresponding performance index is met. The value of C is related to the generalization ability, which is called generalization parameter. The topology of CMAC neural network is shown in Fig. 1.

In general, the n-dimensional component of input vector X is analog quantity. Each element in the virtual storage area A_c only takes two values of 0 or 1. In order to map the points in X space into discrete points in A_c space, it is necessary to quantize the analog quantity $x_i{}^P$ to make it a discrete point of input state space. If each component $x_i{}^P$ of the input vector X^P can be quantified as q levels, then the n-dimensional component can combine the input state space into q^n possible cases. The number of A_c storage unit is not less than the number of states q^n in X space. A_c is equivalent to a virtual memory address, and each address corresponds to a sample point in the input state space. Then, the address space A_c of q^n storage units is mapped to a much smaller physical address space A_p by Hash-coding method.

2.2 Concept Mapping Algorithm

Considering the conciseness of description, this paper takes one-dimensional input vector as an example to describe the concept mapping algorithm. Let the quantization level of one-dimensional vector be $X = [x_1]$ and the generalization parameter C. The m storage units in the virtual storage area are divided into C segments, and the serial numbers of the storage units are 1 to m. Each input sample data is mapped to a cell in each segment. Then the total number of storage units in each segment m_k is

$$m_k = INT \left[\frac{S_1 - k + (C - 1)}{C} \right] + 1 \, (k = 1, 2, ..., C) \tag{1}$$

Where INT is rounding.

Let the quantized value of input vector sample be i. Then i will map C storage units. Its serial number P_k is

$$P_1 = INT \left[\frac{i - k + (C - 1)}{C} \right] + 1 \tag{2}$$

$$P_k = \sum_{g=1}^{k-1} m_g + INT \left[\frac{i - k + (C - 1)}{C} \right] + 1 \, (k = 2, 3, ... C) \tag{3}$$

If the quantization level $q = 6$ and the generalization coefficient $C = 4$, then the 4 storage units corresponding to each quantized value can be obtained according to Eq. (1)–Eq. (3), as shown in the Table 1.

Table 1. Quantizaion level and storage number.

Quantized serial number	1	2	3	4	5	6
4 units with content '1'	1468	2468	2568	2578	2579	3579

2.3 Physical Mapping Algorithm

Physical mapping is a one-to-one mapping. In order to save the actual storage space of the neural network, the physical mapping of CMAC is realized by using the method of division and residue in spurious coding technology. Let the table length of the actual storage space be N and $N \leq m$. The remainder obtained by dividing the element value PK by N is taken as the actual address d_k. So as to realize the physical mapping, i.e.

$$d_k = (P_k \, MOD \, N) + 1 \tag{4}$$

In the above equation, the value stored in the address d_k is the weight of the unit activated by vector X.

2.4 Learning Algorithm of CMAC

CMAC network uses learning algorithm to adjust the weight. Let the expected output vector corresponding to the input sample vector X^p be $Y^p = (y_1{}^p, y_2{}^p, \ldots, y_j{}^p, \ldots y_r{}^p)$. Then the weight adjustment equation is

$$\delta_j = y_{dj} - y_j \tag{5}$$

$$\omega_{ij}(t+1) = \omega_{ij}(t) + \eta(\delta_j/|A_p|) \quad (i = 1, 2, \cdots, n; \; j = 1, 2, \cdots, r) \tag{6}$$

The j-th output value of CMAC network is

$$y_j = \sum_{i \in A_p} \omega_{ij}(j = 1, 2, \cdots, r) \tag{7}$$

Where A_p is the combination of C virtual addresses in the memory.

3 CMAC Neural Network Hardening Method

This system takes EP2C8Q208 chip of Cyclone II series of Altera company as the development platform, adopts the idea of combining VHDL programming and schematic design to harden the software of CMAC control system. For the convenience of description, this paper still takes the hardening implementation of one-dimensional CMAC network as an example. The n-dimensional CMAC network can be extended according to the structure described below. Figure 2 shows the top-level structure of one-dimensional CMAC network. The input and output of the system adopts 8-bit floating-point numbers, including 1 bit sign bit, 3 bit order codes and 4 bit bases. The system is divided into six modules: subsection, addlen, Pk, SRAMadd, SRAM and adder8bit4in. The subsection function is to quantize the input signal in layers. The addlen function generates a constant, which is the length of the storage unit actually used. The Pk function is to calculate the serial number of the storage unit used in the virtual storage area. The SRAMadd function is to calculate the physical address of the storage unit actually used. SRAM function is to write or read weights. Adder8bit4in function is weight accumulation. There are eight groups of input signals in the system, which are addextn, Wren, CLK, DIN, C, s, en and win. Where addextn is the address input when updating the weight memory. Wren is the read-write control terminal of weight memory. clk is the system clock. A din of 8 is a floating-point input signal. C is the size of generalization coefficient. S is the layered quantization number of input signal. en is the enable signal of parallel signal and serial signal conversion module in SRAM module. Win is the input for the update weight. In order to be consistent with the previous description, the generalization coefficient $C = 4$ and the layered quantization number $S = 6$ can be taken.

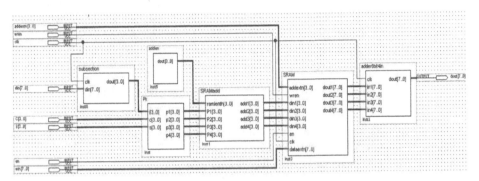

Fig. 2. Top diagram of CMAC.

Figure 3 is the internal structure block diagram of subsection level quantization module in CMAC neural network. The input signal of this system is quantized into 6 layers. For the convenience of description, the input signal is a floating-point number in the range of $[0, 6)$. The hierarchical structure of the system is: when the input signal is $[0, 1)$, the quantization result is 1; when the input signal is $[1, 2)$, the quantization result is 2. Similarly, when the input signal is $[5, 6)$, the quantization result is 6. Because VHDL does not support floating-point number comparison, the idea of hierarchical implementation is to subtract constant from input signal and determine the quantization result according to the positive and negative difference. For example, if the result of subtracting 5 from the input signal is less than zero and the result of subtracting 4 is greater than zero, the quantization result is 5. In the figure, con01to05 module outputs five constants from 1 to 5. fadd is an 8-bit signed floating-point adder. Section judge module is used to judge the number of layers.

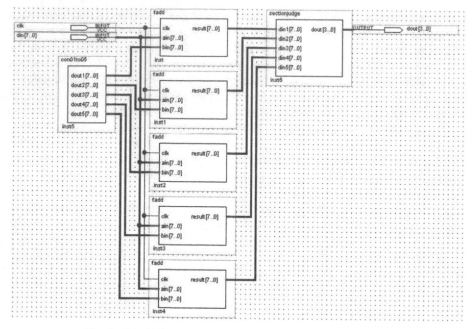

Fig. 3. Block diagram of subsection level quantization module.

The simulation waveform of subsection module is shown in Fig. 4. The six input signals were 0.25, 1.5, 2.5, 3.5, 4.5 and 5.5, respectively. The output signal is delayed by 1 clock cycle and generated by floating-point adder.

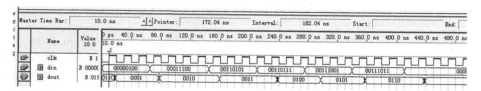

Fig. 4. Simulation waveform of subsection module.

If the quantization result of input signal is set in PK module, then C memory units will be mapped with the serial number of. The function of this module is to calculate the serial number of the used unit in the virtual storage area according to the generalization coefficient C, the quantization level s of the input signal and the quantization value i of the input signal. The calculation principle is shown in Eqs. (1)–(3). In this module, only the quotient of division result is used (i.e. integer part). The simulation waveform of PK module is shown in Fig. 5. The system inputs six kinds of quantization signals, the generalization coefficient is 4 and the quantization level is 6. The results are consistent with Table 1.

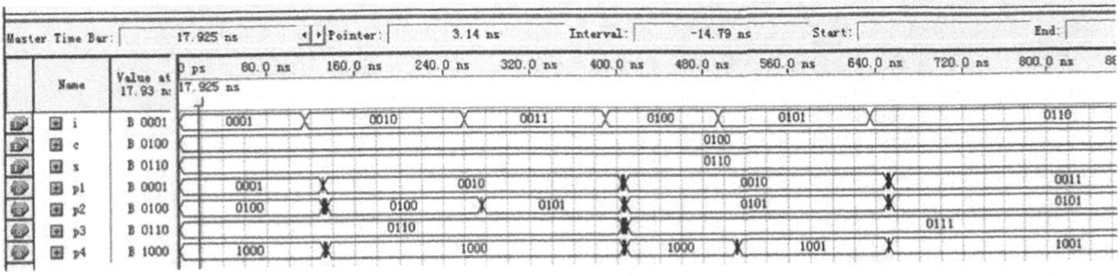

Master Time Bar:		17.925 ns		Pointer:	3.14 ns		Interval:	-14.79 ns		Start:			End:	
	Name	Value at 17.93 n	0 ps 17.925 ns	80.0 ns	160.0 ns	240.0 ns	320.0 ns	400.0 ns	480.0 ns	560.0 ns	640.0 ns	720.0 ns	800.0 ns	8
	i	B 0001	0001		0010		0011		0100	0101				0110	
	c	B 0100							0100						
	s	B 0110							0110						
	p1	B 0001	0001			0010				0010				0011	
	p2	B 0100	0100		0100		0101			0101				0101	
	p3	B 0110			0110							0111			
	p4	B 1000	1000		1000				1000	1001				1001	

Fig. 5. Simulation waveform of Pk module.

The calculation principle of physical storage area mapping address calculation module is the method of division and residue in the scattered hybrid coding technology, as shown in Eq. (4). The divisor, namely ramlenth, is provided by the addlen module in Fig. 1 and is a fixed value. In this system, the physical storage area is 8. The simulation waveform of sramadd module is shown in Fig. 6.

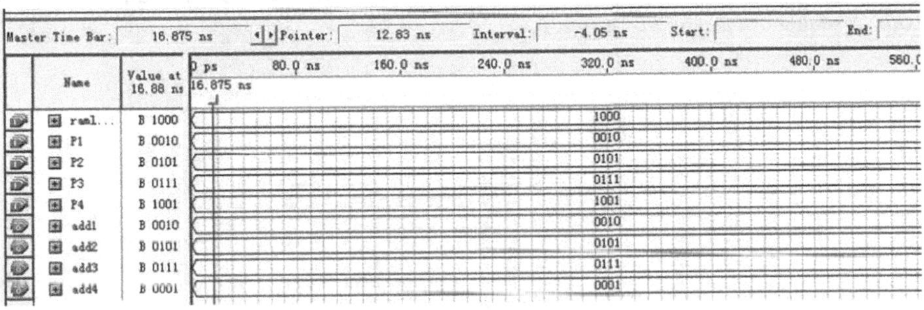

Master Time Bar:		16.875 ns		Pointer:	12.83 ns		Interval:	-4.05 ns		Start:		End:	
	Name	Value at 16.88 ns	0 ps 16.875 ns	80.0 ns	160.0 ns	240.0 ns	320.0 ns	400.0 ns	480.0 ns	560.0	
	raml...	B 1000					1000				
	P1	B 0010					0010				
	P2	B 0101					0101				
	P3	B 0111					0111				
	P4	B 1001					1001				
	add1	B 0010					0010				
	add2	B 0101					0101				
	add3	B 0111					0111				
	add4	B 0001					0001				

Fig. 6. Simulation waveform of SRAMadd module.

The SRAM module structure block diagram is shown in Fig. 7. Where lpm_ram_dq0 is the SRAM module of QuartusII. Since the address and data of the module are serial input and serial output, the parallel data to serial data module should be added at the input end, and the serial data to parallel data module should be connected at the output end. The above two modules are pts and stp module. Addsel module completes the function of SRAM memory address selection and read-write control. When wr is high level, the external address input signal addextn is valid, and the external weight is written into SRAM. When wr is low level, the output signal of pts is used as lpm_ram_dq0 address input. The weight of the input data is read out in the srdqam. en is the reset signal of pts and stp module. en is the reset signal of pts and stp module. en is the reset of pts and stp at high level, while en is the work of pts and stp at low level.

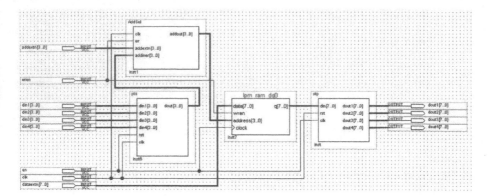

Fig. 7. Diagram of SRAM module.

It is assumed that the eight connection weights of CMAC neural network are set to lpm_ram_dq0 module as follows: 0.5, 0.75, 0.875, 0.9375, 1, 1.5, 1.75 and 1.875, and store in sequence, as shown in Fig. 8.

🐱 w.mif*	Bin	Decimal
Addr	+0	
0	00000100 ◄	► 0. 25
1	00000110 ◄	► 0. 375
2	00000111 ◄	► 0. 4375
3	00001000 ◄	► 0. 5
4	00001010 ◄	► 0. 625
5	00001100 ◄	► 0. 75
6	00001110 ◄	► 0. 875
7	00001111 ◄	► 0. 9375

Fig. 8. Initial weight setting of SRAM.

When the parallel input address of SRAM module is: $din1[3..0] = 2D = 0010B$, $din2[3..0] = 5D = 0101B$, $din3[3..0] = 7D = 0111B$ and $din4[3..0] = 0D = 0000B$, The simulation results of SRAM module based on FPGA are shown in Fig. 9. Obviously, compared with the weight given in Fig. 9, the output result dout1-dout4 [7..0] is correct.

The simulation waveform of one-dimensional CMAC model shown in Fig. 2 is shown in Fig. 9. The input signal din of the system is 3.5. According to the working principle of CMAC, the input signal should be 4 after layered quantization. P1-P4 should be 2, 5, 7, 8 respectively. The actual address of physical storage unit calculated by address mapping of physical storage area should be 2, 5, 7 and 0, and the corresponding weights are 0.875, 1.5, 1.9375 and 0.5. The final theoretical result is 4.75. The simulation result in Fig. 10 is 4.5. The error is due to the small number of floating-point digits.

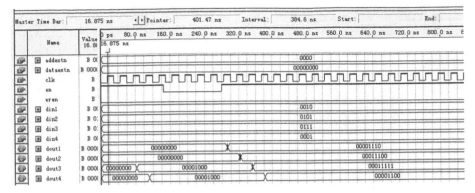

Fig. 9. Simulation waveform of SRAM module.

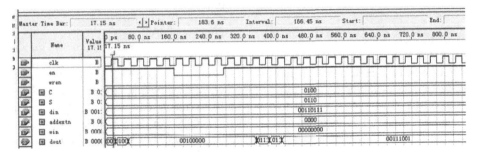

Fig. 10. Simulation waveform of CMAC.

4 Realization of CMAC Neural Network Motor Control System

There is nonlinearity in the servo system of permanent magnet synchronous linear motor for CNC machine tools, and it is easy to be affected by external interference, which leads to control difficulties [4]. Based on its working characteristics, this paper designs a compound control scheme of PID + CMAC linear servo system. The system adopts three closed-loop structure of position loop, speed loop and current loop. PID controller is used as forward channel controller to ensure system stability and suppress disturbance; CMAC controller is used as feed-forward channel controller to accelerate system response speed and reduce overshoot. The three closed loop system and CMAC feedforward compensation structure are shown in Fig. 11.

P* and V* are the given values of position and velocity respectively. P control is used for position adjustment, PID + CMAC control for speed regulation and PI control for current regulation. The detailed structure of speed regulation in the small box at the top of the figure is represented by the large and virtual frame at the bottom of the figure.

The CMAC controller is composed of CMAC calculation module and CMAC learning module in Fig. 9. Two FPGAs and one DSP are used to constitute the control core, and the two FPGAs are used to harden the CMAC network with the same structure. The front online control module is composed of one FPGA and DSP, and the other is background learning module. When the system works, the two FPGAs first learn the prior knowledge

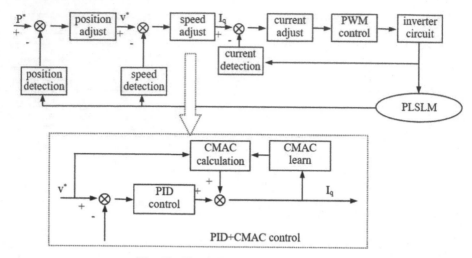

Fig. 11. Simulation waveform of CMAC.

offline. When the performance is close to the preset index, one FPGA and DSP jointly control the linear motor, and the other FPGA keeps learning and adjusting the weights based on the object model and the actual operation of the system, and is ready to update and solidify the down transmitted neural network connection weights at any time. When the controlled object parameters change, the background FPGA with better comprehensive performance can be switched to the foreground for real-time online control, while the FPGA controlled in the foreground can be transferred to the background for learning and updating as a standby. This cycle achieves the goal of self-improvement.

In order to test the performance of the above scheme, ic22-050a2p1 linear motor of Kollmorgen in the United States is selected as the test object to test the characteristic parameters of CMAC neural network control chip realized by ep2c8q208 chip hardening. The test is divided into no-load test and 350 N load test. Figure 12 shows the speed response curve of the linear feed servo system in the starting process without load.

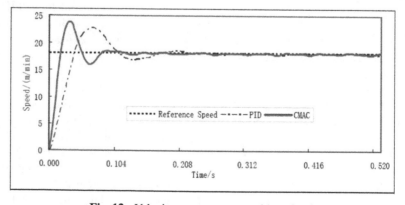

Fig. 12. Velocity-response curve without load.

The experimental results show that: when the system has no load, the speed response of CMAC neural network composite control strategy is faster than that of conventional PID algorithm, and the comprehensive performance of dynamic response is better. The adjustment time of transition process is shortened from 0.208 s to about 0.104 s, which is reduced by half. Although the overshoot increases, it is not obvious.

Figure 13 shows the speed response curve of the linear feed servo system in the starting process when the load is 350N. It can be seen from the test results that the speed response performance of the system is significantly reduced due to the influence of the load, and the system has oscillation due to the inertia of the load. However, compared with the conventional PID control, the CMAC neural network compound control strategy has more obvious advantages. The response curve in the figure shows that the response speed is faster and the oscillation amplitude is smaller, which shows that the algorithm has better generalization ability and application value.

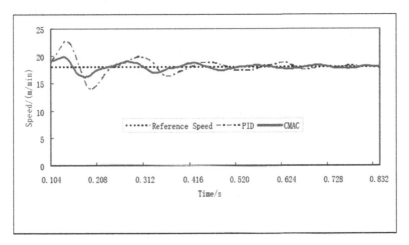

Fig. 13. Velocity-response curve with load.

5 Conclusion

According to the working characteristics of CMAC, this paper proposes a CMAC network hardening control chip, which makes full use of the characteristics of FPGA and overcomes the disadvantages of slow speed and poor performance of traditional software neural network control system. It has been applied in motor control system and achieved good results. The idea proposed in this paper can be extended to similar systems as a general scheme.

References

1. Chen, Z., Peng, L., Guangyu, S., Yijin, G., Bingjun, X., Jason, C.: Optimizing FPGA-based accelerator design for deep convolutional neural networks. In: ACM/SIGDA International Symposium on Field-Programmable Gate Arrays, pp. 161–170 (2015)

2. Chen, J.-L., et al.: FPGA implementation of neural network accelerator for pulse information extraction in high energy physics. Nucl. Sci. Tech. **31**(5), 1–9 (2020). https://doi.org/10.1007/s41365-020-00756-z
3. Andrew, B., Sadegh, Y., Vaughn, B.: You cannot improve what you do not measure: FPGA vs. ASIC efficiency gaps for convolutional neural network inference. ACM Trans. Reconfig. Technol. Syst. **11**(3), 1–23 (2018)
4. Cheng, L., Mankit, S., Hongxiang, F., Shuanglong, L., Wayne, L., Ce, G.: Towards efficient deep neural network training by FPGA-based batch-level parallelism. J. Semicond. **41**(2), 53–64 (2020)
5. Jianhui, H., Zhaolin, L., Weimin, Z., Youhui, Z.: Hardware implementation of spiking neural networks on FPGA. Tsinghua Sci. Technol. **25**(4), 479–486 (2020)
6. Ben, V.B., et al.: A mixed-analog-digital multichip system for large-scale neural simulations. Proc. IEEE **102**(5), 699–716 (2014)
7. Neil, D., Liu, S.C.: Minitaur, an event-driven FPGA-based spiking network accelerator. . IEEE Trans. Very Large Scale Integr. Syst. **22**(12), 2621–2628 (2014)
8. Qiang, L., Ming, G., Tao, Z., Qijun, Z.: Feedforward neural network models for FPGA routing channel width estimation. Chin. J. Electron. **25**(1), 71–76 (2016)

Research on Path Planning of Mobile Robot Based on Deep Reinforcement Learning

Shi Zhan[1]($\boxtimes$), Tingting Zhang[2,3], Han Lei[1], Qian Yin[1], and Lu Ali[1]

[1] School of Computer Engineering, Nanjing Institute of Technology, Nanjing 211100, China
[2] PLA Army Engineering University, Nanjing 210017, China
[3] Southeast University, Nanjing 210096, China

Abstract. Reinforcement learning has been widely used in the path planning of mobile robots, and has gradually become the main technology in path planning research. However, in the process of using reinforcement learning, there are problems such as "dimensionality disaster", slow convergence, and poor generalization. In order to solve these problems, this paper proposes a new learning framework of mobile robots called deep Q learning with experience replay and heuristic knowledge or HDQN in short. In this system, there is a new reward function defined. Then, heuristic knowledge can be designed, which includes knowledge about the target and avoiding obstacles. Finally, experiments can be executed to verify the effect of the HDQN algorithm.

Keywords: Reinforcement learning · Path planning · Q learning · DQN

1 Introduction

With the rapid development of science and technology, intelligent robots play an important role in many fields, including health care, space exploration, military operations, rescue operations, etc. They can always replace humans in performing difficult, high-risk, and time-consuming tasks [1].

In the application of intelligent robotics, path planning has always been one of the core issues in robotics and related artificial intelligence industries. The so-called path planning is that in a certain environment, the intelligent robot avoids all obstacles by calling its many sensors to work together, finds a path from the starting point to the target point, and optimizes this path according to certain criteria [2].

The path planning can be divided into global path planning and local path planning according to the known degree of the robot's working environment. The global path planning masters the information of the whole environment, while the local path planning only masters some or no information of the environment. According to the sensors, the obstacle information around the robot is obtained and the robot kinematics constraints are considered. The robot can complete collision-free movement from the starting point to the target point in a unknown environment. In fact, it is still one of the biggest challenges to be able to generate an effective path from a given starting point to the target point in real time in an unknown environment [3].

© Springer Nature Singapore Pte Ltd. 2021
Y. Tian et al. (Eds.): ICBDS 2020, CCIS 1415, pp. 549–560, 2021.
https://doi.org/10.1007/978-981-16-3150-4_45

Global path planning algorithms include graph-based algorithms and sampling-based algorithms. Among them, graph-based algorithms include A* and Dijkstra [4] algorithms, and sampling-based algorithms include random path graphs (Probabilistic roadmaps (PRM) [5], Rapid exploring rand tree (RRT) [6, 7] algorithm.

Local path planning algorithms can include the artificial potential field method [8–10], algorithms based on velocity space: dynamic window method DWA [11] and elastic band algorithm TEB, etc., and artificial intelligence (AI)) algorithms mainly including neural network algorithm [12], fuzzy logic algorithm [13], etc.

In recent years, reinforcement learning has also been widely used in the path planning of mobile robots, and has gradually become the main technology in path planning research. Through continuous trial and error in the unknown environment, it enables mobile robots to acquire knowledge and adjust their actions to realize obstacle avoidance path planning,

Reinforcement learning Q_learning [14] algorithm does not need to know the robot model and static environment map, which can make the robot learn and train in the process of continuous interaction with the environment to improve its path planning ability. In 2013, the deep reinforcement learning algorithm proposed by Mnih V et al. [15, 16] uses images as output, and its algorithm's ability to play Atari games surpasses humans. In 2015, Schaul T et al. proposed a prioritized experience playback technology [17], improve the learning efficiency of the algorithm. However, in the process of using reinforcement learning, there are problems such as "dimensionality disaster", slow convergence, and poor generalization.

This paper proposes a new learning framework of mobile robots called deep Q learning with experience replay and heuristic knowledge or HDQN in short, defines a new reward function, and designs heuristic knowledge including knowledge about the target and avoiding obstacles. Through experiments, this paper further compares the three methods including the traditional Q learning, deep Q learning based on experience replay (DQN), and deep Q learning based on experience replay and heuristic knowledge (HDQN). Finally, some conclusions is discussed in this paper.

The rest of the paper is organized as follows. Section 2 introduces some basic definitions of reinforcement learning as the preliminaries to Sect. 3, which presents a new DQN algorithm with the heuristic knowledge, called HDQN in short, and uses this algorithm to make a path planning of the mobile robot. Based on the HDQN, Sect. 4 provides simulation and analysis of path planning for mobile robot. Finally, Sect. 5 concludes the whole paper.

2   Preliminaries

Reinforcement learning, like deep learning, belongs to a branch of machine learning. Generally, machine learning is divided into supervised learning, unsupervised learning and reinforcement learning. Reinforcement learning is between supervised learning and unsupervised learning, because it does not need guidance or supervision outside of its own to learn, but its learning process is through the information exchange of the environment, which is based on feedback. So it is similar to unsupervised learning, but also different from unsupervised learning.

Generally speaking, a standard reinforcement learning model mainly contains four basic elements, the reward function, policy, value function and model of environment. The basic principle is to use the feedback generated by the immediate interaction between itself and the surrounding environment to make the evaluation on the actions taken. If the feedback is stronger, it represents the positive reward of the environment for the action, then the tendency of the action will be strengthen; on the contrary, the tendency to execute this action weakens [18].

Figure 1 shows the basic model of reinforcement learning. The agent uses a certain strategy to output an action a and inputs it into the environment. The environment receives this action and generates a reward r which is fed back to the agent, and the agent then returns the reward according to the feedback. r and the current environmental status information e to select the next action, and so on, continuously improving the strategy. Through the iterative cycle process, the strategy corresponding to the largest cumulative environmental reward obtained is obtained, which is the optimal strategy obtained [19].

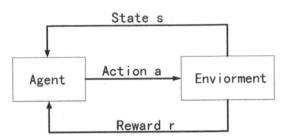

Fig. 1. Basic model of reinforcement learning

3   A Path Planning Method Based on the HDQN Algorithm

There have been many research results of deep reinforcement learning in the path planning of mobile robots. Among them, the DQN algorithm is mostly used in obstacle avoidance tasks. DQN combines neural network and Q-learning, which is an Off-policy learning method, and solves the bottleneck of traditional Q-table reinforcement learning. In fact, with discrete action of the output, the DQN algorithm has many variants used in games, robotic arm control and other fields. However, when the environment becomes complicated, there is a "dimensionality disaster". At this time, the convergence of the algorithm becomes worse and takes a long time to learn. In order to solve the corresponding problems, this section improves the DQN learning system and proposes a new HDQN algorithm, as described below.

3.1   The Structure Framework of the HDQN Algorithm

In order to solve dimensionality disaster of deep reinforcement learning when the environment is complex, the poor convergence of the algorithm, and a long time to learn, this section proposes the learning framework of mobile robots shown in Fig. 2. While, this framework can also solve the problem that the model obtained by deep reinforcement learning has poor generalization and cannot adapt well to other unknown environments.

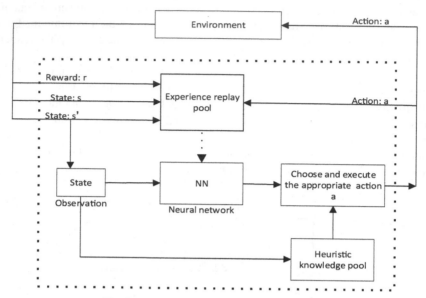

Fig. 2. Learning framework for mobile robots

In Fig. 2, its main components are the environment and mobile robots. In this system, the mobile robot no longer only uses neural networks and experience replay mechanisms, but adds heuristic knowledge, action judgment and selection functions. The input of the neural network is the state S' of the mobile robot, and the output is the expected cumulative reward value of each action in this state. Then, this output of the neural network will be compared with the action generated by the heuristic knowledge pool in the selection and execution module to determine an appropriate action. In this way, when the mobile robot has a state S, it needs to go through a comparison between the output of the neural network and the heuristic knowledge to determine an appropriate action.

In this section, heuristic knowledge is added to the mobile robot system, which can provide effective training data to the neural network. On the one hand, it can guide the mobile robot to choose actions; on the other hand, it can provide characteristic training data for the neural network. With the help of heuristic knowledge, neural networks can converge to the optimal action strategy faster. Therefore, the mobile robot can achieve path planning and obstacle avoidance tasks without worrying about the lack of training data and the dimension disaster.

The mobile robot studied in this paper is equipped with five sonar sensors used to interact with the environment. The distribution of mobile robot sensors is shown in Fig. 3. The angle among each sensor is 30 degree and the measurement data of the sensors are represented by s1, s2, s3, s4, and s5.

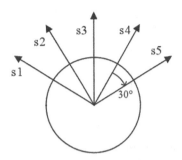

Fig. 3. Sonar sensors installation of the mobile robot

The actions of the mobile robot are divided into three types:

Action 1: Move forward 0.5 m;
Action 2: Rotate 30° to the left;
Action 3: Rotate 30° to the right.

It should be noted that we use the angle β to represent the angle between the moving direction of the mobile robot in the current state and the direction connecting the position of the mobile robot and the target position. Then, the above 5 sonar data and the angle β represent the state s of the mobile robot, the expression is s = (s1, s2, s3, s4, s5, β). And, directly use the distance data measured by the sonar device as the corresponding value of the mobile robot state.

3.2 Definition of Reward Function

In this paper, in order to better implement the reward function, we first define the safe state of the mobile robot, where the subscript safe indicates that this is a safe state variable, and there are four values of it:

Safe state (S). In this state, the mobile robot will not hit obstacles in any action selected;
Dangerous state (D). In this state, the mobile robot may hit an obstacle in the next step;
Collision state (C). It means that the mobile robot has hit an obstacle;
Completion status (F). It means that the mobile robot has reached the target point.
The reward function used in this paper is shown in the following formula. " → " represents the transition of the mobile robot's safe state, AT (away target) means that the mobile robot is far away from the target point; AO (away obstacle) means that the mobile robot is far away from the obstacle; CT (close target) means that the mobile robot

is close to the target point; CO (close obstacle) means that the mobile robot is close to the obstacle.

$$reward = \begin{cases} 200, F \\ 3, D \rightarrow S \\ 2, (S \rightarrow S)\&\&(CT) \\ -1, (S \rightarrow S)\&\&(AT) \\ -1, (D \rightarrow D)\&\&(AO) \\ -2, (D \rightarrow D)\&\&(CO) \\ -3, (S \rightarrow D) \\ -50, C \end{cases}$$

3.3 The Heuristic Knowledge Pool

In order to make the mobile robot learn the expected optimal strategy, it is very important to store sufficient effective experience data for the mobile robot in the experience replay pool. In traditional deep reinforcement learning, in order to make the learning data samples sufficiently diverse and comprehensive, mobile robots are often taken to perform random actions to meet this requirement.

However, objectively speaking, in many specific situations, the randomly selected actions of the mobile robot are completely wrong. The experience data gained from this is put into the learning experience pool. Then, the experience data greatly affect our training process for the mobile robot, and it is very likely to lead to poor learning effects and difficulty in converging training data when the environment is more complicated and the mobile robot can take a wide variety of actions. That is to say, for the neural network, the large amount of collision experience data and the experience data of randomly selected actions cannot make a beneficial contribution to the training of the neural network.

Therefore, this paper introduces heuristic knowledge in the traditional deep reinforcement learning to guide the mobile robot to choose actions, thereby reducing the randomness of the mobile robot. With the help of heuristic knowledge, mobile robots can always choose appropriate actions, provide characteristic training data for neural networks, and accelerate the training process.

1. Knowledge about the target

In order to reduce the blind exploration of the mobile robot, we use target-oriented knowledge to guide the mobile robot to choose actions.

There are two vectors in the map scene where the mobile robot is located: 1) the vector of the mobile robot's direction, 2) the vector connecting the position of the mobile robot and the target position. This paper uses the angle β between these two vectors as the basis for the target-oriented knowledge. The range of the angle value is defined as $-180°$ to $180°$. According to the angle, we can know the relative relationship between the position of the mobile robot and the target point. For example, if the angle is $180°$, it means that the current direction of the mobile robot is opposite to the direction of the target destination. This information can provide accurate guidance for the action selection of the mobile robot.

According to the relationship between the three optional actions of the mobile robot and the above angle β, we design the following target-oriented knowledge:

a. if $120 \leq \beta < 180$, the mobile robot selects action 3;
b. if $90 \leq \beta < 120$, then:

    a) if the mobile robot selects action 1, then continue to select this action;
    b) else the mobile robot selection action 3;

c. if $\beta = (+ -) 180$, then:

    a) if the mobile robot selects action 1, it will not continue to select this action, and randomly select action 2, 3;
    b) else the mobile robot selection action 1;

d. if $-120 < \beta \leq -90$, then:

    a) if the mobile robot selects action 1, then continue to select this action;
    b) else the mobile robot selection action 2;

e. $-180 \leq \beta < -120$, the mobile robot selection action 2.

Target-oriented knowledge can provide a good help for the action selection of the mobile robot, thereby helping to accelerate the training process of the neural network.

2. Knowledge avoiding obstacles

Because the randomness of early action selection in reinforcement learning, the probability of a mobile robot hitting an obstacle is very high. If there is a large amount of experience data generated during collision in the experience replay pool, it will inevitably have a negative impact on the learning of the neural network. It will make the neural network only learn the collision knowledge, which will affect the subsequent training. Therefore, we provide knowledge avoiding obstacles for the mobile robot, which can help the mobile robot avoid obstacles as much as possible.

According to the relationship between the three optional actions of the mobile robot and the distance between obstacles in this paper, we design the following knowledge avoiding obstacle:

If the safety status of the mobile robot is "D", the mobile robot selects action 3.

4 Simulation and Analysis of Path Planning for Mobile Robot

4.1 Simulation Experiment Environment

The training of reinforcement learning is very time-consuming. As the learning task becomes more and more complex, the training process will also become longer. Mobile robots often need thousands of repetitive training to obtain a good behavior strategy, which makes it difficult to directly apply reinforcement learning in real life. Therefore, simulation experiments for reinforcement learning are essential. In this paper, the simulation experiment is performed based on Python programs.

Figure 4 is a map of a simulation experiment environment. The green object in the map represents the mobile robot, the red object represent the target, the blue squares are randomly placed obstacles, and the gray boxes around are the edges of the map. At the beginning, the mobile robot is at its starting point, which is the upper left corner. This map simulates a plane with a size of 19 m * 14 m. In the simulation experiment, there are different maps where the number and position of obstacles, and the initial state of the mobile robot can change, but the mobile robot only knows the location of the start point and the target point, and cannot know the rest of the environment. The task of the mobile robot is to avoid all obstacles in the environment and successfully reach the target from the start point.

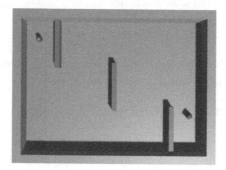

Fig. 4. Map of the simulation experiment environment (Color figure online)

The following Table 1 lists the parameters used in the reinforcement learning and neural network training process.

Table 1. Parameter settings

Parameters	Value
Learning rate	0.5
Rew and Decay	0.9
Size of experience replay pool	2000
Batch size	32
e_greedy	0.9

4.2 Comparison of Algorithms

In the same experimental environment, this section makes comparative experiments on three methods including the traditional Q learning, deep Q learning based on experience replay (DQL + ER), and deep Q learning based on experience replay and heuristic knowledge (DQL + ER + HK), which mainly compare the convergence speed of the training process.

In the experiments, there are two maps with 3 or 4 obstacles respectively, which are labeled Map_1 and Map_2 respectively. The above three learning methods are used in different maps.

When the average reward value of the mobile robot in a round tends to be stable, it is regarded as convergent and the training ends. Figure 5 shows the mobile robot path of the three methods after training on the two maps. Each row is the same map, and each column uses the same method.

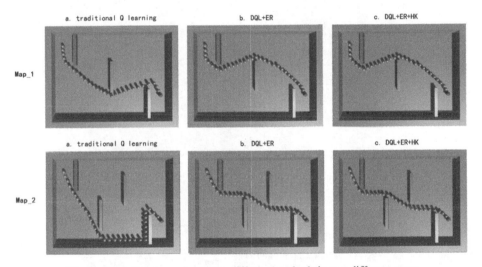

Fig. 5. Path planning using three different methods in two different maps

We choose the average reward value obtained by the mobile robot in a training period as the evaluation index. Figure 6 shows the average reward value of these three algorithms when they are used on the Map_2.

From Fig. 6, we can see that in the early stages of training, the average reward is very unstable. One of the reasons is that when the mobile robot explores the map in the early stages, it may take many steps to reach the target point, which lowers the average reward. Another reason is that, without the help of heuristic knowledge, the mobile robot that uses Q learning and DQL + ER has a greater chance of hitting an obstacle in the previous training period, and gets a negative reward value, which makes the average reward change low. After a period of training, these three methods will eventually converge. In the experiment, DQL + ER + HK can always converge the earliest and obtain the highest average reward.

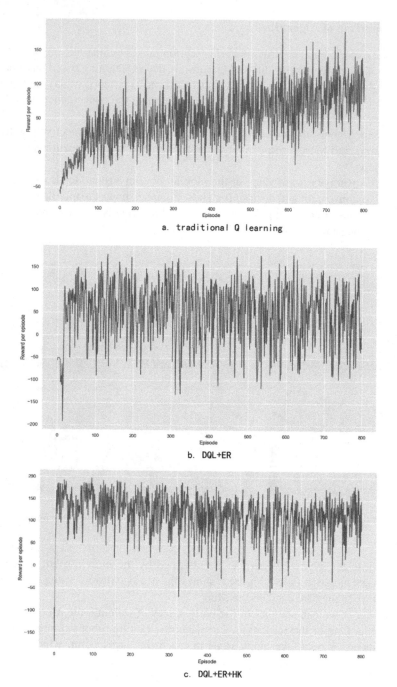

a. traditional Q learning

b. DQL+ER

c. DQL+ER+HK

Fig. 6. The average reward value of each training round of the three methods in Map_2

The experimental results show that the mobile robot using our method has the faster convergence to optimal path than the mobile robot using the other two methods. With the help of heuristic knowledge, the mobile robot can accelerate the learning speed and obtain better strategies.

5 Conclusions

As an important branch of intelligent robots, mobile robots have been used in various aspects such as family, industrial detection, and transportation. In the field of mobile robots research, path planning algorithm is one of the key technologies of its navigation. Different from traditional methods, reinforcement learning theory is applied to the field of robots path planning, which can enable robots to acquire human-like learning capabilities and complete tasks with unknown environments and uncertain factors.

However, as the external environment becomes more complex, the state space and action space of the Markov decision process will also become larger, resulting in a "dimension disaster". At the same time, slow convergence is also a problem faced by reinforcement learning.

This paper is mainly based on the mobile robot equipped with five sonar sensors to perceive the external environment information. Then, it combines deep Q learning with experience replay pool and heuristic knowledge to propose a new path planning method for mobile robots. The method of avoiding obstacles can realize the path planning of mobile robots in unknown environments. On the one hand, heuristic knowledge is used to guide the action selection of the mobile robot in an unknown environment; on the other hand, it provides effective training data for the neural network, thereby it can improve the training speed and enhance the generalization of the model.

Acknowledgments. This work is supported by the Natural Science Foundation of the Jiangsu Youth of China under grant BK20181019, National Natural Science Foundation of China under grant 61802428, and Science Foundation of Nanjing Institute of Technology under grant YKJ201723.

References

1. Abhishek, K., Ashish, K., Deepak, C.: Artificially intelligent robotics: a survey. Int. J. Adv. Eng. Res. Dev. **4**(10), 755–762 (2017)
2. Howard, A., Mataric, M.J., Sukhatme, G.S.: An incremental self-deployment algorithm for mobile sensor networks. Auton. Robots **13**(2), 113–126 (2002)
3. Souissi, O., Benatitallah, R., Duvivier, D., Artiba, A., Belanger, N., Feyzeau, P.: Path planning: a 2013 survey. In: International Conference on Industrial Engineering and Systems Management, pp. 1–8 (2013)
4. Zhan, F.B.: Three fastest shortest path algorithms on real road networks, data structures and procedures. J. Geograph. Inform. Decis. Anal. **1**(1), 69–82 (1997)
5. Kavraki, L., Svestka, P., Latombe, J., et al.: Probabilistic roadmaps for path planning in high-dimensional configuration spaces. IEEE Trans. Robot. Autom. **12**(4), 566–580 (1994)
6. Lavalle, S.M.: Rapidly-exploring random trees: a new tool for path planning. Algorithmic and Computational Robotics New Directions, pp. 293–308 (1998)

7. Palmieri, L., Koenig, S., Kai, O.A.: RRT-based nonholonomic motion planning using any-angle path biasing. In: IEEE International Conference on Robotics and Automation, pp. 2775–2781. IEEE (2016)

8. Koren, Y., Borenstein, J.: Potential field methods and their inherent limitations for mobile robot navigation. In: Proceedings of IEEE International Conference on Robotics and Automation, pp. 1398–1404 (1991)

9. Fujimura, K.: Motion Planning in Dynamic Environments. Springer-Verlag, Berlin and Heidelberg GmbH & Co.k (1991)

10. Ko, N.Y., Lee, B.H.: Avoidability measure in moving obstacle avoidance problem and its use for robot motion planning. In: Proceedings of the IEEE International Conference on Intelligent Robots and Systems, Osaka, Japan, pp. 1296–1303 (1996)

11. Fox, D., Burgard, W., Thrun, S.: The dynamic window approach to collision avoidance. IEEE Robot. Autom. Mag. 4(l), 23–33 (1997)

12. Singh, M.K., Parhi, D.R.: Path optimisation of a mobile robot using an artificial neural network controller. Int. J. Syst. Sci. 42(1), 107–120 (2011)

13. Hong, T.S., Nakhaeinia, D., Karasfi, B.: Application of fuzzy logic in mobile robot navigation. In: Fuzzy Logic - Controls, Concepts, Theories and Applications, pp. 21–36 (2012)

14. Watkins, C.J.C.H., Dayan, P.: Q learning. Mach. Learn. 8(3–4), 279–292 (1992)

15. Mnih, V., Kavukcuoglu, K., Silver, D., et al.: Playing atari with deep reinforcement learning. Computer Science (2013)

16. Mnih, V., Kavukcuoglu, K., Silver, D., et al.: Human-level control through deep reinforcement learning. Nature 518(7540), 529 (2015)

17. Schaul, T., Quan, J., Antonoglou, I., et al.: Prioritized experience replay. Computer Science (2015)

18. Barto, A.G., Sutton, R.S., Anderson, C.W.: Neuronlike adaptive elements that can solve difficult learning control problems. IEEE Trans. Syst. Man Cybern. SMC 13(5), 834–846 (2012)

19. Schwartz, A.: A reinforcement learning method for maximizing undiscounted rewards. In: Proceedings of the Tenth International Conference on Machine Learning. Amherst, MA: Morgan Kaufmann, pp. 298–305 (1993)

Research on K-Means Clustering Algorithm Based on Improved Genetic Algorithm

Lulu Zhang[1]($\boxtimes$) and Yu Shu[2]

[1] Ma'anshan University, Ma'anshan, China
[2] Anhui Business College, Anhui, China

Abstract. Genetic algorithm is the simulation of the natural biological evolution principle, through the selection, crossover, mutation three genetic operators to complete the evolution and inheritance of nature. The advantage of genetic algorithm is its strong ability of global optimization. However, genetic algorithm has premature phenomenon, which makes the algorithm produce sub optimal solution prematurely. In this paper, adaptive strategy is introduced. In the process of algorithm implementation, crossover probability and mutation probability are adjusted dynamically, and population evolution speed is automatically adjusted to ensure that the algorithm finally obtains the global optimal solution.

Keywords: Data mining · Clustering · K-means · Genetic algorithm · Adaptive

1 Introduction

In recent years, with the development of computer technology and database technology, it is very convenient to read and find data and information. However, the important information hidden under the surface data is difficult to obtain through the traditional database query and retrieval technology. Data mining technology involves related knowledge of multiple disciplines, which are integrated and supported by each other. With the help of these knowledge, the given data is analyzed, and then the general rules of knowledge pattern are extracted.

2 Research Status of Data Mining

Data mining technology is accompanied by knowledge discovery, and its development has experienced the following key events.

Domestic scholars study data mining technology later than abroad, and there is a big gap between the research results and foreign countries. At present, data mining research in China mainly includes theoretical research, algorithm research and practical application research. The research work is mainly concentrated in universities, research institutes and some companies. Most of the related research projects are funded by the government, and some data mining software, such as mine MSMiner, dminer and scope, has been developed However, due to various defects, it has not been widely used. Although China & apos;s government and society have spent a lot of energy and financial resources, but has not achieved impressive results, we still have a long way to go.

© Springer Nature Singapore Pte Ltd. 2021
Y. Tian et al. (Eds.): ICBDS 2020, CCIS 1415, pp. 561–571, 2021.
https://doi.org/10.1007/978-981-16-3150-4_46

3 The Common Data Mining Technologies Are as Follows

(1) Decision tree
Decision tree method is a classification mining method based on tree structure. It can divide data into tree structure automatically. The decision tree is classified from the top root node. By comparing the attributes of each node, the next level branch of the node is determined. The end of the branch is the leaf node, which is the final result of classification.

(2) Association rules
It is found that there are general rules and general rules between the data, such as the famous "beer and diaper" event. The two seemingly unrelated things of "beer" and "diaper" are sold together, and they actually get very high profits. This phenomenon reflects the correlation between commodities.

(3) Cluster analysis
A subset of customers or data records with similar characteristics is called a cluster. According to the differences between a batch of data or a group of objects, the data or objects with high similarity are divided into a group as far as possible. This operation process is called clustering.

(4) Statistical analysis
Statistics provides a technique to deal with noise parameters in the process of data preprocessing.

(5) Rough set
Rough set is a kind of set which will be imprecise and has no definite scope. Usually, an object is represented by a known region data [2].

4 Cluster Analysis

As an important classification tool, clustering plays a very important role in the analysis of massive data. With the development of knowledge research, clustering analysis has been introduced into data mining technology, which has become an important technology of data mining technology.

4.1 Classification of Clustering Algorithms and Their Typical Algorithms

There are six types of commonly used clustering algorithms, as shown in Fig. 2 [7], Fig. 1 shows:

(1) Partition based method
The method is based on the database of N data objects, and the final number of clusters K is given. According to the clustering criterion function, the sample data are divided into K clusters, and these clusters are labeled as C1, C2, C3,Ck. In order to ensure the clustering effect, it is stipulated that each cluster cannot be empty, that is, there must be at least one data object in the cluster, and the relationship between the cluster and the data object is one to many. According to the selected number of clusters K, firstly, K sample points are randomly selected from the sample data

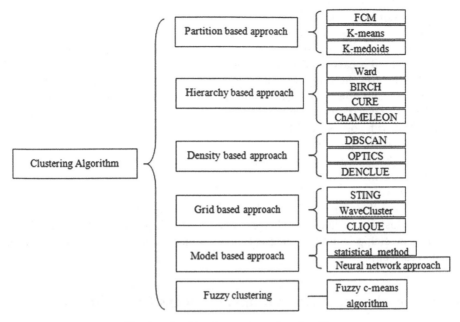

Fig. 1. Classification of clustering algorithm

as the centers of K classes, and then the similarity between other objects and K centers is calculated respectively, and the objects are divided into the class with the highest similarity. Then, the centers of K classes are determined again, and the classes are re divided according to the distance between the rest objects and the centers of each class. The above operations are repeated to make the objects in the class more centralized and the classes more alienated.

(2) Hierarchy based approach

The method divides the sample data into clusters from top to bottom or from bottom to top according to tree structure. The top-down method is also called split hierarchical method, which is implemented from the root node of tree structure to the leaf node, and splits a cluster into multiple until all objects are split; the bottom-up method is also called agglomerative hierarchical method, which executes from the leaf node of tree structure to the root node point, and merges the two clusters until it is merged into a cluster.

(3) Density based approach

As long as the density of a cluster point is greater than a critical value, the point is allocated to the adjacent cluster. Density clustering method is insensitive to the sequence of sample data, effective for any shape of sample data, and can effectively remove noise, but it is necessary to determine the appropriate density parameters and critical value.

(4) Grid based approach

In this method, the sample data is divided into many small grid cells according to certain specifications, and each grid cell is taken as the object of clustering operation. This method is easy to operate, and the clustering time is related to the number of grids. The grid clustering method is not sensitive to the input order; it can deal with large data sets effectively; it does not need to determine the number of clusters in advance; it can discover irregular clusters; it can process high-dimensional data; it can deal with noise successfully.

(5) Model based approach

This method selects a specific sample model and divides the data objects matching the model into a cluster.

(6) Fuzzy clustering

In practice, there are many fuzzy clustering results. Each sample object and class of fuzzy clustering method is no longer a one-to-one relationship, but a certain degree of membership is used to represent the relationship between each sample object and each class.

5   Improved Genetic Optimization K-Means Clustering Algorithm

1. The basic idea of K-means algorithm

K-means algorithm is a segmentation clustering algorithm. It takes the average value as the class center, and takes the similarity as the clustering principle. It divides the data objects into the most similar clusters, so that each data object in the cluster has the closest relationship with the cluster center, so that the generated cluster is as compact and independent as possible.

The algorithm requires users to determine the final number of clusters K for a given set of N data objects, and then randomly select k points from n objects as cluster centers, respectively calculate the distance between the remaining n-k data objects and K clustering centers, divide the objects according to the principle of proximity, and divide each object into the nearest cluster. The new clustering center is calculated according to the current clustering results, and the clustering effect is evaluated by the clustering objective function. According to the clustering objective function value, the objective function value of each iteration result is reduced, the class obtained by each iteration is more compact and dense, and the similarity of objects within the class is greater, and the similarity of objects between classes is smaller.

The clustering algorithm is simple, effective and fast, but it also has the following shortcomings. This method is sensitive to the initial population value and input order, and easy to fall into local optimum.

2. K-means algorithm of genetic optimization

   Combining k-means algorithm with genetic algorithm, this paper uses the global optimization characteristics of genetic algorithm to improve the problem that k-means algorithm is easy to fall into local optimal solution.

   Genetic algorithm simulates the process of biological evolution in nature, and obtains the optimal individual through selection, crossover and mutation operations, showing strong search ability. This combination of K-means algorithm and genetic algorithm is called the K-means clustering analysis method based on genetic algorithm. It combines the easy realization and local characteristics of K-means with the global search ability of genetic algorithm, and has complementary advantages to avoid the adverse impact on the implementation results of the algorithm due to the lack of K-means algorithm and genetic algorithm.

   The improvement of K-means algorithm based on traditional genetic algorithm integrates the basic ideas of K-means algorithm and genetic algorithm [5]. Genetic algorithm is used to optimize k-means algorithm, which does not need to know the experience of parameter setting, so as to avoid obtaining the suboptimal solution due to the rapid convergence of the algorithm. But genetic algorithm also has some shortcomings, premature phenomenon is the most obvious problem. If the traditional genetic algorithm is used to optimize the clustering algorithm, in the later stage of the algorithm implementation, the excellent individual will occupy the dominant position, so that the main operation object of the genetic operator is the excellent individual, and the population evolution speed will slow down or even stop, resulting in the final result of the algorithm is not necessarily the global optimal solution.

3. Design of improved k-means algorithm based on genetic algorithm

   Although genetic algorithm can optimize K-means clustering algorithm, there are still some problems in the actual optimization, such as easy to fall into prematurity and so on.

(1) Chromosome coding scheme

In this paper, floating-point coding is used, that is, chromosomes are encoded by the coordinates of cluster centers. For example, for n-dimensional data object space $\{x_1, x_2, \cdots, x_n\}$, assume that the K initial clustering centers are $(x_{i1}, x_{i2}, \cdots, x_{ik})$, where $i1, i2, \cdots, ik \in n$, the chromosome code is $(x_{i1}^1, x_{i1}^2, \cdots, x_{ik}^{N-1}, x_{ik}^N)$, where $x_i^j, (i \in n, j \in N)$ represents the j-th component of the i-th point. Floating point coding shortens the length of chromosome, accelerates the speed of clustering and genetic operation, and improves the clustering effect of large data sets.

(2) Selection of fitness function

The selection operation is controlled by the fitness value of genetic algorithm, and the fitness function value is required to be non negative, so that the genetic algorithm can be well applied to the problem of clustering analysis. The evaluation results of fitness function decide whether to perform the selection operation, and the evaluation quality of fitness function determines the performance of the algorithm.

In terms of specific clustering analysis, the criterion function E is equal to the sum of the squares of distances between each object in the original data set and the corresponding cluster center of the object. The smaller e is, the better the clustering quality is the criterion function is $E = \sum_{i=1}^{k} \sum_{x \in C_i} |x - c_i|^2$: where c_i is the cluster center, X is the object of the cluster set, and K is the number of clusters.

In the clustering operation, the smaller the distance between similar objects, the better the clustering effect; while the greater the distance between different objects, the better the clustering effect. The purpose of genetic algorithm is to search the best cluster center, which is E-Minimum.

The fitness function f is 1/E, that is, the fitness function is 1/E

$$f(X) = \frac{1}{E} = \frac{1}{\sum_{i=1}^{k} \sum_{x \in C_i} |x - c_i|^2} \tag{1}$$

Where x is the data object set, c_i is the cluster center, X is the object of the cluster set, and K is the number of clusters.

(3) Crossover and mutation operations

Due to the randomness of crossover operation and mutation operation, the excellent characteristics of some individuals in the parent generation can be retained to the next generation, and new characteristics can be added to the new individuals of the offspring, the gene space can be expanded, p_c and p_m the individual diversity in the new species group can be maintained. The crossover probability and mutation probability in genetic algorithm control the speed of genetic operator execution, which directly affects the algorithm results. If the p_c crossover probability is too large, the individuals with high fitness will have greater probability of performing crossover operation, and the probability of gene string being destroyed will be increased, and the probability of obtaining the optimal solution will be reduced. If it is too small, the new individuals will slow down, and even the population evolution will stop. However, when the p_m mutation probability is too small, the new individuals are generated slowly; when p_m the mutation probability is too large, the genetic algorithm becomes a thorough random search algorithm. In this paper, an adaptive genetic algorithm is used. The adaptive strategy can make p_c and p_m change automatically according to the fitness. When the individual fitness tends to be consistent p_c and p_m the population evolution is slow, the adaptive strategy control and appropriate increase; when the individual fitness tends to disperse p_c and the population evolution is rapid, the adaptive strategy control and appropriate decrease [6].

At present, the following strategies are commonly used to change the crossover probability p_c,

$$p_c = \begin{cases} \frac{k(f_{max}-f')}{f_{max}-f_{avg}} & f' \geq f_{avg} \\ k & f' < f_{avg} \end{cases} \tag{2}$$

Where f_{max} is the maximum fitness value, f' is the larger individual fitness value of the two individuals to be crossed, f_{avg} is the average fitness value in the population, and K is the number of clusters.

The following strategies are commonly used to change the mutation probability p_m,

$$p_m = \begin{cases} \frac{k_3(f_{max}-f')}{f_{max}-f_{avg}} & f' \geq f_{avg} \\ k_4 & f' < f_{avg} \end{cases} \tag{3}$$

Where f_{max} is the maximum fitness value, f' is the larger individual fitness value of the two individuals to be mutated, f_{avg} is the average fitness value in the population, and K is the number of clusters.

In the early stage of evolution, the individuals in the population have not undergone multiple selection, crossover and mutation operations, and the changes of excellent individuals in the population are not obvious, p_c and p_m these excellent individuals are not necessarily the global optimal solution, so the value of their sum can not be adjusted immediately. Therefore, using this adjustment method to change p_c and p_m easily make genetic algorithm converge to the local optimal solution will lead to premature problem, so it is not applicable in the early stage of evolution, and adaptive adjustment method can be used to adjust parameters in the late evolution stage.

In this paper, the adaptive genetic algorithm (AGA) is suitable for adjusting the crossover probability and mutation probability of the population in the late evolution stage, but not in the early stage of evolution.

Adaptive adjustment strategy of crossover probability

$$p_c = \begin{cases} \frac{k(f_{max}-f')}{f_{max}-f_{avg}} \cdot \theta_c & f' \geq f_{avg} \\ k & f' < f_{avg} \end{cases} \tag{4}$$

Where G is the total evolution algebra $\theta_m = \frac{1}{3}\left(1 + \sqrt[3]{\frac{g}{G}}\right)$ and G is the current evolution algebra, $g \in (0, G]$.

Adaptive adjustment strategy of mutation probability

$$p_m = \begin{cases} \sqrt{\frac{k(f_{max}-f')}{f_{max}-f_{avg}}} \cdot \theta_m & f' \geq f_{avg} \\ k & f' < f_{avg} \end{cases} \tag{5}$$

Where G is the total evolution algebra $\theta_m = \frac{1}{3}\left(1 + \sqrt[3]{\frac{g}{G}}\right)$ and G is the current evolution algebra, $g \in (0, G]$.

The adaptive algorithm can adjust the crossover probability p_c and p_m mutation probability dynamically in the process of algorithm execution. If the fitness value of an individual in a population is higher than the average fitness value of the population, the sum of the individual should be adjusted to a lower value,p_c and p_m the gene of the individual should be directly retained in the next generation; if the fitness value of an individual is lower than the average fitness value of the population, the sum of the individual should be adjusted to a higher value, p_c and p_m the individual should be eliminated from the next generation. It can be seen that the sum adjusted by adaptive strategy can expand the population at an appropriate time to maintain the diversity of the population, thus ensuring that the genetic algorithm can avoid premature problems.

6   Algorithm Test and Result Analysis

In the experiment, the k-means algorithm, the genetic optimization k-means algorithm (GKA) and the improved genetic optimization k-means algorithm (igka) are implemented on three sample data sets of three kinds of flowers extracted from iris data set of iris plant (as shown in Table 1).

Table 1. Table 1 data sample

Category	Sepal-length	Sepal-width	Pedal-length	Pedal-width
Iris-setosa	4.6	3.2	1.4	0.2
Iris-setosa	5.3	3.7	1.5	0.2
Iris-setosa	5.0	3.3	1.4	0.2
Iris-versicolor	6.2	2.9	4.3	1.3
Iris-versicolor	5.1	2.5	3.0	1.1
Iris-versicolor	5.7	2.8	4.1	1.3
Iris-virginica	6.5	3.0	5.2	2.0
Iris-virginica	6.2	3.4	5.4	2.3
Iris-virginica	5.9	3.0	5.1	1.8

Set the experimental test parameters as shown in Table 2,

Table 2. Test parameters

Parameter name	K	p_c	p_m	p_{size}	T
Value	3	0.9	0.01	150	100

(1) The clustering results of K-means algorithm are shown in Fig. 2

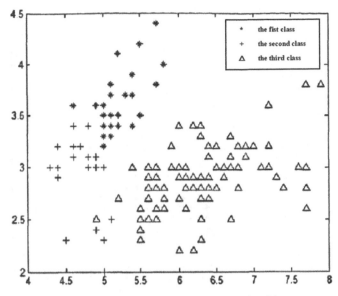

Fig. 2. Clustering results of K-means algorithm

(2) The clustering results of GKA algorithm are shown in Fig. 3

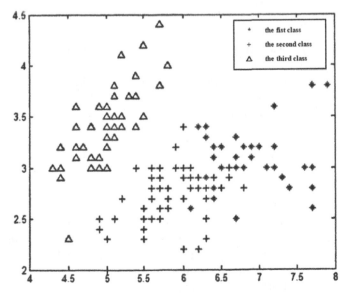

Fig. 3. Clustering results of GKA algorithm

(3)   The clustering results of igka algorithm are shown in Fig. 4

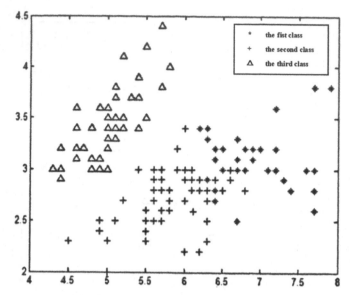

Fig. 4. Clustering results of igka algorithm

According to the execution results of the above three algorithms, the performance is compared, as shown in Table 3.

Table 3. Performance comparison of three algorithms

Clustering algorithm	Clustering accuracy	Jmin
k-means	63%	140
GKA	88%	79
IGKA	89%	79

The clustering effect can be evaluated by the objective function. The more the objective function value is, the more effective the clustering is. The optimal value jmin of the objective function obtained by igka clustering is 79, and the clustering accuracy is 89%. In order to further analyze the implementation of the three algorithms in the process of clustering operation, the average values of the clustering results of the three algorithms are compared. The comparison is shown in Fig. 5.

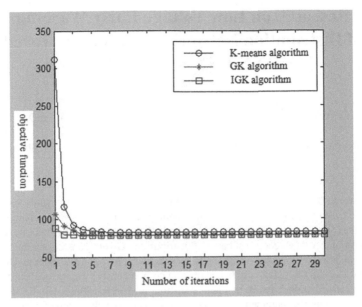

Fig. 5. Change curve of average clustering results

It can be seen from Fig. 5 that after many iterations, the average objective function values of the three algorithms have little difference. However, after careful observation, it can be found that the convergence speed of igka clustering algorithm is faster than that of GKA clustering algorithm and K-means algorithm. Therefore, the performance of igka clustering algorithm is better than that of GKA clustering algorithm and has better clustering results.

References

1. Ming, Z.: Introduction to Data Mining. China University of Science and Technology Press, Hefei (2012)
2. Liangjun, Z., et al.: Data Mining: Practical Case Analysis. China Machine Press, Beijing (2013)
3. Li, W., Suyan, W.: Ten Algorithms for Data Mining. Tsinghua University Press, Beijing (2013)
4. Tan, P.N., Steinbach, M., Kumar, V., Hongjian, M.: Introduction to Data Mining. People & apos;s Posts and Telecommunications Press, Beijing (2011)
5. Zalik, K.R.: An efficient K-means clustering algorithm. Pattern Recogn. Lett. **29**(9), 1385–1391 (2008)
6. Ahmad, A., Dey, L.: A K-means clustering algorithm for mixed numeric and categorical data. Data Knowl. Eng. **63**(2), 503–527 (2007)
7. Ying, W.: Application research of data mining technology based on genetic algorithm. Zhejiang University of Science and Technology (2012)

Research on Low Voltage Early Warning of Distribution Network Based on Improved DNN-LSTM Algorithm

Zeyu Zhang[✉], Xizhong Li, Xuan Fei, Xin Cao, and Qian Xu

Economic Research Institute of State Grid Liaoning Electric Power Co., Ltd., Shenyang, China

Abstract. The voltage control scheme of distribution network is mainly aimed at the current situation, the load of distribution network is constantly changing, and the transformation of power grid has a certain time effect, so it is necessary to evaluate the voltage control scheme of distribution network considering the load growth. Based on the local comprehensive voltage qualification rate index and load voltage sensitivity index, the change of local comprehensive voltage qualification rate of distribution network in a period of time is analyzed. Based on the whole period of time, the increment of unit cost comprehensive voltage qualification rate is calculated, and the effect of low-voltage control of distribution network is evaluated dynamically. The effectiveness is verified by an example, which provides the time efficiency evaluation for low-voltage transformation project of distribution network. Theoretical basis.

Keywords: Low voltage · Predictive model · Neural network · Load-voltage sensitivity

1 Introduction

In recent years, with the rapid development of the economy, the demand for electricity has increased sharply, and at the same time the relative lag of the distribution network has led to endless low-voltage problems [1, 2]. Related scholars have conducted many studies on the prediction of low-voltage in the platform area: Literature [3] proposed a grey relational analysis method based on the weighted improvement of the analytic hierarchy process, screen the main factors that affect the voltage qualification rate, then, a multiple linear regression equation is established to predict the voltage qualification rate. However, due to the use of analytic hierarchy process to determine the weight coefficients of influencing factors, there are large errors due to the influence of subjective factors. Literature [4] proposes a power quality classification early warning threshold setting method considering the characteristics of data clustering, different voltage warning limits are set for the 4 types of monitoring points, and a four-level warning level is established, but this method does not provide early warning for future voltage quality.

According to the current operating conditions of the platform area and the characteristics of load growth, it is of great significance to give early warning to users in the

© Springer Nature Singapore Pte Ltd. 2021
Y. Tian et al. (Eds.): ICBDS 2020, CCIS 1415, pp. 572–584, 2021.
https://doi.org/10.1007/978-981-16-3150-4_47

platform area who may have low voltage. With the popularization of smart meters, massive voltage data and load data of users in the platform area provide a realistic basis for data mining. This paper uses theoretical derivation and big data mining technology to explore the influence of load in the platform area changes voltage in the platform area, puts forward a load-voltage sensitivity index, and establishes a mathematical model of load changes affecting voltage changes.

2 Low Voltage Warning in the Platform Area

Under the current situation that the grid structure of the platform area remains unchanged, the voltage change of the platform area is mainly affected by the load change, so the load-voltage sensitivity index is proposed to characterize the relationship between the load change and the voltage:

$$\delta = \frac{\Delta U}{\Delta P} \tag{1}$$

In the formula, ΔP is load change, ΔU is voltage change.

Predict the trend of load changes based on historical data or planning data. After obtaining load forecast information, obtain the change in voltage deviation through load-voltage sensitivity. If the change rate of voltage deviation plus the original deviation exceeds the low voltage limit, it is judged that the voltage is out of limit. The key is how to determine the load-voltage sensitivity of the platform area.

Aiming at this problem, this paper uses two aspects of equivalent algorithm and data mining technology to study.

3 Based on Equivalent Load-Voltage Sensitivity

3.1 Single Load-Voltage Sensitivity

When the line transmits power, the current will cause voltage loss on the line impedance. At present, the voltage level of the rural distribution network is not high, and the influence of the line to the ground capacitance is ignored. The equivalent impedance of the line is $Z = P + JX$, User voltage is $U_2 \angle 0°$, user load power is $S = P + JX$, the load change is $\Delta P + j\Delta Q$, the components of the voltage drop:

$$\begin{cases} \Delta U = \dfrac{PR + QX}{U_2} \\ \delta U = \dfrac{PX - QR}{U_2} \end{cases} \tag{2}$$

In the formula, ΔU is longitudinal component of voltage drop, δU is transverse component of voltage drop.

So head end voltage U_1: $U_1 = (U_2 + \Delta U) + j\delta U$

Generally speaking: $U2 + \Delta U \gg \delta U$, so ignore δU, then ΔU:

$$\Delta U = U_1 - U_2 = \frac{PL(r_0 + \tan \varphi x_0)}{U_2} \tag{3}$$

In the formula, r_0 is unit resistance, x_0 is unit reactance, L is the total length, φ is power factor angle.

Single user load-voltage sensitivity:

$$\delta = \frac{PL(\Delta P + j\Delta Q)(r_0 + \tan \varphi x_0)}{\Delta U_N} \tag{4}$$

3.2 Load-Voltage Sensitivity Based on Equivalent Load and Line in the Platform Area

The size of the distribution network line load and the location of the connection will affect the line voltage distribution. There are many users in the platform area, and the length from the beginning is inconsistent. Therefore, to calculate the load-voltage sensitivity, it is necessary to obtain the load and the equivalent length [5, 6]. It is assumed that the equivalent load of the platform area is taken as the total load of the platform area; the equivalent length of the line is taken as the equivalent length equal to the maximum voltage drop at the end of the load concentration. Suppose the uniformly distributed load is a resistive load and the power density is p(W/km), wire resistance per unit length is r_0, wire reactance per unit length is x_0, φ is power factor angle, the rated voltage of the line is U_N, the line length is l. The total load size is:

$$P = p \cdot l \tag{5}$$

Total voltage loss on the line with evenly distributed load:

$$\Delta U_{ab} = \iint \frac{p \cdot dx \cdot dx((r_0 + \tan \varphi x_0)}{U_N} = \frac{P \cdot (r_0 + \tan \varphi x_0)}{U_N} \cdot \frac{l}{2} \tag{6}$$

Using the model established above, the load of the platform area is equivalent to the concentrated load, assuming that the initial total power of the line is P, when the line power changes ΔP, the line voltage losses are:

$$\begin{cases} \Delta U_{ab} = \dfrac{P \cdot (r_0 + \tan \varphi x_0)}{U_N} \cdot \dfrac{l}{2} \\ \Delta U'_{ab} = \dfrac{(P + \Delta P) \cdot (r_0 + \tan \varphi x_0)}{U_N} \cdot \dfrac{l}{2} \end{cases} \tag{7}$$

The change in voltage loss caused by power change is:

$$\Delta U'_{ab} - \Delta U_{ab} = \frac{\Delta P \cdot (r_0 + \tan \varphi x_0)}{U_N} \cdot \frac{l}{2} \tag{8}$$

Suppose the load-voltage sensitivity when the load changes is δ, then:

$$\delta = \frac{(r_0 + \tan \varphi x_0)}{U_N} \cdot \frac{l}{2} \tag{9}$$

4 Load-Voltage Sensitivity Based on Big Data Analysis

The load-voltage sensitivity analysis of the platform area based on the equivalent load and the line assumes that the start-end voltage of the platform area is fixed and the load distribution is uniform, so there is a linear relationship. No matter how the platform area load changes, the load voltage sensitivity does not change. In practical projects, the voltage at the beginning of the platform area is affected by many factors such as load size, feeders, and voltage regulation measures in substations, and the power consumption behavior of users in different distribution stations is also somewhat random. Data can retain this information more objectively, and can be more accurately reflected through big data learning.

4.1 Comprehensive Voltage Deviation of Platform Area

Aiming at the problems of interference information in the extracted feature data and the need to consider the timing of feature information, a DNN-LSTM network recognition model based on EMD is proposed.

Since there is no indicator that can be used to measure the voltage quality of the platform area, based on the consideration of a large number of user voltage data, the voltage deviation of all voltage users in the platform area is comprehensively selected as the drop of the platform area voltage, the comprehensive voltage deviation of the platform area, and the specific calculation formula is:

$$\Delta U = \frac{\sum_{i=1}^{n} \Delta u_i}{n} \tag{10}$$

$$\Delta u_i = \frac{u_i - u_N}{u_N} \tag{11}$$

In the formula, Δu_i is the voltage deviation of the i-th user, n is user number, u_i is measured voltage for the user, u_N is the user's rated voltage.

4.2 DNN-LSTM Model Based on EMD

Aiming at the problems of interference information in the extracted feature data and the need to consider the timing of feature information, a DNN-LSTM network recognition model based on EMD is proposed. The method is mainly based on the empirical mode decomposition method to smooth the initial feature data, use deep neural network to perform nonlinear transformation on the feature data, and use long and short-term memory network to analyze the change law between consecutive frames.

Model Principle. EMD has adaptive characteristics, can decompose according to the characteristics of the data itself, and decompose the large-scale fluctuations in the data step by step, and is used to process nonlinear and non-stationary data, and the data whose energy of each component is less than a certain threshold is filtered out to achieve the purpose of data denoising.

The decomposition hypothesis satisfies two conditions: in the entire time series, the difference between the number of local extreme points and zero points of the component is less than or equal to one; At any moment, the upper envelope formed by the local maximum point and the lower envelope formed by the local minimum point have a mean value of zero. The decomposition steps are shown in Fig. 1.

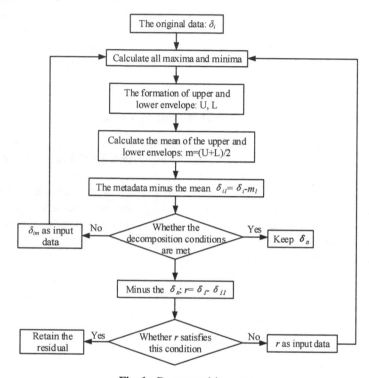

Fig. 1. Decomposition step.

Each component represents a data sequence of characteristic scale. The decomposition process is to decompose the original data sequence into a superposition of various characteristic fluctuation sequences. The energy method is used to select an appropriate threshold M according to the extracted feature data and the energy ratio of each component to process the data to make the feature data more stable to facilitate the subsequent recognition stage.

Calculate the energy of each component:

$$EE_i = \int_0^T |\delta_{i1}|^2 dt \tag{12}$$

In the formula, T is the total number of frames for each action.

Calculate the energy ratio of each component:

$$K_i = \frac{EE_i}{\sum_{i=1}^I EE_i} \times 100\% \tag{13}$$

In the formula, K_i is the energy ratio of the i-th signal IMF component, I is the number of signal components.

After the above processing, the characteristic data can be expressed as:

$$\delta_i = \sum\nolimits_{j=1}^{J} c_j + r_n, (n = J + 1), ki \geq M \tag{14}$$

In the formula, c_j is the j-th component of the original signal, r_n is the residual component of the original signal.

Considering the network performance and generalization ability of the model, increasing the number of network layers can increase the accuracy but will complicate the network. Increasing the number of nodes will reduce the error. Therefore, the deep neural network of the improved model has 4 hidden layers, and each hidden layer has 32 neurons. However, the processing of features by deep neural networks is independent at each moment. The cyclic neural network has a sequential nature in the processing of features. The input of its neuron at the current moment includes the output of the previous layer of neurons at that moment and its own output at the previous moment. The long and short-term memory network adds a gating mechanism to the cyclic neural network, and its cell unit contains input gates, forget gates and output gates.

Consider the smoothed feature data and its corresponding mark as a time series data set $\{(\delta_i, y_i)\}_i^T$ of length T, among them, δ_i is an n-dimensional feature vector, $y_i \in (0,1)$ is the behavior of the current frame, DNN-LSTM model are shown in Fig. 2.

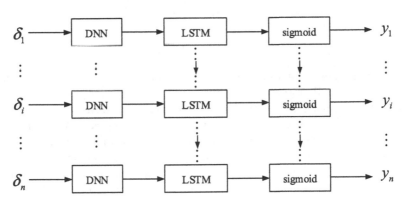

Fig. 2. DNN-LSTM model.

When the deep neural network has l-layer network and its l-1th layer has m neurons in total, the output expression of the j-th neuron in the l-th layer is shown in formula (15).

$$\delta_j^l = \tanh(z_i^l) = \sigma \left(\sum\nolimits_{i=1}^{m} \omega_{ji}^l \delta^{l-1} + b_j^l \right) \tag{15}$$

In the formula, tanh is the activation function of the neuron, σ is the sigmoid function, ω is the weight coefficient, δ represents the input of the current layer, b is the bias vector.

In this paper, the characteristic sequence of sequence frame length N is $\delta = (\delta_1, \delta_2,..., \delta_n)$, the standard LSTM unit is calculated from $t = 1 - n$ in chronological order. The formula is shown in formulas (16)–(21).

The forget gate determines the forgotten information in the cell unit, and outputs a value between 0 and 1 and input to the input gate. The calculation formula is:

$$f_t = \sigma(\omega[h_{t-1}, \delta_j^4] + b_f) \tag{16}$$

In the formula, h_{t-1} is the input of the previous cell, δ is the output of DNN, which is the input of the current cell of LSTM.

The input gate determines the information that needs to be updated and discarded. It is calculated in three steps. σ determines the updated data, and b obtains a new candidate value to determine the proportion of the cell state. The calculation formula is:

$$i_t = \sigma(\omega_i[h_{t-1}, \delta_j^4] + b_i) \tag{17}$$

$$\tilde{c}_t = \tanh(\omega_c[h_{t-1}, \delta_j^4] + b_c) \tag{18}$$

$$c_t = f_t * c_{t-1} + i_t * \tilde{c}_t \tag{19}$$

The output gate is the final output of LSTM. The final output is obtained by first using the decision to update and then multiplying with the obtained new candidate value. The calculation formula is:

$$o_t = \sigma(\omega_o[h_{t-1}, \delta_j^4] + b_o) \tag{20}$$

$$h_t = o_t * \tanh(c_t) \tag{21}$$

DNN outputs more obvious feature vectors and then uses LSTM to analyze its time series characteristics. Perform feature extraction on the load of the platform area and the integrated voltage deviation of the platform area respectively, the number of nodes in the input layer of the model is 8, the number of nodes in the deep network layer is 32, the activation function is *tan h* function, the number of neurons in the long and short-term memory network layer is 64, the activation function is the sigmoid function, the number of nodes in the output layer is 1, and the activation function is the sigmoid function. In order to solve the problem of over-fitting and realize more effective learning to join the Dropout layer, the proportion is set to 0.5. Figure 3 is a diagram of the fused neural network model.

Model Training. Supervised training has both training data and training results in the training process, and the training effect is better. Therefore, the supervised training is used to input the processed features into the model, and the corresponding recognition results are obtained through model processing. The model in this paper uses the mean square error function as the loss function, that is, the predicted value is compared with the actual value, and the loss function is used to calculate the error between the recognition result and the true value. The specific expression is shown in formula (22).

$$MSE = \frac{1}{m} \sum_{i=1}^{m} (h_t - \hat{h_t})^2 \tag{22}$$

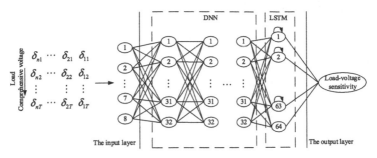

Fig. 3. Network model diagram.

In the formula, h_t is the true value, $\hat{h}$ is the predicted value.

After calculating the loss gradient of the data, the optimization algorithm optimizes the loss. The optimization algorithm used by the model is the Adam optimization algorithm with adaptive learning rate. The first-order moment estimation and second-order moment estimation of the gradient are used to dynamically adjust the learning rate of each parameter. The exponential decay rate of the first-order moment estimation is 0.9, and the exponential decay rate of the second-order moment estimation is 0.999, so that the learning rate of each iteration has a clear interval, the parameters are relatively stable, and the result can be predicted faster.

5 Case Analysis

The steps of using load-voltage sensitivity to predict low voltage in the platform area are as follows:

Step 1: Statistics the voltage data of the user side of the platform area and the platform area load. Calculate the comprehensive voltage deviation of the platform area according to the user-side voltage data, and calculate the platform area load at this time.

Step 2: Use the improved DNN-LSTM for data mining, input the load of the platform area and the voltage deviation of the platform area for sample training, find out the connection, and determine the load-voltage sensitivity of the platform area.

Step 3: Carry out load forecasting based on historical data or planning data. Input the predicted load data into the improved DNN-LSTM model, determine the load-voltage sensitivity at this time, and then calculate the comprehensive voltage deviation of the platform area after the load increases.

Step 4: According to the output integrated voltage deviation of the platform area, assuming that the voltage drop of all users in the platform area is consistent, and the deviation value is consistent with the integrated voltage deviation of the platform area while ignoring the difference in the power consumption of users in the platform area. According to the currently known user-side voltage data, perform a drop simulation for all users to determine whether the user voltage value in the platform area exceeds the limit.

Select IEEE14 node to simulate the low-voltage condition of the platform area. Figure 4 shows the IEEE14 node topology.

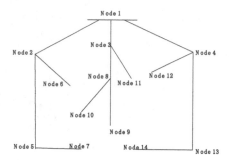

Fig. 4. IEEE14 node topology diagram.

Choose 1000 sets of historical data to verify the effectiveness of the model based on the improved DNN-LSTM algorithm, the commonly used traditional DNN model, LSTM model and DNN-LSTM model are used as comparison models. The comparison test uses the same test data as input, and the comparison results are shown in Fig. 5 and Fig. 6. Figure 5 shows the change in loss of each model as the number of training iterations increases during the entire training process. Figure 6 shows the change in precision. In order to compare the loss and precision of each model more clearly and intuitively, the comparison is made after 30 iterations.

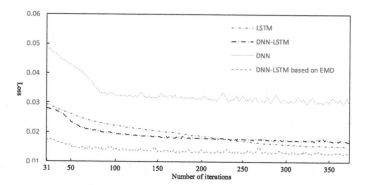

Fig. 5. Training loss graph of each model.

It can be seen from Fig. 5 that during the training process, the network model based on the improved DNN-LSTM algorithm has stabilized after about 150 iterations, and the speed of stabilization is significantly faster than other models, and its loss value is lower than that of the other three models.

As can be seen in Fig. 6, as the number of iterations increases, the precision tends to increase, and the precision tends to be stable when the number of iterations reaches about 100. The network model recognition precision of the improved DNN-LSTM algorithm is significantly higher than the other three models, and the stability is better in the later stage of training.

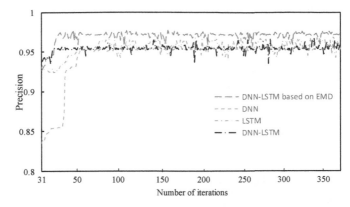

Fig. 6. Precision map of each model.

So the improved DNN-LSTM algorithm has superiority in solving the load-voltage sensitivity of this platform area. Select historical data and input it into the neural network for sample training. The results are shown in Table 1.

Table 1. DNN-LSTM calculation results.

Load in the platform area	Forecast load growth	ΔU	δ
10478	300	1.528%	5.30E-06
10778	77	1.687%	4.92E-06
10855	−208	1.725%	5.56E-06
10647	−250	1.609%	5.18E-06
10397	197	1.479%	5.52E-06
10594	−101	1.588%	5.01E-06
10493	87	1.538%	3.13E-06
10580	182	1.565%	5.278E-06
10762	−353	1.661%	4.62E-06

The improved DNN-LSTM is used to analyze and process the data, the learning rate is selected as 0.1, the maximum number of iterations is 1000, sample training is performed, and the model is established. The current platform area load is 0.5 MW, and the integrated voltage deviation of the platform area is the instantaneous voltage of each node as shown below (Fig. 7):

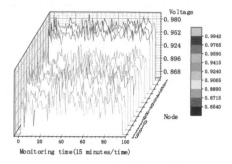

Fig. 7. Voltage curve of each node.

With the continuous increase in power consumption, it is assumed that the load will increase by 20% in the next five years. Input it into the trained improved DNN-LSTM, and get the corresponding load-voltage sensitivity $\delta = 5.3 \times 10^{-6}$ of the platform area under the current load and the increase range. When the total load of the platform area increases by 20%, the overall voltage deviation change rate of the platform area is 1.1%, and it is considered that all node voltage deviations have increased by 1.1%. The voltage curve of each node at this time is as follows (Fig. 8):

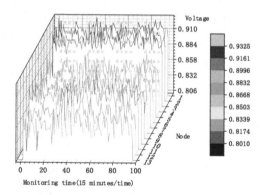

Fig. 8. The voltage curve of each node after the load increases by 20%.

Based on the load-voltage sensitivity, it can be predicted whether the daily voltage deviation of each node in the platform area will exceed the limit at a certain time in the future. Based on this data, the voltage quality of each user can be calculated. Take 3, 4, 5, and 6 nodes as examples,

It can be seen from Fig. 9 that in the current state, each node has not exceeded the limit, and there is no low voltage problem. When the load increases by 20%, the voltage deviation of each node changes by 1.1% on the original basis, then the 3, 4, and 6 nodes will exceed the limit, and there will be low voltage problems, which should be warned in advance. For other nodes in the platform area, early warning should be given to nodes with a daily voltage deviation of more than 8.9%.

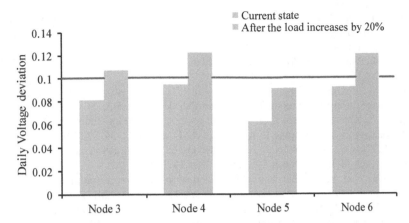

Fig. 9. Daily voltage deviation diagram of some nodes.

6 Conclusion

(1) The prediction model based on the improved DNN-LSTM is used to study the low-voltage prediction technology, and the IEEE14 node is simulated. The model verifies the accuracy of the prediction model.

(2) Through the prediction of the low voltage in the platform area, it will provide some help for the grid company to make early measures to deal with the low voltage problem and plan the distribution network line.

(3) The amount of statistical data in this paper is limited. It is hoped that the model under the rich data structure will be more accurate in judging the type of low voltage in the platform area.

(4) This article only elaborates on the low-voltage problem in the platform area, and it is also available for feeder and substation problems. For the feeder, it is only necessary to treat the distribution transformers under the feeder as a single node, and perform calculations based on the above calculation method. In the same way, low-voltage warning can also be given to the substation.

References

1. Hu, X., Chen, L., Niu, Q., Xing, J., Liu, Y.: Research on the key issues of low voltage management in distribution networks. Distrib. Utilization **34**(02), 35–39 (2017)
2. Wang, J., Duan, X., Li, Y., Zhao, X.: Causes and comprehensive governance measures of low voltage problem in distribution network. Distrib. Utilization **33**(07), 8–12 (2016)
3. Zhang, Y., Bai, X., Zhang, Y., Kuang, C.: The prediction method of voltage qualification rate based on AHP-GCA and multiple linear regression. Electr. Power Sci. Eng. **30**(05), 1–5 (2014)
4. Lu, Y., Gao, M., Zhong, H., Li, F.: Graded early warning threshold setting method of power quality considering the data clustering features. Power Capacitor React. Power Compensation **37**(03), 88–94 (2016)

5. Qin, W., Liu, X., Han, X., Liu, J., Zhu, X., Zhu, X.: An improved control strategy of automatic charging/discharging of energy storage system in DC microgrid. Power Syst. Technol. **38**(7), 1827–1834 (2014)
6. Liu, J., Bi, P.-X., Wu, X.-M.: Equivalent load density models for feeders. Proc. CSEE **23**(1), 70–77 (2003)
7. Zhang, M.: Preliminary analyzing of power distribution transformer power supply area of low voltage management mode. Power Demand Side Manag. **5**(3), 56–57 (2013)
8. Huang, W., Zhang, J., Shen, Z., et al.: Meter reading and line loss management schemes for low-voltage transformer areas. East Chin. Electr. Power **37**(1), 34–37 (2013)
9. Liu, M., Zhou, S., Deng, Y., et al.: An area-decoupled state estimation method for distribution systems. Autom. Electr. Power Syst. **29**(6), 79–83 (2005)
10. Zhang, Y., Tian, J., Yang, L., et al.: Discussion of reactive compensation technology in low voltage distribution. Power Demand Side Manag. **13**(6), 41–43 (2013)
11. Zhang, Y., Shi, H., Xu, L.: Systematic developing program of distribution net-work energy saving potential evaluation. Autom. Electr. Power Syst. **35**(2), 51–55 (2011)
12. Ju, P., Liu, W., Xiang, L., et al.: Automatic post-disturbance simulation based method for power system load modeling. Autom. Electr. Power Syst. **37**(10), 60–64 (2013)
13. Yuan, R., Ai, Q., He, X.: Research on dynamic load modeling based on power quality monitoring system. Gener. Transm. Distrib. IET **7**(1), 46–51 (2013)
14. Li, P., Li, X., Lin, S.: Critical review on synthesis load modeling. Proc. CSU-EPSA **20**(5), 56–64 (2008)
15. Xie, H., Ju, P., Chen, Q., et al.: Electric load modeling for wide area power systems. Autom. Electr. Power Syst. **32**(1), 1–5 (2008)

Cross-Task and Cross-Model Active Learning with Meta Features

Guo-Xiang Li[1], Yao-Feng Tu[1,2], and Sheng-Jun Huang[1(✉)]

[1] College of Computer Science and Technology, Nanjing University of Aeronautics
and Astronautics, Nanjing, China
{guoxiangli,huangsj}@nuaa.edu.cn
[2] ZTE Corporation, Shenzhen, China

Abstract. When the task model or data set changes, the active learning strategies based on heuristics are difficult to perform well all the time. In this paper, we propose a task-agnostic and model-agnostic active learning method based on meta-feature. This method draws on the idea of meta-learning. First, we designed the meta-features of an unlabeled sample at the current learning stage. These designed meta-features have nothing to do with the feature space of the data set or the form of the task model. So our method can be applied to any data set and any model. Second, we regard the active learning query selection procedure as a regression problem. We design a meta regressor that predicts the improvement of model performance for a candidate sample in a particular learning state. And we train the regressor on the experience from previous active learning outcomes. Experimental results show that our method is more stable and effective than the heuristic active learning method.

Keywords: Active learning · Meta learning

1 Introduction

Most supervised learning methods require large amounts of training examples to reach their full potential. Since these examples are mainly obtained through human experts who manually label samples, the labelling process may have a high cost. This can be a critical bottleneck in applying these machine learning methods to practical problems. Active learning is well-motivated in many modern machine learning problems, where unlabeled data may be abundant or easily obtained, but labels are difficult, time-consuming, or expensive to obtain. Active learning mitigates the problem by selectively selecting the most "informative" samples for experts to annotate from an unlabeled dataset. The key idea behind active learning is that a machine learning algorithm can achieve greater accuracy with fewer training labels if it is allowed to choose the data from which it learns.

The core problem of the active learning is how to select the most informative unlabeled data points. There are many active learning strategies designed based on a variety of heuristic ideas. Well-known strategies include heuristics such

© Springer Nature Singapore Pte Ltd. 2021
Y. Tian et al. (Eds.): ICBDS 2020, CCIS 1415, pp. 585–598, 2021.
https://doi.org/10.1007/978-981-16-3150-4_48

as prediction margin [33], uncertainty-based sampling [21], representative and diversity-based [6], query-by-committee [4,12], expected model change [31,35] and combinations thereof [17]. Most hand-designed active learning strategies are either on the basis of researcher's expertise and intuition or by approximating theoretical criteria. They are often tailored for specific applications. Although the heuristic-based active learning strategies can achieve remarkable performance, it is a challenge for most strategies when the data distribution of the underlying learning problems vary. And it is almost impossible to predict in advance which strategy is the most suitable in a particular situation. Empirical studies in [28] show that there is no single strategy that consistently outperforms others in all datasets. Furthermore, they only represent a small subset of all possible active learning strategies. Thus it is hard to pick a perfect active learning strategy, because each strategy is based on a reasonable and appealing but completely different motivation.

To overcome above the limitations mentioned above, it has recently been proposed to design the active learning strategies in a meta learning fashion by learning. There is a novel data-driven approach to active learning LAL [22], its key idea is to train a regressor that predicts the expected error reduction for a potential sample in a particular learning state. They learned the LAL based on experience from previous active learning experiments. But LAL method has strict requirements on the task model, which must be a random forest model. Because all the design features in LAL are related to the random forest model, such as average tree depth of the forest or forest variance computed as variance of trees' predictions. Therefore, the LAL cannot achieve cross-task-model requirements.

In this work, we designed a large number of statistical features of data sets, features of specific task models, and features of a specific unlabeled samples. The most important point is that all the meta-features we designed above do not depend on the specific data set or specific task model, So our method have better generalization performance and can be applied to any machine learning task. To our best knowledge, deliberately designing corresponding meta features for active learning scenarios has not been throughly studied before.

More specifically, follow the idea of meta learning, first, we need to collect meta-data that describe prior active learning tasks and previously learned models. These meta data comprise the meta feature we designed and the model performance changes, such as the increase in accuracy or the decrease in the corresponding task loss function, before and after an unlabeled sample is annotated. Second, we need to train a regressor from this prior meta-data, to extract and transfer knowledge that learn an optimal active learning strategy for new tasks. Then we treat the strategy of active learning as a regression task which scores the amount of information for an unlabeled sample in a particular learning state. In each iteration of active learning, we first calculate the meta-features corresponding to the unlabeled samples, and then use the trained meta regressor to predict the model performance improvement that can be expected by adding the label to that unlabeled sample.

The rest of the paper is organized as follows: In Sect. 2, we briefly review related works. In Sect. 3, we describe the setting of active learning and meta-learning problems. In Sect. 4, the proposed approach is introduced. In Sect. 5, experimental results are reported, followed by the conclusion in Sect. 6.

2 Related Work

2.1 Active Learning (AL)

Many machine learning algorithms require large amounts of high-quality labeled data to reach their full potential. This situation is especially obvious in deep learning. However, high-quality labeled data sets is hard and expensive to obtain, notably in specialized domains, such as medicine, where only experts whose time is scarce and precious can provide reliable labels. This will become a critical bottleneck when machine learning models are applied to the scenarios which involving time-consuming data acquisition or high labeling costs. Furthermore, most fully supervised strategies assume access to samples representing the entire data distribution beforehand, thus making it challenging to handle changes in data distribution over time or adapt the learned model when diverse samples are incrementally included into the training process. Active learning is well-motivated in many modern machine learning problems, where unlabeled data may be abundant or easily obtained, but labels are difficult, time-consuming, or expensive to obtain. [29] provides a general introduction to active learning and a survey of the literature. They include uncertainty sampling [19,29,33,38], query-by-committee [12,18], expected model change [31,35], expected error [20], variance minimization [13], and Bayesian AL [16].

2.2 Meta Learning

The field of meta-learning, or learning-to-learn, has seen a dramatic rise in interest in recent years. When we learn new skills, we rarely, if ever, start from scratch. We start from skills learned earlier in related tasks, reuse approaches that worked well before, and focus on what is likely worth trying based on experience [23]. Likewise, when building machine learning models for a specific task, we often build on experience with related tasks, or use our (often implicit) understanding of the behavior of machine learning techniques to help make the right choices [34]. Meta-learning aims at discovering ways to dynamically search for the best learning strategy as the number of tasks increases [36]. For more meta-learning content, you can read these articles [14,34,36].

Rather than hand-designing a criterion, learning active learning strategies with good generalization has become the trend of active learning research in recent years. Some of them have been proposed to tackle the problem of learning AL strategies instead of relying on manually designed strategies. Motivated by the success of methods that combine predictors, the some of them tried to combine traditional active learning strategies within this paradigm. [17] focus on the traditional active learning strategies and predict the best suitable one using a multi-armed bandits approach. [2,17] used an ensemble containing two of the best known active-learning algorithms as well as a new algorithm. A common limitation of these methods is that they cannot go beyond combining pre-existing hand-designed heuristics. Besides, they require reliable assessment of the classification performance which is problematic because the annotated data is scarce. Others are modelling the data distributions [15,24,30] as a pre-processing step, or similarly use metric-based meta-learning [7,26] as a clustering algorithm. There is another method that use reinforcement learning directly learn strategies from data [1,9,37]. However, these pure reinforcement learning approaches not only require a huge amount of samples they also do not resort to existing knowledge, such as potentially available active learning heuristics. Moreover, training the reinforcement learning agents is usually very time-intensive as they are trained from scratch.

3   Problem Setting

3.1   Active Learning (AL)

In this section we define the settings for the pool-based active learning. A dataset $\mathcal{D} = \{(x_i, y_i)\}_{i=1}^n$ contains n instances $x_i \in R^d$ and labels $y_i \in 1, 2, ..., C$, most or all of which are unknown in advance. At the start of AL, the data set is split between a labelled L and unlabelled $U = \mathcal{D} \backslash L$ set where $|L| \ll |U|$ and a classifier f has been trained on L so far. At each stage of AL iteration, an active learning strategy Q, which is a mapping $Q : L \times U \to U$, selects an unlabeled sample x_i from unlabelled pool U to query its label $(L, U, f) \to x_i$, where $x_i \in U$. Then the selected unlabeled sample x_i is removed from U and added to L along with its label, and the classifier f is retrained based on the updated L. Figure 1 illustrates the active learning process.

3.2   Meta Learning

First, in conventional supervised machine learning, we are given a training dataset $\mathcal{D} = \{(x_i, y_i)\}_{i=1}^n$. We can train a predictive model $\hat{y} = f_\theta(x)$ parameterized by θ, by solving:

$$\theta^* = \arg\min_\theta \mathcal{L}(\mathcal{D}; \theta, \omega) \tag{1}$$

where $\mathcal{L}$ is a loss function that measures the match between true labels and those predicted by $f_\theta(\cdot)$. The condition ω is explicit the dependence of this solution on factors such as hyperparameter for f or choice of optimizer for θ, which denote by ω. Generalization is then measured by evaluating a number of test points with known labels.

The conventional assumption is that this optimization is performed from scratch for every problem $\mathcal{D}$; and furthermore that ω is pre-specified by experts.

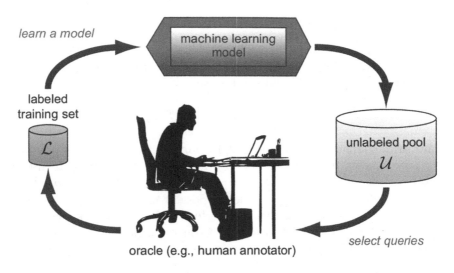

Fig. 1. The active learning process [29].

However, the specification ω of 'how to learn' the θ can dramatically affect generalization, data-efficiency, computation cost, and so on. Meta-learning addresses improving performance by learning the learning algorithm itself, rather than assuming it is pre-specified and fixed.

Meta-Learning aims to improve performance by learning 'how to learn' [32] and learn a general purpose learning algorithm, that can generalize across tasks and ideally enable each new task to be learned better than the last. As such ω specifies 'how to learn' and is often evaluated in terms of performance over a distribution of tasks $p(\mathcal{T})$. Here we define a task to be a dataset and loss function $\mathcal{T} = \{\mathcal{D}, \mathcal{L}\}$. Learning how to learn thus becomes:

$$\min_{\omega} \mathop{\mathbb{E}}_{\mathcal{T} \sim p(\mathcal{T})} \mathcal{L}(\mathcal{D}; \omega) \tag{2}$$

where $\mathcal{L}(\mathcal{D}; \omega)$ measures the performance of a model trained using ω on dataset $\mathcal{D}$. The knowledge ω of 'how to learn' is often referred to as meta-knowledge.

To solve this problem in practice, we usually assume access to a set of source tasks sampled from $p(\mathcal{T})$, with which we learn ω. Formally, we denote the set of M source tasks used in the meta-training stage as $\mathscr{D}_{\text{source}} = \{(\mathcal{D}_{\text{source}}^{\text{train}}, \mathcal{D}_{\text{source}}^{\text{val}})^{(i)}\}_{i=1}^{M}$ where each task has both training and validation data. Often, the source train and validation datasets are respectively called support and query sets. Denoting the meta-knowledge as ω, the meta-training step of 'learning how to learn' is then:

$$\omega^* = \arg\max_{\omega} \log p\left(\omega \mid \mathscr{D}_{\text{source}}\right) \tag{3}$$

Now we denote the set of Q target tasks used in the meta-testing stage as $\mathscr{D}_{\text{target}} = \left\{ \left(\mathcal{D}_{\text{target}}^{\text{train}}, \mathcal{D}_{\text{target}}^{\text{test}} \right)^{(i)} \right\}_{i=1}^{Q}$ where each task has both training and test data. In the meta-testing stage we use the learned meta-knowledge to train the base model on each previously unseen target task i:

$$\theta^{*(i)} = \arg\max_{\theta} \log p \left(\theta \mid \omega^*, \mathcal{D}_{\text{target}}^{\text{train}(i)} \right) \tag{4}$$

In contrast to conventional learning in 2, learning on the training set of a target task i now benefits from meta-knowledge ω about the algorithm to use. We can evaluate the accuracy of meta-learner by the performance of ω^* on the test split of each target task $\mathcal{D}_{\text{target}}^{\text{train}(i)}$. The purpose of meta-learning is to learn a appropriate meta-knowledge ω that can perform well on new tasks. For a more detailed description of the settings of meta learning problem, you can check theses literatures [14, 34, 36]

4 Method

In this section we will introduce our proposed method in detail. We formulate learning a optimal active learning strategy as a regression problem. According to the idea of meta learning, we must first obtain a large amount of empirical data on the previous active learning tasks. In order to make our method applicable to different data sets and task models, we have deliberately designed a series of effective meta-features.

First, we simulate active learning tasks on a large number of labeled source data sets $\mathscr{D}_{\text{source}} = \{\mathcal{D}_{\text{source}}^{(i)})\}_{i=1}^{M}$ to obtain meta data. For each of these data sets, we divide the $\mathcal{D}^k$ into three parts: the initial labeled data set L_0^k, the unlabeled data set U_0^k and the validation set V_0^k, and train an initial model f_0. At current state t, we randomly select an unlabeled sample x_t from U_{t-1}^k and calculate its corresponding meta-features M_t according to the state of the model f_{t-1} and the distribution of the L_{t-1}^k and U_{t-1}^k. Then annotate the sample x_t and add it to the $L_t^k = L_{t-1} \cup x_t$ to retrain the model getting f_t and record the model's performance changes before and after the model on the validation set $\Delta_t = S(f_t, V) - S(f_{t-1}, V)$, where V is the validation set and S is metric quantifying the quality of model, such as accuracy or AUC(Area Under the Curve). So the (M_t, Δ_t) is one record of meta data. In order to capture all possible situations in active learning, such as task model performance rise stage or stable stage, we try to get meta data at different dataset initializations and various sizes of labeled set. After acquiring the meta datasets for active learning task, we model the dependency between the meta-feature we designed and the expected greedy improvement of the model performance: $h : M \rightarrow \Delta$, which is dataset agnostic and task model agnostic. More specifically, we train an appropriate meta-regressor based on the meta datasets. After obtaining a good enough meta-regressor, we can apply the meta-regressor to other new active learning task. According to the score predicted by the meta-regressor h, greedily select the unlabeled sample with the highest score at the t-th iteration. A unlabeled sample with a higher score is more likely to bring more improvements to the model's performance.

4.1 Meta Feature

Meta-learning aims to reason about the performance of learning algorithms across different datasets [5]. Specifically, we collect a set of meta-features and the model's performance changes in active learning tasks from a large number of datasets, where meta-features are characteristics of the current state that help determine which unlabeled sample is more appropriate and can be computed in an efficient manner.

Meta-feature is central to meta-learning and the quality of meta feature design directly affects the effect of meta learning. Rather than the reasoning based on meta-features, meta-features themselves play a more important role to the final performance [10]. However, there is a lack of a principle way to design appropriate meta-features for meta-learning, especially in active learning tasks. Multiple kinds of meta-features from different aspects have been tried and presented in previous meta learning studies, including a) simple meta-features: describe the basic dataset structure [8,11], such as the number of instances, the number of features, etc. b) statistical meta-features [8]: characterize the data viadescriptive statistics such as the kurtosis and skewness; c) PCA-based meta-features [3]: computevarious statistics of the dataset principal components.

To our best knowledge, deliberately designing corresponding meta features for active learning scenarios has not been throughly studied before. In this work, we propose four types of meta features specifically for active learning and define function $MF(x_t, L_t, U_t, f_t)$ to calculate meta features.

- **Dataset-based meta-features:** These features have nothing to do with specific unlabeled samples and can be calculated in advance to improve efficiency. (1) General information: number of instances, number of feature and ration of two characteristic values; and the value after log function transformation corresponding to the above one-to-one; (2) Traditional statistics: the kurtosis of all numerical features and take the maximum, minimum, mean, variance of it; the skewness of all numerical features and take the maximum, minimum, mean, variance of it; (3) PCA Statistic: use the principal component analysis (PCA) to sum the variance explained by each component whose principal component accounts for 95%; and use PCA to reduce the dimensionality of the dataset to one dimension, and calculate the kurtosis and skewness of this feature value; (4) Positive and negative instances ratio: The proportion of positive samples and negative samples in the current labeled data set L_t; According to the predicted label of the current model f_t, the proportion of positive samples and negative samples in the current unlabeled data set U_t;
- **Current dataset distribution meta-features:** First obtain thirty benchmark data points. (1) Use the K-Mean to obtain 10 cluster center points $X_k = \{x_{k1}, \cdots, x_{k10}\}$ on whole dataset D; (2) Select 10 equal points of

labeled dataset according to the predicted probability value of the current model f_t: $X_l = \{x_{l1}, \cdots, x_{l10}\}$; (3) Select the $X_u = \{x_{u1}, \cdots, x_{u10}\}$ on the unlabeled dataset in the same way as (2); Then for a specific sample x_i in the unlabeled set U_t, calculate the distance between it and the thirty benchmark data points mentioned above. And normalize the calculated distance.

– **Model meta-features**: (1) Current model performance: Calculate the confusion matrix of the current model f_t on the labeled dataset L_t to obtain TP, FP, TN, FN; Calculate the mean and variance of the predicted probabilities of the current model f_t at the X_l and X_u; (2) Trends in model performance: Calculate and record the same values of the previous five rounds of active learning iterations in the same way as (1).

– **Model on specific unlabeled sample meta-features**: This meta feature focuses on describing a specific sample x_i in the unlabeled set U_t. (1) Calculate the prediction probability of the current model f_t for the unlabeled sample x_i; (2) Then calculate the difference (not absolute value) from the predicted value of 30 samples, X_k, X_l and X_u; (3) Calculate and record the same values in the previous iterations in the same way as (2).

In this work, we designed corresponding meta features for the active learning task to describe the features of unlabeled samples at different stages using different models on different data sets. Compared with the simple meta features in the previous meta learning, meta features we designed can better reflect the model performance improvement that a specific unlabeled sample can bring at a specific learning stage. Compared to the previous data-driven approach [22], the meta features we designed do not need to restrict the type of model. And these meta features can be used on any task and any model.

4.2 Generation of Meta Data

After designing the meta features, we simulate the active learning process to obtain meta data. Given a large number of dataset with ground truth available, we simulate the active learning procedure using a Monte-Carlo style approach. We aim to learn the meta-knowledge, the mapping relationship between meta feature and model performance changes, from the previous active learning tasks.

More specifically, given the source dataset $\mathcal{D}^k$, divide the into three parts: the initial labeled data set L_0^k, the unlabeled data set U_0^k and the validation set V_0^k, and train an initial model f_0. At state t, we randomly select an unlabeled sample x_t from U_{t-1}^k and calculate its corresponding meta-features M_t according to the method mentioned in the previous section. All data on the source data set have ground truth. Next, obtain the $L_t^k = L_{t-1}^k \cup x_t$ add the label of x_t to labeled set L_{t-1}^k, and get retrained the model f_t. And record the difference in performance of model before and after as the target values, $\Delta_t = S(f_t, V) - S(f_{t-1}, V)$, where V is the validation set and S is metric quantifying the quality of model, such as accuracy or AUC(Area Under the Curve).

Considering the particularity of active learning, the model performance is poor and unstable when there are very few labeled dateset, so it cannot well reflect the amount of information of the unlabeled sample at current learning stage. Therefore, we eliminate the case where the initial task model accuracy is lower than the threshold ρ_l. On the other hand, as the number of labeled samples increases, the task model performance gradually converges to stability. If an unlabeled sample are added to annotate at this time, the model performance will be less improved, but this does not indicate that the amount of information contained in the unlabeled sample is small. Similarly, we eliminate cases where the performance of the current task model is higher than r_h percent of the performance of the model trained with the entire dataset. Inspired by [27] in predicting the size of candidate bounding boxes, the target values is the ratio of the task model performance change compared to the last time, $\Delta(x_t, f_t, V) = \frac{S(f_t, V) - S(f_{t-1}, V)}{S(f_{t-1}, V)}$, instead of the value of the task model performance change. In order to learn to get a more appropriate meta-knowledge, we repeat this process for different datasets, initializations of labeled set, sizes of labeled subset, and randomly selected samples. Algorithm 1 summarizes the steps of meta data generation for a fixed dataset D and a given classifier f.

Algorithm 1. Generation of meta data

1: **Input:**
2:     source dataset D, classifier f, size of labeled set N_l, repeat times M
3: **Initialize:**
4:     Split the D into L_0, U_0 and V, where $|L_0| = N_l$
5:     Train the f_0 on the L_0,
6:     for $t = 1$ to M do
7:         random select $x_t \in U$
8:         update the labeled dataset $L_t = L_{t-1} \cup x_t$
9:         calculate the meta feature of x_t by: $MF(x_t, L_t, U_t, f_t)$
10:        retrain the task model f_t
11:        record the model performance change $\Delta(x_t, f_t, V)$
12:    return $\{MF\}, \{\Delta\}$

After obtaining a large number of meta data, we hope to learn a better mapping h according to the meta feature of an unlabeled sample in the current state to reflect the value of performance improvement of the current task model:

$$h : MF(x_t, L_t, U_t, f_t) \to \Delta(x_t, f_t, V) \tag{5}$$

Therefore, our active learning query strategy is based on the meta regressor predicted value. reedily selects a unlabeled sample with the highest score at active learning stage t:

$$x^* = \arg\max_{x_i \in \mathcal{U}_t} h\left(MF(x_i)\right) \tag{6}$$

5   Experiments

5.1   Datasets

We experiment with UCI datasets including wdbc, ethn, australian, clean1, spectf, blood. All of the above data sets are binary classification tasks. Table 1 gives a summary of all datesets. And we use the logistic regression with its default parameters in scikit-learn [25] as the task model.

Table 1. Statistics on datasets used in the experiments

Datasets	# Instance	# Feature	# Label
wdbc	569	14	2
ethn	2630	30	2
australian	690	42	2
clean1	476	166	2
spectf	349	44	2
blood	784	4	2

5.2   Meta Regressor

In the experiment, we use the neural network model as the meta regressor. The architecture of the meta regressor is a simple four-layer fully connected network, whose layers of size are 1024, 512, 256, 64. The activation function between each layer uses relu. And we use the Adam initial learning rate 0.001 and discount factor $\gamma = 0.99$. The batch size is 128 and the epoch of training is 100.

5.3   Baselines

- **Random** randomly samples data points from the unlabeled pool.
- **US** simply queries the instance with minimum certainty.

In all AL experiments we select samples from a training set and report the classification performance on an independent test set. All results are averages over 5 trials of training and testing dataset splits. Then we report the average test performance as a function of the number of labeled samples to check the effectiveness of active learning query strategies. And we use the conventional accuracy metric to evaluate the task model's generalization performance on test data. In all experiments we use logistic regression classifier as our task model on each data set.

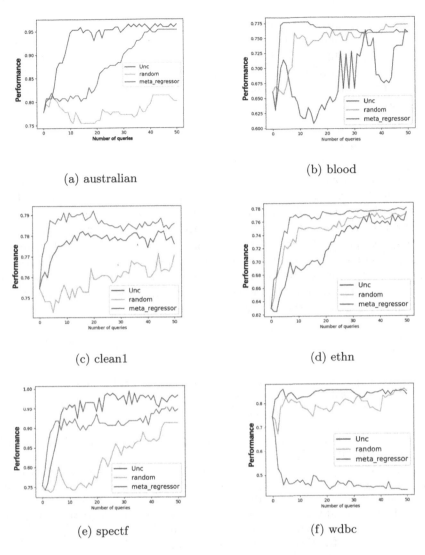

(a) australian

(b) blood

(c) clean1

(d) ethn

(e) spectf

(f) wdbc

Fig. 2. The results of active learning in the experiments

5.4 Results

We use leave-one-out (LOO) setting to conduct experiments to verify the effectiveness of our method. We obtain the meta data from on all data sets other than the test set. Then train a meta regressor based on the meta data and evaluate it on the held out dataset. We denote our method as meta-regressor in the experimental result graph. The total annotation budget is 50 in each experiment. Figure 2 shows the results for the experimental results of active learning at different dataset. In most cases, our method can achieve good results, compared to traditional heuristic active learning methods. One exception is that our method performs very poorly on the wdbc dataset. Generally speaking, as the number of labeled set increases, the performance of the model should only get better. A possible reasonable explanation is that our method selects a large number of noise samples. These noise sample models cannot be learned well by the current task model, so our method believes these noise sample contains more information.

6 Conclusion

Although the heuristic-based active learning strategies can achieve remarkable performance, these strategies are difficult to perform well all the time. Rather than hand-designing a criterion, learning active learning strategies with good generalization has become the focus of researchers. In this work, we propose the meta features specifically for active learning tasks. Compared with the previous method, these meta features can achieve cross-task and cross-model effects. In future work we would like to combine reinforcement learning and use these meta features as description of the state to learn an active learning query strategy that is more suitable for the current data set.

References

1. Bachman, P., Sordoni, A., Trischler, A.: Learning algorithms for active learning. ArXiv abs/1708.00088 (2017)
2. Baram, Y., El-Yaniv, R., Luz, K.: Online choice of active learning algorithms. J. Mach. Learn. Res. **5**, 255–291 (2003)
3. Bardenet, R., Brendel, M., Kégl, B., Sebag, M.: Collaborative hyperparameter tuning. In: ICML (2013)
4. Beluch, W.H., Genewein, T., Nurnberger, A., Kohler, J.: The power of ensembles for active learning in image classification. In: 2018 IEEE/CVF Conference on Computer Vision and Pattern Recognition, pp. 9368–9377 (2018)
5. Brazdil, P., Giraud-Carrier, C., Soares, C., Vilalta, R.: Metalearning - applications to data mining. In: Cognitive Technologies (2009)
6. Chattopadhyay, R., Wang, Z., Fan, W., Davidson, I., Panchanathan, S., Ye, J.: Batch mode active sampling based on marginal probability distribution matching, KDD In: Proceedings of International Conference on Knowledge Discovery and Data Mining 2012, pp. 741–749 (2013)
7. Contardo, G., Denoyer, L., Artières, T.: A meta-learning approach to one-step active-learning. ArXiv abs/1706.08334 (2017)
8. Elder IV, J.F.: Machine learning, neural, and statistical classification (1996)
9. Fang, M., Li, Y., Cohn, T.: Learning how to active learn: a deep reinforcement learning approach. ArXiv abs/1708.02383 (2017)
10. Feurer, M., Springenberg, J.T., Hutter, F.: Initializing bayesian hyperparameter optimization via meta-learning. In: AAAI (2015)
11. Feurer, M., Klein, A., Eggensperger, K., Springenberg, J., Blum, M., Hutter, F.: Efficient and robust automated machine learning. In: Advances in Neural Information Processing Systems, pp. 2962–2970 (2015)

12. Gilad-Bachrach, R., Navot, A., Tishby, N.: Query by committee made real. In: NIPS (2005)
13. Hoi, S., Jin, R., Zhu, J., Lyu, M.R.: Batch mode active learning and its application to medical image classification. In: ICML 2006 (2006)
14. Hospedales, T.M., Antoniou, A., Micaelli, P., Storkey, A.: Meta-learning in neural networks: a survey. ArXiv abs/2004.05439 (2020)
15. Hossain, H., Khan, M.H.A., Roy, N.: Deactive: scaling activity recognition with active deep learning. Proc. ACM Interact. Mob. Wearable Ubiquit. Technol. **2**, 66:1–66:23 (2018)
16. Houlsby, N., Huszár, F., Ghahramani, Z., Lengyel, M.: Bayesian active learning for classification and preference learning. ArXiv abs/1112.5745 (2011)
17. Hsu, W.N., Lin, H.T.: Active learning by learning. In: AAAI (2015)
18. Iglesias, J.E., Konukoglu, E., Montillo, A., Tu, Z., Criminisi, A.: Combining generative and discriminative models for semantic segmentation of CT scans via active learning. Proc. Conf. Inf. Proc. Med. Imaging **2**, 25–36 (2011)
19. Joshi, A.J., Porikli, F., Papanikolopoulos, N.: Multi-class active learning for image classification. In: CVPR (2009)
20. Joshi, A.J., Porikli, F., Papanikolopoulos, N.: Scalable active learning for multiclass image classification. IEEE Trans. Pattern Anal. Mach. Intell. **34**, 2259–2273 (2012)
21. Kapoor, A., Grauman, K., Urtasun, R., Darrell, T.: Active learning with gaussian processes for object categorization. In: 2007 IEEE 11th International Conference on Computer Vision, pp. 1–8 (2007)
22. Konyushkova, K., Sznitman, R., Fua, P.: Learning active learning from data. In: NIPS (2017)
23. Lake, B., Ullman, T.D., Tenenbaum, J., Gershman, S.: Building machines that learn and think like people. The Behavioral and brain sciences **40** (2018)
24. Mahapatra, D., Bozorgtabar, B., Thiran, J., Reyes, M.: Efficient active learning for image classification and segmentation using a sample selection and conditional generative adversarial network. ArXiv abs/1806.05473 (2018)
25. Pedregosa, F., et al.: Scikit-learn: Machine learning in Python. J. Mach. Learn. Res. **12**, 2825–2830 (2011)
26. Ravi, S., Larochelle, H.: Meta-learning for batch mode active learning. In: ICLR (2018)
27. Redmon, J., Farhadi, A.: Yolov3: An incremental improvement. ArXiv abs/1804.02767 (2018)
28. Santos, D.P., Prudêncio, R., Carvalho, A.: Empirical investigation of active learning strategies. Neurocomputing **326–327**, 15–27 (2019)
29. Settles, B.: Active learning literature survey. University of Wisconsin-Madison Department of Computer Sciences, Technical Report (2009)
30. Sinha, S., Ebrahimi, S., Darrell, T.: Variational adversarial active learning. In: 2019 IEEE/CVF International Conference on Computer Vision (ICCV), pp. 5971–5980 (2019)
31. Sznitman, R., Jedynak, B.: Active testing for face detection and localization. IEEE Trans. Pattern Anal. Mach. Intell. **32**, 1914–1920 (2010)
32. Thrun, S., Pratt, L.: Learning to learn: Introduction and overview. In: Learning to Learn (1998)
33. Tong, S., Koller, D.: Support vector machine active learning with applications to text classification. J. Mach. Learn. Res. **2**, 45–66 (2001)
34. Vanschoren, J.: Meta-learning: A survey. ArXiv abs/1810.03548 (2018)

35. Vezhnevets, A., Ferrari, V., Buhmann, J.: Weakly supervised structured output learning for semantic segmentation. In: 2012 IEEE Conference on Computer Vision and Pattern Recognition, pp. 845–852 (2012)
36. Vilalta, R., Drissi, Y.: A perspective view and survey of meta-learning. Artif. Intell. Rev. 18, 77–95 (2005)
37. Woodward, M., Finn, C.: Active one-shot learning. ArXiv abs/1702.06559 (2017)
38. Yang, Y., Ma, Z., Nie, F., Chang, X., Hauptmann, A.: Multi-class active learning by uncertainty sampling with diversity maximization. Int. J. Comput. Vis. 113, 113–127 (2014)

Improved Random Forest Algorithm Based on Attribute Comprehensive Weighting Used in Identification of Missing Data in Power Grid

Yihe Wang[✉], Yufei Jin, Yuancheng Zhu, Xiyuan Li, and Dazhi Li

Economic Research Institute of State Grid Liaoning Electric Power Co., Ltd., Shenyang, China

Abstract. With the rapid development of power grids, data fusion between systems has become a trend. Aiming at the problem of missing data that often occurs in system fusion, this paper proposes an improved random forest algorithm based on attribute comprehensive weighting IRFNNIS (Improved Random Forest-Assisted Nearest Neighbor Interpolation Strategy)'s method of identifying missing grid data. Based on the error expectation, this method firstly proposes an attribute comprehensive weighting strategy based on the error expectation, performs comprehensive attribute calculation on the initial missing set, and generates a complete set of examples; secondly, obtains the similar set according to the attribute comprehensive weighting strategy, and trains the random forest model; Finally, an improved random forest algorithm based on attribute comprehensive weighting can identify missing data and improve the identification accuracy of missing data. The calculation example uses real power grid data to analyze and the results show the feasibility and effectiveness of the method proposed in this paper.

Keywords: Comprehensive weighting · Random forest · Missing data · Identification · Error expectation

1 Introduction

The rapid development of the economy and society has produced a huge amount of information. In the process of collecting these data, some data omissions often occur due to temporary inaccessibility of some data or carelessness in the acquisition process, and it is basically inevitable. However, these missing data items are likely to carry important information of the data object. If these missing data are directly used for data mining or data analysis, the results obtained will have a very serious impact on decision-making, that is, it contains missing data. Value data will cause confusion in the mining process, resulting in reliable output.

At present, there are many filling algorithms. The commonly used algorithms include hot-deck filling, regression filling, KNN filling, and multiple filling. Hot-deck filling mainly includes two steps: (1) The pair does not contain missing values and is related to the value to be filled; (2) From each category, select the appropriate complete data as the donor for filling according to the correlation between the complete data and the missing

© Springer Nature Singapore Pte Ltd. 2021
Y. Tian et al. (Eds.): ICBDS 2020, CCIS 1415, pp. 599–611, 2021.
https://doi.org/10.1007/978-981-16-3150-4_49

data [7]. Literature [8] is based on literature [7], add weights to the donor selection calculation, and propose that the number of times each donor is used for missing value filling is proportional to the weight. Regression filling is a conditional mean filling, which is based on the complete data set to establish missing values and known values. The regression model is based on the parameters learned from historical data to estimate the missing variable value. When the variable is not linearly correlated or highly correlated, it will cause a large deviation between the filled value and the true value. Literature [3, 4] uses a series of linear and nonlinear regression models fill in missing values, literature [1, 2] uses a kernel function to build a regression model. The advantage of regression filling is that it is suitable for both categorical and continuous data. The disadvantage is that the parameter determination of the model is more complicated, and the accuracy of filling is not easy to guarantee. The main idea of KNN filling is to use the weighted mean of the K nearest neighbors of the missing value to replace the missing value. For genetic data, the literature [6] uses Euclidean distance to find the missing value in the data matrix. The most similar K nearest neighbors are then filled with missing values. Literature [9] searches for the K nearest neighbors of missing data based on the degree of gray correlation, and then fills the missing values. Literature [10] proposes partial filling based on KNN, which uses Machine learning and data mining abnormal point detection technology to detect whether the missing value can be filled: if the missing value cannot be filled, the filling is abandoned; if the missing value can be filled, the left and right neighbors of the missing value are used for weighted KNN filling. It can be seen that the filling method does not fill every missing value. In order to further improve the accuracy of filling, literature [11] proposed a non-parametric missing data filling method based on EM, which is similar to the EM algorithm. The difference is that non-parametric models such as KNN or kernel function regression replaces the parametric model in the EM algorithm.

The historical data of power grid has many attribute parameters and the missing data is widely distributed. The above research is generally used to deal with single attribute data missing. For the problem of multiple attribute missing data involving few or obvious performance degradation when applied to multiple attribute missing data, this paper proposes an improved random forest algorithm based on attribute comprehensive weighting. The method firstly proposes an attribute comprehensive weighting strategy based on error expectations, and performs comprehensive attribute calculation on the initial missing set to generate a complete set of examples; secondly, according to the attribute comprehensive weighting strategy, the similar set is obtained, and the random forest model is trained; finally, an improved random forest algorithm based on attribute comprehensive weighting is used to identify missing data and improve the identification accuracy of missing data. Simulation results show that the algorithm can fill in missing values of multiple attributes, which verifies the accuracy and effectiveness of the method.

2   Random Forest Theory

Random Forest Theory is a supervised learning algorithm proposed by LeoBreiman. RF is a supervised ensemble learning algorithm. The main idea is to combine regression decision trees (CART) into a forest through certain rules, and finally pass through the forest.

2.1 CART Regression Decision Tree

A decision tree is a set of rules for classification learning. The classification process is to obtain a tree model with the smallest deviation from the data set. The smallest deviation can be understood as the optimal balance between the training and test set errors, which can be well matched. The training set is fitted and the prediction function of the test set can be realized at the same time. Figure 1 shows the structure of the decision tree:

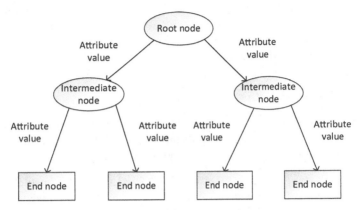

Fig. 1. Decision tree structure.

CART is a data set division strategy based on Gini index (GI) discrimination. By judging all the divisions on the end point, a largest tree is generated, and a decreasing set of subtrees is obtained through the branch reduction strategy. Using the best generalized tree as the target decision tree, the formula of GI is:

$$GI_U = 1 - \sum_{j=1}^{m} p_j^2 \tag{1}$$

In the formula, P_j is the frequency of occurrence of j-type elements, U represents the data set, and m represents the number of categories [11].

For the attribute GI of different individuals, it is required to divide them. For the division of any attribute T, U can be changed to U_1 and U_2. Then the GI of the sample set U of the divided attribute T is shown in formula 2:

$$GI_{U,T} = \frac{U_1}{U} G_{U_1}(U_1) + \frac{U_2}{U} G_{U_2}(U_2) \tag{2}$$

For any attribute, the result of this division can make the attribute generate the smallest GI subset as a split subset. If the $GI_{U,T}$ on the attribute T is smaller, it can be considered that the division effect on the attribute T is better. Therefore, the growth of the entire decision tree can be completed according to this rule.

2.2 Bagging Algorithm Based on Bootstrap Sampling

Although CART has good dividing ability, its prediction accuracy is usually not ideal. The Bagging algorithm was proposed by Breiman L in the 1990s. The biggest feature of this method is the use of the repeated sampling characteristics of Bootstrap to train any CART tree by extracting a subset of the same size from the initial set.. In addition, Breiman L also gave a method to improve the performance of node splitting, which is to randomly extract all attributes to form an attribute subset, and then perform selective splitting. The Bagging algorithm not only improves the performance of a single decision tree in the forest, but also further weakens the association between different decision trees by sampling in the attribute subspace, which plays an important role in reducing the generalization error of the random forest.

2.3 Random Forest Algorithm

Random forest regression (RFR) is an algorithm with high accuracy in machine learning. It can overcome the shortcomings of classification models and single predictions and is widely used in economics, medical, energy and other fields.

Definition 1: The set of all decision trees $\{h(X, \theta_k), k = 1, \cdots N_{tree}\}$ constitutes a random forest f, $h(X, \theta_k)$ means CART without pruning; θ_k is a random vector independently and identically distributed with the k-th decision tree; majority voting is used for classification problems, and arithmetic average is used for regression problems to obtain the final prediction value of the random forest.

Definition 2: Define the edge function $Q(X, Y)$:

$$Q(X, Y) = a_k I(h(X, \theta_k) = Y) - \max_{j \neq Y} a_k I(h(X, \theta_k) = j) \tag{3}$$

X: The input vector, which contains at most three different categories; Y: the correct classification category of the output; j: represents one of the categories; I: indicator function; a_k: average function $(k = 1, 2, \cdots n)$.

It can be seen from formula (3) that the larger the marginal function value, the higher the confidence in the correctness of the classification. Therefore, the generalization error of RFR can be defined as shown in formula (4):

$$E^* = S_{X,Y}(Q(X, Y) < 0) \tag{4}$$

In the formula, $S_{X, Y}$ is the classification error rate function of the input vector X. Using the law of large numbers for formula (4), the following theorem can be obtained:

Theorem 1: For all sequences θ_k, if the number of trees increases, E^* almost converges to:

$$S_{X,Y}(S_\theta(h(X, \theta) = Y)$$
$$- \max_{j \neq Y} S_\theta(h(X, \theta) = j) < 0 \tag{5}$$

S_θ is the classification error rate of set θ. It can be seen from the theorem that the generalization of RFR will converge to an upper bound, and the increase of the tree will not cause overfitting of the prediction result.

Theorem 2: The upper bound of RFR generalization error, as shown in Eq. (6):

$$E^* \leq \frac{\eta(1 - \xi^2)}{\xi^2} \tag{6}$$

η: average correlation coefficient of the tree; ξ: average strength of the tree.

It can be seen from Theorem 2 that with the η decrease and increase of ξ, the upper bound of the generalization error of RFR will be further reduced, which is more conducive to error control. Therefore, the methods to improve the accuracy of RFR prediction are: 1) Reduce the correlation between trees 2) Improve the accuracy of a single decision tree. The RFR algorithm flow is shown in Fig. 2:

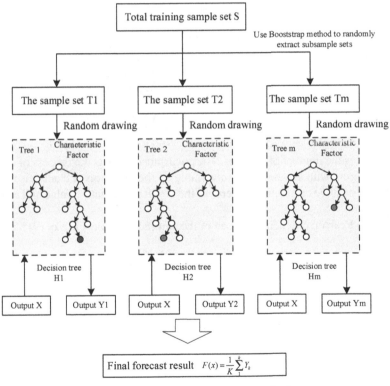

Fig. 2. Random forest algorithm schematic diagram.

3   Attribute Comprehensive Weighting Strategy Based on Correlation Analysis

The random forest algorithm given in the previous section can be used to fill different types of missing data, but the effect of the RFR model depends largely on the data set. In order to improve the training efficiency and training effect of the random forest, how to find the original training set that is more similar to the missing value becomes particularly important. This paper proposes a comprehensive weighting strategy for attributes based on correlation analysis to find a sample set with high similarity to the missing value, which is used to train the random forest model. It can not only ensure the consistency of the input feature quantity, but also simplify the training model.

3.1   Correlation Analysis Based on Pearson Coefficient

Pearson correlation coefficient is a measure of the degree of linear correlation between different random variables. When the Pearson coefficient is used in the overall, as shown in formula (7):

$$\rho_{X,Y} = \frac{\text{cov}(X, Y)}{\sigma_X \sigma_Y} \tag{7}$$

X, Y are two random variables, σ_X, σ_Y is the standard deviation of X and Y respectively, $\text{cov}(X,Y)$ is the covariance, as shown in formula (8):

$$\text{cov}(X, Y) = \frac{\sum_n^{i=1} (X_i - \overline{X})(Y_i - \overline{Y})}{n - 1} \tag{8}$$

n represents the number of samples. The covariance reflects the process of a random variable changing with another random variable. If the direction of change is the same, the result is a positive correlation, otherwise the result is a negative value and a negative correlation.

When the Pearson coefficient is used in the sample, as shown in Eq. (9):

$$r_{x,y} = \frac{\sum_{i=1}^{n} (x_i - \overline{x})(y_i - \overline{y})}{\sqrt{\sum_{i=1}^{n} (x_i - \overline{x})^2} \sqrt{\sum_{i=1}^{n} (y_i - \overline{y})^2}} \tag{9}$$

x_i and y_i are the observation point values of variables X and Y corresponding to i, $\overline{x}$ and $\overline{y}$ are the sample mean values corresponding to X and Y.

3.2 Attribute Comprehensive Weighting Strategy Based on Error Expectation

In order to find the historical data set that has the highest correlation with the missing data of the power grid, it is first necessary to filter all the associated attributes at the moment when the missing data of the power grid is located, and to obtain the associated attributes that are closest to the filling data. The attribute is weighted to obtain the comprehensive weight of the attribute, and finally the historical data set with the highest correlation is obtained by sorting the comprehensive weight. Specific steps are as follows:

1) Select all the corresponding associated attributes of the missing data;
2) Calculate the correlation coefficient between each attribute through Pearson correlation coefficient, select the attribute with the correlation coefficient greater than α (α is a given threshold) and store it in the cross correlation set HG;
3) Further calculate the error expectation $EXPError(X_k, Y_k)$ of all attributes in the HG set;

$$EXPError(X_k, Y_k) = \frac{Cov(X_k, Y_k)}{\sqrt{Var[X_k]Var[Y_k]}} \tag{10}$$

$Cov(X_k, Y_k)$ is the covariance of X_k and Y_k; $Var[X_k]$ is the variance of X_k; $Var[Y_k]$ is the variance of Y_k;

4) If $EXPError(X_k, Y_k) > \beta$ (β is the strong correlation threshold), it is a strongly related attribute, which is retained in the strongly related attribute set QX;
5) The entropy weight method is used to establish the weight between the attributes of each attribute in the set QX, and the weight vector is obtained as follows:

$$W = [w_1, w_2, ..., w_m] \tag{11}$$

m is the number of strongly associated attributes;
6) Comprehensive weighted value of attributes obtained from strong correlation coefficient:

$$SX = W_1 S_1 + W_2 S_1 + ... + W_m S_m \tag{12}$$

7) According to the comprehensive weighted value of each historical section data, sort from large to small, set the selection threshold, and select the sample with the larger threshold as the similar sample set.

The overall flow of the algorithm is shown in Fig. 3:

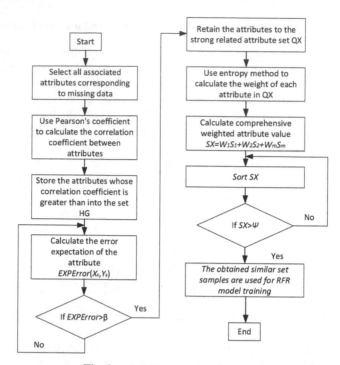

Fig. 3. Algorithm overall flow chart.

4   Improved Random Forest Algorithm Based on Attribute Comprehensive Weighting

In summary, this paper proposes an improved random forest algorithm framework based on attribute comprehensive weighting. By finding the training set most similar to the missing values of the power grid as the training set of the RFR model, the accuracy of the RFR model identification is improved, and the missing values of the power grid are improved. The specific steps are as follows.

Step 1: Obtain the historical data of the power grid, and construct a training sample set and a verification sample set;

Step 2: Use attribute weighting strategy based on error expectation to find similar data set R;

Step 3: Take the similar data set R as input to train the FRF model;

Step 4: Use Bootstrap to resample to form K data sets;

Step 5: Generate K CRAT decision trees;

Step 6: Generate a random forest through K CRAT decision trees;

Step 7: Whether to complete the training of the random forest, if completed, go to step 8, otherwise go to step 6;

Step 8: Use the FRF classifier to discriminate and classify the new data, and use the predicted mean of all trees as the filling result;

Step 9: Evaluate the filling result, if it is within the tolerance range, the filling calculation is completed, otherwise the random forest is retrained.

The overall process is shown in Fig. 4:

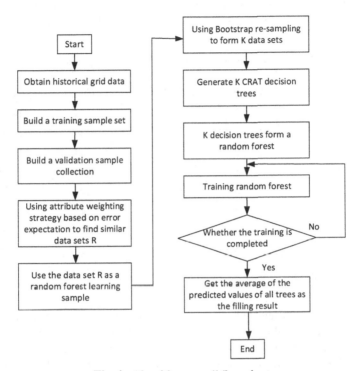

Fig. 4. Algorithm overall flow chart.

5 Case Analysis

This paper selects the historical data of a city-level power grid in the past 1 year as the data set, and selects the grid voltage data as the missing item for filling analysis. In order to better analyze the advantages of the algorithm proposed in this paper, this paper selects the SVM method, the traditional random forest algorithm and the three algorithms proposed in this paper are compared and analyzed, and the filling accuracy of different methods is analyzed.

5.1 Error Analysis Standard

The research object of this paper is the lack of voltage value of the power grid in a certain area. The mining data is selected from the historical database. The sampling period is 5 min. The Pearson correlation coefficient and error expectation (0.5) are calculated for all the attributes in the database. The attributes are: {reactive load, active load, current value}, select strong correlation attributes as the data set field, and then use the attribute comprehensive weighting strategy proposed in Sect. 2.2 of this article (take 0.6), and finally get about 2000 sets of data sample sets, such as Table 1 shows:

Table 1. Locations and capacities of DRSs for minimizing.

Numbering	Active load (MW)	Reactive power load (kvar)	Current (A)	Voltage (kV)
1	10.66	5.33	1.44	10.35
2	10.66	5.33	1.44	10.36
3	10.66	5.33	1.44	10.33
4	10.66	5.33	1.44	10.35
5	10.66	5.33	1.44	10.34
6	10.66	5.33	1.44	10.32
7	10.66	5.33	1.44	10.33
8	10.66	5.33	1.44	10.35
...	...	...	...	...

According to the data selected in the database and combined with the characteristics of the grid voltage data, this paper uses Root Mean Square Error (RMSE) and filling accuracy (Acuracy) evaluation algorithms to evaluate the missing data. σ_{RMSE} indicates the filling error. Obviously, when the value of σ_{RMSE} is smaller, the filling result is better at this time. The formula is as shown in (13):

$$\sigma_{RMSE} = \sqrt{\frac{\sum_{i=1}^{n}(x_r - x_i)^2}{n}} \tag{13}$$

In the formula, x_r and x_i are the true value and the filled value respectively; n is the number of missing values; σ_{RMSE} reflects the gap between the filling value and the true value, the smaller the value, the higher the credibility of the filling result.

Accuracy represents the accuracy of the filling result, the formula of *Accuracy* is shown in (14):

$$Accuracy = \frac{n_r}{n} \times 100\% \tag{14}$$

In the formula, n_r is the correct number of estimates. The tolerance range of *Accuracy* is selected in this article [−8%, 8%], if the value of replacement or filling is finally in the given range, the result of replacement or filling is considered usable.

5.2 Analysis of Filling Results

First, select the missing attributes according to the situation, and construct the missing data sets with the missing rates of 1%, 3%, 5%, 10%, 15%, 20%, 25%, and 30% through random deletion. The IRFNNIS algorithm, the FR algorithm and the IN algorithm are respectively used for experiments under different missing rates, and the experimental results obtained by each algorithm are analyzed and compared based on the root mean square error and filling accuracy.

Taking the missing value of a certain voltage of the actual power grid as the filling target, constructing the missing data set of each ratio, and testing the performance of the three algorithms. In order to fully express the performance of each algorithm, 10 missing data sets are constructed for each missing rate by randomly generating missing values. The results of the algorithm applied to each data set are averaged as the final experimental results, and the experimental results are analyzed and compared.

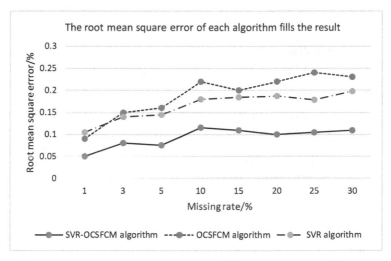

Fig. 5. Comparison of the mean square error of different algorithm filling results.

It can be seen from Fig. 5 that the IRFNNIS algorithm proposed in this paper has the smallest root mean square error at all missing rates and the best filling effect. As the missing rate increases, the root mean square error increases.

The filling accuracy of missing values decreases as the missing rate increases. As shown in Fig. 6, when the missing rate is 1%, the filling accuracy of the three algorithms can reach more than 60%, indicating that each algorithm is missing a small amount of data. The filling performance is better. When the missing rate is 3%–15%, the IRFNNIS algorithm proposed in this paper is significantly better than the OCS-FCM algorithm. When the missing rate is greater than 15%, the accuracy of the SVR and OCS-FCM algorithms is not much different. In all missing cases, the filling effect of IRFNNIS is significantly better than the other two algorithms.

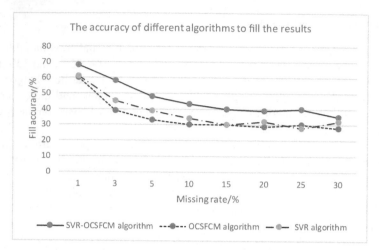

Fig. 6. Comparison of accuracy of filling results of different algorithms.

From the above analysis of root mean square error and filling accuracy, it can be seen that the filling effect of the IRFNNID algorithm proposed in this paper is better than the other two algorithms, in order to show the actual filling effect of the algorithm more intuitively, a data set with a missing rate of 10% is constructed and includes multiple consecutive missing data sets. The algorithm proposed in this paper is used for filling. Figure 7 shows the comparison between the filling results of 27 consecutive missing data and the true value. It can be seen that the filling value has a high correlation with the true value, which meets the data filling requirements.

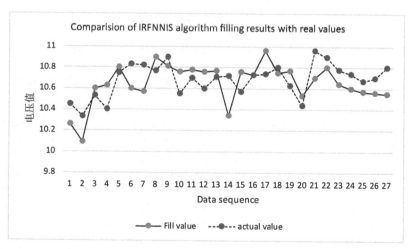

Fig. 7. Comparison and analysis of the algorithm in this paper and the actual algorithm.

6 Conclusion

This article explains the theories related to missing data, including the reasons for missing data and the necessity of missing data processing, and introduces global optimization strategies. In order to improve the efficiency of missing value filling, this paper proposes an improved random forest algorithm based on attribute comprehensive weighting. The method firstly based on error expectation, proposes an attribute comprehensive weighting strategy based on error expectation, and performs comprehensive attribute calculation on the initial missing set to generate complete instance collection; secondly, the similar set is obtained according to the attribute comprehensive weighting strategy, and the random forest model is trained; finally, the improved random forest algorithm based on attribute comprehensive weighting is used to identify missing data and improve the identification accuracy of missing data. The simulation results show that the algorithm can fill in the missing values of multiple attributes, which verifies the accuracy and effectiveness of the method. The algorithm simulation shows that the algorithm proposed in this paper has advantages compared with other algorithms.

References

1. Jiang, Z., Chen, J.: Optimal distributed generator allocation method considering uncertainties and requirements of different investment entities. Proc. CSEE **31**(25), 34–42 (2013)
2. Peng, X., Lin, L., Liu, Y., et al.: Multi-objective optimal allocation of distributed generation considering uncertainties of plug-in electric vehicles and renewable energy sources. Power Syst. Technol. **39**(8), 2188–2194 (2015)
3. Zhang, L., Ye, T., Xin, Y., et al.: Problems and measures of power grid accommodating large scale wind power. Proc. CSEE **30**(25), 1–9 (2014)
4. Xue, Y., Lei, X., Xue, F., et al.: A review on impacts of wind power uncertainties on power systems. Proc. CSEE **34**(29), 5029–5040 (2014)
5. Wang, C., Li, P.: Development and challenges of distributed generation, the micro-grid and smart distribution system. Autom. Electr. Power Syst. **34**(2), 10–14 (2010)
6. Falahi, M., Butler-Purry, K., Ehsani, M.: Dynamic reactive power control of islanded microgrids. IEEE Trans. Power Syst. **28**(4), 3649–3657 (2013)
7. Kekatos, V., Wang, G., Conejo, A.J., et al.: Stochastic reactive power management in microgrids with renewables. IEEE Trans. Power Syst. **30**(6), 3386–3395 (2015)
8. Yuan, X., Huang, C., Zhang, L., et al.: Reliability evaluation of distribution network considering islanded operation of microgrid. Power Syst. Technol. **39**(3), 690–697 (2015)
9. Savier, J.S., Das, D.: Impact of network reconfiguration on loss allocation of radial distribution systems. IEEE Trans. Power Deliv. **22**(4), 2473–2480 (2007)
10. Atwa, Y.M., El-Saadany, E.F., Salama, M.M.A., et al.: Adequacy evaluation of distribution system including wind/solar DG during different modes of operation. IEEE Trans. Power Syst. **26**(4), 1945–1952 (2011)
11. Samadi, P., Mohsenian-Rad, H., Wong, V.W.S., et al.: Tackling the load uncertainty challenges for energy consumption scheduling in smart grid. IEEE Trans. Smart Grid **4**(2), 1007–1016 (2013)
12. Zhu, D., Broadwater, R.P., Tam, K.S., et al.: Impact of DG placement on reliability and efficiency with time-varying loads. IEEE Trans. Power Syst. **21**(1), 419–427 (2006)

Course Classification of Online Learning Platform Based on Sentence-Bert Model

Jiaze He[1], Qian Lu[1(✉)], Ying Tong[2], and Yiyang Chen[3]

[1] Electric Power Research Institute, State Grid Jiangsu Electric Power CO. LTD,
Nanjing, PR China
hzj@js.sgcc.com.cn

[2] School of Communication Engineering, Nanjing Institute of Technology, Nanjing, PR China

[3] MSc Computing and Information Technology, University of St Andrews, St Andrews, UK
chenyiyang2019@udirecter.com

Abstract. A large number of online learning platforms and the explosive growth of the types and quantity of resources on the platform greatly increase the difficulty of learning content selection. Traditional language search uses resource ranking to build index, which cannot meet the needs of professional and accurate search. An intelligent search method is proposed in this paper using Bert language model for pre-training to improve the learning and reasoning ability of the machine. Based on Sentence-Bert model and the concise and effective twin network (Siamese), the sentence vector features are generated to complete the downstream search task. Finally, experiments on the online learning resources of MOOC and the State Grid were analyzed on Google Colab platform, and results show that achieve rapid keyword matching of relevant courseware names.

Keywords: Natural language processing · BERT · Short text · Semantic search · Sentence embedding

1 Introduction

The number of resources of online learning platforms is growing rapidly with the rapid development of the Internet. At the same time, people's demand for more intelligent retrieval of course information on learning platforms is also increasing day by day [1]. With the explosive spread of information, there is an urgent need for effective information screening methods. While searching for relevant information quickly and accurately, discover hidden and higher-value information from the data. In this case, various intelligent search technologies, especially artificial intelligence technologies have been vigorously developed and widely used [2].

Natural language processing in intelligent search is dedicated to the ability of machines to understand and generate human languages. The ultimate goal is to make computers or machines as intelligent as humans in understanding languages [3]. Natural language processing has two research branches, one is based on grammatical rules, and the other is based on probability. Probability-based research methods With the popularity

© Springer Nature Singapore Pte Ltd. 2021
Y. Tian et al. (Eds.): ICBDS 2020, CCIS 1415, pp. 612–623, 2021.
https://doi.org/10.1007/978-981-16-3150-4_50

of finite state machines and empirical methods, coupled with the improvement of computer storage capacity and computing speed, natural language processing has expanded from a few application fields such as machine translation earlier to more fields, Such as information extraction and information retrieval. Various processing techniques based on different rules have also been integrated and used by researchers. The continuous creation of a variety of corpora based on statistics, examples and rules has injected a lot of vitality into the research of natural language processing [4]. Although my country's research on natural language processing started late, the current gap with international standards has been narrowing. Corpora and knowledge bases corresponding to Chinese are constantly being built, and advanced research results on semantic segmentation and syntactic analysis have also been developed. It keeps emerging [5].

Compared with English text classification, the research of Chinese text classification started late, but the speed of development is extremely fast. For decades, many domestic scholars have proposed many excellent classification algorithms when studying Chinese classification, which has laid a solid foundation for the research and development of Chinese text classification. For example, Li Xiaoli and Liu Jimin of the Institute of Computing Technology of the Chinese Academy of Sciences applied the conceptual reasoning network to text classification [8], resulting in a text recall rate of 94.2% and an accuracy rate of close to 99.4%. Literature [9] proposed a hypertext coordination classifier based on the study of KNN, Bayesian and document similarity, with an accuracy rate of close to 80%; Literature [10] studied the text classification of independent languages, and used vocabulary and category The amount of mutual information is the scoring function, considering single classification and multi-classification, so that the recall rate is 88.87%; Literature [11] combines word weights with classification algorithms, which are implemented in closed test experiments based on VSM The classification accuracy rate reaches 97%.

In 2018, the release of the BERT model [6] is considered to be the beginning of a new era in the field of natural language processing (NLP). It broke the records of many tasks in the field of natural language, and showed power in all major tasks of NLP. Gesture. In recent years, the research on Chinese text classification based on the BERT model has received extensive attention from scholars. Hu Chuntao [12] used the transfer learning strategy to apply the model to public opinion text classification tasks, Yao Liang [13] used BERT and domain-specific corpus to classify TCM clinical records, Zhang XH [14] used BERT entity extraction to extract the concept of breast cancer and its attributes; Jwa H [15] proposed exBAKE, which uses the BERT model to analyze the relationship between news headlines and content to detect fake news text. Some studies have also begun to implement pre-training models based on Chinese literature. For example, Wang Yingjie et al. [16] based on the pre-training process of BERT, mainly based on Chinese Encyclopedia, constructed a pre-trained language representation model for scientific and technological text analysis for classification experiments.

Considering that when the BERT model calculates semantic similarity, it needs to enter two sentences into the model at the same time for information exchange, which causes a lot of computational overhead. In this paper, the Sentence-BERT language model is used for pre-training, combined with the concise and effective Siamese network (Siamese), to complete the keyword matching of the generated sentence vector features.

Experimental simulations are carried out on MOOC online learning resources and State Grid online learning resources. The experimental results show that the Sentence-BERT model is better than the BERT model in matching speed and matching accuracy.

2 The Sentence-BERT Model

The Sentence-BERT model [7] is improved based on the BERT (Bidirectional Encoder Representations from Transformer) model. Although BERT and its enhanced models have achieved good results in the regression tasks of sentence pairs such as various sentence classification tasks and text semantic similarity, the excessive overhead restricts their actual application scenarios. In addition, although the BERT model can directly map the sentence vector to the vector space, and then generate a vector that can represent the semantics of the sentence through some other processing, the actual use effect is not ideal, and its own structure makes it similar to the semantics. Unsupervised degree tasks such as degree search and clustering lack applicability. Literature [7] is based on the improvement of the BERT network model and proposes the Sentence-BERT (SBERT) network structure, which uses the twin network or triple network structure to complement the advantages of BERT, so that the generated sentence embedding vector can better represent the semantics Features, and can be applied to large-scale semantic similarity comparison, clustering, and semantic information retrieval.

2.1 Sentence Vector Generation Strategy

The Sentence-BERT model defines three strategies for obtaining sentence vectors, which are mean pooling, maximum pooling and CLS vectors. 1) Mean pooling: all word vectors in the sentence are averaged, and the mean vector is used as the sentence vector of the whole sentence; 2) Maximum pooling: all word vectors in the sentence are subjected to maximum value operation, and the maximum value vector is used as The sentence vector of the whole sentence; 3) directly call the "CLS" mark in BERT as the vector representation of the sentence. Literature [7] gives the experimental results of using three sentence vector generation strategies, as shown in Table 1. It can be seen that the results of the mean strategy are the best on different data sets. Therefore, this article chooses the mean strategy to obtain the feature vector of the courseware name.

Table 1. Experimental comparison of three pooling strategies

Pooling strategy	Natural language inference data set	STS benchmark test set
MEAN	80.78	87.44
MAX	79.07	69.92
CLS	79.80	86.62

2.2 Model Objective Function

Compared with the BERT model, the Sentence-BERT model uses a twin network or a triplet network to update the initial weight parameters of the model, so as to achieve the purpose of the generated sentence embedding vector with semantics. According to different tasks, different objective functions are set.

Classification Objective Function

As can be seen from Fig. 1, the classification objective function inserts sentences passing through the Bert Model and the pooled layer into vectors u and v and the vector difference between them $|u - v|$, splicing them into a vector, and then multiplying it by a trainable weight parameter $W_t \in R^{3n \times k}$, where n is the dimension of the sentence vector and k is the category number. Cross-entropy loss function is used in training optimization. The classification objective function is defined as:

$$o = soft \max(W_t(u, v, |u - v|)) \tag{1}$$

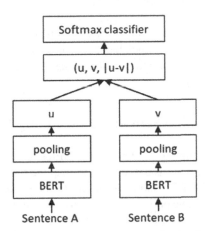

Fig. 1. Flow chart of classification objective function

Regression Objective Function

Calculate the cosine similarity of the embedding vector sum of two sentences, and the calculation structure is shown in Fig. 2. The mean square error loss function is used during training optimization.

2.3 Pre-training and Fine-Tuning of the Model

The SBERT model uses the joint data set ALLNLI, which is composed of two data sets, SNLI and MultiNLI, during pre-training. Among them, SNLI has 570,000 artificially labeled sentence pairs, and the tags are divided into three types: opposition, support and neutral; MultiNLI is an upgraded version of SNLI, which has 430,000 sentence pairs,

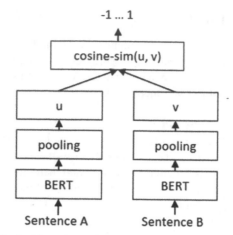

Fig. 2. Flow chart of regression objective function

mainly including spoken and written texts. The format and labels of the two data sets are uniform.

In the experiment, for each iteration, 3 types of Softmax classification objective functions are used to fine-tune SBERT. Each batch size is set to 16, and the Adam optimizer with a learning rate of 2 is used for optimization. The sentence vector generation strategy defaults to the mean strategy.

3   Method of Generating Sentence Embedding Based on SBERT

First, use an existing pre-training model such as BERT to fine-tune the data set using natural language inference and instantiate it, and map the tag vector of the sentence to the embedding layer of BERT for output. Then, for the output access pooling layer, such as the mean strategy or multiple pooling combination strategies, the sentence embedding vector is pooled. In the actual operation process, the sentence vector converter is formed by two modules, word_embedding_model and pooling_model. Each sentence is first passed through the word_embedding_model module, and then the sentence embedding vector with a fixed length is output through the pooling_model module.

Subsequently, we can specify a training data loader, use the NLIDataReader module to read the AllNLI data set, and generate a data loader suitable for training the sentence converter model. To calculate the training loss, Softmax can be used for normalized classification. These generated sentence embedding vectors can be applied to a variety of downstream tasks such as text clustering and semantic similarity analysis.

Among them, we can also specify a verification set to evaluate the sentence embedding model. The validation set can be used for testing on some invisible data. In this experiment, the validation set of the STS benchmark data set is used to evaluate the model.

4 The Experimental Results and Analysis

In this paper, data collection is carried out on the training platform of State Grid and MOOC network of China, and the training course data and MOOC online course data are obtained. In the training course data of State Grid, each course contains 13 data contents such as courseware number, courseware name, production time, and cumulative number of learners. There are a total of 1214 items of statistical course names. MOOC online courses include part of the catalogue of online MOOCs of Chinese universities from 2016 to 2018, with a total of 1352 course name information. For the training course files of State Grid, this article only needs the name information of the courseware. First use the script to take out the name information of the courseware and export it to a new text file named wenben1.txt. As for the MOOC online course catalog file, it can be directly imported into the new text corpus, named wenben2.txt. Part of the course catalog of the two data sets is shown in Figs. 3 and 4, respectively.

课件使用情况统计

课件编号	课件名称	制作时间	累计学习人次	累计学习人数	累计学习时长	完成学习人数	完成学习人对应学时	累计评价人数	课件评分	推送课选
Z93000006	泛在...无所不在	2019-05-08	0	0	0	5385	2692.5	8	5	6089
C0001M00001	交直流混合配电网中关键电力电子装备	2018-12-06	3	3	0	2	2	0	0	0
C020303000007	2018评优_复杂环境下110kV线路开环施工技术	2018-12-05	0	0	0	354	177	4	4.75	2
D0303LM00052	2018评优_老司机带你认识一次主接线及操作联锁条件	2018-11-29	0	0	0	72	14.4	1	5	2
D0302NM00063	2018评优_UPFC关键技术	2018-11-29	0	0	0	253	50.6	3	4.67	4
D0301L01M00005	2018评优_“智能小能手”——110kV智能变电站不同电压等级	2018-11-28	0	0	0	53	26.5	0	0	4
D0302NM00051	2018评优_UPFC应用实例	2018-11-28	336	292	0	235	47	1	5	4
D0302NM00052	2018评优_苏南UPFC建设成果展示	2018-11-28	409	284	0	225	45	1	5	4
D0302NM00054	2018评优_经验推广	2018-11-28	392	328	0	243	48.6	1	5	4
D0302NM00055	2018评优_小无功支撑大直流——什么是同步调相机	2018-11-28	403	328	0	278	55.6	2	5	2
D0302NM00059	2018评优_小无功支撑大直流——冷却系统原理及运维技术	2018-11-28	336	290	0	239	47.8	2	5	2
D0302NM00060	2018评优_小无功支撑大直流——保护及DCS系统运维技术	2018-11-28	324	272	0	236	47.2	2	5	2
D0303LM00029	2018评优_智能站二次设备巡视要点之过程层巡视要点	2018-11-28	284	230	0	207	41.4	1	5	4
D0303LM00030	2018评优_智能站二次设备巡视要点之间隔层巡视要点	2018-11-28	257	224	0	197	39.4	2	4.5	4
D0303LM00031	2018评优_智能站二次设备巡视要点之站控层巡视要点	2018-11-28	245	221	0	200	40	1	5	4

Sheet1

Fig. 3. National grid training course statistics table

The classification of course names in this article belongs to short text analysis. Here, two analysis methods, K-means clustering and semantic search, are used to analyze and research the National Grid Courseware Name Text Data Set and MOOC Online Course Name Text Data Set to further illustrate the effectiveness of the Sentence-BERT model. The hardware experiment environment in this article is built and processed with the help of the Google Colab online computing platform. The software adopts transformers 2.8.0 and above, and installs tqdm and torch1.0.1 and above.

4.1 K-means Text Clustering Experiment Results and Analysis

First, calculate the sentence embedding vector for each course name short sentence in the National Grid courseware text database (wenben1.txt) and MOOC online course text database (wenben2.txt); then, use the first sentence in the python3 package library. The tripartite machine learning module sklearn performs K-means clustering (K is the number of self-clusters, which can be set to different values). Among them, the sentence

1	大学计算机--计算思维的视角
2	工程图学（二）
3	《论语》的智慧
4	物理光学
5	中国传统艺术—篆刻、书法、水墨画体验与欣赏
6	沟通心理学
7	有机化学
8	材料力学
9	现代教育技术
10	概率论与数理统计
11	品读道家智慧
12	经济数学–线性代数
13	经济数学–概率论与数理统计
14	佛教文化
15	金融学基础
16	物流系统工程
17	零基础学Java语言
18	计算机组成原理
19	传感器技术
20	程序设计与算法（一）C语言程序设计
21	大学英语过程写作
22	交互式电子白板教学应用
23	科技与考古
24	现场生命急救知识与技能
25	数学建模
26	走进项目学习
27	管理心理学（下）
28	橡胶与人类
29	用Python玩转数据
30	理解马克思
31	心理学与生活
32	大学化学(上)
33	海洋与人类文明的生产

Fig. 4. Statistics of MOOC online courses

embedding vector is generated by using a trained Sentence Transformer model, and a specific Numpy array containing 768-dimensional embedding is generated corresponding to each sentence information, as shown in Fig. 5.

For the national grid courseware text database and MOOC online course text database, K values were set to 10, 20, and 50 respectively for cluster analysis and comparison experiments. Some experimental results are shown in the figure below. It can be seen from the experimental results that the larger the value K of K-means text clustering is selected, the finer the division of each group of clusters, but too large a value will also make the grouping confused. tendency. This is because the basis of clustering depends entirely on the sentence embedding vector generated above. If the amount of training data in the previous period is not very sufficient, the information will not be fully reflected in the embedded information, and ultimately result in insufficient differentiation density (Figs. 6, 7 and 8).

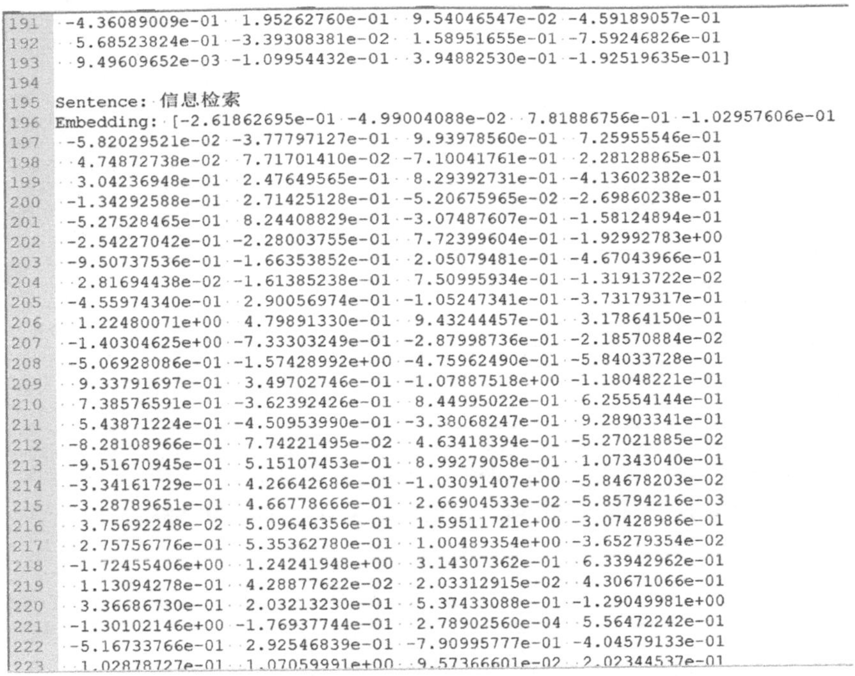

```
191   -4.36089009e-01  1.95262760e-01  9.54046547e-02 -4.59189057e-01
192    5.68523824e-01 -3.39308381e-02  1.58951655e-01 -7.59246826e-01
193    9.49609652e-03 -1.09954432e-01  3.94882530e-01 -1.92519635e-01]
194
195  Sentence: 信息检索
196  Embedding: [-2.61862695e-01 -4.99004088e-02  7.81886756e-01 -1.02957606e-01
197   -5.82029521e-02 -3.77797127e-01  9.93978560e-01  7.25955546e-01
198   -4.74872738e-02  7.71701410e-02 -7.10041761e-01  2.28128865e-01
199    3.04236948e-01  2.47649565e-01  8.29392731e-01 -4.13602382e-01
200   -1.34292588e-01 -2.71425128e-01 -5.20675965e-02 -2.69860238e-01
201   -5.27528465e-01  8.24408829e-01 -3.07487607e-01 -1.58124894e-01
202   -2.54227042e-01 -2.28003755e-01  7.72399604e-01 -1.92992783e+00
203   -9.50737536e-01 -1.66353852e-01  2.05079481e-01 -4.67043966e-01
204    2.81694438e-02 -1.61385238e-01  7.50995934e-01 -1.31913722e-02
205   -4.55974340e-01  2.90056974e-01 -1.05247341e-01 -3.73179317e-01
206    1.22480071e+00  4.79891330e-01  9.43244457e-01  3.17864150e-01
207   -1.40304625e+00 -7.33303249e-01 -2.87998736e-01 -2.18570884e-02
208   -5.06928086e-01 -1.57428992e+00 -4.75962490e-01 -5.84033728e-01
209   -9.33791697e-01  3.49702746e-01 -1.07887518e+00 -1.18048221e-01
210    7.38576591e-01 -3.62392426e-01  8.44995022e-01 -6.25554144e-01
211    5.43871224e-01 -4.50953990e-01 -3.38068247e-01 -9.28903341e-01
212   -8.28108966e-01  7.74221495e-02  4.63418394e-01 -5.27021885e-02
213   -9.51670945e-01  5.15107453e-01  8.99279058e-01 -1.07343040e-01
214   -3.34161729e-01  4.26642686e-01 -1.03091407e+00 -5.84678203e-02
215   -3.28789651e-01  4.66778666e-01 -2.66904533e-02 -5.85794216e-03
216    3.75692248e-02  5.09646356e-01  1.59511721e+00 -3.07428986e-01
217   -2.75756776e-01  5.35362780e-01  1.00489354e+00 -3.65279354e-02
218   -1.72455406e+00  1.24241948e+00 -3.14307362e-01 -6.33942962e-01
219    1.13094278e-01  4.28877622e-02  2.03312915e-02 -4.30671066e-01
220   -3.36686730e-01  2.03213230e-01 -5.37433088e-01 -1.29049981e+00
221   -1.30102146e+00 -1.76937744e-01  2.78902560e-04  5.56472242e-01
222   -5.16733766e-01  2.92546839e-01 -7.90995777e-01 -4.04579133e-01
223    1.02878727e-01 -1.07059991e+00  9.57366601e-02  2.02344537e-01
```

Fig. 5. The generated sentence embedding vector array

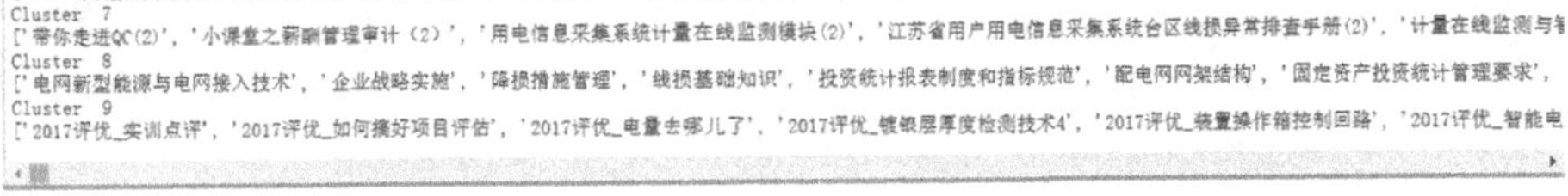

Fig. 6. 10 clustering results of the National Grid courseware text library

4.2 Sentence-BERT Semantic Search Experimental Results and Analysis

Semantic search is the task of finding sentences that are similar to a given sentence. As with cluster analysis, all sentences in the Corpus are embedded with the corresponding sentences, then the input query sentences are embedded with the same method, the Scipy toolkit in Python is used to search the Numpy array of the Corpus to retrieve the content most similar to the query statement, and display the first 8 results.

Cluster 0
['概率论与数理统计', '物流系统工程', '传感器技术', '速解马克思', '概率论与数理统计', '电路基础', '机械制图', '自动化专业概论', '环境污染事件与应急响应', 'c#程序设计', '经典导读与欣赏
Cluster 1
['物理光学', '有机化学', '数学建模', '应用光学', '工程伦理课', '资源经济学', '组织行为学', '广告创意学', '审计学基础', '农业植物病理学', '作物育种学', '普通生物学', '兽医寄生虫学',
Cluster 2
['地下结构数值计算方法', '偏微分方程', '课堂管理的方法与艺术', '东方管理学漫谈', '教学设计原理与方法', '社会调查与研究方法', '教育研究方法', '史学名家的治史历程与方法', '齐鲁名家官方
Cluster 3
['用Python玩转数据', 'Python网络爬虫与信息提取', '大学计算机--Python编程实践', 'Industrial Ecology（产业生态学）', 'Calculus I', '符号计算语言-Mathematica', 'Linux操作系统编程', 'Py
Cluster 4
['中国传统文化', '中国行政故事理及应用', '中国民商案例选读', '中国茶道', '中国现当代文研究', '中华语文与文学', '中国十大传统名曲赏析', '中国传世名画鉴赏', '中国税制', '中国税制'
Cluster 5
['现代数育技术', '线性代数1', '线性代数2', '线性代数习题选讲', '现代工程制图（上）', '高等代数（上）', '西方现代艺术赏析', '线性代数精神与应用案例', '现代企业物流
Cluster 6
['交互式白板教学软件应用', '电子商务', '模拟电子线路A', '模拟电子技术基础', '数字电子技术', '模拟电子电路与技术基础', '孙子兵法的智慧应用', '口腔解剖', '制胜，一部孙子兵阵海', '寄生
Cluster 7
['大学计算机--计算思维的视角', '《论语》的智慧', '中国传统艺术---漆刻、书法、水墨画体验与欣赏', '数字营销，走进智慧的品牌', '大学物理题解析---振动、波动与光学', '民族声乐进阶
Cluster 8
['品读道家智慧', '网络与新媒体应用模式', '新科学家英语、演讲与写作', '数字信号处理', '数据库系统概论（新技术篇）', '计算机通信网络', '网络信息计量与评价', '匠心与创新--一家真行业创
Cluster 9
['程序设计与算法（一）C语言程序设计', '民事诉讼法', '英语语法与写作', '画法几何', '习字书法艺术', '新闻伦理与法规', '刑事诉讼法', '科技英语语法', '画法几何及机械制图', '消费者保护
Cluster 10
['计算机组成原理', '微机原理与接口技术', '犯罪现象，原因与对策', '马克思主义基本原理概论', '经济学原理', '管理学原理', '自动控制原理（二）', '化工原理
Cluster 11
['工程图形学（二）', '沟通心理学', '材料力学', '经济数学---线性代数', '经济数学--概率论与数理统计', '走进项目学习', '管理心理学（下）', '心理学与生活', '大学化学（上）', '大学物理典型问题
Cluster 12
['金融学漫谈', '金属材料及热处理', '公司金融学', '无机非金属材料实验', '营运资金管理', '国际金融', '金融风险管理', '货币金融学', '冶金学', '互联网金融概论', '行为金融学', '金属小说
Cluster 13
['橡胶与人类', '傅泽与人类文明的生产', '航空燃气涡轮发动机结构设计', '认识星空', '微观人体世界', '建筑设计空间基础认知', '飞天、人文与艺术', '无人机设计导论', '《红楼梦》的空间艺术
Cluster 14
['佛教文化', '科技与考古', '现场生命急救知识与技能', '食物营养与食品安全', '博弈论', '营养与健康', '计算思维的结构', '视觉保健康复技术', '基因与健康', '文化差异与跨文化交际', '魅力
Cluster 15
['中国近现史代史纲要', '中国现代文学史（一）', '台湾历史与文化', '中西文明比较', '智圆行方的世界--中国传统文化概论', '设计史话', '《史通》导读', '古籍版本鉴定', '管理思想史', '西方
Cluster 16
['大学英语过程写作', '学术交流英语', '英美诗歌名篇选读', '语统作家英文作品赏析', '商务英语', '职场沟通英语', '英美概况---纵览、博闻', '媒体辅助英语教学', '外经贸英语函电', '大学英
Cluster 17
['毛泽东思想和中国特色社会主义理论体系概论', '工程合同管理', '心理咨询的理论与方法', '会谈技巧', '民法精神与社会文明', '探秘身边的材料--材料与社会', '社会调查与统计分析', '行政职业能力
Cluster 18
['复变函数与积分变换', '概率论与数理统计---习题与案例分析', '电路分析基础', '微积分', '遗传与分子生物学实验', '一元函数微积分', '分析化学', '化工过程分析与合成', '数值分析', '
Cluster 19
['零基础学Java语言', 'Java程序设计', 'Java核心技术', 'Java核心技术（进阶）', 'Java程序设计', 'Java程序设计']

Fig. 7. 20 clustering results of MOOC online course text library

Cluster 7
['计算机组成原理', '导引系统原理', '图像复制原理', '犯罪现象，原因与对策', '马克思主义基本原理概论', '经济学原理', '管理学原理', '自动控制原理（二）', '化工原理（上册）', '数字通
Cluster 8
['学术交流英语', '语统作家英文作品赏析', '商务英语', '职场沟通英语', '外经贸英语函电', '英语演讲', '高级英语写作', '英语耐记', '英语演讲艺术', '英美音乐与文化', '英语听力技能与实
Cluster 9
['用Python玩转数据', 'Python网络爬虫与信息提取', '大学计算机', 'Python语言程序设计', 'Python编程基础', 'Python语言程序设计']
Cluster 10
['电子商务', '模拟电子线路A', '模拟电子技术基础', '数字电子技术', '模拟电子电路与技术基础', '制胜，一部孙子兵法', '卡通动画数字电子技术', '电子商务', '目
Cluster 11
['金属材料及热处理', '无机非金属材料实验', '营运资金管理', '金融风险管理', '互联网金融概论', '金庸小说研究', '股权投资基金与创业投融资', '金融风险管理']
Cluster 12
['现场生命急救知识与技能', '全球卫生导论', '灾害逃生与自救', '卫生技术评估', '城市生态规划', '教育行业创业', '生物材料行行', '海绵城市建设理论与工程应用', '生物演化', '职业生态
Cluster 13
['营养与健康', '视觉保健康复技术', '基因与健康', '运动与健康', '营养与健康讲座', '环境与健康', '音乐与健康', '人体结构功能与健康', '临终中患者的健康管理', '心理咨询与心理健康', '
Cluster 14
['工程图学（二）', '高等数学（一）', '普通昆虫学（二）', '高等数学（一）', '高等数学（一）', '工程图学（一）', '无机化学（下）', '高级物理学', '有机化学（上）', '中级会计学', '高
Cluster 15
['大学化学（上）', '经济地理学', '走进地理学', '大学语文', '书法学堂', '现代遗传学', '地质与地貌学', '走进天文学', '小学语文教学设计', '大学化学', '无机元素化学', '水文地质学基础'
Cluster 16
['走进项目学习', '创业企业法律问题探讨', 'IT项目管理', '广播节目导播与主持', '工程经济与项目管理', '投资项目评估与管理', '工程项目管理']
Cluster 17
['社区管理学', '民法精神与社会文明', '社会调查与统计分析', '社会保障学', '细胞生物学', '细胞社会的奥秘', '法国社会与文化', '英国社会与文化', '遗传学与社会',
Cluster 18
['网络与新媒体应用模式', '新科学家英语、演讲与写作', '数据库系统概论（新技术篇）', '匠心与创新--一家真行业创新创业', '创新思维与战略管理', '创新管理', '美食鉴赏与食品创新设计', '
Cluster 19
['组织行为学', '普通生态学', '兽医寄生虫学', '生物统计学', '生命科学基础', '细胞生物学', '生活药学', '家禽寄生虫病学', '植物生理学', '生命科学与伦理', '恢复生态学', '动物流行病学',
Cluster 20
['复变函数与积分变换', '概率论与数理统计---习题与案例分析', '电路分析基础', '微积分（一）', '偏微分方程', '一元函数微积分', '分析化学', '化工过程分析与合成', '数值分析', '多元统计
Cluster 21
['品读道家智慧', '数字信号处理', '计算机通信网络', '网络信息计量与评价', '商务智能', '信息化教学设计', '光纤通信', '信息论与编码理论', '控制系统仿真与CAD', '会计信息系统', '土木工
Cluster 22
['佛教文化', '科技与考古', '博弈论', '文化差异与跨文化交际', '宠物大鉴赏', '三维形式基础', '自动控制元件', '体育舞蹈与文化', '《文心雕龙》导读', '设计之美', '巴黎文化', '轨道车辆
Cluster 23
['现代教育技术', '线性代数1', '线性代数2', '线性代数习题选讲', '西方现代艺术赏析', '线性代数精神与应用案例', '现代企业物流', '高等代数（下）', '现代煤化工概论'
Cluster 24
['心理咨询的理论与方法', '会谈技巧', '课堂管理的方法与艺术', '教学设计原理与方法', '史学名家的治史历程与方法', '马克思《路易·波拿巴的雾月十八日》导读', '数学物理方法（四）---Leng
Cluster 25
['中国传统文化', '中国十大传统名曲赏析', '中国传世名画鉴赏', '走进中华优秀传统文化', '艺术鉴赏---中国传统绘画鉴赏', '淮影·光阴---早期中国电影导演系列', '中国古典舞与乐器文化

Fig. 8. 50 clustering results of MOOC online course text library

In the same way, semantic search experiments are carried out on the State Grid courseware text library and MOOC online course text library, and the results are shown in Figs. 9 and 10. It can be seen from the figure that, for each query sentence, whether it is a single text or a combination of multiple texts, when calculating the embedded vector of the query sentence, it is treated as a single line of text data for processing and calculation. Under each query sentence, the score is calculated according to the semantic similarity. The higher the score, the more similar the semantics of the query sentence of the retrieval text, and the 8 closest retrieval information texts are given according to the score.

Query: 国家电网
Result:Top 8 most similar sentences in corpus:
国网审计门户考核指标 (Score: 0.9224)
国网江苏电力企业文化及实践 (Score: 0.8964)
国家电网公司企业文化 (Score: 0.8877)
国家电网公司安全生产监督规定 (Score: 0.8706)
全国职工守则-员工职业道德规范 (Score: 0.8684)
什么是企业文化 (Score: 0.8551)
什么是企业文化 (Score: 0.8551)
福利管理审计 (Score: 0.8481)
======================
Query: 变压器 继电保护
Result:Top 8 most similar sentences in corpus:
认识漏电保护器 (Score: 0.9976)
变压器的瓦斯保护 (Score: 0.9594)
高压直流输电及其控制保护系统 (Score: 0.9556)
电力设施保护 (Score: 0.9547)
综合计划基础知识 (Score: 0.9389)
倒闸操作基本步骤 (Score: 0.9364)
审计综合管理系统考核标准 (Score: 0.9310)
实训安全 如何保证实训安全？ (Score: 0.9260)
======================
Query: 电力输送 配电
Result:Top 8 most similar sentences in corpus:
电力企业经营管理制度解析 (Score: 0.9778)
电力电缆故障定位 (Score: 0.9663)
电力企业经营决策和风险管理 (Score: 0.9641)
储能技术现状及其在电力系统应用 (Score: 0.9598)
电力系统实时数字仿真实验室 (Score: 0.9498)
外包队伍安全承载能力专题培训 (Score: 0.9415)
电力设施保护 (Score: 0.9415)
电力系统潮流计算基本理论 (Score: 0.9391)
======================
Query: 智能变电 智能电站
Result:Top 8 most similar sentences in corpus:
智能站关键技术 (Score: 0.9914)
智能站对时系统 (Score: 0.9914)
解剖智能电能表 (Score: 0.9899)
智能配网及新能源实验室 (Score: 0.9546)
智能变电站的概述 (Score: 0.9492)

Fig. 9. Semantic search test results of the State Grid courseware text library

Query: 概率论与数理统计
Result:Top 8 most similar sentences in corpus:
概率论与数理统计 (Score: 1.0000)
概率论与数理统计 (Score: 1.0000)
多媒体技术及应用 (Score: 1.0000)
嵌入式系统与实验 (Score: 1.0000)
电气控制实践训练 (Score: 1.0000)
机械工程控制基础 (Score: 1.0000)
汇编语言程序设计 (Score: 1.0000)
多媒体技术与应用 (Score: 1.0000)
=====================
Query: 大学物理 光学
Result:Top 8 most similar sentences in corpus:
应用光学 (Score: 0.9698)
波动光学 (Score: 0.9698)
物理光学 (Score: 0.9698)
大学物理一振动、波动与光学 (Score: 0.9673)
小学语文教学设计 (Score: 0.9648)
大学物理一电磁学 (Score: 0.9614)
大学化学 (Score: 0.9597)
大学计算机 (Score: 0.9597)
=====================
Query: 大学计算机 数据结构
Result:Top 8 most similar sentences in corpus:
大学计算机实验 (Score: 0.9971)
大学计算机基础 (Score: 0.9971)
大学计算机基础 (Score: 0.9971)
大学计算机基础 (Score: 0.9971)
大学摄影基础 (Score: 0.9912)
大学生职业发展与就业指导 (Score: 0.9846)
大学物理典型问题解析一电磁学 (Score: 0.9826)
大学计算机 (Score: 0.9797)
=====================
Query: 信息检索 文献管理与信息分析
Result:Top 8 most similar sentences in corpus:
信息系统分析与设计 (Score: 0.9872)
信息系统分析与设计 (Score: 0.9872)
文献管理与信息分析 (Score: 0.9835)
信号分析与处理 (Score: 0.9822)
新媒体用户分析 (Score: 0.9374)

Fig. 10. Semantic search test results of MOOC online course text library

Comparing the two sets of semantic search test results, it is found that it is indeed possible to perform semantic matching calculations based on the sentence semantic vector rather than the character matching degree of the phrase in the sentence. However, as the experimental results show, the results of the semantic search are good or bad. The analysis believes that there are two possible reasons: first, the input training corpus text has a low degree of correlation with the text tested in the experiment, and the machine does not learn enough about the information contained in the sentence semantics; second, query and retrieval The amount of sentences in the text is small and the distribution is uneven, resulting in errors in semantic matching.

5 Conclusion

This paper presents an intelligent search method based on natural language processing technology. Sentence-BERT language model is used for pre-training to improve the learning and reasoning ability of the machine. Based on the feature of sentence vector generated by twin network and the embedded vector generated by twin network, clustering and semantic search are carried out respectively. In the Google Colab platform for the two tasks of the application of experimental analysis, achieved short-text intelligent search requirements.

References

1. Wang, Z.: Research and implementation of text categorization based on machine learning. Nanjing University of Posts and Telecommunications (2018). (Chinese)
2. Yang, T.: Application of artificial intelligence technology in information retrieval based on big data. Value Eng. **38**(10), 173–175 (2019). (Chinese)
3. Khurana, D., Koli, A., Khatter, K., et al.: Natural language processing: state of the art, current trends and challenges (2017)
4. Huikun, S.: A method for computing semantic similarity in information retrieval. J. Chizhou Univ. **30**(03), 26–29 (2016)
5. Kui, L.: Research on semantic similarity computation of short tex. Harbin Engineering University (2016). (Chinese)
6. Devlin, J., Chang, M. W., Lee, K., et al.: BERT: pre-training of deep bidirectional transformers for language understanding (2018)
7. Reimers, N., Gurevych, I.: Sentence-BERT: sentence embeddings using Siamese BERT-networks (2019)
8. Xiaoli, L., Jimin, L., Zhongzhi, S.: Conceptual inference network and its application in text categorization. Comput. Res. Dev. **37**(9), 1032–1038 (2009). (Chinese)
9. Yan, F., Enhong, C., Qingyi, W., et al.: Performance Study of hypertext concordance classifier. Comput. Res. Dev. **37**(9), 1026–1031 (2009). (Chinese)
10. Xuanjing, H., Lide, W., Shizaki, Y., et al.: Text classification method independent of languages. Chin. J. Inf. **14**(6), 1–7 (2000). (Chinese)
11. Qian, D., Yongcheng, W., Huihui, Z., et al.: Word weight and classification algorithm in automatic text classification. Chin. J. Inf. **14**(3), 25–29 (2000). (Chinese)
12. Chuntao, H., Jinkang, Q., Jingmei, C., et al.: Application research of public opinion classification based on BERT model. Netw. Secur. Technol. Appl. **11**, 41–44 (2019)
13. Liang, Y., Zhe, J., Chengsheng, M., et al.: Traditional Chinese medicine clinical records classification with BERT and domain specific corpora. J. Am. Med. Inf. Assoc.: JAMIA **26**(12), 12–23 (2019)
14. Xiaohui, Z., Yaoyun, Z., Qin, Z., et al.: Extracting comprehensive clinical information for breast cancer using deep learning methods. Int. J. Med. Inf. **132**, 103985 (2019)
15. Jwa, H., Oh, D., Park, K., et al.: exBAKE: automatic fake news detection model based on Bidirectional Encoder Representations from Transformers (BERT). Appl. Sci.-Basel **9**(19), 32–46 (2019)
16. Yingjie, W., Bin, X., Ningbo, L.: A pre-trained technological language representation for Chinese technological text analysis. Comput. Eng. 12-08 (2019)

Analysis of Economic Loss of Voltage Sag Based on Artificial Intelligence Algorithm

Bo Yang[✉], Bo Jia, Wanchao Jiang, Yongxin Miao, and Yang Wang

Economic Research Institute of State Grid Liaoning Electric Power Co., Ltd., Shenyang, China

Abstract. In order to further simplify the process of economic loss assessment of voltage sag and improvethe applicability and accuracy of economic loss prediction, an estimation model based on DBN-DNN for economic loss caused by voltage sag is proposed. The characteristic factors affecting theeconomic loss of voltage sag are analyzed The 19-dimensional feature vectors are extracted from the saginformation, industrial process information, sensitive equipment information and users' basic information asinput vectors of DBN-DNN prediction model, and the economic loss results are taken as output. Finally, the DBN-DNN model is trained and evaluated based on the actual voltage sag sampling data of alarge electronic industry enterprise in China, which shows the effectiveness of the proposed method.

Keywords: Voltage sag · Economic loss · Deep belief network-deep neural network model · Dropout layer · Data augmentation

1 Introduction

Voltage sags caused by short-circuit faults, startup or switching of large-capacity equipment, lightning strikes, etc. not only seriously threaten the normal operation of sensitive loads in the system, but also cause serious problems such as equipment damage, industrial process interruption, product scrapping and huge economic losses. Effective and accurate assessment of the loss caused by voltage sag is an important prerequisite for solving the problem of voltage sag. It not only provides a strong basis for cost-benefit analysis in the process of voltage sag treatment, but also guides users to make reasonable investment decisions [1–3].

In recent years, scholars at home and abroad have carried out a lot of research on the loss evaluation of voltage sag. The existing methods can be divided into deterministic evaluation methods [4, 5] and uncertainty evaluation methods [6–8]: The deterministic evaluation method is mainly to evaluate the economic loss of specific users through investigation and statistics, which is not very operability in practice; the uncertainty evaluation methods mainly include probability evaluation method [6, 7] and fuzzy evaluation method [8], focusing on studying the response of user-side sensitive equipment or industrial processes to voltage sags, and evaluating losses by calculating the probability of process failure or interruption. In fact, the accurate and easy voltage sag economic

© Springer Nature Singapore Pte Ltd. 2021
Y. Tian et al. (Eds.): ICBDS 2020, CCIS 1415, pp. 624–638, 2021.
https://doi.org/10.1007/978-981-16-3150-4_51

loss assessment has not been well realized. The current mainstream voltage sag economic loss assessment methods generally have the following limitations: ①Economic loss assessment methods are aimed at specific industries and specific production processes, and are not universal and expandable; ②In the process of economic evaluation, loss evaluation formulas are mainly constructed based on human experience. Generally, empirical formulas are subject to scenario limitations. In order to scientifically and reasonably predict the economic loss of voltage sag, it is necessary to construct a mapping relationship from the original input to the semantic information of the abstract layer in different scenarios, and a single empirical formula cannot be used for evaluation to ensure the consistency of the evaluation and the practicability of the method.

This article first explains the working principle of DBN-DNN, then analyzes the key voltage sag economic loss characteristic factors and extracts reasonable and scientific feature vectors, and proposes a DBN-DNN-based voltage sag economic loss prediction model. Aiming at the shortcomings of small sample data, two data enhancement strategies are proposed: Sampling based on the Gaussian distribution density function of each dimension variable and noise processing based on the sample, the sample data is effectively expanded. Finally, the DBN-DNN model is trained based on the actual sampling data of the voltage sag of a large electronic industry company, and the performance is performed on the basis of considering the impact of different random inactivation probabilities, different neuron numbers, and different neural network architecture depths on the economic loss evaluation. The evaluation verifies the effectiveness of the DBN-DNN economic loss evaluation model.

2   DBN-DNN

DBN consists of a stack of several restricted Boltzmann machines. An RBM is composed of a visible layer and a hidden layer, the neurons in the visible layer and the hidden layer are two-way fully connected. On the one hand, DBN retains the original features as much as possible when reducing the dimension of the feature data; on the other hand, when training neural networks, it is inevitable that overfitting will occur, DBN can effectively improve this problem.

Suppose a certain RBM visible layer has V neuronal elements, and the hidden layer has H neurons. For a given state (v, h), the energy function is defined as shown in formula (1):

$$E_\theta(v, h) = -\sum_{i=1}^{V} a_i' v_i - \sum_{j=1}^{H} b_j' h_j - \sum_{i=1}^{V}\sum_{j=1}^{H} v_i W_{i,j}' h_j \tag{1}$$

In the formula, $\theta = \{W', a', b'\}$ is the parameter of RBM, where: W' represents the connection weight between the visible layer and the hidden layer, $W'_{i,j}$ represents the connection weight between the visible unit i and the hidden unit j; a' represents the connection weight of the visible layer Bias, a'_i represents the bias of the visible unit i; b' represents the bias of the hidden layer, and b'_j represents the bias of the hidden unit j.

Based on the above energy function, the joint probability distribution of a given state (v, h) is shown in formula (2):

$$P_\theta(v, h) = \frac{1}{Z_\theta} e^{-E_\theta(v,h)}, Z_\theta = \sum_{v,h} e^{-E_\theta(v,h)} \tag{2}$$

In the formula, Z_θ is the partition function.

Due to the special structure of RBM layers that are interconnected and not connected within the layers, when the state of each neuron in the visible layer is given, the activation state of each neuron in the hidden layer is independent of each other.Similarly, when the state of each neuron in the hidden layer is given, the activation state of each neuron in the visible layer is also independent of each other, so the activation probabilities of the j-th hidden layer neuron and the i-th visible layer neuron are respectively as follows Formulas (3) and 4) show:

$$P(h_j = 1|v) = \sigma(b_j' + \sum_{i=1}^{H} v_i W_{i,j}') \tag{3}$$

$$P(v_j = 1|h) = \sigma(a_j' + \sum_{i=1}^{v} h_i W_{j,i}') \tag{4}$$

In the formula, σ is the activation function.

Traditional activation functions include Sigmid function and Tanh function, but the derivative values of both are in the range of $(0, 1)$. When multi-layer back propagation is performed, the error gradient will continue to attenuate, and the gradient will disappear easily, and the model learning efficiency is low, and some information in the data will be lost at the same time. In this paper, the ReLU activation function is used to train RBM. On the one hand, it can overcome the disappearance of the gradient and most likely retain data information; on the other hand, the activation function will make some outputs 0, making the network sparse and alleviating the problem of overfitting.

Because the distribution function Z_θ is difficult to calculate, the joint probability distribution $P_\theta(v, h)$ cannot be calculated. In 2002, Hinton et al. proposed a Contrastive Divergence algorithm to speed up RBM training and learning. Train RBM through CD algorithm, the update rules of each parameter are shown in formulas (5), (6) and (7):

$$W' = W' + \rho(hv^T - h'(v')^T) \tag{5}$$

$$b' = b' + \rho(h - h') \tag{6}$$

$$a' = a' + \rho(v - v') \tag{7}$$

In the formula, v' is reconstruction of visual layer v, h' is the hidden layer obtained by reconstructing v', ρ is learning efficiency.

DBN pre-training completes feature extraction by learning the coupling relationship of input data features, and provides reasonable initial parameters for DNN training. After

DBN completes the pre-training, the DBN parameters are used as the initial parameters of the corresponding layer of DNN. The network parameters of the last layer of DNN are given randomly. Unlike other layers, the main task of this layer is to use the features extracted from the previous network to complete economic loss prediction for voltage sag. In the training process, there is a certain gap between the predicted value and the actual value. Therefore, the BP algorithm is used to fine-tune the network parameters to improve the accuracy of the prediction.

In the process of training neural networks, over-fitting often occurs, which leads to the network's strong expressive power on the training set, but weaker expressive power on the test set. According to Occam's Razor Law, the more complex the model, the easier it is to overfit. In order to reduce the complexity of DNN and improve the over-fitting phenomenon of DNN, dropout are added: dropout is the process of deep learning network training, the neurons of the neural network are temporarily lost from the network according to a certain probability. Dropout on the one hand simplifies the neural network structure and can reduce training time; on the other hand, each neuron appears with a certain probability, and it cannot guarantee that the same two neurons appear at the same time every time.The weight update no longer depends on the joint action of the fixed relationship neurons, thereby improving the overfitting phenomenon of DNN.

3 Voltage Sag Economic Loss Characteristic Factor

One of the key issues in economic loss prediction based on DBN-DNN is the selection of input feature vectors. Due to the large differences in industrial processes, sensitive equipment tolerance properties, load failure probability distributions, and voltage sag severity included by different users, It often brings great uncertainty to the evaluation of the economic loss of the voltage sag. This article divides the characteristics of voltage sag economic loss into four parts: sag fault information, industrial process information, sensitive equipment information, and basic user information. Feature vector of this composition is used as the input of DBN-DNN. Several important feature vectors are selected for analysis below, and the rest of the feature vectors can be directly obtained through statistics, so I will not repeat them here.

3.1 Severity of Voltage Sag

IEEE Std 1564-2014 The single event indicators describing the severity of voltage sags mainly include voltage sag energy indicators and severity indicators.

(1) Voltage sag energy index.

$$E_{US} = \int_0^T \left[1 - (U(t)/U_{norm})^2\right] dt \tag{8}$$

Among them, E_{US} is the voltage sag energy loss; $U(t)$ is the real-time voltage amplitude during the voltage sag; U_{norm} is the normal voltage amplitude when there is no voltage sag; T is the duration of a single voltage sag event.

(2) The severity index of the voltage sag.

$$S_e = \frac{1 - U}{1 - U_{curve}(d)} \tag{9}$$

Among them, U is the voltage amplitude; d is the duration of the voltage sag; $U_{curve(d)}$ use the reference voltage value corresponding to the abscissa d in the SEMI F47 curve.

3.2 Sensitive Equipment Load Voltage Tolerance Curve

When analyzing the impact of voltage sag events on economic losses, determining the sensitivity of load equipment to voltage disturbances is a very critical step. A large number of studies have shown that the voltage tolerance curve Voltage Tolerance Curve of common sensitive equipment is rectangular, and its uncertainty area is shown in Fig. 1 in the appendix. In the figure, the shaded area (area A, B, C) is the uncertainty area of the voltage withstand capability of typical sensitive equipment. In this area, the equipment may work normally or may be in a fault state. The maximum voltage U_{max}, minimum voltage U_{min}, maximum duration T_{max}, and minimum duration T_{min} corresponding to different devices are different. These parameter values have extremely important guiding significance when evaluating the economic losses caused by voltage sags.

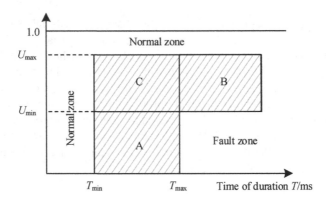

Fig. 1. Uncertainty area of typical equipments responding to voltage sag.

3.3 Process Parameter Immunity Time

When a voltage sag event occurs, because electrical equipment has a certain immunity to disturbance, electrical equipment often does not respond immediately to the disturbance, but has a time delay. C4.110 The joint working group proposed to use the process parameter immune time Parameter Immunity Time to describe the process behavior of the load on the voltage disturbance, It is defined as the process after the equipment is disturbed by a voltage sag of a certain amplitude Parameter overrun time, as shown

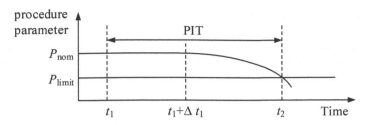

Fig. 2. PIT of process.

in Fig. 2. In the picture, P_{norm} is the rated value of physical parameters; P_{limit} is the acceptable limit value; t_1 is the time when the dip occurs; Δt_1 is the process response delay; t_2 is the time when the physical parameter crosses P_{limit}.

The definition of PIT is shown in formula (10).

$$t_{PIT} = t_2 - t_1 \tag{10}$$

The PIT is proposed to evaluate the economic loss caused by voltage sag. Provides a new perspective, which is also an important input feature of the DBN-DNN model.

3.4 Load Failure Probability Distribution

According to the above analysis, when the state of the load equipment in the power grid is in the areas A, B, and C in Fig. 1, the electrical characteristics of these equipment will no longer be a single definite curve, but will be characterized as a bunch of probabilities estimated by likelihood There are clusters of electrical characteristic curves. At this time, the fault state of the equipment load is usually described by taking the voltage amplitude U and the voltage sag duration T as two statistically independent discrete random variables, and describing the load state through the probability density function, which is:

$$f(U, T) = f(U)f(T) \tag{11}$$

Among them, $f(U)$ is the failure probability distribution of the equipment with respect to voltage sag; $f(T)$ is the failure probability distribution of the equipment with respect to the duration of the voltage sag. According to the difference in sensitivity to voltage sags, typical load devices can be divided into four types: uniform sensitivity, low sensitivity, medium sensitivity and high sensitivity.

(1) Uniform sensitivity equipment.

The load failure probability density function of uniformly sensitive equipment is shown in formula (12), which considers that the failure probability of equipment is only related to U_{max}, U_{min}, T_{max} and T_{min}.

$$f(U, T) = \frac{1}{(T_{max} - T_{min})(U_{max} - U_{min})} \tag{12}$$

(2) Low sensitivity equipment.

Low-sensitivity equipment has a very high immunity to voltage sags. Its failure probability will increase significantly when the voltage sags are relatively large and the duration is longer. The probability density distribution of failures is:

$$f(U, T) = \lambda_U e^{-\lambda_U (U - \mu_U)} \lambda_T e^{-\lambda_T (T - \mu_T)} \tag{13}$$

Among them, λ_U and λ_T are rate parameters; μ_U and μ_T are the standard deviation of voltage amplitude U and duration T respectively.

(3) Medium sensitivity equipment.

The load failure probability density function of medium-sensitive equipment is a two-dimensional joint normal distribution, as shown in formula (14).

$$f(U, T) = \frac{1}{2\pi \sigma_U \sigma_T} e^{-\frac{1}{2}\left[\left(\frac{U - \mu_U}{\sigma_U}\right)^2 + \left(\frac{T - \mu_T}{\sigma_T}\right)^2\right]} \tag{14}$$

Among them, σ_U and σ_T are the average values of voltage amplitude U and duration T respectively.

For moderately sensitive loads, the electrical characteristic curve of the equipment will fall within the area C of Fig. 1 with a greater probability.

(4) Highly sensitive equipment.

The load failure probability density function of highly sensitive equipment decays exponentially as the voltage decreases and the voltage sag duration value increases, and its immunity to voltage sags is very low. The fault distribution density function of highly sensitive equipment is shown in formula (15).

$$f(U, T) = \lambda_U e^{\lambda_U (U - \mu_U)} \lambda_T e^{\lambda_T (T - \mu_T)} \tag{15}$$

The parameter values of the failure probability density model of the four typical load equipment are shown in Table 1, and the parameter values refer to literature [9].

Table 1. Parameters configuration of malfunctions probabilities density function for four typical equipments.

Load equipment type	Parameter value of failure probability density model
Uniform sensitivity	$T_{\max} = 1.1$ ms, $T_{\min} = 1.1$ ms, $U_{\max} = 1.1\,p.u.$, $U_{\min} = 1.1\,p.u.$
Low sensitivity	$\mu_T = 160, \mu_U = 0.70, \lambda_T = 0.013, \lambda_U = 29$
Moderate sensitivity	$\mu_T = 90, \mu_U = 0.78, \sigma_T = 27.25, \sigma_U = 0.015$
High sensitivity	$\mu_T = 15, \mu_U = 0.81, \lambda_T = 0.0125, \lambda_U = 20.07$

3.5   Input Eigenvector of Economic Loss from Voltage Sag

The economic loss caused by the voltage sag is closely related to the voltage sag duration, amplitude, PIT, the voltage boundary of the equipment uncertainty interval, and the duration boundary. In addition, there are related characteristic factors that will not be repeated here. The definitions of the dimensions of the characteristic vectors used in the voltage sag economic loss assessment model and their physical meanings are listed in Table 2.

Table 2. Definition of feature vector used in prediction model of economic loss caused by voltage sag.

Category	Feature	Meaning
Suspended fault information	x_1	Voltage sag duration
	x_2	Voltage sag amplitude
	x_3	Fault clearing time
	x_4	Process interruption time
	x_5	The number of processes involved in operation when the voltage sag occurs
	x_6	Number of affected processes
	x_7	Energy loss E_{US} during voltage sag
	x_8	Severity of voltage sag S_e
Industrial process information	x_9	Number of processes
	x_{10}	Process capacity
	x_{11}	PIT
	x_{12}	Process importance

(*continued*)

Table 2. (*continued*)

Category	Feature	Meaning
Sensitive device information	x_{13}	Minimum voltage U_{min} of equipment uncertainty interval
	x_{14}	Maximum voltage U_{max} of equipment uncertainty interval
	x_{15}	Minimum time T_{min} of equipment uncertainty interval
	x_{16}	Maximum time T_{masx} of equipment uncertainty interval
User information	x_{17}	Annual turnover of the factory
	x_{18}	Maximum load demand
	x_{19}	Product market price

4 Economic Loss Forecast Model for Voltage Sag

4.1 Modeling Process

The modeling process of the DBN-DNN-based voltage sag economic loss assessment model is shown in Fig. 3. The process is mainly divided into data collection and data enhancement, training and test data set division, de-dimensional normalization preprocessing, building DBN-DNN prediction network, Model training, test set forward prediction, performance evaluation and other parts.

4.2 Small Sample Data Enhancement

In order to establish and train the DNN model, it is necessary to collect relevant statistical data to establish a data set. The samples of economic loss events caused by voltage sags need to include all the information in Table 2, but in actual operations they often face the dilemma of small samples. Data augmentation is one of the most effective practical strategies for dealing with small samples [10]. The two data enhancement strategies used in this article are shown in Fig. 4, as follows:

(1) Establish a Gaussian model based on the actual collected voltage sag data samples, and then generate new samples according to the Gaussian parameters (μ and σ) of each feature dimension. The sampling mechanism obeys the Gaussian density function;

(2) Perform Gaussian noise processing on each dimension of the actually collected voltage sag data sample, that is, randomly sample an actual statistical data, and add a noise value that obeys $n \sim N(0, \sigma_i^2/Q)$ to the i-th dimension, among them, σ_i is the standard deviation of the i-th dimension feature; Q is the adjustment factor that controls the noise amplitude.

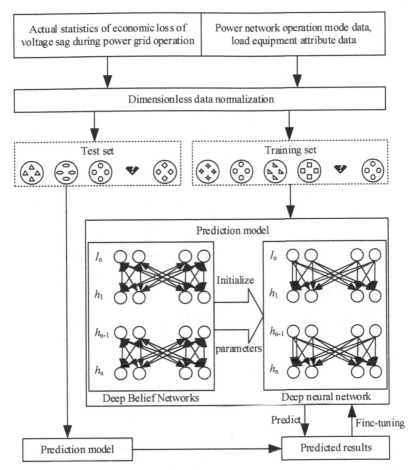

Fig. 3. Modeling flowchart of economic loss estimation for voltage sag based on DBN-DNN.

4.3 Training and Test Data Set Division

In DBN-DNN, the labeled data set needs to be divided into training data set and test data set. The training data set is used to train the parameters W and b in the fitted DBN model, and the test data set is used to evaluate the performance of the trained model. The strategy of dividing the data set is to divide all the labeled data sets into several equal parts, select part of the data subset as the training data set according to the proportion, and the remaining data subset as the test data set.

In this paper, the voltage sag data set is divided into seven equal parts ($k = 7$). In each training iteration cycle, six equal parts are selected as the training set, and the remaining one equal part is used as the performance test set.

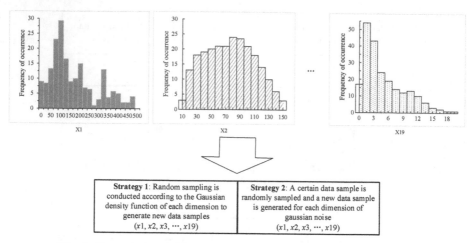

Fig. 4. Two solutions of data augmentation for small size training dataset.

4.4 Eigenvector to Dimensional Normalization

(1) First, calculate the average and standard deviation of each dimension according to the feature vectors of all training samples, as shown in formulas (16) and (17) respectively.

$$\mu_{data} = (\bar{x}_1, \bar{x}_2, \cdots, \bar{x}_m)^T \tag{16}$$

$$\sigma_{data} = (\sigma_{x_1}, \sigma_{x_2}, \cdots, \sigma_{x_m})^T \tag{17}$$

among them, $\_x_I$ is the average of the i-th vector, σ_{xi} is the standard deviation of the i-th vector.

(2) For any eigenvector X, the normalized eigenvector X_{norm} can be obtained according to formula (18):

$$X_{norm} = (X - \mu_{data})/\sigma_{data} \tag{18}$$

After the data is normalized, the influence of the dimension can be removed, and the data distribution can be corrected to near 0, making the feature quantities of each dimension more uniform.

5 Calculation Examples and Result Analysis

5.1 Introduction to Calculation Examples

This paper conducts field survey statistics and analysis of a large electronic industry enterprise in western. The production process of this enterprise mainly includes printing, patching, reflow soldering, aging test, marking, packaging Storage and other links, and there are a large number of voltage sag sensitive devices in each link.

When a company suffers from a voltage sag, the failure of the above-mentioned related sensitive equipment causes a partial or overall interruption of the production process, causing loss of related raw materials and production capacity. In addition, the inability to complete the contract requirements on time resulted in fines for corporate breach of contract, and at the same time decreased customer satisfaction, causing a series of other indirect economic losses. According to statistics, the company suffers 31–35 times of voltage sags annually. The loss caused by a single voltage sag is several hundred thousand yuan, and the cumulative loss is as high as 4.41 million yuan. Using the measured statistical method, 7years of historical data of voltage sags were collected at the 10 kV incoming line of the enterprise, including a total of 195 voltage sag data samples.

5.2 DBN-DNN Model Training and Prediction

The parameter configuration in the model training process is: the original sample number is 195, the sample number after data enhancement is 4120, and the data enhancement method selects strategy 1 and strategy 2 at a ratio of 1:1, based on strategy 1 and strategy 2. The number of samples for data enhancement are 2100 and 2099 respectively; each training period selects 3500 data records as the training set, and the remaining 580 data records as the verification set. The batch scale is 63, of which 54 batches are in the training set. There are 9 batches in the validation set; the model is initialized with a Gaussian randomization method with a mean value of 0 and a standard deviation of 0.01. The number of iterations of model training is 30 Epoch; the model learning rate is e^{-3}.

5.3 Samples Enhance Evaluation Performance

In order to verify the impact of the small sample enhancement strategy on the performance of the DBN-DNN prediction model, this paper compares the performance without data enhancement and with data enhancement. When performing data enhancement, the data enhancement method in Sect. 4.2 is used to expand 3929 samples, and Q is 1, 2, 4, and 6. It can be found that data enhancement has a very significant effect on the small sample data set, and at Q = 4 the average loss function value is 109.74, which is 82.02% higher than the average loss function value 610.35 of the original small sample data.

5.4   Performance Evaluation of 4 Different Network Architectures

In order to compare the effects of different random inactivation probabilities, the number of neurons, and the depth of the architecture on the economic loss prediction model, this paper designs four DBN-DNN models for analysis, and their configuration modes are shown in Table 3. Comparing DBN-DNN1 and DBN-DNN2 models can analyze the impact of different random inactivation probabilities on the accuracy of economic loss prediction;compare the DBN-DNN1 and DBN-DNN3 models to analyze the impact of different neuron configurations on the accuracy of economic loss prediction; compare the DBN-DNN1 and DBN-DNN4 models to analyze the impact of different model depths on the accuracy of economic loss prediction.

Table 3. Model architecture and parameters amount of four different neural networks..

Model	Model architecture	Parameter
DBN-DNN1	$19 \rightarrow 24(\text{ReLU}) \rightarrow 32(\text{ReLU}) \rightarrow \text{dropout}(0.9)$	3579
	$32 \rightarrow 48(\text{ReLU}) \rightarrow 16(\text{ReLU}) \rightarrow \text{dropout}(0.9)$	
DBN-DNN2	$19 \rightarrow 24(\text{ReLU}) \rightarrow 32(\text{ReLU}) \rightarrow \text{dropout}(0.7)$	3579
	$32 \rightarrow 48(\text{ReLU}) \rightarrow 16(\text{ReLU}) \rightarrow \text{dropout}(0.7)$	
DBN-DNN3	$19 \rightarrow 24(\text{ReLU}) \rightarrow 48(\text{ReLU}) \rightarrow \text{dropout}(0.9)$	7109
	$48 \rightarrow 64(\text{ReLU}) \rightarrow 32(\text{ReLU}) \rightarrow \text{dropout}(0.9)$	
DBN-DNN4	$19 \rightarrow 24(\text{ReLU}) \rightarrow 32(\text{ReLU}) \rightarrow \text{dropout}(0.9)$	11052
	$32 \rightarrow 48(\text{ReLU}) \rightarrow 64(\text{ReLU}) \rightarrow \text{dropout}(0.9)$	
	$64 \rightarrow 48(\text{ReLU}) \rightarrow 24(\text{ReLU}) \rightarrow \text{dropout}(0.9)$	

Based on the four neural network architectures in Table 3, this paper trains the data set of economic loss caused by voltage sag, and all four models converge.Among them, the final loss function values of DBN-DNN3 and DBN-DNN4 converged to 122.25, 119.73 and 125.34 125.35 on the training set and validation set, respectively. Compared with DBN-DNN1 and DBN-DNN2, the final convergent loss function values on the training set and validation set are smaller, namely The performance of the voltage sag economic loss prediction model based on the DBN-DNN3 and DBN-DNN4 neural network architecture is better.

Select 9 typical voltage sag economic loss events, and compare their predicted and true values through the prediction model in this paper. The results are shown in Fig. 5. It can be seen from the figure that the prediction performance of DNN3 and DNN4 is equivalent and better than DNN1 and DNN2 has a good reference value for economic forecasting.

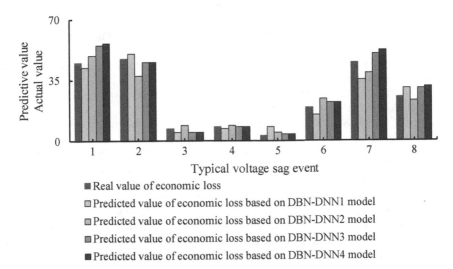

Fig. 5. Comparison of economic loss prediction performance under typical voltage sag events.

6 Conclusion

This paper focuses on the research on the economic loss prediction of voltage sag, and establishes a discrete voltage sag economic loss model based on DBN-DNN. At the same time, in order to compare the effects of different random inactivation probabilities, the number of neurons, and the depth of neural networks on the performance of economic loss prediction, four DBN-DNN architectures are proposed and trained and performance evaluated.

And wo can learn from the model: Supervised learning based on DBN-DNN can scientifically model and reasonably predict economic losses caused by voltage sags. The input feature vectors can be reasonably designed for different industries and different equipment to achieve the final convergence of the model and predict economic losses.

When different random inactivation probabilities are applied to the fully connected layer in the same model, the increase in the random inactivation probability will increase the value of the final convergence loss function of the model, and reduce the accuracy of economic loss prediction; Data enhancement technology can effectively improve the problem of non-convergence or poor convergence on small samples during DBN-DNN training.In this paper, the two methods of constructing new data samples based on Gaussian distribution and adding noise to generate new samples can effectively expand the voltage sag data set.

References

1. Tan, X., Xiao, X., Zhang, Y., et al.: Assessment of economic loss caused by event power quality disturbances based on sensitive process running states. Power Syst. Prot. Control **46**(6), 84–89 (2018)

2. Li, C., Li, H., Liu, B.: Risk assessment based on process immunity uncertainty for industrial customers' financial losses due to voltage sags. Electr. Power Autom. Equip. **36**(12), 136–142 (2016)
3. Chan, J.Y.: Framework for assessment of economic feasibility of voltage sag mitigation solutions. University of Manchester, Manchester, UK (2010)
4. Vegunta, S.C., Milanovic, J.V.: Estimation of cost of downtime of industrial process due to voltage sags. IEEE Trans. Power Deliv. **26**(2), 576–587 (2011)
5. Zhen, X., Tao, S., Xiao, X., et al.: An evaluation model of plant-level economic loss due to voltage dips. Power Syst. Prot. Control **41**(12), 104–111 (2013)
6. Milanovic, J.V., Gupta, C.P.: Probabilistic assessment of financial losses due to interruptions and voltage sags: part I: the methodology. IEEE Trans. Power Deliv. **21**(2), 918–924 (2006)
7. Cebrian, J.C., Kagan, N., Milanovic, J.V.: Probabilistic estimation of distribution network performance with respect to voltage sags and interruptions considering network protection setting: part II: economic assessment. IEEE Trans. Power Deliv. **33**(1), 52–61 (2018)
8. Cebrian, J.C., Kagan, N., Milanovic, J.V.: Probabilistic assessment of financial losses in distribution network due to fault-induced process interruptions considering process immunity time. IEEE Trans. Power Deliv. **30**(3), 1478–1486 (2015)
9. Bai, Y., Li, C., Sun, Z., et al.: Deep neural network for manufacturing quality prediction. In: Proceedings of 2017 Prognostics and System Health Management Conference (PHM-Harbin), pp. 1–5. IEEE, Washington, D.C. (2017)
10. Wang, C., Jiang, P.: Deep neural networks based order completion time prediction by using real-time job shop RFID data. J. Intell. Manuf. **30**(3), 1303–1318 (2017)

Posterior Transfer Learning with Active Sampling

Jie Pan[1] and Yaofeng Tu[1,2(✉)]

[1] Colledge of Computer Science and Technology,
Nanjing University of Aeronautics and Astronautics, Nanjing, China
`panjie@nuaa.edu.cn`
[2] ZTE Corporation, Shenzhen, China

Abstract. Transfer learning has achieved great success on the challenge of learning with insufficient labeled data, mainly by exploiting the knowledge from some other related domains. Common transfer learning methods require to access the data or pre-trained models from source domains, and thus are less applicable to tasks with privacy or security requirements. In this paper, we propose a novel strategy to reuse the posterior probabilities from source domains without data sharing. On one hand, the distribution of posterior probability is regularized by utilizing the source predications as well as limited target data; on the other hand, a sampling strategy based on distribution difference is designed to actively select the most valuable instances for label querying. Experiments on multiple datasets demonstrate that the proposed method can achieve effective performances and requires less labeled data.

Keywords: Transfer learning · Active learning · Maximum mean discrepancy

1 Introduction

Traditional supervised machine learning methods require plentiful labeled instances to train accurate models. However, in many real world applications, such as medical diagnosis, video concept detection etc., there may not be enough labeled data [6]. Transfer learning [31] and active learning [36] are two principle methodologies to address the challenge of learning from insufficient labeled data. Transfer learning tries to utilize the knowledge from related source domains, while active learning tries to get more labels by querying from an oracle.

Inspired by human beings' capabilities to transfer knowledge across tasks, transfer learning aims to leverage knowledge from a source domain to improve the learning performance or minimize the number of labeled instances required in a target domain. Commonly, transfer learning methods try to utilize labeled data from source domains, either at feature level [12,43] or instance level [19,41,49]. However, in many real applications, data sharing is not allowed due to the privacy or security concerns [1]. Federated Learning [25] have been proposed to train a

© Springer Nature Singapore Pte Ltd. 2021
Y. Tian et al. (Eds.): ICBDS 2020, CCIS 1415, pp. 639–651, 2021.
https://doi.org/10.1007/978-981-16-3150-4_52

shared global model under the coordination of a central server, from a federation of participating domains.

As an alternative direction, Hypothesis Transfer Learning (HTL) [4,24,31] tires to improve the target performance by utilizing source models, which can be trained by the data owner, and thus will not leak the privacy. To implement the idea, ensemble technique is commonly used [52] and fine-tuning [28,34] has been successfully exploited in several tasks. But sometimes, well trained models are private properties, which may not be shared. In this case, we find that there is still something containing helpful information that can be used to transfer – the posterior probabilities.

As a different solution to learn with limited labeled data, active learning methods focus on selecting a small set of most informative samples [31], for which they acquire labels from the domain experts. In recent years, there are some studies try to combine the transfer learning and active learning, either in separating stages [27,35] or in one unified framework [21,48]. Common transfer active learning are based on source data or models, which may not ba available.

In this paper, we propose a novel method to reuse the predications of source data, which could be easier to share compared with data and model. Instead of utilize source data or model, the proposed method design a posterior regularization based on common assumption of transfer learning methods. Specifically, to match the joint probability distribution between source and target domains, a unified objective function is proposed to minimize the distance of posterior distributions and empirical loss on target data, where the distribution distance is estimated with Maximum Mean Discrepancy (MMD) [15]. Further, to actively query the most valuable information, a novel criterion based on prediction diversity is proposed to identify the instances with unique information. We test our approach for object recognition on *Office+Caltech* and face recognition on *PIE*. Results on these datasets validate the effectiveness of proposed approaches.

The rest of this paper is organized as follows. We review related work in Sect. 2 and introduce the proposed method in Sect. 3. Section 4 reports the experiments, followed by the conclusion in Sect. 5.

2   Related Work

Among transfer learning methods, Parameters [50,52], instances [6,9], or latent feature factors [30] can be transferred between domains commonly. A few works [45,46,50] transfer *parameters* from source domains to regularize parameters of SVM-based models in a target domain. [24] derived the generalization ability of the regularized least-squares HTL algorithm with the performance of source hypothesis on the target task. [25] extend the formulation in [24] with a general Regularized Empirical Risk Minimization (RERM). [26] views prediction of source models as features and solves HTL as a subset selection problem. In [9,52], a basic learner in a target domain is boosted by borrowing the most useful source *instances*. Various techniques capable of learning transferable *latent feature factors* between domains have been investigated extensively. These techniques include manually selected pivot features [5], dimension reduction [2,3,30], collective matrix factorization [29], dictionary learning and sparse coding [33, 54], manifold learning [13, 14, 23, 44], and deep learning [11, 28, 34, 47, 51, 53].

Many domain adaptative works are based on the assumption that we can embed source and target data into the same joint probability distribution, so that we can learn a model work well on target domain by matching the distributions between source and target domains. For example, [11] try to embed domain adaptation into the process of learning representation, so that the final classification decisions are made based on features that are both discriminative and invariant to the change of domains, i.e., have the same or very similar distributions in the source and the target domains.

As another important solution of insufficient labels, active learning methods focus on selecting a set of instances, and query their labels from the domain experts, aiming to learn better model with lower labeling cost [31]. Uncertainty [37] is a popular criterion, which queries the instance that is most uncertain to the classifier. [20] actively selects unlabeled instances based on informativeness or representativeness. [17] chooses from a candidate set of existing algorithms adaptively based on their estimated contributions to the learning performance on a given data set based on an approach designed for the multi-armed bandit problem.

Many approaches try to combine transfer learning with active sampling to deal with tasks with insufficient labeled data separately. The approach proposed in [39] builds a classifier in the source domain to predict labels for the target domain, and queries the oracle only if the prediction is of low confidence. [27] treats source and target models as committee members, and select informative instances based on QBC strategy. The method in [35] builds a domain separator to distinguish between source and target domain data, and uses this separator to avoid querying labels for those target domain instances that are similar to instances from the source domain. Similar idea is implemented in another work [32].

There are also some studies combining the two tasks in one framework. The method in [48] relaxes the assumption to allow changes in both marginal and conditional distributions but assumes the changes are smooth between source and target domains. The authors incorporate active learning and transfer learning into a Gaussian Process based approach, and sequentially select query points from the target domain based on the predictive covariance. [22] present a principled framework to combine the agnostic active learning algorithm with transfer learning, and utilize labeled data from source domain to improve the performance of an active learner in the target domain. [7] minimizes the distribution distance between labeled source data and unlabeled data, which employs Maximum Mean Discrepancy(MMD) to measure the distribution distance. [21] propose a hierarchical framework to exploit cluster structure shared between different domains, which is further utilized for both imputing labels for unlabeled data and selecting active queries in the target domain. [38] selects instances by traditional active learning, and utilize pre-trained models to filter out unnecessary queries based on prediction confidence.

3 The Proposed Approach

3.1 Notations

We denote by $\mathcal{T} = \mathcal{T}_L \cup \mathcal{T}_U$ the dataset in the target domain, where $\mathcal{T}_L = \{(\mathbf{x}_1, y_1), \cdots, (\mathbf{x}_{n_l}, y_{n_l})\}$ is the labeled set consisting of n_l instances, and $\mathcal{T}_U = \{\mathbf{x}_{n_l+1}, \ldots, \mathbf{x}_n\}$ is the unlabeled set with $n - n_l$ instances. Each instance $\mathbf{x}_t = [x_{t1}, x_{t2}, \ldots, x_{td}]^\top$ is a vector of d dimensions, and $y_t \in \mathcal{Y} = \{1, 2, \ldots, C\}$ is the label in c categories. It is assumed that $n_l \ll n_u$ i.e., labeled data is insufficient in the target domain.

In our setting, there is no data available in the source domains, but the posterior probabilities $\mathcal{P}_S = \{\mathbf{p}_1, \mathbf{p}_2, \ldots, \mathbf{p}_{n_s}\}$ predicted by well trained model, where n_s is the number of source data. The goal is to derive a target model $\mathbf{h}$ by utilizing both $\mathcal{P}_S$ and $\mathcal{T}$, which is expected to perform better than the one learned from $\mathcal{T}$ only.

3.2 Preparations

Before introducing the proposed approach, we firstly introduce a method that can be used to test if two samples are from different distributions and discuss the common assumptation of transfer learning methods.

To measure the difference between two distributions $\mathcal{D}_S$ and $\mathcal{D}_T$, several methods have been proposed, such as Relative Entropy [8] and Bregman Divergence [40]. However, above methods all need to calculate the probability density at a point of different distributions which may be difficult in transfer learning, because it's hard to find enough same instances from both source and target domain. Maximum Mean Discrepancy (MMD) [15] can be applied to this situation. Given two instances sets $S = \{\mathbf{s}_1, \mathbf{s}_2, \ldots, \mathbf{s}_{n_s}\}$ and $T = \{\mathbf{t}_1, \mathbf{t}_2, \ldots, \mathbf{t}_{n_t}\}$ sampled from $\mathcal{D}_S$ and $\mathcal{D}_T$. MMD is definited to be the difference of the expectations after project S and T to Reproducing Kernel Hilbert Space(RKHS) $\mathcal{H}$. The definition and empirical estimation of MMD are as following:

$$\mathrm{MMD}_{\mathcal{H}}(\mathcal{D}_S, \mathcal{D}_T) \triangleq \sup_{\|f\|_{\mathcal{H}} \leq 1} (\mathbb{E}_{\mathbf{s} \sim \mathcal{D}_S}[f(\mathbf{s})] - \mathbb{E}_{\mathbf{t} \sim \mathcal{D}_T}[f(\mathbf{t})])$$

$$\mathrm{MMD}_{\mathcal{H}}(S, T) \triangleq \left\| \frac{1}{n_s} \sum_{i=1}^{n_s} \phi(\mathbf{s}_i) - \frac{1}{n_t} \sum_{i=1}^{n_t} \phi(\mathbf{t}_i) \right\|_{\mathcal{H}}$$

where $f(\cdot)$ is any function in $\mathcal{H}$ and ϕ is the projection from raw data to a high dimensional space decided by f.

Theorem 1 [15]. *Let $\mathcal{D}_S$ and $\mathcal{D}_T$ be the borel probability measure, and $\mathcal{H}$ be a universal RKHS. Then $\mathrm{MMD}_{\mathcal{H}}(\mathcal{D}_S, \mathcal{D}_T) = 0$ if and only if $\mathcal{D}_S = \mathcal{D}_T$.*

By using kernel trick and Theorem 1, the unbiased estimate of $\mathrm{MMD}_{\mathcal{H}}^2$ can be calculated to measure the difference between two distributions. The method is widely used in transfer learning [10, 18, 30].

As previously discussed, by matching the joint probability distribution between labeled and unlabeled domains, we can learn a target model. Usually, the marginal and conditional distributions between source and target domains are considered to be matched by weighting or projecting source and target data. Then the target model would be learned from these matched data. There is an latent assumption in above method, which is that the distributions of posterior probability from source and target domains should be similar. If not, that there is not such a common distribution that we can embed data into to match the distributions. Since past methods show well performance on several tasks, that we think the assumptation is generally hold.

3.3   Transfer Learning with Posterior Probability

In this subsection, we focus on the design of transfer learning method with source posterior probabilities. Let $\mathcal{L}(\mathbf{h}(\mathbf{x}), y)$ be the loss function. With the assumptation that the distribution of posterior probability in target domain should be similar to that of source domains, we can derive our transfer methods. We can use $\text{MMD}_{\mathcal{H}}^2$ to estimate the difference of source and target distributions and regularize the target model by minimizing the loss of difference. Then the objective function can be written as:

$$\min_{\mathbf{h}} \sum_{i=1}^{n_l} \mathcal{L}(\mathbf{h}(\mathbf{x}_i), y_i) + \alpha \text{MMD}_{\mathcal{H}}^2(\mathcal{P}_S \cup \mathcal{P}_{T_L}, \mathcal{P}_{T_U}) \tag{1}$$

where $\mathcal{P}_{T_L} = \{\mathbf{h}(\mathbf{x}_1), \mathbf{h}(\mathbf{x}_2), \ldots, \mathbf{h}(\mathbf{x}_{n_l})\}$ and $\mathcal{P}_{T_U}$ is samely defined. Similar to the conclusion that minimize the distance of conditional distribution is helpful to the robustness [42], it's obviously that the conditional posterior distribution is also helpful to capture the difference between the two distributions. Then we can modify Eq. (1) like that:

$$\min_{\mathbf{h}} \sum_{i=1}^{n_l} \mathcal{L}(\mathbf{h}(\mathbf{x}_i), y_i) + \alpha \text{MMD}_{\mathcal{H}}^2(\mathcal{P}_S \cup \mathcal{P}_{T_L}, \mathcal{P}_{T_U}) + \beta \sum_{c=1}^{C} \text{MMD}_{\mathcal{H}}^2(\mathcal{P}_S^{(c)} \cup \mathcal{P}_{T_L}^{(c)}, \mathcal{P}_{T_U}^{(c)})$$

$$\tag{2}$$

where $\mathcal{P}^{(c)}$ means the set of posterior probabilities taking the maximum value in the cth dimension.

To optimize above objective function (2), since $\text{MMD}_{\mathcal{H}}^2$ can be calculated by using kernel functions which is differentiable, methods based on gradient descent can be selected if $\mathcal{L}$ is differentiable too.

3.4   Active Learning with Posterior Probability

As discussed in Sect. 3.3, in addition to the model transferring from source domains, we may need to query more labels from the target domain to enhance the model with unshared information. To reduce the labeling cost, we actively select the most useful instances from the unlabeled set $\mathcal{T}_U$, and add them the labeled set $\mathcal{T}_L$ after querying their labels.

In the case that we have n_s source posterior probabilities and n_l labeled target data. We would like to select a batch Q of b instances such that the distribution of $\mathcal{P}_S \cup \mathcal{P}_{T_L} \cup \mathcal{P}_Q$ is similar to the distribution of $\mathcal{P}_{T_U - Q}$. The object can be formulated as following:

$$\min_{Q \subset T_U} \mathrm{MMD}_{\mathcal{H}}^2 (\mathcal{P}_S \cup \mathcal{P}_{T_L} \cup \mathcal{P}_Q, \mathcal{P}_{T_U - Q})$$

However, the distributions of $\mathcal{P}_Q$ and $\mathcal{P}_{T_U - Q}$ before and after querying from the oracle could be quite different, which means that it's hard to select the best Q. To solve the problem, we design our strategy from another point of view. We firstly analysis the composition of information. With the transfer of source knowledge, the shared information is expected to be well exploited. Then what we lack are instances meeting the following requirements:

- The information contained in them is different from those in existing labeled data in the target domain.
- The information contained in them is unique in the target domain, and thus can be hardly transferred from source domains.

To select instances satisfying above requirements, we design the following objective functions:

$$\max_{Q \subset T_U} \mathrm{MMD}_{\mathcal{H}}^2 (\mathcal{P}_S \cup \mathcal{P}_{T_L}, \mathcal{P}_{T_L} \cup \mathcal{P}_Q)$$

$$= \left\| \frac{1}{n_s + n_l} \sum_{x_i \in \mathcal{P}_S \cup \mathcal{P}_{T_L}} \phi(\mathbf{x}_i) - \frac{1}{n_l + b} \sum_{x_j \in \mathcal{P}_{T_L} \cup \mathcal{P}_Q} \phi(\mathbf{x}_j) \right\|_{\mathcal{H}}^2$$

$$= \left\| \frac{1}{n_s} \sum_{x_i \in \mathcal{P}_S} \phi(\mathbf{x}_i) - \frac{1}{b} \sum_{x_j \in \mathcal{P}_Q} \phi(\mathbf{x}_j) \right\|_{\mathcal{H}}^2 \tag{3}$$

The first term of MMD is the current target posterior distribution, the second term is the distribution of data will be used in next step. By maximizing the distance of distribution, the instances in Q are strongly possible to meet above two requirements. That is if the predication of an instance leads to big distribution difference, there are two possible scenarios: (1) The true posterior is consistent with current target distribution, which means we make a mistake on this instance. That is what we should query and it matches the first requirement. (2) The true posterior is not consistant with current target distribution, which means it's unique in the target domain and satisfies the second requirement.

To optimize above object (3), we define a binary vector $\mathbf{w}$ of size n_u where each entry w_i indicates whether the data $\mathbf{x}_i \in T_U$ is selected or not. If a point is selected, the corresponding entry w_i is 1 else 0. Then the objective function can be written as:

$$\max_{\mathbf{w}} \left\| \frac{1}{n_s} \sum_{\mathbf{x}_i \in \mathcal{P}_S} \phi(\mathbf{x}_i) - \frac{1}{b} \sum_{\mathbf{x}_j \in \mathcal{P}_{T_U}} w_j \phi(\mathbf{x}_j) \right\|_{\mathcal{H}}^2,$$
$$\text{s.t. } \mathbf{1}^\top \mathbf{w} = b, w_i \in \{0,1\} \tag{4}$$

Replacing the inner product between $\phi(\cdot)$ by kernel function, we can find that is a MIQP problem and may be hard to optimize. A common strategy is to relax the integer constraint to transform it into a QP formulation. In this paper, we can optimizing it by replacing the constraint $w_i \in \{0,1\}$ to $w_i \in [0,1]$. We name proposed method Active learning based on Posterior Divergence(APD for short).

4 Experiments

4.1 Data Sets and Settings

The proposed methods are evaluated on *Office+Caltech* [13] and *PIE* [16][1]. We select four domains on each dataset. For each domain, we test our methods by taking it as the target domain and the others as source domains. All the experiments are performed on a PC with Intel Core i5-8400 processor.

 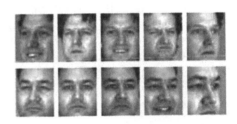

Fig. 1. Example images from four different domains with the same category "monitor" on *Office+Caltech*.

Fig. 2. Example images from facial expression dataset *CMU Multi-PIE*.

(1) *Office+Caltech dataset*: Four domains: Caltech(1123), Amazon(958), Webcam(295) and DSLR(157) are included in the dataset. In fact, this dataset is constructed from two datasets: Office-31 (which contains 31 classes of A, W and D) and Caltech-256 (which contains 256 classes of C). There are 10 common classes between the two datasets. Even for the same category, the data distribution of different domains is rather different. Example images from 4 domains validate this fact in Fig. 1. The SURF features are 800-dimensional. We also have the raw image data.

---

[1] https://github.com/jindongwang/transferlearning/blob/master/data/dataset.md.

Table 1. Accuracy(%) of methods on *Office+Caltech*, from above to below are different settings with $\{10\%, 20\%, 30\%\}$ labeled data. Standard deviation is used as error bar.

Domain	LR				Resnet-18			
	None	L2	PDM	L2 + PDM	None	L2	PDM	L2 + PDM
Amazon	51.8 ± 3	$\mathbf{56.0 \pm 3}$	51.3 ± 2	54.4 ± 3	65.7 ± 5	55.2 ± 7	$\mathbf{70.4 \pm 4}$	67.7 ± 4
Caltech	38.2 ± 1	$\mathbf{43.2 \pm 2}$	38.1 ± 3	41.1 ± 3	62.1 ± 2	51.1 ± 1	61.9 ± 3	$\mathbf{63.1 \pm 3}$
Webcam	49.0 ± 4	53.8 ± 3	50.3 ± 3	$\mathbf{56.0 \pm 3}$	74.4 ± 5	73.2 ± 5	$\mathbf{74.9 \pm 5}$	72.0 ± 5
DSLR	37.5 ± 5	$\mathbf{55.5 \pm 5}$	35.1 ± 6	41.9 ± 3	68.0 ± 7	69.3 ± 6	68.4 ± 4	$\mathbf{70.0 \pm 5}$
Amazon	61.0 ± 2	$\mathbf{63.2 \pm 3}$	60.5 ± 2	63.2 ± 2	$\mathbf{74.1 \pm 4}$	71.9 ± 2	74.1 ± 3	71.5 ± 5
Caltech	46.6 ± 1	$\mathbf{48.0 \pm 2}$	45.4 ± 1	45.6 ± 1	$\mathbf{61.7 \pm 2}$	57.1 ± 2	59.2 ± 3	56.6 ± 1
Webcam	60.3 ± 3	$\mathbf{70.4 \pm 3}$	63.1 ± 4	67.5 ± 4	75.5 ± 7	73.6 ± 6	$\mathbf{75.8 \pm 3}$	71.9 ± 3
DSLR	46.8 ± 5	$\mathbf{55.0 \pm 4}$	46.3 ± 4	50.9 ± 3	70.2 ± 5	68.8 ± 9	$\mathbf{73.0 \pm 5}$	72.7 ± 4
Amazon	65.3 ± 1	$\mathbf{67.2 \pm 2}$	65.1 ± 2	66.2 ± 2	$\mathbf{78.5 \pm 2}$	77.1 ± 2	78.4 ± 2	78.4 ± 4
Caltech	49.5 ± 1	$\mathbf{50.6 \pm 1}$	47.9 ± 1	48.5 ± 2	$\mathbf{69.6 \pm 2}$	65.6 ± 2	66.5 ± 2	65.5 ± 2
Webcam	69.9 ± 2	$\mathbf{75.4 \pm 3}$	68.7 ± 2	74.3 ± 4	$\mathbf{82.5 \pm 4}$	82.2 ± 6	81.7 ± 4	80.4 ± 4
DSLR	51.6 ± 2	$\mathbf{62.2 \pm 4}$	49.6 ± 6	55.1 ± 5	77.2 ± 4	75.8 ± 8	$\mathbf{80.5 \pm 6}$	80.0 ± 3

(2) *PIE dataset*: The CMU Multi-PIE itself is a facial expression dataset which contains more than 750,000 images of 337 people taken from fifteen directions, and in nineteen illumination conditions, as some example images shown in Fig. 2. In this experiment, four domains generated from Multi-PIE (each corresponding to a distinct pose) from 68 individuals are used. Specifically, four subsets, i.e., PIE05(3332, left pose), PIE07(1629, upward pose), PIE09(1632, downward pose), PIE27(3329, front pose), are constructed and the face images in each subset are taken under different illumination and expression conditions. These subsets are based on SURF features and the dimension of features is 1024.

4.2 Experiments on Transfer Learning

Before starting the experiment, we learn the source posterior probabilities based on 10 fold cross validation. Notice that, we use the posterior probabilities predicted by same kind of source models as target, when we perform experiments about transfer learning. We randomly divide each target domain data into two parts: $\{10\%, 20\%, 30\%\}$ as train set and $\{90\%, 80\%, 70\%\}$ as test set. Among the training examples, a small set is randomly selected as the labeled data. Since that we can't find existing method based on posterior distribution, we select some common algorithms to be compared in our experiments, which is enough to show the effectiveness of proposed method. We name proposed transfer method Posterior Distribution Matching(PDM for short). The parameters α and β are chosen among 9 values between 10^{-2} and 10 on a logarithmic scale.

Table 2. Accuracy(%) of methods on *PIE*, from above to below are different settings with $\{10\%, 20\%, 30\%\}$ labeled data. Standard deviation is used as error bar.

Domain	LR				SVM	
	None	L2	PDM	L2 + PDM	L2	L2 + PDM
PIE05	69.0 ± 2	66.8 ± 3	70.8 ± 2	**72.0 ± 3**	77.5 ± 1	**80.1 ± 2**
PIE07	47.3 ± 3	45.5 ± 2	48.5 ± 1	47.9 ± 4	**60.5 ± 2**	58.3 ± 3
PIE09	**50.6 ± 2**	46.9 ± 3	48.2 ± 3	49.2 ± 2	**63.8 ± 3**	62.4 ± 2
PIE27	68.8 ± 2	68.0 ± 4	**71.2 ± 3**	69.8 ± 3	77.6 ± 2	**80.8 ± 2**
PIE05	82.3 ± 2	78.4 ± 3	**83.2 ± 2**	82.2 ± 2	90.3 ± 1	**90.4 ± 1**
PIE07	**68.1 ± 3**	62.4 ± 4	67.4 ± 4	66.3 ± 2	72.9 ± 3	**75.8 ± 3**
PIE09	67.9 ± 3	67.5 ± 3	**70.9 ± 2**	69.1 ± 3	76.6 ± 2	**77.4 ± 2**
PIE27	82.3 ± 2	78.8 ± 2	**84.4 ± 1**	82.6 ± 3	**90.1 ± 1**	89.7 ± 1
PIE05	88.3 ± 1	89.7 ± 1	**91.6 ± 3**	87.2 ± 2	93.4 ± 1	**93.5 ± 1**
PIE07	**76.3 ± 2**	74.8 ± 2	68.8 ± 3	68.0 ± 2	**81.5 ± 2**	81.1 ± 1
PIE09	**80.0 + 3**	76.3 ± 2	75.6 ± 3	75.9 ± 3	84.2 ± 2	**84.9 ± 2**
PIE27	**89.4 ± 2**	88.3 ± 1	86.8 ± 3	86.2 ± 2	92.4 ± 2	**93.2 ± 1**

Because there are too few instances on *webcam* and *dslr*, we use the whole set for test for all methods. The data partition is repeated randomly for 10 times, and the average balanced accuracies are reported.

As shown in Tables 1 and 2, we compare the classification accuracies of several methods on two datasets. In Table 1, we use SURF features for LR and raw images for Resnet-18. We can conclude that PDW is helpful for the robustness of model in most case. In Table 1, the L2 regularization is always better than our method with base model LR. We think it's because of the poor performance of model's predictions. The posterior distribution isn't well learnt and the matching of distributions may not be helpful. This can be proved by other experiments in Tables 1 and 2, we can find that PDW performs well when the model is good enough. When the model is complex or the number of instance is big, L2 regularization could have a negative effect, but PDM can still work in this situation.

4.3 Experiments Combing Transfer and Active Learning

In this subsection, we examine the effectiveness of the proposed APD algorithm for active sampling. We test the performance of different active strategies with PDM regularization. SVM is selected to be the base model. The experiments are performed on *PIE* because there are enough examples to serve as the unlabeled pool for active querying. For each domain, we randomly divide each target domain data into two parts: 50% as train set and 50% as test set. The initial size of labeled data is 68. The batch size is set to 1 and the budget is 300. The data partition is repeated randomly for 10 times, and the average results are reported. The following strategies are compared in our experiments:

- **Random**: randomly selects unlabeled instances.
- **Uncertainty**: [37] selects the most uncertain instances based on prediction entropy.
- **APD**: the proposed method.

The performance curves with the number of labeled instances increasing are plotted in Fig. 3. It can be observed that with PDM regularization, the proposed APD strategy performs well on most case. Random strategy is usually worse than other methods. The performance of PDM+APD looks good.

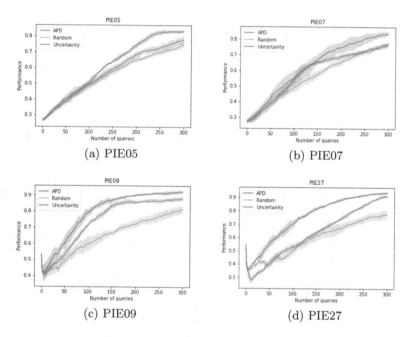

(a) PIE05

(b) PIE07

(c) PIE09

(d) PIE27

Fig. 3. Comparison of different active sampling methods on *PIE*. Standard deviation is used as error bar.

5   Conclusion

In this paper, we find the latent assumption of transfer learning and try to utilize it when data and models can't be shared from source domains due to security or privacy concerns. By minimizing the distance of posterior distributions between source and target domains, we implement the transfer of source knowledge without source data or model. Furthermore, a novel active sampling strategy is proposed to query labels for the most valuable instances from the target domain, and thus to save the labeling cost. Experiments on multiple datasets validate the effectiveness of the proposed methods. In future work, we plan to extend the approach to other transfer learning scenarios.

References

1. Albrecht, J.P.: How the GDPR will change the world. Eur. Data Prot. L. Rev. **2**, 287 (2016)
2. Baktashmotlagh, M., Harandi, M.T., Lovell, B.C., Salzmann, M.: Unsupervised domain adaptation by domain invariant projection. In: Proceedings of the IEEE International Conference on Computer Vision, pp. 769–776 (2013)
3. Baktashmotlagh, M., Harandi, M.T., Lovell, B.C., Salzmann, M.: Domain adaptation on the statistical manifold. In: Proceedings of the IEEE Conference on Computer Vision and Pattern Recognition, pp. 2481–2488 (2014)
4. Ben-David, S., Urner, R.: Domain adaptation as learning with auxiliary information. In: New Directions in Transfer and Multi-Task-Workshop@ NIPS (2013)
5. Blitzer, J., McDonald, R., Pereira, F.: Domain adaptation with structural correspondence learning. In: Proceedings of the 2006 Conference on Empirical Methods in Natural Language Processing, pp. 120–128 (2006)
6. Chattopadhyay, R., Fan, W., Davidson, I., Panchanathan, S., Ye, J.: Joint transfer and batch-mode active learning. In: International Conference on Machine Learning, pp. 253–261 (2013)
7. Chattopadhyay, R., Wang, Z., Fan, W., Davidson, I., Panchanathan, S., Ye, J.: Batch mode active sampling based on marginal probability distribution matching. ACM Trans. Knowl. Disc. Data **7**(3), 1–25 (2013)
8. Cover, T.M., Thomas, J.A.: Entropy, relative entropy and mutual information. In: Elements of Information Theory, vol. 2, pp. 1–55 (1991)
9. Dai, W., Yang, Q., Xue, G.R., Yu, Y.: Boosting for transfer learning. In: Proceedings of the 24th International Conference on Machine Learning, pp. 193–200 (2007)
10. Duan, L., Tsang, I.W., Xu, D.: Domain transfer multiple kernel learning. IEEE Trans. Pattern Anal. Mach. Intell. **34**(3), 465–479 (2012)
11. Ganin, Y., et al.: Domain-adversarial training of neural networks. J. Mach. Learn. Res. **17**(1), 1–35 (2016)
12. Gong, B., Grauman, K., Sha, F.: Connecting the dots with landmarks: discriminatively learning domain-invariant features for unsupervised domain adaptation. In: International Conference on Machine Learning, pp. 222–230 (2013)
13. Gong, B., Shi, Y., Sha, F., Grauman, K.: Geodesic flow kernel for unsupervised domain adaptation. In: 2012 IEEE Conference on Computer Vision and Pattern Recognition, pp. 2066–2073. IEEE (2012)
14. Gopalan, R., Li, R., Chellappa, R.: Domain adaptation for object recognition: an unsupervised approach. In: 2011 International Conference on Computer Vision, pp. 999–1006. IEEE (2011)
15. Gretton, A., Borgwardt, K., Rasch, M., Schölkopf, B., Smola, A.: A kernel method for the two-sample-problem. Adv. Neural Inf. Process. Syst. **19**, 513–520 (2006)
16. Gross, R., Matthews, I., Cohn, J., Kanade, T., Baker, S.: Multi-pie. Image Vis. Comput. **28**(5), 807–813 (2010)
17. Hsu, W.N., Lin, H.T.: Active learning by learning. In: Twenty-Ninth AAAI Conference on Artificial Intelligence **29** (2015)
18. Huang, J., Gretton, A., Borgwardt, K., Schölkopf, B., Smola, A.: Correcting sample selection bias by unlabeled data. Adv. Neural Inf. Process. Syst. **19**, 601–608 (2006)
19. Huang, S.J., Chen, S.: Transfer learning with active queries from source domain. In: IJCAI, pp. 1592–1598 (2016)

20. Huang, S.J., Jin, R., Zhou, Z.H.: Active learning by querying informative and representative examples. IEEE Trans. Pattern Anal. Mach. Intell. **36**(10), 1936–1949 (2014)
21. Kale, D., Ghazvininejad, M., Ramakrishna, A., He, J., Liu, Y.: Hierarchical active transfer learning. In: Proceedings of the 2015 SIAM International Conference on Data Mining, pp. 514–522. SIAM (2015)
22. Kale, D., Liu, Y.: Accelerating active learning with transfer learning. In: 2013 IEEE 13th International Conference on Data Mining, pp. 1085–1090. IEEE (2013)
23. Kandemir, M.: Asymmetric transfer learning with deep Gaussian processes. In: International Conference on Machine Learning (ICML) (2015)
24. Kuzborskij, I., Orabona, F.: Stability and hypothesis transfer learning. In: International Conference on Machine Learning, pp. 942–950 (2013)
25. Kuzborskij, I., Orabona, F.: Fast rates by transferring from auxiliary hypotheses. Mach. Learn. **106**(2), 171–195 (2017)
26. Kuzborskij, I., Orabona, F., Caputo, B.: Scalable greedy algorithms for transfer learning. Comput. Vis. Image Underst. **156**, 174–185 (2017)
27. Li, S., Xue, Y., Wang, Z., Zhou, G.: Active learning for cross-domain sentiment classification. In: Twenty-Third International Joint Conference on Artificial Intelligence (2013)
28. Long, M., Cao, Y., Wang, J., Jordan, M.: Learning transferable features with deep adaptation networks. In: International Conference on Machine Learning, pp. 97–105. PMLR (2015)
29. Long, M., Wang, J., Ding, G., Shen, D., Yang, Q.: Transfer learning with graph co-regularization. IEEE Trans. Knowl. Data Eng. **26**(7), 1805–1818 (2013)
30. Pan, S.J., Tsang, I.W., Kwok, J.T., Yang, Q.: Domain adaptation via transfer component analysis. IEEE Trans. Neural Netw. **22**(2), 199–210 (2010)
31. Pan, S.J., Yang, Q.: A survey on transfer learning. IEEE Trans. Knowl. Data Eng. **22**(10), 1345–1359 (2009)
32. Rai, P., Saha, A., Daumé III, H., Venkatasubramanian, S.: Domain adaptation meets active learning. In: Proceedings of the NAACL HLT 2010 Workshop on Active Learning for Natural Language Processing, pp. 27–32 (2010)
33. Raina, R., Battle, A., Lee, H., Packer, B., Ng, A.Y.: Self-taught learning: transfer learning from unlabeled data. In: Proceedings of the 24th International Conference on Machine Learning, pp. 759–766 (2007)
34. Romero, A., Ballas, N., Kahou, S.E., Chassang, A., Gatta, C., Bengio, Y.: FitNets: hints for thin deep nets. Comput. Sci. (2014)
35. Saha, A., Rai, P., Daumé, H., Venkatasubramanian, S., DuVall, S.L.: Active supervised domain adaptation. In: Gunopulos, D., Hofmann, T., Malerba, D., Vazirgiannis, M. (eds.) ECML PKDD 2011. LNCS (LNAI), vol. 6913, pp. 97–112. Springer, Heidelberg (2011). https://doi.org/10.1007/978-3-642-23808-6_7
36. Settles, B.: Active learning literature survey. Technical Report. University of Wisconsin-Madison Department of Computer Sciences (2009)
37. Settles, B., Craven, M.: An analysis of active learning strategies for sequence labeling tasks. In: Proceedings of the 2008 Conference on Empirical Methods in Natural Language Processing, pp. 1070–1079 (2008)
38. Shi, F., Li, Y.: Rapid performance gain through active model reuse. In: Proceedings of the Twenty-Eighth International Joint Conference on Artificial Intelligence (2019)

39. Shi, X., Fan, W., Ren, J.: Actively transfer domain knowledge. In: Daelemans, W., Goethals, B., Morik, K. (eds.) ECML PKDD 2008. LNCS (LNAI), vol. 5212, pp. 342–357. Springer, Heidelberg (2008). https://doi.org/10.1007/978-3-540-87481-2_23

40. Si, S., Tao, D., Geng, B.: Bregman divergence-based regularization for transfer subspace learning. IEEE Trans. Knowl. Data Eng. **22**(7), 929–942 (2009)

41. Sugiyama, M., Nakajima, S., Kashima, H., Buenau, P.V., Kawanabe, M.: Direct importance estimation with model selection and its application to covariate shift adaptation. In: Advances in Neural Information Processing Systems, pp. 1433–1440 (2008)

42. Sun, Q., Chattopadhyay, R., Panchanathan, S., Ye, J.: A two-stage weighting framework for multi-source domain adaptation. In: Advances in Neural Information Processing Systems, pp. 505–513 (2011)

43. Tan, B., Song, Y., Zhong, E., Yang, Q.: Transitive transfer learning. In: Proceedings of the 21th ACM SIGKDD International Conference on Knowledge Discovery and Data Mining, pp. 1155–1164 (2015)

44. Tan, B., Zhang, Y., Pan, S.J., Yang, Q.: Distant domain transfer learning. In: Thirty-First AAAI Conference on Artificial Intelligence (2017)

45. Tommasi, T., Orabona, F., Caputo, B.: Safety in numbers: learning categories from few examples with multi model knowledge transfer. In: 2010 IEEE Computer Society Conference on Computer Vision and Pattern Recognition, pp. 3081–3088. IEEE (2010)

46. Tommasi, T., Orabona, F., Caputo, B.: Learning categories from few examples with multi model knowledge transfer. IEEE Trans. Pattern Anal. Mach. Intell. **36**(5), 928–941 (2014)

47. Tzeng, E., Hoffman, J., Darrell, T., Saenko, K.: Simultaneous deep transfer across domains and tasks. In: Proceedings of the IEEE International Conference on Computer Vision, pp. 4068–4076 (2015)

48. Wang, X., Huang, T.K., Schneider, J.: Active transfer learning under model shift. In: International Conference on Machine Learning, pp. 1305–1313 (2014)

49. Xiao, M., Guo, Y.: Feature space independent semi-supervised domain adaptation via kernel matching. IEEE Trans. Pattern Anal. Mach. Intell. **37**(1), 54–66 (2014)

50. Yang, J., Yan, R., Hauptmann, A.G.: Adapting SVM classifiers to data with shifted distributions. In: Seventh IEEE International Conference on Data Mining Workshops (ICDMW 2007), pp. 69–76. IEEE (2007)

51. Yang, Y., Zhan, D.C., Fan, Y., Jiang, Y., Zhou, Z.H.: Deep learning for fixed model reuse. In: Thirty-First AAAI Conference on Artificial Intelligence (2017)

52. Yao, Y., Doretto, G.: Boosting for transfer learning with multiple sources. In: 2010 IEEE Computer Society Conference on Computer Vision and Pattern Recognition, pp. 1855–1862. IEEE (2010)

53. Yosinski, J., Clune, J., Bengio, Y., Lipson, H.: How transferable are features in deep neural networks? In: Advances in Neural Information Processing Systems, pp. 3320–3328 (2014)

54. Zhang, L., Zuo, W., Zhang, D.: LSDT: latent sparse domain transfer learning for visual adaptation. IEEE Trans. Image Process. **25**(3), 1177–1191 (2016)

Author Index

Printed in the United States
by Baker & Taylor Publisher Services